THE
PRESENT STATE
OF
EUROPE;

EXPLAINING

The INTERESTS, CONNECTIONS,
Political and Commercial

V I E W S
Of its Several POWERS,

COMPREHENDING Alſo,

A clear and Conciſe Hiſtory of each COUNTRY,
ſo far as to ſhew the Nature of their

PRESENT CONSTITUTIONS.

The FOURTH EDITION.
Reviſed, correƈted, and continued by the AUTHOR.

L O N D O N:

Printed for THOMAS LONGMAN, and CHARLES HITCH, in
Pater-noſter-row; JOHN and JAMES RIVINGTON, in St.
Paul's Church-yard; and ROBERT DODSLEY, in *Pall-mall*.

MDCCLIII.

First Published 1753
Reprinted 1970

LIBRARY OF CONGRESS CATALOG CARD NUMBER:
73-124782

PRINTED IN THE UNITED STATES OF AMERICA

PREFACE.

THE same Indulgence which the Public vouch-safed to this Performance at its first Appearance, has brought it in a very short Time to a Fourth Impression, which requires not only the most grateful Return of Thanks, but our utmost Endeavours to render it worthy of their Favour. We hope the Alterations and Additions with which it now appears, will in some measure acquit us of that Duty; and it would have given us infinite Pleasure, if the Systems of the several Courts mentioned therein could have been rendered more perspicuous than they are.

We were in hopes, when we first began to revise it, that we should have been able to have pronounced clearly as to the State of Things in the North, which notwithstanding remains still in a great Degree of Obscurity. In this, however, we have Reason to think ourselves happy, that nothing has fallen out in those Parts, either contrary to, or inconsistent with the Conjectures that we advanced.

A 2

Nor

Nor is there any great Probability that they have any such Tendency at present. The Change of Kings in Sweden *has made no Alteration in the System, and the Diet which sat last Year was of the same Complexion, but more unanimous than those that went before it.*

In Germany *there is no great Alteration, notwithstanding many long and laborious Negotiations. We were, when this Book appeared last, in Expectation of a great Event, and we are yet filled with the same Expectation. In this the Princes of the Empire act slowly, and with great Sagacity; for the very Consumption of Time, while it contributes to keep Things in Peace and good Order, answers a very important End. But beside all this, it attracts the Eyes of* Europe, *as well as the Attention of all Ministers, and becomes by this means productive of Measures not unprofitable to particular Interest, or inconsistent with the common Good.*

In speaking of France *we should have been glad to have found ourselves more at Liberty to express our Sentiments than the present Situation of Things, Motives of Prudence considered, will allow. But we may well bring ourselves to submit to some Restriction in that Respect, when it is evident, that*
those

those who have superior Lights art not altogether unembarraſſed. It is more than probable that the Time is at hand when theſe Clouds will be diſpe"ed, and we ſhall find ourſelves once more in a Condition to ſee and ſpeak freely.

Spain ſtill remains in poſſeſſion of her old Character for tedious Negotiations. That which ſuſpended our Judgment in the laſt Edition is half adjuſted, and we once flattered ourſelves that a little Delay would have furniſhed us with the Reſult of the ſupplemental Treaty, which has been ſo long upon the Carpet; but perhaps that, which was denied to this, may be reſerved for the Embelliſhment of the next Edition.

Whenever that ſhall happen, we ſhall be likewiſe in a better Condition to judge of the future State of Italy, where Things are ſtill ſubject to thoſe Apprenhenſions, the Cauſes of which have coſt us no ſmall Labour to explain.

There is another Point upon which we muſt more particularly inſiſt, to prevent the Reader's cenſuring us without Grounds. As our Alterations and Additions were made while the Book was in the Preſs, we may be thought chargeable with ſome Omiſſions in the firſt Chapters, from the mention of more re-

cent

cent Facts in the latter Pages of the Work: But when the Reader considers, that what was already printed was out of our Power, he will in Justice acquit us of any Neglect. This is a Circumstance unavoidably incident to every Undertaking of this Kind, which in representing Transactions of a fluctuating Nature, can only give a true Picture of Things for the present; and tho' ever so happily executed, must, like those that have preceded it, become gradually out of Date from the very same Causes that constitute its immediate Value. Almanacks last but for a Year, Political Present States claim a longer, and yet not a much longer Existence; but notwithstanding this hard Circumstance, both are very necessary, to prevent common Men and common Politicians from making Mistakes.

That such a Work was very far from being inexpedient, will appear sufficiently to all who have perused and considered the Treatises of the same Nature formerly written by the Duke of Rohan, Mr. Bethel, Baron Puffendorff, and the later Endeavours of such as have republished, continued, or augmented these Pieces in Holland; and we hope it will sufficiently appear, that we have also made a proper Use of their Performances, without transcribing them; which to say the Truth was impossible,

con-

considering that the following Sheets have been composed upon quite another Plan, without any Bias in favour of a particular System, or the least View of recommending it to the Favour of any Party, the Satisfaction of the Public being our sole Aim, as the Protection of the Public is that alone upon which we depend. This perhaps might have been in some meausre bespoken by a large Display of Authorities, and the Facts contained therein might have been supported by a pompous Train of Citations; but as we have dealt very little in secret Histories, and have founded most of our Observations upon Transactions of public Notoriety; this, whatever it might have appeared, would in reality served rather for Show than for Use, and therefore was omitted, to save the Reader as much Trouble and Expence as possible.

After professing a Desire to avoid wasting the Reader's Time in perusing this Work, it would be preposterous to tire him with a long Preface; and therefore let us conclude with this Reflection, that it is from Events, and the public Occurrences that shall hereafter happen, the Value of a Book of this Kind must be known; for it is not arguing right or wrong in the Opinion of any Set of Men whatever, which can give either Merit or Reputation to a Work that pretends to represent the Political

State

State of Europe. *He who will think justly upon this Subject, must form his Thoughts from the mature Consideration of Facts; and how far he has performed this, can appear from Facts only; for as in Law, so in Politics, the Worth of an Opinion does not consist in its being happily expressed, or handsomely maintained, either by logical Deductions, or Authorities learnedly quoted, but in its Conformity to* Truth : *If it fails in this, the* Lawyer *is mistaken, and the* Politician *deceived, let the Parts of the one, or the Abilities of the other, be what they will. And tho' in these Cases it is a great Hazard that a Man runs, yet there is this Comfort attends it, that there is a* certain Criterion *which decides with regard to the* Rectitude *of his* Notions *beyond all* Dispute.

THE

THE

PRESENT STATE

OF

EUROPE.

INTRODUCTION.

HERE is nothing clearer to such, as have taken the Pains to make themselves Masters of the History of Learning, than that every Age has its peculiar Taste; perhaps a Writer, like *Montaigne*, would call it Humour; from whence it follows, that Authors who are the Objects of Admiration in one Age, become the Ridicule of the next. In that which preceded the present, SYSTEMS were in great Esteem, and nothing recommended a Writer more, than his being very copious, and very methodical. From this Spirit proceeded voluminous *Systems* of History, Law, Physick, Mathematicks, and Divinity; but the very Learning which this kind of Writing furnished, being sufficient to discover its Imperfections, and to enable the Readers to see that it was contrived rather to circumscribe, than to extend his Views; there can be no Wonder that it grew into Discredit, or that after being thoroughly and warmly exposed, People run by Degrees into the opposite Extream, were for banishing Systems, and for contracting as much as possible, so as to bring the Elements and first Principles of Knowledge into a narrow Compass, by which the *Folio's* of

B

the

the laſt Age were in the Beginning of this reduced into *Duo-decimo's.*

It has been ſince found, that this way of Writing has alſo its Inconveniencies, that theſe *Abridgments* were not always made with that exquiſite Judgment, that it required to render them uſeful; that ſome Things falſe or uncertain were retain'd, and others of great Weight and Importance omitted; which obliged ſuch as were deſirous of being thoroughly Maſter of a Subject, to have recourſe to thoſe larger Works, that had been ſo much decry'd, in order to extract from them ſuch Particulars as were truly valuable, and ſerved to explain and elucidate thoſe Principles of Learning that were obſcure and unintelligible without them. For the facilitating this, Men of great Induſtry, and who had Time upon their Hands, began to collect and range theſe Paſſages in a new Order; and from hence aroſe the modern Invention of DICTIONARIES, I mean not ſuch as explain Words, but Things, which are now become very numerous. Theſe, without doubt, are convenient Tools in the Hands of able Workmen; but there is one SCIENCE which is very important, indeed abſolutely neceſſary towards forming the Mind of an accompliſhed Gentleman, in which neither the *Compendium* nor the *Dictionary* can be of any uſe at all.

The SCIENCE I mean is POLITICKS; by which I underſtand a comprehenſive Knowledge of the fundamental Maxims of Policy, grounded upon the actual and real Intereſts of the ſeveral *Governments* of EUROPE; and this is not only a polite as well as uſeful kind of Learning, the Study of which may be therefore recommended without Pedantry, but is in Reality a Point of great Conſequence; becauſe without this Knowledge it will be a Thing very difficult, if not impracticable, for a young Gentleman to qualify himſelf for the Service of his Country; in the preſent Times more eſpecially, when to be able to have a thorough Notion of the *Intereſts* of *Great Britain,* it is not barely expedient, but abſolutely neceſſary to have a clear Inſight into the *Concerns* of *all* the *European* Powers.

Thoſe certainly are much in the Wrong who pretend to treat this as a *Misfortune,* and would perſuade us, that it would be at leaſt much to the Advantage, if not for the Credit of our Country, if our Affairs were drawn into a narrower Compaſs, and our Attention ſtrictly confined to our own Concerns. This never was, indeed never can be the Caſe of a great, a free, and a trading Nation, and more eſpecially of a Maritime Power, which is, and I hope will ever be, the Characteriſticks

racteristicks of the BRITISH PEOPLE, as long as they continue a PEOPLE. While we are in this State, we must be respected, courted, and applied to upon many Occasions by Foreigners; and therefore it must be as I have stated it, absolutely necessary that at least such as manage our Affairs, and while we continue to enjoy our *Liberties*, this will take in a very large Number; should be thoroughly conversant with *Foreign* Interests, that from thence on certain Occasions, they may have a right Notion of their *own*. Without this they will be liable not only to be outwitted by their Enemies, but to be the Dupes also of their Allies; they may be drawn into Quarrels in which they have no Concern; and where they have a Concern they may very possibly mistake it, and engage very improperly, if not on the wrong Side.

One might easily illustrate this by many Examples; but perhaps that would be an invidious Task, because it would engage a Man either to espouse, or to oppose the established *Doctrine* of *Parties*, which is not only contrary to my own Inclination, but to the very Design of this Work, in which I hope there will appear no Leaning or the smallest Bias of that kind; for such Doctrines are of the Nature of Systems in Physick, and Philosophy, they serve to establish a popular Reputation upon the Ruins of Justice and Truth. The great Business in this Case, is to distinguish where *Right* lies, and then to embrace it, let it lie where it will. The latter is not without its Difficulties; but the former is embarrassed with them in a much greater Degree; for to acquire just Sentiments of the political Views, and real Interests of foreign Nations, is no easy Matter, nor are the Helps to it readily found.

It may be expected that the Foundation of this sort of Knowledge, ought to be laid from the Perusal of Books relating to the Constitutions, Laws, and Government of the respective Countries, not without an Insight also into their Antiquities. But if we consider first how laborious as well as how tedious an Undertaking this would be; and next how very little those Men are, generally speaking, skilled in the political Interests of their respective Countries, who are best versed in their Laws and Constitutions, or deepest read in their Records and Antiquities, we shall very easily discern, that as this Method would be in a great measure impracticable; so allowing it to be never so easy, it would nevertheless be very wide of answering the Purpose. Yet I am very far from asserting, that it ought to be totally disregarded; so far from it, that if a Man has Leisure, Opportunity, and Abilities, to look into these Things, he will hardly have Occasion to complain, that his Time has been mis-spent,

B 2

or

or that Nations are fo much altered in a long Courfe of Ages as to become quite a different fort of People; for in general I believe the contrary of this will be found true, and that the Climate, the Soil, the Cuftoms, and Examples of their Anceftors, have a very ftrong Effect upon moft Nations; but this is a Philofophical Refinement upon Politicks, which it requires a very nice Judgment to apply, tho' by fuch it may be fometimes very happily applied even in refpect to modern Tranfactions, as well in the Cabinet as in the Field.

Reading the general Hiftories of all Nations, but more efpecially thofe that are moft in Efteem, is a readier, an eafier, and a much better Help than the former; but this muft be ufed with Caution. It will indeed ferve to give us tolerable Notions of great Events, diftinguifhed Characters, important Revolutions, and their Confequences. But we muft always remember, that the Hiftorian has a natural, and perhaps a laudable Partiality for his Country; and that to be clearly Mafter of the Truth, one ought to compare his Accounts with thofe that are given by the Writers of other Nations, which is likewife a Work of much Labour and Fatigue. We fhould likewife reflect, that in general Hiftories the Compafs, with refpect to Time and Facts, is fo large, that the Springs and Motives, which is what a Politician chiefly looks for, are feldom fet down; and that where they are, it requires much Skill and great Circumfpection to difcern whether they are wholly, or if not, how far they may be depended upon. Yet this Way has its Ufes; and there is in Reality no better Method of forming a right Idea of the Spirit, Genius, and Temper of a Nation, than by perufing their Hiftories; for by knowing what a Nation has done or fuffered, when that comes to be the Point under Confideration, we may beft judge what they can atchieve, or to what Degree they will bear.

The private Memoirs of able Statefmen and illuftrious Captains is another Source from whence this Sort of Knowledge, in the Opinion of moft People, is likely to be drawn; yet here again great Penetration is requifite, and much Caution is to be ufed. For Perfons of that Rank being fo deeply engaged in Affairs themfelves, endeavour for the moft part to reprefent Things as much as poffible in a Light the moft favourable for their own Reputation; and if, upon particular Occafions, they give us evident Marks of their Sincerity, we cannot conclude from thence that they are always conducted by the fame Spirit; for fometimes thefe very Strokes are intended to furprize our Confidence, and to engage us in an implicit Belief of all they fay. Befides, even thefe great Men, being but Men, are
liable

liable to be deceived, and consequently may deceive us, without designing It, which makes it necessary for us to get the best Lights we can as to the Temper, Views, and particular Foibles of such Writers. For want of being acquainted with these, we may be carried into a wrong Road, and bewildered at the very Time when we imagined we were near our Journey's End. It is however right to make use of this Sort of Reading, provided we are very attentive, reflect upon what we read, and set up a Resolution not to be borne down by the Credit of our Author ; since in reading the Memoirs, as well as in conversing personally with great Men, we are naturally apt to receive Impressions from them, which we cannot easily shake off ; and the greater their Abilities, the greater our Danger is in this Respect, an Ascendency once established being very hardly if ever shaken off, by the most vigorous Understanding.

The Perusal of Polemical Writings upon Points of high Consequence, is another, and indeed a very considerable Help, more especially, if the Controversy be between Nations ; for then not only the ablest Writers are usually employed on both Sides, but we are pretty sure of having the Truth in some Measure struck out between them. Thus in the Writings of SELDEN and GROTIUS, we see almost all that can be said upon that famous Question *of the Dominion of the Sea* ; in the Pieces published upon the late *French* King's claiming, in Right of his Queen, the most valuable Provinces in the *Low-Countries*, and the Answers to them, the Doctrine as to *Successions* and *Renunciations* is fully explained ; and the Paper-War between the late CZAR and his Rival CHARLES XII. let us into many Secrets that otherwise would never have been known. All Collections therefore of this Kind, are highly valuable ; and provided we can but preserve a steady Attention, and are secure of our own Impartiality, we have a very fair Opportunity of reaping much Improvement by this Sort of Study. In Domestick Disputes between Factions it is quite otherwise ; for very often the Case is misrepresented alike by both Parties ; and tho' we are ever so well versed in the *Controversy*, it is a very great Chance, whether we ever get Sight of the *Truth*, at least if we have not a Hint of it some other Way.

GAZETTES and NEW-PAPERS, in respect to the Story of present Times, are not to be neglected ; it is true they are but indifferent Evidence, but generally speaking they are all the Evidence we have, and with much Attention and a reasonable Degree of Sagacity, we may discover Truth from Falshood, even in them. Indeed it is chiefly with regard to the Uses that are to be made of these, that the ensuing Work was composed ; for

by

by having a general Knowledge of the System of Affairs in *Europe*, and of the political Views and Interests of the particular Kingdoms and States therein, we may be enabled to make a right Application of that Kind of Reading, and to form a just Notion of what is passing in the World, notwithstanding the Disguises under which Facts appear in some Papers ; and which is a commoner Case, the Incorrectness with which, for want of having proper Lights, they are related in others. Almost every Country in *Europe* has its GAZETTE, or Paper by Direction, in which we are sure to find every thing set forth with such Colourings as may best suit the Interests of that Power from which the Paper derives its Authority. The PARIS GAZETTE, for Instance, has been very well characterized by a Writer of that Nation, that *it is the best written, and the least read of any in* Europe. The Language is very correct and pure, the Facts are well told, and ranged in their proper Order ; but we may be sure that nothing finds a Place there injurious to the Interest, or repugnant to the Sentiments of the *French* Ministry. We may sometimes learn from it Things of Consequence, with regard to other Countries ; but as to those of *France*, nothing appears but the News of the *Court*, without either Reasoning or Reflection. The latter Part of this Character belongs to most other GAZETTES by Authority; that is to say, we can depend upon nothing in them but the Dates and Facts, nor upon the Circumstances of the latter, if they are of any Importance ; but by the Comparison of these GAZETTES with each other, and a due Attention to the Partiality of each, we may, generally speaking, collect the Truth. In respect to other Papers of Intelligence, a very short Acquaintance with them will let us into the Character, Spirit, and Views of their Writers ; and from thence we are to judge of the Credit due to their respective Relations.

To facilitate this critical Kind of Reading, by which alone we can be enabled to judge of what passes in *our own Times*, and what Alterations happen in the Power, the Influence, the Connection, the Interests, and the Views of the several STATES of EUROPE, we must constantly keep in Mind the general Scheme, and the particular Plan before mentioned. To furnish the Reader with which, is the simple and sole Design of the following Sheets, in which they are as fairly and as succinctly set down as possible. One must however allow, that general *Collections* of *Treaties*, and a *Tincture* of the Law of *Nations*, which may be collected from GROTIUS and PUFFENDORF, and a general Notion of the *Geography* and *History* of Countries, are also necessary ; but these making always

ways

ways a Part of polite Education, which is a Structure we suppose already raised, and by no Means undertake to lay within so narrow a Compass; what we have to offer is accessory only; and this it was necessary to premise, that Things might not be taken in a wrong Light, or more be expected from the following Treatise than it was ever intended to contain. It is infinitely better to keep our Promises within Bounds, and to perform them strictly, than to endeavour to raise vast Expectations in the Reader; and then frustrate those very Expectations we have been at so much Pains to raise. Arts like these are sometimes used, in order to make Way for Sequels or second Parts, which is not at all in our Intention, as they flow from the Vanity of a Writer, whose Affection for his own Abilities magnifies to himself alone, the Merits of his Performance; and of this too it is hoped, that nothing will appear in this Treatise, since we are equally sensible of the Difficulty of the Task, and of our own Deficiencies; but to break the Ice, and to give an Opening to what may be made useful and valuable, ought to stand us in some Stead with the Publick, and defend from Censure what was never meant to acquire Applause. The being serviceable to Mankind gives infinitely more Satisfaction to an honest Mind than either Admiration or Praise.

To set this Matter in a still clearer Light, it may not be amiss however to observe, that there is a wide Difference between a *Geographical* Description, or an *Historical* Account of a Country, and a *Political View* of its *State* and *Interests*. The latter cannot indeed be known, without having some Idea of the former; but this may be brought within much narrower Limits than is commonly imagined. The Manner at present in Use for conveying the Principles of these Sciences, is much more expanded, and consequently more tedious and troublesome than is necessary; and may very well be reckoned one of the chief Causes, why so few apply themselves to the Study of them with that Steadiness and Attention, which is requisite to become Masters of what is practicable and useful; that is, what every Day's Occasions call for, and which may be as speedily applied. But it is one Thing to endeavour the setting these Matters in such a Light as is requisite for those who are wholly unacquainted with them, and quite another to range the Heads requisite to such a *Political Introduction* in their natural Order, so as to refresh the Memories of such as are already acquainted with them, and enable the Reader to connect Events with each other, and with the general System of Things, in the gradual Progress of his own Inquiries and cursory Observations on the Course of publick Affairs.

In

In order to make the general Method of this Discourse evident, as well as the Dependence of its Parts upon each other, it is requisite that we should acquaint our Readers with the Rules observed therein. In the first Place then, we take Notice of those principal and leading Parts in POLICY, that are, as it were, the Keys by which Men of Penetration unlock the Cabinets of Princes, discover the true *Maxims* of their Politicks, and thro' the Varnish of outward Colourings pierce into their most secret Resolutions, and distinguish their pretended from their real Views. We proceed next to the *General State of* EUROPE, and give, as near as we can, a clear and concise Detail of the relative Force of its several Parts, of the Ties by which some of these are united one to another, of the complicated Powers arising from thence, with the Proportion between them, and whatever else regards the Title of the Chapter, and extends to the Powers of *Europe*, collectively considered. The Way being thus paved for setting out the present State and particular Interests of its several Powers respectively, we begin with the Northern Potentates, and proceeding in the plainest and most natural Manner possible, we speak of each Kingdom and State, its Forces, Interest, and Maxims, as they stood upon the Conclusion of the late Treaty, by which the *Peace* of EUROPE has been so far restored, as to enable the judicious *Reader* to gain a rational Prospect of what may ensue during the remaining Part of the present Century.

CHAP. I.

Of the Universal Principles of POLICY, or General Interests of every GOVERNMENT.

IT is a just and sensible Remark of a great *Spanish* Writer, that " as the Motives of Submission are the same in all Societies whatever, so from thence certain *Principles* arise, " from the various Combinations of which, according to the " Nature of Times and Tempers of Men, different Systems of Rule, and various Methods of administring these " Systems, become necessary, or at least expedient." If, therefore, we are well acquainted with these, and accustom ourselves to reflect on the Manner in which they have been or may be combined, what at first Sight, for Want of this Consideration,

appears

appears myfterious and inexplicable, becomes by Degrees intelligible and familiar. It is the Notion that the governing Part of any Community has of this kind of Science, that in one Senfe is properly ftiled INTEREST, and in this Senfe it is that an illuftrious and able *French* Politician fays truly, and with great Spirit, that Kings govern Nations, and Intereft governs Kings : *Les Princes commandent aux Peuples, & l'Intereft commande aux Princes.*

According to the Form of Government that prevails, this *Maxim* is to be underftood. In abfolute Governments, if the Monarch has real Abilities, his *Senfe* of publick Affairs is the *Intereft* of the Body Politick, of which he is the Head ; and if he wants Abilities, it is, generally fpeaking, the Sentiment of his Prime Minifter that occupies that Place. In limited Governments, *Intereft* depends upon the Notions of thofe, who according to the Conftitution are vefted with fupreme Power ; and in fuch Governments their Notions may be very eafily known, becaufe their firft Maxim is, that what is for the general Benefit fhould be generally underftood, In *Ariftocratic* States, or Commonwealths governed by the Nobility, their Senfe of Things is looked upon as the *Publick Intereft*. In free States again, where the People, or all who have a certain Degree of Property, are confidered as the fupreme Power, the *Genius* of the Nation, by which I mean their general Temper and Difpofition, is the Index that points out their *Intereft*. The firft Thing therefore that is requifite to be underftood in practical Politicks, is the true State of the Government fubfifting in any Country. I fay the true State ; for the exterior and nominal Conftitution is to be found in every Compendium of Geography or Hiftory. But if an arbitrary Monarch confides in a *Junto*, his Government is, in effect, an *Ariftocracy*. If a limited Prince either governs, or is governed by the *Heads* of a *Party*, the Conftitution becomes from that Moment an *Oligarchy* ; and this is alfo the Condition of a *Popular State*, where by any fudden Revolution, or by the gradual working of a deep-laid *Intrigue*, the like Change is brought about.

But this is to be confidered only as the *accidental* Intereft of any Country ; for befides this, there is a *real* Intereft which arifes from the Principles before mentioned ; and the wife or weak, the good or ill, the fteady or fluctuating Adminiftration in every Government, is owing to the Harmony or the Oppofition between its actual and its real Interefts. The former we have fhewn is no otherwife to be difcovered than by Inforformation, as to the Hands in which Power is intrusted; and this may be derived either from Intelligence from those who have lived long under, or had an Opportunity to be well acquainted with, any Government; or it may be the Fruit of Observation. For if we consider the Conduct of any Nation, in respect to a few capital Points, and compare it with the real Interest of that Nation, we shall very speedily, and with great Certainty, discern the true Spirit of its Government. And this in most Cases will be found the safest Way of judging, or at least it will enable us to correct the other Mode of Information, by shewing us what Part of our Intelligence is worthy of Credit, and what ought to be rejected, let it come from what Authority it will. We know this is an infallible Maxim, *Ye shall judge by their Fruits.*

But we come now to the great Point of all, which is that of separating and distinguishing the Principles upon which the *real* Interests of all Nations are founded; and this, as in the other Art of decyphering, depends upon five great Points, which may be metaphorically stiled *Political Vowels.* Of each of these in their Order we will speak as succinctly as possible, because we are aware, that to some Readers this Part of the Work may seem tedious, which is common to the elementary Parts of all Sciences; and yet without due Attention to them, no Branch of Learning can be fully or thoroughly understood. To these there is a frequent Necessity of having recourse; and no Man is ever Master of any Kind of Study, till he feels the Advantage, and is fully satisfied as to the Use of its fundamental Principles. For then, to resume the former Comparison, he first spells with little Trouble, and at length reads fluently and without Hesitation, what one would have thought him an *Oedipus,* who should have been able to unriddle.

The *first* Principle tending to demonstrate the *real* Interest of a People, is their RELIGION; for that will always have its Weight. It is true, that the Reality and Importance of this appeared stronger in the last Age than in the present, when perhaps there was a sincerer Sense of it in most Countries; but it is still of Consequence enough to maintain its Post. For how moderate soever Men may be in their Professions, how lukewarm soever in their Practices, yet either from Principle, from worldly Motives, or from Custom, they will have a Readiness to unite with such as declare themselves of the same Belief, and an Eagerness in opposing those who differ from them. In short, Infidel, Bigot, and Heretick, remain still

Terms

Terms of Enmity ; and though they have not the fame Strength as heretofore, each of them has yet its Meaning, and carries a large Proportion of Refentment with it.

Next to *Religion*, the *natural Grounds* of Friendfhip, Alliances, or Amity, is a leading Principle. In Monarchies this fometimes arifes from Nations being governed by the fame Family. As for Inftance, in *France*, *Spain*, and *Naples*, we have feen, and in all Probability we fhall fee, that this has a great Effect ; and that the Meafures of the Head of the Houfe will be, generally fpeaking, acquiefced in by all its Branches. Sometimes it arifes from Intermarriages ; but very little Strefs is to be laid upon this, where the Princes are equal, but a very great Weight where it is otherwife. For a great King, or his Heir apparent, marrying a Princefs, Daughter to an inferior Prince, attaches the latter to his Intereft : And this without Doubt was the Motive to a late Match, that need not be mentioned. Sometimes it proceeds from an Identity of Interefts, as between the Maritime Powers, whom Refpect to mutual Safety keeps clofely united. At other times it arifes from having like Views ; which was formerly the Cafe between *Sweden* and *France*, and has been of late that of *France* and *another* Power, as in Reafon it ought to be between the Emprefs *Queen* and the King of *Sardinia*. There is alfo a Kind of Connection that fprings from the Similarity of Government ; whence we fometimes hear of the common Caufe of Kings, and the joint Intereft of Republicks ; but this feems rather for a Colour than a Principle.

The *third* general Head is, that of *Situation*. Our own is a pregnant Inftance of this ; a great Part of our Politicks are, or at leaft ought to be, dictated to us from our Pofition as an *Ifland*, which makes a martial Spirit univerfally diffufed amongft our People, and a great maritime Force, our natural Strength ; as Commerce, not Conqueft, is our true Principle of Acquifition. As to the Effects of Situation upon the Continent, they will be naturally explained in that Part of the following Work, where we fpeak of the *Balances* of *Power*, I mean of the Inferior Balances which arife chiefly from Vicinity, and that Neceffity which weaker Neighbours feel of living in Union, to prevent their being oppreffed or fwallowed up by fome fuperior Power, that can be only kept in Awe by fuch an Union.

The *relative State* of a Nation is the *fourth* Principle, by which is meant its being in a better or a worfe Condition than formerly. For if any People are flufhed with Succefs in War, in Commerce, or from the Change of their Government to a milder from a feverer Form ; their Courage naturally rifes, their

their Refolutions are quicker taken, and executed with unufual Vigour. On the other Hand, if People are dejected by frequent Loffes, torn by inteftine Factions, or any other way internally diftreffed, their Deliberations are confufed, their Refolutions flow, and an apparent Languor is vifible, whenever they attempt to carry their Refolutions into Execution.

The *laft* Principle in general Politicks, is that of *Claims* or *Pretenfions*; for there is always a Diffidence, or an Incompatibility of Interefts, between fuch Powers as have Pretenfions upon each other, of which, in the Courfe of the laft and prefent Age, we have feen fo many flagrant Inftances, that to infift upon it would be needlefs. It fhall fuffice therefore to obferve, that where thefe feem to be got over, and a temporary Conjunction is brought about, it is always weak and unfound; and, like all unnatural Motions, however violent, is never lafting. The Alliance between the Courts of *Vienna* and *Madrid* is a modern as well as memorable Proof of it: *Europe* was fcarce alarmed by their Conjunction, before its Fears were quieted by their Separation.

It requires great Force of Mind, much Application, and a large Compafs of Knowledge, to apply thefe general Principles to each particular State. A fuperior Genius, capable of this in its utmoft Extent, and with the higheft Degree of Perfection, becomes a confummate Statefman; one fit not to affift only, but even to direct the greateft Monarch. And therefore the Emperor CHARLES V. who was at once the wifeft and moft fortunate Prince of the Age in which he lived, had Reafon to fay to his Son PHILIP II. when he introduced to him his Secretary *Erafo*, the Day after he had refigned to him fo many Kingdoms, and recommended him to his Service; " The Prefent I make " you now, is greater than that which I made you yefter- " day; *Quanto os hé dado efte dia, no es tanto que daros efte* " *criado.*

CHAP. II.

A View of the prefent State of EUROPE *in general.*

THAT *Europe* is, beyond all Comprehenfion, the moft happy and valuable Quarter of the Globe, is a thing fo much taken for granted, that perhaps few would think a Man
much

much in the Wrong who should conceive himself under no Obligation to prove it; but I must confess this has never been my Sentiment; since, in order to judge right, I am persuaded that in Politicks as well as Philosophy we should not admit any Thing till it is proved, because there is no Reasoning with the smallest Degree of Certainty, where we are not satisfied that our Principles are sound. In the first Place then, these high Prerogatives are not derived to *Europe* from its Size, since it is the least of all the four Parts into which the Globe is divided; and, as it may be of some Use to know these Proportions, and because I do not remember to have seen them set down any where with tolerable Exactness, I think it may not be amiss to give them here.

If we suppose the whole habitable World to be divided into three hundred Parts, *Europe* will contain of these twenty seven, *Asia* one hundred and one, *Africa* eighty two, and *America* ninety. In respect to People, though she certainly excels *Africa* and *America*, yet she falls very far short of *Asia*, if we may depend upon the Accounts that have been given us by the best and most judicious Travellers. In reference to Riches, her Gold and Silver Mines are not to be compared with those in the other Quarters of the World; she has few or no precious Stones, strictly speaking, found in any of the Countries which she contains; and as to Spices and Perfumes, we know very well from whence they are brought.

At first Sight these Remarks may seem to destroy the common Opinion, but when more closely examined they will be found to confirm it; for when we say one Country is greater, more powerful, and more considerable than another, we mean that it is so in Respect to the Condition of its Inhabitants; and in this Sense we may very safely affirm it of *Europe*.

For with regard to Territory, if we consider what the *Spaniards*, the *English*, the *Portuguese*, the *French*, and the *Dutch* possess in other Parts of the World, we may venture to assert, that it is equal, if not superior to *Asia*; and if it contains not so many People within its own Bounds, yet it may be truly said to command more. As to Riches, it is notorious that the *European* Nations enjoy, in Consequence of their Trade, all that Nature has bestowed upon the other Parts of the World. Thus we see, that without any Prepossession in Favour of that Part of the Globe in which we are seated, we have good Cause to maintain that it surpasses all the rest; and that we may with Reason admit for Truth what Custom has taught us to believe, that *Europe* is indeed the happiest, the most powerful, and in respect

respect to Arts, Arms, and Trade, by very far the most confiderable Portion of the Globe.

After settling this Point, it is natural to descend to those general Heads, whence the Grandeur, and, which is of no less Consequence, the Stability of the Government of *Europe* arise, and on which the Power and Safety of its several Parts depend ; which, that we may not multiply such Articles beyond what is necessary, we shall confine to three Heads, *viz.* Religion, Trade, and the Union of Political Interests ; and when we have treated particularly of these, the general State of *Europe* may be thoroughly and perfectly understood, and a right Judgment formed of the Views and Force of the several Parties therein, and of the Nature of those Controversies which from Time to Time arise amongst them, and which, as Experience will shew, may be easily referr'd to one or other of these Subjects.

To begin then with Religion : Tho' it is true that there are some *Pagans* in the *Swedish* and *Muscovite Lapland*, a vast Multitude of *Jews* scattered through almost every Country, and that the *Mahommedan* Religion has the Sanction of publick Authority in the Grand Seignior's Dominions ; yet the prevailing Religion is Christianity, divided indeed into a great Number of Sects, but falling under the three following capital Distinctions ; *viz.* Christians of the *Greek Church*, Christians in Communion with the Church of *Rome*, and Protestants. I must confess it has always appeared to me in the Light of the most difficult Task, to settle the Weight and Proportion of these different Interests ; and yet this is a Point that ought not to be hurried over ; because the supporting, promoting, and extending their several religious Systems, makes a great Part of the Business, and is a principal Point in the Policy of most of the *European* Powers ; and without a competent Understanding of the Question I proposed, as to the Strength or Weight of each Party, the State of *Europe* can never be thoroughly or justly understood ; and therefore how thorny or perplexed soever this Point may be, it is incumbent upon me to discuss it.

As to the Christians of the *Greek* Church, they have for their Head whoever wears the Imperial Diadem of *Russia* : The Princes of *Moldavia* and *Wallachia* are also of this Religion, and so are the greatest Part of the Christians subject to the Grand Seignior, besides Multitudes that are scattered through *Hungary*, *Poland*, *Transylvania*, and some Parts of *Germany*. On the whole, after the strictest Computation, and most mature Reflection, I am apt to believe that the People of this

Persuasion

Perfuafion are at leaft equal in Number to the Papifts. If any one fhould object, that there are many great Kingdoms, the Inhabitants of which are in Communion with the Church of *Rome* : I muft reply, that the Extent of their Dominions taken together, Is not more than half of the Territories poffeffed by the Czarina in *Europe* only ; and though it be true, that thofe are thinly inhabited, and that her *Ruffian* Majefty's Subjects are of all Religions, yet furely the *Greek* Chriftians under the Yoke of the *Turk*, if they were removed into her Countries, would go near to render her Empire as populous as any of the Kingdoms governed by Popifh Princes.

I might add fome other Confiderations upon this Subject, fuch as, that we are lefs acquainted with the Countries inhabited by the Chriftians of the *Greek* Church, than with thofe inhabited by Papifts, which may render us lefs capable Judges of this Queftion. But the Reafon of the Thing, when ftrictly confidered, will overcome all thefe Prejudices, and convert every competent Judge to my Opinion. The Importance of this Enquiry will be the better underftood, if we reflect a little on the Difputes that fo frequently happen between the *Ruffians* and *Turks*. The former are certainly by much the moft dangerous Enemies that the *Ottoman* Empire hath to fear, becaufe the beft Part of its *Chriftian* Subjects are naturally inclined to the *Ruffians*, whereas they are much better pleafed to live under the Power of the *Turks* than to fall under that of the *Auftrians*, merely becaufe the latter are Papifts, which implies a Difpofition to perfecute, reftrained by nothing but the Vicinity of fo formidable a Power as the *Turk* ; but when the domeftick Affairs of the *Mufcovites* are once fettled, and the Houfe of *Holftein* in peaceable Poffeffion of the Imperial Throne, as well as of that of *Sweden*, it is very eafy to difcern the firft fair Opportunity that offers will endanger the Fall of the *Turkifh* Empire, or at leaft the Lofs of her Dominions in *Europe*, chiefly from the Crown of *Ruffia*'s being confidered as the Remnant of the old *Conftantinopolitan* Empire, and the ancient and natural Head of the *Greek* Church.

We come now to examine the Strength and Power of the *Romanifts*, which is certainly very great, and the common Opinion is, that it daily gains Ground. If there be any Truth in this, it muft be principally owing to their having a vifible Head, I mean the POPE, cloathed with that Sort of Authority, which is fitteft to fupport and extend the Tenets of Religion. The Reformation, though it has much weakened the fpiritual Power and temporal Strength of the Holy Father, has, notwithftanding, withstanding, furnished him with many Advantages of another kind; or rather the Policy of the Church of *Rome* hath turned the Views of Protestants to her own Advantage, by affecting a paternal Care for the Princes and States of her Communion, assisting the Authority of the State in Times of Peace, and interposing her Authority as a common Mediator whenever Wars break out amongst them. This is certainly a Benefit to them; and from their being convinced of this, springs the Respect paid to his Holiness by the wisest Administrations in all Popish Countries. It is from the same Principles that the Propagation of the Popish Religion is looked on by them as the highest Point of Policy, from which they are sure never to depart; and therefore we need not wonder that they have made, and continue still very likely to make, considerable Acquisitions.

It may be look'd upon however as a Thing certain, that notwithstanding all the Endeavours that have been used, during the last two Centuries, to weaken the Protestant Interest, it is still very considerable, very able to support itself against the Force, at least, if not the Frauds, of all its Enemies; neither, after all, is it so much weakened as some out of Fear, and others from worse Intentions, have asserted; for we are to consider, that the Countries in which the Reformed Religion is professed, are most of them very populous, carry on a great Trade, and have many Colonies, by which means they propagate their religious Sentiments almost without attending to it.

We must confess however, that the Want of a Head, the disclaiming the Doctrine of Persecution, and the maintaining the opposite Sentiment of the Right of private Judgment, are great Disadvantages to the Protestant Cause, consider'd in a political Light. We are the more sensible of this of late Years, because the Zeal and Spirit which formerly appeared in several Princes and States for the Support and Encouragement of Religion, is in a manner lost from the prevailing of a Spirit of Licentiousness, not more dangerous to the Concerns of the Church than of the State, which, by Degrees, may revive the old Spirit, especially as the Encroachments of Popery become more and more visible. The famous *Gustavus Adolphus*, King of *Sweden*, owed all his Power and Grandeur to his assuming the Character of *Protector of the Protestant Interest in Germany*; and when he comes thoroughly to consider his Situation, there is great Reason to believe that the present King of *Prussia* will fix also on that Character at last, as the most proper to preserve the Dominions and Power he has already obtained, as well as to extend them; and while the Protestant Interest is effectually secured in *Germany*,

many, it is certain that it never can decline in other Parts of *Europe*. We shall next enter into a short Comparison of the Weight of these two Interests, and then proceed to another Subject.

In computing the Strength of the *Papists*, it is usual and indeed proper to reckon the Emperor first, because he precedes all the Princes of that Communion, and adds somewhat to the Credit of this Religion by his Authority in *Germany :* Yet having few or no Subjects as a Monarch, he ought not to be considered as having, in this respect, any Weight comparable to the lofty Title of Emperor of *Germany*, and King of the *Romans*. The next Popish Power is *France*, then *Spain*, and next *Portugal*; though the King of *Poland*'s *European* Dominions are more extended than *Spain* and *Portugal* taken together. After them follow the King of *Sardinia*, the *Pope*, the Princes and States of *Italy*, with such of the *Swiss* Cantons as are Papists; and this brings us back again to *Germany*, where we find all the Dominions of the Queen of *Hungary* and *Bohemia*, together with the Electors *Bavarian* and *Palatine*, besides the Spiritual Electors, and other Princes and States of the same Communion.

Of the Protestant Powers WE are without Doubt the most considerable. Next follow *Sweden*, *Denmark*, and *Prussia*, the *United Provinces*, the *Swiss* Cantons and their Confederates; then the Subjects of the Elector of *Saxony*, though their Prince be a *Papist*; the Elector of *Hanover*, the Duke of *Courland*, and all the lesser Princes and States of *Germany* of our Communion. According to the nearest Computation that can be made with respect to Territory in *Germany*, the Proportion between *Papists* and *Protestants* may be as Ten to Eight, but in Point of Number of People, I apprehend the Protestants are at least equal; and throughout the rest of *Europe*, I conceive the Proportion in Point of Territory to be as Eight to Seven; but as to People, I think there is good Reason to believe that the Protestants are rather more numerous than the Papists, because the Protestant Countries are incontestably much fuller of People.

In the North, for Example, though *Poland* be very populous, yet it is certain that one half of the People are not Papists, and at least one third of them Protestants, whereas in *Sweden* and *Denmark* there are few or no Papists; in *Germany* again all the great trading Cities, tho' crouded with Inhabitants, are Protestants. In *Italy* indeed the Papists are in a Manner without Mixture; but this is ballanced by the Number of People in *Great Britain*. In order to cut the Matter short, and to set this Point in the clearest Light possible, I shall here present the Read-

C   er

er with a very curious Table, which will serve to regulate his
Judgment not only in respect to this, but with regard to many
other Subjects of Importance.

The Proportion of the several Powers in Europe to Great B ritain.

Ruſſia	10,	13	*Portugal*	0,	36
Germany	3,	53	*Spaniſh Netherlands*	0,	18
Sweden	3,	63	*United Provinces*	0,	11
Poland	3,	39	*Switzerland*	0,	17
France	1,	7	*Denmark*	1,	49
Spain	1,	81	*Italy*	1,	19
Turkey	3,	18			

In order to explain this, I need only say, that the Proportion
between *Ruſſia* and *Great Britain* is as 10—13, to 1 ; that is,
Ruſſia is ten times as large as *Great Britain*, and 13 Parts of 100
more ; and at the same time it points out the comparative
Strength of *Britain* to other Nations, it also shews the Proportions of all these Countries to each other.

The next Thing to be considered is the Trade of *Europe*,
which has undergone in the Course of Ages very great Alterations. Upon the Fall of the *Roman* Empire it seemed to be
in some Measure extinguished, but very soon revived again
among the *Saxons*, who, when they became Masters of this
Island, established a vast Maritime Power here, which however did not continue very long, the *Danes* making themselves Masters of this Country by their Superiority in this respect. After some Ages, Commerce and Maritime Power retired Southward, and were, in a Manner, wholly possessed by
the *Italian* States, particularly the *Venetians* and the *Genoese*,
who had shared between them the Traffick of the East, which
enabled them to draw the Wealth of all other Nations to themselves.

But in the thirteenth Century, several free Cities in *Germany*
began to combine together for the Support and Maintenance
of their Trade, and soon made their Confederacy known to
the World, by the Title of the *Hanseatic* League : But as
their Commerce brought them in immense Wealth and Power,
so this rendered them haughty and insolent, which, by Degrees,
brought on their Ruin, to which, however, other Circumstances

stances also contributed; for in the fifteenth Century the *Portu-guese* perfected a new Route to the *East Indies* by the Cape of *Good Hope*, and about the same Time the *Spaniards* discovered *America*, which threw the Trade of *Europe* and its chief Naval Power into the Hands of those Nations, who, if they had known how to cultivate it with Skill, and to use it with Moderation, might have raised it much higher, and have made it much more lasting than it proved, especially when both the Trade of the *East* and *West Indies* was in the Hands of the Subjects of the same Prince, which happened by the Accession of King *Philip* II. of *Spain* to the Crown of *Portugal*.

But as almost all Evils point out and in time produce their own Remedies, so the boundless Ambition and cruel Oppression of the *Spaniards*, constrained the *United Provinces* to throw off their Yoke, and engaged their Inhabitants, and the *English*, to endeavour by their Expeditions into both *Indies* to share in those Riches, which were the great Source of the *Spanish* Tyranny, and this raised up those that are now called the Maritime Powers. The Progress of the *Dutch* was amazingly quick; for in the Space of little more than half a Century, from having hardly any Ships at all, they came to have more than all the rest of *Europe* put together.

But since that Time the Inhabitants of *Great Britain*, by extending their Commerce, and especially by cherishing and augmenting their Colonies, have certainly raised their Maritime Force to an Equality at least in every respect with the *Dutch*, as all intelligent Writers, and particularly Foreigners, agree. And this of late induced the Partizans of the *French* Court to suggest to the *States*, that they are in more Danger from the growing Trade and Naval Power of *Great Britain*, than from the ambitious Designs of any of their Neighbours besides.

Yet the *French* themselves have of late Years laboured with great Diligence not only to raise a Maritime Force, but to extend their Trade into all Parts of the World, in which they have been very successful; for though the two last general Wars in a great Measure ruined their Navy, yet their Commerce is even at this Juncture, or was at least before the breaking out of the last War, in a better Condition than ever. So that the Maritime Affairs of *Europe* have in this last Century suffered a very great Change, though very probably they may suffer still a greater before its Period.

The like Attention to Commerce and Maritime Power has, within this fifty Years, appeared in almost every other Nation in *Europe* : The *Swedes* and *Danes* have set up *East-India* Com-

panies;

panies; the *Ruffians* have opened a new and advantageous Traffick, as well on the *Caspian* as on the *Black* Sea. The House of *Auftria* fhewed a great Defire of reviving the antient Commerce of the *Low Countries*; and when that was found impracticable, made fome excellent Regulations in Theory at leaft at *Triefte* and *Fieume*. The *Genoefe* have within thefe few Years erected a Company of Affurance, on purpofe to encourage their Subjects to venture upon long Voyages, and, if poffible, to recover their old Reputation as a Maritime Power. Nay, even the *Spaniards* themfelves, who in this refpect have flept for fuch a Number of Years, have at laft opened their Eyes, erected fome, and have under Confideration the erecting feveral other Companies, for the Encouragement and Extenfion of Trade through their *European* and *American* Dominions.

We may, I think, fafely infer from thefe Inftances, that the Navigation and Shipping of the *Europeans* in general, is, within the laft fifty Years, greatly increafed; and, as a farther Proof of this, we need only confider the numerous Fleets and great Embarkations of different Powers, fuch as the *Ruffians, Swedes,* and *Danes* in the North, the Invafion of *Sicily* and *Africa* by the *Spaniards,* and many others. Sir *Walter Raleigh* made a very ingenious Calculation of the Maritime Power of *Europe* in his Time; and Sir *William Petty,* from better Lights, gave us another Calculation, which has been confidered as the Standard ever fince. He thought the *Dutch* had about 900,000 Ton in Shipping, *Great Britain* 500,000; *Sweden, Denmark,* and the trading Towns in *Germany* 250,000; *Portugal* and *Italy* 250,000 likewife; and *France* about 100,000. But fince that Time, Things have alter'd very much, both with refpect to us and other Powers, infomuch that I am fully perfuaded, that our Shipping was, before the breaking out of the laft War, at leaft double to what it might be at the Conclufion of the Peace of *Utrecht.* It is, I muft freely acknowledge, a very difficult thing to pretend to give, with any Degree of Exactnefs, the prefent Proportions of Maritime Power; however, till a better can be formed, I flatter myfelf the following Table may have its Ufes.

If the Shipping of *Europe* be divided into *Twenty* Parts, then

Great Britain, &c. hath - - - - - - -	6
The *United Provinces* - - - - - - - -	6
The Subjects of the Northern Crowns - - -	2
The trading Cities and Sea Ports of *Germany* and the *Austrian Netherlands* - - - - - - - -	I
France - - - - - - - - - - - -	2
Spain and *Portugal* - - - - - - - - -	2
Italy, and the rest of *Europe* - - - - - -	I

The Grounds upon which this Calculation ſtands, would require a great deal of Room to explain. And after all, it might prove no eaſy Thing to perſuade ſuch as are acquainted with the Commerce only of this or that particular Country, to admit that the Computation is fairly made; but however, it will, I dare ſay, be found, that ſuch as are concerned for any particular Country, will allow the Table to be right enough as to the reſt, which is as much as any one can well expect. Beſides ſhewing the State of Commerce at this Day, there is another great Uſe to which this Computation may be applied, and that is by way of Standard, to ſee how far one Power riſes, or another ſinks in this Reſpect; for if ever it ſhould come to paſs that theſe Proportions ſhould vary conſiderably, it is plain that this muſt produce very great and ſenſible Alterations in the general State of Affairs.

Thus, for Inſtance, if the Houſe of *Bourbon* ſhould ever acquire as great a Proportion of Trade and Naval Force as either of the Maritime Powers, it would be an Acquiſition of much more Conſequence than any they have hitherto made in Point of Territories or Dominion; but at the ſame time we muſt be aware of another Thing, which is this, not only the Proportions, but the Total of Maritime Power may alter, and in that Caſe the Growth of any particular State, though advantageous to itſelf, would not render it more formidable to others.

This Computation likewiſe ſhews how much it is the Intereſt of the Maritime Powers to ſuſtain their Characters in that reſpect at all Events; ſince by this Means only they can pre-

ſerve

ſerve their Independency, protect their Subjects wherever they may be ſettled or diſperſed, and aſſiſt their Allies, notwithſtanding the ſuperior Power as well as boundlſs Ambition of any aſpiring Neighbour. We need not wonder then, at a common Notion which prevails, as if we had a Right to preſcribe to ſome other Nations the Bounds of their Naval Greatneſs. I will not pretend to vindicate the Exerciſe of ſuch a Prerogative; but, methinks, it would be no ill Stroke of Policy, ſhould any State, really Miſtreſs of ſuch a Power, exert it upon extraordinary Occaſions; but under ſuch Colours and Pretences, as might effectually hide it: for this may be laid down as a Thing certain, that nothing is ſo dangerous to a Maritime Power as Pride, and, in conſequence of that vicious Principle, making an ill Uſe of it.

What we have before ſpoken of Trade or Commerce, may very well anſwer the Ends expected from it in an Hiſtorical Light, and teach us to judge tolerably well of the Nature, Extent, and comparative Strength of what is ſtiled Maritime Power. But in a Political Senſe, this will not by any Means ſuffice. If we will really judge of Things as they are, we muſt be thoroughly acquainted with their Inſides, and not content ourſelves with the bare Conſideration of Appearances. We ſee and know that whatever State or Power is poſſeſſed of extenſive Trade, muſt have a great Naval Force, the Effects of which will render her conſiderable; yet it is very requiſite to know how this ariſes, and why the Strength and Dominion of a Maritime Power is firmer and more durable than that which is collected from a great Extent of Territory, Multitudes of Subjects, or rich and fruitful Countries, which is what I ſhall endeavour to explain in very few Words, and then apply it to ſome very material Purpoſes.

Firſt then, Trade is extremely ſerviceable to any Nation, let the Form of its Government be what it will, becauſe it introduces Induſtry and Arts, by which the Manners of a People are entirely altered; for it is not abſolutely the Number of Subjects, but the Number of uſeful Subjects, that make any State powerful. In the *next* Place, it introduces Property, for without Security as to that, it is impoſſible that Trade ſhould flouriſh; and in this reſpect, it leſſens ſome, and takes away many Inconveniencies, to which every kind of Government is from its Nature liable. And *laſtly*, it draws an almoſt inconceivable Flux of People, wherever it is thoroughly fixed.

Hence we may very eaſily aſſign the true Cauſes of the long Duration of Republicks famous for Trade, ſuch as *Tyre* and *Carthage* in ancient Times, and the *Venetians* and *Genoeſe* in later Ages.. It is impoſſible that a Nation active and induſtrious, rich and populous, and at the ſame time living under a mild Government,

ment, fhould not exert a greater Force when employed in attack-ing others, and have much greater Refources in Cafe fhe is at-tacked herfelf, than other States that want thefe Advantages ; hence it will appear how the State of *Holland* rofe to fuch vaft Power in fo fhort a Time, and how her Subjects have been able to thrive and grow rich under Taxes and Impofitions, which muft have beggar'd them long fince in any other Situation than that of a trading Republick.

Secondly, Trade quite alters the comparative Strength of States and Kingdoms, becaufe wherever it refides, it creates fo many and fo great Advantages, and begets fuch Relations and Con-nections, as render a Trading State infinitely fuperior to her Neighbours. For fuch a State, if on the Continent, can fortify her great Towns fo as to refift a Power ten times ftronger, in refpect to People ; fhe can maintain, if it be requifite, great Num-bers of Regular Troops, and on any Emergency can hire more from her Neighbours, befides what fhe may be able to do by the Help of her Maritime Force. Hence arifes that great Strength and real Power fhewn by Trading Republicks, when attacked, either by ambitious Princes, or even by powerful Confederacies.

Thus the *Venetians* have often been too hard for the *Turks* ; the *Genoefe* for the moft potent Princes in *Italy*; and in earlier Times, the *Lubeckers* for the greateft Powers in the North. Hence the famous League of *Cambray*, which was formed for the Deftruction of the State of *Venice* in 1509, came to nothing, though the greateft Princes of that Time engaged in it, though the *Venetians* themfelves were guilty of fome Indifcretions, and though they had been very much exhaufted by former Wars. Thus alfo the famous Confederacy between *France* and *Great Britain* againft *Holland* in 1672, proved abortive, though at the firft, even the *Dutch* themfelves thought their Affairs defperate ; but ftill their Love of Liberty encouraged them to refift, and their Trade furnifhed them with the Means of getting tolerably out of that War.

Thirdly, Trade has not only a very great Influence on the par-ticular Affairs of Nations feparately confidered, and is almoft the fole Caufe of a comparative Difference in the Strength and Forces of moft of the Powers in *Europe*, but is alfo of infinite Advan-tage to this Quarter of the Globe in general ; keeps us free from all Apprehenfions of being over-run by thofe barbarous Empires which the *Mahommedan* Religion has eftablifhed in the World, and likewife brings us every thing that is rich and coftly, every thing that is curious and valuable, even from the remoteft Quar-ters of the Earth ; fo that to Trade alone is, ftrictly fpeaking, due, that Superiority which at the Beginning of this Difcourfe we

attributed

attributed to this Part of the World over the reft. In a Word, it is to Commerce that the People of *Europe* owe their Freedom and Independency, their Learning and Arts, their extenfive Colonies abroad, their prodigious Riches at home; and above all, that Naval Power, which fo much furpaffes any thing of the fame Kind in other Parts of the World, and whatever was attempted in that Way in former Ages.

But there's one thing more, with refpect to Trade, which I have not yet obferved, and which, for any thing I know, has not hitherto been confidered by any political Writer. It is this: That the reciprocal Connections refulting from Trade, have quite altered the State of Things, and produced within thefe two, or at moft thefe three Centuries paft, a kind of new Syftem in *Europe*, or in the Chriftian Parts of *Europe* at leaft, by which every State is led to have a much greater Concern than formerly for what may happen to another: an Inftance will make my Meaning perfectly intelligible.

In former Ages, a Quarrel in the North could only have affected the North, but in the laft Century Things were totally altered. Both the *Dutch* and we fent our Fleets into the *Baltick*, upon the Quarrel that happened between the *Swedes* and *Danes*, a little before the Reftoration of King *Charles* II. Not long after this, the Crown of *Sweden* became a contracting Party in the famous Triple-Alliance for maintaining the Peace of *Europe*, preferving the *Spanifh Low Countries*, and fetting Bounds to the Power of *France*. After the Revolution, towards the Clofe of the Reign of King *William*, both the Maritime Powers fent their Fleets again into the *Baltick*, with the fame View and the fame Succefs, and the like has been done more than once fince. The Pretence in all thofe Cafes was, the Love of Juftice, and an exact Performance of Treaties, in which alfo there was fomewhat of Truth; but the great and real Defign was, to prevent thofe Inconveniencies which muft have befallen the Maritime Powers, if either *Sweden* or *Denmark* had been entirely undone by thofe Wars. We may therefore fafely fay, that the *Ballanfe of Power* (in the ftrict Senfe of that Phrafe) was created by Trade, and muft continue to be the Object more especially of Trading Countries, fo long as they preferve their Commerce and their Freedom.

It is from a Senfe of this, that whenever any Power attempts to opprefs another, or betrays a vifible Defign of heightening its own Strength by attacking or conquering its Neighbours, other Potentates are ready to interpofe; from a quick Senfe, not only of the Inconveniencies that muft arife from the Incroachments made by fuch a Power, but from the juft Apprehenfions that this may,

and

and indeed muſt, prove extremely prejudicial to Commerce in general, and to that of ſeveral Nations in particular ; who, to prevent this, will not ſcruple to take up Arms, as was the Caſe in the two general Wars againſt *France*, as well as in this laſt. Thus it appears, that the *Ballance* of *Power* is not an empty Name, or an idle Thing, but a very juſt and ſignificant, though a new and figurative Expreſſion.

By it we mean the preſerving the ſeveral Governments of *Europe*, as far as may be, in their preſent Condition, and the hindering any Potentate whatever from acquiring ſuch a Degree of Grandeur, as may be dangerous or fatal to thoſe reciprocal Intereſts beforementioned, which as they took Riſe from, are abſolutely neceſſary to the Continuance of Commerce ; and any Attempt upon which, is conſequently felt by every Nation that has any Share of Trade, and in the higheſt Degree as they have moſt Trade, and make the moſt of their Trade, by the *Maritime Powers*. This, when he has attentively conſidered it, the ingenious and judicious Reader will allow to be a fair as well as free Account of a Matter of great Importance ; which, unleſs thoroughly, clearly, and perfectly underſtood, no View of the preſent State of *Europe* can be exhibited worthy of Credit, or capable of anſwering that End which we propoſe.

But notwithſtanding we have ſhewn, without any great Difficulty, how this Political Ballance ariſes ; yet it is not quite ſo eaſy to explain wherein it truly conſiſts. For with reſpect to this, it is very certain that even the ableſt Writers find it a very hard Thing to diveſt themſelves of their Prejudices. As for Inſtance : A *French* Politician takes it for granted that this Ballance ought to be held by the King his Maſter ; and never ſo much as ſuſpects that this will, or ought to be diſputed. At *Vienna* again, there is nothing clearer than that the Right of holding the Ballance is in the Imperial Court, and he who ſhould treat this as chimerical, would be thought as deficient in Senſe, as in good Manners. The moſt judicious and ſenſible Authors that I have met with upon this Subject, are the *Italians*, and particularly the *Venetians* ; for do but grant them that the Sea as well as Land is ſubject to Dominion, and that their Republick has an indubitable Right to the Sovereignty of the *Adriatick*, and they will very readily grant you all that can be deſired in Favour of other Princes and States.

The Struggle therefore for the *Ballance* of *Power*, is in reality a Struggle for Power ; and ſuch as from the different Methods of treating this Queſtion, preſume to ſhew their Sagacity by doubting whether there is any ſuch Thing at all, rather ſhew their Weakneſs ; for though it be true, that in learned Diſputes Men
often

often differ merely about Words, yet it is otherwise in political
Quarrels, for Nations very seldom fall out about nothing. The
last Part therefore of our Task is the hardest, for it consists in
shewing truly where this Ballance lies, which requires more Penetration and Impartiality than we can boast; but, however, we
will do the best we may, and leave the rest to be supplied by the
Observations and Reflections of the judicious Reader.

In the first Place, it is certainly the Interest of all the Powers
in *Europe* to support each other's Independency, and to prevent
any thing that has the Appearance of an Universal Monarchy,
or the introducing the Influence of one Court over the greatest
Part of the rest; because this must be detrimental to the whole,
and prejudicial to the Freedom, Learning, Arts, Manufactures
and Commerce of *Europe* in general.

This we learn not only from the Principles of true Policy, but
also from the unerring Lights of Experience; since it is impossible to assign a Time when the Powers of *Europe* in general
made so mean a Figure as when the Emperor *Charles* V. or his
Son *Philip* II. were nearest the Accomplishment of their ambitious Views, and had in a Manner all the other Potentates
at their Mercy, or at their Devotion.

But besides the general Ballance of Power, there are three particular Ballances which ought to be attended to and supported;
because if any of these be weakened or destroyed, it will be almost impossible to preserve the rest. The first of these is the
Ballance of the *North*, where the Power of *Russia* is chiefly to
be apprehended. There is no answering for the Views of any
Court, because they are perpetually changing; the only Security
that can be had, must result from the prescribing proper Bounds
to all; and in the present Case, this chiefly depends on the Maritime Powers, who are always able and ought to be ever willing
to maintain that Equilibrium there which subsists at present. In
this they have Reason to expect, if she is true to her own Interest, the Concurrence of *France*, to whom an absolute and overbearing Power in the North would be as fatal as to any other
State, because she must become dependent upon it for her Naval Stores, and find her Grandeur in other Respects greatly diminished.

The second Ballance of Power is in *Germany*, where, for the
common Peace and Safety of *Europe*, it is necessary the Constitution of the Empire should be maintained; which however
cannot be done, if either the Imperial Dignity be transferred to
a House more potent than all the rest, or if any other Power be
permitted to give Laws to the Emperor and Empire. At present,

fent, the Ballance of *Germany* feems to depend upon poifing properly the two great Houfes of *Auftria* and *Brandenburgh*, and preventing either from giving a new Form to Things in that Country, which, confidering the Intereft which feveral of its Princes have in other Parts, muft from its Confequences neceffarily throw all *Europe* into Confufion.

The third Ballance is in *Italy* ; where the feveral Princes and States feem to underftand their own Interefts the beft of any Upon this Principle, it feems reafonable to preferve both the Houfes of *Auftria* and *Bourbon* in the Poffeffion of their Dominions in that Country, fince if either fhould be expell'd, the other would foon be abfolutely Mafter of the whole ; for the fame Reafon it is expedient that the firft Branch of the Houfe of *Bourbon* fettled there, fhould not only be Sovereign, but altogether independent, which, in the Courfe of a few Years, would neceffarily change the Face of Affairs there, and bring that Power to act under the fame Political Maxims with the reft of the Princes and States of *Italy*.

It feems likewife requifite for the Security of this Ballance, that the Power of his *Sardinian* Majefty fhould be extended, becaufe every Acceffion of Territory to him, muft fix him more effectually to thofe Principles which conduce to the Peace and Profperity of *Italy*; and tho' Accidents may happen, and for a Time perhaps oblige him to temporize, or it may be act inconfiftently in regard to this Ballance ; yet it is certain nothing but real Neceffity, and being reduced to downright Defpair, can carry him into an Alliance fatal to his own Independency, as well as to the Interefts of his Subjects, and the common Good of *Chriftendom*.

I think it would be needlefs to infift farther upon this Subject, or to enter into a long Difcuffion of the Rights the other Princes of *Europe* have to reduce *that* which would give Law to them all, fince this is fufficiently guarded againft by my firft Principle ; and therefore I fhall only obferve, that Peace and good Neighbourhood, the Encouragement of Arts and Sciences, and the Purfuit of Manufactures and Commerce, as they are agreeable to the Intereft of every particular State, fo they are beft for the whole, and would contribute to render every particular Country of *Europe* infinitely more populous, and the People in all Countries much more happy, than any vain Endeavours to aggrandize particular Families at the Expence of the Human Species,

CHAP. III.

The present State *and* Political Interests *of the* RUSSIAN EMPIRE, *truly aad succinctly represented.*

THERE is nothing more natural in a Work of this Nature than to begin with the Northern Kingdoms of *Europe* ; for in treating of these we shall have an Opportunity to explain thoroughly, and to enforce fully, those Considerations that have been already mentioned, and the political Principles that have been laid down, as well in regard to Nations in general, as to that particular *Ballance* of *Power* which has been for several Ages, and which is like to continue the System of the Northern Crowns. Amongst these, as the Imperial Diadem of *Russia* is by far the most considerable, so there can be nothing more just than to allow it Precedence.

It is not at all requisite that we should enter into the ancient History of this Empire, and, in truth, this is a Circumstance much in our favour ; for nothing was ever covered with deeper Obscurity than that Period of Time amongst the *Russians.* All we know with Certainty is, that about *Eight hundred* Years ago they were converted to Christianity, when their Sovereign married the Sister of one of the *Greek* Emperors ; but after this, they fell under great Difficulties, were absolutely subdued by the potent Monarchs of the *Tartars,* and were scarce heard of or known in *Europe* as a considerable Nation, 'till about the middle of the *fifteenth* Century.

They were then governed by *John Basilowitz,* a Prince justly stigmatized for his Tyranny, but at the same time a Prince who wanted not either a Head or a Heart: he found himself acknowledged the Sovereign of a very large Tract of Country, tho' at the same time the Exercise of his Authority was confined within very narrow Bounds ; for absolute Power has been in all Times, and in all Places, a Thing so terrible, that many different Methods have been used, even in Countries where it is the acknowledged Constitution, to keep it within some Bounds. Amongst the *Russians,* the *Czar,* or supreme Lord, was treated with a Degree of Reverence that favoured not a little of Divine Honour ; but, notwithstanding this, the hereditary Governors of Provinces retained the essential Exercise of Power in their own Hands, and except those extravagant, shameful, and, at the same time, useless Marks of Submission, they left very little more to the supreme Monarch, than the Revenues of the Territory

tory

tory of *Moscow*, for the Support of his Houshold ; whence he was ftiled by Strangers *Grand Duke* of *Muscovy*, a Title never owned by, and indeed hardly known to his Subjects.

But *John Bafilowitz* was not of a Difpofition to be fatisfied in any Degree with this fantaftick Greatnefs ; and therefore, having begun by fowing Jealoufy and Difcord among thefe inferior Princes, he, by Degrees, reduced them all, and, at length, made an Irruption into *Livonia*, pretending it was held of him by the Knights who were in Poffeffion of it, which had terrible Effects. It was in order to cover themfelves from the Oppreffion of fo dreadful a Power, that Part of this Country fubmitted to the *Swedes*, and the Grand Mafter *Gotofred Kettler*, renouncing that Title, fubmitted to the Republick of *Poland*, and accepted as a Fief the *Dutchy* of *Courland*, which he had before held in Sovereignty.

We may form a tolerable Idea of the Loftinefs, and ridiculous Pride of this Conqueror, and fome of his Succeffors, from the following Circumftance ; that they would not vouchfafe to treat with the Kings of *Sweden*, or to have any Intercourfe with them whatever directly ; but left all Tranfactions with that Power to the Governor or *Novogorod* ; upon which ftrange Piece of Vanity, even the late Czar *Peter* I. valued himfelf not a little, in the Manifefto's which he publifhed againft *Charles* the *Twelfth*, during the long War that fubfifted between them.

In the fixteenth Century, the Troubles in the *Ruffian* Empire gave great Advantages to the *Swedes*, who made themfelves Mafters of feveral of the Diftricts nearest to their own Dominions, as well as extended their Conquefts in *Livonia*, which, at laft, humbled the Pride of the *Ruffian* Monarchs fo much, that towards the Clofe of that Century, they were glad to conclude a Peace with *Sweden* ; by which all Pretenfions were given up to *Livonia* and *Efthonia*, the *Swedes*, at the fame time, quitting the Province of *Carelia*, which, together with *Ingria*, they exprefsly acknowledged to be dependent upon the Government of *Novogorod*.

But this Peace lafted not long; for inteftine Divifions breaking out again in *Ruffia*, the *Swedes* made their Advantage of them, as before ; and at laft, having the Czar in a Manner at their Mercy, they were with much ado prevailed upon, by an *Englifh* Minifter fent by King *James* I. to liften to Terms of Accommodation, which produced a Peace figned *February* the twenty-feventh 1616, in the Village of *Stolbowa*, by which the *Ruffians* not only quitted all Claim to *Livonia* and *Efthonia*, but likewife gave up the Provinces of *Ingria* and *Carelia*, together with all the adjacent

cent Country, as far as the River *Neva*, and the Islands at the Mouth of that River.

Thus the Reader sees, how the *Russian* Empire was deprived of those Provinces, she has since recovered from the *Swedes*; which is a Point of great Consequence to be remembered. Nor will it be amiss, to observe here, that it was an established Maxim with the *Swedes*, and indeed, with all the rest of the Northern Powers, to keep the *Russians* as far as possible from the *Baltick*, that they might have no Communication with other *European* Powers; having a just Foresight of those Inconveniencies that might produce, and which they have since felt very severely. It was with this View, that they inserted express Clauses in some of their Treaties with the *Hanse* Towns trading to *Riga*, *Nerva*, and other Places in that Neighbourhood, that they should not furnish the *Muscovites* with any Kind of Arms offensive or defensive, or with any Sort of Military Stores or Ammunition whatever; so apprehensive they were of the internal Strength of that Power, which the rest of the *European* Crowns were scarcely acquainted with, and of which, without Question, they had but very imperfect and indistinct Notions.

The Treaty last mentioned, by which such important Cessions were made to the Crown of *Sweden*, was concluded with *Michael Foedorowitz*, the first Prince of the present reigning Family, who was the Son of a Patriarch of the *Greek* Church, by a Daughter of *John Basilowitz*. He ascended the Throne in 1613, and reigned many Years; during which, the Empire recovered in a great Measure from that deplorable Condition in which he found it. He was succeeded by his Son *Alexius Michaelowitz*, who had some Thoughts of recovering the Provinces torn from his Dominions by the *Swedes*, and with that View entered into a War with *Charles Gustavus*, King of *Sweden*, in which, at first, he had some Success; but a Rebellion breaking out in the Kingdom of *Astracan*, he was obliged to give up his Conquests to the *Swedes*, that he might have Leisure to suppress that Rebellion, which he happily accomplished.

This Monarch died in 1675; he had by his first Wife two Sons, *Fedor*, and *Iwan*, and three Daughters, *Sophia*, *Mary*, and *Catharine*; by his second Consort *Natalia Kirilowna*, the Daughter of his Prime Minister *Kirili Poluchrowitz Narifkin*, he had a Son and a Daughter, *viz. Peter Alexowitz*, born *June* the Eleventh 1672, and *Natalia*. *Fedor* the eldest Son succeeded his Father, and being of a sickly Constitution, was assisted in his Administration by his Sister *Sophia*. He died in 1682, and knowing his Brother *Iwan* to be yet less capable of governing, than himself, he nominated *Peter*, his younger Brother, for his Successor;

Succeffor ; but by the Intereft of the Princefs *Sophia*, after *Fedor*'s Demife, the elder Brother was alfo affociated with him in the Government ; but by Reafon of his Incapacity, never had any confiderable Share in the Adminiftration.

This was that *Peter Alexowitz* juftly furnamed *the Great*, the Father and Founder of that *Ruffian* Empire, which makes fo glorious a Figure at this Day, and which will be known, as one of the greateft Powers in the World, to lateft Pofterity. At the Time of his Acceffion, he found the greateft Part of his Dominions mere Defarts, fprinkled here and there with a few great Cities, and fcarce defended by any Fortreffes of Confequence. The Port of *Archangel* was almoft the only one in his Territories ; at leaft, that was frequented by Strangers : He was not only very little refpected, but on many Occafions infulted, by his Neighbours, amongft whom the barbarous, but martial Nation of *Crim Tartars*, entered his Territories at Pleafure, and had formerly been Mafters of his Capital. The *Turks* looked upon him as their Dependent ; the *Poles* were more than a Match for him ; and the *Swedes* contemn'd him. But at the Time of his Deceafe, he left Things in quite another Condition. He had torn from *Sweden* fome of her beft Provinces, or rather recovered thofe of which his Anceftors were defpoiled ; and in them he erected his new Capital of *Peterfburgh*. He taught, not his Neighbours only, but all *Europe* to refpect him ; and eftablifhed not barely a new Power in the North, but a new Maritime Power, created by his own Skill ; and I may fay literally, wrought with his own Hands ; for he knew how to build Ships, as well as to command them ; and was not only a Soldier and Seaman, as well as Statefman, but was all thefe in Perfection. He was called, and which was a much higher Honour, he deferved to be called, the Father of his *Country*. He affumed the Title of EMPEROR, and left it to his Confort, and his Family, who now enjoy it without Difpute, as an Inheritance purchafed by his Virtue.

This great Monarch died in the Beginning of the Year 1725, and was fucceeded by his fecond Confort, the Emprefs *Catharine*, a Lady whom he had raifed to his Bed, purely from the Confideration of her Merit. She governed this great Empire on the fame Principles by which it was founded ; and during her whole Reign was refpected by her own Subjects, and by all the Powers of *Europe*, as the worthy Succeffor of fo great a Monarch. Yet fhe enjoy'd this high Dignity but for a very fhort Space, dying in the Month of *May* 1727, and leaving the Empire to the Grandfon of her deceafed Lord. *Ruffia*, from being governed by a Woman, fell under the Dominion of a Child, who was the Emperor *Peter* II. Grandfon to *Peter the Great*, the laft

Heir

Heir Male of his Family, and in the Hands of an ambitious Statesman, Prince *Menzikoff*, the Favourite of *Peter*, and no less so of the late Czarina *Catharine*.

We may easily conceive that the Czar *Peter* I. had laid the Foundations of the *Russian* Monarchy deep, when we see, that it not only continued to subsist, but to flourish also, notwithstanding these Accidents, than which none could be more dangerous in their Nature to a new-raised Government. Prince *Menzikoff* was a Man of boundless Ambition, and at the Time of the young Emperor's Accession, had the whole Power of the Empire in his Hands. He had framed a Design of raising his Daughter to the Rank of Empress; and it is not improbable that he might have succeeded in this View, if he had not by an Act of Insolence incurred the young Emperor's Displeasure, who tho' he was but twelve Years old at his Accession, yet had so much Sense and Spirit, that he disgraced and banished this too powerful Subject, and confiscated all his Estate. He afterwards raised the Princes *Dolgorouki* to the highest Employments in the Empire, and actually espoused the Princess *Catharine*, Daughter to Prince *Alexis*, and Sister to the Princes *Sergius* and *John*; but before the Marriage was consummated, he was seized with the Small-Pox, of which he died on the 19th of *January* 1730.

The History of the Imperial Family is, in this Country, the History of the Empire; which is the Reason that we insist upon it; and from thence alone the Reader may collect what is of greatest Consequence towards understanding the publick Occurrences in *Russia*. Upon the Death of the Emperor *Peter* II. the regular Succession in that Empire was at a stand. According to the Will of the Empress *Catharine*, her eldest Daughter *Anne Petrowna*, Dutchess of *Holstein*, ought to have been called to the Throne, but she died the Year after her Mother, and left behind her a Son, who was at that Time about two Years old; and therefore the Senate and Nobility of *Russia*, to avoid so tedious a Minority, resolved not to adhere to this Will; for which they established this Pretence, that it was vacated by the Declaration of the late Emperor upon his Death-bed, who had appointed another Successor, though at first they could not agree among themselves who they should declare this Successor to be; by which it was very manifest, that notwithstanding their Assertions, the young Emperor in reality made no such Declaration.

It has been reported, that some of the principal Nobility had Thoughts of changing the Government into a Republick, but that finding this would be impracticable, they framed a new Scheme of Rule, which was, to govern the Empire themselves, felves, allowing only the Name and Enfigns of Sovereign Authority to one of the Imperial Family. The next Confideration was, who this Perfon fhould be, and after fome Debate, they caft their Eyes upon the Princefs *Anna Iwanowna*, Dutchefs of *Courland*, of the Imperial Line indeed, but out of all the Rules of Succeffion. She was the fecond Daughter of the Emperor *Iwan* or *John*, elder Brother to *Peter the Great*, and who, as we before obferved, was for fome time his Affociate in the Empire; but then fhe had an elder Sifter *Catharine Iwanowna*, who was married to the Duke of *Mecklenbourg*, to whom, if the Succeffion was to devolve firft on the Daughters of the elder Brother, the Imperial Crown fhould have come, but her Hufband was engaged in a kind of Civil War with his Nobility; and therefore it was given out, that for fecuring the Peace and Tranquillity of his Subjects, the young Emperor *Peter* II. paffing her by, had called her younger Sifter to the Succeffion, which, foon after his Death, fhe was invited to accept.

The Princes *Dolgorouki* and their Faction, who took upon them the Management of this Affair, affigned the new Emprefs a Council, framed a new Conftitution for the Empire, and limited her Authority as they thought proper; to which Regulations fhe readily confented. But as foon as the *Czarina* was fixed upon the Throne, fhe cancelled all thefe Limitations, and banifhed the Authors of them. She made choice of grave and wife Men for her Minifters, and gave the Command of her Armies to very able and experienced Generals, which enabled her to govern with great Reputation, and to maintain the Credit of her Empire, with regard to the reft of *Europe*, in as high a Degree as any of her Predeceffors. She afforded the late Emperor of *Germany*, *Charles* VI. powerful Succours againft the Houfe of *Bourbon*; fhe feated the prefent King of *Poland* upon the Throne of his Father, notwithftanding all the Arts, and in Spite of the Arms of *France*; fhe made War againft the *Turks* with great Succefs, and in the Courfe of the War totally ruined the Power of the *Crim Tartars*. In a Word, fhe made her Government as much revered as from the Power of her extended Dominions it ought to be, and concluded fuch Alliances with Foreign States, as were moft proper for maintaining that Syftem of Government, which fhe laboured to eftablifh.

She brought to her Court her Niece, the Princefs *Ann* of *Mecklenbourg*, the Daughter of her eldeft Sifter, and married her to Prince *Anthony Ulric* of *Brunfwick Beveren*, refolving to call the Iffue of this Marriage to the Succeffion. The only Error in her Government was, the confiding almoft wholly in Strangers, and

D   particularly

particularly *Germans*, with whom she filled her Councils and Armies, which raised a strong Spirit of Envy and Resentment in the *Russian* Nobility, who could not bear with Patience, living in a State of Subjection to Foreigners. This Disposition began to shew itself with great Vehemence towards the latter End of the Life of the Empress, who in order to extinguish it, had recourse to extraordinary Acts of Severity, which were so far from having the desired Effect, that they highly increased it, insomuch that the *Czarina* became very apprehensive of the Consequences, for defeating of which she made the best Provision that was in her Power.

The Princess of *Mecklenbourg* was delivered of a Son, on the Twelfth of *August*, whom the *Czarina*, according to the *Russian* Constitution established by *Peter the Great*, named her Successor, and directed that the Prince his Father, and the Grand Dutchess his Mother, should be his Guardians; she likewise appointed a Council about the young Emperor, whom she thought the most capable of sustaining the Weight of Affairs, and of preserving Things in that Condition wherein she intended to leave them. At the Head of this Council, with the Title of Regent, was the then Duke of *Courland*, her great Favourite, whom she had raised to that Dignity, and who had the principal Direction of Affairs in her Reign. Baron *Osterman*, High Chancellor of *Russia*, had the Rank of Prime Minister, a Person of great Experience, and through whose Hands, whatever related to Foreign Affairs, had passed for many Years. Count *Munich*, who had served with so much Reputation against the *Turks*, was at the Head of the Army, with the Title of Field-Marshal; so that there seemed no great Reason to doubt the Government might be carried on as well as in the former Minority; and flattered with these fair Hopes, the Empress *Anna Iwanowna* died in *October* 1740.

The Emperor was immediately owned by the Senate and People in his Cradle, and the Marquis *de la Chetardie*, the *French* Minister, made his Imperial Majesty a long Speech upon the Occasion, in which he assured him of the sincere Friendship of *Louis* XV. to *Iwan*, or *John*, Sovereign of all the *Russians*. But as if Professions of *French* Friendship were ominous to all Princes, it was not long before it appeared, that this Government could not subsist in the Form in which it stood by the late Empress's Will. The Prince of *Brunswick* and the Grand Dutchess themselves ventured upon a great Alteration; for they thought fit not only to remove from his Share in the Government, but to seize on the Person of the Duke of *Courland*, and to banish him and his Family into *Siberia*. This was a great Stroke, and yet

yet it was managed with so much Address and Dexterity, as not to occasion any great Stir of Bloodshed in the Execution, and hardly any Noise or Tumult in its Consequences, which tho' at that Time regarded as a very favourable Circumstance, served, if not for a Precedent, at least for a Prelude to a Revolution of far greater Importance, with a succinct Account of which we shall conclude our Historical Memoirs of this Empire.

Peter the Great left behind him a Daughter, whose Name was *Elizabeth Petrowna*, a Lady of distinguished Accomplishments, and now about thirty-eight Years of Age. She had lived at Court, during the last Reign, in a Manner and under Circumstances far enough from being suitable to her Birth : and the Prudence of her Behaviour, joined to that Magnanimity with which she had supported her Misfortunes, had such an Influence on all who beheld her, that she had long reigned in the Hearts of her People, while others reigned upon the Throne. At last, the whole *Russian* Nation, Princes, Nobility, Senators, Soldiers, and even the Populace, testified such an Affection for her, that some who had served her Father with Fidelity, and now enjoyed the Rewards of their Services, resolved to hazard all for her Deliverance, and to risque every thing to recover her just Rights. They attempted it, and Providence gave a Blessing to the Attempt; this Revolution happened in a single Night. On the fifth of *December* the Princess *Elizabeth* was a kind of Prisoner in the Imperial Palace, and on the sixth she was seated on the Imperial Throne, and, the Tongues of her Subjects being set at Liberty, saluted Empress of all the *Russians* by the unanimous Voice of all the People.

The Empress *Elizabeth* was no sooner possessed of the Crown of her illustrious Ancestors, than she gave the highest Marks of those Virtues which render'd her worthy of that Elevation, and which her former Circumstances had conceal'd. She rewarded beyond their Expectations such as had contributed to this great Revolution, and she suffer'd those who had persecuted her under the former Reign, to escape much better than they had Reason to expect. She caused many of the Abuses that had been committed in the Management of the Affairs of the Empire to be redressed. She restored the great Families of *Russia* to their just Ranks, and entrusted them with the principal Employments in the Government. As to the Conduct of Foreign Affairs, they suffered little Alteration ; for the Empress did not affect to change all, but only such Measures of the preceding Government as were not calculated for the Benefit of her Subjects; and by this wise and moderate Behaviour, she secured Respect to

her

her Government abroad, as by her Tenderneſs and maternal Affection for her People, ſhe diffuſed the moſt perfect Serenity through all her Dominions.

But her Conduct appeared in nothing more wiſe and amiable, than in the Care ſhe took for ſettling the Succeſſion, which ſhe knew muſt be fixed, before ſhe could hope to ſee her Government firmly eſtabliſhed. She therefore reſolved to ſend for her Nephew, the young Duke of *Holſtein*, who was the preſumptive Heir to the Imperial Crown, under the original Eſtabliſhment of the Emperor *Peter the Great*. The Name of this young Prince is *Charles Peter Ulric*, born the Tenth of *February*, 1728, who ſoon after his Arrival at *Peterſburgh*, was declared Grand Duke of *Ruſſia*, and Heir Apparent of the Empire, in which Quality he has been acknowledged by the Senate, as well as by all the Nobility of that great Empire, with the utmoſt Chearfulneſs poſſible.

This Deduction will give the Reader a clear Idea of the preſent Situation of Things in *Ruſſia*, and of the Motives which have induced the *Czarina* to provide with ſo much Diligence for the Eſtabliſhment of the Houſe of *Holſtein*; which will very ſoon occupy all the Thrones in the North, and conſequently appear one of the moſt conſiderable Families that has been known in *Europe*. The Houſe of *Oldenbourg*, of which are the preſent Royal Family of *Denmark*, is the ſame with that of *Holſtein*. The King of *Sweden*, who certainly owes his Dignity to the Interpoſition of the *Czarina*, is the near Relation, and as ſuch was Adminiſtrator of the Dominions of the Duke of *Holſtein*, now Grand Duke and Heir of *Ruſſia*. Prince *Auguſtus* of *Holſtein* may poſſibly obtain the Dutchy of *Courland*, and if that ſhould ever happen, this Houſe will be truly formidable; and if all its Branches unite their Intereſts, muſt neceſſarily have a great Influence on the general Affairs of *Europe*. Such an Influence as our modern Politicians ſeem not to have ſufficiently conſider'd, but which I conceive will daily diſplay itſelf more and more.

The Hiſtory of *Ruſſia* thus diſpatched, we come next to the Government of this great Empire; a Subject very little underſtood, but which may be, however, explained in a very few Words. The Czar, *Peter the Great*, was the Legiſlator of his Dominions; and though no Prince was more abſolute than himſelf, yet it is certain that he aimed at ſetting ſome Bounds to the Power of his Succeſſors; and for this Reaſon he eſtabliſhed a Senate, in which it is thought that he had the Government of *France* in View, and that he meant this ſhould

resemble

resemble the Parliament of *Paris*, which it does in many Respects, and in none more than this, that it serves to sanctify and give the Form and Authority of Laws to Acts that spring from the Will of the Prince.

But still the old Constitution prevails, and the true Government of *Russia* is what it always was, despotic. In Minorities indeed, and in other Conjunctures, such as in the late Revolutions, there seems to be an actual Power attributed to the Senate, which to People at a Distance may represent the Form of Rule in *Russia* as a limited Government; but when we come to examine it more closely, we shall perceive so strict a Conformity between the Will of the Prince and the Decrees of this Assembly, as must sufficiently convince us of the Truth of what has been before laid down, *viz.* that the Imperial Power is rather strengthened than controuled by their Proceedings. As to the several Colleges, as they are stiled in *Russia*, or as they are called by us, Boards; to which the various Branches of the Administration are assigned; though the Form is *German*, yet the Thing is *French*; and *Peter the Great* contrived them after the Model of the several Councils in *France*. The High Chancellor is generally considered as the Prime Minister, and the Vice Chancellor as his Coadjutor. The present Chancellor is the Count *de Bestucheff*, a Man of moderate Views, indefatigable in Business, and very easy of Access. The Vice Chancellor is Count *Woronzoff*, who spent some time in making a Tour to the principal Courts in *Europe*.

The Political Interests of *Russia*, with respect to foreign Nations, are not either so many, or so complicated, as might be expected, considering the Extent and Situation of the Empire, which gives a Right to its Monarchs, of being considered as *Asiatic* as well as *European* Powers. The Northern Parts of the Empire, from the Frontiers of the *Swedish* Dominions to those of *China* and *Japan*, are guarded in such a Manner as to be secure not only from Danger, but from Apprehensions; having on that Side a Sea, hitherto impenetrable, and through which, if any Passage could be found, it must turn to the Benefit, but can never prove of any Disadvantage to the Subjects of *Russia*; which is a Point of great Consequence, and, as I take it, is a Blessing scarce known to any other Country than this. The Frontiers of the Empire towards *China* are also inaccessible, as consisting of Desarts impenetrable by Armies, but which yield a tolerable Passage for Caravans; so that the *Russians* may always reckon on the Friendship of the *Chinese*; and whenever they apply themselves seriously thereto, may make

make this Friendſhip turn to their Advantage. The *Tartars* inhabiting the Countries between *Ruſſia* and *Perſia*, are no longer formidable to the firſt-mentioned Empire; on the contrary, they all reſpect it, and many of them have willingly ſubmitted, and become Vaſſals to it. The *Caſpian* Sea, and the Dominions which the *Ruſſians* have on that Side, give them a fair Opening into *Perſia*, which they have already improved ſo as to gain to themſelves a very advantageous Trade, and this by Degrees may be extended perhaps as far as the *Eaſt-Indies.*

It will always be the Intereſt of *Ruſſia* to cultivate a good Underſtanding with the *Shâh*; but in caſe of a Rupture, ſhe would not have much to fear, ſince the Frontiers of *Perſia* being open, ſhe might ſoon make an End of the War, by leting looſe upon them the *Tartars*, who are her Tributaries; the *Turks*, and their Aſſociates the *Crim Tartars*, are more dangerous Enemies, but at preſent, the Circumſtances of the *Porte* are ſuch as will ſcarce allow her to break with the *Ruſſians*, if ſhe had concluded a Peace with *Perſia*; and we ſhall hereafter ſee, that *Ruſſia* can never want the Power of defending herſelf on this Side, or even of making the *Turks* ſenſible of the Folly of breaking with her wantonly, and without juſt Provocation. The two great Chriſtian Principalities dependent upon that Empire, have always a Bias in Favour of the *Ruſſians*; and therefore, as we have ſhewn in diſcourſing of the Religions in *Europe*, the *Turks* run a greater Hazard by making War with this, than with any other Nation.

The Intereſts of *Ruſſia* in *Europe*, are not hard to aſſign: As to *Sweden*, it is of great Conſequence to live upon good Terms with that Crown; and, on the other Hand, the Superiority of *Ruſſia*, when forced into a War, has been of late rendered ſo apparent, that there are good Grounds to expect the *Swedes* will continue quiet on that Side for a long Series of Time, even ſuppoſing that no Streſs ſhould be laid on the natural Connections between the two Branches of the Houſe of *Holſtein*, when they ſhall come to govern theſe Nations. As it is requiſite for the Court of *Peterſburgh* to be well with the *Swedes* on one Side, ſo it imports them no leſs to be upon good Terms with the *Poles* on the other; for which Reaſon we ſee the late *Czarina* omitted nothing to ſet the preſent King *Auguſtus* upon the Throne of *Poland*, well knowing that his Intereſts were of ſuch a Nature, as muſt without Treaties bind him effectually to hers.

There ſeems to be no great Cauſe of Intercourſe between *Ruſſia* and *Denmark*, farther than what reſults from Attention

to

to the Ballance of Power in the North, which will always incline a wise Administration in this Empire, to keep the Scales as even as may be between this Crown and that of *Sweden*; of late indeed, there is another Ground of Connection arising from the Disputes between the House of *Holstein* and the Crown of *Denmark*, in relation to the Dutchy of *Sleswick*, for accommodating of which we are told there is a Treaty now on Foot, and pretty far advanced.

The Interests of *Russia* with respect to the House of *Austria*, are its most material Concern; for while these Imperial Houses are united, not only by general Alliances, but by a due and hearty Regard for each others Prosperity, neither has much to fear from the *Turks*; but if they are divided, and the *Ottomans* should recover their ancient Power, they may be formidable to both. As to *Prussia*, of late Years great Regard has been due, and in succeeding Times it is like to claim a greater; but certainly if these two Powers pursue their true Interests, and are not misled by ambitious Views, they are not like to fall out. The Maritime Powers are the natural Allies, and hitherto have been, and are like to be fast Friends to *Russia*. As to the other Potentates of *Europe*, their Dominions lie at too great a Distance for *Russia* to have any great Intercourse with them of either sort: and with respect to the House of *Bourbon*, as the Court of *Petersburgh* has never had any Cause to like, so in spite of all its Power, there is no Probability of its ever seeing much Reason to fear it.

We have hitherto considered the Interests of this Empire in the most favourable Point of View, but it must be allowed, that she is not altogether free from Dangers and Apprehensions. It is not at all impossible, that Disputes may arise about the Succession: The Party of the late Emperor *John*, though at present seemingly extinct, may hereafter revive; and it is very likely that in such a Case, some neighbouring Powers that are jealous of *Russia* may likewise interfere. It may also happen, that the Imperial Prince may have no Issue, and in that Case the Succession must devolve upon the young Prince *John* beforementioned, who is the last Heir Male of the Imperial Line; besides, it is not altogether impossible that such a Confederacy might be formed in the North, as would greatly distress the *Russians*; but then we suppose, that *Sweden, Denmark, Poland,* and *Prussia,* should unite, and continue united in this League, which is far from being probable.

The Reader may possibly wonder, considering the present State of things, that I should venture to lay down these Points in such clear and precise terms, when, by making use of general

Expressions,

Expreſſions, I might, in all Appearance, guard better againſt the Danger of Contradiction. But, in Anſwer to this, let me obſerve, that in the very ſame Proportion an Author ſhews his Tenderneſs for his Character in this Reſpect, he ſhews a Diſregard for his Readers. The Value of political Principles muſt appear, by their Compariſon with future Events; for, if they give us no Light into theſe, where is their Uſe? It is very certain, that the great Power of the *Ruſſian* Empire, and her cloſe Connection with the Houſe of *Auſtria*, has excited a Spirit of Suſpicion and Jealouſy in the North, to which alſo the particular Views of ſeveral Powers have not a little contributed; but notwithſtanding this, what has been before laid down remains not at all the leſs certain.

It does not follow, that becauſe both Sides have armed and entered into Alliances, in caſe of a War, that therefore a War muſt neceſſarily enſue; or, even if that ſhould fall out, that it muſt create an extraordinary Alteration in the State of Things either one way or the other. In reference to the firſt, it muſt be evident to all competent Judges, that the Scales are pretty even, and therefore, notwithſtanding theſe terrifying Appearances, it is ſo far from being impoſſible, that it is very far from being improbable, a pacifick Negotiation may yet diſſipate theſe Clouds, and once more procure fair Weather in the North. But if, all Negotiations failing, a War ſhould actually break out, the Turn of that War muſt remain very uncertain, ſince the Force of the *Ruſſian* Empire is really much greater than is commonly imagined, and would be found ſo in ſuch a Caſe.

We may add to this, that as Winds are neceſſary to purge the Air, and as the Emotions of Human Paſſions, provided they are not too violent, exhilarate the Spirits, and contribute to bodily Health; ſo in great States, more eſpecially when there is an Appearance of bad Humours, Wars are ſo far from being inconvenient, that on the contrary, they are both ſalutary and expedient. We may from hence form a Judgment of the Abilities of thoſe Miniſters, who direct at preſent the Councils of this Empire, and who, by ſhewing an unſhaken Steadineſs in purſuing that Syſtem which they have eſtabliſhed, have at leaſt raiſed the Credit of their Government to a very high Degree, and for ſome time made this Empire not only the Arbiter of all Differences in the North, but have likewiſe extended its Influence to the moſt diſtant Parts of *Europe*; ſince it is univerſally confeſſed, that the March of the Auxiliaries was the Meaſure that contributed moſt to the Concluſion of the Definitive Treaty at *Aix la Chapelle.*

Before

Before we conclude this Chapter, it will be proper to put the Reader in mind of some things that regard the future State of this Empire. If the Imperial Prince should have Issue, there is very little Reason to doubt, that sooner or later the present King of *Sweden* will consider the Interests of the House of *Holstein*, and the great Advantages that may result from pursuing them with Steadiness and Vigour, as shall be more fully shewn in its proper Place. On the other hand, if the Imperial Prince of *Russia* has no Issue, it may open a Way to the settling the Succession of this Empire in a Method very agreeable to the natural Laws of Hereditary Monarchies, and to the mutual Satisfaction of all Parties : Neither can it be supposed, that political Points so obvious in themselves, and so important in their Natures, should not be taken into the Views of all the Potentates, who interest themselves in the Affairs of the North ; and tho' for a Season, and in consequence of the Humours of reigning Princes, accidental Interests may direct all things ; yet, in process of Time, and in consequence of the Alterations that must necessarily make, the real and permanent Interests of every Government will prevail. By the Way, it deserves the Reader's Notice, that in the present State of Things, the true Interests of this Empire will certainly be the Rules of the reigning Czarina's Government ; for remaining single, and having no particular Desires or Designs to gratify, the Peace and Prosperity of her Government can depend on nothing else.

In consequence of this, a constant and firm Adherence to that System, best calculated to promote the Good of her Subjects, and the Glory of the Empire, will be the standing Maxim in the Czarina's Councils. As such a Conduct cannot fail of having a strong Tendency to promote Peace and Satisfaction at home, and to secure the Attachment of the Allies of *Russia*, by maintaining the Credit of the Administration abroad ; there are no Grounds to apprehend, at least in our Times, any great Inconveniencies or extraordinary Alterations should ensue. We may likewise add, that Things remaining, as they are like to remain, in their present Posture, for a few Years, the Advantages of these Measures will become more and more perceptible, and a proper Sense of Loyalty and Gratitude diffuse itself through the Inhabitants, even of the remotest Provinces of that wide Empire, which is certainly in a very thriving Condition, and will, by Degrees, in consequence of the Improvements that are daily making, come to extend its Power and Influence much farther than those who are unacquainted with or unattentive to political Principles can possibly conceive.

C H A P.

CHAP. IV.

The Present State, *Modern* History, Constitution, Interests, *and* Political Views *of the Crown of* SWEDEN.

THE next of the Northern Potentates after *Ruffia* is *Sweden*. In the laft Age, the Monarchs of this Country were very juftly efteemed the moft powerful in thefe Parts, and indeed, fometimes their Power was fo great, as to enable them to act againft, or at leaft, not to be borne down by the Confederacy of all the other Northern Powers taken together. The Kingdom of *Sweden*, and the Great Dutchy of *Finland*, with the Territories dependent upon them, ftretching from the Coafts of the *Baltick* on one Side, to thofe of the Northern Ocean on the other, are Countries of a large Extent: And tho' in many Places they are little better than Defarts, Moraffes, or impenetrable Forefts; yet, amongft the Mountains and Woods there are found many fair and fruitful Spots. Their great Lakes are full of Fifh, and their craggy Rocks, and even their rudeft Hills, produce the richeft Mines of Iron and Copper; fo that as on the one hand they want not the Neceffaries of Life, (for with proper Cultivation and Care, they may well procure Corn and Cattle fufficient for their own Ufe) fo on the other, they are not deftitute of valuable Commodities, for the fecuring a Trade fufficient to fupply them with the Conveniencies of Life from other Nations, feated in richer Soils, and in more agreeable Climates.

But as nothing can be had in this Country without Labour, as the Air is cold and fharp, and the Soil generally fpeaking rugged and ungrateful, the common People are confequently a Race of Men as hardy, patient, and robuft, as any in *Europe*; and preferve in full Vigour their Abilities both of Body and Mind to a very advanced Age. They have been always very juftly efteemed a martial People; but for many Ages this Country was torn with civil Diffentions, to fuch a Degree, as that the Inhabitants rather exercifed their Valour upon themfelves, than upon their Neighbours; fo that they made no great Figure in the World, and were fo far from being confidered by the reft of *Europe*, that their Force was very little known, and lefs regarded. The famous Duke of *Rohan*, one of the greateft Politicians, as well as one of the moft judicious Writers of his Time, gives us a fingular Inftance of this. He obferves, that the Chancellor of *Navarre* having written a Treatife to vindicate the Claim of his

Mafter,

Master, afterwards HENRY IV. to the Crown of *France*, and finding some Objections made against it, which he thought very trifling and insignificant, expressed himself to the following Effect, *viz. That such kind of* Notions *might probably pass for Arguments in* Egypt, *or in* Sweden, *tho' they could scarce be considered as such in* France. This great Man, who had both Parts and Learning, had however very little Foresight, that in the Space of Half a Century, *Sweden,* which he considered in so contemptible a Light, would become one of the most considerable Powers in *Christendom,* and an Ally, of all others, of the greatest Use to *France,* as well as the most dangerous Enemy to the House of *Austria.*

Thus we see, of how great Consequence it is, to have an accurate and perfect Idea of the State of those Countries that make a small, as well as of such as cause a great Noise in the World ; for sometimes a single GENIUS changes intirely the Condition and Circumstances of a whole Nation, as *Peter the Great* did the *Russians,* and *Gustavus Adolphus* the People of whom we are now speaking. It has likewise fallen out, that the deep Distress of a Nation becomes the Cause of its future Prosperity, as happened in the Case of the Inhabitants of the *United Netherlands,* who owe all their Greatness to that Spirit of Industry and Trade, of Patience, Fortitude, and Diligence, by which they became for a Time, the first Maritime Power in *Europe,* to the galling Oppression of the *Spanish* Yoke. In the very same manner, the *Swedes,* who in the last Century rendered themselves so powerful and conspicuous, by their military Virtues and their Conquests, finding themselves weakened and exhausted by the continual Wars of the late *Charles* XII. and all Hopes of Recovery check'd by the superior Power of the *Russian* Empire, found themselves under a Necessity of improving their Country, and extending their Trade, in order to repair in some Measure the Losses they had sustained. And though for a Time this was looked upon rather as a right Intention, than a Scheme likely to be attended with any great Success, yet it is now certain, that they have prosecuted both these Views with surprizing Advantage ; and if the hot Fit of Ambition had not returned upon them too soon, might have grown both wealthy and formidable, without any Opposition from their Neighbours.

To obtain a tolerable Degree of Light into these Matters, and to put ourselves into a Condition of forming a just Idea of the Strength and Forces of this Crown, so as that we may be able to see what Progress it is capable of making, in succeeding Times, we must look a little into the Causes of those remarkable Changes in her Circumstances, as a Nation, that have been
already

already briefly mentioned; which can be only done, by taking a short Survey of the principal Events that have happened in this Country, and their Consequences. By this Method we shall not barely gain a competent Knowledge of the *Swedish* History, and of its Connection with the general Affairs of *Europe*; but, which is of at least as great, or even greater Importance, we shall obtain a thorough Acquaintance with the Genius, Temper, and Spirit of the People. For, as by attentively considering the Works of great Artists, we may not only discover the Nature of that Skill and Knowledge by which they were contrived, but also derive some Intelligence of the Tools and Instruments with which they were wrought; so in contemplating the Atchievements of great Princes, we do not simply distinguish the Strength of their Abilities, but the Temper also, and Virtues of their Subjects, by whose Assistance those mighty Actions were atchieved; since in Politicks, and in War, as well as in other Things, there must be either a natural, or an artifical Aptness in the Materials, before any great Structure can be raised, or any extensive Conquests attained.

There is no need, however, to go higher in this respect than *Gustavus Adolphus*, who ascended the Throne of *Sweden* in 1611. He was a Prince of great Abilities, which manifested themselves so clearly in his Youth, that the States thought fit to give him the entire Administration of Affairs soon after his Accession to the Crown, though he was then but Eighteen. He found his Kingdom the Lowest and Weakest, as he left it the Greatest and most Powerful, in the North. He had two Wars upon his Hands in the earliest Part of his Reign, and he ended them both with great Prudence; for perceiving that the Forces of his Kingdom were not at all proportioned to its Occasions, he very wisely purchased a Peace with *Denmark* at the Expence of one Million of Crowns, for the Payment of which there was a Time limited, which he very honestly discharged when his Affairs were mended, and when, if he had been so inclined, he wanted not plausible Pretences for refusing to comply with that Treaty. He recovered by this Means those Fortresses which the *Danes* had taken, and laying hold of this favourable Opportunity, he turned his Arms against the *Russians*, from whom he took great Part of *Livonia, Ingermania*, and the City of *Kexholm*, the Possession of which he secured by a Treaty concluded under the Mediation of *Great Britain*.

He turned his Arms next against the *Poles*, with whom he maintained a long War, which proved very advantageous to *Sweden*, and procured for her the remaining Part of *Livonia*, and the important City of *Riga*. In this War the *Poles* were assisted fifted by the Emperor, which gave sufficient Provocation to *Gustavus* to declare himself against the House of *Austria*, the Power of which was then formidable to all *Europe*, and which neverthelefs he broke in a short space of Time, and with a very small Force. He was called into *Germany* by the Proteftants, and on the 24th of *June* 1630, he landed at the Mouth of the *Oder* with an Army which confifted of only sixteen Troops of Horfe, and ninety-two Companies of Foot, making in all but eight thoufand Men. He soon made himfelf Mafter of *Stetin*, and a great part of *Pomerania*; upon which all the Proteftants in *Germany* declared for him, and in the Beginning of the fucceeding Year he concluded a Treaty of Alliance with the Crown of *France*.

King *Gustavus* soon after took the City of *Francfort* upon the *Oder*, and sent his Deputies to the General Aflembly of the Proteftants at *Leipfick*, where they quickly difcovered that the Elector of *Brandenburgh* was diffident, and the Elector of *Saxony* jealous of the King their Mafter. *Gustavus* being determined to finish what he had so happily begun, forced the former to put into his Hands fuch Places as were neceflary to secure him a Retreat, and left the latter to be diftreffed by the *Imperialifts*, till he was conftrained to call him to his Affiftance, which on *Sep.* 7, 1631, produced the glorious Battle of *Leipfick*, in which he routed the famous Count *Tilly*, who commanded 40,000 old Troops, killing 7,000 upon the Spot, making 5,000 Prifoners, and taking above an Hundred Colours and Standards. After this he carried the War into *Franconia*, and leaving there a Part of his Army, he with the reft marched into *Bavaria*, where in the Paffage of the *Lech* Count *Tilly* was killed with a Cannon-fhot: After which the King drove the *Imperialifts* out of all the open Country, and made himfelf Mafter of *Munich*.

He not long after attacked Count *Wallestein* in his Intrenchments, but was repulfed with lofs. He augmented however his Conquefts after this, till the Elector of *Saxony* called him again to his Affiftance, which that Monarch did not refufe, though it was entirely owing to his fluctuating Conduct that the War had not being ended long before. On his advancing towards the *Imperialifts*, the King sent Orders to Prince *George* of *Lunenburgh* to join him with the Forces under his Command; but being informed that the *Imperial* General had detached Count *Pappenheim* with some thoufand Men, he refolved to attack him without waiting for the Duke of *Lunenburgh*; which he accordingly did in the Plain of *Lutzen*, on the 16th of *Nov.* 1632; in which Battle the

Swedifh

Swedish Foot having routed the *Imperialists*, and seized their Cannon, the King thinking the Horse did not advance fast enough to the Pursuit, put himself before them in passing a small River, on the other Side of which he was found dead, having his Arm broke by one Musket-shot, and another entering his Back, had passed through his Body.

There were great Suspicions of Treachery in this case, some imputing it to Persons hired by Cardinal *Richlieu*, but *Puffendorf* fixes it expressly upon the Duke of *Saxe-Lawenburgh*. However it was, the King's Death was soon known, which instead of abating, heightened the Courage of the *Swedes* into Fury, so that when Count *Pappenheim* returned with his Detachment, and rallied the *Imperialists*, they again attacked, and again defeated them, which Circumstance does the highest Honour to the *Swedish* Troops. Thus fell this Great Conqueror in the Arms of Victory; and it was very remarkable, so formidable he was become, that his Death was no less grateful to his Allies, than to his Enemies; but his Courage, Virtue and Fortune, having raised him to the highest Pitch of Greatness and Glory, his Memory will be always revered by such as are well-affected to the Protestant Religion and the Liberties of *Germany*, both which he saved from Destruction, by his incomparable Wisdom, and his successful Arms.

As *Gustavus Adolphus* extended the Dominions, and raised the Reputation of *Sweden* Abroad, so he likewise acted the Part of a Legislator at Home, and reduced the Constitution of his Country into Order, which he would certainly have improved if he had lived to return into his own Dominions. In Virtue, however, of his Regulations, the Crown, which was before intailed only on the Male Line, descended to his Daughter *Christina*, a Child of six Years old; which Minority, though it seemed to threaten the Ruin, proved, in reality, the great Security of *Sweden*; for the King of *Denmark* and the Elector of *Brandenburgh* remained firm to the Engagements into which they had entered with *Gustavus*, and the rest of the Allies became less apprehensive of the Power of that Crown, than they had been in the Life-time of that King.

The Chancellor *Axel Oxenstiern*, to whom the whole Management of Affairs in *Germany* was committed, made so right a use of these favourable Circumstances, and managed all Things so wisely and so well, that at the close of the War which lasted several Years, the *Swedes* were possessed of above one hundred fortified Places, and had an Army on foot of upwards of an hundred thousand Men, which enabled them so effectually to

maintain

maintain their Pretensions, that on the Conclusion of the Peace of *Munster*, they had the Country of *Pomerania*, with the Dutchies of *Bremen* and *Verden*, the City of *Wismar*, a Vote in the Diets of the Empire and Circle of *Lower Saxony*; together with a Million of Crowns in ready Money, as a Satisfaction for their Services.

As the War was glorious to the Arms, so the Peace was no less honourable to the Counsels of *Sweden*; and the young Queen *Christina* was esteemed and courted by all the Powers of *Europe*. She had a great deal of Learning, and a very extensive Capacity; but with these great Qualities, there was a Mixture of many Defects. Her Subjects would willingly have seen her married to her Cousin Prince *Charles Gustavus*; to which, however, neither she nor that Prince were inclined, and therefore she very wisely chose to content all Parties, by resigning to him the Crown, which she did in an Assembly of the States, held at *Upsal* in the latter End of *May*, 1654, reserving only a Pension to herself for the Support of her Dignity; and having embraced the Popish Religion, she retired to *Rome*, where she lived with great Magnificence to the Time of her Decease, which happened *April* 9, 1689.

Charles Gustavus, or *Charles* X. of *Sweden*, who ascended the Throne by the Abdication of Queen *Christina*, was the Son of *John Casimir*, Prince Palatine of the *Rhine*, and *Catharine* of *Sweden*, Daughter of *Charles* IX, and Sister to *Gustavus Adolphus* Queen *Christina*'s Father. He found the Affairs of his Kingdom in a very indifferent Posture at his Accession; but he soon put them into so good a Condition, that the Year following he made War upon *Poland*, to revenge the Affront done to him in protesting against his Admission to the Crown. His Progress at first not only surprized *Poland*, but alarmed all *Europe*; for in three Months Time he had taken all *Prussia*, except *Dantzick*, a great Part of *Lithuania*, the Cities of *Warsaw*, *Cracow*, and other Places in the Greater and Lesser *Poland*; most of the People of these Provinces swearing Allegiance to him, as being deserted by King *Casimir*, who was fled into *Silesia*.

But this Career of Prosperity did not long continue. The first Consternation being over, the *Poles* were as ready to fall from him, as they had been to embrace his Party. Besides the Emperor, *Muscovy* and *Holland* became his Enemies, as did *Denmark* also, which gave the King of *Sweden* an honourable Occasion of quitting *Poland*, where he could not long have subsisted. Having therefore left his Brother Prince *Adolph* Governor of *Prussia*, he hastened to *Denmark*, which he

soon

foon reduced to a neceffity of begging Peace at the Price of the Provinces of *Schonen*, *Halland*, and *Bleaking*, which was con-cluded in the Spring, but the War broke out again in the Space of a few Months. In the Summer enfuing, which was that of 1658, the King having conceived frefh Jealoufies againft the *Danes*, fuddenly landed with his Army in the Ifland of *Zeland*, and while General *Wrangel* befieged *Cronenburgh* at the Entrance of the *Sound*, he attacked *Copenhagen*.

Thefe Sieges had very different Events; for *Cronenburgh* was foon taken; but the *Danes*, encouraged by the Prefence of their King in the Capital, made an obftinate Defence, which gave Time for the *Dutch* Fleet to come to their Relief; and the *Swedifh* Navy being defeated, the King was forced to change his Siege into a Blockade, which continued all that Year, and the beft Part of the next, in which the *Swedes* met with fo many Misfortunes, that the King was forced to return Home in order to make the neceffary Preparations for carrying on his Enter-prize with Vigour in the Spring; but while he was intent on his Affairs he was furprized by a Fever, which foon carried him off. And at his Death, which happened on the 13th of *February*, 1660, he left his Son, who was but five Years old, engaged in a War againft fix of the greateft Powers in *Europe*. Such was the End of this great Monarch, whofe Courage and Virtues had enabled him to make fo great a Figure, as not only to maintain the Credit which the Crown of *Sweden* had acquired, but to carry it even higher than it had rifen under his glorious Prede-ceffor, the famous *Guftavus Adolphus*, but then it was built on the Foundation which he had laid.

Charles XI. was chiefly governed in his Minority by his Mother, who was Sifter to the Duke of *Holftein*, a very wife and prudent Princefs, who by the Advice of the principal Perfons in the Kingdom, brought about a very advantageous Treaty of Peace, called from the Place where it was con-cluded, the Treaty of *Oliva*; by which the King of *Poland* renounced his Claim to the Crown of *Sweden*, and the Re-publick all her Rights to *Livonia*. The *Swedes* made Peace at the fame Time with *Denmark*, and Things were kept in tolera-ble Order till the Clofe of the King's Minority; when by a very unhappy Turn in his Counfels, he was engaged to take Part with *France* in the War which preceded the Peace of *Nime-guen*, wherein he met with very indifferent Succefs, and loft a great Part of his Dominions in *Germany*; which however were reftored to him by a feparate Treaty concluded a little before the general Peace laft mentioned, in the Negotiation of which he acted as a Mediator.

In

In 1680, being about twenty-five Years of Age, he chose for his Confort the Princefs *Ulrica Eleanora*, Daughter to *Frederick* II. and Sifter to *Chriftian* V. Kings of *Denmark*; and thenceforward applied himfelf with greater Diligence to the Government of his Kingdom than any of his Predeceffors, or indeed than any Prince of his Time. The firft Effect of this, was his detaching himfelf entirely from the *French* Intereft; which he looked upon as dangerous to his Authority, and not at all compenfated by the paltry Subfidies granted by that Crown, which ought to be a ftanding Leffon to his Succeffors.

He next inquired after and corrected all Abufes that had crept into the Civil Government, whilft former Kings of *Sweden* trufting all Things to their Minifters, minded nothing but War; and looked particularly into Law-Suits, fitting himfelf in the Supreme Court, and difpatching there more Caufes in feven Years than before had been decided in twenty. By this Means he gained the Love of his Subjects to fuch a Degree, that the States of the Kingdom confented, at his Requeft, to take away a great Part of the Power, which till then the Senate had enjoyed; and made afterwards fuch farther Alterations in the Government, as rendered the King as abfolute as any Monarch in *Europe*. They enabled him likewife to reunite to the Crown fuch Eftates as had been alienated from it, and to pay off the publick Debts, by raifing the Value of the Coin. They fettled the Militia alfo in fuch a Manner, that he had always feventeen thoufand Horfe, and forty-three thoufand Foot, kept up at the Expence of his Subjects. Befides all this, they granted him large Sums of Money which were raifed by heavy Taxes; but fuch was his Conduct, that the People being fatisfied that all they gave was either laid out, or laid up for their Service, they thought they could never do too much for him; and indeed his Reign is the ftrongeft Proof, that the fureft Way for a Prince to make his Will the Law, is to govern by Law.

He was remarkably addicted to the Religion of his Country, and not only ftrict in his Morals, but fevere; and though not uxorious, yet his Chaftity was never fo much as fufpected. He humbled his Nobility, but was very obfequious to the Clergy, kind to the Citizens, and very tender of the common People. He took a proper Care of Foreign Affairs, though he avoided making War; but he did not fuffer his Love for Peace fo far to influence him, as to allow any of his Neighbours to prejudice either the Crown of *Sweden*, or her Allies; for when the King of *Denmark* feized the Duke of *Holftein*'s Dominions, he without Delay interpofed, and began to make fuch Preparations for

E

doing

doing Right to that Prince, as produced the Treaty of *Altena*, which was signed on the tenth of *June*, 1689, and by which the Duke was restored to his Dominions.

After this he entered into a close Alliance with the *Danes* for preserving the Peace of the North ; and in the first general War against *France* he lent the *Dutch* six thousand Men, and offered the Emperor as many more, yet without declaring War against *Lewis* XIV. who was so well satisfied with his Behaviour, or rather was so much afraid of him, that he forbid all *French* Privateers molesting *Swedish* Ships ; and thus by a steady and prudent Management, he supported his own Power at home, and maintained the Credit of the Crown of *Sweden* abroad to the Time of his Decease, which happened on the fifth of *April*, 1697, at the Age of forty-two. He left behind him three Children ; *viz.* *Hedwig-Sophia-Eleanora*, who espoused the Duke of *Holstein-Gottorp*; *Ulrica Eleanora*, Consort to the late King of *Sweden*; and his only surviving Son and Successor

Charles XII. who in his Minority was governed by the same great Princess with whom the Affairs of the Kingdom were intrusted in that of his Father, I mean the Dowager of *Charles* X. assisted by five Senators, and they were to administer the Government till her Grandson came to the Age of Eighteen. But the States thought fit to abridge that Term, and to declare him Major before he reached Sixteen ; and in half a Year afterwards the general Peace of *Ryswick* was concluded under his Mediation. His Neighbours taking Advantage of his Youth, formed a Confederacy for attacking him on all Sides, and this without the least Provocation. The Confederates were *Frederick* IV. King of *Denmark*, *Augustus* II. King of *Poland*, and the Czar *Peter the Great*, all esteemed as wise Princes as any of their Time ; but influenced in this by their Ambition, and the Prospect they had of dividing amongst themselves the late Acquisitions of *Sweden*.

Charles penetrated this Scheme, and as soon as he saw the *English* Fleet in the *Baltick*, as Guarantees of the Treaty of *Altena*, determined to begin with that Prince of the Confederates who broke with him first, and make him feel the whole Weight of his Power. Accordingly he landed an Army in *Zealand*, and besieged *Copenhagen*, reducing in a very short Time the King of *Denmark* so low, that he was constrained to make Peace upon reasonable Terms, and desert the Confederacy, by a Treaty which was signed at *Travendahl*, *August* 8, 1700. The very same Year he relieved *Narva*, that was besieged by the Czar, and obtained on the 20th of *November* the most compleat Victory

with

with the greateſt Inequality of Forces that is recorded in modern
Hiſtory.

He turned his victorious Arms next againſt the *Poles*, forced
them to depoſe King *Auguſtus*, and make Choice of a new
King, which they did the fifth of *May*, 1704, in the Perſon of
Staniſlaus Leſzinſki, Palatine of *Poſnania*, and Son to Count
Leſzinſki, Great Treaſurer of the Crown. He puſhed this
Reſentment of his ſtill farther, by following *Auguſtus* into his
hereditary Dominions of *Saxony*, where he exhauſted the
Country by exceſſive Contributions, and impoſed very hard
Conditions on that Monarch himſelf, by the famous Treaty
which was concluded at *Altranſtadt*, a Village within two Miles
of *Leipſick*.

While the King of *Sweden* was in *Saxony*, he took an Opportunity of ſhewing the Emperor *Joſeph*, who then reigned,
ſome Marks of Diſtaſte at the Conduct which he had purſued,
and obliged him to do Juſtice to his Proteſtant Subjects. We
may truly affirm the Year 1708 was that in which the Glory of
Sweden roſe to its utmoſt Height. *Charles* had then the Ballance of *Europe* in his Hand, and might have preſcribed Terms
to all its Powers, from the critical Situation of his own Affairs
and theirs; but his boundleſs Ambition, heated, perhaps, by
the artful Praiſes of an *Engliſh* General, whoſe Eloquence was
as victorious as his Sword, threw him very ſoon into a different
Condition. For deſirous of compleating his Plan, towards
which there wanted but one Stroke, he marched through the
Ukraine into *Ruſſia*, reſolved to drive the Czar out of his Territories, as he had forced the *Dane* to ſave his Capital by a
Peace, and the *Poles* to depoſe the King who was his Enemy.
A great and glorious Project if it had been practicable!

This produced the famous Battle of *Pultowa*, which coſt the
Swedes 30,000 Men, and forced the King to take Shelter in
Turky with a handful of People. This fatal Engagement hap-
pened on the twenty-ſeventh of *June*, 1709, and opened a
Paſſage for the Enemies of this Crown to execute the Projects
they had formed ten Years before, which was an Opportunity
they none of them let ſlip. The King of *Denmark* once more
declared War, and made a Deſcent upon *Schonen*; the King of
Poland entered again into Poſſeſſion of his Dominions; the
Ruſſians repoſſeſſed themſelves of the moſt valuable Part of the
Swediſh Territories on the *Baltick*; and though at firſt the Confederates kept ſome Meaſures in *Germany*, yet at laſt they attacked and divided the *Swediſh* Territories there; the *Pruſſians*
got the better Part of *Pomerania*, and *Bremen* and *Verden* falling
into

into the Hands of the *Danes*, they difpofed of them to the Elector of *Hanover*.

His *Swedifh* Majefty returned into his Dominions in *November*, 1714, and very foon made his Enemies fenfible of his Prefence. He found his own Territories exhaufted, his and his Predeceffors Conquefts loft, and fcarce any Friend or Ally left; yet he maintained his abfolute Power over his own Subjects, and profecuted the War with inflexible Refolution. He perfifted in his former Notions of deftroying or depofing every Prince with whom he was difpleafed. He meditated a Defcent upon *Zealand*, with a View once more to befiege *Copenhagen*, in which he failed; he engaged in fome dark Defigns for difturbing the Peace of *Great Britain*, which were difconcerted; his laft Attempt was an Invafion upon *Norway*, where he was fhot before *Frederickfhall*, on the firft of *December*, 1718, dying as he lived, ill treated, but unconquered.

Upon his Demife the States of *Sweden* declared his Sifter the Princefs *Ulrica Eleanora* Queen, and her Hufband the Hereditary Prince of *Heffe-Caffel* Generaliffimo; for the War ftill continued. In 1720 that Prince having embraced the *Lutheran* Religion, was raifed to the Throne of *Sweden*, and foon after Peace was made with all the Powers with whom *Sweden* had fo long contended; that with *Denmark* took place in *June* 1720; that with *Pruffia* on the 11th of *January*, 1721; and that with the Czar was concluded at *Newftadt* in *Finland*, on the 19th of *Auguft*, in the fame Year. By thefe Treaties the *Swedes* recovered part of *Pomerania*, and the Town of *Wifmar* : But the King of *Pruffia* kept the Dutchy of *Stetin*; the Dutchies of *Bremen* and *Verden* were left to *Hanover*, and the Czar kept in general all his Conquefts. In 1729 the Kings of *Sweden* and *Poland* were reconciled.

In confequence of thefe Steps the Face of Affairs in *Sweden* has been entirely changed, and from being one of the moft abfolute, it is again become the moft limited Crown in *Europe*; the Senate has recovered all its ancient Privileges, the States have refumed and even extended their Powers; fo that the King can do nothing of Confequence without their Approbation. While the Miferies of the late War were frefh in Remembrance, the *Swedes* continued firm to their new Syftem, maintained a clofe Correfpondence with *Ruffia*, remained on good Terms with all their Neighbours, and feemed very little difpofed to rifque any new Alterations in their Government, by admitting the Claim which the Duke of *Holftein*, only Son to the Queen's eldeft Sifter, kept up to the Succeffion; they likewife entered into very ftrict Engagements with the Crown of

Great

Great Britain, and shewed a great Respect for the House of
Austria; whence it was conceived that all Things in the
North would go on in this Channel; and that nothing was to
be feared from the Intrigues of France in that Nation, which
formerly had so great an Influence on the Affairs of Europe in
general.

But those who knew the Disposition of the Swedes best, always foresaw, that any Alteration in the Power and Conditions
of their Neighbours would still produce extraordinary Effects
amongst them; in short, that this long Calm would be followed
by a high Storm: and the Event very fully proved that their
Conjectures were but too well founded.

It was in 1738 that this great Change in the Politicks of
the Swedes began to discover itself. The Diet that assembled
that Year, of which Count Tessin was chosen Marshal, soon appeared to be composed of Persons of very different Sentiments,
who in a little Time, however, were distinguished into three
Parties. The first and most vigorous were for reviving the old
System, and for trying to recover, if possible, part of the Dominions yielded to Russia, and therefore they inclined to martial Measures; these were called the Hats. The Party directly
opposite to them, declared absolutely for Peace, for the Maintenance of the present System, and for endeavouring to promote
the domestick Welfare of the Nation; these were stiled the
Night-Caps. The third Party was a kind of flying Squadron,
who were for keeping in a middle Way; and were from thence
denominated the Hunting-Caps. It was not very long before
the first Party appeared to have a great Majority; but as it required Time to execute their Designs, the Diet, contrary to
Custom, continued sitting eleven Months, and before they rose,
turned out five of the Senators that had been most concerned in
renewing the Treaty with Russia.

In 1739, a French Squadron of five Sail, commanded by the
Marquis D'Antin, arrived in the Baltick, and anchored in the
Road of Stockholm: With what View this Squadron came, has
been rather guessed at than known; but there was one Circumstance attended it, which deserves particular Notice. The King
of Sweden presented the Sword he wore at the Time the Marquis had his Audience to that Officer, with this extraordinary
Compliment; I give you this, Sir, with the greater Pleasure,
because I am sure, you will draw it on all Occasions for us, as I
and my Subjects will draw ours for France. Another Event
happened in this Year, which likewise made much Noise;
the States had taken care to discharge the Debts contracted by
the late King Charles XII. in Turky, and had employed for

that

that Purpofe, as well as for fome others perhaps of much greater Importance, one Major *Malcolm Sinclair*, who in his Return was murdered by a *Ruffian* Officer near *Naumbourg* in *Silefia*, on the 6th of *June*, and all his Papers taken from him, which contributed to heighten the Refentment of the *Swedes* againft that Nation, notwithftanding the *Czarina* difowned in the moft folemn Manner, her having any Concern in that Matter.

The very fame Day Major *Sinclair* was murdered, died *Charles* Duke of *Holftein-Gottorp*, who always confidered himfelf as prefumptive Heir to the Crown of *Sweden*. The next Year died the Emperor *Charles* VI. and *Anne* Emprefs of *Ruffia*, which facilitated the Defigns of thofe who endeavoured to bring the *Swedes* to declare that War againft the *Ruffians*, which at laft broke out in the Month of *July* 1741, the Confequences of which are too well known to be dwelt upon here. It was attended with nothing but Misfortunes from the Beginning; and while things went fo ill on the Frontiers, there happened a very unlucky Event at *Stockholm*, which was the Death of the Queen the latter End of *November* 1741. The *Swedes* were in hopes that things would have gone better after the great Revolution in *Ruffia*, which placed the Emprefs *Elizabeth* upon the Throne; but after various Negotiations, the War broke out again with greater Heat than ever; and the *Swedes*, who had fo often in former times beat the *Ruffians*, were now beaten by them over and over, the beft Part of their Army made Prifoners, and all the Country of *Finland* loft, which reduced them to the hard Neceffity of making Peace upon the beft Terms they could obtain.

While this was under Confideration, the Diet, which was again affembled, proceeded in the great Affair of the Succeffion to the Crown, the eftablifhing of which they hoped would contribute to change the melancholy Face of their Affairs. But for the prefent this occafioned new Divifions, and ftill greater Confufions. There were four Candidates for the Succeffion; the firft was the young Duke of *Holftein-Gottorp*, fupported by many of the Nobility, and by a ftrong Party amongft the Burgeffes, as well as by the whole Order of Peafants; the fecond was Prince *Frederick* of *Heffe-Caffel*, Nephew to the King, for whom all the Clergy declared; the third was the Prince of *Denmark*, who had a very confiderable Party; and the fourth the Duke of *Deuxponts*, who is alfo of the Royal Family of *Sweden*, and had but a fmall Party. After very warm Debates, the Duke of *Holftein* was declared Succeffor, in the Month of *October* 1742, by a Majority of two Votes only;

and

and Deputies were named to offer him on certain Conditions the Reversion of the Crown, in hopes he might induce the *Czarina* to restore the Grand Dutchy of *Finland*. But before they arrived at *Petersburg*, he had embraced the *Greek* Religion, with a View to the Succession of *Russia*, to which also he had a Claim of Hereditary Right.

This Scheme having failed of producing its desired Effect, was followed by Consequences that were equally unavoidable and unexpected; for the Peasants that had expressed such unanimous Affection for the House of *Holstein*, began with the same Zeal and Unanimity to espouse the Interest of the Prince of *Denmark*, to whom the Clergy were attached; they likewise insisted on the calling to a severe Account the Generals that had commanded the Forces in the two last Campaigns; and those very Persons that had shewn the greatest Warmth in promoting the War with *Russia*, were now equally warm in demanding the Punishment of all such as were the Managers of that War, to whom they imputed its Want of Success.

Yet in the midst of these domestick Disputes, Peace appeared as precarious as ever, and the Diet seemed equally unable to bear the Thoughts of losing *Finland* entirely, or falling upon any Expedient for recovering it; except receiving it as an Equivalent from the Hands of the *Czarina*, with which View his *Britannick* Majesty having offered his Mediation, the Conferences were continued at *Abo*. These, at last, ended in a Treaty, by which *Russia* consented to restore all that had been taken in this War from *Sweden*, except a small District in *Finland*, and to renew the Peace between the two Nations, in case the States of *Sweden* should elect Prince *Adolphus Frederick*, Administrator of *Holstein* and Bishop of *Lubec*, Successor to the Crown; and in this Case the young Duke of *Holstein*, whom they had already elected, and who was now become hereditary Prince of *Russia*, offered to make a solemn Resignation of all his Claim and Right to the *Swedish* Diadem.

When this Treaty came to be considered in the Diet at *Stockholm*, there arose very high Debates; but at last the Consideration of those immediate Advantages which were to arise from the Election of the Bishop of *Lubec*, and the Prospect of continual Disputes in case they elected any other Successor, brought over all the Orders of the States to this Proposition; and Duke *Adolphus* was accordingly chosen hereditary Prince and Successor of *Sweden*, on the 23d of *June* 1743. But while the Diet was thus providing for their present Peace and future Safety, the *Dalecarlians* took up Arms and marched directly to the City of *Stockholm*, under Pretence of supporting the Interest of the Prince

of

of *Denmark*, in which they perfifted, notwithftanding the King took all poffible Methods to reduce them by fair Means to their Duty. At laft the Malecontents attempted to overturn all to which the King and the States of *Sweden* had confented. This obliged his Majefty, much againft his Will, to employ Force, even in his capital City; where after a fharp Engagement, in which one of his Senators at the Head of the King's Troops was mortally wounded, the Rebels were totally defeated, obliged to lay down their Arms, and fubmit to the King's Mercy, which was extended to them in the moft ample Degree, notwithftanding the Blacknefs of their Crime.

But this extraordinary Inftance of Royal Clemency, did not foften the Refentment of the Peafants againft two unfortunate Noblemen, *viz.* Count *Loeuwenhaupt* and Baron *Buddenbrok*, who to fatisfy them, had been condemned for want of Succefs in the two laft Campaigns, and whofe Execution was now demanded with fuch Heat, that the moft merciful Monarch in the World could not refufe it. Lieutenant General Baron *Buddenbrok* fuffered firft, on the 16th of *July* in the fame Year; but Field Marfhal *Loeuwenhaupt* made his Efcape, yet was foon after retaken; and notwithftanding the Nobility and Clergy were inclined to fpare his Life, the Peafants remained ftill inflexible; and to fatisfy them, he was according to his Sentence beheaded. The King retired to his Country Palace, till thefe melancholy Scenes were over, and the Peafants, gratified in their Revenge, confented to the Election, which being fignified to Duke *Adolphus*, he went foon after to *Stockholm*, where he was received with univerfal Acclamations.

The late King of *Denmark*, who for Reafons that will appear in the next Article, had many Motives to diflike this fudden and extraordinary Elevation of the Houfe of *Holftein*, and who befides was not a little mortified on the fcore of his Son's being fet afide to make way for the Bifhop of *Lubec*; began to make fuch vaft Military Preparations as feemed to befpeak a Defign of invading *Sweden*, and which for fome Months not only amufed the *North*, but all *Europe*; yet the *Czarina* found means to lay this Storm, by declaring roundly to the Courts of *Stockholm* and *Copenhagen*, that fhe would maintain the Election fhe had promoted, with the whole Force of her Empire. To eftablifh the Peace of the Kingdom more effectually, it was thought highly requifite, that the new Prince Succeffor fhould marry, and accordingly he efpoufed the Princefs *Louifa Ulrica*, Sifter to the King of *Pruffia*, by whom he has already three Sons.

The

The prevailing Party of this Kingdom, are thought to have been diſappointed in their Views as to the Succeſſion; in reference to which it has been ſtrongly ſuſpected, that they inclined rather to the Duke of *Deuxponts*, than to Prince *Adolphus* of *Holſtein*; but after this great Point was once ſettled, and the Prince Succeſſor arrived in *Sweden*, they made their Court to him with ſuch Succeſs, that it was not long before the World became ſenſible, that either his Royal Highneſs had embraced their Principles, or thought proper to wear the Appearance of having adopted them, in order to render himſelf popular. In this, it may be, he went farther than was neceſſary, ſince it is agreed that his own and his Conſort's Behaviour has been ſo full of Rectitude and Affability, that without eſpouſing any Party Maxims, they might have attracted the Eſteem, and ſecured the Affections of the People. But Count *Gyllenburgh*, who was the Head of the Country Party in *Sweden*, was a Man of ſo great Parts, and knew how to place the Notions he had eſpouſed in ſo fair a Light, that we need not wonder he gained an Aſcendant over a Prince, whoſe Virtues, Sincerity, and Candour, made him the more ready to believe, what with great Addreſs was repreſented to him as the true Intereſts of the Nation. Another Incident contributed not a little to fix him in theſe Opinions, and that was the Reſolution taken by the governing Party in *Sweden*, to fall in with the Views of his *Pruſſian* Majeſty; in order to which, a Treaty was ſet on foot between the two Crowns, which has been ſince concluded and ratified by the Conſent of the Diet, and to which the Crown of *France* has alſo acceeded.

It was very natural that this Conduct in the Prince Succeſſor ſhould not be well reliſhed in *Ruſſia*, where from the Jealouſies entertained firſt of the Marquis *de Botta*, next of the Marquis *de la Chetardie* and Baron *Mardefeldt*, and laſtly of Mr. *D'Allion*, it was very apparent that ſo cloſe an Intercourſe with the Courts of *Verſailles* and *Berlin*, muſt of neceſſity create Suſpicions. But notwithſtanding every Method poſſible has been tryed by Letters from the *Czarina* and the Imperial Prince, to give another Turn to his Royal Highneſs's Sentiments, he remained firm to the Party he embraced ſo early; tho' at the ſame time he in the moſt publick Manner acknowledged his Obligations to the *Czarina*, and profeſſed the higheſt perſonal Regard and Eſteem for her Imperial Majeſty, conſiſtent with his Duty and Intereſt in purſuing the Welfare of the *Swediſh* Nation. It was thought, that upon the Death of Count *Gyllenburgh*,

lenburgh, some Alteration might have happened; but the long Illness of that great Minister, who in the midst of bodily Pains and Infirmities retained not only his Abilities, but his Party-Engagements to the very last, gave him an Opportunity of preparing every thing in favour of Count *Teffin* his intended Successor.

It is true, that the Court of *Ruffia* took a very brisk Step to prevent the Promotion of this Nobleman, by charging him with being an Enemy to the Harmony and good Understanding between the two Crowns, which however had not the Success that was expected from it. For the Diet being at that Time sitting, Count *Teffin* assumed in appearance a Resolution of quitting all his Employments; previous to this, he desired his Conduct might be examined by the States, in which he shewed himself as wise and able a Man as his Predecessor, since he foresaw that this must either open a Way to a safe and honourable Retreat, or else bring the States of the Kingdom to espouse his Interest as their own, and make his Elevation to the Post of President of the Chancery an Act of the Diet.

To push this more effectually, the Discovery of a new Plot was set on foot, to which the wild and unguarded Expressions of an inconsiderable and desperate Man, gave a Colour of Truth; and this was so well managed, that after a formal Tryal and Conviction, this Person was executed *August* 9, 1747, at *Stockholm*; and others who were stiled his Accomplices were likewise punished, but not with so great Severity. At length the Report of the secret Committee having been made entirely in his Favour, Count *Teffin* was raised to the Post beforementioned, with all the Circumstances of Honour and Reputation that a Subject could receive. All Things from that Time went in the Channel into which they were turn'd by Count *Gyllenburgh*; and to interest all Ranks and Degrees of People in the Nation more effectually in support of the new System, three Orders of Knighthood were instituted or revived, *viz.* the *Seraphim*, the *Sword*, and the *North Star*; so that it is not easy to conceive a political Plan, either better contrived, or more discreetly executed than this has been. His *Swedish* Majesty, then the oldest Monarch in *Europe*, was rather passive in these extraordinary Transactions than forward, agreeable to the Calmness of his Temper, to the unsettled State of his Health, and to his declining Years; but all along behaved in a manner that preserved to him the utmost Respect, as well as the most sincere and hearty Affections of his People.

His

His Reign was one of the mildest with which this, or indeed
any other People were ever blessed ; he discovered a true Concern for whatever related to the Good of his People; promoted,
to the utmost of his Power, every Project that tended either to
heighten or to secure their Felicity ; and never discovered any
Backwardness or Want of Spirit, but when he was unwilling
to lend the Colour of his Authority to those Acts of Party Violence, which as a wise, a good, and an humane Prince, he
could not but in his Heart disapprove.

We need not wonder therefore that this Monarch was so much
considered by his Neighbours, so highly reverenced by the
Prince who was to succeed him, or so much beloved by his
Subjects, more especially when we consider that they had all a
very great Interest in his Life, created by an Opinion that generally prevailed, as if his Demise would be attended with some
Alteration in the Government, and with some Disturbance in
the publick Tranquillity ; and yet this was not at all justified by
the Event. His *Swedish* Majesty , whose Death had been long
looked for, and more than once published, died at length somewhat unexpectedly, *April* the fifth 1751, when he was very
near seventy-five Years of Age, and when he had worn the
Crown near thirty Years, deservedly and universally regretted.
The next Day the new King was proclaimed, and in the Afternoon went to the Senate, and there signed and swore to the
following solemn Act.

" Whereas the united States of the Kingdom of *Sweden*, of
" their own Motion, and by a free and voluntary Choice,
" elected me Successor to the Kingdom of *Sweden*, of the *Goths*,
" and of the *Vandals* ; I should be wanting in a suitable Return
" to the Confidence they reposed in me on my Advancement
" to the Throne, which is devolved to me by the Disposal of
" the Almighty, and by the free Election which they made,
" if I did not in the most solemn Manner confirm the Assu-
" rance I have given to support them at the Expence of my
" Life and Blood, in the Exercise of the pure Doctrine and
" Religion they profess, and to preserve and defend the Liber-
" ties and Privileges they have acquired. And as my Desires
" are far from every thing which might bear the least Shadow
" of Constraint, I declare by this publick Act, which I swear
" to observe upon my Royal Word and Faith, that I not only
" intend to govern my Kingdom according to the Laws of
" *Sweden* and the Form of Regency established in the Year
" 1720, as well as in Conformity with the Assurance I gave
" the States of the Kingdom in the Year 1742 ; but also that I
" shall

" I fhall regard as the moft dangerous Enemies to me and the
" Kingdom, and treat as Traitors to their Country, all fuch
" as fhall either in publick, or under any Pretence foever un-
" dertake, or endeavour to introduce into this Kingdom, de-
" fpotick Power or arbitrary Government, wherein God affift
" me."

Signed,

Stockholm, April 6,
1751.   ADOLPHUS FREDERICK.

This new Monarch likewife wrote immediately to the Emprefs of *Ruffia*, with his own Hand, to notify his Acceffion to
the Throne, and to acquaint her Imperial Majefty with the
Sentiments of Refpect and Friendfhip, which he had ever retained and ever meant to retain for fo good an Ally, and of his
fincere Intentions to fupport the Promifes contained in that Act,
which was the firft of his Reign, and which accompanied this
Letter. Thefe were fent by a Perfon of Diftinction, who, by
the Rigour of the Seafon, and other Accidents, was much retarded in his Journey ; but, upon his Arrival at *Peterfburgh*,
was extremely well received, had the Honour of prefenting his
Letter to the Emprefs, who not only returned a fuitable Anfwer,
but publifhed likewife a Declaration that correfponded in its
Contents with his *Swedifh* Majefty's Act at his Acceffion. In
this State Things are at prefent ; fo that the Death of the late
King has not hitherto produced any thing like a Rupture, and
it may be that the Refolutions taken in the Diet, which will
very fpeedily meet, may remove all Fears and Apprehenfions :
For as all thngs in this World are variable, fo we ftate this as
a Matter probable, and without fuggefting that the contrary is
at all impoffible.

Thus we have given a large Account of the Affairs of
Sweden, from that Æra, at which fhe firft began to make a Figure
amongft the Powers of *Europe*, down to the prefent Times ;
and have fhewn how fhe extended, and how fhe loft her Dominions, how fhe changed her Conftitution, and from being
limited, became an abfolute, and now a limited Monarchy
again. All which Circumftances the Reader will find not only
requifite to the underftanding what we have to fay of the Political Interefts of this Nation, but alfo highly ufeful in refpect to
the remaining Hiftory of the *North*, inafmuch as almoft every
remarkable Event therein, at leaft for feveral Ages paft, is fome
way or other connected with the Affairs of this Kingdom ;
fo that the Room we have taken in this, will enable us to be

more

more concise in the succeeding Articles, without rendering them from that Circumstance in the least obscure.

As there was no Way of learning the Interest of *Sweden*, but by consulting the History, so it is impossible to form a right Notion of its Government, without being acquainted with the Manners of the Inhabitants. The *Swedes* have, like other Nations, good and bad Properties; they are unquestionably as brave, as hardy, and as patient as any People in the World, which qualified them for making excellent Soldiers; and as they were disciplined and intermixed with Foreigners of all Countries, who had either signalized themselves by Skill or Courage in Service, this in the Space of a few Years rendered their Armies justly famous; and though their Force is much reduced, yet the Troops they have are as good as ever. They are likewise most sincerely zealous for the Protestant Religion, according to the *Lutheran* Doctrine, which is not only the Faith by Law established, but the only one tolerated in that Kingdom. The Nobility, Gentry, and better sort of People, have all a Tincture of Learning, and very few have more; they have always been esteemed loyal to their Princes, and have generally shewn themselves hearty Friends to Liberty, though they have been sometimes mistaken about it, and yet have persisted obstinately in their Mistakes.

As to the Vices of the *Swedes*, they are at least as conspicuous as their Virtues; they have a Fickleness in their Tempers, equally fatal to them in the Pursuit of Politicks or Learning; they have a great Proportion of Vanity, which displays itself particularly in Furniture and Equipage; for as to those Expences that make no Shew, these People are by Nature little addicted to them. But the Vice most predominant among them is Envy, directed more especially against Strangers, who if they thrive in Trade, at Court, or in the Army, fill the People with an unaccountable Malice and Displeasure. And the same bad Turn they are apt to take, even against their own Countrymen, more especially if they spring from a low Beginning, or rise at too quick a Rate. They are not much inclined to Manufactures, nor have they any true Genius for Trade, though they have good Ships and skilful Seamen; but they are suspicious, especially where Foreigners are concerned, and so very impatient if things do not immediately succeed, that there seems to be no great Reason to apprehend their very soon acquiring an extensive Commerce, or consequently their becoming a Maritime Power; but on the other hand, it may be presumed, they will not neglect that Naval Strength which they have already acquired, and for the Support of which, as well as for all other
things

things ufeful or neceffary to the Publick, the Laws have made a competent Provifion in *Sweden*.

After confidering this fair and impartial Character of the *Swedifh* Nation, we need not be at all furprized at the various Revolutions to which their Government has been fubject. The Love of Freedom, to fay the Truth, was their reigning Paffion; and not being always able to fee fo diftinctly how thofe Evils might be cured, which they well enough difcerned it did not become a brave Nation to endure, they took fuch Methods as were dictated by their own Defpair, or were advifed to by fuch as undertook to procure their Deliverance. But ftill there were fome fhort Maxims, and fome fundamental Articles of Government, from which they never departed, and upon which they grounded that Conftitution, which took Place after they fhook off the Yoke of *Denmark*, and beftowed the Crown upon *Guftavus Vafa*, from whom their Kings are defcended. Amongft thefe fundamental Points, the two moft material were, the preferving the Legiflative Power entirely to the States of the Kingdom, and fo much of the Executive as was thought expedient for the publick Good in the Hands of the Senate; upon which two Columns they conceived the Structure of their Common-wealth might always reft, without Danger of Subverfion.

As for the States of the Kingdom, the ufual Time of their Affembly is once in three Years, or oftener, if the Affairs of the Kingdom require it. The Letters mandatory for calling them together are fent to the Governors of the feveral Provinces, into which the Kingdom is divided; who thereupon write to each Nobleman and Gentleman of their Province, and to the Bifhops, who caufe the fame to be publifhed in all the Parifh Churches. The Body of the Nobility and Gentry are reprefented by one of each Family, of which there are above a thoufand in *Sweden*, and with them, that is in the Chamber of Nobles, the Colonel, Lieutenant-Colonel, Major, and one Captain of each Regiment, fit and vote. For the Clergy, befides the Bifhops and Super-intendants; in each rural Deanery, or Diftrict containing ten Parifhes, one is chofen and maintained at the Charge of the Electors; thefe make a Body of about two hundred. The Reprefentatives of the Burghers are chofen by the Magiftrates and Common Council of each Corporation, of which *Stockholm* fends four, other Places two, and fome one, who make in all about one hundred and fifty. The Peafants of each Diftrict chufe one of their own Quality to appear for them, whofe Charges they bear, and give him Inftructions about fuch

Matters,

Matters, as they think need Redress; they are, generally speaking, about two hundred and fifty.

At their first Meeting the King is present with the Senate, and the President of the Chancery makes them a Speech on the Part of his Majesty, in which he gives them a short Account of what has happened since their last Meeting, and of the principal Points they are called together to consult about; and after an Answer given by the Speaker of each of the four Orders, they withdraw to their respective Houses, where each elects out of its own Body a certain Number of Members to make up the secret Committee, that prepare and digest Matters for the Consideration of the States. Each of the several Orders has a negative Voice, but in their respective Houses the Majority of Votes absolutely decides the Business.

The Reason that the Military Officers have in Right of their Commission a Seat in the Diet is, because the Army makes a Part of the Constitution; the Officers are for Life, and have Estates in Land, which are let at Rents equivalent to their Pay; and being generally Men of good Families beside, there are no Inconveniencies to be feared from their having Seats in the Diet. As there are no Dissenters in *Sweden* of any Denomination whatever, this obliges their Princes to court the Clergy very much. The House of Burgesses is commonly well-affected to the Crown, and remarkably moderate in their Proceedings. The Peasants, on the contrary, are often very warm and very obstinate; and they may be considered, to use a Phrase adapted to our own Constitution, as the Country Interest in *Sweden*, or rather, as the mere, modern Expression is, the Landed Interest; and on that Account have great Regard paid them. Each of the Houses have a Right to represent their respective Grievances to the King, who gives separately such Answers as he thinks proper; and at the Conclusion of the Diet every Member of the Orders of the Clergy, Burgesses and Peasants, has an Extract given him of their whole Proceedings, and the King's Answer to their Grivances, which he carries home to his Constituents.

The Senate hath not only Authority to advise the King in all Business of Importance, but may likewise admonish, and even over-rule him, in case he attempts any thing contrary to Law; and without the Concurrence of the Senate he can undertake nothing of Importance. They take an Oath of Fidelity to the Kingdom, and are accountable for their Conduct to the States, who, in case they disapprove the Behaviour of any of them, may, though it be very seldom done, remove them. In the three last Reigns but one, their Power was much

lessened,

leſſened, and in ſome meaſure taken away, but it is now re-ſtored, and made a fundamental Part of the Conſtitution They have the Direction of the Revenue, and in caſe of the King's Abſence from his Dominions, they have the executive Power entirely in their Hands. The King appoints all Military Offi-cers under the Degree of Colonel; but in appointing Officers of that, or of a ſuperior Rank, he muſt have the Conſent of the Senate; and the ſame is neceſſary in framing and publiſhing Proclamations and other Acts of State.

It appears clearly from hence, that the Royal Power in Swe-den is as much limited as in any Country in the World; and the annulling all Pretence to arbitrary, independent, or abſolute Power in the Crown, is alſo become a fundamental Law. So that the Incroachments of Charles XI. who made uſe of the States to weaken and controul the Senate, and of Charles XII. who ſlighted and diſregarded the States themſelves to ſuch a De-gree, as to talk of ſending one of his old Boots to direct them in their Deliberations, have proved the Means of reſtoring the old Government to its full Vigour, and taught the Swedes to put their Conſtitution on as right as well as regular an Eſtabliſh-ment, as any that occurs either in ancient or modern Hiſtory.

The Revenue of the Crown, or rather Kingdom of Sweden, has been very much leſſened by the repeated Misfortunes ſuf-tained during the long War in the Reign of Charles XII. and that which happened under the late King againſt Ruſſia. But however, as the Expences of the Government have alſo been leſſened, there ſtill remains a competent Proviſion for the King's Civil and Military Liſts, and whatever elſe is requiſite for the Publick Service; ſo that while their Finances are regularly and frugally managed, they will always be able to maintain their Government in ſuch a Condition as not to ſtand at all in need of Subſidies from Foreign Courts, or to be apprehenſive in any Degree of Invaſions from their Neighbours.

They are likewiſe in leſs Danger of ſuffering by a long Peace than moſt other Nations, becauſe they conſtantly keep up a great Body of regular Troops, and that without any Danger to their Liberties. For the Army in Sweden is the Army of the King-dom, and every Foot Soldier is maintained by his own Free-hold, aſſigned by the Conſtitution; and from hence, as has been obſerved, is derived the Right of their Officers to ſit and vote in the Diet, becauſe they are poſſeſſed, as Officers, of ſo large a Landed Property therein, an Eſtate for the Maintenance of a Colonel being worth three hundred Pounds Sterling a Year, and ſo in Proportion. From whence we may eaſily diſcern, that no Argument can be drawn from this Practice in Sweden, to coun-

tenance

tenance the admitting military Officers into the Diets, States or Parliaments of other Countries, where their Circumstances are quite different.

There is another Convenience which results to the *Swedes* from this wise Settlement of their Militia, which is, that the Laws are guarded by the Soldiers ; who, as they derive their Property from their present Constitution, will be always Friends to it, and Enemies to such as shall labour to overturn it, whether Ministers or People, as appeared plainly in the Case of the last Insurrection, when the Army remained firm to their Duty, and will very probably appear in direct Opposition to his Measures, if any Prince hereafter should attempt to extend his Power beyond the Limits of the Laws. Let us next look to her Situation abroad, and in regard to other Countries.

The Interests of *Sweden* are so changed at present from what they were at the Time Baron *Puffendorf* wrote about them, that how excellent soever his Discourses might be in those Times, they can now be of little Use ; and, perhaps, instead of being serviceable they contribute to mislead us. The *Swedes*, who in former Ages had very little to do with the *Turks*, are bound at present to maintain the Engagements they have entered into with them, in order to secure their Friendship in case of a War with *Russia*. Their Interest with regard to the last mentioned Power cannot easily be stated. As long as the *Swedes* are inclined to think Peace absolutely necessary, they will live in strict Correspondence with this Empire ; but if ever they should entertain different Sentiments, and desire to recover those fine Provinces which formerly were annexed to their Kingdom, and made the most valuable Part of their Dominions, they may possibly find some favourable Opportunity of breaking with the Court of *Petersburgh*; yet this must be done with great Caution, and such an Opportunity, as Things now stand, looks as if it was at a very great Distance.

But as to any Danger that the *Swedes* are in from the present Power of the *Russians*, it seems to be much magnified by those who would be thought to apprehend it, since it is very evident, that the *Russians* are more concerned to improve what they have, than to acquire new Countries. Besides, the very Losses of the *Swedes* on the Side of *Russia*, have been attended with some Advantages elsewhere. In the first Place they have left no Room for Disputes between them and the *Poles* ; they have given the King of *Prussia* a new Interest, so that it is highly probable he will rather contribute to preserve the *Swedish* Dominions in *Germany*, than endeavour to get them into his own Hands, as having more to hope from the Friendship of the

F   *Swedes,*

Swedes, than from the small Accession of Strength which would accrue to him, by getting what they still have in *Pomerania* added to his Territories. It is the same thing in respect to *Denmark*; and though there has been a long Hatred between the People of those Kingdoms, yet they now begin to see, that this has rendered them both unconsidered; and that the only way for them to be respected, is to live in the closest and strictest Friendship, which while they do, no Foreign Power will be able to hurt, or inclined probably to provoke them.

The *Swedes* have for a long Series of Years had a very close Connection with the *French*, grounded chiefly on Treaties of Subsidy, and a supposed Correspondence between their Interests; but at the bottom this Union has been of the highest Prejudice to *Sweden*, as creating much larger Expences than the *French* Subsidies amount to, and being attended with many other and those too great Inconveniencies; and in respect to the latter, as the Power of the House of *Austria* is so much declined, and her Views so manifestly altered since the Beginning of the present Century, the *Swedes* can have nothing to fear from her on that Account, or to expect from *France*, which can be useful in no Conjuncture but this.

Their Obligations to the Maritime Powers, but more especially to *Great Britain*, have been frequent and considerable; so that Experience, as well as general Maxims of Policy, will probably incline them to a constant Cultivation of that Friendship which has so long subsisted with those Powers, and which will be always necessary, considering the great Effects their Squadrons are capable of procuring whenever they appear in the *Baltick*.

The Interest which *Sweden* had in *Germany* is much lessened, but perhaps it is still as useful, and of as great Consequence to the Nation as ever, since they yet preserve a Seat in the Diet of *Ratisbon*, are highly considered by the Protestant Powers in the Empire, and have, or may have for their fast Friends now, those who were formerly their bitterest Enemies. As to *Spain*, *Portugal*, *Italy*, and other distant Countries, tho' their Alliances may be honourable, yet they can hardly be very useful to the Crown of *Sweden*, unless her Commerce were more extensive.

On the whole we may venture to assert, that in her present Circumstances *Sweden* can only follow one of these *three* Courses. She may, if she pleases, attend to restoring the inward Strength of her People, increasing their Manufactures and enlarging their Trade, in which case she must study to preserve Peace with all her Neighbours, which may be easily effected; and will perhaps prove the safest, surest, and speediest Way of repairing her Losses,

and

and restoring her Credit, without being obliged to *France*, or any other Nations for Subsidies, which have always produced Factions and Divisions in that, and indeed all other Countries.

She may attach herself to *Russia* in support of the Interest of the House of *Holstein*, and in that case she will perhaps be able to extend her Trade through that Empire to *Persia*; and may likewise reap other Advantages from her Assistance, if any Change should happen in the present Circumstances of the Powers of *Europe*.

Or, lastly, she may throw her Weight into the opposite Scale, and in Conjunction with *Denmark*, *Prussia*, *France*, and perhaps *Poland*, establish a Ballance of Power against *Russia*, which is not impossible may likewise be attended with some Advantages. But without doubt, the first is the wisest Course : and to say the Truth, if all the Powers of the North were united, it would not only prove for their common Benefit, but great Advantages would likewise result from thence to every State in particular, and to none greater than to *Sweden*. Time will shew how far these Maxims are understood in that Country, and will, I dare say, abundantly justify the Reasonableness of these Conjectures as to the *future*, and the Impartiality of the Account we have given of the *present* Interests of this Crown and Nation.

C H A P. V.

The Revolutions that have happened in DENMARK ; *the modern History, the present Constitution, political Interests, and particular Views of that Crown.*

AS the Kings of *Sweden* affect to stile themselves Kings of the *Goths* and *Vandals*, to perpetuate the Memory of those great Nations that were once so formidable in the World, so the *Danish* Monarch might assume the Title of King of the *Cimbrians* and *Teutons*, the former of which had almost overturned the *Roman* Commonwealth when in the Zenith of its Power, and the latter established themselves in *Germany* and *Gaul*. After the Irruption of these Nations the *Jutes* took Possession of their old Territories, who bestowed their Names upon that Part of the Continent which remains under the Power of the *Danish* Kings, and is from thence stiled *Jutland*. It was towards the Close of the tenth Century, that these People became Christians. *Swenon*,

or,

or, as we call him, *Swain* King of *Denmark*, made himself Master of a great Part of *England*, and left a very extensive Monarchy to his Son *Canute*, or, as the *Danes* call him, *Knute*, sirnamed the *Great*. His Son *Harold*, who from his extraordinary Swiftness had the Sirname of *Hare-foot*, was King of *England*, but by an Error very common amongst Northern Nations, the *Danes* lost their Dominions by dividing them. *Waldemar* the First, who was crowned *Anno Dom.* 1157, took the Title of King of the *Vandals*, and made himself Master of the greatest Part of *Pomerania*. His Son *Canutus* VI. conquered *Livonia*, and introduced the Christian Religion there. He was succeeded by his Son *Waldemar* the Second, who conquered a great Part of the *Lower Germany*, but held it not long; for the Inhabitants of *Pomerania* and *Mecklenburgh* revolted; the People of *Holstein* elected a Prince of their own; and the *Teutonic* Knights made themselves Masters of *Esthonia* and *Livonia*; after which, the Power of this Kingdom was in a great measure broken, as well by civil Wars amongst themselves, as by the Advantages gained over them by their warlike and potent Neighbours.

But notwithstanding this Reverse of Fortune, it once more recovered its former Grandeur, and this by the Abilities of a Woman, who from the Power attained by her Wisdom has been justly stiled the *Semiramis* of the North. Her Name was *Margaret*, and her Son *Olaus* VI. King of *Denmark*, and Heir Apparent to *Sweden*, dying without Issue, she succeeded him in the Possession of one Kingdom, and in his Pretensions to the other. It is true, that she was opposed by *Albert*, who took the Title of King of *Sweden*; but having defeated him, and made him Prisoner, she compelled the *Swedes* to acknowledge her for their Queen. This great and wise Princess, *Anno Dom.* 1395, assembled at *Calmar* the States of *Sweden*, *Norway* and *Denmark*, and there persuaded by her eloquent Harangues, they framed and settled that Constitution which has been since stiled the UNION of CALMAR. It consisted of three principal Articles: *First*, That these three Kingdoms should for the future constitute one elective Monarchy, and upon the Demise of the reigning Prince the Successor was to be chosen by the equal Suffrages of all three Nations; the *Second*, That each Kingdom should be governed by its own Laws, defended by its own Troops, by whom all the principal Fortresses were to be garrisoned, and no Stranger to be preferred to a civil or military Employment from any Motive, or upon any Pretence whatever; the *Third*, That the General Diet, composed of the States of all the three Kingdoms, should be held for the future at *Helmstadt*, in the Province of *Halland*. This Constitution, which was intended to unite in-

2   separably

separably the Interests of the Northern Crowns, proved (so uncertain a thing is human Policy) the Cause of greater Dissention, and in consequence of that, of more cruel and bloody Wars than even those which from a Spirit of Conquest had been excited in former Ages.

These lasted for about two hundred Years, when the *Danes* having elected *Christiern* I. Count of *Oldenbourg*, he was also through the Intrigues of the then Archbishop of *Upsal*, elected King of *Sweden*, by which the Union of *Calmar* was revived ; but it was not long before the *Swedes* threw off the *Danish* Yoke again ; and this Prince dying, left his Dominions and Pretensions to his Son *John*, who after a troublesome Reign of thirty-two Years, in which he was never able to reduce the *Swedes*, deceased *April* 12th, 1513. He was succeeded by his Son *Christiern* II. who for his Luxury, Cruelty, and other abominable Vices, was justly stiled the *Nero* of the *North*. He vindicated the Claim of his Family to the Crown of *Sweden* with great Warmth, and at length, partly by Force, and partly by Favour, actually obtained the Possession of that Kingdom, and on the 1st of *November*, 1520, was solemnly crowned at *Stockholm*. In order to secure himself from all future Rebellions, he took Advantage of that Solemnity, and caused the whole Nobility of *Sweden* to be massacred at once. This rendered him so generally hated by the *Swedes*, that it was not long before they forced him to retire out of their Country. Upon his Return to *Denmark*, his Debauchery, his Oppression, and his bloodthirsty Disposition, excited such an universal Abhorrence, that several Provinces, and more especially *Jutland*, which was the most considerable in his Dominions, revolted, and at length the States unanimously resolved to depose this tyrannical Prince as an Enemy to Mankind.

The present Royal Family of *Denmark* was raised to that Dignity in the Year 1523, by the free Choice of the People, when they drove out their King * *Christiern* II. before mentioned, and placed *Frederick* Duke of *Holstein*, his Uncle, on the Throne of *Denmark*, who by confirming the great Privileges of the Nobility and Clergy, maintained himself in Possession of the Kingdom to the Time of his Death, which happened after a Reign of ten Years, and left the Crown to his Son *Christiern* III. in whose Time the Reformation took place, and the *Lutheran* Religion was established by Law in this Country. *Frederick* II. succeeded his Father in 1558, and was engaged in a long War

F 3   with

---

* The *Danes* write this Name *Christiern*, but other Nations usually write it *Christian*.

with *Sweden*, which ended however in 1570, by a Peace concluded under the Mediation of the Emperor, and the Kings of *France* and *Poland*; he died in 1588, when his Son *Christiern* IV. ascended the Throne. This Monarch governed much longer than any of his Predecessors, and in Times full of Calamity and Trouble. He first engaged himself in the Wars of *Germany* against the House of *Austria*; and in the latter part of his Reign he broke with the *Swedes*, but was very unfortunate in that War, which was terminated by a Peace made in 1645, whereby the *Danes* were obliged to give up the Province of *Halland* to the *Swedes* for thirty Years, and were also constrained to abate the Toll, which the *Dutch* paid for passing the *Sound*, in consideration of the Assistance furnished them by the Republick; after which unlucky Dispute the King governed in Peace till the Year 1649, in which he deceased.

Frederick III. was engaged by the *Dutch* to break with the *Swedes* in 1657, which had like to have proved fatal to him, as has been already shewn in the Reign of *Charles Gustavus* of *Sweden*, who besieged *Copenhagen*; and if it had not been for the powerful Interposition of the *Dutch*, had very probably taken the City, which he reduced to great Extremities. At this Juncture however it was, that the King, who notwithstanding his Misfortunes, was certainly as wise and brave a Prince as any of his Time, found Means to change the Constitution of *Denmark*, and from one of the most limited and precarious, made it the most absolute Sovereignty in *Europe*. According to their old Form of Government, the whole Power of the Nation was lodged in the Gentry or Nobility, for between these, there was in those Times no Distinction. Every Gentleman was a kind of Prince in his own Estate, and the Farmers and Countrymen were very little better than Slaves. They sent, however, their Representatives to the General Diet, where they had scarce any thing more to do than to give their Consent to Taxes, by which they were oppressed to such a Degree, that they might be justly esteemed the most wretched People upon Earth.

The Nobility formed a distinct Body in the States of the Kingdom, and without their Advice the King could no nothing of Importance; so that in Time of Peace he was very little better than President of the Council, and in Time of War no more than General of the Army. The Succession of the Crown too was very precarious; for though the Son succeeded the Father, yet as it was by the Consent of the Nobility, the Monarchy was strictly speaking elective, tho' in appearance hereditary. It is not at all wonderful that a King should be extreamly uneasy in such

Circum-

Circumstances, or that he should desire to fix himself and his Family in an easier Situation, but it is truely amazing, that after losing a great part of his Dominions, and under Circumstances of the greatest Distress, a King should be able to do this without any Foreign Force, without Bloodshed, and in less than a Week's Time; which however was what this Prince projected and happily atchieved. As this is by far the most remarkable Event in the whole Compass of the *Danish* History, it is necessary it should be considered more particularly.

In the Year 1660, immediately after Peace was restored, when the Nation was almost undone by the Misfortunes attending a tedious and bloody War, a Diet of the States was called to consider of the proper Means for re-establishing Affairs, and enabling the People to recover their Losses. The Means of doing this was far enough from being facile, and the King foresaw there would be Disputes upon the Subject in the Diet; he therefore took care to have it insinuated to some of the Clergy, and to the President of *Copenhagen*, Speaker of the Commons, that the Thing might be well enough brought about, if every body would do their Part, as they had seen the King do in the Time of the Siege. The Commons therefore by their Speaker laid before the Nobility the wretched Condition of the Kingdom, and the Impossibility there was of finding Money even for necessary Expences, if they did not consent to bear their Proportion of them, which was so much the more reasonable, as they were the great Gainers.

The Nobility, who were very numerous, and not at all apprized of the Intrigue, dealt with the Commons very roundly; they told them, that it was very high Presumption to enquire into their Privileges, and that it shewed great Ignorance of their own Condition; for their Vassals they were, and their Vassals they should remain. The Speaker of the Commons then rose up, and told the Lords, that since they would do nothing towards preserving their Privileges, they were unworthy to enjoy them; that their Answer to the reasonable Request of the Commons, was equally insolent and cruel; and that though they could not make themselves noble, the Nobility should find to their Cost, they could bring the Weight of Subjection to fall as heavy upon other People as hitherto it had lain upon themselves.

After saying this, he went out, followed by the Commons and the Clergy to a Man, retiring to a Hall in the City which had been provided for that Purpose, where they came to a quick Resolution of devolving their own Authority upon the King.

They

They went accordingly to Court, and demanded an Audience of his Majesty, to which they were immediately admitted; a Bishop and the Speaker of the Commons, having set forth that the present Constitution did not in their Opinions answer the End of Government, they were therefore resolved to make the Crown hereditary in his Majesty's Family, and leave the Administration entirely in his Hands, because they were sensible he had done all that was in his Power for the Good of his People; and would have done much more, if more had been in his Power. The King thanked them for their good Intentions, but at the same time told them, that the Consent of the Nobility was necessary to render that effectual which they had proposed. At the same time, under pretence of securing the City from any Disorders that might arise from this Ferment in the Diet, he ordered the Gates to be shut, and having the Army entirely in his Power, posted Guards wherever he judged it necessary, so that it was impossible for any body to go out of *Copenhagen* but by his Leave, which brought Things to a speedy Conclusion.

The Nobility quickly discerned the Error of which they had been guilty; but discerned it too late, as producing no other Fruit than the knowing that it was irreparable. They sent and offered the King to entail the Crown upon his Heirs Male, and to encrease his Power considerably; but the King gave them to understand that this would not answer the Purpose, and consequently would never content the Clergy and People. After this fruitless, and dishonourable Struggle, the Nobles found themselves obliged to comply; and three Days after, the King, the Queen, and Royal Family, appeared on a Kind of Theatre erected for that Purpose; and being seated in Chairs of State under rich Velvet Canopies, received the Homage of all the Senators, Nobility, Clergy, and Commons, in the Sight of the Army. And thus the Gentry of *Denmark*, in the Face of their Country, divested themselves of Right as well as Power, and made a formal Surrender of their Liberties to the Crown. The King governed after this with great Wisdom and Prudeuce, ten Years, and died universally beloved by his Subjects, whose Affections he gained by many Acts of Liberality, and by taking Care that Justice should be duly and speedily admininstred.

His Son *Christiern* V. succeeded in 1670, and having put his Affairs into very good Order, and made several powerful Alliances, he resolved to lay hold of this Opportunity to recover part of what his Predecessors had lost to the *Swedes*. But that he might be in a better Condition to do this, he

resolved

resolved to make himself Master, first, of the Person of the Duke of *Holstein*, in which he succeeded, but with very little Advantage to his Reputation; for the Duke suspecting nothing, in 1675 came to *Rensbourg* to visit him, and was there seized and put under a Guard, till such Time as he consented to relinquish the Advantages he had gained by the Treaty of *Roschild*; after which the King made himself Master of *Tonningen*, the strongest Place in his Dominions, and pursuing his Advantage likewise reduced *Wismar*.

He had also some Success in the Beginning of the next Year, but his good Fortune did not continue long; for being defeated by the *Swedes*, in the famous Battle of *Lunden*, he was from that time never able to do much against them by Land, though by Sea he was fortunate, but at last made Peace with that Crown upon equal Terms. He afterwards employed his Forces against the City of *Hamburgh*, upon which the Kings of *Denmark* always had Pretensions, which twice in his Reign he made turn to good Account. In the Year 1694, on the Death of the Duke of *Holstein-Gottorp*, his *Danish* Majesty formed new Claims upon that Family, which were for some time adjusted by the Mediation of the Emperor, and the Kings of *Great Britain* and *Sweden*; that is to say, *William* III. and *Charles* XII. whose Sister the Duke of *Holstein* had espoused. But in the last Years of his Life these Disturbances broke out again, and Things were on the Point of coming to a Rupture, when the King died in the Month of *September* 699.

His Son and Successor *Frederick* IV. acted precisely on his Father's Principles, and resolved to compel the Dukes of *Holstein* to remain dependent on the Kings of *Denmark* for the future; in order to which, he over-ran that Country, and undertook the Siege of *Tonningen*, which gave occasion to that long War in the North at the Beginning of the present Century, of which so much has been said in the former Article. The *English* and *Dutch*, as Guarantees of the late Peace, sent a powerful Fleet into the *Baltick*, and the King of *Sweden* at the same time besieged *Copenhagen*, so that the *Danes* were obliged to conclude the famous Treaty of *Travendahl*, on the 18th of *August* 1700. It was stipulated in this Treaty, that the House of *Holstein* should for the future enjoy the same Rights with other Sovereigns; that the Duke should be at liberty to raise Troops and build Forts in his own Dominions, provided they were two Miles distant from any Fortress belonging to the *Danes*, and at least a Mile from their Frontiers. It was likewise agreed, that the Crown of *Denmark* should pay
the

the Duke of *Holstein* two hundred and sixty thousand Crowns, and that the Chapter of *Lubec* should be at liberty to elect a Prince of *Holstein* for their Bishop.

It was hoped by the Maritime Powers that this Peace would have been lasting, and that no farther Debates could arise, but the very next Year however produced a new Dispute : Part of the Chapter of *Lubec* having elected the Brother of the Duke of *Holstein*, and Part the Prince of *Denmark*, Coadjutor and Successor to their then Bishop. In 1705 the Bishop died, and then the Debate ran so high, that the Maritime Powers were forced again to interpose, not indeed by Force of Arms, but by Dint of Money; in consequence of which it was agreed, that the Prince of *Holstein* should remain Bishop of *Lubec*, and that the Prince of *Denmark* should receive from the Crown of *Great Britain* a Pension by way of an Equivalent. In 1708 the King of *Denmark* made the Tour of *Italy*, and the next Year he attacked the *Swedes*, by whom he was roughly handled in *Schonen*; but in the latter End of the Year he had better Success by Sea. In 171., in Conjunction with the King of *Poland*, he fell into the *Swedish Pomerania*, where he took *Domgarten*, but failed in two other Enterprizes the same Year.

In 1712 he made himself Master of the Town of *Stade* and the Duchy of *Bremen*; but the same Year his Army was beaten by the *Swedes*, who afterwards burnt the fine Town of *Altena* to the Ground. In 1714 and 1715, he had great Success against the *Swedes* both by Sea and Land; and in 1716, he drove them entirely out of the Places they had conquered in *Norway*, and in Conjunction with the *Prussians* reduced *Wismar*; after which he did not push the War with the same Vigour for many Reasons, but chiefly because he saw that his Success would be less advantageous to himself than to his Allies. This made him the more inclinable to Peace, which was concluded under the Mediation of *George* I. King of *Great Britain*, in 1720.

By this Treaty his *Danish* Majesty obtained all that he could reasonably expect, and which to him was a Matter of great Consequence, he procured the Guarantee of the King of *France* for the Possession of the Duchy of *Slefwick*, and the King of *Great Britain* renewed his, which had been given before. After the Conclusion of this Peace, the King passed his Days in Ease and Quiet, and met with only one Accident to disturb him, the Burning of his Capital, which happened in 1728; but it has been rebuilt with great Magnificence since. This Monarch was in himself inclined to promote the Welfare and Trade of his Subjects, and willing

to

to promote every thing that might contribute to their Benefit ; but towards the End of his Life, it was thought he listen'd too much to Projectors, who induced him to enter upon Schemes which were not always attended with the Consequences he expected from them. He died however greatly regretted on the second of *October* 1730, when he had attained the Age of sixty compleat.

His Son, the late King *Christiern* VI. ascended the Throne of his Ancestors with universal Reputation. He had in his Father's Life-time been very attentive to the Concerns of the *East-India* Company, and had been in a great measure the Support of it ; which induced the People to hope that a particular Regard for Trade would be the principal View of his Reign ; and so indeed it proved. At his very Accession to the Government he made many Changes, but all of them such as gave great Satisfaction to his Subjects, who were particularly pleased with his abolishing a Farm that had been established in his Father's Time, for the sole vending Wine, Brandy, Salt, and Tobacco, which was very burthensome to the Subjects, however advantageous to the Prince. Such as were interested in the Farm offered to advance larger Sums, if it might be continued ; but the King answered, *It brought in too much, since his Subjects complained of the Exactions which it occasioned.* A Sentence worthy of perpetual Memory and Admiration !

This was not an Act done hastily, and in the Honey-moon of his Government ; but his whole Administration was of a Piece, so that he became justly reputed one of the wisest Crown'd Heads in *Europe*. In 1732 he acceded to the Treaty between the Courts of *Vienna* and *Petersburgh*, by which he obtained their Guarantee for his own, and became himself Guarantee for their Dominions, and of the Pragmatick Sanction. In virtue of a separate Article of this Treaty, the King obliged himself to pay the Duke of *Holstein* a Million of Rix-dollars, provided he renounced his Pretensions on the Duchy of *Sleswick*. It was in consequence of this Treaty, that in the Year 1734 he marched six thousand Men for the Emperor's Service, in the War that happened on account of the Succession to the Crown of *Poland*. In 1736 he terminated the old Dispute between the Crown of *Denmark* and the City of *Hamburgh*, and thereby obtained half Million of Marks of Silver from that City, as well as some other Concessions which were very advantageous to his Subjects. He soon after erected a Council of Trade, whose Business is to examine all Proposals made for extending it, in order to give such Encouragement as may be necessary for carrying them into Execution. He

like-

likewise sent for Workmen out of *Holland* and other Countries at his own Expence, to establish Manufactures in *Denmark*, and took every other Step for their Encouragement that his People could desire or expect. Amongst others he erected a Royal Bank, which has been attended with many advantageous Consequences; was always careful to keep his Fleet and Army in a proper Condition to render him respected by his Neighbours; and to prevent the Expence occasioned thereby from becoming burthensome to his People, he concluded from time to time Treaties of Subsidy with Foreign Powers, which brought in large Sums without exposing him to the Necessity of taking any Share in any of the Quarrels, either in the North or in *Germany*.

Yet this prudent and pacifick Conduct never hindered him from making Use of vigorous Measures when they appeared really necessary, as was evident in the Case of the Territory of *Steinhorst*, when he differed with the Electorate of *Hanover*, and in that of the *Iseland* Fishery, which occasion'd a Quarrel with the *Dutch*; in both which Instances he behaved with so much Firmness as to carry his Point, and that too without entering into a War. It was solely from the great Reputation he had acquired by his wise and upright Administration, that induced the *Swedish* Nation to cast their Eyes upon his Son, the Hereditary Prince of *Denmark*, when they were about to chuse a Successor to their late King; and though he did not prevail in that Point, yet he carried it much farther than could be well expected, and extricated himself at last from the Difficulties into which it brought him, with Honour.

In the beginning of the late War he was very strongly sollicited to take part with the House of *Austria* and her Allies, but could never be prevailed upon to break through that Neutrality, which appeared to be so beneficial to his Subjects. He found himself most of all embarrassed by the Pretensions of the House of *Holstein*, which having now the Countenance and Support of the *Russian* Empire, he had great Reason to apprehend that even the powerful Guarantees he had procured, might prove ineffectual for his Support. In this Situation he acted with such Prudence and Circumspection, and shewed so great a Disposition to compromise Matters upon moderate Terms, discovering at the same time by the Armaments made upon the Occasion just mentioned, that he was in a Condition, in case he was attacked, to defend himself; that after all he procured his Peace with *Russia* to be prolonged, without entering into the Discussions of the Points in Debate with
the

the House of *Holstein*; and thereby gave a Lesson to his Son, who has renewed that Treaty very lately. In fine, during the Course of sixteen Years that he reigned, he never fell into one false Step against the Interests of his Crown, or to the Prejudice of his Subjects; so that as no Prince of his Time was more beloved or better obeyed while living, hardly any at their Death have been more sincerely or universally lamented.

His Son *Frederick* V. the present Possessor of the Throne, succeeded to it *July* 26, 1746, in the twenty-third Year of his Age; he espoused about three Years before, the Princess *Louisa* of *Great Britain*, by whom he has an Heir apparent, born *January* 18, 1749. Upon his first taking the Reins of Government into his Hands, he thought fit to make a few Alterations very judicious in themselves, and acceptable to his Subjects. He has steadily pursued his Father's Maxims in maintaining Peace, improving the Trade, and encouraging the Industry of his Subjects; his Application to Business, joined to a constant and well-regulated Œconomy, has enabled him not only to live within the Bounds of his Revenue, but to make very considerable Savings. In this however, he has conducted himself as a wise and good Prince, or rather in such a Manner as to become a Model to those of his own Rank, who generously aspire to so sublime a Character; for he has demonstrated that this did not arise from Avarice, or a natural Nearness of Temper, but from a noble and truly royal Principle of doing whatever might contribute to the Publick Good. For in those Provinces of his Dominions that have suffered by inevitable Calamities, such as the Mortality among their Cattle, and the Inclemency of Seasons, he has remitted even his just Rights. He has expended very considerable Sums for encouraging and promoting new Manufactures, and he has discharged a large Debt which was due from the Crown.

This, though in itself very extraordinary, considering the Sum and the short Time he has reigned, has been attended with a Circumstance too singular to be omitted, even in this succinct Recapitulation of Events; in which we pretend not to give the History, but a few historical Remarks only upon the late Reigns. The Creditors of the Crown, as soon as they were informed of his Majesty's Design, endeavoured to prevent it, by humbly representing that if he was displeased at the Largeness of their Interest, they were content to accept of Four instead of Five *per Cent*. which had been hitherto paid them; but his *Danish* Majesty answered, that having the

Money

Money in his Coffers, where it could be of no Service to the Publick, he chose to discharge their Obligations; but that he would take it as a Favour done to himself, if they would lend the Money he now paid them at a low Interest to his Subjects, which might enable them to extend their Commerce, and improve the new Manufactures.

It is incredible to what a Degree his own and his Father's peaceable and prudent Administration have contributed to the Benefit of the Countries belonging to the Crown of *Denmark*; and how much the Face of Affairs is changed within so short a Time. New Ports have been opened, which has been owing to the opening new Channels of Trade; the Shipping of the *Danes* has been more than doubled, and the Revenues of the Crown have increased in the same Proportion within that small Space. The Court is splendid without Profusion, the King rich without Oppression, the Ministers attentive to the Duties of their respective Stations, not only from the Example of their Master, but from the Sense they have that a contrary Behaviour would infallibly draw upon them immediate Disgrace. Adored at home, and respected abroad, the King is only attentive to preserve and promote the Happiness of his Subjects, in which he places his own.

It is a Pleasure to insist upon a Subject of this Nature, and it is at the same time the Duty of a Political Writer, to shew that he has a Pleasure in bestowing just Praises, and in paying where Truth directs that Tribute of Applause which is due to good Princes, from all who have Occasion to enquire into, and are thence enabled to become acquainted with their Characters. Besides, it serves to illustrate that great and leading Maxim in Politicks, that where the actual and real Interests of any Government are the same, that is, where the particular Views of the Prince coincide with the Publick Good, the Progress made is equally swift and great. Yet this is a Remark that is commonly left to distant Historians, from an unaccountable, and at the same time a most unwarrantable Propensity to commend past, and to condemn our own Times, whereas we ought to shew the same Impartiality with respect to both. It is by adhering to this honest and equitable Spirit only, that an Author can hope to render any Service to his Reader, and to make his Writings esteemed useful rather than agreeable Amusements; which, how much soever they may entertain for a Day, from the Neatness of their Dispositions, the Sprightliness of their Sentiments, or the Elegance of their Language, cannot fail of sinking speedily into Oblivion; since, as the immortal Master of the *Roman* Elo-

quence

quence long ago obferved, Opinion is a fleeting Thing, but Truth and Reality fubfift without feeling the Effects of Age.

The *Danes* have been formerly efteemed a very warlike Nation, and though from their Misfortunes in their Wars with the *Swedes*, their Power is much diminifhed, yet the Credit of the *Danifh* Troops is ftill very good. The Forces the King keeps up are very well paid and difciplined, and are numerous enough to fecure his Dominions againft any Invafion, more efpecially as his Fleet is in excellent Order, and as the *Danifh* Seamen and the *Norwegians* are juftly reputed the beft in the North. His Revenue amounts to between two and three Millions of Rixdollars, which the prefent King has fo prudently employed as to have always Money in his Coffers, and to defray all the Charges of Government, without loading his People with extraordinary Taxes, fo that we need not wonder he is fo univerfally beloved. The Clergy, though they have but fmall Livings, are as much confidered in *Denmark* as in any Country in the World ; becaufe fince the great Change in their Government beforementioned, the Tranquillity of the Nation depends very much upon their Influence over the People, which they have hitherto conftantly exerted in Favour of the Crown.

The Laws of this Country have been defervedly in Reputation, as lying within a very narrow Compafs, a moderate Quarto containing them all ; and the Adminiftration of Juftice is fo well looked after, that Suits in this Country are but few, and thofe very fpeedily determined. The King makes and repeals Laws as to him appears neceffary for the Good of his Subjects, but the Crown has always ufed this Power with much Moderation and Difcretion : fo that as *Denmark* may be truly faid to be the only legally abfolute Government in *Europe*, perhaps in the World, the People have had lefs Reafon to regret the Change made by themfelves than could well have been expected ; and if their Monarchs copy after the Example of their prefent King, the *Danes* will feel fewer Evils from the Want of Liberty, than in other Nations are produced by the Abufe of it.

What has been already faid, fufficiently explains the domeftick Interefts of this Nation, which having fuffered extreamly by the warlike Temper of many of its Princes, as well as by the too great Power of the potent Families of their Nobility in former Times, muft be content to aim at repairing their paft Miftakes by an induftrious and frugal Conduct for the future. Titles were not formerly in ufe here any more than in *Sweden* ; but of late thofe of Baron and Count have
been

been introduced, and about thirty or forty Families have been honoured with them by the Crown.

The Kingdom of *Norway*, which still remains united to that of *Denmark*, is of great Consequence; and under the last and present Reign there have been great Improvements made in its Trade, and the Inhabitants have been used with more Indulgence than formerly. The same thing may be said in regard to *Iseland*, and other Islands belonging to the Crown of *Denmark*, which have been of late Years put in all Respects into a much better Condition than they were; so that their Commodities come to a better Market, their Manufactures are in a much more flourishing Condition, and the Number of their Inhabitants, Towns, and Shipping, is continually increasing; whereby, in the Space of another Century, if no Wars break out, or unforeseen Confusions happen, the *Danes* will become quite another People, and their Monarchs make a greater Figure than they have done for some Ages past; which will probably be owing to the Necessity they must find themselves under of living upon good Terms with *Sweden*, that they may not be in any Danger from the Power of *Russia*: for it has been the perpetual Quarrels between the *Swedes* and *Danes* that have kept both Nations low; as the Extinction of this Humour would infallibly render them both great, or, which is perhaps better, secure.

In respect to the Empire, *Denmark* has not much either to hope or to fear; for if she can but preserve the peaceable Possession of *Sleswick*, it will be a sure Barrier to her Dominions on the Continent; and with regard to her Islands, as the Princes of the Empire have no great Maritime Power, she cannot be much in Danger on that Side. As to her Disputes with the House of *Holstein*, they can be only dangerous to her from the Support that Family may receive from the Interest it has at present in *Russia*, which though at first Sight it may appear very formidable, yet, when closely examined, the Scene will be much changed. For in the first Place, there are but very few Powers in *Germany* that would be pleased to see the *Russians* in that Country; and the Powers that have guaranteed *Sleswick* to *Denmark*, would not fail in such a Case for their own Sakes to interpose. Besides, it is really more for the Interest of the House of *Holstein*, to receive a good Equivalent for its Pretensions to that Duchy, than to enter again into the Possession of it, unless with a View to facilitate the Conquest of *Denmark*, which would bring on them all the Powers of the North at once.

The

The Hereditary Claim which the Kings of *Denmark* have upon the City of *Hamburgh*, cannot in all human Probability ever furnish them with the Means of bringing that City under their Power ; becaufe all its Neighbours, who are much fuperior in Force to the Crown of *Denmark*, are in Interest concerned to preferve it, and fo indeed is the whole *Germanick* Body. But it is not at all unlikely that future Quarrels, like the paft, may enable the Crown of *Denmark* to draw from time to time confiderable Sums from the Inhabitants of this rich City ; though after all, as the Trade of *Denmark* increafes, the true Intereft of that Kingdom will be beft promoted, by entertaining a fair Correfpondence with the *Hamburghers*, who, by taking Quantities of their *Indian* Goods, will render them more real Service in their prefent independent State, than if (which I faid before is very improbable) the *Danes* fhould ever obtain Power enough to bring them into Subjection. Befides, the Crown of *Denmark* will always find it requifite to live upon good Terms with their *German* Neighbours, that in cafe of War either with *Sweden* or *Ruffia*, fhe may depend upon their Affiftance, without which fhe will fcarce be able to defend herfelf.

The Interefts of *Denmark* with regard to *Sweden*, are very much changed from what they were. The *Danes* remembering their ancient Power when their Kings were poffeffed of the whole North, have very often attempted to re-conquer *Sweden*, and continued thefe Endeavours fo long and fo unfuccefsfully, that, without the Affiftance of her Allies, *Denmark* was in the utmoft Danger of being conquered in her Turn. In thefe Difputes the *Danes* loft fome of their beft and moft fruitful Provinces to the *Swedes*, which was a new Caufe of Difcontent, and in reality, produced two or three of the laft Wars, which however favourable the Conjunctures might be when they were undertaken, yet did not by any Means prove fortunate in this Refpect, the *Swedes* ftill retaining thofe Dominions conquered from *Denmark*, though they have fuffered feverely elfwhere.

At prefent, Things have quite altered their Appearance, and the fudden and furprizing Increafe of the *Ruffian* Power has taught the *Swedes* and *Danes* to open their Eyes a little to their true Interefts. We may therefore reafonably expect, that for the future thefe Nations will be better Neighbours, and inftead of aiming at the Conqueft one of the other, will make it their Study, by living in a clofe Conjunction of Interefts, to preferve the Independency of both, which may be effectually done, if the old Rancour between the

G   two

two Nations can be but thoroughly extinguished. This seems to be in a great Measure done already, from the Influence which his late *Danish* Majesty shewed he had over the Commons of *Sweden*, who were almost unanimously in the Interest of his Son. But though such a defensive Alliance may effectually answer the End before mentioned, yet there seems no Reason to believe that the *Swedes* and *Danes* will engage in an offensive War against *Russia*, or that they would have any great Success therein, if they should.

As to the Interests of *Denmark* with respect to that potent Empire, they certainly consist either in maintaining so strict and close a Friendship therewith, as to prevent thereby all Apprehensions of Danger, which however can scarce this Way be done ; or by allying herself in such a Manner as to have no Reason to fear any Attempts from *Russia*, which may very easily be done ; because it is very natural for all the Neighbours of a superior Power to unite against her for their own Security ; and besides, if it should at any time so fall out, that the *Russians* should prove too hard for such an Alliance, the Maritime Powers would certainly interpose to preserve the Ballance in the North, which Ballance so nearly concerns them, and which of all others, by exerting only their natural Strength, they are most able to keep even.

It is for this Reason that it imports *Denmark* above all things to maintain her Friendship unimpaired with the Maritime Powers, who are both of them her natural Allies : His *Britannick* Majesty being bound in both Capacities, I mean as King and Elector, as well by Interest as by Treaties, to support the *Danes*. On the other hand, the *Dutch* have been always fast Friends to *Denmark*, and must be so as long as they continue a free State ; there seems no room therefore to doubt that *Denmark* will constantly use her utmost Endeavours to cultivate a good Correspondence with Nations from whom she hath so much Good to expect, and from whom it is not probable she can ever have any thing to fear.

The remote Situation of *Denmark* in respect to the Southern Parts of *Europe*, has hitherto hindered any great Communication between them ; but that is not likely to continue long the Case, since his present as well as his late *Danish* Majesty is intent on extending the Commerce of his Subjects, particularly into the *Mediterranean* ; with which View he hath not only obtained various Concessions from the Court of *Vienna*, but has entered into some Negociations with the Court of *Spain* likewise ; and has lately concluded a Treaty of Commerce with the King of the *Two Sicilies*.

The

The great Thing which has hitherto deterred the *Danes* from attempting the Trade of *Italy*, and other Countries adjacent, was the Apprehension of having their Ships continually taken by the *Algerines* and other Piratical States of *Barbary*. But the late King, to remove these Difficulties, was pleased to equip a small Squadon for the Protection of the *Danish* Merchant-Men in those Seas ; and declared that he would continue to send such a Squadron every Spring, which at the same time that it exercised the Seamen in his Service, and secured the Trade of his Subjects, made the Flag of *Denmark* known and respected in those Parts, and thereby promoted that Prince's capital Design of being considered as a Maritime Power. Whether the present Monarch will be soon able to carry this into Execution, will depend upon the general Turn of Affairs in *Europe*, of which it is certain that no Prince is more capable of forming a true Judgment, or making a right Use. The War, while it continued, proved also favourable to those Views, as it afforded the *Danes* an Opportunity of disposing of dried Fish, and other Commodities carried usually into the *Mediterranean* by other Nations. It is also more than probable, that the Hopes of vending *East India* Goods in those Countries, may have some Share in these Projects, though hitherto nothing can be affirmed on this Head with Certainty, because the Treaties relating to these Points are, at least most of them, as yet but in Embryo. But as a Peace has been concluded with the Piratical States in *Africa*, there is now no longer occasion to send annual Squadrons into the *Mediterranean*.

It has been suggested by some Writers, that the *Danes* may have it in their Power to supply the *French* and other Nations with Beef, Butter, and other Provisions, upon as easy Terms as they can be had from *Ireland*, which would certainly prove a very great Advantage to them, and no small Prejudice to us ; but it has fallen out unluckily for them during the Course of the last War, that a contagious Distemper prevailed amongst their Cattle, which prevented those Experiments from being made, by which this Matter might otherwise have been determined. However it is very certain, that *Denmark* and *Norway* can furnish a Multitude of Commodities of Value in the Southern Parts of *Europe* ; and wherever they fix their Trade, it will necessarily occasion a Connection of Interests, and thereby render the Crown of *Denmark* more considerable than she has hitherto been ; more especially if there be any Truth in what has been suspected, that the late revoking the Treaty of Commerce with the *Dutch*

by

by the Court of *Versailles*, was with a View to make Trial of
what might be done by encouraging a Fish Trade from the
Danish Dominions. This the *Dutch* themselves have apprehended ; and it is one of the principal Reasons why they have
taken so much Pains in negociating with the Court of *France*,
in order to get that Edict recalled, from a Jealousy, that how
indifferently soever this Trade may answer at first, yet in
Time all Difficulties may be removed, especially where two
absolute Monarchs are concerned, who can oblige their Subjects
to do and bear what they please ; which is a very high
Advantage towards carrying either good or bad Measures into
Execution.

I shall conclude this Article with endeavouring to explain the
Conduct that *Denmark* ought to pursue, and that which the
present King has all along pursued with regard to *France*. It is
certain that formerly the close Connection between the *French*
and the *Swedes* made the *Danes* jealous of the former, and attached them more closely to the Maritime Powers ; but the
present King of *Denmark* seems in some measure to deviate
from this Point of Policy, and has, of late Years especially, been
careful to maintain a good Correspondence with *France*. We
must not however persuade ourselves from thence, that this
Monarch has deserted his old Principles, or that he is not as
much convinced as any of his Predecessors of the Importance
of his Friendship with *Great Britain* and *Holland*.

The Truth is, that the State of Things between *Sweden*
and *Denmark* being very much altered, the King of *Denmark*
has the less Reason at present to be jealous of the *French* Influence there. Besides this, we ought to consider, that as it
was not either the Interest or Intention of his *Danish* Majesty
to take any Share in the War lately determined, or to part
with his Forces to any of the Powers engaged therein ; so his
receiving Subsidies from *France* to do this, that is, to keep an
exact Neutrality, which is also all that *France* desires, is really
receiving them for nothing ; and it ought to be considered as
a Master-piece of Policy, that his *Danish* Majesty has found
Ways and Means to oblige the *French* not only to pay these
Subsidies, but also to grant his Subjects very considerable Advantages in Trade for acting in such a manner, as the Maxims of his Government would have led him to act independent
of these Motives.

But if Affairs should alter, there is no doubt the King of
Denmark will alter his Conduct ; for we may with greater
Certainty reckon on the Behaviour of this Prince, than we can
upon

upon almost any other ; because we are sure that he will always do what is fit for him to do, and neglect nothing that is suitable to his Dignity, to his Love for Peace, and his Regard for the true Interests of his Subjects.

CHAP. VI.

A brief View of the present State, modern History, legal Constitution, political Interests, and particular Views of the Crown and Republick of POLAND.

THERE is so great a Mixture of Truth and Falshood in the Notions commonly received as to the Power and Circumstances of this Government, that at the same time it becomes extreamly necessary, we find it also highly difficult to separate and distinguish them. This Perplexity arises from a peculiar Cricumstance, which will be at large explained hereafter, but of which we are also obliged to say somewhat here. The dominant Power in *Poland* is not a King, a Minister, a Council, or Senate, but the whole Body of the Nobility ; and the ruling Passion of this dominant Power, is to preserve this Prerogative, which for the Sake of giving it a good Name, they are pleased to stile *Liberty*, in its full Extent. This therefore may be considered as the accidental Interest of *Poland*, that is, in contradiction to its real Interest ; which, as in all other Countries, is no other than the Good of the whole.

But here lies the Misfortune, that, as the Persons who pursue this accidental Interest have a constant Succession, there is but very little Ground to hope that the real Interest will ever prevail. Now this Circumstance makes the common Opinion of the Fickleness, Imbecility, and Instability of the *Polish* Government really true ; whereas, if any Method could be fallen upon to bring the *Poles* to understand, to vindicate, and support their true Interest, nothing would be more false ; for they would then have a fixed and proper System, which they have a Force more than sufficient to maintain ; and instead of being one of the weakest and least respected, *Poland* would become one of the most powerful, and in consequence of that, one of the most considered Kingdoms in *Europe*.

If the Reader will reflect upon this Remark, which is strictly founded in Truth, he will be very seldom at a Loss

for the Caufes of the principal Events whieh occur in the
Hiftory of *Poland* in Times paft, or make at this Day the
Subjeét of our Gazettes. To render the Ground of our Af-
fertion clearer, it may be proper to infift on a few Points relative to this Country in general. If we confider *Poland* with
regard to its Extent, we fhall find it thrice as big as *France* properly fo called ; in its Figure it is nearly round, fo that all its
Provinces conneét with each other, and are confequently capable of contributing to their mutual Defence. It muft indeed
be owned, that the Fruits of *Spain*, the Flowers of *Italy*, and
the Vines of *Hungary*, are not to be found in any Part of *Poland* ; neither can it be affirmed that the Cities and great Towns
approach in Size to thofe of *Germany*, or have any relation in
point of Neatnefs to fuch as we meet with in *Holland* ; but notwithftanding this, the Country is far from being barren or
thinly peopled.

We may judge how plentifully it is ftored with Corn, from
its being ftiled the Granary of the North, and from the vaft
Quantities of that Commodity annually exported from *Dantzick* ; it abounds alfo in Cattle, without any Exaggeration beyond moft Countries in *Europe* ; its Forefts furnifh Timber of
all Sorts, and for all Ufes, and that in a Degree more than fufficient for the Confumption of its Inhabitants, notwithftanding
that they employ frequently Timber to thofe Purpofes, for
which in other Countries they make ufe of Brick and Stone.
Its Lakes are full of feveral Kinds of excellent Fifh, and in
the Woods and Heaths there is variety and plenty of Game.
Some Mines there are, more efpecially of Salt, which are in-
exhauftible. The Climate is in Winter pretty fevere ; they have
great Rains in the Autumn, but their Summers are generally
fpeaking warm and pleafant.

The *Poles* are naturally aétive, hardy, and robuft ; the Gentry have many Virtues, they are open, generous, and hofpitable,
very civil to Strangers, and for the moft part Men of Honour ;
their greateft Failing is Vanity, and a ftrong Inclination to live
after their Manner in a wild kind of Magnificence. As for the
Polifh Ladies, they are Women of exemplary Piety and Virtue ;
and as to the meaner Sort of People, they are confeffedly lazy
and ignorant, which however is rather to be charged on the
Conftitution of their Government, than any Defeéts in their
Country ; for where the Law has rendered Peafants incapable
of poffeffing Property, one cannot fuppofe they will take pains
to acquire it. Their having no Ports ftriétly fpeaking, except
Dantzick, is the Reafon that they have little Commerce with
their Neighbours ; but this Deficiency muft be alfo charged
upon

upon their Government; for when they were in a better Condition in that Respect by their being in Possession of *Livonia*, they shewed no great Inclination to improve them. Their Turn in general is to Arms and good Fellowship; but from domestick Feuds and Animosities their Valour is mostly experienced upon each other, and by their intestine Divisions they have often become a Prey to those Nations, whom if they had been united, they had Strength sufficient not only to repulse but to conquer.

This makes them very good Neighbours, for their Ambition has never tempted them, at least for some Ages past, to make any Attempts upon others; but then the Power of their Nobility is so great, that the People are apt to shew but little Vigour in the Support of it; nor can this be wondered at in any Nation where the People cannot be properly said to defend themselves. The *Polish* Armies, as we shall see hereafter, have fought with Success and Glory against the *Turks* and *Tartars*; but this was owing to their Nobility mounting on Horseback, and deciding the Business in one or two Campaigns. The same thing that we collect from their Victories, we may infer also from their Defeats; they have suffered deeply from their Wars with the *Swedes*, and of late have been greatly awed by the *Russians*; in both Cases however this has been owing to their having to do with regular Forces, which a Crown Army composed of thin Battalions under a bad Discipline and poorly paid could never resist.

While their Monarchs had a reasonable Degree of Power, they protected them from such Misfortunes, as we shall see hereafter, by the establishing a proper Militia, to whom they assigned Lands in lieu of Pay; but through Errors in Government those Regulations have been long subverted, and the *Cossacks* who in former times were the Defence of *Poland*, act now on the Side of their Enemies. But after all, perhaps none of these Mistakes are irretrievable; and if the present Weakness and Distress of that Kingdom, which is greater than ever, should at last inspire them with a true Notion of their Errors, and incline them to Amendment, it might still appear their Case is not past Remedy; tho' if nothing of this kind happens, it will be very soon. Their Neighbours have already encroached upon them in such a manner, as nothing but their Factions could have encouraged, and nothing but their Folly and want of publick Spirit could have brought a brave Nation to bear. But it is now time to pursue our ordinary Method, and to enter upon a Series of Facts necessary to render these, as well as our subsequent Reflections intelligible.

There

There are few Histories more confused than that of *Poland*, insomuch that we know little or nothing with Certainty, or at least with Certainty enough for our Purpose, before the Reign of *Jagellon*, who mounted the Throne in the latter End of the fourteenth Century. He was Grand Duke of *Lithuania* and a Pagan; but on his being elected King of *Poland* he became a Christian, and took care to make his Subjects so; he also united the whole of his hereditary Dominions to those of *Poland*, which induced the *Poles* to have such a Regard for his Memory, as to preserve the Crown in his Family until his Male Line extinguished in *Sigismund Augustus* in 1552.

After much Confusion and a long Struggle between the two Factions, *Henry* Duke of *Anjou*, Brother to *Charles* IX. of *France*, was elected King of *Poland*, in preference to *Maximilian* of *Austria*; but before he had enjoyed the Crown four Months, his Brother died, and *Henry* returned privately into *France*, which Kingdom he governed by the Name of *Henry* III. and this Election and short Reign introduced the Correspondence between the *French* and the *Poles*, which has subsisted ever since, but very little to the Advantage of the latter.

At first, the Nobility of *Poland* expressed prodigious Resentment at the Usage they had met with; King *Henry* having taken the Advantage of a dark Night to make his Escape and to desert that Throne, to which, not without much Trouble and Sollicitations, he had been admitted; and therefore upon his Abdication, the Party which had espoused the Cause of *Maximilian* of *Austria*, endeavoured to revive his Pretensions, and to place upon his Head that Diadem which his Rival had quitted; but however they were not able to carry their Point, the Majority of the *Poles* being inclined to chuse a Prince that they were sure would reside amongst them; a Thing they could no more expect from *Maximilian* than from *Henry* of *Anjou*, considering the Views the former of these Princes had in *Germany*.

It was for this Reason, more especially, that they made Choice of *Stephen Batori*, Prince of *Transilvania*, who had already gained a great Reputation by his Courage. He found notwithstanding some Difficulties to struggle with in the beginning of his Reign; for a considerable Party declared against him, and seized upon the City of *Dantzick* on the Behalf of *Maximilian*. King *Stephen*, however, took the wisest Way to establish himself on the Throne of *Poland*, by marrying *Anne* the Sister of *Sigismund Augustus*, of the Royal House of *Jagellon*, which procured him the Affection of all his Subjects. After reducing *Dantzick*, he engaged in a War against the

Muscovites,

Muscovites, from whom he recovered all that they had taken from the *Poles*; and his Success in this War enabled him to settle the *Ukrain*, which in the *Polish* Language signifies the Frontiers, which before his Time had been a wide and wild Desart.

He was likewise the Author of the Military Tenures among the *Poles*, by which he rendered them the best Cavalry in the World. But because he very well knew that Horse alone was not a Strength sufficient to defend such a Kingdom; and was sensible also that the Nobility would never serve on Foot, he devised a new Militia composed of the *Cossacks*, a rough and barbarous Race of People, who had hitherto been the Plague and Scourge of *Poland*, and on whom he bestowed the *Ukrain*, where he settled them in such a manner, that the *Poles* might always command a great Body of Infantry, without being at any more than an easy Expence. Thus he wisely provided for the interior Security of the Kingdom on one hand, and for its Protection against the *Muscovites*, *Tartars*, and *Turks* on the other. For these People being in part settled in the Islands of the *Borysthenes* or *Nieper*; they from thence made the most dreadful Incursions by the *Black Sea* into the Territories of the *Turks*, taking and burning the Cities *Sinope* and *Trebisonde*, and even pillaging the Suburbs of *Constantinople*.

This great King died in 1586, at a Time when he was engaged in a War with the *Turks*, and left behind him a Reputation as great as that of any Prince of his Time, and bequeathed to the *Poles* as a Legacy, such a Military Establishment, as duly attended to would have always defended them from the Ambition of their Neighbours; but which by their Seditions, Factions, and Corruptions, gradually decayed, and is now in a great measure lost.

The Peace and Prosperity of *Poland*, as it was restored by King *Stephen*, seemed to be destroyed at his Death; for though at all the *Polish* Elections, Discord and Confusion had been and still are common, yet we read of none so great as at this Time, the Nation being equally involved in Religious and Political Disputes; so that on one side the *Lutherans* came into the Field with ten thousand Men, and on the other the Senate had a great Body of good Troops to support the Catholick Cause. The Competitors for the Crown were three, each supported by a numerous and powerful Faction.

The first was *Theodore*, Czar of *Russia*; the second *Maximilian*, Archduke of *Austria*, who now for the third time pretended to the Crown; the third was *Sigismund*, Prince of *Sweden*. It was argued in favour of the first, that if he was

elected

elected he would render *Poland* the moſt powerful Monarchy in *Europe*, by adding thereto all the Dominions of *Ruſſia.* The perſonal good qualities of the ſecond were chiefly inſiſted upon, and which is pretty ſingular, he was ſupported by the *Pope*'s Nuncio and the *Lutherans.* As for the laſt, he was the Son of the Sſter of their late King *Sigiſmund*, and conſequently the Heir Male of the Family of *Jagellon*, and for this Reaſon chiefly, by the Aſſiſtance of the Senate, was choſen on the ninth of *Auguſt* 1587.

The Archduke *Maximilian* however marched with an Army into *Poland* to diſpute this Election, but was routed in two Engagements ; and in the laſt being made Priſoner, was obliged to renounce all his Pretenſions, to the Crown of *Poland.* By this Means *Sigiſmund* III. became the peaceable Poſſeſſor of the Kingdom, but was diſappointed in the Deſign he formed of keeping that of *Sweden* alſo : for as he was a violent Papiſt, the *Swedes* refuſed to acknowledge him, and therefore placed upon the Throne the Duke of *Sundermania*, which occaſioned a long War between the two Kingdoms. He reigned forty-four Years, and in that Time gave ſignal Proofs of his Courage and Conduct, particularly againſt the *Turks*, tho' in the Wars againſt the *Swedes* he was very unfortunate.

He was ſucceeded, tho' not without a great Struggle, by his eldeſt Son *Uladiſlaus* VII. who was choſen the 13th of *November* 1632. This Monarch proved very ſucceſsful in the Beginning of his Reign againſt the *Ruſſians*, *Turks*, and *Swedes* ; forcing each of them to make Peace with the *Poles* upon Terms advantageous to that Nation. But in the Year 1637, Diſturbances broke out with reſpect to the *Coſſacks* ; for the *Poliſh* Nobility having acquired great Eſtates in the *Ukrain*, prevailed upon the King to take away from that Militia the Privileges granted them by King *Stephen*, which proved of very bad Conſequence to the Nation ; that Diſpute laſted beyond the Date of that King's Life, which determined on the 20th of *May* 1648.

He was ſucceeded by his Brother *John Caſimir*, who had aimed at the Crown when *Uladiſlaus* was choſen, afterwards became a Jeſuit, and was promoted to the Rank of a Cardinal; which he reſigned in hopes of the Crown. After his Election he married his Brother's Widow, a *French* Woman ; to whoſe Intrigues were chiefly owing all the Misfortunes that attended his Reign. We have in our Account of the Kingdom of *Sweden* ſhewn how he was driven out of his Dominions by King *Charles Guſtavus*, but how he got Poſſeſſion of them again

'is

is a Point of History so little known, that it may not be amiss to insert it here. The *Danes* having attacked the *Swedish* Dominions, King *Charles* offered to give up all his Conquests in *Poland* for 800000 Rixdollars, which Offer was readily accepted; but the *Poles* found it very difficult to raise the Money. The Elector of *Brandenburgh*, who had called in the *Swedes*, perceiving that he was likely to lose their Assistance, privately proposed to the *Poles* to pay this Money and to assist them against the *Swedes*, if they would renounce the Sovereignty of the Ducal *Prussia*, which he held as a Vassal to the Crown of *Poland*: this was accepted and performed on both Sides, and ratified in the famous Treaty of *Oliva*, by which the *Poles* ended all their Differences with their Neighbours.

This Circumstance Sir *Robert Southwell* declared, at a Meeting of the Royal Society, he had from the Mouth of the Elector of *Brandenburgh*. After this King *Casimir* might have reigned in Peace, if he had not formed a Project to render himself absolute, in order to which he raised an Army of thirty thousand Men, most of them *Germans*. But this Design being discovered, Prince *Lubomirski*, the Crown General, at the Head of the *Polish* Troops, fell upon the King's Army, defeated them totally, and made their General, who was a *Frenchman*, Prisoner.

We need not wonder that after such a Blow as this, the King should be out of Humour with his Subjects, or that his Subjects should have no longer any Confidence in such a Prince; but the Methods he took to be revenged on them deserve to be made known, more especially as they proceeded from the Advice given him by his *French* Queen, and those of her Nation, whom she procured to be admitted into his Council. In the first place, he excited the *Cossacks* to rebel, and to throw off their Subjection to *Poland*, a Thing so base as would never have been believed, if he had not been weak enough to have written a Letter under his own Hand to their Generals for that Purpose, which they produced, and thereby proved it incontestably.

Another Scheme of his, still meaner than the former, answer'd his End more effectually. He pretended to be very sorry for the Mischiefs he had occasioned, and having called a Diet at *Leopold*, he there proposed redressing publick Grievances, and paying the Army. The best Expedient that could be found to effect this, was to call in the Gold and Silver of the Kingdom, and recoin it. But this having been found deficient, the States consented to have vast Quantities of Copper coined, which

before

before had been very scarce in the Country, and to raise its intrinsick Value to almost double the common Standard. With this Money the King paid the Publick for what they brought in, as likewise the Arrears of the Army, but kept all the Gold and Silver, which he afterwards remitted into *France*, and soon followed himself, when he had beggared the Nation, for which the *Poles* abhor his Name even to this Day.

He had now reigned twenty Years with very little Quiet, and less Credit ; he saw plainly that it was impossible for him to enjoy the One, or recover the Other in *Poland*; and therefore he resolved to resign the Crown, which he accordingly did in the Church of St. *John* at *Warsaw*, *Sept.* 16, 1668 ; and afterwards retiring into *France*, died at *Nevers* in *December* 1671. But as he was Abbot of St. *Germains* near *Paris*, he was buried there under a magnificent Tomb of Brass, with a pompous *Latin* Inscription, attributing to him many Virtues which he never had, and in which there is not the least mention of those Follies and Vices by which he lost his Honour and his Crown.

This Resignation threw the Kingdom of *Poland* into fresh Distractions, for immediately four Candidates declared themselves ; the first was the Great Prince of *Russia*, on whose behalf the *Czar* his Father made large Offers. The second was the Duke of *Newbourg*, supported by the *French* Interest. The third was the Duke of *Lorrain*, who had the *German* Faction for his Friends. The fourth was the Son of the Prince of *Conde*, espoused by many of the Nobility out of Respect to his Father. The first and the last of these Candidates were soon laid aside, but the Factions of the other two were of such equal Strength, that a Civil War was apprehended.

The Palatine *Opalinski* however changed the whole Face of Affairs by a Speech, in which he told them, that it was a Shame they should either admit of a Foreign Prince, or suffer Foreigners to prescribe to them who should be their King; that their Ancestors did not act in this manner; but when they found themselves in such a Situation, made choice of their Countryman *Piastus*, distinguished only by his Virtues, who governed them so prudently, that tho' he lived to be one hundred and twenty, his Death was as much regretted as if he had been cut off in the Flower of his Age. This Speech was so well received that the whole Assembly cried out, A *Piast!* A *Piast!* which is since become a Phrase to express a *Polish* Candidate in Opposition to a Stranger.

At the next Meeting the same Palatine was called upon to name one of the Nobility worthy of the Crown ; upon which he made another Speech, at the Close of which he proposed poled Prince *Michael Wiesnowiski*, who was descended from a Brother of *Jagellon*. He was not remarkable for Parts, for Courage or Fortune; and it was generally suspected that he was mentioned to make way for some other powerful Nobleman; but it so fell out, that as the Palatine pronounced his Name, a Swarm of Bees flew over his Head, upon which the People cried out unanimously, *God save King* MICHAEL! That Prince, who was himself present, broke out into Tears, declared that he was very unfit for a Crown, and begged they would proceed to a new Election, but it was to no Purpose; the Diet persisted in their Choice, so he became a King whether he would or not.

Michael Wiesnowiski having thus had the Crown forced upon him by the plainer and honester part of the Assembly, was crowned on the seventeenth of *September* 1670: He had been, while a Youth, one of the Lords of the Bedchamber to the Emperor *Leopold*, who notwithstanding consented very readily to his Marriage with the Princess *Eleonora* of *Austria* his Sister, which at first raised some Jealousies and Discontents amongst the Nobility, who were afraid he made this Match with a View to enlarge his Power at the Expence of the public Liberty; but the Easiness of his Temper, and his Readiness to consent to whatever they asked, very soon convinced them, that their Fears were groundless; and that they had nothing to dread from this Monarch on the Side at least of his Ambition.

But in the Year 1672, the *Turks* under Pretence of having taken the *Cossacks* under their Protection, invaded *Poland*, and very soon made themselves Masters of *Kaminieck*, the Capital of *Podolia*, a Place till then esteemed impregnable; and so much superior their Forces appeared to any that he could raise against them, that the King resolved to make the best Peace he could, which however proved a very indifferent one; for by it he covenanted to give them a great Sum of Money for sparing that City and its Inhabitants, and stipulated besides, that he would pay the *Turks* a constant Tribute of 22,000 Gold Ducats *per Annum*. As advantageous as this must appear, the *Turks* nevertheless were not long before they renewed their Hostilities, which obliged the Crown-General *Sobieski* to venture a Battle under great Disadvantages, in which however he gained a compleat as well as unexpected Victory. But the King did not live to receive the Pleasure of this News, dying suddenly on the sixteenth of *November* 1673, not without strong Suspicions of Poison. He was thirty-two Years of Age, a Man of much Mildness, Moderation, and Piety; but one who was

far

far enough from having the great Qualities requisite to fill the Throne with Dignity, more especially in such a Country as *Poland*.

The next Diet of Election was attended as usual with great Confusion; the Candidates were the Czar of *Muscovy*'s youngest Son; the Prince of *Transilvania*; the Elector of *Brandenburgh*'s eldest Son; the Duke of *Lorrain* and the Prince of *Conde* were also named, with some others. At last there were three Factions form'd; the first of the *Lithuanians*, who were for the Duke of *Lorrain*; the second of the *Polish* Nobility, who were most of them for the Duke of *Neuburgh*'s Son; and the Army, who pretended to be for the *French* Prince, who tho' not named, was understood as (I have said) to be the Prince of *Conde*. By Degrees all the Factions were reduced to two, one for the Duke of *Lorrain*, and the other for the *French* Prince.

In the End however, this Election, like the former, was decided suddenly by a Speech. The Palatine of *Russia* stood forth and said, "That the *Lithuanians* had dishonoured their "Country, by protesting so violently as they had done against "a *Piast*, or Native of *Poland*; that it was dangerous at this "Juncture to choose a *German* Prince; and that for his part "he would speak his Sentiments plainly. That they were on "the Point of sinking into the lowest State of Contempt, if "they had not been delivered by the late Victory over the "*Turks*, and that as it was won by the Crown-General *Sobieski*, "so he only deserved to be *King*, by whose Courage and Con- "duct they still remained a *People*." This did the Business effectually; for tho' the *Lithuanians* protested against it that Day, yet they recanted the next, and so the Election became unanimous, which was the more singular as it was perfectly just and reasonable.

John Sobieski being thus raised to the Crown, was desirous of prosecuting the War against the *Turks*, in which he was very indifferently seconded by the Nobility, who tho' they before promised an Army of 60,000 Men, yet made a Difficulty of furnishing him with 40,000 after he was elected. The King, notwithstanding this, carried on the War, and in the Year 1675 obtained the greatest Victory the *Poles* ever had to boast; for in the Neighbourhood of the City of *Leopold*, with 5000 Men in an open Plain he defeated 60,000 *Turks* and *Tartars*, who fled in one Night as many Leagues as they had marched in three Days; and afterwards with an Army of 15,000 Men he drove above 100,000 *Turks* and *Tartars* out of *Podelia*.

2   When

When he had thus secured the Peace of the Kingdom, he returned to *Cracow*, where on the second of *February* 1676, he was crowned with great Magnificence. He made a very honourable Peace with the Infidels not long after, which lasted till the Year 1683. In that Year they invaded *Germany*, and besieged *Vienna*, to the Relief of which the King of *Poland* marched with 20,000 Men ; and having joined the Electors of *Bavaria* and *Saxony*, and the Duke of *Lorrain*, who had about the same Number, he on the twelfth of *September* attacked the Grand Vizir, who had an Army of near 200,000, entirely defeated them, forcing them to raise the Siege, and fly with the utmost Precipitation. The King made his Entry into *Vienna* through the Breach, with the great Standard of the *Turks* taken by his Troops carried before him.

He afterwards continued the War for some time longer, tho' he thought himself but indifferently treated by the Emperor. On his Return to *Poland*, he met with much Uneasiness and Discontent ; the Nobility apprehending that he intended to make the Crown hereditary in his Family, and that it was with this View he hoarded up so much Money ; for it was computed that in the Space of twenty Years, he saved near two Millions Sterling. His Cares and Fatigues brought on a Complication of Distempers, which carried him off the seventeenth of *June* 1696, in the sixty-sixth Year of his Age, and twenty-second of his Reign. At the Time of his Decease, he was the Oldest, the Richest, and for personal Courage the most renowned Monarch in *Europe*.

After the King's Death, Cardinal *Radziouski*, Archbishop of *Gnesna*, and Primate of the Kingdom, took the Administration of the Government, as is usual, upon him, and notified the King's Death to Foreign Princes, and to all the Governors of the Provinces, and advised with the Senators that were then at *Warsaw*, as to the most proper Method and the fittest Time to chuse a new King. They fixed upon the twenty-ninth of *August* 1696, for the Convocation of the grand Diet ; but there appearing several Competitors, and these too supported by powerful Factions, it was thought necessary to take more Time to appease the Dissentions of the Nobility ; for which Reason the Overture of the Diet was deferred to the fifteenth of *May* 1697.

They then chose the Sieur *Belinski* for their Speaker, whom they call *Marshal*. The chief Competitors were Prince *James* of *Poland*, and his Brother Prince *Alexander*, the Prince of *Conti*, Don *Livio Odeschalchi*, and Prince *Lewis* of *Baden* ; but at last the Elector of *Saxony* unexpectedly came to the
Frontiers

Frontiers of *Poland* with 8000 Men, and declared himself a Candidate, having a Twelvemonth before privately abjured his Religion to qualify himself for this Crown, which procured him the Interest of the Pope and Clergy ; so that at length no considerable Party appeared but for him, the Prince of *Conti*, and Prince *James*.

The Cardinal Primate, with a great Number of the Palatins, supported the Interest of the Prince of *Conti*, the *French* having for several Years before given a great Character of his Merit and Valour, which made the King of *Franec* believe that he would undoubtedly carry that Crown, as it is probable he would have done, had he been in Person as near the Place of Election as the Elector of *Saxony* was ; for on the 26th of *June*, being the Day of Election, the Diet drew out into the Field, and he had that Day more Votes than either the Elector of *Saxony* or Prince *James*, which the Primate observing, went with his Party and immediately proclaimed him King.

But the two other Parties knowing that this could not be legally done, without the unanimous Consent of the Diet, protested against it ; and Prince *James* perceiving his Party to be the weakest, and having always been in the Interest of the House of *Austria*, as being married to the Sister of the Empress and Queen of *Spain*, resigned all his Interest to the Elector of *Saxony*, who was likewise supported by the Emperor. These two Parties being thus united, were more numerous than that of the Prince of *Conti* ; and therefore coming next Day into the Field, they got the Bishop of *Cujavia*, after the Primate had refused it, to proclaim *Frederic Augustus* of *Saxony* King of *Poland*, and sent Ambassadors to desire him to accept of the Crown ; he accordingly entered the Kingdom with his Forces, and marched directly to *Cracow*, where he was crowned.

The other Party endeavoured however to maintain their Election ; but the Prince of *Conti*, who came from *Dantzick*, finding he should have no more Friends in *Poland* than he purchased with his Money, and that they would continue so no longer than they were supplied with it, determined to quit his Claim, as he did, and so left the peaceable Possession to King *Augustus* ; who notwithstanding this was far enough from meeting with that Duty and Respect which he hoped for ; so that new Disturbances were on the Point of arising immediately, if they had not been prevented by the Wisdom and Moderation of the King.

In the Beginning of the Year 1700, he had brought Things into some tolerable Degree of Order, and might very pro-
b..bly

bably have reigned peaceable enough, inasmuch as with all the great Qualities that could be wished for in a Prince, he had an Affability and Freedom in his Behaviour that was very engaging, and withal an almost boundless Generosity, which is a Quality much esteemed in all Countries, but more especially acceptable in *Poland*. I say, notwithstanding what was past, he might have reigned as quietly as any of his Predecessors, if he had not a little rashly embarked himself in a Quarrel with the King of *Sweden*, in the Manner we have already related in some of our former Articles.

This it was that gave an Opportunity to that Faction which had supported the Prince of *Conti*, once more to make head against the King, under Pretence that he had violated the Laws by bringing in his *Saxon* Troops, and by taking other Steps that were inconsistent with the Convention into which they had entered at the Time of his Election, and which, according to their Constitution, was to be the sole Rule of his Government. The King of *Sweden* encouraged this Party, and even went so far as to hint to them, that the only Way to make themselves easy and gain his Friendship, was to declare the Throne vacant, and elect a new King; which when they saw that Monarch in a Condition to support them, they made no Scruple of doing, and accordingly they made choice of *Stanislaus Leczenski* Palatine of *Posnania*, a young Nobleman about the same Age with the King of *Sweden*, who on the fourth of *October* 1705 was crowned at *Warsaw*.

The next Year his Confederate *Charles* XII. of *Sweden* entered *Saxony*, where he reduced King *Augustus* to such extreme Distress, that he was glad to make Peace upon such Terms, as were imposed on him by his Enemy, amongst which the hardest was this, that he should acknowledge the Title, and write a Letter of Felicitation to *Stanislaus* as King of *Poland*. In the succeeding Year the last mentioned Prince was acknowledged by all the Powers in *Europe*; but the Year following, that is, in 1708, the King of *Sweden* being defeated in the famous Battle of *Pultowa*, it soon became evident, notwithstanding these Recognitions, that *Stanislaus* would lose his Kingdom almost as soon as he had acquired it. He had indeed a Body of *Swedish* Troops about him, with which for some time he endeavoured to maintain himself in Possession; but at length found he was under a Necessity of quitting his Country, and following the *Swedish* Monarch into the Dominions of the Grand Signor.

In 1709 King *Augustus* resumed the Sovereignty, and before the End of the Year the *Swedes* were obliged to retire absolutely out of the Kingdom. In 1710, King *Augustus* held a

H   Diet

Diet at *Warfaw*, where he was congratulated by the Senate and Nobility on his Return, and the neceffary Refolutions taken to fecure his peaceable Poffeffion of the Throne; but the Meafures which beft fecured him were thofe taken by himfelf, by keeping near his Perfon a confiderable Body of his faithful *Saxons*, and acceding to the Treaty concluded between the Czar and the *Turks*, which delivered the *Poles* from the Dangers of a Foreign War, 'tho' it was far enough from extinguifhing their domeftic Factions.

In the Year 1713, there was a Confpiracy formed againft the King, but it was happily difcovered and prevented. He thought fit thereupon, after making the neceffary Difpofitions for fettling the Affairs of the Kingdom, to retire for fome time into *Saxony*, whence he did not return till the Year following, when he found new Symptoms of Jealoufy and Difcontent in that Country, with which he was much offended; becaufe to purchafe the Good-will of the *Poles*, he had voluntarily pardoned two of his greateft Enemies, remitted a third Part of the Taxes granted for the Support of the Army, and had ordered thirteen Regiments of his *German* Troops to leave the Kingdom.

Some of the difcontented Senators demanded a Diet on Horfeback, which his Majefty refufed to call, becaufe he forefaw it could anfwer no End, but that of giving Rebellion the Colour of a legal Proceeding. There were however fome of the Nobility who actually began to mount, and fhewed a Difpofition of holding fuch an Affembly without the Royal Licence; but the King prevented this, by declaring pofitively that he would treat as Rebels all who fhould prefume to meet together without fuch an Authority as the Conftitution had rendered requifite; and to incline thefe People to hearken more readily to Reafon, he recalled his *German* Troops; and having alfo renewed the Peace with the *Turks*, he began to enjoy more Quiet than he had done from the Time he firft afcended the Throne.

In the Year 1724 happened the unfortunate Affair of *Thorn*, which had like to have plunged the Republick into a War with moft of the Proteftant Powers in *Europe*. The City of *Thorn* is one of the moft confiderable in that Part of *Pruffia* which belongs to *Poland*, and is generally fpeaking inhabited by Proteftants. There were however fome Papifts, and they had invited a few Jefuits thither to educate their Children. Some of their Scholars quarrelled with the Townfmen, this occafioned a Riot, and the pulling down a Part of the Houfe in which the Jefuits lived; upon which, the Magiftrates not interpofing in time, fome other Exceffes were committed. Upon
this

this a Tribunal was erected, composed of some Grandees and Senators of *Poland*, who after examining into the Affair, caused the chief Magistrate Mr. *Reusner* to be beheaded, and some of the Townsmen to be hanged and their Bodies burnt; they likewise changed the Magistrates of the Town contrary to the Treaty of *Oliva*, which obliged the Crowns of *Great Britain*, *Sweden*, and *Prussia*, to interpose, as Guarantees of that Treaty, in favour of the Protestants; but the Affair being drawn into a Negotiation, the bad Effects that were apprehended from those violent Proceedings were prevented, though the Protestants had not that Justice done them, which from the Nature of that Treaty, and the Power of those Courts that interposed on their Behalf, they had just Reason to expect.

There followed not long after another troublesome Affair, which because it may hereafter be revived and create new Disputes, it is necessary we should consider more at large. The Dutchy of *Courland*, which was anciently a Part of *Livonia*, was a Fief of the Crown of *Poland*, and had been held as such by the Family of *Ketler*, from the Year 1561. *William* Duke of *Courland* married, in the Year 1710, the Princess *Ann* of *Russia*, Daughter to the Czar *John*, and Niece to the Czar *Peter*, but died without leaving any Children of that Marriage: By his Demise the Dutchy descended to his Uncle *Ferdinand*; but the Dutchess Dowager took Possession of it by Force, and the Duke was obliged to live at *Dantzick* in very indifferent Circumstances.

The King of *Prussia* laboured to procure this Country for the Margrave of *Brandenburgh Swedt*, who offered to pay the Debts with which it was charged; but the Grandees of *Poland* were strongly inclined to let it remain no longer a separate Dutchy, but rather to unite and incorporate it with the rest of *Poland*, to be governed in the same manner as other Parts of the Kingdom. The Nobility of *Courland*, who are very numerous, were extremely alarmed at this, and therefore in the Name of Duke *Ferdinand* called a general Diet in order to elect a Successor, in which they chose Count *Maurice* of *Saxony*, the natural Son of King *Augustus*, afterwards so well known to the World by the Title of Marshal *Saxe*. But Duke *Ferdinand* having disavowed the Edict by which the Assembly was called, and the *Poles* highly resenting this Election, King *Augustus* was forced to declare against his Son, and he was, tho' not without Difficulty, compelled to retire by the *Russian* Troops.

H 2   This

This was in the Year 1728, and from that Time *Poland* grew more and more uneafy, from an Apprehenfion that the King intended to fecure the Crown to the Electoral Prince on his Deceafe, which they pretended was a high Violation of their Conftitution; tho' their Election of this very King rather than Prince *James Sobiefki* was the firft Inftance that ever happened in *Poland* of the deceafed King's Son being fet afide; their Crown, tho' always elective, having gone in a direct Line for eight hundred Years. King *Auguftus* laboured all he could to fatisfy the Nobility, and to compofe their Differences, but to no Purpofe.

His Sicknefs hindered him from holding a Diet at *Grodno* for that Year, and the next the Factions were fo high that no Diet could be held; upon which the King retired much diffatisfied into *Saxony*, and the *Lithuanians* drew up a ftrong Proteft againft his leaving the Kingdom without the Confent of the Senate, and fpecified therein alfo feveral other Grievances. The King called another Diet in 1730, which broke up without coming to any Refolution. In 1732, he called a third extraordinary Diet at *Warfaw* with no better Effect. He fummoned however a fourth extraordinary Diet in the Beginning of 1733, but was prevented from holding it, by Death. His Deceafe happened on the 27th of *January* that Year, and left the Affairs of this Country in great Confufion.

It is recent in every one's Memory, that the Death of King *Auguftus* of *Poland* gave rife to a bloody War between the Houfes of *Auftria* and *Bourbon*; but how this came about, and what were the Meafures taken by the different Parties from the Beginning of that Affair to the End, is not fo generally underftood, and yet there is nothing that deferves to be better known than the Myftery of this whole Tranfaction.

The late Emperor, *Charles* the VIth, was very far from being fatisfied with the Conduct of King *Auguftus* in the latter Part of his Reign, becaufe he fufpected, not without Grounds, that he had fome Engagements with the Courts of *France* and *Bavaria*, far from being favourable to the Pragmatic Sanction; for which Reafon the Imperial Intereft was employ'd in *Poland* rather to traverfe than promote the King's Views with refpect to the Succeffion.

But when his *Polifh* Majefty was dead, and the Imperial Court found his Son the prefent King very tractable with refpect to its favourite Point the Pragmatic Sanction; this gave a new Turn to the Councils of the Court of *Vienna*, and engaged them to favour that Meafure which they had hitherto impeded.

On

On the other hand, *France* from first to last openly supported the Interest of King *Stanislaus*, whose History, from the Time of his being driven out of *Poland*, is, in few Words, this. His generous Friend the King of *Sweden* assigned him his paternal Inheritance the little Dutchy of *Deux Ponts* for his Subsistence, which he held so long as that Prince lived, but upon his Demise the next Heir took Possession, and King *Stanislaus* was forced to retire to *Strasburgh*, where he lived on the Bounty as well as under the Protection of his Most Christian Majesty, who in the Year 1725 married the Princess *Mary* his Daughter; which consequently interested *France* extremely in his Favour. His numerous Alliances, his shining Virtues, and his being freer from Vices than almost any Prince of his Time, had preserved him many Friends in *Poland*; so that is was no difficult Matter for the Marquess *De Monti*, the *French* Ambassador in that Kingdom at the Death of King *Augustus*, in Conjunction with the Primate, to form a potent Faction in his Favour, more especially as they were both Men of great Abilities.

But the Electoral Prince of *Saxony* being supported by the Courts of *Vienna* and *Petersburgh*, a double Election ensued. King *Stanislaus*, who passed into that Country immediately after the Throne became vacant, went to *Warsaw*, where he was received and treated as King, but was very soon driven out again by the *Russian* Army commanded by Count *Munich*, and obliged to retire to *Dantzick*, in which he sustained a long Siege, ran great Hazards, suffered many Hardships, and at last with infinite Difficulty made his Escape to *Koningsberg*, where he was honourably protected by the late King of *Prussia*.

In the mean time the Crowns of *France* and *Spain* broke with the Emperor, upon Pretence of this Dispute, and of his having supported King *Augustus* III. and prosecuted that War with great Vigour in *Germany* and *Italy*; till at last having carried their Point, and forced the Emperor to a Peace, all the Care that was taken of King *Stanislaus* was, that he should enjoy the Title of King of *Poland* and the Possession of the Duchy of *Lorrain* for Life, and on the other hand *France* and *Spain* acknowledged King *Augustus*.

It was very clear from their whole Management of this Affair, that the Court of *Versailles* was never in earnest in the Support of *Stanislaus*'s Title to this Crown; but made use of it only as a Colour, first of engaging in a War against the House of *Austria*, and next for obtaining an immediate Possession of *Lorrain* under his Name, which otherwise they could never have gained. After this Peace was thus conclud-

H 3   ed

ed there broke out a War between the late Emperor, affifted by the late *Czarina*, againft the *Turks*, in which, notwithftanding the Share thofe two Powers had in raifing him to the Throne, King *Auguftus* took no Part ; and indeed the miferable Condition his Kingdom was in from a fhort but fevere Civil War, might very reafonably exufe it.

He has ever fince continued in the peaceable Poffeffion of his Dominions, and the *Poles* have had nothing to difturb them but Broils and Difputes among their great Families, from which they never were, or indeed are ever like to be free ; fince from a miftaken Notion of Liberty, they look upon the unbounded Power of their Nobility as the moft valuable Part of their Conftitution, and thereby fuffer themfelves to be cheated by the *Sound* of *Freedom* out the *Thing* itfelf.

Frederick Auguftus III. King of *Poland*, Elector of *Saxony*, was elected to the firft of thefe Dignities, *September* 23, 1733, in the forty-feventh Year of his Age. He had long before efpoufed his prefent Queen *Maria-Jofepha*, of the Houfe of *Auftria*, Daughter to the late Emperor *Jofeph*, which attached the Court of *Vienna* fo clofely to his Interefts, as to make great Conceffions in the beforementioned Treaty in 1736, for the fake of procuring his Election to be acknowledged by thofe who had difputed it. Yet on the breaking out of the laft War on the Score of the late Emperor's Succeffion, he was fo far from making ufe of the Difpofition of the *Poles* to affift the Queen of *Hungary*, that he entered into the Views of the Houfe of *Bavaria*, and, as Elector of *Saxony*, marched a Body of Troops into *Bohemia*, in Conjunction with the *French* and *Pruffians* as Auxiliaries of the Emperor *Charles* VII. But after the Treaty of *Breflau*, he went over again to the *Auftrian* Intereft, and by an Alliance concluded at *Warfaw*, undertook to fend a Body of Troops into *Bohemia*, for the Service of the Queen of *Hungary*.

He likewife endeavoured to draw the Republick into an Augmentation of its Forces to give Weight to the fame Caufe ; but by an unforefeen Accident the Diet fell into great Confufion, and rofe without coming to any Refolution. The King of *Pruffia* (who has always had both good Intelligence and great Influence in *Poland*) not fatisfied with defeating his Views in that Country, attacked him in his Hereditary Dominions in the following Winter, made himfelf Mafter of *Drefden*, and forced him to a Peace on his own Terms, fince which his Conduct has been again very different from what it was before.

In

In the Spring of the Year 1746, his *Polish* Majesty thought fit to make some Promotions in that Kingdom, which it was believed tended to a Coalition of Parties, and very soon after it was obferved that fome of the *Polish* Lords, who, tho' they were preferred by the reigning Family, had never been confidered as very warmly attached to it, Interefted themfelves extreamly in removing the Prejudices of fuch as had continued for many Years in an avowed Oppofition. The *Polish* Minifter at the Court of *Peterfburgh* alfo began to confer clofely with fome Ambaffadors and Envoys, whom till then he had avoided. There grew alfo a Difference, or at leaft a Difagreement with the Court of *Vienna*, on account of the Sums that were expected to indemnify his *Polish* Majefty for the great Expences occafioned by the Stay of the *Auftrian* Forces in *Saxony*. The like Syftem of Politicks prevailed the next Year, and notwithftanding the Allies were in want of Troops, and fhewed a great Inclination to take a Body of *Saxons* into their Pay, which appeared alfo a Meafure not at all improper for the Court of *Drefden* to have complied with upon advantageous Terms, it was waved notwithftanding, or rather flighted.

This occafioned many Speculations, till about the Middle of that Summer a double Marriage was concluded with the Houfe of *Bavaria*, in confequence of which the Electoral Prince of *Saxony* efpoufed on the 9th of *June*, 1747, the Princefs *Maria-Antonietta*, Daughter to the late Emperor *Charles* VII. and in lefs than a Month after the Elector of *Bavaria* married the Princefs *Mary-Ann* of *Saxony*. The World had fcarce Time to reflect on the Confequences that might follow from fo clofe a Junction between thefe two Courts, when their Attention was farther awakened by the Report of a Marriage of ftill greater Importance. The Dauphinefs, Daughter of their Catholick Majefties, dying in Child-bed of a Princefs, it was forefeen that the Dauphin could not long remain a Widower, and within as fhort a Space as Decency would allow, the Marriage of that Prince was declared with the Princefs *Maria-Jofepha* of *Saxony*, which took Effect in the Month of *February* following.

It is true that thefe Matters belong rather to the Affairs of *Germany* than to thofe of *Poland*, but inafmuch as they feem to have operated very powerfully in that Kingdom, no great Inconfiftency will appear from our treating of them in this Chapter. The Court of *Ruffia* having granted a Body of Auxiliaries to the Maritime Powers, they traverfed *Poland* about this Time in their Paffage to *Moravia*; and though they met with no Interruption, yet it did not remain a Secret to the World, that fome

Intrigues

Intrigues tending that Way had been set on Foot amongst the *Polish* Grandees, by the Count *Da la Salle*, a *French* Officer, who had been in the *Russian* Service, and was now charged with a Commission, or at least had a publick Character given him from his most Christian Majesty to the City of *Dantzick*; but being a little slow in producing his Letters Credentials, though he had been brisk enough in his former Negotiations at *Warsaw*, he was at the Request of the *Czarina*, arrested by the Magistrates of *Dantzick*, and confined in their Citadel. This occasioned a great Noise, more especially upon his being retaken after making his Escape, which did not hinder his attempting it a second Time with better Success, and then taking his Rout through *Prussia* he arrived safely in *France*, where for Form Sake, he was arrested. This produced some Altercations between the Courts of *Petersburgh* and *Warsaw*, that at first threatened extraordinary Consequences, but by Degrees have been buried in Oblivion.

His *Polish* Majesty in the next Spring caused the necessary Preparations to be made for holding of a Diet, of the Success of which there were great Hopes, more especially after the King's coming to *Warsaw*, where he resided upon this Occasion longer than at any Time during his Reign. This however, like the former Diet, proved ineffectual; but the Nobility having shewn an Inclination to see Prince *Xavier*, his *Polish* Majesty's second Son, settled in that Capital, it is believed their Sollicitations will not be slighted, nor is it at all improbable that the utmost Endeavours will be used to recommend this young Prince to the Affections of the *Poles*.

In the mean Time the Affair of *Courland* was again brought upon the Carpet, and the States of that Country encouraged to proceed to a new Election, though there were then no less than three Princes who flattered themselves with having each a Title to this Duchy ; *viz.* the Marshal Count *Maurice* of *Saxony*, formerly elected by the States ; the Duke of *Biron*, once in Possession, and now deposed; and Prince *Lewis* of *Brunswick Wolfenbuttle*, who was elected when the former Duke was deprived. It is not easy to discover what Turn this Affair, which is still depending, though the Number of Candidates is lessened by the Death of Marshal *Saxe*, will take, or what Measures the Court of *Poland* will think proper to pursue in so nice and critical a Business. But there is very little Reason to doubt the Decision of this Affair will instruct us what to think of the Views of his *Polish* Majesty and his Ministers, and whether there is any Reason to credit that Report which for some time prevailed, of *Poland*'s entering into an Alliance with the Courts

of

of *Vienna* and *Peterfburgh*, and the Maritine Powers, for maintaining the Tranquility of thofe Parts, or to another Rumour of a very different and even oppofite Nature, which however is not althogether deftitute of Probability.

There are few Political Conftitutions fo little known to the reft of *Europe*, as that of *Poland*; and- yet it deferves to be very well underftood, becaufe, taken altogether, it is fuch a Conftitution as bears no Refemblance to any other, ancient or modern. Thofe who live under it have a King, and yet the Government is ftiled, and that with Propriety enough, a Republick. In many Cafes, the King feems to be no more limited than another Prince; and yet Experience fhews that he can do little or nothing. The Nobility of *Poland* are the moft Powerful and Independent of any perhaps in the whole World; and yet they hate an Ariftocracy, becaufe that would make them fubject to fome of their own Body, whereas they account themfelves equal. They are paffionately fond of Liberty, and yet they feldom enjoy it; for either they are Penfioners to Foreign Crowns, the Creatures of their own Prince, or are engaged in fome Faction or other, fo that they are often governed by Intereft, as often by Prejudice, and feldom or never by Principle or Reafon.

They are indifputably as brave as any People in the World, and *Poland* alone has brought one hundred thoufand Horfe into the Field; yet no Army has been fo often beat, no Country fo frequently over-run. They are generally fpeaking far from being rich, and yet they are the only Nation in the World afraid of Commerce, and that provide by Law againft the raifing a naval Power. They have been for fome Ages declining, and yet they have feldom or never taken any Step to prevent it. Their Political Conftitution has been the continual Source of their Misfortunes, and yet they are fond of it to a Degree of Enthufiafm, and which is ftill more extraordinary, are moft zealous for thofe Points of it, by which they have fuffered moft. This is a fair and juft Reprefentation of the State of *Poland*; and whoever confiders it will be certainly of Opinion, that the Caufes from which fuch ftrange and remarkable Events flow, deferve to be enquired into, and made known; for though in general, there are few People ignorant of the Facts before ftated, yet the Fountains from whence they fpring have not been fo clearly difcovered as they deferve.

The only Diftinctions in *Poland*, are Peafants, Citizens, and Nobility. As to the firft, they are the moft miferable People on the Earth, for they belong abfolutely to their Lords;
they

they have no Poſſeſſions, nor can they have any; they work three or four Days in a Week for their Maſters, without Meat or Wages, and employ the reſt of their Time to gain a poor Subſiſtence for themſelves. What they hold is at the Will of their Lords; and if one of theſe gives a Piece of Land to a Peaſant, he orders his other Peaſants to build a Houſe for him, and to furniſh him with a Cow, Hens, Geeſe, and as much Rye as will keep him a Year. As they labour for their Lord in Time of Peace, ſo if he is diſpoſed to quarrel, they muſt fight for him likewiſe, and they do both willingly and chearfully. They are conſidered by their Maſters, and conſider themſelves as their abſolute Property; and therefore if ill treated they bear it, and if well uſed they are thankful.

Learning is the only Road to Liberty, and if a Peaſant he ordained a Prieſt he is free; but then no Man can ſend his Son to School, or the Univerſity, without his Lord's Leave: This low Condition abaſes their Minds, and puts it pretty much out of their Power to revolt. The People in Towns are in a Condition very little better; they may indeed purchaſe, which a Peaſant cannot, but then this extends only to a few Houſes, and to a certain ſmall Quantity of Ground within a League of the Place in which they live. The Citizens of *Dantzick*, and of ſome other Places in *Pruſſia*, as well as thoſe of *Cracow*, *Leopold*, and *Vilna*, are exempted from theſe Reſtrictions, and live in ſome meaſure like other People.

With reſpect to the Nobility of *Poland*, every Gentleman or Nobleman has his Coat of Arms granted by the Republick; but then he, or ſome of his Family, muſt have an Eſtate there in Land. They are capable of the greateſt Offices in the Kingdom, and may buy Lands where they pleaſe; and have each of them a Right to be elected King, if their Credit and Intereſt can procure it. Every Gentleman is a Sovereign Prince in his own Lands, and has Power of Life and Death over his own Tenants, who have no Laws or Privileges to protect them. They dare not leave his Lands to reſide in others on Pain of Death, unleſs he ſells them, and if he do, his Tenants paſs with his Lands; but if their Lords raviſh their Wives or Daughters, the Tenants may leave his Service.

If one Lord kills another's Peaſant, he is not puniſhed for it, but obliged only to give him another in his Room, or as much Money as will buy one, and to maintain the Family of him that is killed. If he kills one of his own Slaves, he only pays a ſmall Fine; nay, if one Gentleman kills another, he cannot be apprehended or impriſoned, unleſs convicted

by

by a Court of Juſtice, which gives him Time enough to eſcape; and when condemned, he cannot be executed without the King's Conſent. No Soldiers can be quartered upon the Gentry; if any Officer does it, the Diet either ſentences him to die, or declares him infamous. The Houſes of the Nobility are Sanctuaries, ſo that no Delinquent can be taken thence by Force, though he ſhould be arreſted, and fly thither afterwards.

All the Gentry of *Poland* are equal by Birth, and therefore they do not value Titles of Honour, but think that of a Noble *Pole*, or Gentleman of *Poland*, the greateſt they can have. Neither the King or Republick beſtow the Title of Prince, which belongs only to the Sons of the Royal Family: For though ſome *Poliſh* Nobles are made Princes of the Empire, and as ſuch enjoy the Title of Prince, they have no Precedency upon that Account; nor have they any Dukes, Marquiſſes, Counts, Viſcounts or Barons, but what have Foreign Titles, which the reſt generally deſpiſe; for they do not value any borrowed Character, or lofty Denomination, but ſay it is intrinſick Worth and Services done to their Country that deſerve Preferment.

King *Sigiſmund* III. eſtabliſhed an Order of Knighthood of the *Immaculate Conception*, created ſeveral Knights, and allowed them Privileges and Superiority above others; but they were ſo much undervalued and deſpiſed by the reſt of the Gentlemen of their Country, that the Order ſoon came to nothing. Theſe great Privileges make the *Poliſh* Gentry powerful. Many of them have alſo large Territories, with a deſpotick Power over their Subjects; ſome of them have Eſtates of five, ſome of fifteen, ſome of twenty, and ſome of thirty Leagues in Extent. But the pooreſt Gentry have their Votes in the Diet as well as the richeſt; ſome of them are Hereditary Sovereigns of Cities, with which the King has nothing to do. Prince *Lubomirſki* poſſeſſes above four Thouſand Towns and Villages; ſeveral of them can raiſe five, ſix, eight, and ten thouſand Men, and maintain them at their own Charge.

After all this, which is collected from Books, it is requiſite to inform the Reader, that notwithſtanding what all Writers tell us of the Grandeur of the *Poliſh* Nobility, it is to be underſtood with great Reſtrictions, for they are moſt of them very little better in fact than our Highland Chiefs; and though it be true that they can raiſe and maintain conſiderable Bodies of Troops, yet it is generally ſpeaking to be underſtood in their own Country, where inſtead of ſerving to any good Purpoſe, they

O;

only prove a Means of difturbing the State, and hindering the Execution of Juftice. There are indeed twelve or fifteen great Families, that may be confidered rather as Princes than Nobility, which have great Revenues, large Territories, and exorbitant Power; as for Inftance, Prince *Lubomirfki*, who has at leaft fixty thoufand Pounds *Sterling* a Year, and who has fometimes had feven thoufand Horfe, Foot, and Dragoons in his own Pay.

The *Radzivil* Family were formerly very powerful; fo were alfo the Princes of *Sapieha*; and the Families of *Czartorifki*, *Jablonowfki*, *Pryzemfki*, *Lipfki*, and *Poniatowfki* are fo now. The King of *Poland* might formerly enoble any Man, but at prefent he only propofes fuch, and they are enobled by the Diet; but whoever is raifed to the Magiftracy in *Cracow* or *Vilna*, is thereby enobled for himfelf and his Pofterity. Nobility may be alfo forfeited various Way, as by committing an infamous Crime, by exercifing any Retail Trade; but as for the Products of their own Eftates, the *Polifh* Nobility may fell and export them Cuftom-free. Their Honours are likewife forfeited by bearing any Office in Cities or Towns that are not privileged.

The Government of this Country is entirely in the Hands of the Clergy and Nobility. The Archbifhop of *Gnefna* is Primate of the Kingdom, and the Pope's Legate *born*, that is, in Virtue of his Office; he has a Gold Crofs carried before him when he goes to the Diet, or to the King; and when he fits, his Chaplain holds it behind his Chair. He is the firft Subject in the Kingdom at all Times, but during the Interregnum he may coin Mony in his own Name; all the Officers of the King's Houfhold attend him, and he enjoys the Revenue of the Crown for that Time. There are befides fixteen Ecclefiaftical Senators, and the Number of Lay Senators is one hundred and twenty-eight.

In order to underftand this perfectly, it is neceffary to obferve, that the whole Kingdom is divided into *Palatinates*, each of which is governed by a *Palatine*, who is in the Nature of a Lord Lieutenant, appointed by the King for Life; and the Office of Senator is annexed to his Dignity. It belongs likewife to the Governors of moft of the ftrong Places in the Kingdom, who are called Caftellans. The Governors of Cities are ftiled Starofts, but very few of them are Senators. An Example will make this Matter clearer than all that can be faid about it. *Great Poland* is divided into two Provinces: *Poland Proper* and *Cujavia*; of thefe, the former contains five Palatinates, and the latter two. The firft Palatinate in

Poland

Poland is that of *Poſnania*, which contains two Cities, *Poſ-nan* and *Gneſna*, and twelve large Towns; the Senators from this Palatinate are the Archbiſhop of *Gneſna*, the Biſhop of *Poſnan*, the Palatine, and the Caſtellan of that City, and ſix other Caſtellans. The City of *Gneſna* has a Caſtellan, but he is not a Senator; and the City of *Poſnan* has a Starolta or Mayor, who is choſen annually, and while he is in Office bears the Title of General of *Great Poland*, but he is no Senator for all that.

All the Senators take an Oath to preſerve inviolable the Rights and Liberties of the Republick, and the King can do nothing of Conſequence without their Conſent. Four of theſe Senators always attend their Prince wherever he is, and have a Right to examine into every thing, and to give him what Advice they think right. Once in three Years the King is obliged to call a Diet, or an Aſſembly of the States; but he may, by the Advice of the Senate, call a Diet at any other Time, but then it is ſtiled an extraordinary Diet. It is a fundamental Point of their Conſtitution, that their ordinary Diet ſhall meet twice at *Warſaw*, and once at *Grodno* in *Lithuania*.

When the King reſolves to aſſemble the States, he ſends his Circular Letters of Summon, which are ſtiled *Univerſalia*, to each Palatinate, ſix Weeks before the Day of Meeting, in which he expreſſes the Time, Place, and Matters to be con-ſulted upon. Then the Leſſer Diets are convened in each Palatinate, in which the Nobility meet to chuſe their Deputies, or *Nuncios* as they are called; of whom *Poland* ſends one hundred and ſeventy-eight, and *Pruſſia* ſeventy. Theſe Mem-mers are not elected by Plurality of Voices, but unanimouſly; and if this cannot be brought about, they break up in Confu-ſion. The Grand Diet conſiſts of the upper and lower Houſe; the Former is compoſed of the *Senators*, the Latter of the *Nuncios*. The firſt Step to be taken is for the lower Houſe to elect a Marſhal of Speaker, about which they frequently diſagree, and ſo break up in Confuſion, and there ends that Diet.

But if this Point be once well got over, they then enter upon Buſineſs, and Bills are brought in; but as every Nuncio has a Negative Vote, it is eaſy to conceive that there can be nothing more difficult than to conduct an Affair of any Conſequence through ſuch an Aſſembly; yet when this can be done, five Days before the Cloſe of the Diet the Nuncios go into the Upper Houſe, and there with the Senators reviſe and ſettle all that has paſſed in the Seſſion. The utmoſt
Time

Time the Diet can fit is fix Weeks, and if Bufinefs cannot be done in that Time, it is left undone, let the Confequence be what it will; as in 1649, when the *Turks* and *Coffacks* had almoft over-run the whole Kingdom. Before they rife, the Marfhal or Speaker goes in their Name to take Leave of the King, which he does by a civil or faucy Speech, juft as he is in the Humour. The Reafon why the Seffion is confined to fo fhort a Time, is this: The Nobility bring with them fuch a Number of Guards and Domeftics, that they are by that Time eat up, and cannot really afford to ftay any longer.

The King, during the Time the Diet fits, doubles his Guards, that he may be fecure againft any Infults; for without doubt, there is no Affembly in the World where Diforders rife to fuch a Height as in a *Polifh* Diet; for there the Deputies not only take the Liberty to fpeak freely of the King's Government, but will even abufe him to his Face.

When the Throne becomes vacant by Death, Depofition, or voluntary Abdication, the Archbifhop of *Gnefna* acts as Inter-Rex, iffues Circular Letters to acquaint the Provinces with it, and to fummon a general Convocation of the Gentry to meet at *Warfaw*. Before this Meeting the little Diets or Dietines take Care to fecure the Roads from Thieves, and to guard the Frontiers againft Invafions, and Spies are fent into all Neighbouring Countries to difcover their Defigns. They fuffer none to go out or come into their Kingdom till the Election is over; all Foreign Letters, though to Senators, are intercepted; the Highways are block'd up with Trees, and Ambufcades are placed about them. None muft write to the Army during this Time; the Ufe of Fire-Arms is forbid to the People, and all Taverns are fhut up. The Diet confifts of the Archbifhop of *Gnefna*, who reprefents the King, and the other Senators, with the Deputies of the Province.

In the firft Place they fend fome of the Senators to the Army, to direct the Affairs of War; others have the Charge of the Treafure; and till a King is elected, the Senate claims the Title of Serene from Foreign Governments. The Diet for ordering Affairs relating to the Election fits only a Fortnight, during which Time all Courts of Judicature ceafe, except that of the Marfhal. Moft crown'd Heads, Princes, and States, fend Ambaffadors at fuch Times to the Senate, and the Pope fends his Nuncio. A Gentleman is appointed to attend every fuch Foreign Minifter, to prevent their corrupting the Electors with Money. But this Precaution is of little Ufe now. When the Diet ends, the Deputies retire to their refpective Provinces,

vinces, acquainting their Conftituents with the Proceedings and the Day appointed for the Election; and then the Gentry advife among themfelves what is fit to be propofed in the Diet.

This Diet of Election, before the Union of *Poland* with the Great Duchy of *Lithuania*, was held at *Petrico*, but fince that Time it is held in a Field half a League from *Warfaw*, near the Village *Wola*, and muft not continue above fix Weeks. There is a great Hall of Boards erected here for the Senate. They firft go to Church to pray to God to direct them in their Choice; then the Nobility chufe their Speaker, who takes an Oath that he will receive no Bribes, keep no Correfpondence with any of the Competitors, and do nothing without the Confent of the Republick. The Deputies fit in the open Field. After they have appointed a Court of Juftice during the Inter-regnum, all the Senators and Deputies take an Oath on their Knees, adminiftered by the Primate, to maintain Union among themfelves, and to acknowledge none for King but him that is lawfully and unanimoufly elected; and fwear to preferve the Rights and Privileges of the Republick. They annual all Decrees of Tribunals, and all the Statutes of Kings, that intrench on their Liberties; and the Generals are fworn to remove their Forces from the Place of their Diet; then the Diet gives Audience to Ambaffadors from the Competitors or others, who are very liberal to the Deputies, by giving Prefents, and keeping an open Table, &c.

After the Ambaffadors have had Audience, they proceed to the Election. If the Votes be unanimous, the Primate demands three times, if the Exorbitances and Grievances be redreffed; and if anfwered in the Affirmative, he declares the King elect, which is alfo done by the Marfhal of the Crown and the Marfhal of the great Duchy, and then *Te Deum* is fung. At the Time of the Election, the Diet form an Act for the Security of their Liberties, which is ftiled the *Pacta Conventa*, and is in the Nature of a Contract between the King and the Republick, which is figned by the Ambaffadors from the Prince elected, who take an Oath to obferve them in his Name. He afterwards fwears to them in Perfon, before he is recognized, and again at his Coronation. As this *Pacta Conventa* is the Rule of the King of *Poland*'s Government, and contains the Maxims which he is obliged to follow, the Reader will not be difpleafed to fee the common Form of it, efpecially as we have reduced it into a narrow Compafs, though without any Detriment to the Senfe.

The

The standing Points of the *Pacta Conventa*, or the Royal Capitulation, are: " That the King shall not appoint any " Succeffor, but preferve all the Laws for the Freedom of " Election; that he shall pretend to no Right of coining Mo- " ney, but leave that in the Hands of the Republick; that " he will ratify and confirm all the Treaties made with Fo- " reign Princes; that he will maintain the Tranquility of the " Publick; that he will not declare War againft any Prince, " bring Foreign Troops into the Kingdom, or fuffer any to go " out, nor levy any new Troops, without the Confent of the " Diet; that all Field-Officers shall be either *Poles, Lithua-* " *nians*, or Natives of thofe Provinces depending on the Crown " of *Poland*; that all Officers of the Guards shall be either " *Poles, Lithuanians*, or Natives of thofe Provinces depending " on the Crown of *Poland*, and their Colonel a *Polish* Noble- " man; and all fwear to be fubject to the Grand Marshal; " that he shall not ufe his Privy Seal in Affairs that concern the " Republick; that he shall give no Man more Places than " the Law allows; after a Place has been vacant fix Weeks, " he shall beftow it on fome well qualified *Polish* Gentleman; " that he shall not marry without Confent of the Senate, " who shall affign his Queen what Revenue they pleafe; that " by the Confent of his Council he shall regulate the Num- " ber of his Troops, and preferve good Difcipline; that he " shall build no Fleet without the Advice of the Senate; " that he shall not diminifh his Treafure in the Caftle of " *Cracow*, but rather encreafe it; that he shall borrow no " Money without the Confent of the Diet; that he shall al- " ways adminifter Juftice by the Advice of his Senators; that " he shall be content with the Revenue of his Predeceffors; " that no Strangers be introduced into his Councils, and that " he shall beftow no Offices or Dignities upon them; that " he shall not diminifh any of the Offices at his Difpofal; " that he shall maintain and defend all Rights, Liberties, and " Privileges granted by former Kings to the *Poles* or *Li-* " *thuanians*, or to any of the Provinces that depend on " thefe two Nations." To thefe Articles they add others occafionally, according to the Circumftances of Time, or the Quality of the Perfon elected.

We have feen how much the Power of this Monarch is limited, and how inpracticable it is for him, if he was ever fo much inclined to it, to make any fuccefsful Attempt upon their Liberties. We will now mention the Advantages he receives from his high Dignity. In the firft Place it muft be allowed that his Dominions are ftill very large and extenfive,

though

though several Provinces have been cut off from them by powerful Neighbours, and that his Subjects are a very brave and generous People. His Revenue is very considerable, arising from Customs, the Tribute paid by the *Jews* and *Tartars*, the Revenue drawn from the Salt Mines, and from the Crown Lands; which with various other Branches, make up all together better than one hundred and fifty thousand Pounds *per Annum*. He bestows all Employments, Offices, and Preferments that are in any Country in the Power of the Crown, Ecclesiastical, Civil, or Military; but he can resume none; so that though he may do much by Hope, yet he has none of that Influence which arises from Fear; for those who are preferred by him, very often desert him: And what may be thought very strange in some Countries, is very frequent in *Poland*; the shortest Road to Preferment, is that of Opposition, which is attended with many Inconveniencies, and is the principal Cause that the Crown and the Nation both are sunk so low as at present; when, if it were not for the Noise of their domestick Distractions, the rest of *Europe* would scarce know any thing of them, or what they are doing.

The King swears to protect four Religions, *viz.* the *Romish*, the *Protestant*, the *Greek*, and that of the *Jews*, for which the latter pay about twelve thousand Pounds a Year. In the great Duchy of *Lithuania* there are many Thousands of *Tartars*, who are allowed the Exercise of the *Mahometan* Religion; and on the Frontiers there are still some *Pagans*. As to the Military Affairs of the Country, there are two standing Armies kept in constant Pay, each under the Command of two Generals, distinguished under the Titles of Great and Little. The first, which is the Crown Army of *Poland*, consists of 36,000 Men, and that of *Lithuania* of 12,000; but they are very indifferently subsisted, and worse disciplined; so that they seldom make any great Figure, which is chiefly owing to the Badness of their Infantry; to qualify which they have some Foreign Troops in their Pay, and heretofore they had their *Cossacks*, who, though they might not be as good Troops as any in *Europe*, though they are so stiled by many Authors, were much better certainly than any that could be brought against them; but most of these have now put themselves under the Protection of *Russia*, which is a great and indeed an irreparable Loss to the *Poles*.

The Reader, after perusing this Account, will very probably wonder how under such a Constitution the Wheel of Government can be at all kept in Motion, or how it is possible that Men of Sense and publick Spirit can be so strangely

I

fond

fond of a Constitution, productive of so many disastrous Consequences; we will therefore endeavour to give some Account of both.

As to the first, when the King finds he can do nothing in the Diet for the publick Service, he has recourse to what is called a *Senatus Consilium*, which is exactly the same thing with what we had formerly here in *England*, under the Title of the *Great Council of the Peers*; yet the Acts of this Assembly are but of doubtful Authority in *Poland*; however they are better than none, and have often done great Service to the State. On the other hand, if the Nobility think themselves at any time oppressed or aggrieved, they form what are called *Confederacies*, which are so far legal, that I don't find in their History such as have taken Steps of this Natuae, have been often treated as Rebels.

As to the latter Point, the *Polish* Nobility are fond of their Constitution, first, because it preserves their Power, which though they are not a tenth Part of the Inhabitants of *Poland*, they are pleased to call Liberty, that their particular and exorbitant Privileges may pass for publick Blessings. In the next Place, they like this Form of Government, because every Gentleman of *Poland* knows that there is a Possibility of his Posterity's wearing the Crown; and lastly, they are attached to this Form of Rule, because every Election brings half a Million Sterling into their Country, and a great Part of that Sum into their Pockets. But then, instead of avowing these Principles, they are pleased to alledge, that their Constitution obliges Kings to govern by Law, secures the Nobility in the Enjoyment of their Rights, defends them from the Inconveniencies that attend a Minority, and keeps them from being Slaves, like the *Turks*, *Tartars*, and some of their Neighbours.

The Interest of *Poland* with respect to Foreign Powers, lies in a very narrow Compass, since as Things stand at present, they seem to be in no great Danger of being involved in a War with any of their Neighbours. The Power of the *Russians* might justly alarm them, if his *Polish* Majesty was not so closely connected with the *Czarina*. The *Turks* were very formidable to them heretofore, and so were the *Tartars*, but their Alliances with the *German* and *Russian* Empires secure them from all Apprehensions now. They were anciently very jealous of the House of *Austria*, as apprehending she was desirous of obtaining their Kingdom in the Manner she had done those of *Bohemia* and *Hungary*; and this it was that made them incline to the *French*, who have spent large Sums

of

of Money to keep up a Faction in that Country, and perhaps their Piſtoles find a Way thither ſtill.

The King of *Pruſſia* is a Prince with whom the *Poles* ought to live upon good Terms ; as we ſhall ſhew hereafter, there are many Reaſons to induce that Monarch to live upon good Terms with them. With the *Swedes* they have now very little to do, the *Ruſſians* having taken from them the Provinces they conquered from the *Poles* ; ſo that unleſs the Face of Affairs ſhould change in the North, *Poland* is like to continue quiet enough, at leaſt till her Throne becomes once more vacant.

We might conclude from hence, the Tranquillity of *Poland* ought to be greater than ever, as it is undoubtedly more ſecure from the Views of ambitious Neighbours. We might likewiſe conceive that in a Time of ſo much Serenity and Safety, the true Patriots in this Country would examine into the Defects, and apply proper Remedies for reſtoring the Vigour of their Government ; and we might be farther tempted to hope they would carefully uſe their utmoſt Precautions to prevent the Revival of publick Diſturbances amongſt them, before they are inevitably brought on them by every new Vacancy of the Throne.

In Juſtice however to Truth, it muſt be confeſſed that their preſent Situation is as remote from this as can be well imagined ; their Diviſions are far from being healed, the Condition of publick Affairs is as bad or worſe than ever ; all this is repreſented to the States, and to the whole World at the meeting of every Diet, where proper Remedies are ſuggeſted, methodized, and reaſoned upon with great Force and Spirit, yet in the End there is nothing concluded, but all things are ſuffered to run from bad to worſe ; ſo that in reality, no Nation was ever in a more hapleſs, helpleſs, or hopeleſs Condition.

In this Situation of Things, the preſent King ſeems to have acted with all the Temper and Moderation poſſible, ſo that the *Poles* are obliged to take the Weight of their Misfortunes upon themſelves, and cannot ſo much as find a Colour of imputing it to their Prince, or his Miniſters. It is however thought that his Majeſty has ſome Views, as we have before hinted, for engaging the Nobility to elect his ſecond Son Prince *Xavier*, a Scheme in itſelf very rational, and which ſeems to promiſe as great Advantages to the Nation as to the Royal Family ; for that Prince would be then entirely ſettled in *Poland*, and could have no other Views than for the Welfare and Glory of that Kingdom. It is however very poſſible that this Deſign may be traverſed by that foreign Influence, which for many Years paſt

I 2　　　　　　　　　　　　　　　has

has divided, diſtracted, and deſtroyed the Force, the Credit and Happineſs of the *Poliſh* Nation.

In order to enter into the Reaſon of this, we muſt call to mind the Principles laid down at the Beginning of this Section, and remember that if the real Intereſt of *Poland* was to be purſued, it is ſtill capable of becoming one of the greateſt and moſt conſiderable Powers in the North ; which however if ſome of its potent Neighbours can prevent, it never will be. The Hints thrown out by the *French* Emiſſaries as to the Inſults that have been offered to this Nation, and the contemptuous Manner in which they have been treated, from the miſerable Circumſtances into which they have brought themſelves, tho' proceeding, as the Intrigues of theſe Sort of People ever proceed, from very bad Motives, are not however altogether void of Truth. To ſpeak freely and honeſtly upon this Subject, the Language of falſe Patriots is not always to be diſregarded, for the very worſt of Men by being obliged to diſſemble their bad Intentions, very frequently ſay Things that might become the beſt ; and it is Prudence to diſtinguiſh between wholeſome Suggeſtions, which are a kind of gilded Wrappers, and the Poiſons they are meant to convey.

In ſhort, if there be any latent Remains of Virtue, Principle, or publick Spirit among the *Poles*, and if there be ſtill amongſt them any great Men of able Heads and warm Hearts, they may poſſibly take Advantage from this diſmal Poſture of Affairs, to excite a general Concern in the Nation to provide at leaſt for the Safety and Security of themſelves, if not for the Recovery of that Power and Glory which once diſtinguiſhed their Anceſtors. They may be prompted to ſuſpend at leaſt in one extraordinary Diet, the Tribunitian Power of the *Liberum Veto*, and thereby put it out of the Capacity of any ſingle perfidious, ambitious, or ſplenetick Nuncio to diſturb and counter-act the rational and laudable Deſigns of Men, who have the Good of their Country at Heart. They may by this Means recover the Exiſtence of a real active and well-intentioned Government, which would reſtore their Independency, and remove the Misfortune and Reproach of being influenced in their moſt important Concerns by the Intrigues of their Neighbours, whoſe Intereſt it is, or at leaſt who take it to be their Intereſt, to keep them in a State of Feebleneſs and Inactivity.

But all this is in the Womb of Time, we muſt patiently wait to ſee what ſhe will bring forth ; poſſibly the convulſive Motions that are at preſent felt in the North may be attended with good Effects, and after a few ſharp Pangs *Poland* may

be

be delivered of a new and ſtable Government. It is alſo poſſible that her Strength may be already ſo weakened and exhauſted as not to endure this, and that the People may rather incline to fall back into the ſame drowſy State, in which they have continued uſeleſs to themſelves, and contemptible to the reſt of the World. We muſt acknowledge that there is much of Obſcurity, and little of Certainty in theſe Obſervations; but this ariſes from the Subject, and it is better to ſhew the Reader how little can be ſaid upon it with Confidence, than to miſlead him, by a bold Pretence to Lights we neither have nor can have. For who can penetrate the Secrets of a State that has no Secrets? Who can diſtinguiſh the Views of a Nation that are really without Views? Or who can pretend to ſay what will be the future State of a People, who as to that ſeem to be abſolutely careleſs themſelves? The preſent Policy of *Poland*, like the World of *Epicurus*, is directed by Accident and Chance; ſo that Time only can ſhew us what theſe will produce.

CHAP. VII.

A ſuccinct Account of the Modern Hiſtory, Political Intereſts, and real Views of the Crown of PRUSSIA.

THIS, though one of the lateſt, is very far from being the leaſt conſiderable Kingdom in *Europe*, ſeems to be every Day riſing in Power, in Extent, and in Reputation, and will probably mount as high in the next Age as *Sweden* did in the laſt; which are the Reaſons that we judged it neceſſary to treat of it, and of its Concerns, independent of thoſe of the Empire; in as much as we have already ſeen the King of *Pruſſia* conſidered of late as one of the greateſt Powers of the North: And there is the higheſt Probability, that they will hereafter become more conſpicuous in that Character, and take a much larger Share in the general Syſtem of Affairs in *Europe*, than they have hitherto done.

We ſhall not pretend to aſcend higher in the Hiſtory of the Houſe of *Brandenburgh*, than the Beginning of the laſt Century; but ſhall content ourſelves with obſerving, that no Houſe in *Germany* has produced more great Princes, or Princes of greater Merit than this. Some have been diſtinguiſhed by their Valour

and

and Military Skill, that frequently placed them at the Head of the Empire, which besides contributing to their own Glory, added likewise to the Extent of their Dominions, and to the Happiness of their Subjects. Some again have been no less distinguished for their consummate Knowledge in Politicks, for their making the best Use of their Abilities in that respect, towards promoting the Peace and Welfare of *Germany*, as well as increasing and adding to their own Dominions, by the dexterous Management of their Affairs in the most critical Conjunctures. Others have been celebrated for their great Learning, extensive Science, and admirable Eloquence; all which remarkable Qualities they applied for the Benefit of their Subjects, and for the Improvement of their Territories.

As Proofs of this, we need only observe that *Albert* of *Brandenburgh*, who flourished in the fifteenth Century, was stiled by the Pope the *Achilles* of *Germany*, but the *Germans* themselves called him their *Ulysses*. His Successor *John* had the Title of the *German Cicero*; and *George the First*, Elector of *Brandenburgh*, in the Middle of the sixteenth Century, was so renowned for his Probity, that the Dukes of *Mecklenburgh* and *Anhalt*, and the Elector of *Saxony*, appointed him by their Wills, Tutor to their Children, which Trust he executed with the highest Justice; so that it may without Flattery be said, that the present Greatness of his illustrious House is not the Work of Chance, or the Effect of any remarkable Flow of good Fortune; but of the Valour, Wisdom, Justice, Prudence, and Piety of a long Succession of able Princes.

John Sigismund, Elector of *Brandenburgh*, embraced the reformed Religion, and introduced it into his Territories. After the Extinction of the ancient Family of the Dukes of *Cleve*, he, in Conjunction with the Elector Palatine, made himself Master of that Succession, notwithstanding the Expectative that had been granted the Duke of *Saxony*, and by this Means added a very considerable Country to his Dominions. His Right to which was thus founded: He had married the Princess *Anne*, eldest Daughter to *Albert Frederick* of *Prussia*; and *Mary Eleanor*, eldest Sister of the last Duke of *Cleve*. Upon the Death of his Father-in-law, he took Possession also of the Duchy of *Prussia*, of which he obtained the Investiture from the King of *Poland*, notwithstanding the warm Opposition made thereto by the Grandees of *Poland*; and died in full Possession of these Dominions, in the twelfth Year of his Reign, and the forty-seventh of his Age, *A. D.* 1619.

He was succeeded by his Son *George William*, who entered into the Possession of the Electorate in a very difficult

I   Conjuncture,

Conjuncture, when the Troubles of *Bohemia* had spread the Flames of War through the Empire, and threatened the Safety of his Dominions, which however he protected by his great Wisdom and Moderation. He was a very zealous Protestant, and laboured earnestly to have united the *Lutherans* and *Calvinists*; in order to which, he caused a general Assembly to be held at *Leipsick*, which, through the Peevishness and private Views of Churchmen, came to nothing. Upon the March of *Gustavus Adolphus* into *Germany*, his Dominions suffered greatly, and he was obliged to put the Fortress of *Spandau* into the Hands of that Monarch, as we have elsewhere shewn, in order to obtain his Assistance for the Relief of *Magdebourg*, then besieged by the *Imperialists*, who notwithstanding made themselves Masters of it, and with unexampled Severity cruelly destroyed that City.

Count *Tilly* who commanded them, falling afterwards into *Saxony*, our Elector joined his Troops to the *Saxons*, and had his Share in the famous Victory of *Leipsick*. But after the Death of *Gustavus* King of *Sweden*, when the Elector of *Saxony* thought fit to make Peace with the Emperor, by the Treaty of *Prague*, the Elector of *Brandenburgh* took care to be included therein, which freed him from a very expensive and burthensome War, and left him Leisure to look after his own Affairs, and to provide for the Peace and Welfare of his Subjects, which he had always much more at Heart than making Conquests. In 1637, the Family of the Dukes of *Pomerania* extinguishing in *Bogislaus* XIV, that Country ought to have descended to the Elector, by virtue of a Treaty made for that Purpose with the House that was extinct; but however, the *Swedes* seized and kept it by Force, to which the Elector was obliged to submit; and the Sense of this and the Misfortunes of *Germany*, contributed to shorten his Days; so that deceasing in 1640, he left his Dominions to his Son,

Frederick William, Elector of *Brandenburgh*, the second of that Name, who was one of the greatest and most distinguished Princes of his Time, both for Wisdom and Courage; which were always properly employed for his own Security, and the Benefit of his People. He too entered upon the Government when the Affairs of *Germany* and his own were in a very difficult and embarrassed Situation, and therefore he provided for the Ease of his Subjects, by a Treaty of Neutrality with the *Swedes*, who by the Peace of *Munster* were obliged immediately to evacuate *Pomerania*, and the Marquisate of *Brandenburgh*, but the *Swedish* Deputies delayed it till 1653;

nor

nor could it then be procured, but by the Electors's quitting that which is now called the *Swedish Pomerania*, and several Bailiwicks, with the Isle of *Rugen*, to the *Sweds*, for which he had, but much short of an Equivalent, the Archbishoprick of *Magdebourg*, the Bishopricks of *Halberstat* and *Camin*, and the Principality of *Minden*, with their Dependencies.

He offered two Millions of Crowns, and all those Dominions, for that Part of *Pomerania* he was obliged to yield, but in vain. He strenuously maintained the Prerogatives of the Electors, as to the Ceremonial of the Diet of *Franckfort*, and was very zealous in supporting the Interest of Religion, and particularly of the *Calvinists*. In 1656, he was obliged for the Preservation of *Prussia* to join with the *Swedes* against the *Poles*; but the King of *Denmark* having declared War against *Charles Gustavus* of *Sweden*, he was compelled to leave *Poland* to defend his own Country; so that the Burthen of that War falling upon the Elector, he compromised Things by a Treaty with the *Poles*, by which they released him from the Homage due to their Crown from *Prussia*, and quitted to him the Fiefs of *Lawenberg*, *Botow*, and the Town of *Elbing*, on Condition that he should restore the latter on their paying him four hundred thousand Crowns.

After the Death of *Ferdinand* III. in 1657, the *French* were for advancing the Elector of *Bavaria* to the Imperial Throne; but the Elector of *Brandenburgh* adhering to the House of *Austria*, the Emperor *Leopold* of *Austria* was chosen, though the Elector of *Bavaria* had beforehand gained three Votes. He afterwards took part with the *Poles*, but not being seconded by the *Dutch*, as he expected, a Treaty was concluded at *Oliva*, in 1660. After this he applied himself to Affairs of Peace, to reconcile himself to the Princes at Variance with him; and making an Alliance with *France* and *England* for his own Security. The *French* King having seized the Principality of *Orange*, the Elector being Tutor to the young Prince, sent an Ambassy to demand its Restitution.

In 1666, he made a definitive Treaty with the Prince of *Neuburg*, about the Succession of *Juliers* and *Cleves*; and afterwards got the latter perpetually secured to his own Family. He assisted the Emperor against the *Turks*, made Peace by his Mediation between the Dukes of *Lunenburg*, who had fallen out amongst themselves, and likewise between the *English*, the *Dutch*, and the Bishop of *Munster*. In 1672, the *French* having declared War against the *Dutch*, he sent Assistance to the latter, and his Troops joined those of the Emperor under General *Montecuculi*, who disapproving of
the

the Elector's Measures, they did little more during this Campaign than make a bare Diverſion.

The Elector finding that he was in great Danger of loſing Part of his own Dominions, by a War in which he had engaged purely for the Sake of his Neighbours ; reſolved in 1673, to make a Treaty with *France* upon the beſt Terms he could, which he accordingly did at *Voſten,* upon Condition that the *French* ſhould reſtore to him all that had been taken from him in the ſeveral Countries of *Cleves, Marck,* and *Ravenſberg,* excepting only the Towns of *Weſel* and *Rees,* in which the King ſhould be permitted to keep a Garriſon till the Concluſion of a Peace, when they were to be reſtored to the Elector ; and his Majeſty farther agreed to pay him eight hundred thouſand Livres for the Expences of the War. As advantageous as this Treaty was to the Elector, and notwithſtanding the *French* yielded up to him the Places before mentioned, ſooner than they need have done, yet obſerving their pernicious Deſigns, and that they were reſolved to oppreſs the *Dutch,* he the very next Year renewed his Alliance with the *States* againſt *France,* and marched into *Alſace* with twenty thouſand Men ; but the Imperial General *Bournonville* thwarting his Meaſures, little was done that Campaign.

In the mean time the *Swedes,* at the Sollicitation of *France,* invaded *Pomerania,* and the Marquiſate. Upon which the Elector returned from *Alſace,* and turned his Arms againſt the *Swedes,* over whom he gained a compleat Victory at *Feght-Berlin,* and took from them the Iſle of *Wolen, Wolgaſt,* and *Anclam,* one of the ſtrongeſt Forts of *Pomerania.* He alſo took *Stetin* after a famous Siege, which laſted many Months. In 1678, he made himſelf Maſter of the Iſle of *Rugen,* took *Stralſund,* and *Gripſwald,* and drove the *Swedes* entirely out of all *Pomerania.* They, to divert him, invaded *Pruſſia* ; but the Elector, in the middle of the Winter, paſſed the Lake of *Courlund,* which falls into the *Baltick,* with his Army and Artillery upon the Ice, where it was three Miles broad, ſurprized and defeated them ; ſo that of ſixteen thouſand ſcarce five thouſand eſcaped. After the War of 1672, he was left out of the Treaty of *Nimeguen,* and Peace being concluded among the other Princes, and the *French* joining with the *Swedes,* he was obliged by the Treaty of St. *Germains,* to quit all his Conqueſts to them ; for which the *French* King by a ſecret Article paid him three hundred thouſand Crowns towards the Charges of the War, which, though all he could obtain, was a very poor Satisfaction.

In

In 1680, this great Prince took such a Step as was entirely worthy of his Character. The Court of *Spain* was largely in his Debt for the Succours furnished in the last War, by which, in all Probability, she saved her *Low Countries*; but no Persuasions, no Applications, no Letters from the Elector, no Memorials from his Ministers had any Weight, either because the Court of *Spain* was very negligent in her Administration, or that her Treasures where absolutely exhausted. At last, when his Catholick Majesty's Ministers could find nothing to say that looked like an Answer, they had recourse to an Artifice, not to be excused or justified; they promised the Elector's Ministers Payment, and gave them Bills upon Merchants in the *Low Countries*, which in Consequence of their Collusion were protested. This left no Room to hope for any future Redress; the Elector therefore saw himself reduced to the Necessity either to sit down with the Loss, or to take some hitherto untried Method for Redress; he chose the latter; and having Imformation of a very rich Ship that was expected in one of the *Spanish* Ports of *Flanders*, he fitted out eight Privateers to seize her, and the Design was conducted with such Diligence and Secrecy, that the first News the *Spanish* Court had of his Project, brought that of its Execution.

At first the *Spanish* Ministry took up the Matter very warmly, and would hear of nothing but Restitution of the Vessel, and Satisfaction for the Affront; yet after some Time, when they saw the Elector was determined, and that the Forces of *Spain* could make no Impression on any of that Prince's Territories, they were content to listen to his Excuses, which without doubt the Elector was willing enough to make, for putting a Million eight hundred thousand Ducats into his Pocket. The same Year *Augustus* of *Saxony*, Administrator of *Magdebourg*, deceased, upon which the Elector added that Country to his Dominions as a secularized Duchy, agreeable to the Treaty of *Westphalia*.

He was on the Point also of annexing the Principality of *Querfurt* as a Fief of that Duchy, which consisted of four Bailiwicks; but this was contested with him; and in the Year 1687 he compromised the Matter by accepting of the Bailiwick of *Bruck* as a full Satisfaction for his Pretensions upon all four. In the succeeding Year, he came to an amicable Conclusion with the Emperor, in relation to a Dispute that had long subsisted, concerning the Principality of *Jagerndorf*, which the Emperor hast re-united to the Kingdom of *Bohemia*, notwithstanding the Claim always made to it by

our

our Elector, in Compensation for which he had the Territory of *Schueibusin*, or the Northern Part of *Silesia*, yielded up to him, which the Emperor afterwards found Means to obtain back from his Son and Successor, as we shall hereafter more largely explain.

This excellent Prince shewed himself as compleatly qualified for Government as any of his Rank in that Age, and this from his first taking the Reins of the Administration into his Hands, to the time that they were taken from him by Death. His Personal Courage appeared in several Actions in which he was present; his Steddiness in the Siege of *Stetin*, one of the most memorable that ever happened in *Europe*, and of which particular Accounts have been published in almost all Languages; his glorious Zeal for Liberty, in his generously assisting the *Dutch* in 1672, and on many other Occasions.

He gave also various, and those very signal Instances of his Abilities as a Statesman, in chusing the fairest Opportunities for asserting his Rights, and in being content to wave them when he found it would be difficult or dangerous to maintain them. He arrived at much greater Authority than his Predecessors, and enjoyed it without seeming to aspire to it; and this by studying the Good of his Subjects to such a Degree, that they looked upon his Acquisition of Power as an Advantage to themselves, and indeed it proved so; for not content with giving Audience to all who desired it, and doing Justice upon the Spot after hearing both Parties, he set apart certain Hours for reading Letters from every Place in his Dominions, so that the meanest of his Subjects might depend upon his Notice; and the greatest of his Ministers were not secure, if they behaved ill, from being both detected and punished.

He was very kind to the *French* Protestants, and not only permitted, but invited them to settle in his Dominions; he bestowed on their Gentry Commands in his Army, or Posts in his Court; he provided for the poorer Sort either as Mechanicks in great Towns, or as Peasants in *Prussia*; to the Former he gave Houses, and to the Latter Lands. He did this with so good a Will, that when one of his Ministers insinuated that these Liberalities might produce Inconveniencies, his Answer was, that he would sell his Plate to feed them. He said upon another Occasion, he now understood how both Parties might gain by the same Bargain, for that his Lands in *Prussia* were formerly worth nothing to him, but that by giving them to the poor Protestants, both he and they had

acquired

acquired good Eftates, and were under mutual Obligations to each other.

He built a new Town at *Berlin*, and by uniting five irregular Boroughs compofed a fine City, which he embellifhed with publick Buildings, and ftrengthened by regular Fortifications. He put his Dominions into better Order than they had ever been in the Days of his Predeceffors, by eftablifhing new Regulations where they were neceffary, and abolifhing old Cuftoms where Experience fhewed they were pernicious. He gave up to his Subjects a Land-Tax, that was a heavy Burthen on their Eftates, for an Excife, which was a more equal, tho' perhaps as profitable an Impofition. In order to improve Trade, he built a noble Fortrefs on the Coaft of *Guinea*; and at Home he cut a Paffage or Canal between the *Spee* and the *Oder*, for the Conveniency of the Merchants of *Silefia* trading to *Hamburg*, or into his own Dominions.

In a Word, he was not fo careful of any one Thing as to neglect another; or fo much fet upon diftinguifhing himfelf in a fingle Point of Character, as to flight the reft, but knew what became a great Prince, and practifed it in every refpect. His Juftice and Beneficence rendered him beloved by his Subjects; the Splendor of his Court drew the Refpect of Strangers; and his keeping on foot a great Body of well-difciplined Troops made him confiderable in the Eyes of his Neighbours. His Religion was warm and fincere, but had nothing in it of Bigotry: And after a Reign of forty-eight Years, and when he had lived fixty-eight, he died with as high a Reputation as the moft ambitious Prince could defire, regretted by his Allies, and lamented by his Subjects.

This Elector was twice married; firft to *Louifa Henrietta*, Daughter to *Henry Frederick*, Prince of *Orange*, from which he claimed a Right to that Succeffion; his fecond Princefs was *Dorothy*, Daughter of *Philip* Duke of *Holftein Glucksbourg*, by whom he had three Sons, whofe Pofterity are ftill living. *Frederick* III. who fucceeded him, *Philip William* who was Governor of *Magdebourg*, and died in 1711, and *Albert Frederick* Governor of *Pomerania*. The former left two Sons and a Daughter, the latter three Sons, all Princes of the Blood in *Pruffia*, which is a Point neceffary to be known, becaufe we fhall have Occafion to fpeak of thefe Princes hereafter.

Frederick III. fucceeded his Father in the Electorate of *Brandenburgh* on the nineteenth of *April* 1688, and, like feveral of his Predeceffors, entered upon the Adminiftration of Affairs at a Conjuncture which required a Prince of great

Parts

Parts to conduct them to Advantage. He gave a very early Proof of his having inherited the Virtues as well as the Dominions of his Ancestors, by concurring with the Elector of *Saxony*, the Duke of *Hanover*, and the Landgrave of *Hesse-Cassel*, in settling some Matters of Importance relating to their respective Dominions, and in assisting the Prince of *Orange* in his Design upon *England*, which had been principally concerted with the late Elector his Father. He professed a great Esteem for *Lewis* XIV. whom he considered as a very wise as well as magnificent Prince; and whose Example he followed in many Respects, but was far enough from embracing the whole System of his Politicks, or suffering himself to be deluded into implicity following his Measures.

On the contrary, when his most Christian Majesty attacked the Empire, he immediately took up Arms, and in the Year 1689 recovered the Towns of *Keiserswert* and *Bonn*, in which last Expedition he very narrowly escaped being made Prisoner by a *French* Detachment, and, what did him great Honour, his Escape was entirely owing to his personal Courage. In 1690, King *William* having succeeded in his Expedition, sent him the Order of the Garter by the late *James Johnson*, Esq; afterwards Secretary of State for *Scotland*. In 1693 his Troops distinguished themselves at the Battle of *Landen*, under the Conduct of his Brother Prince *Philip*, of which King *William*, as a Mark of Respect, sent him an ample Account under his own Hand.

In 1694 he sent Assistance to the Duke of *Savoy* under his Brothers, Prince *Philip* and Prince *Albert*. In 1695 his Troops contributed greatly to the taking of *Namur*, of which King *William* gave him also an Account under his own Hand; upon which the Elector came to the *Hague*, to congratulate his Majesty, whom, with the Duke of *Zell*, he entertained splendidly at *Cleves*. After King *Augustus* was chosen King of *Poland*, the Elector seized the Town of *Elbing* by way of Security for the Money due to his Father. But this Affair was afterwards settled by Treaty, according to the Maxim of this great Prince, who was always willing to compromise any Differences he had with his Neighbours, as he had before done with the Elector of *Saxony* in respect to certain Pretensions, and thereby instead of a large Claim, added the Provostship of *Quedlimbourg*, the Bailiwick of *Petersberg*, and some other Places, to his Hereditary Dominions.

In the Year 1700 our Elector having adorned and improved his capital City of *Berlin*, added several fair Countries to those which descended to him from his Ancestors, filled Part
of

of those Countries, that were before but thinly peopled, with Inhabitants, who were invited thither by the Kindnesses shewn, and the Privileges granted them by his Father and himself; took the Resolution of assuming the Royal Dignity, which some however have suggested arose from seeing King *William* seated in an Arm-Chair, at the splendid Congress of Princes, who were engaged in the first grand Alliance; yet that seems rather fit to be inserted in private Memoirs, than to stand recorded in History.

But whatever his Motives were, the Fact is certain, that about this Time he resolved to take the Title of King of *Prussia*; and that he applied himself to the Imperial Court to be acknowledged in this Quality, concerning which likewise the Dealers in secret History tell us a very remarkable Story, which is, that when his Negociation was in no very good Train at the Court of *Vienna*, he was advised by his Minister there in a Letter, written in Cypher, to make use of the Interest of a certain Prince; but the Sense of the Letter being mistaken by their Names beginning with a Letter; he instead of the Prince had recourse to the Father Confessor, who was a Jesuit; and so much struck with the Honour done him by a Protestant Elector, that by his own Interest, and that of his Order, he quickly accomplished all that was desired of him.

I will not make myself answerable for the Truth of this, since it appears very probable to me that the Elector took his Measures upon much surer and better Grounds. The War was just then broke out, on Account of the *Spanish* Succession. The House of *Austria* stood in great need of his Assistance, and he might well expect they would not differ with him about a Title. But however the Matter was, there is no Doubt, that in the Month of *January* 1701 *N. S.* he was crowned King of *Prussia* at *Koningsberg*, and was acknowledged as such by the Emperor *Leopold*, and all his Allies; in Consideration of which the new King furnished him with a numerous Body of Auxiliaries, who served with great Credit in different Parts of *Europe*, during the whole Course of that long and glorious War.

The Year following proved remarkable for the Death of *William* III. King of *Great Britain*, to whom his *Prussian* Majesty accounting himself Heir, immediately took possession of the County of *Lingen*, the Principality of *Meurs*, and some other Lordships which had belonged to the Deceased, tho', as we shall hereafter see, he was willing to give Satisfaction to the Prince of *Nassau Frise*, who took the Title of *Orange*. In the Year 1707, upon the Death of the Duchess

of

of *Nemours*, the Sovereignties of *Neufchatel* and *Valingen* became vacant, to which, as the Heir of the Prince of *Orange*, his *Prussian* Majesty put in his Claim amongst many others. The Right to those Principalities was to be decided by the States of the Country; and as the *French* King supported one of the Candidates, so the Queen of *Great Britain* espoused the Cause of his *Prussian* Majesty, who carried his Point notwithstanding the Threats of the *French*; and about the same Time it was that he purchased the County of *Tecklenburgh*.

At the Diet of *Franckfort*, which assembled for the Choice of an Emperor, the Abbot *Albani* assisted on the Part of the Pope, and it was said that he had a particular Commission to protest against the new Title of the King of *Prussia*, which coming to the King's Ears, he declared, that if such a Step was taken, he would order his Troops then in *Italy* in the Service of the Allies, to take Quarters in the Ecclesiastical State at Discretion, as in an Enemy's Country; but the Ambot *Albani* prevented this, by sending Word to the *Prussian* Minister at the Diet, that he had no such Commission, and that it never so much as entered into his Thoughts to question the King's Title; which, whether true or false, gave his Majesty entire Satisfaction.

At the Close of the War, this Monarch concluded with the rest of the Confederates a Treaty of Peace with *France*, which consisted of thirteen Articles; the most remarkable of which were, that he was confirmed in the Possession of *Upper Guelderland* in full Sovereignty; he had likewise the Country of *Kessel*, and the Prefecture of *Kriekenbeck*, and was acknowledged as Sovereign Lord of *Neufchatel* and *Valingen* by *France*, in Consideration of his quitting his Pretensions to the Principality of *Orange*. There were two separate Articles to this Treaty; by one of which, the most Christian King acknowledged him as King of *Prussia*, and agreed to give him the Title of Majesty.

He likewise interposed in favour of the Protestants of *France*, to whom he had always been a Friend and Protector; and it is highly probable they would have felt the Effects of his Interposition, if he had not been taken off by Death in the Middle of these Negotiations, in the fifty-sixth Year of his Age, leaving behind him the Character of being one of the most magnificent Princes of his Age; and who knew as well as any of his Predecessors, how to serve himself of every Occasion that offered for augmenting his Power, or enlarging his Dominions.

Frederick

Frederick William, Prince Royal of *Pruffia*, and Electoral Prince of *Brandenburgh*, succeeded his Father in all his Dominions, finished the imperfect Negotiation of Peace in which that Prince was engaged at the Time of his Demise, and entered into a closer Correspondence than most of his Predecessors with the Court of *France*. He had not been long seated on the Throne, before he found himself involved in some Disputes with the Crown of *Sweden*, occasioned chiefly by the marching of Troops through different Parts of his Dominions, as well by the *Swedes*, as by the Powers engaged in a War against them. His *Pruffian* Majesty endeavoured first to have compromised Matters amicably; but that being found impracticable, he perceived himself at last obliged to enter into that War in Conjunction with other Princes confederated against *Sweden*; which ended in driving the *Swedes* almost entirely out of *Germany*, and depriving them of all that *Guftavus Adolphus* and his Successors had acquired in the Empire.

But notwithstanding this great Success, his *Pruffian* Majesty consented, under the Mediation of his late *Britannick* Majesty King *George* I. to certain Preliminary Articles for a Peace with *Sweden*, which were signed the eighteenth of *Auguft* 1719, and afterwards digested into a Treaty, that was concluded at *Stockholm* between the two Crowns, *January* 10, 1720. By the third Article of which Treaty, the Crown of *Sweden* yields in Perpetuity to his *Pruffian* Majesty, his Heirs and Successors, the City of *Stetin*, the District between the *Oder* and the *Rhine*, with the Islands of *Wallin* and *Ufedom*, with all the Rights granted to the Crown of *Sweden* by the Emperor and Empire to the said Places, by the tenth Article of the Treaty of *Weftphalia*. And by the nineteenth Article of this Treaty, the Crown of *Sweden* yields farther the Towns of *Dam* and *Golnaw*, on the other Side the *Oder*, with the Territories respectively belonging to them.

In Consideration of these Cessions, his *Pruffian* Majesty undertook no longer to assist the Enemies of *Sweden*, to promote to the utmost of his Power the intended general Peace between her and her Neighbours, to satisfy the Mortgages and Incumbrances on all the Places yielded to him, which had been formerly contracted by the Crown of *Sweden*; as also to pay two Millions of Rix-Dollars to that Crown at three different Payments. By this Treaty his *Pruffian* Majesty acquired a great Accession of Territory, to which, as we have shewn before, his Family had very fair Pretensions as Successors to the Dukes of *Pomerania*; and by this Acquisition gained a free Communication with the *Baltick*, which was of as great or

greater

greater Confequence than the Revenue of all the Places thus acquired; and contributed highly to the Benefit of other Parts of his *Pruffian* Majefty's Dominions.

The fame Temper and Difpofition which his *Pruffian* Majefty fhewed in the Management of this important Affairs, appeared in all the fubfequent Tranfactions of his Life; that is to fay, he was in every Inftance careful to maintain and fupport his own Dignity, to fecure his Dominions, to make himfelf refpected by his Neighbours, to keep his Troops and Fortreffes conftantly in fuch a Pofture as might prevent his being hurt by any unforefeen Accident; and give him an Opportunity, where the Circumftances of Things would permit it, of turning any fuch Accident to his Advantage. It was with this View, that he kept always on foot between eighty and a hundred thoufand regular Troops, well paid, and perfectly well difciplined; at the fame time that he was no lefs careful of his Revenues, as being thoroughly fenfible, that if ever a War became neceffary, Treafure would be to the full as needful as Troops.

This Conduct of his, though it expofed him to the Cenfure of fome fhallow Politicians, was perfectly agreeable to his own Circumftances, and to the general Syftem of Affairs in *Europe*. It preferved all his Dominions, though feparated and detached from each other, from running any Rifque; it made him confidered as the moft powerful Potentate in *Germany*, next to the Houfe of *Auftria*; and it gave him an Opportunity of promoting his Intereft upon every Variation of the Ballance of Power, without actually engaging in a War. Upon thefe Motives he entered into the famous Treaty of *Hanover*, concluded the third of *September* 1725, with their moft Chriftian and *Britannick* Majefties; and tho' the Bounds of this Article will not allow us to enter into Particulars, yet we may fafely venture to affirm in general, that he managed that, and the many fubfequent Negotiations which quickly followed from it, with great Dexterity, and fo as to turn every Incident as much as it was poffible to his own Advantage.

We have already fhewed the Pretenfions formed by the Houfe of *Brandenburgh* on the Succeffion of King *William* III. as Prince of *Orange*; and have taken notice of the Difpute occafioned by the Will of that Monarch, in favour of his Coufin the Prince of *Naffau Frize*, which fubfifted for many Years; and for terminating of which, a Negotiation was fet on Foot in 1722, which ended ten Years afterwards, in a Treaty concluded at *Berlin*, *May* 13, 1732. By this Treaty the Principality of *Orange* and all the Dominions of

K   the

the Family of *Chalons* in *France*, are yielded to his *Pruſſian* Majeſty, and all Ceſſions thereof by him to the King of *France*, by the Treaty ſigned at *Utrecht*, the firſt of *Auguſt* 1713, are confirmed by the Prince of *Naſſau Frize*, late *Stadtholder*.

It is agreed that his Highneſs ſhall take the Title and Arms of *Orange*, but without Prejudice to the Royal Houſe of *Pruſſia*, by whom the Title and Arms of that Principality are to be likewiſe borne. His *Pruſſian* Majeſty was by this Treaty to have for himſelf, his Heirs and Succeſſors, as his Share of the Succeſſion beforementioned, the Principality of *Meurs*, the County of *Lingen*, the Diſtrict of *Montfort*, the Lordſhip of upper and lower *Swaluwe*, the Lordſhips of *Naltwick*, *Hoendorland*, *Wateringen*, *Orange-Polder*, and *s'Graveſand*, the Cuſtoms of *Gennep*, the Barony of *Herſtal* entire, the Lordſhip of *Turnhout*, the Houſe at the *Hague* called the *Old Court*, and the Houſe of *Honſlaardyck*.

All the reſt of the Succeſſion was left to the Prince of *Orange*, who charged himſelf with all the Debts of the Family; and all the Penſions payable to certain Perſons therein mention'd, and all the Demands of the Houſe of *Orange* on the Crown of *Spain*, for an annual Penſion of fiſty thouſand Florins, as well as a Debt of one hundred and twenty thouſand Crowns, are aſſigned to the Prince, with the King's Promiſe to aſſiſt him with his Intereſt at that Court, to procure a Satisfaction for them. This definitive Treaty, by which an End was put to a very tedious as well as a very perplexed and troubleſome Affair, was ratified by his *Pruſſian* Majeſty on the thirtieth of *May*, by the Prince of *Orange* on the thirtieth of *June* following; and ſoon after notified to their High Mightineſſes the *States General*, who had charged themſelves with the Adminiſtration of the ſaid Succeſſion, in due Form, and who were conſequently deeply intereſted therein.

The Deſire his *Pruſſian* Majeſty had to preſerve the Peace of his Dominions, and to avoid, as far as he was able, taking any Share whatever in the Diſturbances of *Europe*, induced him to act with great Caution and Reſerve when the War broke out between his late Imperial Majeſty *Charles* VI. and the Kings of *France* and *Spain*, in Reference to the Election of the King of *Poland*. There is no doubt, that both the Houſes of *Auſtria* and *Bourbon* were extremely preſſing in their Inſtances to his *Pruſſian* Majeſty to enter into this Diſpute, by which, in all Probability, the Scale muſt have turned, according to his Pleaſure; ſince it was very apparent, that if the Election of King *Staniſlaus* had been immediately ſupported by a tolerable Force, the Affection of the *Poles* would have engaged

them

them to have shewn themselves much more effectually than
they did ; and on the other hand, it is no less evident, that if
the King of *Pruſſia* had declared absolutely on the other Side,
the Party for King *Staniſlaus* could not have made any Resistance at all, but must have submitted immediately, and that too
upon any Terms.

But no Intreaties could prevail upon that wise Monarch to
act on either Side in this Dispute, by which, no doubt, he was
a very considerable Gainer. It is true, that tho' he did not give
King *Staniſlaus* any Assistance in support of his Pretensions, yet
after the Ruin of his Affairs, and the close Siege of the City
of *Dantzick*, he suffered that Prince to take Shelter in his Dominions, where he was treated with all the Respect due to
a crown'd Head ; and with the Remittances he received from
France kept up a great Court, and lived at a vast Expence,
which was of considerable Use in that Part of his *Pruſſian*
Majesty's Dominions.

There were many People, who from their Attachment to the
House of *Auſtria*, treated this Conduct of his as unworthy of
a King, and inconsistent with his Obligations to the Emperor ;
but such were certainly too hasty, and had not sufficiently reflected, that the Obligations of a Prince to his Subjects are
infinitely superior to those he contracts with his Allies; and
that with respect to the Safety of his Dominions, and the true
Interest of the Crown of *Pruſſia*, he was not at all bound to
interfere farther than by good Offices in this Dispute; so that
the Measures he took as a Sovereign and independent Prince
were certainly right. As to the Engagements he was under,
as a Member of the Empire, they were so punctually complied
with, that even his Imperial Majesty himself had no Reason
to complain.

The same Method in respect to all other Affairs his Majesty
of *Pruſſia* constantly pursued, shewing himself alike prepared
for War and inclined to Peace : for tho' he made his Troops
his Delight, and led all his Days rather a Military than a Court
Life, yet this was more with a View to save Expence, to keep
his Troops in Motion, and to maintain strict Discipline, than
with any Thoughts of distressing or disturbing his Neighbours.
In the latter Years of his Life the King was dropsical, and in
a very bad State of Health ; so that he was frequently thought
near his End, and yet in some Measure recovered.

At last he was carried off by a short Illness, on the 31st of *May*
1740, in the fifty-second Year of his Age ; and tho' like other
Princes, he had his Faults and Failings ; among which the
Love of Money, and draining it by various unpopular Methods

K 2 out

out of the Purses of his Subjects was the chief; yet in respect to his great Regard for Justice, his prudent Œconomy, strict Frugality, and Easiness of Access, he was much to be and here therefore is commended; since with regard to the general Maxims of his Politicks, they are like to do his Memory more Credit, than they acquired him Glory while living.

This Monarch espoused in his Father's Life-time the Princess *Sophia Dorothea* of *Hanover*, Sister to his present *Britannick* Majesty, who was born the 16th of *March* 1687, and is now Queen Dowager of *Prussia*, by whom he left a numerous Issue, *viz.* *Charles-Frederick* his Successor, *William-Augustus* Prince Royal of *Prussia*, born *August* 9th 1722, who espoused the Princess *Louisa-Amelia* of *Brunswick Wolfenbuttle*, by whom he has already two Sons; *Frederick-Henry* Prince of *Prussia*, born *January* 8th 1726; *Augustus-Ferdinand* Prince of *Prussia*, born *May* 23d 1730; *Frederica-Augusta* Princess Royal of *Prussia*, born the 3d of *July* 1709; and who on the 20th of *November* 1731, espoused the Hereditary Prince of *Brandenburgh Bareith*; *Frederica-Louisa* Princess of *Prussia*, born *September* 28th 1714, who on the 30th of *May* 1729, espoused the Margrave of *Anspach*; *Dorothea-Sophia*, Princess of *Prussia*, born the 26th of *January* 1719, and married the 10th of *November* 1734, to the Margrave *Frederick-William* of *Schwed*; *Louisa-Ulrica* Princess of *Prussia*, born *April* 24th 1720, who on *July* 17th 1744, married *Adolphus-Frederick* Duke of *Holstein-Eutin*, elected Successor to the Crown of *Sweden*, and now in Possession; *Anna-Amelia* Princess of *Prussia*, born *November* 9th 1723, and who remains still unmarried.

Charles-Frederick, the present King of *Prussia* and Elector of *Brandenburgh*, was born *January* 24th 1712, and consequently was in the twenty-ninth Year of his Age when he mounted the Throne; and in his Father's Life-time espoused the Princess *Elizabeth-Christina* of *Brunswick Wolfenbuttle*, born *November* 8th 1715. He began his Reign with an Act of the greatest Generosity; for whereas it was publickly known that his Marriage was a pure Act of Obedience to his Father, absolutely against his own Consent, and therefore never consummated, every body expected that his first Care would have been to have taken the Opinion of some of the Protestant Universities in *Germany*, in order to have procured its Dissolution.

But when that Princess, in Company with the Queen-Dowager, came to compliment him upon his Accession, he addressed her in the following Terms: *You are sensible, Madam, that your becoming Princess Royal was contrary to my Inclination; but having observed the Amiableness of your Behaviour,*

viour, and the Regard that you have shewn for my Person, I find myself under a Necessity of making you suitable Returns; and now therefore that I am a King, I acknowledge you for my Queen-Consort, and the lawful Partner of my Throne and Bed. It is impossible to express the Surprize and Joy of the whole Court upon this Declaration; a Declaration which every body desired, but no body expected; and which gave the greatest Hopes of a Reign that opened with so extraordinary a Mark of Justice, Tenderness, and Generosity.

The very Dawning of this young Monarch's Government, drew the Attention of all *Europe*, and gave his Neighbours very just Ideas of what might be expected in the Progress of it. He had been but indifferently treated in his Father's Lifetime; and there were many who dreaded his Resentments; but he punished no body except the Councellor *Eckard*, whom he ordered to depart his Dominions, because he had been a constant Deviser of Taxes, and the principal Instrument of the late King in laying Burthens upon his Subjects; so that in his Manner of treating him, the new Monarch shewed that he could avenge the Wrongs done to his People, tho' he was at the same time patient under his own. He was no sooner possessed of the Crown, that he declared himself a Protector of Learning; and by a Letter written with his own Hand invited the famous Mr. *Maupertuis* from *Paris*, to take upon him the Direction of the Academy of *Berlin*; or, as the King himself elegantly expressed it, to graft the Slips of true Science on the wild Stocks in the North.

But I forget the proper Business of this Article, while I pretend to draw the Picture of a Prince, whose great Qualities are so numerous, that they would require more Room than I have left, should I attempt their Description. I will content myself therefore with a bare Detail of the principal Facts of his Administration, that I may keep within due Bounds.

In the succinct Account which has been given of his Father's Reign, it has been shewn, that tho' he took care to put his Army on a better Foot than any of his Predecessors, yet he was very far from being inclined to War, which probable arose from the Circumstances of the Affairs of *Europe* in his Time; but whatever his Motives were, most certain it is, that he was rather careful in ascertaining his Rights, than vigorous in asserting them, as appears from his suffering the Bishop and Prince of *Liege* to continue in the Possession of the Barony of *Herstall*, which had been yielded to the King as a Part of the Succession of the late King *William*, and offering to compromise his Dispute with that Prelate for 100,000 Florins, which however he could not obtain.   K 3   But

But upon his Son, the new King's coming to the Possession of his Dominions, and going to receive the Homage of the Duchy of *Cleves*, he demanded the same of the Inhabitants of *Herstall*, who positively refused it, alledging that they were, and had been always Subjects to the Prince of *Liege*. The King, to cut this Dispute short, sent a Body of his Forces into that Bishoprick, who took Possession of *Maseyk*, and who declared they had their Master's Orders to live at Discretion, till he had received Satisfaction for his Barony of *Herstall*. It was on the 14th of *September*, 1740, that the *Prussian* Troops entered his Territories, upon which the Bishop of *Liege* published a long Manifesto, setting forth the great Injury that had been done to him, but confessing at the Close, that the Price set by the late King of *Prussia* was very moderate; and that he had offered to pay him Interest for that Sum at the Rate of Four *per Cent.* which in his own Opinion was better than so much ready Money.

He remonstrated at the same time to the Courts of *Vienna* and *Paris*; but while he was thus busy in drawing Memorials, and making Complaints, the *Prussian* Troops lived on his Subjects at Discretion; so that at last he was forced to send two Deputies to *Berlin*, to put an End to this Dispute, who were obliged to consent that his *Prussian* Majesty should receive 200,000 Florins for his Pretensions upon *Herstall*; and this Money being paid on the 23d of *October* in the Evening, the *Prussian* Forces evacuated *Maseyk* the next Morning. Thus, according to his new Method, the King ended this Controversy without the Formalities of a Law-suit.

It was not only with the Bishop of *Liege* that his Majesty had Disputes; for about the same time the Duke *de Chevreuse*, and the Marquis *de Nesle* set up their respective Claims to the Principality of *Neufchatel*, against what they were pleased to call the King of *Prussia*'s Usurpation; and the former sent an Advocate of the Parliament of *Paris*, the latter two Advocates of the Parliament of *Besançon*, to assert their Claims; but the Governor of *Neufchatel* decided the Matter presently, by directing that they should all quit the Principality in twenty-four Hours, on Pain of being treated as Criminals. This, however, was but a Prelude to the great Stroke of all, by which his Majesty added a great Part of the rich and fruitful Country of *Silesia* to his Dominions; which, inasmuch as it has been considered as the Occasion of the late general War; the Reader will very naturally expect that we should be a little more particular in the Account of this singular Transaction.

We

We have already shewn that the House of *Brandenburgh* had a very fair Title to the Principality of *Jagerndorf*, and other Territories in that Country, which the Emperor notwithstanding united to the Kingdom of *Bohemia*; but as the Elector still kept up his Claim, and the House of *Austria* had great Need of his Assistance, it was found necessary to give him some Satisfaction; and accordingly a Treaty was set on foot at *Berlin* in 1686, whereby it was stipulated, that the Elector should renounce all the Pretensions of this House to the Principalities of *Jagerndorf*, *Lignitz*, *Brieg*, and *Wolau*, upon Condition that the Emperor should yield to the Elector the Territory of *Schwibus*. The Baron *de Frytag*, who managed this Negotiation for the Court of *Vienna*, with the Elector *Frederick* II. set on foot at the same time another clandestine Treaty with the Electoral Prince *Frederick*, who was afterwards *Frederick* III. Elector of *Brandenburgh*, though he is generally called *Frederick* I. because he was the first King of *Prussia*.

The Nature of this secret Negotiation was very dark; for there were some Family Disputes, in which the Emperor threatened to take Part against the Prince, if, at the same time his Father subscribed the Treaty before mentioned, he did not subscribe an Obligation to give up, as soon as it should be in his Power, the Territory of *Schwibus* for a small Sum of Money. Accordingly when he became Elector of *Brandenburgh* the Money was offered, and the Territory demanded; but all the Counsellors of the new Elector advised him not to part with it, as he had been compelled to make this Agreement, which in its own Nature therefore was void; but the Emperor *Leopold* insisting upon it, and threatening to use Force, he yielded up the Territory, but refused to confirm the Renunciation made by his Father of his former Rights. Upon this Occasion he expressed himself to his Ministers in these Words: " I shall yield the Territory of *Schwibus*; it be-
" comes me to be as good as my Word; I must and I will do
" what I promised. As to prosecuting my Rights to *Silesia*, I
" leave that to the Care of my Posterity, whose Hands I cannot,
" I will not bind under my present Circumstances, when it is
" necessary for me to submit to this Injustice. If Providence
" and Time do not suffer the Thing to take another Turn,
" the only Way is to be quiet; but if God orders it otherwise,
" my Descendents will know what they have to do."

Thus the Reader sees in few Words the Nature of the King of *Prussia*'s Claim; he represented both *Frederick* II. and *Frederick* III. consequently the Rights of both were in him;

him; and as the House of *Auftria* had taken away the Equivalent, he conceived he had a juft Title to the Territories formerly in the Poffeffion of his Family, *viz.* the Principality of *Jagerndorf*, and other Countries, of which he refolved immediately to take Poffeffion. He had two Reafons for acting in this Manner, without any previous Declarations made to the Court of *Vienna*; the firft was, that the Male Line of the Houfe of *Auftria* being extinct, and the Power of that Family thereby weakened, he thought this a favourable Opportunity of doing himfelf Juftice; 'and that he fhould be wanting to himfelf and his Pofterity, or Succeffors, if he neglected it. His fecond, that the Elector of *Bavaria* and the King of *Spain* forming Pretenfions upon the Emperor's Succeffion, he was defirous of reconciling his View of doing himfelf Juftice to the Inclination he had of affifting *Maria Therefia*, Queen of *Hungary*, in maintaining her Rights to her Father's Dominions, agreeable to the Pragmatic Sanction.

At the fame time therefore that he ordered his Troops to march into *Silefia*, which was in *December* 1740, he declared to the Court of *Vienna*, that notwithftanding this Step he was difpofed to promote the Election of the Duke of *Lorrain* to the Imperial Dignity; that he was willing to advance the Queen of *Hungary* two Millions of Florins; and that he was ready to employ all his Forces in defending her Dominions againft all her Competitors. But thefe Propofitions were abfolutely rejected, upon which a War enfued. It is to be obferved, that in this Article I am ftating the Claims, Pretenfions, and Meafures of his *Pruffian*-Majefty, as Matters of Fact, and am very far from taking upon me to decide whether the former were well or ill founded, and confequently whether the latter were right or wrong; but thus much I think I may be allowed to fay, that if the Court of *Vienna* had accepted his Propofal, the War in *Germany* had been prevented, and the Emprefs Queen had not yielded more to the King of *Pruffia* than he is poffeffed of at prefent, after all the Blood and Treafure fpent on both Sides in this fatal Quarrel.

His *Pruffian* Majefty carried his Point in the firft Inftance, that is to fay, he made himfelf Mafter of *Silefia* without much Oppofition, and the *Auftrians* having brought a great Army into that Country, under the Command of Field-Marfhal Count *Nieuperg*, in the Beginning of the next Spring his *Pruffian* Majefty gave that Army Battle, the tenth of *April*, 1741, at *Molwitz*, in which, though with great Effufion of Blood, he gained the Victory. In the fucceeding Year having

marched

marched to the Affiftance of his Allies the *French, Bavarians,* and *Saxons,* into *Bohemia,* after being bafely deferted by them, he, *May* the twenty-fourth, 1742, fought the famous Battle of *Czaflaw,* in which he alfo claimed the Victory; but both Parties being now weary of the War, a Treaty of Peace was negociated between his Majefty on the one Part, and the Queen of *Hungary* on the other, which was concluded and figned *June* 11th, at *Breflaw* in *Silefia*; by which the greateft Part of that Dutchy, and the whole County of *Glatz* were yielded to his Majefty.

But this valuable Ceffion did not hinder him from entering into the League of *Frankfort,* in fupport of the Emperor *Charles* VII. in Confequence of which, he invaded *Bohemia,* and took the City of *Prague September* 6th, 1744, which obliged Prince *Charles* of *Lorrain* to march from the *Rhine* to the *Elbe,* with the *Auftrian* Army; upon whofe Approach his *Pruffian* Majefty retired with his Forces towards *Silefia,* but Prince *Charles* preffing hard upon him in his Retreat, a Battle enfued at *Friedberg, June* 4th, 1745, in which his *Pruffian* Majefty gained a clear and very compleat Victory. It was believed that this Action would have made an End of the War; but the *Auftrians,* who were now joined by the *Saxons,* and had formed great Views of diftreffing the King of *Pruffia,* continued their Military Operations with the utmoft Vigour; and on the thirtieth of *September,* by a forced March, furprized that Prince near *Stadentz,* and plundered his Baggage; but by the great Military Skill and inimitable Prudence of the King, his Troops were foon brought into Order, the Battle renewed, and a glorious Victory obtained.

Yet the *Auftrians* ftill perfifted in continuing the War, prefuming on the Diverfion to be made by a great Body of *Ruffian* Auxiliaries, which it was fuppofed would have marched through *Poland* into his Territories. But his *Pruffian* Majefty took Advantage of the Seafon, and while his Enemies were pleafing themfelves with the Hopes of invading and ruining his Country, the old Prince of *Anhalt Deffau* with a *Pruffian* Army entered theirs. The King of *Poland* was obliged to abandon his Hereditary Dominions, and to retire to the Frontiers of *Bohemia* for Safety. *Leipfick* opened her Gates to the Conqueror, and though a numerous Army of *Saxons* and *Auftrians* interpofed to preferve *Drefden,* yet *December* 4th, 1745, they were totally defeated by the Prince of *Anhalt Deffau,* with half their Number of *Pruffian* Troops.

The King entered *Drefden* in Triumph, and having overcome all his Enemies, on the fourteenth of the fame Month

over-

overcame his Provocation and Refentment, and in the full
Warmth of Victory gave them a fair and equitable Peace. By
which *Silefia* was again folemnly yielded to him; the *Saxons*
gave him one Million of Crowns for the Expence of the War;
his Majefty acknowledged the Emperor, guaranteed the Dominions of the Emprefs Queen, and included his Ally the Elector
Palatine in the fame Treaty, which was negotiated under the
Mediation of his *Britannick* Majefty, and the Conclufion of
which once more fettled the Tranquillity of *Germany*.

The Interefts of this Monarch, if they were to be confidered
at large, would require a confiderable Treatife; but we fhall
reduce them into a narrow Compafs, and treat of them with as
much Perfpicuity as we are able. In Quality of King of *Pruffia*, he is one of the greateft Powers in the North; and therefore it is his Intereft to fee the Ballance in that Part of *Europe* kept exactly even; with this View, there is no doubt, that
he will have a conftant Eye to the Meafures purfued by *Sweden*
and *Denmark*, pay ftill more Attention to the Behaviour of *Poland*, and be moft affiduoufly watchful of the increafing Power
of *Ruffia*. Upon his Diligence and Succefs in thofe Points, the
Security, Welfare and Grandeur of his own State will depend.

How far it is poffible to manage all thefe with fuch Addrefs
as to draw fome Advantages from feveral of thofe Powers, and
to be in no Danger from any of them, may beft be known
by confidering the Practice of the prefent King, who has actually carried this Scheme into Execution in the moft difficult
Conjuncture. The late Revolution in *Ruffia* changed the
whole Syftem of his Affairs with refpect to that Empire; inftead of a clofe Conjunction, it brought about a Divifion of
Interefts, and from an intimate Union, created a diftant Civility intermixed with fome Degrees of Jealoufy, fo much harder
to be removed becaufe they were natural, as being derived from
his clofe Alliance with the excluded Family. The Power of
Ruffia alfo was vaftly increafed, for by the Election of the Succeffor of the Crown of *Sweden*, that Kingdom came in fome
Meafure to depend upon her: *Denmark* was aw'd by her fuperior Force, and by the old Differences between that Royal
Family and the Houfe of *Holftein*; while *Poland* was firmly
tied, as well by the Intereft of the reigning Prince, as by a long
and uninterrupted Alliance.

But the admirable Policy of the *Pruffian* Monarch has got
the better of all thefe Connections. By marrying his Sifter to
the then Succeffor, and now King of *Sweden*, he gain'd an Intereft in that Country which is daily increafing. *Denmark* is

bound

bound to live upon good Terms with him as a Neighbour, at the same Time that she needs his Affistance as an Ally. He has always kept a good Correspondence with the Republick; and notwithstanding their late Quarrel, has now as good a Correspondence with the King of *Poland*; so that he has exactly modelled the *North* to his Mind: And notwithstanding the vast Power of *Russia*, has nothing to fear from her Jealousy, and still less to apprehend from her Influence; which easy Situation of his on this Side, is entirely owing to his own great Parts as a Politican; and must, to every competent Judge, raise his Character, in that respect, to the greatest Height.

As a Prince of the Empire, he plainly considers himself as the Guardian of the *Germanick* Constitution; and as he has all Things to hope, and nothing to dread from the Independency of all the Members of the Empire, he has very wisely shewn as warm and steady a Concern for their Rights as for his own. At the very Beginning of his Reign he compromised the Disputes which had so long subsisted between his Family and the Elector *Palatine*, upon very equal and moderate Terms; he embraced the Friendship of the House of *Bavaria* when it was necessary to him; and he gave the highest Proofs of his Fidelity to the Interests of that Family, when they stood in the greatest Need of his Friendship.

In a Word, he has lost no Ally in the Empire, but has gain'd many; he has restored the Credit of the Diet of *Ratisbon*, by giving Power to the Princes of the Empire to send their Ministers thither, to speak their true Sentiments, and explain themselves freely, instead of submitting implicitly to the Imperial Decrees, as in Times past they were wont to do. In short, he has so conducted his Affairs, as to be universally considered as a *German* Patriot; that is, as one resolved to maintain the Essence of the *Germanick* Constitution, and to preserve the Liberty of its Members from all interior Influence, as well as foreign Subjection; and what Effects this may produce, Time has already, and will hereafter declare.

As one of the principal Powers of *Europe*, the present King of *Prussia* seems to have formed to himself a Design of establishing a more effectual Ballance than has been hitherto known, in Virtue of that Increase of his own Dominions, which has put it into his Hands. This Point was never sufficiently considered by any of our Politicians, or to speak plainly, has never been considered by them at all. The Situation of *France* enabled her formerly to preserve the Ballance against the House of *Austria*; the Situation of his *Sardinian*

dinian Majesty's Dominions, enables him to hold the Ballance of *Italy*, and to keep it even between the Houses of *Austria* and *Bourbon*; but with respect to the King of *Prussia*, he has no less than three Ballances in his Hands, that of the North, that of *Germany*, and the great Ballance of Power against *France*.

It is very true, that during the Course of the last War, he acted in Confederacy with *France*; but, as we have shewn before, this was absolutely against his Will. If the Court of *Vienna* and the Allies of that Court had not considered his Expedition into *Silesia* as an Infraction of the Pragmatick Sanction, in which Light he never regarded it himself, or thought it would be regarded by others; he had certainly taken the contrary Side, as having no Reason to be a Friend of *France* longer than he has the House of *Austria* for an Enemy. He shew'd in his last Treaty with the King of *Poland*, Elector of *Saxony*, a true Zeal for the Protestant Religion, and without Doubt it is his Interest to put himself at the Head of the Protestants in *Germany*; he is too clear-sighted a Prince not to see this; and it is upon this admirable Faculty we ground all our political Doctrines in this Section.

But it will be objected, that some of the Admirers of the present King of *Prussia* have magnified his Power to a Degree much beyond what he is ever like to acquire, have promised many Things for him which he is never likely to perform, and have kept such a Silence in reference to the Points he has really pursued, as might induce the World to suspect their having very dark Notions of that Monarch's Forces, Inclinations or Interests. In answer to this I must intreat the Reader to observe, that there is no such thing as mathematical Certainty in Discourses of this Nature; and therefore those are equally in Fault who pretend magisterially to decide what such a Prince will attempt, or what he may be able to atchieve; and those who on the other hand expect that every thing should fall out exactly according to a Plan laid down from Conjectures.

But still this Art of foreseeing future Events from prudentially applying the Knowledge of human Nature, the Forces of Government, and the Lights of Experience, ought not to be despised. Physicians cannot always cure, because they cannot always form a right Judgment from their Acquaintance with the human Œconomy, and their Skill in discerning Symptoms of the Nature of Diseases; and yet none but Fools disparage the Study of Physick, or decry the Knowledge of Physicians. There is no Doubt that Statesmen derive vast Advantages from secret Intelligence; but it was a very wise Saying of *Lewis* XIV. that he was much less in Pain about what his Enemies might learn

learn by this Method, than from the Hints they received from the *Dutch* Gazettes. It is difficult indeed, but not impossible, to guard against the Effects of Influence or Money, in penetrating the Transactions of a Cabinet; but it is far more difficult, and borders more closely upon Impossibility, to hinder speculative Politicans from prying into even the closest Designs, by the Knowledge they have of Men and Things. To be convinced of this, we need only consider what sanguine Promises were made by the Statesmen in some Countries, before the opening of every Campaign during the last War, and the bold Judgments passed by undignified Politicians, that few or none of those Promises would ever actually be fulfilled.

It would be no difficult Thing to shew the Reader, that the Revolutions in *Russia*, in *Sweden*, and in *Holland*, were foreseen and foretold some Years before they happened; but we will confine ourselves at present to the Points immediately before us. And tho' all the World allows that there never was a Cabinet more impenetrable than that of the present King of *Prussia*, yet we shall endeavour to shew, that as our past Conjectures have not been altogether vain, so we are able to guess at what his Politicks may produce in Time to come. We were inclined to think that upon the Conclusion of a general Peace, that Monarch might have been induced to change his System; but upon seeing the Peace concluded at *Aix la Chapelle*, and considering the Conduct of other Powers, we are clearly of Opinion, that Time is not yet come. We are satisfied that the Schemes formed for abasing or circumscribing the Power of this Monarch will have a contrary Effect, and that instead of diminishing, there is the highest Probability that they will increase his Power. We were always and are still of Opinion, that he might be detached from *France*, and that he will never be the Dupe of *France*; but we see no Ground for supposing that proper Measures have been taken to bring about the former, or that by the Steps he is now taking, he is in Danger of falling into the latter.

He has great Forces, large Revenues, a Genius capable of conducting both, and a Moderation that will restrain him from Attempts superior to these. He knows perfectly well the Grandeur of the Sovereign must be established upon the Welfare of the Subject, and this has excited him to shew the same Regard for the Happiness of his People, as for the Extension of his own Power, or rather has induced him to make the latter always subservient to the former. He is known to have an Inclination to become a Maritime Power, or which is the same thing in other Words, to enable his Subjects to increase
their

their Wealth by their Induſtry, through the Channels of foreign Trade. Now though there are many, and amongſt them perhaps ſome Stateſmen, who treat this as a Chimera, yet we hold the direct contrary, and are inclined to think, that this Monarch and his Succeſſors will actually carry that Point; and we think ſo, becauſe there is no great Improbability in ſuppoſing that they may be ſome time or other Maſters of a Sea Coaſt four or five hundred Miles in Extent. It would require more Time and more Room than we have at preſent to beſtow, to endeavour the Explanation of this, ſo as to bring it within the Reach of every Capacity: but whoever will conſult the Maps, conſider the preſent State of Things, and the vaſt Improvements in the Power of an abſolute Monarch to make, who knows what he is doing, and what is to be done to carry a favourite Point, which is at the ſame time his People's Point as well as his own; I ſay, whoever will reflect upon theſe Things, will not conſider what we have advanced as a viſionary Deluſion.

His Views might certainly have been altered, his Meaſures changed, and his Deſigns otherwiſe directed than they are. But then this did not depend entirely upon him; there muſt have been a Concurrence in other Powers to have brought this about; for to manage a wiſe Prince, and one true to his own Intereſts, it muſt be ſhewn, that thoſe who deſire to have him for a Friend and Ally have no Intention to reſtrain, no Inclination to defeat the Meaſures he takes for that Purpoſe, while they are not deſtructive or dangerous to them. To manifeſt a Diſpoſition contrary to this, is ſufficient to give another Biaſs to his Councils; and when we ſee a Prince of the King of *Pruſſia*'s Turn continue armed at an immenſe Expence, we muſt conclude that he has ſome great Enterprize in View, which whenever Time ſhall diſcloſe, it will alſo diſcover that he took proper Meaſures for carrying that Point, whatever it is, which thoſe Armaments were meant to compaſs.

The Situation of his *Pruſſian* Majeſty's Territories is ſuch, as obliges him for Reaſons that have been before aſſigned, to have a conſtant Eye to the Affairs of the North, where no Power was ever predominant, but his Predeceſſors ſuffered for it, and their Dominions and Eſtates. With reſpect to the Dukes of *Courland*, they have been, generally ſpeaking, cloſely allied to the Houſe of *Brandenburgh* by Marriage, which as it ſhews the ancient Connection of their Intereſts, diſcovers alſo the Reaſon why this Prince is ſtill ſo attentive to the Choice which the *Courlanders* are ſtill to make of a new Duke. The Province of *Samogitia* in *Poland*, with the Duchy of
Courland,

Courland, divide the Ducal *Pruſſia* from the Territories of the *Czarina*; and therefore in the preſent State of Things, it is but natural that the King of *Pruſſia* ſhould deſire to ſee the Hands of the *Polanders* ſtrengthened, and the Inhabitants of *Courland* ſet intirely free; becauſe he might then flatter himſelf, that in caſe at any time hereafter the Troubles of *Germany* ſhould revive, his Territories would be ſafe from any ſudden Invaſion by the *Ruſſians*, with which he was threatened but a few Years ago, when his Concerns were in a very critical Situation.

It is alſo very likely, that he would be glad to annex what the *Swedes* ſtill retain in *Pomerania*, to the reſt of that Country which is already in his Poſſeſſion; not from any Jealouſy of the *Swedes*, or from a Deſire of aggrandizing himſelf at the Expence of his Neighbours and Allies, but on the Score of Convenience, and the better Connection of his Eſtates. We may from thence infer, that he will never ſeek to procure this in any other than an amicable Way, and with the Conſent of the *Swedes*, in Conſideration of ſome kind of Equivalent or other, which may be alſo more acceptable to them. It may be this Acquiſition is ſtill at a great Diſtance, and it may be alſo that the Meaſures which this great Monarch has concerted in reference to the Affairs of the North, will bring this about ſooner than is generally imagined. But be that as it will, there is no Queſtion that whenever it is effected, the Power of *Pruſſia* will be very much augmented thereby, and the Liberties of the Empire will then ſtand in need of no Guardian without the Limits of *Germany*. While theſe Deſigns attract the Thoughts, and employ the Hands of this active Prince, he will certainly maintain a good Correſpondence with all thoſe Powers that are Neighbours to him, in reſpect to the reſt of his Dominions, which will leave the Inhabitants of the United Provinces at full Liberty to redreſs their own Grievances in their own manner, and to recover the ancient Strength and Vigour of their Government, in Conſequence of reſtoring that Form under which it was firſt conſtituted, and for a long Series of Years happily flouriſhed.

But whenever thoſe Struggles for Power, which at preſent embarraſs and diſtract the Potentates of the North, ſhall be by Negociation or otherwiſe compoſed, we have very little room to doubt that his Majeſty of *Pruſſia* will again turn his Views towards the Countries of *Cleves* and *Gueldres*, and the Principality of Eaſt *Frieſland*, where he has the very important and commodious Port of *Embden*, to facilitate the Schemes he may form in favour of the Commerce of his Subjects, to which there is no doubt that he will apply himſelf with equal

3 *Induſtry*

Induſtry and Spirit, whenever the Tranquillity of *Europe* ſhall be ſo thoroughly ſettled, as that he has no reaſon to ſuſpect his Neighbours may force him ſuddenly into a War, while his Councils are wholly taken up in cultivating the Arts of Peace. His erecting an *Aſiatic* Company demonſtrates what we have advanced to be Truth.

He will by that Time have ſerved himſelf to the utmoſt of whatever Aſſiſtance *France* may have found it her Intereſt to give him, for more than that ſhe will never give; and his Senſe of this will engage him not to perſiſt any longer in the Proſecution of Meaſures acceptable to the Court of *Verſailles*, than they are conducive to the Extenſion or Eſtabliſhment of his Power and Influence. He will then ſee that Independency, and being at the Head of the Proteſtant Intereſt in *Germany*, is ſufficient to gratify his utmoſt Ambition, and to raiſe him to the higheſt Point of Authority, by making him courted and reſpected by all his Neighbours, and as Occaſions offer, the Umpire of all their Differences.

Theſe are indeed but Suppoſitions, but then they are built upon ſolid and rational Foundations; whereas thoſe who fancy that he will be ſome time or other ſwallowed up by a Confederacy of powerful Neighbours, or deſpoiled of a great Part of his Territories, are not able to offer either Facts or Arguments to countenance their Opinion, ſince hitherto we have never ſeen him attempt beyond his Strength; nor has it appeared after many Months ſpent in Regulations, freſh Eſtabliſhments, new Diſcipline, and other military Improvements, that the Power moſt concerned, or which thinks herſelf moſt concerned, to traverſe the Deſigns of *Pruſſia*, has been able to do it with any great Effect, even in Conjunction with a very uſeful Ally, who after being once ſacrificed, will moſt certainly take care to prevent being involved again in the like Quarrel. In Points of this Nature it is inexcuſable to miſtake twice.

Theſe are all the Reflections we dare hazard at preſent upon this Subject, and perhaps there are very few political Writers who would have ventured to ſay ſo much; but as we have only the Reader's Advantage in View, it was not neceſſary for us to be ſo nice in that Particular, ſince whether our Conjectures are juſtified or refuted by Events, the Advantage to the Reader will be the very ſame; for as in one Caſe he will have an Opportunity of diſcerning in what manner probable Judgments may be drawn from political Principles, ſo in the other, the Detection of thoſe Errors will contribute not a little to the Increaſe of his Sagacity. We are ſo far from pretending to Infallibility, that what we offer is only in the na-

ture

ture of an Essay, which must be submitted to those Corrections that all Writings of this kind require, and in Consequence of which only, they can be brought at length to a tolerable Degree of Certainty and Perfection.

C H A P. VIII.

In which is comprehended a clear though concise Account of the Rise and Progress of the Power of the House of AUSTRIA, *the Opposition it has met with from that of* BOURBON, *and the present State of the first-mentioned House.*

THE Disputes between the Houses of *Austria* and *Bourbon*, having been the principal Causes of those Troubles that have disturbed the Peace of *Europe* for several Ages past, and there being but too just Grounds to believe that these Debates will be no less fatal to the Tranquillity of succeeding Times; it may be easily conceived from hence, that nothing can contribute more to the forming a just Idea of the present State of Things, and of the Maxims of Policy, by which the several Powers of *Christendom* regulate their Views, than a clear and distinct Account of the Acquisitions, Pretensions, Interests, Controversies, and Connections of these two great Families.

It is indeed true, that this is so wide, and so ample a Field, that it might well afford Matter sufficient for several large Volumes; but our Business is to contract it, to select from the Materials proper for so large a History, those Particulars that are fittest for the Purposes before mentioned, and by ranging these in right Order, to afford the Reader such a Prospect of this Subject, as it would be very difficult for him to obtain, even from so large a History, though written with all the Skill and Accuracy possible. This Attempt indeed is hardy and difficult, but then it is both rational and requisite; there is no proceeding in our Plan without it, and he who aims at pleasing the Publick, and who has already received Marks of their Willingness to be pleased with his Endeavours, will never think any thing hard or impracticable, which he is convinced is necessary for their Service.

L   With

With this View, and with these Hopes, let us begin with the History of the *House* of *Austria*, and use our utmost Care and Diligence to free those Circumstances that are most suited to our Design, from that Obscurity, and Embarrassment, in which they have been hitherto involved; chiefly from the Prejudices and Prepossessions of almost all the Historians, who have undertaken to afford us Light into these Matters; and who, instead of representing Things as they really were, have made it their Business to misrepresent them in such a Manner, as might bring the World in general to embrace for Truth their particular Opinions.

As to the Original of this great and flourishing Family, there is no need of troubling ourselves, or our Readers, with the Disputes of various Writers about it; these very Disputes incontestably prove its great Antiquity, and the different Sentiments that have been published about it, are pregnant Evidences of a Desire to entitle many antient and illustrious Houses to the Honour of being allied to this. The most probable and best attested of these Accounts, make *Rodolph* Count of *Hapsbourg*, generally reputed the Founder, because he was the first Emperor of this Family, to be descended by his Father's Side from the Counts of *Tierstien*, near *Basil*, in *Switzerland*; and by the Mother's Side from the antient Counts of *Hapsbourg*.

He enjoyed from his Father the Landgravate of *Alsace*; and the Glory with which he extricated himself from several unjust Wars that were made against him by his Neighbours, induced the Cantons of *Uri*, *Schwitz*, and *Underwald* to demand his Protection; the Cities of *Zurich* and *Fribourg* did the like; the Counties of *Kyburgh*, *Lentzburgh*, and *Baden*, came to him by the Death of his Cousin; and some other Lordships were added to his Dominions in Right of his Consort.

The Extent of his Reputation exceeded by very much that of his Territories; and the Prudence with which he governed them, induced *Ottocarus* King of *Bohemia*, to make Choice of him for his Prime Minister; which Dignity he enjoyed with the Title of Great Master of his Houshold. In this Situation of Things, the Empire became vacant by the Death of *Henry* II, and the Affairs of *Germany* fell into the greatest Confusion; for some endeavoured to raise *Alphonso* King of *Castile*, others *Richard* Earl of *Cornwal*, to the Imperial Dignity. Indeed both took the Title, but neither enjoyed the Authority of Emperor.

During the Time of these Disputes, three of the most antient Families extinguished; by which the Duchy of *Swabia*, and the Margravates of *Austria* and *Thuringia* were without Sovereigns

or

or lawful Princes, which increased the Disorders in *Germany* to such a Degree, that several great Cities had no other Way to secure themselves from those Bands of Thieves and Plunderers, that ravaged whole Countries with Impunity, than to enter into a League from mutual Defence, in some measure to supply the Want of that legal Government, by which they had been formerly protected.

At last, in the Year 1273, when this Scene of Confusion had wearied out even those by whom it was occasioned, the Elector of *Mentz* suggested, as the only Remedy for these Disorders, raising *Rodolph* of *Hapsbourg* to the Imperial Dignity; this Proposal was immediately embraced, and the Electors of *Saxony* and *Brandenburgh* not only gave their Votes, but, to strengthen his Interest, and to render him more able to support his new Dignity, they each of them married one of his Daughters. It was not long after his becoming Emperor, that he formed a Resolution of obliging *Ottocarus* King of *Bohemia* to submit himself to the Laws of the Empire. This Prince relying on his Power, and taking Advantage of the publick Calamity, had seized the Duchy of *Swabia*, and the Margravate of *Austria*; but *Rodolph* soon forced him to give up the Duchy to his second Son; and even insisted, as he had a Right to do, upon his rendering him Homage for the Kingdom of *Bohemia*; which was extreamly mortifying to the proudest, and most ambitious Prince of his Time; who could not forget that the Emperor had been once Master of his Houshold.

At length however he submitted to what could not be declined, but upon Condition that he should do Homage to the Emperor in his Tent, and before the great Officers of the Empire only. *Rodolph* condescended thereto; but when, according to the Ceremony, the King was on his Knees with his Hands upon the Gospels that lay open in the Emperor's Lap, the great Officers of the Houshold who were present, threw themselves flat upon their Faces, and the Sides of the Tent being drown up, exhibited this extraordinary Scene to the whole Imperial Army, ranged in two Lines on each Side of the Tent for that Purpose. This provoked the King so much, that at the Persuasion of his Queen he renewed the War, in hopes of recovering *Austria*, *Stiria*, and *Carniola*; bnt instead of this, in the first Battle he fought, he lost the Victory and his Life together.

The Emperor *Rodolph* gave another Instance of the Quickness of his Wit, and his great Presence of Mind, in the Ceremony of his Coronation at *Aix-la-Chapelle*, when the Electors made some Difficulty because the Scepter was wanting:

There

There is a Crucifix yonder, said the Emperor, *let us use that for a Scepter*. There was no rejecting this Expedient, so that they were obliged to do their Homage, and receive the Investiture of their Dominions, which they held as Fiefs of the Empire, by laying their Hands on the Crucifix instead of the Scepter. He answered in all other Respects the Expectations of those who had raised him to the Empire; for he restored its Domestick Tranquillity, and its Reputation with regard to Foreign Nations; by suppressing such as made use of their Power to harrass and disturb their Neighbours, as well as by giving new Vigour to the Laws for the Punishment of lesser Offenders every where throughout the Empire.

It is true, that he took great Care of his own Family, obliging *Henry* Duke of *Bavaria* to restore him the Towns of *Weltz*, *Lintz*, *Steyr*, and other Places upon the River *Ens*, mortgaged to him by *Ottocarus* King of *Bohemia*, which the Duke parted with to prevent being punished for the Assistance he had given that Prince against the Empire. It is also said, that the Emperor *Rodolph* sold several Rights of the Empire in *Italy*, and made many of the Cities free. But in doing this, he conceived that no Prejudice was done to the Empire, since he never affected to be powerful in *Italy*, and therefore declined being crowned King of the *Romans* by the Pope, or of *Lombardy* by the Archbishop of *Milan*, which his Predecessors affected at a vast Expence.

He thought an Emperor might become powerful enough by minding his Affairs in *Germany*; and that their frequent Journeys into *Italy* had been prejudicial to the *Germans*. Until this Emperor's Time all Acts of State, all Laws, and all Proceedings in Courts of Justice, had been written in *Latin*; but he changing that Custom, used the *German* Language himself, and established this Usage for the future; in a Word, he laid the Foundation of the Power and Grandeur of the *German* Empire, as well as of the House of *Austria*; and after a glorious Reign died in 1291, leaving behind him two Sons, *Albert* Duke of *Austria*, and *Rodolph* Duke of *Swabia*.

After the Decease of this Prince, the Archbishop and Elector of *Mentz* procured *Adolphus* of *Nassau* to be elected Emperor, with an Intention of governing the Empire under his Name; but finding that Prince of too high a Spirit to bear such a Treatment, he deserted him, and engaged other Electors to do the same, who soon after took upon them to depose him, and to elect *Albert* Duke of *Austria*, Emperor. This produced a civil War, which was ended in the Year 1298, by a decisive Battle, in which *Albert* was not only victorious,

victorious, but also killed his Competitor *Adolphus* with his own Hand, and thereby secured to himself the Possession of the Imperial Dignity.

The Elector of *Mentz* in a very little Time grew as uneasy in Regard to him, as he had been in respect to *Adolphus*; and relying on his own great Power and the Influence he had over the Electors, had the Insolence to tell him once, when they were hunting together, that he had nothing more to do, than to blow his Horn, which hung at his Side, and immediately there should start up another Emperor. But in this he shewed his Vanity and Ambition, more than either his Wisdom or his Interest; for *Albert* had immediately recourse to Arms, and forced him and the Electors who sided with him, to a speedy Submission. He was a powerful and prudent Prince, and, like *Rodolph* his Father, alike careful of the Concerns of his Family, and the Interests of the Empire.

But with many great Qualities he had (and indeed what Prince has not?) some Mixture of Vices. His Ambition was boundless, and his Government arbitrary. The Governors he sent into *Switzerland*, which belonged to him, oppressed the People to such a Degree, that the Cantons of *Uri*, *Schwitz*, and *Underwald*, resolved to make themselves free; in order to which they entered into a Confederacy in the Year 1307 for ten Years, which afterwards they renewed in 1315, and made perpetual: And this was the Origin of the *Switz* Republick, which has since made such a Figure in *Europe*. For tho' the Emperor neglected nothing to reduce them again under his Dominion, yet it was in vain; for partly by the Situation of their Country, and partly by the Bravery of the People, they preserved their Liberty in spite of all his Endeavours.

He married his eldest Son *Rodolph* to *Blanche* the Daughter of *Philip* the *Fair*, King of *France*, by which he gained some Advantages to his Family. After her Decease he espoused *Isabella*, Queen Dowager of *Bohemia*, and in her Right acquired that Kingdom, which now for the first Time was possessed by the House of *Austria*; but he dying soon after, they lost it again. As for the Emperor *Albert*, he continued to govern the Empire with great Honour and Reputation several Years, in which Space he lessened the Power of the Clergy, made several good Laws, and endeavoured to fix the Imperial Authority upon a firmer Foundation than it had hitherto stood.

But while he was meditating this, and other great Designs, an Act of Injustice he had committed, brought him to an

untimely

untimely End; for having undertaken the Tutelage of his Nephew *John*, the Son of *Rodolph* Duke of *Swabia*, he refused when of Age, to put him in Possession of his Country, which provoked him to such a Degree, that he took an Opportunity when the Emperor was hunting, to assassinate him on the first of *May* 1308, in a Place where the Monastery of *Koningsfield* was afterwards built by his Widow the Empress Dowager *Isabella* or *Elizabeth*.

By the premature Death of this great Monarch, the House of *Austria* lost the Imperial Dignity, which they did not recover for one hundred and thirty Years; though her Chiefs continued all that Time to be reckoned amongst the greatest and most powerful Princes of the Empire; and this notwithstanding their Dominions were divided into several distinct Principalities, the Possessors of which frequently differed amongst themselves. At length, *Albert* surnamed the *Magnanimous*, having married *Elizabeth*, the Daughter of the Emperor *Sigismund*, revived the Glory of his House; for on the first of *January* 1438, he was elected King of *Hungary*; on the sixth of *May* the same Year, he became King of *Bohemia*; on the twenty-sixth of *June* following, was elected Emperor. He was one of the bravest, and at the same Time one of the most prudent Princes of his Age. He met with great Difficulties in maintaining the many Dignities to which he was raised; but by degrees he found Means to bring the *Hungarians* to Submission; he next drove *Uladislaus* King of *Poland* out of *Bohemia*, by which he reduced that Country into a State of Tranquillity; and afterwards engaging in a War against the *Turks*, he forced their Emperor *Amurath* to raise the Siege of *Belgrade*, when he had lain before it a Year.

He would undoubtedly have performed still greater Things, if he had not been removed by sudden Death on the twenty-sixth of *October* 1439. He left behind him a posthumous Son called *Ladislaus*, who had the Titles of King of *Hungary* and *Bohemia*; but he never enjoyed either, though the *Hungarians* were desirous enough of putting him into Possession of their Country, if his Cousin, who succeeded his Father in the Empire, would have consented to it; but whether through Ambition, or from some other Point of false Policy, he kept him at *Vienna*, where at last he died about the Age of eighteen, not without great Suspicion of Poison.

Frederick, surnamed the *Peaceable*, was elected Emperor on the Death of *Albert* II. in the Year 1440, and two Years afterwards he married the Infanta *Eleonora*, Daughter of *Edward* King of *Portugal*, by whom he had his Son and Successor ceffor *Maximilian.* He interpofed his Authority at the famous Council at *Bafle,* by which he prevented a Schifm, when at the very Point of breaking out; he reformed the Laws of the Empire, and digefted thofe relating to Fiefs into one Code, which prov'd very beneficial to all the Members of the *Germanick* Body. He engaged in feveral Family Difputes, which ended in a War; but by Degrees, and by dint of Patience and Prudence, he extricated himfelf out of numberlefs Difficulties, not with Safety only, but in almoft every Inftance with Advantage.

He was a very faving Prince, which drew upon him the Reproach of being covetous; but in reality Frugality was to him a very neceffary Virtue; for his Predeceffors in the Empire having poffeffed with it the two rich Kingdoms of *Hungary* and *Bohemia,* were confequently able to fpend liberally, and to keep very magnificent Courts. But as he held neither of thofe Kingdoms, and drew but a fmall Revenue from his own Territories, he could not live with the fame Splendor that they had done. He was very flow in his Meafures, but withal very fecure, and with great Prudence eftablifhed the Grandeur of the Houfe of *Auftria* upon that Bafis on which it has hitherto fubfifted, notwithftanding all the vigorous and repeated Efforts of its numerous Enemies.

There were two Things that contributed extreamly to this Eftablifhment: the firft was the Length of his Reign, which exceeded half a Century, and gave him an Opportunity of doing greater Things for his Family, than hitherto any Prince had done: And on the other, the Marriage of his eldeft Son *Maximilian* to *Mary* Duchefs of *Burgundy,* the greateft Heirefs in *Europe,* by whom the Houfe of *Auftria* acquired an immenfe Treafure in ready Money, and thofe that are ftill called the *Auftrian Netherlands,* with the Provinces which have fince compofed the *Dutch* Republick, included. This Match enabled the Emperor alfo to procure his Son to be elected King of the *Romans* in his Life-time, which was a very wife Precaution, fince after a Reign of fifty-three Years, this Monarch was taken off fuddenly; for having eat plentifully of a Melon after Dinner, and drank too much Water upon it, this proved the Caufe of his Death, on the 14th of *Auguft* 1493.

Maximilian I. fucceeded his Father, having been chofen King of the *Romans* in 1486. He was in his Temper one of the moft generous, as well as in his Perfon one of the handfomeft Princes of his Time. The former gained him the Affection of his Subjects, as the latter had procured him the Heirefs of *Burgundy,* to whom all the great Princes on the Continent had pretended. It may not be amifs to obferve,

that

that it was this Lady who brought the large Lip into the *Austrian* Family, at *Brantome* obferves on the Authority of *Eleanor* Queen of *France*, who was Sifter to *Charles* V, who told it that Gentleman.

Befides the other Bleffings he poffeffed, *Maximilian* was one of the moft extraordinary Princes of his Age in refpect to his natural Abilities, and conquered many fignal Difadvantages which would have weighed down an inferior Genius. He could fcarce fpeak plain at ten Years old, and afterwards fpoke fo faft, that he could hardly be underftood. His Father put him under the Care of *Peter Englebert*, who was a downright Pedant, and behaved towards him in fuch a Manner as gave him a Difguft to Learning; but as he grew up, he corrected thefe Errors by his own Care and Diligence, and became not only extreamly eloquent in his own Language, but fpoke alfo the *Latin*, *French*, and *Italian* Tongues with the greateft Purity.

After the Death of *Mary* of *Burgundy*, he projected a fecond Marriage with *Ann* of *Bretagne*, which if it had taken Effect, would have been no lefs beneficial to him than the former, but he was fupplanted in this by the *French* King *Charles* VIII. Upon this Difappointment he married *Blanche* Daughter to the Duke of *Milan*, with whom he had a prodigious Sum in ready Money, which enabled him to recover that Part of *Auftria* that had been conquered by *Mathias Corvinus* King of *Hungary*. His Care of his own Concerns did not hinder him from being very attentive to thofe of the Empire; for in the Year 1495, he eftablifhed, in a Diet at *Worms*, the famous Conftitution for the Security of the publick Peace, and at the fame Time created an Imperial Chamber, for hearing and determining in a legal Manner the Differences and Difputes between the Princes of the Empire, which before his Time had been feldom decided any other Way than by the Sword. He continued the War which his Father had begun againft the *Swifs* Cantons; but after being defeated in eight Battles, concluded a Treaty of Peace with them in 1499.

The Year following he fettled a Council for the Government of the Empire; and at the fame Time divided it into Circles, of which there were originally but fix, *viz. Franconia*, *Bavaria*, *Swabia*, the *Rhine*, *Weftphalia*, and Lower *Saxony*; but in 1512, there were four other Circles added; *viz.* thofe of *Auftria*, *Burgundy*, the Lower *Rhine*, and Upper *Saxony*. Authors are very much divided, as to the Time in which *Auftria* was erected into an Arch-Duchy; and there are good Authorities which afcribe this to five feveral Princes; but however the moft probable Account is, that *Maximilian*

gave

gave it this Title, to diftinguifh it from all the other Principalities of the Empire and of *Europe*.

The *Venetians* having refufed him a Paffage thro' their Territories, he was offended with it to fuch a Degree, that he engaged the Pope and the King of *France* in the League of *Cambray* againft that Republick, which was very near being fatal to it. The Lofs of the Battle of *Agnadel* had infallibly drawn after it that of all their Territories upon the Continent, if fome Mifunderftanding had not arifen between the Powers embarked in that Alliance. The *Venetians* themfelves were fo aftonifhed when they faw the Emperor become Mafter of *Verona*, *Brefcia*, *Bergamo*, *Padua*, *Vicenza*, *Lodi*, and other fortified Places, that they offered him an annual Tribute of fifty thoufand Ducats to be taken under the Protection of the Empire; and without doubt it was the greateft Miftake in his Reign, that he neglected this Offer: for the Republick, recovering from their Fright, and having prevailed upon *Lewis* XII. of *France* to quit the League, foon brought moft of thefe Places again under their Obedience; fo that except *Riva* and *Roveredo*, the Emperor kept nothing at the Peace, which he fold the *Venetians* for two hundred thoufand Ducats, one half of which Sum was paid by *France*.

In this War the Emperor had the Affiftance of the *Swifs*, in virtue of the hereditary Convention he had made with them; fo that he found them more ufeful to him as Allies, than he could have made them as Subjects. In 1515, he united the County of *Goritz* to his Dominions, upon the Death of the laft Count without Heirs. He received with great Magnificence, *Sigifmund* King of *Poland*, and *Uladiflaus* King of *Hungary*, at *Vienna*; at which Interview he renewed the Treaty of Succeffion with the laft of thefe Princes, by which he gained the Kingdom of *Hungary* for his Pofterity. His Reign, though fhort in Comparifon of his Father's, was glorious for himfelf, very ufeful to the Empire, and exceedingly happy for his Family. He died at *Wells* in *Auftria*, on the twelfth of *January* 1519.

This great Monarch had only one Son, *Philip*, who died before him; he efpoufed *Jane* the Daughter of *Ferdinand* of *Arragon*, and *Ifabella* of *Caftile*, who brought him the whole Kingdom of *Spain* for her Fortune. Don *Juan Antonio de Vera*, a *Spanifh* Hiftorian, gives us this Character of him: " His Temper and his Manners, fays he, gained him not only " the Love of his Subjects, but alfo of his Enemies; he was " very beneficent, but his Gifts were fmall, and like thofe of
" a private

" a private Man, for he had not Time to shew that he had the
" Soul and Generosity of a King. His Queen was so fond of
" him, that his Death, which happened in the Year 1506, cost
" that Princess her Senses; she directed his Body to be embalm-
" ed, and carried it every where about with her; a memorable
" Example of conjugal Tenderness! and though in itself an
" Act of Folly, has been admired by Men of the best Sense."

King *Philip* left behind him two Sons, *Charles* born the
twenth-fourth of *February* 1500, and *Ferdinand* born the
tenth of *March* 1503. He had likewise four Daughters;
Eleonora, who espoused Don *Emanuel* King of *Portugal*, and
afterwards the *French* King *Francis* I. *Isabella*, who married
Christian II. King of *Denmark*; *Mary*, who espoused *Lewis*
King of *Bohemia* and *Hungary*; and *Catharine*, first promised
to *John Frederick* Elector of *Saxony*, and afterwards married to
John III. King of *Portugal*.

Philip made a Treaty with *Lewis* XII. of *France* for the
Division of the Kingdom of *Naples*; and by his last Will
directed, that he should have the Tuition of his eldest Son,
desiring that he would provide some able Man to have the
Care of his Education, which that Prince faithfully fulfilled,
by appointing *William de Croy* of the House of *Chievres* to that
Employment, who was one of the wisest and best-bred Men of
his Time, and who laid the Foundation of his Pupil's Fortunes, by an excellent Education.

This young Prince *Charles*, whom his Grandfather *Maximilian* I. could not prevail upon the Electors to choose King
of the *Romans* in his Life-time, succeeded him after his Decease, and became Emperor by the Name of *Charles* V. chiefly
by the Influence of the Electors of *Mentz* and *Saxony*. He
yielded to the Arch-Duke *Ferdinand* his Brother, all the Dominions belonging to the House of *Austria* in *Germany*, reserving to himself the Successions of the Kings of *Spain* and
Dukes of *Burgundy*. He added to the *Low Countries*, the
Lordships of *Utrecht* and *Over-Yssel*, which came to him by
the Donation of *Henry*, Bishop of *Utrecht*. He afterwards acquired the Duchy of *Gueldres*, and the County of *Zutphen* on
the Death of their last Duke *Charles*. The Countries of *Frieze*
and *Groninguen*, he purchased from *George* Duke of *Saxony*,
for one hundred and fifty thousand Florins in Gold. He annexed likewise the Towns of *Cambray* and *Lingen* to those
Provinces; and for their Security, incorporated the whole into the Empire, under the Title of the Circle of *Burgundy*. He
had in the Course of his Reign many Wars, and was in most
of them very successful.

In

In the Year 1521, he entered into a League with Pope *Leo* X. in Consequence of which he made himself Master of *Parma*, *Placentia*, and *Milan*, which last he restored to Duke *Francis Sforza*. He raised to the Papacy *Adrian* VI. who had been his Preceptor. The Constable of *Bourbon* quitting the Service of his natural Prince, and entering into his, he made an Irruption into *Provence*, where he took the Cities of *Aix* and *Toulon*, but was obliged to raise the Siege of *Marseilles* by the steady Resistance of the Inhabitants. He afterwards repassed the *Alps*, which encouraged the *French* King *Francis* I. to invade the *Milanese*, and lay Siege to *Pavia*, which by making an obstinate Defence, gave the *Imperialists* Time to collect their Forces ; and the King, against the Sentiments of his principal Officers, having ventured to give them Battle, not only lost it, but with it his Liberty.

This could not but give the Emperor much Satisfaction, since King *Francis* had been Competitor against him for the Imperial Dignity ; and perhaps it was in some measure owing to this, that he sent him Prisoner into *Spain*, where he remained under a hard Captivity for three Years, and even then did not obtain his Liberty, but upon very severe Terms ; for the Performance of which he gave his Children as Hostages. A Proceeding that does this Emperor's Memory no great Honour.

On his Return into his Dominions however, the *French* King enter'd into a League against the Emperor with the then Pope *Clement* VII, and the *Venetians* ; which so provoked *Charles*, that he ordered his Forces under the Command of the Constable of *Bourbon*, to enter the Ecclesiastical Territories, where he soon carried all before him, took and sacked the City of *Rome*, and besieged his Holiness in the Castle of St. *Angelo*, while by an unaccountable Strain of Popish Bigotry and Hypocrisy, they were making solemn Processions in *Spain* for his happy Deliverance.

The Doctrines of *Luther* prevailing in *Germany*, the Emperor, who at first did not give much Attention to them, or perhaps inclined in his own Mind to a Reformation, surmising afterwards they might prove dangerous to his Authority, resolved to extinguish them ; and for that Purpose assembled a Diet at *Spire*, and by a Decree dated the 13th of *October* 1529, directed that the *Lutherans* should be proceeded against ; upon which, several Princes who had embraced those Sentiments, protested in favour of their Religion, and so they came to be called *Protestants*, and the Doctrine of *Luther* was thenceforward stiled the *Protestant Faith*.

The

The same Year the Emperor concluded a Peace with *Francis* I. at *Cambray*, but it did not last long; for the Duke of *Milan* having caused, as it was said, a *French* Ambassador to be killed in his Dominions, King *Francis* raised a great Army in order to revenge this Affront; but the Duke of *Savoy* having refused him a Passage through his Territories, he turned his Arms against him, and took from him without any Pretence, but that of superior Force, all his Countries.

In the mean time the Duke of *Milan* died without Issue, upon which the Emperor entred into Possession of that Country, as devolving to him in the nature of a Fief; which kindled a new War in *Italy*, and in the *Low Countries*; however in the Year 1537, a Truce was concluded for ten Months at *Terouanne*; which was prolonged soon after at *Nice* for ten Years. It was in this Space, that upon a popular Insurrection in the City of *Ghent*, the Emperor demanded, and was permitted to pass through *France*, where he received very great Honours, and was treated with much Generosity by *Francis* I. to whom it is said he promised on that account to restore the Duchy of *Milan*; which however it is certain he neither did, nor intended to do; which, with some other Grievances, engaged the *French* King to break the Truce, and enter into a War with the Emperor; who thereupon made a League with the King of *England*, whose Assistance at that Time was of great Consequence to him.

Yet the *Imperialists* being defeated near *Carignan*, and the Emperor being afraid that the *French* would take Advantage of the Religious Disturbances in *Germany*, resolved to conclude a Peace in Time, which, tho' some Years after, was accordingly done at *Crespy*. There never lived a Prince who had a better Title to the high Characters of a great Captain and a consummate Politician, than *Charles* V. He gained every Advantage by his Arms that it was possible to gain by them; and he very soon saw when these Advantages were no longer in his Power, and then he had recourse to Treaties, in which no Monarch knew better how to manage his Interest than he did, or gained more in the Course of several intricate Negotiations.

The Protestants were now become extreamly formidable in *Germany*; for upon publishing the Decree of the Diet of *Spire*, they formed, as it was very natural for them to do, a Confederacy for their own Preservation; which, from the Place where it was concluded, had the Title of the League of *Smalcald*, and makes a great Figure in the *German* History. The Emperor going to *Bologna* to be crowned by the Pope, had a very serious Conference with him upon this Subject; in which he he pressed him to call, before it was too late, a general Council for the Reformation of the Church, as the sureft and most effectual Means for remedying these Disorders; the Mischiefs attending which he foresaw, and represented in the strongest Colours. But his Holiness was of a different Opinion; he thought that this was being too complaisant to Hereticks; and therefore insisted that they should be compelled to Obedience, in which the Emperor acquiesced, but resolved to do it in his own Method.

On his Return therefore to *Germany*, he summoned a Diet to be held at *Augsbourg* on the eighth of *April* 1530; where the Proteftants appeared, and presented a Confession of their Faith, shewing plainly that they adhered to the true Church of *Chrift*; and that they rejected only the Superftitions of the Church of *Rome*, which were of late Date, and, so far from being authorifed by, that they were incompatible with the Gospel. This however was so far from having the designed Effect of procuring Peace and due Liberty of Confcience, that it brought about quite the contrary, through the Emperor's Management.

For in that Diet an Edict was framed for reftoring all Things to their former State, and for maintaining the Church, that is, the Church of *Rome*, by the Secular Arm; so that the Proteftants saw themfelves obliged either to part with their Religion or to fight for and defend it, and they chose the latter. This opened a long and bloody War in the Empire; in which at firft the Emperor was fuccefsful; for in the Battle of *Mulberg* he defeated the Confederate Army, and made the famous *John Frederick* Elector of *Saxony*, who was at their Head, Prifoner, which gave the Proteftants a dreadful Blow.

He foon after got into his Hands the Landgrave of *Heffe*, by an Artifice of the famous Cardinal *Grenvelle*, a great Politician, but one of the wickedeft Men of that Age; who by changing the Letter in the fafe Conduct given to that Prince, furnifhed the Emperor with a Pretence for detaining him; which pitiful Artifice, how much foever it might be for his Intereft, was highly and will be ever detrimental to his Honour. He carried those two illuftrious Princes about with him, and thereby so terrified the Proteftants, that they began to fall off from their League; by drawing over Prince *Maurice* of *Saxony* to his Party, through Hopes of granting him the Inveftiture of his Coufin's Dominions, under Pretence that his War againft the Elector was founded on Motives of State, and not of Religion, he divided them ftill more; and by befieging fome of the Imperial Cities that had taken their Part, he frighted them into fuch Compofitions, as coft them much more Money than

would

would have been neceſſary to ſecure their Freedom, by ſupporting the Confederacy into which they had entered for that Purpoſe.

The City of *Magdebourg* alone remained firm to thoſe Engagements, its Inhahitants reſolving to hazard their Lives and Fortunes rather than their Conſciences; and thoſe generous Sentiments of theirs enabled them to make a long and vigorous Defence, which afforded the Proteſtants time to recover their Spirits, and to conſider of Ways and Means for reſtoring their Affairs, and obtaining the free Exerciſe of their Religion. This was the firſt great Criſis of what was called the new, but which in reality deſerved better to be ſtiled the old Religion; and if the Inhabitants of *Magdebourg* had been leſs zealous, or to ſpeak plainly, if Providence had not enabled them to triumph by their Conſtancy over all the Fury, as well as over the ſuperior Forces of their Enemies, Papal Authority would have regained by the Sword all that it had loſt in Conſequence of that general Reception the Arguments of *Luther* and his Followers had met with throughout all *Germany*.

From hence by the Way, the Reader may diſcern two Points of very great Conſequence in Politicks. The *firſt* is, that religious Principles are much more capable of ſuſtaining and ſupporting a firm and determined Courage, than either political Notions or Views of Intereſt; which ſhould induce Stateſmen to be very cautious of running down Religion in general, which can never have any better Effect than corrupting and daſtardizing ſuch as are deluded into theſe looſe Sentiments; for this is an infallible Maxim, that he who does not think himſelf accountable to God, will never do any thing worthy of a Man. The *ſecond*, that Firmneſs and Reſolution, with any competent Degree of Strength, will, generally ſpeaking, command Succeſs, and that frequently beyond the Reach of Probability; ſo that in a good Cauſe, Men ought ſeldom or never to deſpair, but rather conſider how they may diſcharge their Duty to God and their Country, and leave the Iſſue to Providence, by which they are to be protected here, or rewarded hereafter. But to proceed with our Hiſtory.

The *French* King *Henry* II. ſaw the falſe Step he had taken in not ſupporting the Proteſtants in time, and therefore reſolved to repair his Error if it was poſſible, by ſending them powerful Succours, provided he was ſure they would not come too late. He firſt enter'd into Intrigues with their Chiefs, and finding they were beginning to recover their Spirits, and that they were yet able to raiſe great Numbers of Men, he furniſhed them with conſiderable Sums of Money; and next attempted the

Fidelity

Fidelity of *Maurice*, to whom the Emperor had given the Inveftiture of the Electorate of *Saxony*, and who then commanded his Army before the City of *Magdebourg*. That Prince was a great Politician, and forefeeing the Dangers to which he might be expofed, in cafe the Proteftants were crufh'd, he refolved to affift them; with much Secrecy at firft, by protracting the Siege, and, when they had gathered Force fufficient to fupport him, to declare openly in their Favour.

He executed this Scheme with fuch Dexterity and Succefs, that he conftrained the Emperor to retire into *Tyrol*, and was very near feizing his Perfon at *Infpruck*; from whence he was obliged to make his Efcape with the utmoft Precipitation to *Villaco*, in the Dominions of the State of *Venice*. The *French*, who affifted the Proteftants merely with a View to their own Intereft, in hopes of recovering the Duchy of *Milan*, and feizing fome Places that lay conveniently for them in *Germany*, found themfelves deceived in their Expectations by the Wifdom of the Emperor, and the publick Spirit of Prince *Maurice* of *Saxony*; for the former having given full Powers to *Ferdinand* King of the *Romans*, to treat of Peace upon the beft Terms on which it could be had, it was very foon concluded, by a Treaty figned the 2d of *Auguft* 1552, which, from the Place where it was negotiated, received the Title of *the Pacification of Paffau*; and the *French* were entirely excluded, of which they complain'd highly, and charged Prince *Maurice* with the greateft Perfidy.

But the Truth of the Matter is, that when the Elector difcovered the real Defigns of the *French*, and faw at the fame Time how much they tended to the Ruin of *Germany*, he thought that no Engagements could bind him to concur in Meafures tending to the Deftruction of his Country; in which he certainly acted like a good Patriot and a Man of Senfe, deceived the Deceivers, put an End to the Troubles of the Empire, and fecured to the Proteftants what they fought for, the Freedom of their Confciences, and the Liberty of exercifing their Religion.

The Refentment which the Emperor had of the Behaviour of *France* upon this Occafion, engaged him in a War with that Crown; and, which plainly fhewed his great Capacity, he brought over to his Service the greateft Part of that very Army, by which he had been driven into *Tyrol*; and having done this, he march'd directly to recover *Metz*, which was one of the Places the *French* had feized, and into which the Duke of *Guife* threw himfelf with an Army, rather than a Garrifon; by which the Place was preferved, and the Emperor forced to retreat; which put him in Mind of a Defign he

had

had form'd when at *Infpruck*, of quitting all his Dignities, and retiring for the Remainder of his Days to a private Life. This, one would have thought, might have been eafily executed; but the Emperor judged otherwife.

He refolved to fhew himfelf in that, as well as in all other Things, a Hero and a Statefman; and therefore there were many Points which he refolved to fee fettled before he abdicated the Thrones of the Empire and of *Spain*. He was contriving in his own Mind, how to weaken the Force of the Proteftants; but before he had fix'd upon a Scheme, that was likely to be attended with Succefs, the Proteftants did his Work without his Interpofition; for the Hatred between *Maurice* of *Saxony* and *Albert* of *Brandenburgh* rofe to fuch a Height, that it came at laft to a decifive Battle, in which the Army of the former gained the Victory, tho' their Chief was killed; and *Albert*, who was defeated, found no other way to preferve himfelf but by Flight. His Brother *Auguftus*, who fucceeded *Maurice* in the Electorate of *Saxony*, became fo firmly attach'd to the Emperor, that he had no longer any Caufe to be apprehenfive of Dangers in *Germany*.

He then march'd into the *Low Countries* with a powerful Army to expel the *French*; and while he was carrying on the War there, he meditated and accomplifh'd another great Defign, which was the Marriage of his Son *Philip* with *Mary* Queen of *England*, and Daughter to *Henry* VIII. which took Effect in *July* 1554, and confirm'd the Emperor in the Refolution he had taken to refign his Dominions to his Son, in order to which he was willing to have concluded a Peace with *France*; but finding that, after a long Negotiation, impracticable, he refolved to proceed to what was entirely in his own Power, and to make an Exchange of Splendor and Power, for Retirement and Peace of Mind.

It is neceffary, for the Sake of Perfpicuity, to treat this Affair of his Refignations more at large, becaufe many Writers confound their Readers Notions about it, by reprefenting it as a fingle Act; whereas the Emperor made three diftinct Refignations, which all of them deferve to be confidered. In the firft, which was perform'd with great Solemnity at *Bruffels* on the 28th of *October* 1555, he declared his Son Grand Mafter of the Order of the Golden Fleece, and Sovereign of the Seventeen Provinces of the *Low Countries*. In the fecond, two Months after, he refigned to him all his hereditary Dominions; but ftill referved to himfelf the Empire, with a View to have fecured that likewife, if it had been practicable, for King *Philip*; and the Method by which he propofed to fucceed in his Defign, was this:

He

He labour'd to persuade his Brother *Ferdinand*, King of the *Romans*, to consent that *Philip* should be elected to that Dignity, in Consideration of his resigning the Empire to *Ferdinand*. But this Project, tho' managed with great Secrecy and Address, fail'd of Success by the Assiduity of the Archduke *Maximilian*, Son to King *Ferdinand*, who traversed all the Emperor's Endeavours for that Purpose, and secured the Succession to himself. A whole Year was spun out in this manner; and then the Emperor sent *William* Prince of *Orange*, attended by the Vice-Chancellor of the Empire, and his own Secretary, to carry his Resignation to his Brother *Ferdinand*, which put an End to that Affair. *Charles* soon afterwards made a Voyage to *Spain*, where he resolved to spend the Remainder of his Days in a Monastery.

At *Valladolid* he pass'd a few Days in taking Leave of the Ladies, and some Persons of Distinction, who came on so strange an Occasion to pay their Respects to him. Amongst the rest came his Fool, or Jester, *Pedro de San Erhas*, who, upon seeing the Emperor make a low Bow, could not help saying, *Sire, you are very complaisant to pull off your Hat to me; is it to shew that you are no longer Emperor? No*, Pedro, answered that Prince gravely, *it is because I have now nothing in my Power to give you, save this Mark of Civility*. We may collect from this Answer, that he began already to be chagrin'd on the Subject of his Abdication. He retired however, as he proposed, to a Convent of *Hieronomites*, where he died on the 21st of *September* 1558, at the Close of the second Year after his Resignation. By the Manner in which he parted with his Dominions, he created two distinct Branches of the House of *Austria*, viz. the *Spanish* and the *German*. Of the former we shall speak in its proper Place, at present it is our Business to pursue and finish the History of the latter.

Ferdinand I. the younger Brother of the Emperor *Charles* V. was born in the Year 1503, and was a Prince of a mild Disposition, very learned himself, and a Lover of learned Men. He married the Princess *Ann*, Daughter of *Uladislaus* King of *Hungary*; and in her Right, on the Death of her Brother *Lewis*, who was kill'd in the Battle of *Mohatz*, he claim'd that Crown, as well as the Diadem of *Bohemia*, in 1526. He obtained the Possession of the latter immediately; but the Party which opposed him in the former call'd in the *Turks*, which gave Rise to a long and bloody War. In 1531, his Brother *Charles* procured him the Title of King of the *Romans*, notwithstanding a vigorous Opposition made thereto by the Elector of *Saxony*. The two Brothers, however, considered this

Election

Election in very different Lights. *Charles* intended that his Brother should hold it no longer than till his own Son *Philip* was of Age; whereas *Ferdinand* look'd upon this Promotion as the first Step to securing the Imperial Dignity, not only for himself during Life, but for his own Family.

He was in this Respect a very wise and cautious Prince, and never neglected any Opportunity of enlarging his Dominions. In Conjunction with the other Princes of the Empire, he had expell'd *Ulric* Duke of *Wirtemberg* from his Dominions; but in 1534, by the Assistance of the Landgrave of *Hesse*, he recover'd the Possession of them; and the same Year *Ferdinand* came to an Agreement with this Prince, that in Case his Family in the Male Line should fail, his Duchy (one of the most considerable in the Empire) should fall to the House of *Austria*.

When *John-Frederick* Duke of *Saxony* was depriv'd of his Electorate, and put under the Ban of the Empire, the Emperor at the same Time keeping him close Prisoner, *Ferdinand* form'd Pretensions upon several Cities in his Dominions, which he pretended belonged of Right to his Kingdom of *Bohemia*; and tho' he did not prevail so far as to keep those Cities, yet *Maurice* Elector of *Saxony* found it requisite to yield the Duchy of *Sagan* in *Silesia* to this Monarch, by way of Equivalent.

In 1550, the Emperor *Charles* V. pressed him very hard to resign the Title of King of the *Romans* to his Son *Philip*, and actually held a Diet for that Purpose. But *Ferdinand* had acquired so great an Interest amongst the Princes of the Empire, that his Brother could not have carried his Point, even if he had forced him to resign. In the Year 1555, he settled the Religious Disputes in the Empire, at a Diet held for that Purpose at *Augsbourg*. The Year following he succeeded, by his Brother's Resignation, to the Imperial Dignity; which was confirm'd by a kind of second Election at *Franckfort* in the Month of *March* 1558.

Paul the Vth, who was then Pope, took this very ill, and absolutely refused to acknowledge him for Emperor, which however had not the Effect that he expected; for *Ferdinand* being inform'd that he had denied Audience to his Ambassadors, he sent them Instructions to leave *Rome* in three Days, in case the Pope continued in that Disposition, which they accordingly did. But his Successor *Pius* IV. as soon as he ascended the Pontifical Throne, own'd the Emperor, and so put an End to that Dispute; which however gave such a Wound to the Papal Authority as hath never been cured, all subsequent Emperors having treated the Recognition of the Pope

as

as a thing of little or no Consequence, and by its having taken Place constantly since, is now in reality become so.

He govern'd the Empire with great Wisdom and Mildness; and by his smooth Conduct procured many considerable Advantages still in the Possession of the House of *Austria*, to the Year 1564, in which he died, in the 61st Year of his Age, and the ninth Year of his Reign.

He had three Sons, *Maximilian, Ferdinand*, and *Charles*. The first had the Kingdom of *Hungary* and *Bohemia*, and the Duchy of *Austria*; the second, *Tyrol* and the Exterior *Austria*; the third, *Stiria, Carinthia,* and *Carniola. Ferdinand* married a Lady much beneath him in Birth, by whom he had two Sons, *Charles* and *Andrew*, who for that Reason were excluded the Succession; only *Charles* had the Marquisate of *Burgaw*; and *Andrew* becoming an Ecclesiastick, obtain'd the Bishoprick of *Constance*, and afterwards a Red Hat, with the Title of Cardinal of *Austria. Maximilian* and *Charles* divided the *German* Line of *Austria* into two Branches, *viz.* that of *Bohemia*, and that of *Stiria*.

Maximilian II. was a Prince of Spirit and Vigour. He governed *Spain* in Quality of Viceroy, when he received the News of his Uncle's endeavouring to procure his Son *Philip* to be elected King of the *Romans*; upon which he hasten'd into *Germany*, together with the Infanta *Maria*, whom he had espoused, and was very instrumental in defeating that Design. In 1562, he brought his own Election to bear in the Diet of *Franckfort*; and the same Year was crown'd King of the *Romans*, of *Bohemia* and *Hungary*. He succeeded his Father two Years after, and govern'd the Empire with great Wisdom and Equity. His War with the Prince of *Transilvania* brought on another with the *Turks*, in which he was not very successful; which inclined him to admit of a Truce, or Cessation of Arms, with their Emperor *Solyman*, which he faithfully adher'd to; and could not be brought, either by the Arts and Insinuations of the Pope or the *Venetians*, to break it.

He was naturally inclin'd to a peaceable Life, and was very far from desiring to oppress any of the Princes or States of the Empire, which he thought unworthy of his Dignity. Yet he was forced into a War with *John-Frederick* Duke of *Saxe-Gotha*, on a very singular Occasion. There was one *William de Grombach*, a Man of a noble Family in *Franconia*, who had served in the Troops of *Albert* of *Brandenburgh*, and afterwards became a kind of Soldier of Fortune; and either from Motives of Interest or Ambition, was guilty of a very black Action, in assassinating *Melchior de Zoebel*, Bishop of *Wurtzbourg*.

M 2

His

His Goods were feiz'd, and his Eftate confifcated on this Account, and he obliged to conceal himfelf, fometimes in one Part of *Germany*, and fometimes in another, to avoid further Punifhment. At laft, grown weary of this Vagabond Life, he affembled a Body of Men, in Circumftances as defperate as his own, furpriz'd the City of *Wurtzbourg*, difarm'd the Inhabitants, pillag'd the Churches, ravifh'd the Nuns; and, after all thofe Acts of Violence, forced the Gentry and Clergy to affemble, and declare him innocent of the Bifhop's Murder, and to reftore him to his Eftate both perfonal and real; as alfo to take an Oath to defend him againft all who fhould attempt any thing to his Prejudice, even if it were the Emperor himfelf.

Maximilian looked upon this as an Indignity done to the Empire, and therefore procured a Refolution in the Diet of *Augfbourg*, that all who had any Concern in furprizing *Wurtzbourg*, fhould be delivered up to legal Punifhment; for this Action was done in the Time of his Father *Ferdinand*, and he had put *Grombach* under the Ban of the Empire, who thereupon retired to the Duke of *Saxe-Gotha*, who not contented with giving him Protection, declared him his Privy-Counfellor; upon which the Emperor put the Duke likewife under the Ban of the Empire, and committed the Execution of the Sentence to *Auguftus* Elector of *Saxony*; who, after trying fair Means to no Purpofe, at length befieged *Gotha*, and took it. The Duke being fent Prifoner to the Emperor, was depriv'd of his Dominion, and fentenced to be confin'd for Life; a Judgment fevere in itfelf, but fo juft, that it drew no Imputation upon *Maximilian*, whofe Unwillingnefs to proceed to thefe Extremities was known and acknowledged.

He was far from being a Bigot in Religion, as appears from his granting the free Exercife of their Religion to his Proteftant Subjects in *Auftria*, and by his publickly blaming the *Parifian* Maffacre, tho' committed by the Authority of his Son-in-Law *Charles* IX. of *France*. His Juftice and other Royal Virtues induced many of the *Polifh* Nobility to elect him for their King; but *Stephen Batori* Prince of *Tranfilvania*, having a ftronger Party, fupplanted him, and held that Kingdom, notwithftanding all the Endeavours of the Emperor to recover his Rights. He died in the Year 1576, at *Augfbourg*, where he had affembled a Diet, of a violent Palpitation at the Heart; which, it is fufpected, was occafioned by a Dofe of Poifon given him by the Cardinal *de Granvelle*, whom we have mentioned before, as a Man very capable of fuch an Action.

This Monarch, by the Infanta *Maria*, Daughter to *Charles* V. had a numerous Pofterity: *viz Rodolph*, who fucceeded him; *Erneft*, Governor of the *Low Countries*, born in 1553,

and

and who died in 1595; *Matthias*, who succeeded his Brother *Rodolph* in the Empire; *Maximilian*, Great Master of the *Teutonick* Order, afterwards elected King of *Poland*, who died in 1618; *Albert*, born in 1597, who was first an Ecclesiastick, and obtained a Cardinal's Hat, which afterwards he resign'd; and marrying the Infanta *Clara Isabella Eugenia*, Daughter to *Philip* II. King of *Spain*, was made Governor of the *Low Countries*, and died in 1621, without Issue; *Ann*, born in 1549, and married in 1559 to *Philip* II. King of *Spain*; *Elizabeth*, born in 1554, and married in 1570 to *Charles* IX. King of *France*; *Margaret*, born in 1567, who lived a Nun, and died in 1633, and *Eleonora* born in 1563, and died in 1581.

Rodolph II. was a Prince of an excellent Disposition, very learned himself, and a great Encourager of Learning, to a Degree, in the Opinion of many, prejudicial to his Affairs; because it led him to spend more of his Time amongst his Books, and with his learned Friends, than the Affairs of Government would permit; but in other Respects he was a very wise and worthy Prince, one desirous of living quiet himself, and of maintaining the Peace of the Empire, without attempting upon the Rights of others. He was King of the *Romans* at the Time of his Father's Decease, and so succeeded of Course, without any new Election; and had been crown'd King of *Hungary* in 1572, and of *Bohemia* in 1575, so that his Power was great, and his Dominions very extensive.

He came to the Empire in a very difficult Juncture, because of the Differences about Religion. He forced *Gerhard Trusches*, Archbishop of *Cologne*, who turn'd Protestant, and married *Agnes* Countess of *Mansfield*, to quit his Dominions. By a Truce of fifteen Years he prevented the Consequences of the Quarrel betwixt the Cardinal of *Lorrain*, and *John-George* Marquis of *Brandenburgh*, who were both chosen Bishops of *Strasbourg*; the former by the Popish Canons, and the latter by the Protestants. After the Death of Count *John Manderscheid*, to prevent the War that might have been occasioned by the Succession of *Juliers*, he would have sequester'd that Duchy; but the Pretenders to the Succession opposed it. The Protestants concluded an Association, which they call'd THE UNION, in 1609, of which *Frederick* V. Elector *Palatine*, was Chief. The Papists made a Confederacy for nine Years among themselves at *Wurtzbourg*, which they call'd THE LEAGUE, and thus the *German* were on the Point of arming against each other.

The Imperialists were engaged in a War with the *Turk* from 1549 to 1606, when they took several Towns, and com

mitt

mitted great Ravages. *Rodolph* demanded Affistance of the Princes, and made a League with the Prince of *Tranfilvania*, which had very untoward Confequences. His Army however engaged the *Turks*, who had taken *Agria*, and defeated them; but being too intent upon the Plunder, the *Turks* rallied, and deftroyed many of them. During this War *Philip-Emanuel* of *Lorrain*, Duke of *Mercœur*, General of the Imperial Army, made the famous Retreat of *Canifa*. His Imprerial Majefty granted the free Exercife of their Religion to the Proteftants of *Bohemia*, at the Requeft of the Elector of *Saxony*; but he took away the fame Privilege from his Subjects in *Auftria*, which, as we have obferved, was granted them by his Father; but it was believed this proceeded from Political rather than Religious Motives.

He would have taken Advantage of the Difputes about the Succeffion to the Duchy of *Cleves*, in order to have fecured it to his own Family; and with that View fent his Coufin, the Archduke *Leopold*, to take Poffeffion of it; but the Princes of *Germany*, and the neighbouring Power, concurr'd to defeat this Defign; fo that the Succeffion was preferved to the Families of *Brandenburgh* and *Newburgh*, tho' the Emperor made a Decree in Favour of the Houfe of *Saxony*. But what chiefly difturb'd the Emperor's Repofe, was the Party form'd againft him by his Brother the Archduke *Matthias*; who perfuaded himfelf that the Emperor intended to defeat him of his Succeffion, in Favour of his Coufins the Archdukes *Ferdinand* and *Leopold*, who were Princes exceedingly dear to him.

Being full of this Jealoufy, he form'd fuch a Faction againft *Rodolph*, that in 1608 he found himfelf obliged to yield up *Hungary* and *Auftria* to the Archduke; which was fo far from procuring that Quiet which he defired, that on the contrary it made the Archduke more uneafy and importunate; fo that in 1611, he forced from him the Kingdom of *Bohemia*; and then forming a Party, in order to his being elected King of the *Romans*, this had fuch an Effect upon the neglected and difconfolate Emperor, that he died in *January* 1612, of a broken Heart. He was never married, but had feveral Natural Children. His Inclination to Books, and great Application to Chymiftry, tho' they difturb'd his Affairs, were far enough from exhaufting his Coffers, in which he left a larger Treafure than any of his Predeceffors had poffefs'd, or any of his Succeffors have been fince able to collect, amounting in ready Money and Jewels to feventeen Millions of Florins.

Matthias King of *Hungary* and *Bohemia* fucceeded his Brother, notwithftanding that a ftrong Party was formed againft him.

him. His Reign was a continual Scene of Troubles and Uneasiness, occasioned chiefly by Religious Disputes: for there were now three powerful Factions in the Empire, all covering their private and ambitious Views with the plausible Pretence of Religion. The *Papists* formed what they called a *Catholick League*, at the Head of which was the Elector of *Bavaria*. The *Protestants* of the *Augsbourg* Profession, or *Lutherans*, had for their Head the Elector of *Saxony*; and the *Calvinists*, or as they stiled themselves the *Reformed*, finding there was no Security to be had but by some such League, framed a Confederacy likewise, to which they gave the Title of the *Evangelick Union*, at the Head of which were the Elector *Palatine* and the Landgrave of *Hesse*.

The Emperor now fully experienced all those Difficulties which he had taken Pains to excite in the Days of his Brother, and found it a very unpleasant Task for himself to go through, as being able to shew no Countenance or Favour to any Party without inflaming and exasperating the rest; neither was it long before these Religious Differences, which disturbed and distracted the Empire, begun to spread themselves into his Hereditary Dominions; to which the Haughtiness of his own Spirit, and the Errors of his Government, gave but too much Encouragement, and afforded the Malecontents may just Grounds for Complaint. Instead of being more vigilant and active from these threatning Circumstances, *Matthias* grew more averse to Business, and left it altogether in the Hands of Cardinal *Klesar*, who was his Chief Minister and Favourite.

He disputed the Right of naming the Prince of *Transilvania* with the *Turkish* Emperor *Amurath*; but at last made a Peace with him for twenty Years. He preferred the Archduke *Ferdinand* his Cousin, to *Philip* III. of *Spain*, who was his Nephew, to be his Heir, out of his natural Aversion to the *Spaniards*, a Point which deserves great Notice. He regulated the Succession at *Prague* in 1617, by the Advice of the Archduke *Maximilian* his Brother; and at the same Time a secret Treaty was made betwixt *Philip* III. of *Spain* and the Archduke *Ferdinand*; by which *Philip* quitted to *Ferdinand* and his Heirs Male, the Hereditary Countries that should fall to him by the Emperor's Death, on Condition that the Daughters of the Branch of *Spain* should be preferred to those of the House of *Germany*. At this Time happened the Revolt of *Bohemia*, because the Emperor's Ministers invaded the Laws and Privileges granted them by *Rodolphus* the Second, for securing their Religion and Liberty.

The

The Emperor affembled the States at *Prague*, where his Minifters fo provoked the People, that they threw, them out of the Windows of the Caftle; by which however they received no Hurt. After that they chofe new Magiftrates, took up Arms, and publifhed a Manifefto to juftify their Proceedings. The Emperor publifhed another, and his Council, in order to accommodate Matters, were for turning out his Favourite *Klefar*, who was hated by the *Bohemians*. But the Emperor being againft it, the Archdukes *Maximilian* and *Ferdinand* fent him Prifoner to *Tirol* by their own Authority. The Emperor however went on with the War, but the *Bohemians* being much more diligent, raifed thirty thoufand Men under Count *Mansfield*, and took feveral Towns; upon which the Emperor's Troops entered the Country, and committed fuch Cruelties as moved feveral neighbouring Princes and States to pity the *Bohemians*, and intercede for them in the Name of all the *Proteftants* of the Empire; who alfo laid their Grievances before him, and complained that he gave the Command of his Army to Strangers, fworn Enemies to their Religion, which fhewed there was a Defign rather to deftroy them than to redrefs their Complaints.

They made Application to feveral of the Electors to endeavour to procure an Accommodation. But the Duke of *Bavaria*, who loved to fifh in troubled Waters, prevented it. The Emperor at laft began to grow weary of the War and Fatigue, and refign'd the Kingdom of *Hungary* and *Bohemia* to his Coufin the Archduke *Ferdinand*. Soon after by his Grief for the Lofs of the Archduke *Maximilian* and the Emprefs, he fell into a Diftemper, and died the twentieth of *March* 1619; leaving his Succeffor embroiled in a War of thirty Years Continuance, which almoft exhaufted *Germany*.

The Emperor *Matthias* efpoufed *Ann* of *Auftria*, Daughter to the Archduke *Ferdinand*, by whom he had no Iffue; fo that all the Pains he had beftowed in endeavouring to fecure the Empire to his Pofterity, were vain and to no Purpofe. But he was more fuccefsful in his Endeavours on the Behalf of the Archduke *Ferdinand*, whom he procured to be elected King of *Bohemia*, and afterwards of *Hungary*, and thereby made Way for his fucceeding in the Empire, tho' he was not a little jealous of his Power; and therefore ftipulated that he fhould not meddle with the Affairs of the Empire during his Life; whence it may be juftly affirmed, that as he made it his Bufinefs to trouble his Brother's Reign on the Score of his own Pretenfions, fo he enjoyed as little Peace while he held the Imperial Dignity, the Power of which

he

he laboured greatly to extend, and thereby increased those Troubles with which *Germany* was vex'd in his Time, and which rose still higher after his Decease, as the Reader will see in the Account of the next Reign.

Ferdinand III. mounted the Throne at a very critical Conjuncture, and became Emperor of *Germany* at the very Instant almost, that the *Bohemians* determined that he should no longer be their King. They charged him with the most flagrant Breaches of the Laws, with violating the Privileges of his Subjects, and thereby losing all Title to rule over them; for which Reason they solemnly deposed him, and offered their Crown to the King of *Denmark*, the Duke of *Saxoy*, and the Elector of *Saxony*, who all very wisely refused it; but *Frederick* V. Elector Palatine, being pressed thereto by his Wife, the Daughter of our King *James*, accepted it, in hopes of being assisted by several great Princes.

But engaging unluckily in a decisive Battle with all his Forces, he was totally defeated at *Weisenberg* near *Prague*, on the 18th of *November* 1620. This Defeat not only cost him his new Kingdom, but his Hereditary Dominions, which were given by the Emperor to *Maximilian* Duke of *Bavaria* in 1623. The Protestants, astonished at this Blow, began to form a Confederacy for their own Security; the Princes of the Lower *Saxony* also joining themselves to the King of *Denmark*, ventured to act openly against him; upon which the Emperor's General Count *Tilli* attacked that Prince, and routed his Forces, prosecuting his Victory with such Effect, that the King of *Denmark* was glad to make his Peace upon the best Terms he could obtain in 1629, which were indeed very indifferent.

The Emperor's good Fortune had an Effect but too common amongst Princes, it induced him to flatter himself with the Hopes of erecting an absolute Power in *Germany*; and therefore the very same Year, he published an Edict, that the Protestants should restore all the Ecclesiastical Livings they had seized since the Pacification of *Passaw*. The History of these Troubles, and of this War, is a Point of the greatest Importance towards a thorough Understanding of the History of *Europe* even at this Day; for it changed the whole Face of Affairs, and produced a new System, which it is absolutely requisite the Reader should comprehend, in order to his becoming Master of those Disputes in the Empire, which then engaged the Attention of all *Europe*, and have never failed to engage them as often as they have been renewed from that Time to this, which has been in almost every Reign.

The

The Emperor, who as we before observed, had given the Palatinate to the Duke of *Bavaria*, supposed that he had most effectually secured him and all the Papists to his Interests; and he also thought, that by giving the Marquisate of *Lusatia* to the Elector of *Saxony*, he had secured him likewise, and so had the rest of the Protestants at his Mercy. In all Probability he would scarce have been deceived in his Expectations, if the latter had not called to their Assistance a Prince, of whom he had then but little Jealousy or Apprehension.

They held for this Purpose a general Assembly at *Leipsick*, in which after mature Deliberation on the distressed State of their Affairs, they came at last to a Resolution of applying themselves to the King of *Sweden*, at that Time the brave *Gustavus Adolphus*, who had various Reasons to listen to their Proposals: For in the first Place, the Imperialists had already carried their Arms as far as the *Baltick*, so that they were become formidable to him as Neighbours; next, they had assisted the *Poles* during the Time in which he was engaged in a War against them, and so were his Enemies; and besides these and some other inferior Motives, as a zealous Protestant he could not be a calm Spectator of the Ruin of that Interest in the Empire. Upon these Motives therefore, and the Assurances he had received of Assistance both from the *French* and *Dutch*, who with great Reason were become very jealous of the then exorbitant Power of the House of *Austria*, he determined to enter *Germany* with an Army, which accordingly he did in 1630, tho' that Army was very small.

The Elector of *Saxony* seeing plainly, that his Ruin must be included in that of the Protestants, fell off from the Emperor, and his Forces having joined the *Swedes*, in Conjunction with them attacked and defeated the Imperial General *Tilli*, in the first Battle of *Leipsick*, by the Loss of which the Emperor was at once deprived of the Fruits of all those Victories which he had obtained in the Space of ten Years. After this, the *Swedes* marched towards the *Rhine*, and, as we have shewn in a former Article, had all the Success that could be expected; but the Elector of *Saxony* did not prosecute the War with that Vigour which he ought to have done, and this gave the Imperialists Time to recover themselves, and to gain some Advantages in their turn. *Gustavus* however, leaving all Things safe behind him, marched directly into *Bavaria*, where he attacked Count *Tilli* at the Head of his numerous Army, and after an obstinate Engagement defeated it, chiefly by his own wise Conduct, and the great Intrepidity of the *Swedish* Troops, which were excellent, both Horse and Foot.

In

In this Battle Count *Tilli* was dangerously wounded, and being carried to *Ingolſtadt*, died there four Days afterwards. The Emperor, whoſe Affairs were now in a very dangerous Condition, gave the Command of his Armies to Count *Wallſtein*, the ableſt General in his Service, who marched with a new Army into *Bavaria*, in hopes of ſurpriſing the *Swedes* and their Allies; but *Guſtavus* wiſely entrenched himſelf in a ſtrong Camp, within a League of *Nuremberg*, where he amuſed the Imperialiſts till he was joined by the Duke of *Saxe-Weimar*, and General *Banier*, and then divided his Army into three Corps, marching himſelf towards *Winſheim*. *Wallſtein* thereupon pretended to move towards *Bamberg*, but turned ſhort of a ſudden, and marched back into *Saxony*. *Guſtavus* foreſaw this, and by very haſty Marches came up with them at *Lutzen*, a ſmall Place in *Saxony* between *Leipſick* and *Weiſenfels*. He would not fight that Day, that his Army might have Time to recover their Fatigue: but the next, which was the ſixteenth of *November* 1632, he gave them Battle, and though in the Beginning of the Action he loſt his Life, yet his Troops obtained a ſignal and complete Victory, which did inexpreſſible Honour to their Courage and Diſcipline.

The Proteſtants were ſo much dejected by the Loſs of this Conqueror, that they began to act with leſs Vigour; but the *Swediſh* Generals *Horn* and *Banier* continued to behave with great Spirit and Reſolution, which contributed to reſtore by degrees the Affairs of their Party, as well as an Accident that could ſcarce be foreſeen, which was the Neceſſity the Emperor found himſelf under of cauſing *Wallſtein*, whom he had made Duke of *Fridland*, to be aſſaſſinated, on Account of his having form'd a Deſign to make himſelf Maſter of the Kingdom of *Bohemia*; and as he was an Officer of the greateſt Reputation in his Service, this could not but have a very bad Effect upon his Affairs, eſpecially at ſo critical a Seaſon as that in which it happened.

The Emperor had declared his eldeſt Son *Ferdinand* King of *Hungary* in 1625, two Years after he was crowned King of *Bohemia*; and being a young Prince of great Parts and Expectation, his Father put him at the Head of his Armies, after *Wallſtein* had been taken off in the Manner before mention'd. He recover'd the Towns of *Ratiſbon* and *Donawert*, and afterwards beſieged *Nordlingen*; to the Relief of which the Proteſtant Princes, having join'd their Forces to the *Swedes*, march'd with all the Diligence poſſible, in hopes of reſtoring their Affairs by the Defeat of that young Monarch. Upon their Approach he intrench'd his Army, raiſed ſeveral Batteries of Cannon,

non, and made the beft Difpofitions poffible for giving them a vigorous Reception.

The Confederates however attack'd him; but, after a long and obftinate Engagement, they were totally defeated; the Imperialifts quitting their Lines as foon as the Enemy began to break, and improving their Advantage to the utmoft, cut off the greateft Part of the Confederate Army, and took Marfhal *Horn* Prifoner. This decifive and important Action happen'd *November* 16, 1634, and was by far the greateft Defeat the *Swedes* had received from the Time of their entering *Germany*. The Effects of it were fuch as might well have been expected; for feveral of the Proteftant Princes fell off from the League, particularly the Elector of *Saxony*, and concluded a feparate Peace with the Emperor at *Prague* in the Year 1635; the principal Articles of which were, That the Reftitution of the Eftates of Ecclefiafticks fhould be fufpended for forty Years; that *Magdebourg* fhould be reftored to Duke *Auguftus* of *Saxony*, and *Halberfted* to the Archduke *Leopold*; fo that now the Emperor though he had the Proteftants once more at his Mercy, and behaved accordingly.

The greateft Princes and the ableft Politicians are fometimes miftaken in their Views, which was the Cafe of the Emperor *Ferdinand* III. in relation to this great Victory gain'd by his Son at *Nordlingen*. He treated the *Swedes*, and thofe that ftill remain'd firm to their Alliance, as abfolutely within his Power, and to whom he might prefcribe what Terms he pleafed; whereas, if upon fuch reafonable Terms as they would glady have accepted he had made Peace at that Time, he might certainly have kept the Conditions of it only as far and as long as he pleafed. War is a hazardous and dangerous Thing, and, till it is abfolutely over, there is no knowing who has the better. The *Swedes* had at that Time a Statefman, whofe Abilities faved them and their *German* Confederates: This was Count *Oxenfteirn*, who undertook to draw the *French* into the Difpute, and, which was more extraordinary, render them firm and faithful in ne Profecution of it; in which he fucceeded fo well, that the Emperor finding himfelf at laft quite tired out, and his Subjects in a manner abfolutely exhaufted, refolved to confent to a Peace upon the beft Conditions that the Circumftances of the Times, and a Train of unexpected Events, would allow.

The *Swedes*, on the other hand, were alfo much difpofed to a Negotiation, becaufe their own Armies being entirely worn out, they had now only *German* Troops under *Swedish* Officers to fight their Battles, and they knew not how foon thefe People might grow weary of ruining their native Country,

try, and fighting for them againſt their Countrymen. The Troubles that about this Time broke out in *France*, made that Crown likewiſe very inclinable to Peace; which being the ſole End and Aim, from the Beginning of the War, that the Proteſtant Princes in *Germany* propoſed to themſelves, they omitted nothing on their Sides that was neceſſary to bring it to a ſpeedy Concluſion. It was this Diſpoſition in all the Parties that brought about, in 1648, the famous *Treaty of Weſtphalia*; by which a reaſonable Satisfaction was given to all that had been concern'd in the War, and conſequently a Foundation was thereby laid for a ſolid, laſting, and honourable Peace.

As the Intention of this hiſtorical Deduction is to give the Reader, from the Conſideration of paſt Events, a perfect Inſight into the preſent State of Things, it is abſolutely neceſſary that we ſhould inſiſt more particularly upon this Treaty, than upon any thing of the ſame Nature that has gone before; becauſe it entirely changed the Face of Affairs not only in *Germany*, but throughout all *Europe*. When we ſpeak of it generally, and in its full Extent, it is called the *Peace* of *Weſtphalia*, tho' ſtrictly ſpeaking, there be really no ſuch Treaty exiſting; and therefore, to underſtand this perfectly, the Reader is to obſerve, that the Diſputes with *Sweden* were firſt regulated by a Treaty concluded at *Oſnabrug* the 16th of *Auguſt*, 1648, by which that Crown acquired certain Provinces in the Empire, a Seat in the Imperial Diet, and a conſiderable Sum in ready Money: Satisfaction being likewiſe given to the Elector of *Brandenburgh* for his Pretenſions, as has been already ſhewn in the Articles of *Sweden* and *Pruſſia*: And at the Time this Treaty was concluded, there was a Proviſo inſerted, That it ſhould be of no Force till another Treaty, then negotiating, was likewiſe ſign'd and concluded.

This other Treaty was carried on at *Munſter* between the Empire and *France*; which was alſo brought to Perfection, and ſign'd the 25th of *October* the ſame Year. By this laſt Treaty a great Variety of Intereſts were ſettled. The Emperor reſtored to the Elector of *Treves* all that had been taken from him. The Electoral Dignity was confirm'd to the Duke of *Bavaria*, and he had alſo the *Upper Palatinate* given him; but the *Lower Palatinate* was reſtored to the Elector *Palatine*; who, as we have before ſhewn, had been deprived by the Emperor, and a new Electorate was created in his Favour. The three Biſhopricks, and beſt Part of *Alſace*, were yielded to *France*; and, on the other hand, that Crown reſtored a great Part of her Conqueſts.

But

But the moſt material Points, of all that were regulated by theſe two Treaties, were the Civil and Religious Rights of the States that compoſe the Empire. The latter we ſhall have Occaſion to mention more at large hereafter; but with reſpect to the former, the ſhorteſt Method that can be taken is to tranſcribe the eighth Article of the Treaty of *Oſnabrug*, which runs thus.

" For preventing any Diſputes that may ariſe for the future
" in the Political State, all and every of the Electors, Princes,
" and States of the *Roman* Empire, ought to be ſo confirm'd
" by Virtue of this Treaty, in their ancient Rights, Prero-
" gatives, Freedom, and Privileges, in the free Exerciſe of
" their Territorial Rights, in Matters Eccleſiaſtical and Politi-
" cal in their Dominions, in their Rights of Regale, and in
" the Poſſeſſion of all theſe Things together, that no Perſon
" may have it in his Power or Choice to give them actual
" Moleſtation, on any Pretence whatſoever. They ſhall,
" without any Contradiction, enjoy the Right of Suffrage in
" all Deliberations concerning the Right of the Empire, par-
" ticularly when Laws are to be made or interpreted, War
" to be declared, Contributions to be impoſed, Levies of
" Troops to be made, and their Quarters regulated; new For-
" treſſes to be erected in the Name of the Publick in the
" Territories of the States, or Garriſons to be placed in the
" old ones; as alſo, when any Treaties of Peace or Alliances
" are to be concluded, or any other Affairs of this Nature to
" be treated; none of theſe, or others of the like Kind,
" ſhall be undertaken or permitted without the Suffrage and
" free Conſent of all the States of the Empire aſſembled in
" the Diet. They ſhall have, above all Things, the perpetual
" Right of making Alliances between themſelves and Foreign-
" ers, for their own Preſervation and Security; provided ne-
" vertheleſs, that ſuch Alliances are not directed againſt the
" Emperor and Empire, againſt the publick Peace, or againſt
" the preſent Tranſaction in particular; and that they do not,
" in any wiſe, infringe the Oath which they have all taken to
" the Emperor and Empire."

It is to be obſerved, that the Cities of *Oſnabrug* and *Munſter* are both in *Weſtphalia*, and the two Treaties being united by the Proviſo before mention'd, are from thence ſtiled the *Peace* of *Weſtphalia*; but when they are quoted more particularly, the Articles are mention'd from the reſpective Treaties. Hence it is ſaid, that the Peace of *Weſtphalia* is a fundamental Law of the Empire, and with great Propriety; for it may be truly ſtiled the *Magna Charta* of *Germany*: and therefore we need not wonder that the *French*, who were principally concerned in making this Treaty, had afterwards the Vanity

to

to strike a Medal upon this Subject; in which the Genius of *France* is reprefented standing by an Altar, on which is a *Caduceus* supported by two Horns of *Plenty*; In one Hand, which leans upon the Altar, fhe holds an *Olive Branch*; and in the other a *Ballance*, having in one Scale the Imperial Crown, and in the other the Crowns of the Electors and Princes of the Empire, fo that they hang exactly even. Under her Feet is a *Yoke*. The *Legend* is LIBERTAS GERMANIÆ, and the *Exergue* contains thefe Words, PAX MONASTERIENSIS; MDCXLVIII. implying, that Liberty was reftored to *Germany* by the Peace of *Munfter*.

It may not be amifs to remark, that the Liberty of *Germany* and the Slavery of *France* were the Work of the fame Hand, or rather of the fame Head; I mean that of the famous Cardinal *Richlieu*, who contrived this Scheme to keep the Houfe of *Auftria* within Bounds, and to hinder her from ever becoming too powerful for that of *Bourbon*. The Reader will likewife fee, for this very Purpofe *France* took fo much Pains to aggrandize the Crown of *Sweden*; and this will lead us to underftand the true Motives which induce the *French* to be fo complaifant at prefent to the King of *Pruffia*; the Power of that Prince, in refpect to the Empire, or rather in refpect to the Houfe of *Auftria*, ftanding her in the fame Stead as *Sweden* did formerly, when fhe was more powerful than fhe is at prefent. This Obfervation, which is very fhort, and from the Hiftory we have given of this War and this Peace, very clear and convincing, is the true Key to the modern Syftem, and very fully explains the prefent Situation of Things in *Germany*, and that Connection between two great Powers, which has been hitherto held equally unnatural and furprizing, but which will now appear in quite another light.

The Emperor having thus reftored the Peace of *Europe*, as well as of the Empire, applied his whole Care to the fettling the Tranquility and Welfare of his Dominions, and the Authority of his Family. The former gain'd him the Affection of his Subjects, and he had all the Succefs he could wifh for in the latter. He procured his Son *Ferdinand*, already King of *Hungary* and *Bohemia*, to be elected King of the *Romans* at *Augf-bourg* in 1653. But when he thought his Felicity effectually fecured, he found it leaft fo; for on the 4th of *July*, in the Year following, that young Prince died, which ftruck the Emperor with a deep Melancholy, from which he never afterwards recovered.

He acted however as to publick Affairs with much Dignity and Spirit; thus he gave powerful Affiftance to the *Poles* againft

the

the *Swedes*, who would otherwise have over-run their Country; and it was by this Means also, that the *Danes* were engaged to take the same Step, and to break with the *Swedes*; but he did not live to see the Issue of this War, dying of a Consumption, occasioned, as has been said, by his Concern for the Loss of his eldest Son, on the 2d of *April*, 1657. He was in every Respect a very wise and great Man, in most Things a very fortunate Prince, and if his Ambition had been less, his Authority had been greater; but the too great Warmth he discovered in Matters of Religion, and the Desire he had to extend the Imperial Power beyond the Bounds prescribed to his Predecessors, induced the Protestant Princes of the Empire to take such Measures for their Security, as in the End, notwithstanding all his Victories, proved in that Respect very effectual.

Leopold I, the younger Son of the Emperor *Ferdinand* III. did not immediately succeed his Father, because he was under Age; he was originally intended for the Church, but upon the Death of his Brother *Ferdinand*, he was crown'd King of *Hungary* on the 25th of *June* 1655, and King of *Bohemia* on the 14th of *September* the same Year. On the 18th of *July* 1658, he was elected Emperor, and on the 5th of *August* following, was crown'd at *Franckfort*. In the beginning of his Reign, the War, which lasted so long betwixt the *Swedes*, the *Danes*, the *Poles* and the *Brandenburghers*, was concluded by the Treaty of *Oliva* in 1660, under various Guaranties.

A War broke out soon after betwixt the Emperor and the *Hungarians*, who complained that their Privileges were invaded; that the *German* Troops maintained there on Pretence of defending them, which they were able and willing to do themselves, committed all Sorts of Violence and Cruelty; that the *Hungarians* in Possession of Offices were not suffered to discharge them; that the Liberty of Religion, which had been allowed them by several Diets, was denied, their Churches taken from them, and their Ministers banished, because they were not of the Religion of their Prince. That the Nobility, who ought to be try'd by their own Judges, were brought to answer before *Germans*; that tho' the Revenue was more than sufficient to maintain the Troops, yet they were not paid, but lived by Extortion, or invading the *Turks*, who made severe Reprisals on the peaceable Inhabitants of the Country.

The Grand Seignior improved this Difference, and the Emperor taking Part with the Prince of *Transilvania*, set up without his Consent, he therefore gave that Title to Prince *Abaffi*. The *Turks* defeated the Imperialists at *Clausenbourg*,

and

and took *Newhensel* in 1663, but were routed at *Levents*, where they lost 6000 Men; and afterwards at St. *Gothard*, where they lost above the same Number, and many General Officers, which brought on a Peace. The *Hungarians* finding that their Privileges were not restored according to the Emperor's Promise, being oppress'd by *German* Troops, and the Office of *Palatine* being abolished, which had continued many hundred Years; they joined with the *Transilvanians* to obtain Help from the *Turks*. The very Monks preached that their Yoke was easier than that of the *Germans*; for this Insurrection the Counts of *Serini*, *Frangipani*, and *Nadasti* were put to death, which hinder'd Prince *Ragotski*'s taking Arms; and Count *Tekely* dying in his Castle, just as the Imperialists had invested it, they were left without a Head, till young Count *Tekely*, who was then but fifteen Years of Age, and from his Prison escaped to *Transilvania*, came to espouse their Cause; for a bare Suspicion of being well-affected to which, he had been treated with much Severity.

He was received by this exhausted Nation with the utmost Joy, and the Revolt of the *Hungarians* became almost general; but however, the *German* Forces in that Kingdom soon reduced them to the Necessity of repining in secret against the Emperor's Measures, instead of openly taking up Arms, as they certainly intended.

His Imperial Majesty's Thoughts, which were entirely turned towards the Settlement of his own Dominions, without the least Inclination to incroach on, or disturb his Neighbours, were called off by the ambitious Views of a Monarch who spent his whole Life in disturbing the Peace of *Europe*; for in 1672 the *French* invaded *Lower Germany*, and over-run most of the *United Provinces*. The Elector of *Treves* having no Force to oppose to these Troops, was obliged to allow them a Passage through his Dominions. And the Archbishop of *Cologne*, and the Bishop of *Munster*, joined with them in this Expedition against their Country. The Elector of *Brandenburgh* demanded Assistance of the Emperor to protect his Duchy of *Cleves*, but the *French* over-run it before he could procure any.

The *French* in 1673 entered *Alsace*, where they took several Towns, and laid part of the Palatinate under Contributions. The Duke of *Lorrain*, who commanded the Emperor's Army, would have joined *Caprara*, but was prevented by M. *Turenne*, which occasion'd the ineffectual Battle of *Sintsheim*. The Elector *Palatine* was so much provoked at the ravaging his Country, that he sent M. *Turenne* a Challenge, which he would not accept, without Allowance from the *French* King, his Master. These Things, with the taking

of

of *Treves*, obliged the Empire to declare War, and assemble more Troops ; upon which M. *Turenne* repassed the *Rhine* and entrenched near *Philipsbourg*.

In 1674 the *Germans* fought the *French* Army commanded by Marshal *Turenne* near *Moltsheim*, where both Sides claimed the Victory. In 1675 the *French* defeated the *Germans* near *Colmar* ; but *Montecuculi* succeeding the Duke of *Bournonville* in the Command of the *German* Army, he was a more equal Match for *Turenne*, who being encamped near him, and going to an Eminence to reconnoitre his Army, was kill'd by a Cannon Ball, which put an End to his Glory, that was tarnished before by his turning Papist. After the Battle of *Altenheim*, the *French* repassed the *Rhine*, where the Duke *de Duras*, Nephew to *Turenne*, acquired much Reputation by retiring with but little Loss in Sight of the Enemy from a very disadvantageous Camp.

In 1679, the War between the Empire, the *French* and the *Dutch*, was concluded by the Treaty of *Nimeguen*, where the King of *Sweden* was Mediator, by which *France* got *Fribourg* and the *Burgau* in lieu of *Philipsbourg*, and the *Swedes* recovered the Provinces they had lost in the War. After the Peace of *Nimeguen*, the *French* King began to erect Chambers of Reunion at *Metz* and *Brisac*, where by Sentences of his own Judges, several Princes were required to surrender those Provinces and Cities that were adjudged to be dependant on his new Acquisitions ; and such as would not comply were compell'd by Force, particularly the Elector Palatine, and the Elector of *Treves*.

The *French* also still kept Possession of those Places, they had stipulated to surrender to the Empire by the Peace. The Emperor's Ministers gave in a Memorial to the *Diet* at *Ratisbon* of these Proceedings, and the States assembled there unanimously resolved that they were directly contrary to Treaties ; but *Holland* and *Brandenburgh* were not inclined to a new Rupture with *France*. In 1680 the *French* surprized *Strasbourg*, by the Treachery of some of their new Magistrates. The King of *France* likewise endeavoured to get the Dauphin elected King of the *Romans*, but miscarried in it. In 1681 he made a Treaty with Count *Tekely*, who had a strong Party of Malecontents in *Hungary*, was in high Esteem with the Grand Seignior, and engaged the *Turks* to invade *Hungary* before the Emperor was aware of it.

In 1683 the Duke of *Lorrain* besieged *Newheusel*, but was obliged to break up from thence on the Grand Vizier's marching towards him. At the same Time three thousand *Tartars* harassed the Country, and the *Germans* with great Difficulty

retired

retired towards *Vienna*; for three thousand *Turks* and *Tartars* fell upon their Baggage, took it, and killed most of the Convoy; but at length Prince *Lewis* of *Baden* rescued some part of the Baggage. The News of this occasioned an incredible Consternation at *Vienna*. The Emperor removed to *Lintz*, and most of the Citizens were for leaving the City; but the Approach of the Duke of *Lorrain* next Day encouraged them; so that they began to repair the Fortifications, and the Garrison was reinforced, there not being above two hundred regular Forces in the City at this Time.

The *Turks* opened their Trenches the fifteenth of *July*; the Garrison under Count *Stharemberg* disputed every Inch of Ground, and by frequent Sallies cut off great Numbers. In the mean time, the Duke of *Lorrain* defeated *Tekely*, took his Baggage, and relieved *Presburg*, that was ready to have fallen into his Hands. The Duke engaged him a second Time on the Borders of *Moravia*, and forced him to retire. The Siege of *Vienna* continued to the twelfth of *September* with all the Fury imaginable; and the Besieged behaved themselves with the utmost Intrepidity, till they were relieved by the Confederate Army of eighty thousand Men, consisting of *Imperialists* and *Poles*, and as fine Troops as any in *Europe*.

The Right Wing was commanded by *John Sobieski*, King of *Poland*, the Left by the Elector of *Bavaria* and the Duke of *Lorrain*, and the main Body by the Elector of *Saxony* and Prince *Waldeck*. They forced the Enemy's Entrenchments, and during the Engagement the Duke of *Lorrain* detached Prince *Lewis* of *Baden*, with a Body of Horse, Foot and Dragoons, to relieve the City; which he did, and killed most of the *Turks* that were employed in the Assault. Upon this the *Turkish* Horse fled, and left their Foot and Camp to the Mercy of the *Christians*, who gained a signal Victory, with the Loss of about one thousand Men. The *Turks* lost about seventy-five thousand, with their Baggage, and one hundred and twenty Cannon; and the Garrison about six thousand Men during the Siege, which lasted fifty-nine Days open Trenches.

After the taking of *Buda*, Prince *Abaffi* began to temporize with the Emperor. But the Duke of *Lorrain* entered *Transilvania*, as Count *Tekely* had foretold him, and obliged that Prince and the States to a Submission; forcing them to surrender their Fortresses, and conclude a Treaty very advantageous to the Emperor; upon which the Prince retired to *Forgats*. About this Time the strong Fortress of *Agria* surrendered to the *Imperialists*, and *Mohammed* IV. Emperor of the *Turks*,

was

was depofed, and his Brother fet up in his Stead. The Emperor's good Succefs put him upon getting his Son, the Archduke *Jofeph*, crown'd King of *Hungary*.

He went himfelf to *Prefburg* upon this Occafion, where he affembled the States, and told them, He would have the Crown made hereditary. The States took it into Confideration ; reprefented their Grievances as ufual, and faid they were willing to elect the Archduke ; but defired their Freedom of Election might be continued, and that the Crown fhould not become hereditary : That the *German* Troops might be recalled when Peace was made with the *Turks*, and all their Grievances redreffed before the Coronation. The Emperor allowed them fourteen Days to deliberate and draw up their Grievances ; but told them he had been at more Charge to defend their Kingdom againft the *Turks* than it was worth, and therefore had a Right to look upon it as one of his hereditary Countries. A ftrange Inftance of boundlefs Ambition founded in falfe Politicks !

There were great Debates about this in the Diet ; and Count *Drafcowitz*, the chief Judge of the Kingdom, having reprefented the Confequences of it, they moft humbly prayed the Emperor not to make fuch an Alteration in their Conftitution. But the Count being found dead in his Bed fome Days after, no body knew how, thofe of his Sentiments durft not mention it any more. Some defired they might be at Liberty to chufe any fuch Prince of the Houfe of *Auftria* as they fhould think fit ; but this was alfo rejected with Difdain.

There were two other Points which for fome time retarded the Coronation ; the firft was, that according to an Article of King *Andrew*'s Declaration, any of the three Eftates had a Right to oppofe the King when he acted againft the Laws of the Kingdom, without being guilty of Treafon : But the Emperor would not allow of that. The fecond was, that the Proteftants, who had joined with the Court to get the Crown made hereditary, thought it a proper Seafon to demand that they fhould be maintained in their ancient Privileges : That the Churches and States which had been taken from them fince 1667 fhould be reftored : That they fhould have Deputies in every Diet : That the Jefuits fhould not meddle in Affairs of State, or what related to the Proteftant Religion : That they fhould not be allowed to fettle in any other Place than where they then were : And that Count *Caraffa*, who had got many innocent People cut off upon Pretence of Plots, fhould be turned out of his Places and the Miniftry.

But the States did not think it a feafonable Time for the Proteftants to infift on thefe Things. And thus, on the twenty-ninth of *December*, the Kingdom was declared heredi-tary, and the Power of the Prince became in a manner abſolute, ſo that the People could do nothing but ſigh for the Loſs of their Liberty : For Count *Tekely*, who had formerly acquired ſo much Glory, had failed of late in moſt of his Attempts, and was not able to keep up their Spirits, or afford them any pro-bable Hopes of Relief.

The War againſt the *Turks* was ſtill proſecuted with various Succeſs for ſeveral Years, notwithſtanding that the *French* in 1689 fell into *Germany* with a great Army, and committed ſuch Outrages as were inconſiſtent with the Laws of War. This Conduct of theirs ſo totally deſtroyed the Intereſt they had among the *German* Princes, that in 1690 the Emperor procured his Son the Archduke *Joſeph*, who was already King of *Hungary*, to be elected King of the *Romans* ; and the Year following, the *Turks* were defeated by the *Imperialiſts* in the Battle of *Salankeman*, in which they loſt their Grand Vi-zier *Cuperli*, and twenty thouſand Men. The War continued notwithſtanding, chiefly from the Encouragement given to the Infidels by the *French*, and the vaſt Efforts they made in their Favour. The *Turks* likewiſe did all that lay in their Power to ballance the former Succeſſes of the *Imperialiſts* ; but in 1697, Prince *Eugene* defeated one of the moſt powerful Armies the Infidels ever brought into the Field, at *Zanta*, in which deci-ſive Action no leſs than 25,000 *Turks* periſhed.

The *French* perceiving that this Blow had put it out of the Power of their good Allies to do any thing more for their Ser-vice, reſolved to get out of the War in Time, and make the beſt Peace for themſelves they could ; which they accordingly did at *Ryſwick*, whereby they quitted all their Re-unions in *Alſace* : But the Popiſh Religion was to remain where they had ſettled it. The Elector Palatine was reſtored to his Territories, on paying 200,000 Livres *per Annum* to the Ducheſs of *Orleans*, till her Pretenſions were decided. *Dinant* was reſtored to the Biſhop of *Liege* ; *Straſbourg* reſigned to *France* ; and *Fort-Kiel*, *Fribourg*, *Star-fort*, *Old Briſac*, and *Philipſbourg* reſtored to the Empire.

The *French* were to demoliſh the Fortifications over-againſt *Hunningen* and *Fort-Lewis* ; the Caſtles of *Traerbach*, *Ebren-burg*, *Kirnburg*, and the Fortreſs of *Mont-Royal*, were to be demoliſhed and given to their right Owners. The Duke of *Lorrain* was reſtored to his own Country, and to *Nancy* ; and the Caſtles of *Bitſch* and *Homburg* were to be razed. The Proteſtant Princes of the Empire gave in a Memorial againſt eſtabliſhing Popery in *Alſatia*, becauſe contrary to the

fundamental

fundamental Laws of the Empire, *i. e.* to the Peace of Religion made in 1588, to that of *Westphalia* and to that of *Nimeguen*, which were the Basis of this Treaty : And that this Article was likewise contrary to the Capitulations of the Emperor and the King of the *Romans*, by which the said Peace of Religion was secured ; but this Remonstrance was without Effect.

The *Turks*, finding themselves abandoned in this manner by those who drew them into the War, and who had more than once hinder'd them from making Peace upon reasonable Terms, resolved to accept the Mediation of the Maritime Powers, and to conclude a Peace with the Emperor and his Allies on the best Terms that, in their present Circumstances, could be had. Accordingly, after great Pains taken by Lord *Paget* and Mr. *Collier*, who conducted this Negotiation, on *January* 26, 1699, a Truce was sign'd for 25 Years between the Emperor and the *Turks* at *Carlowitz*. The chief Articles of which were, That *Transilvania* should remain intire to the Emperor, but the Province of *Temiswaer* to the *Turks* : That the Emperor should demolish *Carensebeis*, *Lippa*, *Zenwock*, *Berske*, and *Sabla*, and never re-fortify them. The Islands of the Rivers *Save* and *Morosch* were to belong to the Emperor, but the Use of those Rivers to both : All Prisoners taken during the War to be exchanged, or ransomed : No Protection on either Side to be given to Rebels and Malecontents : The Papists in the *Turkish* Territories were to have the free Exercise of their Religion. The *Czar*, the King of *Poland*, and the Republick of *Venice*, were comprehended in this Treaty ; but Count *Tekely* was excluded. The Grand Seignior made him, by way of Compensation, Prince of *Weddon*, *Carensebeis*, and *Lugos*, with their Dependencies, that he might still retain him in his Interests.

At the Time the great general War broke out on the Score of the *Spanish* Succession, the Affairs of the Emperor *Leopold* were but in a very indifferent Condition. He saw plainly, that without the Assistance of the Empire it was impossible for him to act effectually against *France* ; and he saw at the same time, that it would be very difficult to engage the Princes and States of *Germany* in a War, with which they had no farther Concern, than as *Philip* V. King of *Spain* had taken Possession of the Duchy of *Milan*, which was a Fief belonging to the Empire ; and the Dukes of *Savoy* and *Mantua* declaring against the Emperor, whose Vassals they were. Yet so great an Interest his Imperial Majesty had, that by degrees he engaged all the Circles to enter into the Alliance he had form'd with the Maritime Powers, which was brought to bear in the

Year

Year 1701, when it was agreed that the Empire should raise an Army of 120,000 Men; which, however, were never assembled but upon Paper.

The Elector of *Bavaria* sided with *France*; as did also his Brother the Elector of *Cologne*: The former arm'd in his own Dominions, and the latter admitted *French* Troops into his Towns. The Duke of *Wolfembuttle* also raised Troops for the Service of *France*; but before they were in a Condition to act, the Elector of *Hanover*, our late Sovereign, surrounded his Forces, and obliged them to enter into the Imperial Service; which was a Point of very great Importance at that Time, and so acknowledged to be by the Emperor.

In 1702, the Elector of *Bavaria* seized the City of *Ulm*. The Army of the Empire, under Prince *Lewis* of *Baden*, was beat at *Fridlinghen*; and *France* took Possession of the Duchy of *Lorrain*, and the greatest Part of the Electorate of *Treves*. In 1703, the Elector of *Bavaria* defeated another Imperial General, made himself Master of the City of *Ratisbon*, and seized there all the Ministers assembled at the Diet of the Empire. He afterwards made an Irruption into *Tirol*, out of which he was driven by the Inhabitants: But upon his Return into *Germany*, being join'd by M. *Villars* with a Body of *French* Forces, he defeated the Imperialists at the first Battle of *Hochsted*, and soon after made himself Master of *Augsburg*. This Year also Prince *Ragotski* raised an Insurrection in *Hungary*; and by these several Misfortunes the Emperor was driven to the last Degree of Distress; the *Bavarians* being on the Frontiers of his Dominions on one Side, and the Malecontent *Hungarians* making Inroads to the very Gates of *Vienna* on the other. In the midst however of all these Difficulties, his Imperial Majesty declared, in the Month of *September*, the Archduke *Charles* King of *Spain*, by the Name of *Charles* III. who in that Quality, was acknowledged, received, and supported by the Allies, the Court of *Vienna* having nothing to give but the Title.

In 1704, the Duke of *Marlborough* form'd the glorious Resolution of delivering the Emperor and Empire at once; with which View he advanced with the Army of the Allies into *Suabia*, and on the 2d of *July* forced the Lines at *Schellenberg*, which open'd his Army a Passage into *Bavaria*. On the 13th of *August* following he defeated the *Bavarians* and *French*, in the second Battle of *Hochsted*, or *Blenheim*; in which, with the Loss of about 5000 Men, he kill'd 12000 of the Enemy, took as many Prisoners, together with all their Artillery and Baggage; after which he drove the *French* intirely out of *Germany*, and return'd with his victorious Army into the *Low*

Countries,

Countries. The Emperor was no lefs fuccefsful againſt the *Hungarian* Malecontents; fo that, as this was the laſt, it might be accounted the moſt glorious Year of his Life. He died at *Vienna* on the 5th of *May* following, in the 64th Year of his Age, and 46th of his Reign. He was thrice married; firſt to *Margareta Thereſa,* Daughter to *Philip* IV. King of *Spain*; fecondly to *Claudia,* Daughter to the Archduke *Ferdinand* his Coufin; and thirdly to *Eleanora,* Daughter to the Elector *Palatine,* by whom he left two Sons and three Daughters.

The Emperor *Joſeph* who fucceeded his Father, was in the Flower of his Age; being at that Time about Twenty-five, and a Prince of as great Hopes as any in *Europe.* It was believed, that at the very Beginning of his Reign an End might have been put to the War, by the Recovery of *Lorrain,* and entering that way into *France*; and it was likewife propofed to bring about an Accommodation with the *Hungarians.* The former was defeated by Prince *Lewis* of *Baden*'s failing the Duke of *Marlborough,* whom he ought to have join'd; and the latter came to nothing through the Obſtinacy of the Malecontents, who tho' they might be beaten, could never be humbled.

In the Beginning of the Year 1706, there happened a kind of general Infurrection among the Peafants in *Bavaria,* out of meer Loyalty to their Sovereign, at that Time an Exile in *France*; but it was fuppreffed, tho' not without vaſt Effufion of Blood; fome thoufands being kill'd in the Field, and many afterwards hanged, in order to terrify the reſt. This only ferved to fharpen the Emperor's Refentment; who, on the firſt of *May,* proceeded to put the Electors of *Bavaria* and *Cologne* under the Ban of the Empire. The *French* not only relieved *Fort Lewis,* but alfo recover'd *Drufenheim* and *Haguenau,* which they had loft the Year before; and in the laſt-mention'd Place they became Maſters of a fine Train of Artillery, which drew a Sufpicion upon Prince *Lewis* of *Baden,* as if he had left it there for them; but his Highneſs dying foon afterwards, and the military Affairs of the Empire going then rather worfe than before, convinced the World that he had been afperfed, and the Loffes under his Command owing to Misfortune, and not any Fault in him.

In 1707, the *French,* under the Command of Marſhal *Villars,* forced the Imperialiſts in their Lines, and over-ran all *Suabia* and *Wirtemberg,* raiſing moſt dreadful Contributions, for which that General was ever famous: And it is very highly probable he would have puſh'd ſtill farther into the Empire, if

he

he had not been prevented by the Siege of *Toulon*; so that none of the Allies reap'd so great Profit from that Expedition as the Emperor, who was most against it. The Negotiations with the *Hungarians* went on, but to no Purpose; tho' the Maritime Powers offered their Mediation, and laboured all they could to have brought about a Peace on equitable Terms.

In the Beginning of 1708, there happened a Dispute between his Imperial Majesty and the Pope, in which the latter was reduced to submit to such Terms as were prescrib'd him, and amongst others obliged to acknowledge the Archduke *Charles* in Quality of King of *Spain*, and consequently of *Naples*, much against his Inclination. In *Flanders* the *French* were beat at *Oudenard*, and lost *Lisle*; but the Army of the Empire was able to do nothing.

In 1710, the Emperor proposed sending to that Army 11000 of his own Troops, and to contribute a large Sum of Money towards the Expences of the Campaign; yet these Promises were so indifferently comply'd with, that the Elector of *Hanover*, who was to have commanded the Army of the Empire, thought fit to return into his own Dominions. In *Hungary* however, the Malecontents were so effectually beaten, that their Chiefs thought fit to retire; and in all Probability an End had been put to the Troubles in that Kingdom, if the Emperor had not died of a very short Illness on the 17th of *April* 1711, in the 33d Year of his Age, and at the Close of the sixth Year of his Reign; leaving by his Empress, who was a Princess of the House of *Hanover*, no Male Issue, which produced those Events which have exercised the Politicks of *Europe* ever since.

Charles VI. the late Emperor's only Brother, and the sole Heir Male of the House of *Austria*, was elected his Successor in the Month of *August* the same Year, and was crowned in *December* following. By his Return out of *Catalonia*, he lost all Hopes of recovering the Kingdom of *Spain*; and the Peace of *Utrecht*, in the following Year, put it out of his Power to carry on the War in the *Low Countries*. On the 22d of *May* 1712, he was crown'd King of *Hungary* at *Presbourg*, and began to employ all his Thoughts on settling the Succession in the House of *Austria*, in case he should die without Issue; and in finding out Ways and Means for carrying on the War with *France*.

In respect to the former, he declared the eldest of his Nieces his sole Heiress; and in regard to the latter, he marched a great Body of Forces into the *Low Countries*; but was soon after forced to employ all his Troops in securing the Frontiers of the Empire, which were again attack'd by the

French;

French; who, before the Close of the Year 1713, reduced the strong Fortress of *Fribourg*; which, with other Misfortunes, forced him to make a Peace with *France*, that was sign'd at *Radstadt* on the 6th of *March* 1714, chiefly on the Plan of the Treaty of *Westphalia*.

In the following Year he declared War against the *Turks*, in Favour of the *Venetians*. Prince *Eugene* commanded the Imperial Armies, as he had done against the *French* and *Spaniards*; and on the 5th of *July* 1716, totally defeated the Infidels at *Peterwaradin*, where the Grand Vizier and ten Bashaws were kill'd upon the Spot; their intire Train of 170 Pieces of Cannon, their military Chest, and all their Baggage falling into the Hands of the Imperialists. The important City of *Temeswaer* surrender'd on the 13th of *October*, which added a very considerable Country to the Emperor's Dominions, in Quality of King of *Hungary*.

The next Year Prince *Eugene*, at the Head of the Imperial Army, invested *Belgrade*; to the Relief of which the *Turks* march'd as great an Army as it was in their Power, under the Command of the new Grand Vizier; which Army, however, was defeated on the 15th of *August* 1717, after an obstinate Engagement of five Hours. In this Action the *Turks* lost 131 Pieces of Brass Cannon, 37 Mortars, 52 Colours, and nine Horse-Tails. On the 17th of the same Month *Belgrade* capitulated; and soon after the *Turks* consented to a Peace, or rather to a Truce, for twenty-five Years, which was concluded at *Passarowitz* under the Mediation of the Maritime Powers.

While this War lasted, King *Philip* V. of *Spain* had attack'd the Island of *Sardinia*, which had been left to the Emperor by the late Treaty of Peace; and was very near making the Conquest of the Island of *Sicily*, which had been yielded to the Duke of *Savoy*, with the Title of King. But the great Powers of *Europe*, perceiving that these Disputes would bring on a new general War, resolved to cut them short; and to this End the Quadruple Alliance was concluded between the Emperor, *France*, *Great Britain* and *Holland*. By which both *Sardinia* and *Sicily* were recovered out of the Hands of the *Spaniards*; and the former given in Exchange for the latter, to the Duke of *Savoy*, who has ever since been stiled King of *Sardinia*. In order to prevent future Debates, and to induce *Spain* to accede to this Treaty, it was agreed that the Issue of his Catholick Majesty *Philip* V. by his second Queen *Elizabeth*, Daughter to the Duke of *Parma*, should succeed to the Dominions of this Prince, if he died without Male Issue; which Concession has been the Cause of all the Troubles that have since happened in *Europe*.

Spain

Spain was with much Difficulty forced to accept of thefe Terms, or rather to fubmit to them ; and his Imperial Majefty was not very well fatisfy'd even with this, which occafioned the holding in the Year 1724 a Congrefs at *Cambray*, where while *France* and the Maritime Powers were taking all imaginable Pains to comprife thefe Difputes, and fix the general Tranquility of *Europe* upon a folid Bafis, the Courts of *Vienna* and *Madrid* entered into a private Negotiation, which terminated foon after in two feveral Treaties of Alliance and Commerce between the two Courts, fo much to the Advantage of the Emperor, and fo utterly inconfiftent with the Intereft of *France* and the Maritime Powers, that they found themfelves under an abfolute Neceffity of entering into a Treaty for their own Security, which was accordingly figned and concluded in 1725 at *Hanover*, and this foon changed the Face of Affairs again.

After fome Hoftilities between *Spain* and *England*, another Congrefs was held at *Soiffons*, in which *Spain* demanded and obtained from the *Hanover* Allies, that inftead of fix thoufand *Swifs* Troops, which were to be put into the Duchies of *Parma*, *Placentia*, and *Tufcany*, to fecure the eventual Succeffion of thofe Countries to Don *Carlos*, fix thoufand *Spaniards* fhould be employed, to which the Emperor refufed to confent. This in 1729, produced the Treaty of *Seville*, concluded by the *Hanover* Allies with his Catholick Majefty, in order to force the Emperor to fubmit to the Condition before mentioned ; but before this could be brought about, the Duke of *Parma* died, which made a confiderable Alteration in the State of Affairs ; inafmuch as it gave Don *Carlos* an immediate Right to his Dominions, even in Virtue of thofe Treaties which had been concluded with his Imperial Majefty. However, he took Care to put all Things into fo good a Pofture, in his *Italian* Dominions, that the Allies of *Seville* were able to do nothing by Force.

There could be no other Method found out to induce his Imperial Majefty to give way to the Alteration made in the Treaty of *London* by that of *Seville* ; except the Promife of guarantying the Succeffion, which he had eftablifhed in his Family, when he faw there was no longer any Probability of his having Male Iffue. This Point was effectually fecured thro' the Treaty of *Vienna* in 1731, by which the Emperor confented to the Introduction of Don *Carlos* in the Manner that had been defired. But this was fo far from hindering, that it really brought about a War, which the Emperor flattered himfelf self would not have been at all prejudicial to his Interest, supposing that his Alliances would have secured him effectually even against the whole Power of the House of *Bourbon*.

He depended in the North upon the *Czarina*, and her placing on the Throne of *Poland* the present King *Augustus* III. He looked upon the Empire's declaring in his Favour as a Thing of Course, he depended upon the King of *Sardinia*, and had not the least Scruple about the Maritime Powers. Yet for all this fair Prospect, that War had very near cost him all his Dominions in *Italy*. The Empire did indeed assist him, but unwillingly. The Elector of *Bavaria* kept a kind of armed Neutrality. The Elector Palatine desired to be excused from contributing to the War, an Account of what his Dominions suffered by it. In short all the Princes of the Empire were as slow as ever ; and some of them suspected. The King of *Sardinia* entered into the Alliance against him. The *Dutch* took care of themselves, by a Neutrality, which made it unfit and unreasonable for *Great Britain* to engage in the War ; but after a great deal of Blood spilt, and the almost total Ruin of the Countries contended for, the War was concluded in 1735, by a Peace as favourable for the Emperor as he could well expect.

He lost indeed the Kingdoms of *Naples* and *Sicily*, which were given to Don *Carlos*, and the Duke of *Lorrain* made an absolute Cession of his Country to *France*, but then the Emperor had *Parma* and *Placentia* in Exchange ; the Duke of *Lorrain* had *Tuscany*; which by his Marriage with the Archduchess, was to become part of the hereditary Dominions of the House of *Austria*. *Augustus* III. was left in the peaceable Possession of the Kingdom of *Poland*, and *France* guaranty'd the Pragmatick Sanction. As soon as this War was over, the Emperor most unaccountably engaged in another with the *Turks*, in Conjunction with the *Czarina*, tho' he had no Quarrel with them of his own ; in which he was very unfortunate ; and at last, by the Interposition of *France*, made an indifferent Peace at the Expence of *Belgrade*, which was given up to the Infidels.

He saw, when it was too late, the Error he had committed, and the Consequences that would attend it, against which he endeavoured to provide in the best Manner he could ; and the War which broke out between *Great Britain* and *Spain*, might possibly have given him an Opportunity of doing it effectually, if in the Midst of the Political Measures he was taking for that Purpose, he had not been cut off by Death, after

after a few Days Illness, on the 20th of *October* 1740, leaving behind him only two Daughters; one married to the Duke of *Lorrain*, then stiled Grand Duke of *Tuscany*; the other intended for his Brother Prince *Charles*, whom she afterwards espoused, tho' she did not long survive.

The late Emperor *Charles* VI. Father to her present Imperial Majesty, having had Time sufficient to consider the Misfortunes that might arise from his Want of Issue Male, in Case the Succession in his Family was not effectually settled before his Decease, resolved according to the Custom of his Ancestors, to publish a *Pragmatick Sanction*, or perpetual Edict for that Purpose, which was accordingly done in 1713; and afterwards proclaimed with great Solemnity at *Vienna*, in the Month of *December* 1724; and on the 15th of *May* 1725, at *Brussels*, that is, in the Capitals of his hereditary Countries.

By this Pragmatick Sanction all the Dominions of the House of *Austria* were entail'd on the eldest Daughter of his Imperial Majesty, the Archduchess, now the reigning Empress *Maria Theresa*, and afterwards on her Issue; next, to her Sister; and then to the Nieces of his Imperial Majesty; with due Preference to the Heirs Male. The sole Design of this Settlement being to preserve the Possessions of the House of *Austria* entire, this Succession was accepted and confirmed in his Imperial Majesty's Dominions. But as the Emperor very easily discerned this Affair of the Succession of the House of *Austria* regarded not only his own Subjects, but all the Princes of the Empire, and indeed all the Princes and States of *Europe*; he consequently judged that it would be necessary to obtain their Consent likewise, by Way of Guaranty of the Pragmatick Sanction before mentioned.

It was with this View, that he took the Advantage of every favourable Conjuncture that offered, to carry this Point with his respective Allies; and was so fortunate to obtain, at different Times, all that he proposed to himself from the great Powers of *Europe*, viz. From *Russia*, *Sweden*, and *Denmark*, by particular Treaties: From *Spain*, by the famous Treaty of *Vienna*, in Consequence of the close Alliance then subsisting between the two Courts: From *Great Britain* and *Holland* in 1731, in Consequence of the Emperor's consenting to the Regulations stipulated by the Treaty of *Seville*: From the States of the Empire assembled in the Diet of *Ratisbon*, in the same Year: And from *France*, on the Conclusion of the Peace which followed the War in *Italy*.

As we have already spoken particularly of each of these Periods, it is not necessary that we should enter more largely

into

into them at present; but it may not be amiss to observe, that throughout this whole Transaction there was not so much as a single Step taken but what was perfectly regular, as well as strictly agreeable to Justice and Equity,

The Emperor, as the last Heir Male of the House of *Austria*, was bound in Justice to himself, his Family, and his Subjects, to regulate the Succession to his Dominions in his Life-time, which he did in the same Manner as his Predecessors had done, agreeable to the constant Maxims of the House of *Austria*, the Rights of his Descendants, and the Interests of his People, to whom his Intentions were made known in the most publick Manner, and by whom they were received with the utmost Marks of Joy and Satisfaction, as well as Obedience and Consent.

The Northern Potentates had many Reasons to wish the Power of the House of *Austria* might remain undiminished, as a Thing necessary to their own Security; and therefore we need not wonder that they gave his Imperial Majesty in this Respect such Testimonies of their Satisfaction, as were equally consistent with his Views and their Interests.

As to the Princes and States of the Empire, they were thoroughly persuaded that nothing was of greater Consequence to the Safety of the *Germanick* Body, than the maintaining undiminished the Strength of so considerable a Power, which had been always a Bulwark against the Infidels, and indeed against all the Enemies of *Germany*. *Spain*, no doubt, had her solid and substantial Reasons for guarantying this Succession, exclusive of her imaginary Hopes of procuring a Marriage between the Archduchess *Maria Theresa* and Don *Carlos*, now King of the *Two Sicilies*.

The Maritime Powers had always looked upon the House of *Austria* as the proper Ballance against *France*, which she could not be otherwise, than by keeping her Dominions entire, and in the Hands of the Heiress of that Family; so that what they did was the plain and natural Consequence of those Maxims, upon which they had acted for a Century past. As for *France*, as she professed at that Time an inviolable Attachment to a pacifick System, and the maintaining the general Tranquility of *Europe*, there was nothing strange in her Behaviour upon this Occasion; and by this Time perhaps that Crown may be convinced she had pursued her own Interest most effectually by adhering to, as well as granting her Guaranty.

Thus, we see, it is no very difficult Thing to shew how and why this Settlement was made; but it will not be quite so easy to distinguish the true Reasons why so many great Princes concurr'd in endeavouring to defeat it, and why so few of the Powers who guaranty'd the Pragmatick Sanction, in the Course of the late War, took up Arms in its Defence. The maintaining this Order of Succession was indeed agreeable to the Will of the late Emperor *Charles* VI. and for the Glory and Benefit of the House of *Austria* ; but at the same time it was calculated to preserve the Tranquility of *Europe*, and to hinder the Independency of the *European* Powers from being violated ; and in this Light it really was and ought to have been regarded as a common Concern.

The Archduchess *Maria Theresa* of *Austria*, Consort to the Great Duke of *Tuscany*, caused herself to be proclaimed Queen of *Hungary* and *Bohemia*, as well as Sovereign of all the Countries belonging to her August Family, immediately after her Father's Death, which happened, as we said, on the 20th of *October* 174c, and a few Days afterwards she associated the Grand Duke of *Tuscany* her Husband in the Government of all her Dominions, under the Title of *Co-Regent*. Thus the Pragmatick Sanction seemed to have operated without Trouble or Dispute ; and indeed upon her first Accession, her Titles were acknowledged by some of those Powers, from whom she had most Reason to expect and afterwards met with the greatest Opposition.

The *French* King made at this Time no Difficulty of owning her Titles ; and the King of *Prussia* was so far from questioning her Rights, as established by the Pragmatick Sanction, that on the contrary, he made the strongest Professions of Friendship to her Majesty, and of his earnest Desire to assist and support her in the Possession of all the Hereditary Dominions of the House of *Austria*. It has been alledged that there was very little Sincerity in this, and that it was the Fallacy of this Declaration which occasioned all the succeeding Disputes. We have already set this in its true Light, and shall only add here, that his *Prussian* Majesty's Demands, tho' they affected the *Austrian* Succession, had nothing to do with the Pragmatick Sanction ; that at the same time his *Prussian* Majesty attacked *Silesia*, he declared his Readiness to perform his Guaranty, and, that it is very certain this was his Interest.

The Queen herself, from the Moment she ascended the Throne, display'd all the Virtues worthy her Rank, agreeable to her Sex, and suitable to her Condition. She took care to assemble the States of *Hungary*, *Bohemia* and *Austria*, as soon as it was possible ; and it appeared from the Resolutions taken in those Assemblies, that she reigned far more absolutely

absolutely in the Affections of her Subjects, than over their
Persons. Her Government was just, prudent, and gentle;
her Behaviour firm, equal, and constant; but the Zeal of
her Subjects was boundless. She desired a reasonable Supply
for the Necessities of her Administration, and they made her
a ready Tender of their Lives and Fortunes. Leaving it to
the Wisdom of their Sovereign to settle as her Occasions required, the Instances she might expect of the Sincerity of
their Offers; and they complied with her Demands, when
known, with that Chearfulness and Alacrity, which shewed how
much they were in earnest, when they made those warm Professions of Duty.

She caused all her Troops to be compleated before any
Necessity appeared for employing them, and it was to this
wise Precaution that she owed the Preservation of her Dominions; for it became quickly evident, that the Enemies
of the House of *Austria* were resolved not to let slip this
Occasion of lessening the Authority of that Family, and disturbing the Peace of *Germany*. The single Error committed
at this Time, was neglecting to comprise the Disputes with
Prussia, for if this would not have extinguished the Rancour
of other Powers, it would very probably have hindered its Irruption.

The late Elector of *Bavaria*, a Prince of great Qualities
and greater Virtues, was so far misled by his Ambition, as
to form immediate Pretensions on the *Austrian* Succession, in
Virtue of the Will of the Emperor *Ferdinand* I. made in the
Year 1543; and of a Codicil added to that Will, dated the
4th of *February* 1547, in favour of his eldest Daughter *Ann*,
married to *Albert* of *Bavaria*. This Will was in the Nature
of a Pragmatick Sanction; and not only the Spirit of that
Instrument was clearly in Favour of the Queen of *Hungary*
and *Bohemia*, but the very Letter of it gave her a prior Right
to the Elector of *Bavaria*, if the Expressions therein were so
to be understood, as to make the Will and Codicil consistent
with each other, and with the plain Intention of the Emperor
to preserve the Dominions of his Family entire, for the Sake
of its Safety, Benefit, and Grandeur.

At first it looked, as if the Elector of *Bavaria* alone
meant to contest the Queen's Title, under the Pragmatick
Sanction; but it very soon appeared, that he was not without Hopes of being supported by other Powers. While this
Dispute was confined only to Paper, the King of *Prussia*
attacked *Silesia* in the Manner before mentioned, purely, as he
gave out, to secure to himself what of Right belonged to him.
This

This Incident produced the War not long since ended ; for the Queen of *Hungary* and *Bohemia* resolving to defend her Territories, and looking upon this as an Infraction of the Pragmatick Sanction, demanded on that Account, and in Virtue of their Guaranty, the Assistance of her Allies,

By this Requisition of Succours, an Opportunity was given for the *French* to interfere ; who had it always in their Intention to support the Claim of the Elector of *Bavaria*, tho' they were perplexed about the Manner of declaring it. His *Prussian* Majesty seeing himself exposed to the Danger of losing not only what he had acquired by his sudden Irruption into *Silesia*, but much more, *if* Fame *speaks* Truth, resolved at last to take that Step which hitherto he had declined ; and on the seventeenth of *August* 1741, concluded with *France* a Treaty, to which the Elector of *Bavaria*, and the King of *Poland*, Elector of *Saxony*, acceded. By which, it is said, the following Agreement was made : *viz.* That the Kingdom of *Bohemia*, with *Upper Austria* and *Tirol*, should be given to the Elector of *Bavaria* ; *Upper Silesia* and *Moravia* to the Elector of *Saxony* ; and *Lower Silesia*, with the Town and Territory of *Neiss*, and the City and County of *Glatz*, to the King of *Prussia*.

As soon as this Alliance was made, the *French* began to be in motion ; and his *Britannick* Majesty, in Quality of Elector of *Hanover*, having augmented his Forces, and shewn his Willingness to assist the Queen of *Hungary*, as he was bound by Treaty to do, tho' she was then attacked only by the King of *Prussia* : The first Step that was taken by the new Allies, was to put this out of his Power ; in order to which, the *French* marched a great Army into *Westphalia* on one Side of the Electorate ; and at the same Time his *Prussian* Majesty assembled a numerous Body of Troops upon the Frontiers of that Electorate on the other ; which produced what it was intended to produce, and which indeed it was impossible at that Season it could fail of producing, a Treaty of *Neutrality* for that Electorate for a small Time only.

Things at this Juncture looked as if the Allies must necessarily have carried all before them ; for the *French*, besides their Army in *Westphalia*, sent another to the Assistance of the Elector of *Bavaria*, which enabled him to march directly into *Austria*, at the same Time that the *Prussians* and *Saxons* were in the Field ready to execute what they had undertaken, and thereby secure the Shares that had been allotted them out of the Spoils of the House of *Austria*. Her Majesty, the Queen of *Hungary*, in the mean time, found it requisite to

retire

retire into that Kingdom from *Vienna*, in Sight of which her Enemies were now arrived ; but in the midst of this Distress, than which no Princess had felt a greater, she preserved her Prudence and Firmness of Mind, relying always on the Protection of the Almighty, and the Loyalty of her Subjects, Resources on which all good Princes may well depend.

The Application of the Allies to their Military Operations, did not hinder them from attending to another Point of equal, Consequence, which was the Election of an Emperor. The Queen of *Hungary* and her Allies intended to have set up the Grand Duke of *Tuscany*, as a Candidate for that supreme Dignity ; but it very quickly appeared that this would have been at that Conjuncture to little or no Purpose.

The Ecclesiastical Electors were inclined to the Duke of *Bavaria*, one of them (*viz.* the Elector of *Cologne*) being his Brother; the King of *Prussia* as Elector of *Brandenburgh*, had engaged by Treaty to give him his Vote; the King of *Poland* as Elector of *Saxony*, was under the like Obligation ; the Elector Palatine had entered early into these Measures ; and his *Britannick* Majesty as Elector of *Hanover*, was oblig'd to act in the same Manner, by the Neutrality which he had concluded, for the Reasons before mentioned.

Thus the Election was secure : but the Allies not contented with this, were resolved that it should be likewise unanimous ; and in order thereto, they suspended the Vote of *Bohemia*, which tho' prejudicial to the Queen of *Hungary*'s Interest, was a tacit Acknowledgment of her Right ; since otherwise the Elector of *Bavaria*, now stiled King of *Bohemia*, might as well have voted for himself by that Title. This Scheme being well laid, was attended with all imaginable Success ; for upon the 24th of *January* 1742, the Elector of *Bavaria* was chosen Emperor at *Frankfort*, and crowned there on the 13th of *February* following, by the Name of *Charles* VII, to the general Satisfaction of the Princes and States of *Germany*.

The Joy of the Allies on this Occasion was very great, but it was soon lessened by the News of the Capitulation of *Lintz*, where 10,000 *French* and *Bavarians* had been surrounded by the glorious Count *Kevenhuller*. This was followed by a long Train of Successes in *Bavaria*, by which the Face of Affairs was very soon changed, and the Queen return'd in Triumph to *Vienna*. In the Month of *May* the same Year, was fought the famous Battle of *Czaslaw*, between the *Austrians* and *Prussians*, which about three Weeks after produced the Peace of *Breslaw*, between the same Powers.

The

The *French* that were in *Bohemia*, having received several confiderable Checks, and being deferted by the *Pruffians* and *Saxons*, from whom, however, they had firft feparated; contrary to all the Rules of Policy and War, fhut themfelves up in *Prague*; from whence they afterwards made an happy Efcape under the Command of Marfhal *Belleifle*, with about one fourth Part of the Forces they had brought into *Bohemia*. A Circumftance that in all Probability will deter them from venturing, at leaft in our Times, to attempt the carrying into Execution Schemes of fuch vaft Extent as thefe, which are always liable to Difappointments; and in which Difappointments are not barely fatal but irreparable.

The fucceeding Year, *viz.* 1743, was no lefs glorious to the Queen of *Hungary* and her Allies. The *Spaniards* had invaded the *Auftrian* Dominions in *Italy*, his Catholick Majefty *Philip* V. claiming the whole Succeffion of the Houfe of *Auftria*, without fo much as any plaufible Pretence, and in direct Breach of the feveral Treaties concluded by himfelf with the late Emperor *Charles* VI. at *Vienna*, as well as his folemn Guaranty of the Pragmatick Sanction,

But the Queen of *Hungary*, with the Affiftance of her unalterable Ally, the King of *Sardinia*, defeated all the Attempts of the Duke *De Montemar*, one of the greateft and moft fortunate Generals (before this Time) in the *Spanifh* Service; and after he was recalled, the Field-Marfhal Count *Traun* defeated, or at leaft repulfed, his Succeffor, the Count *De Gages*, an excellent Officer likewife, at *Campo Santo*. Prince *Charles* of *Lorrain*, in the latter End of *April* beat the *Imperialifts* and *French* at *Braunau*; and on the 16th of *June*, his *Britannick* Majefty gained the famous Battle of *Dettingen*, which forced the *French* to think in earneft of abandonning their military Operations in *Germany*.

In 1744, the *French* and *Spaniards* were worfted in *Italy*, and Prince *Lobkowitz* drove the Latter into the Kingdom of *Naples*, and block'd up his *Sicilian* Majefty, the Count *De Gages*, and all their Forces, in *Veletri*. Prince *Charles* of *Lorrain* paffed the *Rhine*, and drove the *French* before him into *Alface*, till recalled by a new Irruption of the *Pruffians* into the Kingdom of *Bohemia*, from whence upon his Return he foon expell'd them with very great Lofs on their Side.

In 1745 a new Treaty was made with his *Pruffian* Majefty; and the Emperor *Charles* VII. dying of a broken Heart, the Queen of *Hungary* and *Bohemia* compromifed all Differences with the young Elector of *Bavaria*, his Son and Succeffor, by the Treaty of *Fueffen*; and on the 15th of *September*, her Confort *Francis* Grand Duke of *Tufcany* and *Lorrain*,

was

was elected Emperor at *Frankfort*, and crowned on the 4th of *October* following.

In the Progress of this glorious War, *Munich* the Capital of *Bavaria* was thrice taken by the *Austrians*; the City of *Prague*, the Capital of *Bohemia*, twice recovered from the Enemy, the *French* entirely driven out of *Germany*, and this Year out of *Italy*; the *Austrians* and *Piedmontese* penetrated likewise into *Provence*; so that the Seat of War was removed from the Gates of *Vienna* and *Turin*, into the most fruitful Provinces of *France*; and the Republick of *Genoa*, that took part with the Enemy, was now reduced to lie absolutely at the Mercy of the Empress Queen, who was also Mistress of the Dominions of the Duke of *Modena*, and had it in her Power to conquer those of the King of the Two *Sicilies* whenever she pleased. A Change so surprizing that it was altogether unforeseen.

But as nothing is more uncertain than the Events of War, in the Year 1747 Affairs begun to run retrograde in *Ita'y*, and the Successes of the common Enemy, which had already rendered them Masters of a great Part of the *Austrian Low Countries*, still continued, notwithstanding all the Measures that were taken to prevent them. The Revolt of the City of *Genoa* in the preceding Winter, was the principal Cause of all the Misfortunes that happened on that Side.

At first this was ascribed entirely to the Madness of the Populace, the Nobility and the Republick pretending to adhere to the Capitulation they had made with the Marquis *de Botta*; but when they were powerfully supported by the *French*, who upon this Occasion exerted themselves with all the Vigour imaginable, and at length sent the Duke *de Boufflers* to command their Forces in that City, it was no longer necessary to retain the Mask; and therefore the *Genoese*, without either Scruple or Ceremony, resumed their former Sentiments, and not only acted offensively against the *Imperialists*, but attacked them whenever Occasion offered, with inexpressible Fury.

It was to this Situation of Things that the Disappointment in *Provence* was chiefly owing, for tho' General Count *Brown* maintained himself in that Country all the Winter, yet it was not without Difficulty; and tho' the very important Fortress of *Savona* surrendered to the King of *Sardinia*, and by affording him a safe Port and a strong Place, enabled that Prince to send frequent Supplies to his own and the Imperial Troops that had entered *France*, and notwithstanding the Islands upon the Coast were reduced, yet Count *Brown* found it impracticable to extend his Conquests, or even to reduce *Antibes* for want of a proper Train of Artillery, and a necessary Quantity of Military Stores, before the *French* were in a Condition to act offensively.

Marshal

Marshal *Belleisle* who commanded their Forces on that Side, behaved with all the Military Skill and Caution possible, and did not attempt any thing of Consequence, till he had acquired such a Superiority of Force, as rendered it utterly impossible for Count *Brown* to think of venturing an Engagement, in which, if he had had the worst, it would not only have been decisive, with respect to the Army he commanded, but must have ruined the Affairs of *Italy* entirely. He therefore very wisely chose to make a timely and prudent Retreat, and having raised the Siege of *Antibes*, repassed the *Var* in the Sight of a much superior Army, without any Loss either of Troops or Credit.

In the mean time the Imperial Army in *Italy* under the Command of Count *Schulemberg*, formed the Siege of *Genoa*, in which he was greatly assisted by the *English* Fleet, which had also contributed as far as could be expected to the Support of Count *Brown*, while he remained in *Provence*. But the *Genoese*, prompted by Necessity and Despair, and at the same Time thoroughly supported by *France*, who will be always solicitous for the Safety of her Allies, when upon that alone her own Security depends, defended themselves so obstinately, that when Marshal *Belleisle* passed the *Var*, and advanced again into the County of *Nice*, the *Imperialists* found themselves obliged to retire, that they might provide against that double Invasion which the Enemy meditated, and which, as shall be elsewhere shewn, was happily defeated.

The Campaign this Year in the *Low Countries*, tho' it promised fair at the Beginning, and some plausible Hopes there were that *Antwerp* would have been recovered, was notwithstanding very unfortunate in its Conclusion. The *French* King in Person commanded his Army, and under him those two great Officers who owed their Fame and Fortune to that War, and to the Manner in which they conducted it, having the Address to procure by the King's Presence such an extraordinary Attention to all their Demands, as seldom fails to render any Army victorious.

They had already ruined the Barrier, and not only taken but destroyed those important Fortresses which had been considered as the Bulwark of the Imperial and *Dutch* Territories, and in that Light were likewise held of the highest Consequence to *Great Britain*. They now fell directly upon the *Dutch* Territories, and having gained an Advantage over the Allies in the Battle of *Maestricht*, formed the Siege of *Bergen-op-Zoom*, and with a prodigious Expence of Men, as well as by improving the fatal Mistakes in the Conduct of the *Dutch* Officers, made

them-

themſelves Maſters of that ſtrong Place, and gave ſuch a Turn to Affairs on that Side, as made a Peace very deſirable.

There had been a Negotiation for that Purpoſe at *Breda*, in which however it did not appear that the Houſe of *Bourbon* was much in earneſt. But notwithſtanding this, towards the Cloſe of this Year, the Courts of *Verſailles* and *Madrid* ſeemed to change their Sentiments, and finding all their Efforts for dividing the Allies, and making a ſeparate Peace ineffectual, they began to think in Reality of reſtoring the general Tranquility, which was now become to the full as requiſite for them, as for thoſe whom they had forced into a bloody and expenſive War, in ſupport of publick Faith and the Liberties of *Europe*.

Before theſe pacifick Meaſures could be put into a regular Train, it was requiſite to provide for the Continuance of the War, in ſuch a Manner, as that the Houſe of *Bourbon* might perceive, that the Houſe of *Auſtria* and her Allies were in a Condition to inſiſt upon reaſonable Terms, and to expect that this ruinous and expenſive War ſhould not end in a precarious and ill-concerted Pacification. At leaſt this, which would have been a very right and prudent Meaſure, was very ſtrongly given out, and many Engagements mentioned as entered into for this ſalutary Purpoſe, neither is it impoſſible that theſe Suggeſtions were of Uſe.

With this View a Convention was actually ſigned for aſſembling a formidable Army in the *Low Countries*, which might procure Time for a Body of *Ruſſian* Auxiliaries to make the long March neceſſary before they could arrive at the Scene of Action, and afford thereby a moral Certainty of putting a Stop to the *French* Conqueſts, or even giving a new Turn to Affairs on the Side where they had hitherto gone worſt, and where any Turn once given muſt have thrown the Concerns of the Houſe of *Bourbon* into the greateſt Confuſion. But notwithſtanding this Convention, the *French* knew how to profit by their immediate Superiority, and taking the Field earlier than could be expected, by a lucky Temerity inveſted the Fortreſs of *Maeſtricht* before the Allies were in a Condition to offer them Battle.

Affairs in *Italy* however were more upon an Equality, and tho' the Duke *de Richlieu* commanded the Succours of the Houſe of *Bourbon* in the Room of the Duke of *Boufflers*, which were very conſiderably reinforced, yet the Imperial Generals in *Italy* threatened the Dominions of *Genoa* with another Invaſion, and that Capital with a freſh Siege. It is true that Marſhal *Belleiſle* on one Side made ſuch Diſpoſitions in the County of *Nice*, as ſeemed to foretel a freſh Irruption into the *Sardinian* Territories; and on the other, the Motions of his *Sicilian* Majeſty's Troops on his Frontiers looked as if he was inclined to aſſiſt the *Genoeſe*;

Genoese; but then his *Sardinian* Majesty was in a Condition to stop the Progress of the *French*, and there were just Reasons to believe that the King of the *Two Sicilies* would hardly commit another Breach of that Neutrality, which had been obtained for his Dominions by the Interest of his *Polish* Majesty.

The Negotiations for the general Peace, agreeable to what has been before intimated, were opened as early as the Campaign, at *Aix-la-Chapelle*; and tho' the House of *Bourbon* and its Allies had not acknowledged the Emperor in that Quality, and for this Reason opposed the admitting an Imperial Minister at *Breda*; yet now that Scruple was no longer insisted upon, and the Count *de Kaunitz Rittberg* in Quality of Minister Plenipotentiary from her Imperial Majesty, assisted at this Congress; to which the Earl of *Sandwich* was sent on the Part of the King of *Great Britain*, the Count *de Chavannes* for the King of *Sardinia*, and Count *Bentinck*, with four other Plenipotentiaries, from the States; his Most Christian Majesty entrusted the Care of his Interests with the Count *de St. Severin d'Arragon*; the Plenipotentiary of his Catholick Majesty was Don *Jaques de Soto Major*; and the Duke of *Modena* and the Republick of *Genoa* sent their Plenipotentiaries also.

Things went very leisurely there at first, but the Siege of *Maestricht* being pushed in a very extraordinary Manner by Marshal *Saxe*, who is said to have flattered himself with the Hopes of over-running *Holland* before the *Russians* (notwithstanding the boasted Expedition of their March) could join the Allies; quickened the Pace of the Plenipotentiaries, and that to such a Degree as to produce the Plan of a general Peace under the Title of Preliminaries, which were signed very unexpectedly *April* the 30th 1748, N. S. by the Plenipotentiaries of *France*, *Great Britain*, and *Holland*, to which their respective Allies thought proper soon after to accede.

There were indeed some Exceptions taken at the Manner in which this great Affair was concluded, as well as to the Matter of the Preliminaries; but upon the whole, as the Necessity of this Measure at that Juncture excused the former, so the Advantages that were expected from the restoring publick Tranquility, were in the End judged a sufficient Equivalent for the latter; and therefore the Negotiations of Peace proceeded, and a Cessation immediately took place in the *Low Countries*, as the March of the *Russian* Auxiliaries, who by this Time had reached the Frontiers of the Empire, was on the same Account likewise suspended.

In *Italy*, by the Dilatoriness of the *Genoese*, arising from some Cause hitherto concealed, the Operations of the War still

went

went on, till that Republick found sufficient Reason to repent her languid Manner of acting, and to claim the Benefit of those Preliminaries which she seemed to accept with Reluctancy; in this Situation Things continued for about five Months, notwithstanding some Impatience expressed by the Publick, for the Delay of a Blessing which they expected with so much Ardour. Yet if we consider how many Difficulties there were to get over, what a Variety of Interests to reconcile, and how hard it must have been to make the particular Schemes of certain Courts bend and give way to a general System calculated for the common Advantage, we shall rather wonder at their Expedition than entertain a Doubt that any Time was lost. The Defensive Treaty was signed *October* 18th 1748. and was concluded in the same Manner with the Preliminaries, that is to say, *France*, *Great Britain*, and *Holland*, as being now most interested, were the only contracting Parties, and the rest of the Powers at War acceded thereto.

This Method proved very agreeable to the Sentiments of the Court of *Vienna*, where, notwithstanding all that had been suffered by the War, and all the Evils that were to be feared from the Continuance of it, the Sacrifices to be made by this Peace made it relish but indifferently. It was particularly thought hard, that as the Peace itself was to be purchased by an Establishment for the Royal Infant Don *Philip*, at the Expence of the Empress Queen, she should also be obliged to adhere to those Cessions that were made by the Treaty of *Worms* purely to avoid this Necessity, and to prevent the giving any such Equivalent. But tho' at first Sight, and more especially upon the View of a certain Paper made publick upon this Occasion, there seems to be great Force and Weight in this Objection; yet, when thoroughly weighed and candidly considered, it will not perhaps to impartial Judges appear so conclusive as to induce an Opinion, that her Imperial Majesty departed in the least either from her Dignity or her true Interest in complying with it.

For as to the Establishment, the real Expediency of granting it was altogether independent of the Treaty of *Worms*, so far as regarded his *Sardinian* Majesty, to whom certain Cessions were made by that Treaty, and who was to suffer by this as well as her Imperial Majesty; on the other Side, his *Sardinian* Majesty having complied with his Stipulations in that Treaty, and by this Means contributed to the great Successes in *Italy*, had from thence a very clear Title to the Advantages derived to him from that Treaty, more especially when it is considered how deeply his Dominions had suffered during the Course of the War, into which he had entered merely from a Principle of publick Spirit, and out of which he might at any Time have

extri-

extricated himself with equal, not to say greater Advantages, than he was to reap by this Definitive Treaty.

But having now deduced Things as low as can be expected in this Chapter, we shall conclude it by taking a short View of the Alterations made by this Definitive Treaty, in respect to the Possessions of the Empress Queen, and the Advantages in consideration of which those Alterations were admitted ; for this being done, we shall have a distinct Idea of the present State of the House of *Austria*, with Respect to its Power and Influence, and be from thence in a better Condition to judge of its true Interests in Time to come. In the first Place then we are to observe, that by the twenty-second Article of the Definitive Treaty, the Duchy of *Silesia* and the County of *Glatz* are guarantyed to his *Prussian* Majesty by all the contracting Parties ; which however is not to be considered as an original Concession by this Treaty, but as a Confirmation of what had been yielded to him by her Imperial Majesty in former Treaties, and more especially by that of *Dresden*.

By the thirteenth Article, her Imperial Majesty stipulated to restore to his Serene Highness the Duke of *Modena*, the Fiefs he possessed in the Kingdom of *Hungary*; which was also no new Concession, but a bare Restitution of what her Imperial Majesty had seized, upon that Prince's entering into a War against her. By the twelfth Article, her Majesty confirmed to the King of *Sardinia* the Cessions formerly made him, as well as those granted by the Treaty of *Worms* in the Year 1743; and this likewise was no new Concession by the Definitive Treaty, but a Confirmation of what was yielded before.

In the thirteenth and fourteenth Articles, her Imperial Majesty consented to restore the Duchy of *Modena*, and all its Dependencies, to the Duke its lawful Sovereign ; and undertook to give the same Prince Satisfaction for his Rights to certain allodial Estates in the Duchy of *Guastalla* ; and all these except the last, which was a Point of Equity, are barely Restitutions, as is also what is farther stipulated in the same Articles with respect to the Republick of *Genoa*.

But in the seventh Article, her Imperial Majesty makes an entire Cession of the Duchies of *Parma*, *Placentia*, and *Guastalla*, to the Infant Don *Philip*, to be held by him and the Heirs Male of his Body born in Marriage, till such Time as he or his Descendants shall obtain the Possession of the Kingdom of the *Two Sicilies*, or of *Spain*, when those Duchies are to revert to their former Possessors, and consequently except what was formerly granted to his *Sardinian* Majesty, to the Empress Queen or to

her

her Defcendents. This is the great, one may fay the only Con-
ceffion, that for the Sake of Peace and the Reftitution of the great
Towns, ftrong Fortreffes, and large Diftricts that had been taken
from her in the *Low-Countries*, her Imperial Majefty has made.

How far thefe Ceffions infringe the Settlement of the *Auftrian*
Territories by the Pragmatick Sanction, and in what Degree
the Lofs of them affects the Power of the Houfe of *Auftria* in
Italy, will be fhewn in another Place ; let us obferve at prefent,
that thefe Ceffions are but temporary, and that the fame Guarantees which fecure the Eftablifhment of the Royal Infant Don
Philip, fecure likewife the Reverfion of this Eftablifhment to
the Emprefs Queen, or to her Heirs ; we may likewife venture
to affert, without pretending to the Gift of Prophecy, that the
recovering the Poffeffion of thofe Countries will be then effected without involving *Europe* in a new War.

As to the Advantages which arife to her Imperial Majefty
and her Auguft Houfe, from the Definitive Treaty of *Aix-la-
Chapelle*, we are firft to reckon the Acknowledgment of his Imperial Majefty in that Quality, tho' ftrictly fpeaking this was an
Effect of the Preliminaries ; we may next give place to the fecond Article, by which the Treaties of *Weftphalia*, *Nimeguen*,
Ryfwick, *Utrecht*, *Baden*, the Quadruple Alliance, and the Treaty
of *Vienna*, are renewed. By the fixth Article it is ftipulated,
that all the Conquefts made by the *French* in *Flanders* fhould be
reftored ; and by the twenty-firft Article, the Pragmatick Sanction made by the late Emperor *Charles* VI. *April* 19th 1719, is
again moft folemnly guarantyed by all the contracting Parties,
except in the Alterations made by the Definitive Treaty itfelf.

On the whole therefore it appears, that confidering the high
Demands made at the breaking out of the War, the formidable
Alliance by which thofe extraordinary Demands were fupported, and the Backwardnefs fhewn by feveral Powers (exclufive
of thofe who actually attacked the Queen of *Hungary*) to maintain their Guaranties of the Pragmatick Sanction, that the
Power of the moft Auguft Houfe of *Auftria* has not fuffered any
confiderable Diminution ; and if we reflect upon procuring
the Imperial Crown for the Grand Duke of *Tufcany*, and the
conciliating the Affections of the *Hungarian* Nation, we fhall
run no Hazard of being refuted if we affert, that its Luftre and
Credit were rather augmented than diminifhed ; and how cava-
lierly foever this Remark when firft made was treated, the Confequences have fince made the Truth of it very evidently appear.

It will pafs with fome for a high Piece of Imprudence to
add any thing farther upon this Subject ; but as the profeffed
Defign of this Work is to fhew, that human Prudence alone

is

is very capable of penetrating, in some Degree, into future Events, we will venture to own it is in our Opinion highly probable, that the Establishment of the House of *Austria* will, within the Compass of the present Age, grow more solid, and become more firmly rooted, than ever it has been esteemed in our Times; and will consequently have a stronger Influence, as it must always retain the same Interest in supporting the Ballance of Power in *Europe*, upon which its Fame and Authority, and, what is still more, its Safety, will always depend. In saying this, we oblige ourselves to assign the Reasons of this Opinion; for in political Treatises nothing is to be asserted from Motives that must be concealed: Such as predict Things from their Knowledge of what was formerly stiled Occult Philosophy, claimed a Privilege of this Sort; but no such Claim will ever be put in by any one who either is, or believes himself to be a Politician.

There are then three Causes that have led us to this Assertion; we will first state them freely and fairly, and then leave the Reader to approve or censure them as he thinks fit. In the first Place, it is highly likely that the Guaranties contained in the Definitive Treaty will be punctually performed, and that for many Reasons; let us only mention a few: The Breach of good Faith in that respect was attended with such fatal Consequences in the last War, that it will teach the Statesmen in all Courts and Countries, to discern that nothing great or good can flow from such a Conduct. The Parties are reciprocally interested, and any Chicanery upon one Point of the Guaranty would afford a Precedent fatal to the whole; and therefore tho' there may be Courts not over tender of the Concerns of their Neighbours, they will neverthelefs be unwilling to take such Measures as in their Consequences may be dangerous to their own. It is not improbable that certain Powers, whose Goodwill in the Performance of their Stipulations there is most Reason to suspect, may have the first Occasion to recur to the general Guaranty in this Treaty, for their own Security. More might be advanced upon this Subject, but, to the Intelligent, what has been already said will certainly be sufficient.

The second Cause is this, That their Imperial Majesties have a numerous Issue, and as these Princes and Princesses grow up, they will certainly contract Alliances by Marriages, that cannot but strengthen the Power of the House of *Austria* exceedingly; and this is so fair a Prospect, that whoever considers it attentively, and compares it with the different View in which that August House was considered from the Beginning of the present Century, as well as with the Light in which another
House

House at present stands; whoever, I say, coolly and attentively contemplates this, cannot fail of perceiving, that we have not guessed at random.

The third Cause is, the Discovery, that this last War has made of the real and inherent Strength derived to this illustrious Family from its hereditary Dominions, and the new Turn that this has given to the Politicks of the Court of *Vienna*, where no longer regarding the antiquated Maxims of those who would make the Customs of former Ages, whether reasonable or not, the Laws of the present, it is now thought necessary to employ Men in the Cabinet for their Abilities, for their military Virtues in the Field, and for their eminent Integrity on the Benches of Justice, where the Piety of their Imperial Majesties heightens the Lustre of their secular Stations, and where their own Examples, in Point of Virtue, Vigilance, and Clemency, merit the universal Approbation and Applause of their Subjects, and seem to have attracted the Blessing of God upon their Counsels, and that in a Degree very conspicuous even to the People of this Age, who amongst all their numerous Follies, are not justly chargeable with Credulity, at least upon this Head.

After so ample Detail as this, of the History of the House of *Austria*, from the Time of its becoming possessed of the Imperial Scepter, down to the present, we are next, according to our Plan, to consider its Interests; and these will fall naturally under five several Heads. The First, in regard to the Imperial Dignity, so happily restored to this august Family; and what we have to say upon this Head, may be reduced within a very narrow Compass. As it is the Interest of the Princes and States of the Empire, for preserving a Bulwark against the Infidels, a proper Ballance of Power against *France*, and the Tranquility of *Germany*, to continue the supreme Power in this Family; so on the other Hand, it is certainly the Interest of the House of *Austria*, while possessed of the Imperial Dignity, to maintain the Freedom and Independence of the Empire, together with the Privileges and Immunities of all its Members.

This Conduct can alone secure to that House the Support of the Empire upon all Occasions, and which though from past Experience Politicians may possibly consider as a Thing rather of Shew than Consequence, yet it may become of very great Efficacy and Importance. For as the Interests of the Emperor and Empire are always the same, so if they were constantly and firmly united, it is very evident that the *Germanick* Body would be always an Equal, if not an

Over-

Over-match for *France*, without the Affistance of any other Power whatever.

A gentle and mild Administration therefore, that may conciliate the Hearts of the *German* Princes, so as to bring them to feel juft and warm Sentiments of their own Intereft, will be the moft eafy and expeditious Means of inducing them to confide in and pay a proper Refpect and Duty to the Head of the Empire, will detach them from *France*, and from every other Foreign Power, none of which ever had or can have any any Influence over them, but from their real or imaginary Apprehenfions of the Ambition and Power of the Houfe of *Auftria*.

This once removed, the Emperor would become the greateft and moft formidable Prince in *Europe*, that is, confidered in a defenfive Light, if attacked without Reafon or juft Provocation, and would therefore be revered by his Neighbours, inftead of being dependent upon them ; and be capable of protecting his Allies, without ever falling under the Neceffity of feeking beyond the Limits of *Germany* for any Affiftance. At prefent this will to many appear a Doctrine very ftrange and improbable ; but to fuch as examine carefully and attentively, it muft feem very juft and reafonable, and at the fame time no lefs eafy and practicable.

The Emperor by his Prerogative has many Opportunities to benefit and oblige moft of the Princes and States of the Empire, and can always defend and protect them. This Power therefore, wifely and feafonably exerted, may fuffice to bring about all that I alledge might be expected from it; in the mean time I defire it may be underftood, that I do not fpeak abfolutely, but conditionally. I do not fay this *will*, but affirm only that it *may* very well happen, of which the Reader muft be convinced when he has read and confidered what we have to offer in Relation to the Kingdom of *Hungary*.

The next Point that claims our Regard, is the Intereft of the Houfe of *Auftria*, as a Member of the *Germanick* Body. As to this it is apparent, that her Power is already fufficiently great, and that it cannot be for her Advantage to endeavour to increafe it at the Expence of her Neighbours, which indeed is the fole Thing that has hitherto turned, or can at any Time turn to her Prejudice. While fhe remains fatisfied with her Poffeffions, and forms no Pretenfions to the Dominions of others, it is highly probable, that as the War is now over, fhe may find her Neighbours difpofed to live with her upon Terms of Friendfhip and Refpect.

If

If she is ever inclined to enlarge her Territories, it ought to be those that lie without the Empire, and even this must be done with very great Caution; for at present there is such a Spirit of Jealousy in all Powers, that they cannot with any Patience see Acquisitions made, which increase the Strength of their Neighbours, and consequently alter that Proportion between them, upon which they conceive their own Safety in a great measure depends. Yet the House of *Austria* may, without any Hazard, augment her real and internal Force, while she is content to preserve the antient Limits of her Dominions. Almost all her Hereditary Countries are capable of great Improvements; the Kingdom of *Bohemia*, and the Provinces that border on the *Adriatick* more especially.

The reviving of Trade in those Parts, and encouraging the mutual Commerce of the Subjects in all her Dominions, might render the Empress Queen a much richer, and consequently a more powerful Sovereign than she is at present. Some of those Nations that in the late War were famous for furnishing her Armies with Irregulars, are known to have a great Turn for Trade; and if properly encouraged, would not fail of rendering her as essential Services in Peace as in War. The only Check in this Respect, that hitherto has hinder'd their Genius from appearing, is the Want of Religious Liberty; since it must be owned the House of *Austria* has in some measure picqued itself on a Zeal for the Popish Faith, that bordered upon Bigotry: And yet through the Course of the two last Wars, the Court of *Rome* has been so far from making any proper Returns, that she has actually shewn a manifest Partiality in Favour of the House of *Bourbon*.

Any Relaxation in this Kind, arising from Christian Charity, sound Policy, or the Gratitude of the Court of *Vienna*, would have wonderful Effects, for it could not fail of rendering all the Countries under her Obedience more populous, and consequently more rich and fruitful than they are at present. Neither ought this Liberty of Conscience to extend only to the *Lutherans* and the Reformed, but to the Members of the *Greek* Church, to the *Moravians*, and indeed to Christians in general; for this would draw Multitudes out of the *Turkish* Dominions into those of the House of *Austria*, and contribute at once to strengthen the Hands of the Empress, and to weaken those of her Enemies.

As Sovereigns of *Hungary*, the House of *Austria* is extremely powerful; and it is with great Pleasure we can observe her present Majesty has taken such Measures, as ought to be a Rule to all her Successors. On the 25th of *June* 1741, she was crowned at *Presbourg* with all the Ceremonies usual in that Kingdom,

Kingdom, having first confirmed to the Protestants the future Enjoyments of all their Rights with regard to Religion, and agreed to the Capitulation drawn up by the Diet, of which the following were the chief Articles.

I. That the Kingdom shall never be without a Palatine; and that after the Death of the Veldt-Marshal Count *Palfy*, the Diet shall be convoked in order to chuse one out of the four Persons that the Queen shall propose.

II. That in case the Queen dies (which God forbid) before the young Archduke is out of his Minority, the Palatine shall be his Guardian in this Kingdom.

III. That the Employments in this Realm shall be given to none but *Hungarians*.

IV. That such of the Noblesse as have purchased Estates of Peasants (or Roturiers) which only are liable to be charged with Imposts, shall pay none for the said Estates.

It was by these Concessions, and by the most gracious and popular Speeches on all Occasions publick and private, that her Majesty, while she remained in that Kingdom, changed the Face of it entirely, and procured such Succours from thence, as enabled her to make head against all her Enemies : Neither was it for once, or from a sudden and passionate Expression of their Affection and Loyalty, moved by the Goodness and the Distress of the Queen, that this Assistance was received ; but it continued through the whole War as constant and regular as her Occasions required, to the just and immortal Honour of that brave and generous Nation.

We have already pointed out in the Course of this History, the sad Condition of this Country in former Reigns, and the mean Opinion her Imperial Majesty's Grandfather had of the Fidelity and Power of the *Hungarians*, when he affirmed that he had spent more in defending them than their Kingdom was worth ; and which if it did not belong to him as a Conqueror, ought to be reputed his as a Purchaser, as much as any of his hereditary Dominions. Notions inspired, no doubt, by Jesuits and self-interested Statesmen, who had nothing in view but to make their court to his Imperial Majesty by a false Shew of Zeal for his Family, at the sad Expence of a gallant and loyal, but then dejected and oppressed Nation : A Nation equally exposed to continual Invasions from Infidels abroad, to the subtil Intrigues of false Patriots, and the base Complacency of false Courtiers at home.

But the present Queen, when except this, she had scarce any other Territories left, was able to draw from it Resources sufficient for the Recovery of all the rest : And thence to demon-

strate

ſtrate to all the World, that it is not an abſolute Prince, but a Prince governing a free People according to their own Laws, that is the moſt powerful, the moſt formidable, the moſt Maſter of the Lives and Fortunes of his or her Subjects. We cannot therefore doubt that the ſame Maxims will for the future be purſued; in conſequence of which, from being thought the leaſt conſiderable, *Hungary* will from henceforth be reputed one of the moſt potent Monarchies in *Europe*.

It may not be amiſs to obſerve in this Place, it was from that unexpected Support the Empreſs received from the People of *Hungary*, ſuch an additional Weight has been thrown into the Scale of the Houſe of *Auſtria*, as none of our Politicians have duly conſidered, and which notwithſtanding ought to be looked upon as one of the moſt ſingular Events produced by the late War. In all probability it has been the real Cauſe why the *Turks* have never attempted to interfere, or to give the leaſt Diſturbance to her Imperial Majeſty, though continually prompted to it by *France.* They ſaw that the Union which reigns in that Country between the Sovereign and her Subjects, has reſtored the ancient Vigour of the *Hungarian* Militia; ſo that if a War ſhould happen, the *Hungarians* alone would be able to make Head againſt their whole Force, and perhaps make ſome Impreſſion on the *Ottoman* Empire itſelf, at a time when from the Diſorders in the Adminiſtration of the Government, its Credit and Forces are equally weak.

Beſides, even in regard to *France*, the State of Things is very much changed, in conſequence of the Alteration which happened in *Hungary*; for when at a very ſmall Expence, the *French* kept up a Malecontent Party there, which was always ſure of private Support, if not of open Countenance from the *Turks*, they were ſecure of a Diverſion on that Side; and have ſometimes carried this ſo far as to bring ſome of the bold Irregulars, who now ſerve with ſo much Reputation in the Imperial Armies, as hoſtile Plunderers into the Suburbs of *Vienna*. A wonderful and happy Change this! from a divided, diſcontented, and diſtracted, to a united, loyal, and well-principled People; from being the Terror, to become the Protectors of the *Auſtrians*; from being ſcarce ſeen, to make, as they now do, ſo great a Figure in their Armies. In ſhort, this Advantage, which has been the Reſult of the War juſt concluded, may be conſidered as ſome Equivalent for the Danger and Expence of it.

The Houſe of *Auſtria* is alſo to be regarded as one of the greateſt Powers in *Italy*; and it will be certainly its Intereſt to ſecure the Ballance in that Country, by remaining firmly
united

united to the king of *Sardinia*; for while this Union sub-
fists, it is impossible that the House of *Bourbon* should bring
any of her ambitious Projects to bear. The Neutrality of
Tuscany, the keeping a Court at *Florence*, and the maintaining
the Privileges of *Leghorn*, as a free Port, are Measures so right
in themselves, and which seem to be so well understood by the
Court of *Vienna*, that we can have no doubt of their being
constantly pursued.

Another Advantage that will result from her Territories in
this Country to the House of *Austria*, is, the having it in
her Power to provide for the younger Branches of the Family by the considerable Governments she has to bestow; and
by this means she will take at once the most effectual Measure for the Security of these Provinces, and for the suitable
Support of the Princes and Princesses of the Imperial and Arch-
ducal House without any additional Expence, and this too
in the Manner most agreeable to the Genius and Temper of
her Subjects, as well as the most capable of defeating either the
open or secret Designs of her Enemies. So that on the whole,
nothing can contribute more to the reviving and restoring the
Lustre of the House of *Austria*, than such a Disposition of her
Italian Territories.

We now come to the last Article, which is the Interest of
the House of *Austria*, as Sovereign of the *Low Countries*, a Point
of the greatest Consequence to that Family, and indeed to
all *Europe*. It is by her being in possession of these Provinces, that she becomes the natural and perpetual Ally of the
Maritime Powers, who have never failed to shew the utmost
Readiness to support her Interest. By her being in possession of
these Countries, she covers the Republick of *Holland* from the
Power of *France*; and may be likewise said to form a Barrier
against that dangerous and ambitious Power, in favour of *Great
Britain* also.

Whilst she preserves these Countries, she cannot fail of
preserving the unalterable Affection of her Neighbours; and
therefore it is her Interest to be as tender of these Provinces
as of any part of her Dominions. She sees by fatal Experience,
what dreadful Consequences follow the neglecting her Frontiers
on that side, and therefore she will certainly avoid committing
the like Mistake for the future. It is a visible Error, to suppose that these Provinces may be absolutely trusted to the
Care of the Maritime Powers, and to imagine that this may be
some Excuse for being less mindful of their Security. The contrary is very plain; if the *Austrian* Garrisons in those Countries
were kept complete, and their Fortresses in a proper State of

P   Defence,

Defence, the *Dutch* would have nothing to apprehend from the Power of *France*, and would consequently act upon all Occasions with Dignity and Spirit; whereas a contrary Conduct leaves them so open to their Enemies, and gives such Opportunities to the Emissaries of *France*, and to the discontented Party in that Country, as must necessarily weaken, or, which is worse, intimidate, a popular Government.

On the other hand, the Conduct of the *Dutch* in all such Conjunctures, must have such an Influence upon that of *Great Britain*, that in respect to both, it will be certainly found the Interest of the House of *Austria* to manifest the utmost Concern for these Provinces, by the Justice of her Government, by encouraging the Commerce of the Inhabitants, by applying the Revenues for their Defence, and by keeping every thing in such a Condition, as that *France* shall never be tempted to think it most for her Advantage to attack her Imperial Majesty on this Side. Thus from a clear and impartial View of the present State and Interest of the House of *Austria*, it is fully and plainly shewn that she has emerged from the late War greater, more powerful, and in a Condition of being a more effectual Ballance against the House of *Bourbon*, than she has been during the present Century. The Imperial Dignity is restored to her; her Power in *Germany* is very little impaired; the Kingdom of *Hungary* is become of infinitely greater Consequence to her than it was; her Dominions in *Italy* are safe, and it is in her own Power, by taking suitable Measures for their Defence, to obtain from her Allies whatever Assistance is necessary to preserve the *Low Countries*. This is all that is requisite to make her as secure as herself can desire, as much respected as her Friends can wish, and as powerful as the present System of *Europe* requires she should be.

Thus this Article stood in the last Edition of the Book, before there was any Rumour of electing the Archduke *Joseph* King of the *Romans*. A Point decisive in favour of these Reflections; and as to which, tho' a Matter of the last Importance, there is no Difference but as to the Means and the Manner. His *Prussian* Majesty professes in the strongest Terms, that the highest Respect is due to that Candidate, when an Election shall become necessary; but he has hitherto shewn rather a Distaste than an Approbation of the Method proposed for elevating that young Prince to the Throne. He seems to apprehend, that tho' a certain Majority may be sufficient when they come to an Election; yet with respect to the previous Question, as to the Necessity, there ought to be Unanimity. On the Vacancy of the Imperial Throne the Necessity is apparent; and there is nothing

absurd

abfurd or unreafonable in fuppofing, that it ought to be apparent alfo when the King of the *Romans* is elected during the
Life of the Emperor. An apparent Neceffity infers Unanimity ;
for Difficulties and Doubts, more efpecially, if fupported by
any thing that looks like Argument, is a direct Proof that the
Neceffity is not apparent. Be this as it will, the propofing
this Prince in fo tender an Age, and the Manner in which that
Propofition has been received, even by thofe who feem not at
prefent difpofed to clofe with it, clearly demonftrates all that
I have contended for; *viz.* That the Figure and Confideration,
that is, in exprefs Terms, the Power of the Houfe of *Auftria*, is
augmented; for in a Government like that of the Empire, Figure and Confideration is actual Power, as the future Courfe
of Events will fully explain.

There has been this Year a Dyet held in *Hungary*, the Conclufion of which, tho' at fi ft Sight it feems otherwife, is notwithftanding wholly in Favour of the Principles advanced in
the foregoing Part of this Section. Certain Demands were
made on the Part of the Sovereign, and certain Claims on Behalf of the People; but as the latter could not be fully adjufted,
the former were not complied with in their full Extent. But
a Palatine was chofen according to Law, many other Things
were done for the Satisfaction of the Nation, and the Clofe of
her Imperial Majefty's Speech at the rifing of the Dyet was
exactly agreeable to the C nftitution, which, becaufe I have not
feen it publifhed, I will fubjoin in her Imperial Majefty's own
Words; *Majore expectav:mu, equidem erga nos, fiduciam ac promp-
titudinem a cara Gente, quam femper diftinguimus*, Hungarica, *cui
& plura & nova præ reliquis maternæ noftræ benevolentiæ dedi-
mus argumenta. Deponite igitur in Matrem & Reginam veftram
diffidentiam, & fatagite omnes definitiones diætales folerter exequi,
& mereri, ut priftina fiducia & gratia redeat:* That is, " We
" did indeed promife ourfelves great Confidence and Alacrity
" on the Part of a Nation fo dear to us; from the *Hungarians*,
" whom we have always diftinguifhed, and to whom we have
" given many, and thofe too, late Proofs, in Preference to all
" others, of our maternal Affection. Banifh therefore all Dif-
" fidence of your Mother and your Queen; be punctual, be
" affiduous in carrying into Execution the Meafures taken in
" this Dyet for the Benefit of your Conftituents, and merit
" thereby the full Return of our former Confidence and Fa-
" vour." This is not the Language of Artifice or Flattery;
much lefs of Pride and arbitrary Power; but the candid Sentiments of a gracious Princefs, careful of the Interefts, and therefore jealous of the Affections of her Subjects, defirous of reign

ing in their Hearts, and of augmenting her Authority by extending her Benevolence.

From the Measures that have been taken to settle and secure the Territories in the Possession of this august Family in *Italy*, of which we shall have occasion to speak more at large in another Place, all Suspicions of new Dangers on that side are removed. We are likewise told that a Congress will be very speedily opened at *Brussels*, in which the Business of the Barrier, and whatever else regards the Safety and Welfare of the *Austrian Low-Countries*, will be regulated, with the Consent, by the Advice, and under the Inspection of her Allies. We have good reason therefore to felicitate ourselves upon the Events that have already happened, and have no Grounds for Dissatisfaction with respect to the future Prospect of Things. We do not pretend to answer for, or to struggle with, Events that are in the Womb of Time; but we may venture to affirm, that if Negotiations are evenly and fairly managed, with a just Regard to the Constitution of the Country in which, and with a becoming Respect for the Princes with whom they are carried on, all things we can reasonably desire or expect, may be fully, and in due Time, accomplished. But the noblest Designs, the best concerted Plans, are not Proof against private Views, indirect Measures, or precipitate Attempts, if they should ever enter into the Heads of those who are employed either to direct or conduct them.

C H A P. IX.

The genuine Constitution, real Power, and natural Interests of the GERMANICK *Body, impartially stated from the best and most authentick Writings of their own Lawyers.*

THE *Germanick* Body is a Term with which we are very well acquainted in *Britain*, and the Notion we have of it is in the general right enough; but when we come to speak of it more closely, it does not appear, at least from general Conversation, that People enter into it very strictly, comprehend it very clearly, or are able to satisfy themselves whether Propositions relating thereto, are consistent with,

with, or oppofite to Truth, or even whether they are probable or improbable. This, if we confider it as a Branch of Political Learning, is indeed of very great Importance; but it is of ftill greater Importance, when we remember that it is a Point which often concerns the immediate Safety of our own Country.

Men of great Parts, and wholly devoted to the Service of this or that Faction, frequently introduce the *Germanick* Body into their Debates, and either exalt or deprefs, heighten or weaken it, at pleafure. Sometimes we hear it magnified as one of the greateft Powers in *Europe*, as more than a Ballance for *France*, and as capable of itfelf to fecure and maintain the Equilibrium, not on the fide of *Germany* only, but in refpect to the North, and to the Houfe of *Bourbon*: By others, perhaps by the fame Men when another Purpofe is to be anfwered, we are told that it is a vaft, unwieldy, and languid Power, unconnected in its Parts, flow in its Refolves, and dilatory in the Execution of them.

It is to free this Subject from all Embaraffment, and to fet it in a clear and natural Light, that we have given place to this Article; and as it is very poffible to do this within the Compafs of about an Hour's reading, it is hoped that the pains taken thereon will merit the Approbation of the Publick; the rather becaufe it will appear from our manner of treating it, that there is not the fmalleft Mixture of Prepoffeffion or Prejudice, but that we really mean to render the thing as intelligible as it is in our Power to make it.

The Empire of the *Weft*, of *Germany*, or as it is commonly ftiled, the *Holy Roman* Empire, was founded by *Charles* the Great; and under him and his Son the Government was Monarchical; and the Dominions of thofe Princes being very large, and accruing to them by different Titles, they were governed either by Perfons vefted with Powers from the Emperor immediately, or by their natural Princes, Vaffals to the Emperor; and both thefe kind of Governors were ftiled *Dukes*. In refpect to Spiritual Affairs, they were adminiftered by Bifhops, and as there was a great Spirit of Religion in thofe Days, this render'd thofe Prelates very confiderable.

The Care of Juftice within the Diftricts into which the large Provinces were divided, belonged to an Officer called in *Latin Comes*, from whence the Word *Count* is derived; but in the *German* Language he was ftiled *Grave*. From thefe Courts there was an Appeal to that of the Emperor, and therefore the Chief-Juftice or Prefident of the Imperial Court,

was

was ſtiled *Gomes Palatinus*, that is, *Count Palatine*, *i. e.* of the Palace, or in *German*, *Palſgrave*. The ſame Reaſon of State introduced other neceſſary Offices, ſuch as a Governor of the Frontiers or Marches, then ſtiled *Marquis*, and by the *Germans*, *Margrave*, anſwering to our Lord *Warden* of the *Marches*; the *Landgrave* was an Officer of the ſame Nature with the *Grave*, or *Count*, but had a greater Extent of Country, and that generally in the Heart of the Empire; the *Burgrave* was the Emperor's chief Officer in Towns and Caſtles, that is to ſay, that which immediately belonged to the Emperor, and in which, when he came into the Country where they lay, he was wont to reſide, for in theſe only he kept ſuch an Officer.

We may from hence plainly ſee, that except the Dukes, who were Vaſſals, there were none of the Officers but what depended upon the mere Pleaſure of the Emperor, and had not the leaſt Colour to expect that their Offices ſhould become ſettled and conſtant, much leſs hereditary. But Diviſions in the Imperial Family, Civil Wars, and the ſinking of the Imperial Dignity, ſoon brought about a Change. In ſome Caſes the Dukes themſelves took ſuch Meaſures, that it was ſcarce in the Power of the Emperor to diſpoſſeſs them, or hinder their Sons from ſucceeding; in others it became the Intereſt of the Prince to continue this Power to them and their Deſcendants, in order to attach them more effectually to his Family; and thus the modern Conſtitution came in, of diſtinct Principalities, owning the Emperor for their Head.

All Beginnings are rude, and ſo was the Commencement of the *Germanick* Body; but it is neceſſary to aſcend to the Origin of Things, if we will underſtand them; and when this is once fixed in our Minds, it is a very eaſy Thing to follow the Channel from its Source. Beſides, taking Matters thus high, ſaves time in many other Reſpects, by explaining in the familiar and perſpicuous Way of Narrative, a variety of Terms that would ſeem harſh and unpleaſant in the dry Mode of Interpretation, and introduced without that Caution, might eaſily be miſtaken, or remain for ever obſcure.

But it was not long that Things continued in this Situation, and theſe new Princes in a State of doubtful Authority; for upon the Extinction of the Imperial Line, and the ſetting *Conrad*, Duke of *Franconia*, upon the Throne by an Election, the Rights of the Emperor and of theſe Princes came to ſtand upon the ſame Foot, which was about the Beginning of the tenth Century. His Succeſſor, *Henry* of *Saxony*, had indeed

a No-a Notion of exerting the old Imperial Authority, to which the Princes thought he had no Title; and this produced great Disturbances in his Reign, and a very opposite Conduct in his Son and Successor *Otho* I. who courted the Princes, and might have made himself the most powerful Monarch of his Age, if the Divisions in his own Family had not prevented it.

By the Conquest of *Lombardy*, and annexing the Imperial Dignity to the Crown of *Germany*, he in some measure extended the Power of his Successors; but at the same time brought in certain Inconveniencies, which were not felt before. The Emperor thenceforward claimed the Right of approving the Bishop of *Rome*; and the Popes, who were then much more powerful than they have been since, formed, in their Turns, Pretensions to name or to approve the Prelates; and the Disputes which this occasioned, joined to the Confusions that naturally happen in Elective Governments, brought the Empire into such a Condition, that, as we have shewn in the Beginning of the last Article, it was found necessary to offer the Imperial Dignity to Count *Rodolph* of *Hapsburgh*, in the Beginning of the XIIIth Century: And the Disturbances that happened after the Exclusion of the House of *Austria*, for some time made the *German* Princes very willing to raise *Albert* II. to the Throne in 1437.

Himself and his Successors yielded to several Regulations that were favourable to the *Germanick* Body; more especially the Emperor *Frederick* III. the least powerful, and the least respected of the Princes of the House of *Austria*; who notwithstanding laid the Foundation of its Power, and gave Form and Credit to the *Germanick* Constitution, which was improved by the Emperor *Maximilian*; who, in the Beginning of his Reign, was very well inclined to remedy the Disorders that had been either created or permitted by his Predecessors. Upon his Demise, before *Charles* V. was admitted to the Imperial Dignity, the Electors thought fit to secure themselves against the Effects of his great Power, by a new Step, which has been since constantly followed; I mean, the swearing the Emperor elect to certain Articles of Government, stiled the Imperial Capitulation. In the foregoing Articles we have shewn the Attempts made by the Emperors to enlarge their Authority, the Measures taken by the Princes and States of the Empire to prevent their extending it, the calling in the *Swedes* and the *French* for that Purpose, and the settling all the Pretensions on both Sides, for ever, by the famous Treaty of *Westphalia*.

As the Imperial Dignity was originally absolute and hereditary, and as those Monarchs had very great Powers, their

P 4   Suc-

Successors have always kept up a Claim to, and sometimes, that is, as often as they were able, have exercised such Prerogatives. Those Emperors, being Protectors of the *Roman* Church, the Popes thought it for their Interest to make them greater than any other Princes, and therefore stiled them the Temporal Heads of the Christian World. It was from hence they assumed to themselves Precedence of all Kings, and even claimed a Power of making Kings, not by bestowing Territories, but by granting that Dignity or that Title to such as had them already, but with an inferior Stile. They pretended also to other Rights, even in the Territories of Princes without the Bounds of the Empire; more especially of granting Dignities to their Subjects, which however was frequently controverted, and particularly by our Queen *Elizabeth*.

It was also a long time before they gave the title of *Majesty* to other Kings, whom they treated with that of *Serenity* only; but those Notions are now almost wore out, except in *Germany*; and setting aside the point of Precedence, they have scarce any other Prerogative superior to other Monarchs. In the Empire, indeed, they have, upon particular Occasions, very high Marks of Reverence paid them; and very powerful Princes not only submit to, but contend for the Right of acting as their menial Servants; which, at first sight, may seem to be inconsistent with their own Dignities; but when closely examined, this seeming Humility is really founded on a Principle of Ambition.

All the Electors have great Offices; and those Offices are not only annexed to their Dignities, but seem to have been the Occasion of them, which is the Reason of their being so tenacious in this Respect; and as they are capable of being elected, as well as of electing, as they stile themselves *Coimperantes*, and in the Time of a Vacancy exercise a part of the Imperial Authority, it is no wonder that they are for raising it in point of Stile and Prerogative as high as they can; especially as the Emperors, in return, employ that very Authority in their Favour, and would have the Electors, considered in that Quality, stand upon the Level with Kings. But it is necessary to see who and what these great Princes are, and how they have acquired their Right of Election, which, tho' now long since settled and incontested, was not always so; the Election of the ancient Emperors differing in many respects from that Form of Election which has prevailed for some Ages past, and which, being now made a Part of the *Germanick* Constitution, is like to remain as long as that shall endure.

The

The Kings of *Germany* were always elective; but originally this did not depend upon the great Officers of State intirely, but also on other Princes: And in process of Time the Deputies of the Imperial Towns repaired to the Diet of Election, and gave at least their Approbation to the new King before he was proclaimed; but, however, the great Officers, by their being always about the Court, had great Advantages of being earlier present at such Diets, and so came to have a considerable Influence over the Members.

In the troublesome Times, when *Henry* of *Thuringia*, *William* Earl of *Holland*, *Richard* Earl of *Cornwall*, and *Alphonso* King of *Castile*, were chosen, the Princes and great Towns had scarce an Opportunity of attending; and this gave such a Countenance to that Right, the great Officers of the Houshold had assumed of electing, without consulting any other Members of the Empire, that *Gregory* X. either conceived they had such a Right, or was willing to favour their acquiring it; which induced him to direct a Bull to those great Officers, in which he exhorted them to elect an Emperor, and thereby put an End to the Troubles in *Germany*; since which they have been considered as the sole Electors.

To secure the Possession of that Dignity, they, in the Reign of *Lewis* of *Bavaria*, entered into a League amongst themselves, which was called the *Electoral Union*, and which was confirmed by the Emperor, and ratified afterwards by the famous Constitution of *Charles* IV. so well known to the World by the Title of the *Golden Bull*; by which also it was provided, that the Territories, with the great Offices annexed to them, and by the Possession of which the Electoral Dignity was obtained, should descend according to the Right of Primogeniture, and be absolutely indivisible, that the Right of each Elector might be the better known, and the more effectually secured.

By this Constitution the Number and Titles of the Electors, and the Manner of Election, were fully settled in the following Manner: The Archbishop of *Mentz*, as Great Chancellor of the *German* Empire; the Elector of *Cologn*, as Great Chancellor of the Empire in *Italy*; the Elector of *Triers*, as Great Chancellor of the Empire in *Gaul* and *Arles*; the King of *Bohemia*, in Quality of Cup-bearer; the Count *Palatine*, as High Steward; the Duke of *Saxony*, as Grand Marshal; and the Margrave of *Brandenburgh*, as Grand Chamberlain, were the Seven Electors.

The Duke of *Bavaria*, tho' in every Respect as powerful a Prince as any of these, was not thought of upon this Occasion, as having none of the great Offices; but he being of the same
House

House with the Counts *Palatine*, demanded to share the Quality of Elector with them; and on this it was actually settled by Treaty, that the Chiefs of the two Houses should exercise that Right alternately; but of this there is no mention made in the *Golden Bull*. When the Emperor thought fit to deprive the Elector *Palatine*, *Frederick* V. of that Dignity as well as of his Territories, the Duke of *Bavaria* came into Possession of it, and kept it, even by the Peace of *Osnaburgh*; by which an Eighth Electorate was erected in Favour of the Elector *Palatine*; and that he might not be without an Office, the Dignity of Arch-Treasurer was conferred upon him.

In 1692, the Emperor *Leopold* erected a Ninth Electorate, in favour of *Ernest-Augustus* Duke of *Lunenburgh*, Grandfather to his present *Britannick* Majesty, which occasioned very high Disputes; but at length all Things were amicably settled. On the putting the Elector of *Bavaria* under the Ban of the Empire, in the last general War, the Post of Arch-Treasurer was given to the new Elector, the Elector *Palatine* getting Possession again of his antient Title of High Steward, which the Elector of *Bavaria* had kept. But upon the Peace of *Baden*, the Elector of *Bavaria* came again into Possession of the Electoral Dignity, and that of High Steward; and the Post of High Treasurer is ever since claimed by both the Electors of *Palatine* and *Brunswick*.

As for the Election of a new Emperor, it is so effectually settled, that there cannot now be any Disputes about it. The Elector of *Mentz*, in Quality of Great Chancellor of the Empire, is to summon the rest of the Electors upon the Demise of an Emperor, within the Space of one Month after he receives Notice of it; and the Day fixed for Election is to be within the Compass of three Months from that of his Summons. The Electors are not bound to attend in Person, but may send their Ambassadors, as they generally do; and they commonly name three of these; but if they neglect to come in Person, or to send an Ambassador, they lose the Right of Election for that Time. The Place of Election is *Frankfort* upon the *Maine*; but that is not a Thing indispensible, yet so that the Right of the City of *Frankfort* must be always saved, in case the Election is at any Time made elsewhere.

As soon as the Diet of Election is met, they begin to settle the Capitulation, to which the Emperor, when elected, is to swear. This is done by the College of Electors, but the College of Princes claim a Right of approving it; which however is a Point in Dispute. When the Capitulation is fixed, the Elector of *Mentz* appoints the Day for the actual Election,

up-

upon which the Gates of the City are shut, and the Keys delivered to that Elector.

The Electors, or their Ambassadors, repair in great Pomp to Church; and when the Mass is over, at which the Protestants are not obliged to be present, they take a very solemn Oath to chuse without caballing, or a View to private Interest, the Person that appears to them the most fit for the Imperial Dignity: This done, they retire to the Sacristry, where the Elector of *Mentz* asks if there be any Impediment known why they should not then proceed to an Election; and next he exacts a Promise, that the Person shall be owned and admitted for Emperor who shall be chosen by the Majority; and the Declarations of the Electoral Ambassadors upon these two Heads are recorded by two Notaries of the Empire: After which all the Witnesses are commanded to withdraw.

After this, the Elector of *Mentz* collects the Suffrages, which are given *viva voce*, and last of all he gives his own. It is necessary that the Person chosen should have a Majority of the whole Body, and not a bare Majority of Votes; for supposing there were three Candidates, and one had four, another three, and another two Voices, this would be no Election; but any of the Electors who has Suffrages for him, may add his own to make up the Majority. When this is over, the Witnesses that were present at the Beginning of the Transaction, are again called in, and the Elector of *Mentz* declares to them the Person whom the Electors have chosen.

The new Emperor however is not proclaimed, till himself, if present, or his Ambassador, if absent, has sworn in his Name to the Capitulation; and then the Election is looked upon as intirely compleat. There have been several Attempts made to settle a perpetual Capitulation; and the doing this is looked upon as a Point of great Consequence to the Empire; but the Debates it has hitherto occasioned in the Diet of the Empire, has hindered it from being brought to a Conclusion.

The Emperors were formerly stiled only Kings of *Germany*, from the Time of their Election to the Time of their Coronation at *Rome*; and this serves to explain a Passage before made use of in respect to the Emperor *Otho*, and his annexing the Imperial Title to the Crown of *Germany*; agreeable to which the *Golden Bull* declares, That the Electors ought to chuse a King of the *Romans* for their future Emperor. In respect to this, the Reader will observe, that the Office was conferred by the Election, and only the Title by the Coronation: Sometimes the Popes encouraged, and were very fond of this; at other
Times

Times they were uneasy at the Emperor's Presence: At last the Inconvenience grew so great on both Sides, that the Emperor *Maximilian* I. declined going to *Rome*; and the Pope was so far from taking this ill, that he granted him a Bull, which enabled him to take the Title of Emperor on his being crowned in *Germany*.

It remained long an Article in the Capitulation, that the Emperor should endeavour to be crowned in that City; but at the Election of the Emperor *Leopold*, this was left out as a Thing needless, as being cancell'd by Disuse. His Coronation in *Germany* however is still required by the Capitulation, and it generally follows the Election as soon as may be, that the Electors who are obliged to be present at it, to perform their arch, or great Offices, may not be obliged to give a double Attendance. The Place appointed by the *Golden Bull* is the City of *Aix la Chapelle*, in regard to the Residence of *Charlemagne*; but notwithstanding this, he may be crowned in any other City, saving the Right of *Aix la Chapelle*.

By the *Golden Bull*, the Coronation of the Emperor belongs to the Archbishop and Elector of *Cologn*; but that is upon a Supposition that the Emperor is crowned at *Aix*, which is within his Diocese; and therefore when he is crowned elsewhere, the Ceremony is performed by the Elector of *Mentz*, if the Place which happens to be made choice of for that pompous Solemnity, is situated within the Diocese of *Mentz*; and in the Cities that are in neither of their Dioceses, he and the Elector of *Cologn* enjoy this Honour by turns. When the Emperor is seated on the Throne, the Elector of *Saxony* puts into his Hand the Sword of *Charles the Great*, with which he makes some Knights of the Holy *Roman* Empire, of his own Motive, and is obliged also to make others who are nominated by the respective Electors.

When he comes to dine in the great Hall, he has the Table to himself, which is raised two Steps higher than those of the Electors, and is served by Counts of the Empire; whereas the Electors, who have each of them his Table, are served only by the Gentlemen of their respective Courts. Such of them as assist at this Ceremony in Person, sit and eat at their own Tables; but those who are represented by their Ambassadors, have only Tables covered for them with empty Plates, at which the Ambassador does not sit down. The Coronation of the Emperor is not only a great Ceremony, but a very significant one also; for it keeps up all the great Offices, and serves to raise the Authority and Dignity of the Emperor, by shewing him in such

such high Lustre to all who are present upon the Occasion, at his Entrance upon his Government.

We are now to speak of the King of the *Romans*, which is a Title that has had two very different Significations, as relating to two different Persons. From the Time of his Election to that of his Coronation, the Person vested with the Imperial Dignity is stiled King of the *Romans*; and the Presumptive Successor, elected in the Life-time of the Emperor, is also stiled King of the *Romans*; but since the Emperors are no longer crowned at *Rome*, this Distinction is lost; and we mean now by the King of the *Romans*, only the last mentioned Person: And the only Reason I mention the Distinction here, is to let the Reader see, that the King of the *Romans*, mentioned in the *Golden Bull*, is not the last, but the first of these Persons: For as to a Successor, and his Election during the Life of the Possessor, there is no Direction at all given in this Bull, but it came afterwards by an Agreement between the Emperor and the Electors, for the common Benefit of the Empire.

At present the King of the *Romans* is chosen, generally speaking, at the Request and for the Ease of the reigning Emperor, with all the Ceremonies that the *Golden Bull* requires for the Election of an Emperor; and yet this Election gives rather a Title than an Office; for the King of the *Romans*, by an express Article in his Capitulation, promises not to intermeddle with the Affairs of the Empire during the Life of the Emperor; but upon his Demise, he becomes Emperor upon his Coronation, without any second Election. It is true, that in the Capitulation sworn to by the Emperor *Matthias*, there was an Article inserted, that if the Emperor, being duly requested by the Electors to yield to the Choice of a King of the *Romans*, should refuse, without rendering a solid Reason, they should be at Liberty to elect a King of the *Romans* without his Consent: But since that Time this Article has been omitted; probably, because it was ambiguous, and could be of little use, since there was no Judge to determine whether any Reason the Emperor thought fit to assign, was a solid Reason or not.

When therefore there is no King of the *Romans*, and by the Demise of the Emperor the Throne becomes vacant, the *Golden Bull* has provided for the Administration of the Government, by the Electors *Palatine* and of *Saxony*, who have the Title of *Vicars* of the Empire; and this they seem to have in Right of their respective Offices, the one of Count Palatine, the other of Arch-Marshal of the Empire; but when it is said, that these

Provi-

Provisions are made by the *Golden Bull*, it does not follow that they did not exist before, but only that they were ascertained and confirmed by it.

The Disputes between the Electors of *Bavaria* and *Palatine* have interfered very much in this, both claiming to be Vicars, and both in their Turns have enjoyed it ; but at present, this Difference is adjudged by an Agreement between the two Families, so that the Empire suffered no Prejudice from it in the two last Vacancies. Each of these Vicars has his District, and they have likewise an Aulic Council, which is called the Tribunal of the Vicariate; and it is provided by the *Golden Bull*, that the Acts of the Vicars of the Empire, during the Vacancy, shall be valid and binding; but to prevent Disputes, and for the greater Security, Care is taken to insert an Article in the new Emperor's Capitulation, by which he promises to ratify and confirm in the fullest Manner possible, whatever the Vicars of the Empire have done during the Time of the Vacancy.

We sometimes meet in the *German* History, with Vicars of the Emperor as well as Vicars of the Empire; and indeed these Offices differ widely : For, by Virtue of his Imperial Dignity, the Emperor may, if he pleases, delegate his Power to any Prince in the Empire, when it so happens that he is not in a Condition to execute it himself. But then this Vicar is very far from having the Powers of a Vicar of the Empire ; for, in the first place, he is accountable to the Emperor, who may revoke or annul whatever he has done by Virtue of that delegated Power ; and besides this, his Office depends entirely upon the Pleasure of the Emperor, who may resume or determine it whenever he pleases.

There is also a Vicariate of the Empire in *Italy*, which has been generally executed by the Dukes of *Savoy* ; but as this is a Matter of some Perplexity, does not immediately relate to our present Subject, and may be considered hereafter in another Place, there is no Occasion for dwelling on it here ; only it may not be amiss to remark, that from the latest Practice, in case of the Vacancy of the Empire, it seems, that the Affairs of *Italy* fall under the Direction of the Vicars of the Empire appointed by the *Golden Bull* ; and as to any Power granted to the Duke of *Savoy*, or any other Prince, by a reigning Emperor, that can only make him the Emperor's Vicar in *Italy*, and does not vest him with the Quality of Vicar of the Empire; which Offices, as the Reader will now clearly perceive, are very distinct and different Things.

It

It will also appear, from what has been said, that unless an Emperor is desirous of having a Successor appointed in his Life-time, there can be no solid Reason assigned for the Electors giving him an Associate under the Title of *King of the Romans*, since the Emperor, if he pleases, may devolve any Part of his Authority, for his own Ease and the Good of the Empire, upon any Prince he thinks proper, with the Character of his Vicar; and with this additional Advantage, that he may be called to account for his Adminstration in that Quality, which in the other Case might not be so easy.

This Distinction between the Emperor and the Empire is necessary also in many other Cases; and that we may know how to make it, where and whenever it becomes necessary, we will endeavour to explain the Relation there is between the Members of the Empire and its Head; or, in other Words, the Emperor and the Princes and other Powers of the Empire. This the very best Authors on the *Publick* or *Constitutional Law*, as it is stiled in *Germany*, own to be a very difficult thing, and it appears the more so from their differing about it.

But if we consider that the Empire was first hereditary, and that the Territories held by Lords of all Ranks and Denominations were *Fiefs*, granted to those Lords by *Investiture*; and if we farther reflect, that when the Race of *Charlemagne* ceased to govern *Germany*, the Princes and Lords of their own Motive preserved the ancient Constitution, and resolved, by giving themselves a Head, to continue the Empire, we shall understand this Matter clearly. Their Sovereignty appears in this Resolution: If they had been under any Master, they could not have taken it; but being under none, they associated themselves in a certain Manner, and on certain Conditions; the Performance of which includes all that is properly called Duty to the Empire.

But as this Constitution implies some Center of Dignity, some Head or Chief, by which the Majesty of the Empire may be rendered visible, and its Laws be put in Execution, they agree to chuse an Emperor for this Purpose. In consequence of this Choice, they are to receive from him, or before his Throne, the Investiture of their Dominions; that is to say, Electors and Princes are to do this; for as to Counts and free Cities, they obtain their Investitures from the Aulic Council; but this marks no more than their Submission to the Empire; since as it is their Duty to demand, it is no less the Emperor's to bestow; and this he promises upon Oath, amongst other Articles in his Capitulation.

The

The Members of the Empire therefore, are dependent upon it, that from their Union they may derive Protection; and they are dependent on the Emperor, because in him resides the Majesty of the Empire; in all other Respects they are independent and free. We may hence discern, that every thing done against a Prince wearing the Imperial Crown, is not done against the Emperor. For such a Prince may have other Dominions and other Titles, and what concern him in respect to them does not concern him as Emperor; and therefore nothing relating to Things or Persons out of the Empire, can be construed to the Prejudice of any Prince or Power of the Empire.

But to act against the Emperor in quality of Head or Chief of the Empire, is a Crime against the Nature of that Confederacy, which constitutes the Empire, and renders the Member committing it liable to Punishment for it, according to the Laws of the Empire. Yet this is no Infringement on the Sovereignty of such a Member, because he acquires and enjoys it under the Covenant of being true and loyal to the Empire; and if he continues so, must be secure of their Assistance, which is an Equivalent for the Duty expected from him.

This Account, simple and easy as it is, of the Relation between the States composing the sacred *Romish* Empire, sufficiently explains the Reasonableness and Justice of proceeding against any Prince or State of the Empire, wanting in his or its Duty, or departing from their Fidelity, by putting them under the BAN of the Empire. This at first sight seems to wound even mortally the Notion of Sovereign Authority in these Princes; for if Sovereigns, how shall they be judged? But when more closely examined, this Objection will not appear so weighty. The Sovereignty of these Princes springs from that Union which constitutes the Empire, and therefore this Power is necessary for the Preservation of the Empire, so that the Subjection arises from the Consent of these Sovereigns, and the Punishment is suitable to this Notion of the Thing; *viz.* Deprivation of those Territories which render such Princes Members of the Empire.

It is very true, that there are some old Examples of putting Persons to Death for Treason against Emperors, but this extended no farther than Counts of the Empire. It is also true that *Charles* V. not only deprived the Elector of *Saxony*, and the Landgrave of *Hesse*, of their Dominions, but also passed Sentence of Death on the former, though he forebore to put it in Execution. But this was done, not in the old legal Way,

by

by an Affembly of the adjacent States, but by the Aulic Council eftablifhed by the Emperor *Maximilian*, and was confidered as one of thofe Stretches of Power which brought on the fucceeding Civil War.

The Deprivation of the Electror *Palatine* on the Score of the War in *Bohemia*, had fomething more of Formality in it, but ftill was far enough from being legal, or from being confidered as fuch by the unbiaffed Powers of the Empire; who therefore took the firft Opportunity of doing the Defcendent of that Prince Juftice, by reftoring him to his Dignity and Dominions.

Since that Time, and indeed in our own, the Electors of *Bavaria* and *Cologne* have been put under the Ban of the Empire with far greater Reafon, and with much more Shew of Juftice ; and yet the States of the Empire were not fatisfied, but provided by an exprefs Article in the Capitulation of the Emperor *Charles* VI. that no Member of the Empire fhould be put under the Ban without being heard, and without the Opinion and Confent of all the Electors, Princes, and States of the Empire firft had and obtained, &c. Thus it appears clearly, that the Ban of the Empire is a Punifhment founded in the Nature of the Government, derogates little or nothing from the Sovereignty of Princes, who derive their Sovereignty from and are fupported therein by that Conftitution, and is now fo effectually regulated as to be no longer liable to Abufes.

The Emperors themfelves are not above Law, or free from the Danger of feeling its Effects, if they digrefs from their Duty. The Electors have claimed, and even executed a Right of depofing as well as choofing Emperors, and the fame Thing has been done other Ways. At prefent we fee the Capitulations are drawn up and fworn to, in order to prevent fuch a rigorous Method of Proceeding, from whence, how well founded foever, vaft Inconveniencies muft enfue ; but if in Breach of this Capitulation a *German* Emperor fhould attempt to fubvert the Conftitution, there is not the leaft Doubt that the College of Electors have a Right to remonftrate againft his Conduct, and if that has no Effect (in Conjunction with the Diet) to apply proper Remedies to reftrain him.

But after infifting fo long on the fuperior or fupreme Jurifdiction, it is very natural to defcend to the ordinary Tribunals of Courts of Juftice. According to the original Conftitution of the Empire, there was the greateft Care imaginable taken for the Diftribution and Execution of Juftice by the Counts, within their Jurifdictions ; and by Appeals from them

in

in the Emperor's Courts, before the Count Palatine. When the Power however of the Emperors came to decline, this Diftribution of Juftice, which depended entirely thereupon, came to be interrupted. This Mifchief was foon perceived, but not fo foon remedied; various Attempts indeed were made, but all proved partial, moft of them ineffectual.

At laft, the Inconveniencies grew fo many and fo great, that the States folicited the help of feveral Emperors, for conftituting a Court which might anfwer the End propofed, of having Juftice impartially adminiftered in great, as well as in fmall Caufes. *Ferdinand* III. abfolutely refufed his Confent, but in the Reign of his Son *Maximilian* I. this great Point was fettled, and fuch a Court erected under the Title of *The Imperial Chamber*, at *Worms*, in 1495, removed to *Spire* 1533, and after the *French* had barbaroufly ruined the Palatinate, to *Wetzler* in 1696. The Members of this great Court of Juftice were, a Judge of the Chamber, four Prefidents, and fifty Affeffors; but in 1719, this Number was leffened by one half, and thefe are to be part Proteftants, part Papifts.

The Reafon why the Emperors were averfe to the forming fo neceffary a Tribunal, was, becaufe they had always Hopes of recovering this laft Flower of their Prerogative, by bringing all Caufes in the laft Refort before a Tribunal of their own appointing, whereas the Emperor names only the Judges and Prefidents of the Imperial Chamber. What former Emperors had endeavoured in vain by Authority, *Maximilion* obtained by Policy. He forefaw that the large Expence of the Imperial Chamber, which fell entirely on the States of the Empire, would make them unattentive to their new Tribunal; and fo it fell out. They knew the Importance of it, they ftruggled to obtain it, but they neglected its Support.

The wife Emperor, to provide for the Adminiftration of Juftice, at fuch Times as thefe Accidents kept the Imperial Chamber clofe, revived his *Aulic Council*; and to fhew his Moderation, defired the States to add to the Number of Affeffors eight, though the Emperor allows Salaries to them all. By this Means he drew all the Caufes before his own Tribunal, by keeping it ever open, and the Seats well filled; and by taking care to fee the Sentences pronounced, duly and fpeedily executed.

The Princes and States of the Empire quickly faw their Error, and that the Emperor had made ufe of their Negligence to fecure what, if they had not loft their Opportunity, muft have always depended upon them. They did not fail to remonftrate and expoftulate on this Subject, and to reprefent it as an Infringefringement on the *Germanick* Conftitution, by which the *Imperial Chamber* ought not only to be the fupreme, but the fole Tribunal of that kind.

To this, however, the Emperor returned very plaufible Anſwers. He obſerved, that in erecting the Imperial Chamber he had complied with the Deſire of the States; and by eſtabliſhing the *Aulic Council*, he had provided for the conſtant Adminiſtration of Juſtice; he inſiſted that he had performed his Duty in both Reſpects, that he was not at all accountable for the Want of Judges in one Court, and that he deſerved Thanks for the Pains he took to fupply the Deficiency of one Tribunal by the other.

After all theſe Diſputes therefore, theſe two fupreme Courts ſubſiſt, and that too in ſome meaſure with equal Authority; for which firſt poſſeſſes a Cauſe, thereby retains it; but ſome Points, ſuch as the reſerved Rights of the Emperor, belong to the *Aulic Council*, but both receive Appeals from inferior Juriſdictions, and decide dubious Titles. The Sentences in both Courts are ſubject to a Reviſion, and in caſe of Injuſtice there may be a Complaint made to the Diet.

In this Circumſtance alone, theſe Tribunals differ, *viz.* that the Imperial Chamber ſubſiſts during a Vacancy of the Throne, when Juſtice is done in the Name of the Vicars of the Empire; but the *Aulic Council* is immediately diſſolved by the Death of the Emperor, and a new one cannot be named till an Emperor is elected.

But before we part with this Subject, it may not be amiſs to ſay ſomewhat more particular of this *Aulic Council*, which conſiſts of a Preſident, a Vice-Preſident, and ſeventeen Aſſeſſors, of whom ſix are Proteſtants; the Vice-Chancellor of the Empire hath alſo a Right to a Seat therein, and all the Decrees iſſuing from hence, paſs through his Hands, and are directed by him to thoſe who are to put them in Execution. It is by the great Weight and extenſive Influence of this Court, that the Emperors are enabled to make their Authority more felt than one would imagine was poſſible, conſidering the Conſtitution of the *Germanick* Body, and the Stipulations about this Matter in the Treaty of *Oſnaburgh*.

The Papiſts and Proteſtants both complain of the too great Authority of this Tribunal, and the latter, with too much Reaſon, of its Partiality; but hitherto they have not been able to agree upon the Means of repreſſing or reſtraining it within Bounds, and thereby reſtoring to the true Court of the Empire, *viz.* the *Imperial Chamber*, its original and legal Juriſdiction.

But

But if the Princes and States have an Interest one Way, the Emperor has no less visibly an Interest the other; for by Virtue of Appeals from the Tribunals of other Princes, he finds Means to draw out of it a kind of coercive Authority. We are however to observe, that the Electors, and even some other Princes of the Empire, such as the Archdukes of *Austria* and the Duke of *Saxony*, are exempted from this Dependence; that is to say, their Subjects have no Right at all to those Appeals: Ecclesiastical Causes in like Manner are exempted, and so are Criminal Causes, because of the many Inconveniencies and Delays that must necessarily attend such Appeals in both.

By this Court, and the Exercise of his reserved Rights, the Emperor's Power appears, and by a dextrous Use of them he avails himself of his Dignity, notwithstanding all the Restrictions by which it is bounded. By reserved Rights, are meant the Prerogatives annexed to the Imperial Dignity, and are chiefly these, *viz.* Granting to all the Princes the Investiture of their Dominions, which has been explained; conferring Titles, such as Princes and Counts of the Empire, making Cities, founding Universities, granting Fairs, and other such like Advantages; in giving Dispensations with respect to Age, that Princes may the sooner come to govern their own Dominions, without waiting the Close of tedious Minorities, which are always destructive; in deciding Disputes about Rank and Precedency, and granting for once only a vacant Seat in every Chapter of the Empire, which is stiled the Right of *Primæ Preces*, and is equivalent to the Prerogative of the Primacy called an *Option*.

In none of these Points however he is absolutely at Liberty; for as to Fiefs, he is bound to bestow Investitures as the Laws direct; as to Titles, he promises to bestow them only on worthy Persons, and who have Estates sufficient to support them; and when bestowed, they only give Name and Respect. To acquire Power and Privileges, these Princes and Counts, after their Creation by the Emperor, must have the Consent of their respective Bodies, in order to be admitted to sit and vote; yet some Titles are of great Consequence, as for instance, ennobling Ladies that are inferior by Birth to Princes, who incline to espouse them, and thereby legitimating their Descendents; who otherwise, on account of that Inequality of Birth, are considered as incapable of Succession. In Cases of Minority, no Wrong must be done to the natural Guardian of the Prince, and in all the other Cases many Cautions are to be used; notwithstanding all which, such are the Politicks of this Court, that these Imperial Prerogatives are attended with many, and those too very considerable Advantages.

After

After reviewing separately the Powers of the Emperor and Princes of the Empire, we are next to regard them as acting conjunctly in the Diets, or Assemblies of the States of the Empire, where the *Germanick* Body appears in its full Lustre, and in which the Legislative Power of the Empire resides. It would be needless to detain the Reader with an Account of the Differences between the ancient and modern Diets, as the Diet is now become necessary and perpetual, this that now subsists having sat since 1653; neither is it requisite to dwell on the Manner of convoking and opening this Assembly, as these are not at all like to occur in our Days; and therefore let us content ourselves with observing, that every Prince and State, every Prelate, Count, and free City of the Empire, has a Right to a Seat in this Diet, which the Princes claim before Investiture, the Prelates before they receive their Bulls, and the Guardians of young Princes during the Minority of their Wards.

The Emperor, when present at the Place where the Diet is held (usually at *Ratisbon*, but may be held in any City of the Empire) presides there in Person; when absent, he does so virtually by his Commissary, or first Commissioner, who lays before the Assembly whatever he receives Orders from his Master to propose, which is done by the Communication of what is called the *Commissorial Decree*.

The Director, or as we would phrase it, the Speaker of the Diet, is the Elector of *Mentz*, in Quality of Chancellor of the Empire; and therefore he has a Chancery there, to which all Things are addressed that are to come before the Diet; and these are made known and published by the Secretary of the Elector of *Mentz* reading the Papers, which are to be communicated to the Secretaries of the other Ministers of the States at the Diet; and this is what they call *per Dictaturam*, whence the Expression of transmitting Memorials or other Papers of State to the *Dictature* of the Empire.

It is common in all the Accounts we have of the Debates in the *German* Diets, to find mention made of several Colleges; and this makes it proper to take Notice, that the Diet or general Assembly of the States is considered as divided into or forming three distinct Colleges, each of which has its particular Director. The first is that of the Electors, in which the Elector of *Mentz* directs, not in Quality of Chancellor of the Empire, but as being the first Elector, or as some phrase it, Dean of the College.

The second is stiled the College of Princes, in which sit not only the spiritual and temporal Princes of *Germany*, but

the

the Prelates also, who are not confidered as Princes, and the Counts of the Empire; but with refpect to their Votes, there is a wide Difference; for the Princes fpiritual and temporal, vote diftinctly, that is, each of them has a fingle Vote; but the Prelates and Counts vote by Benches, each of thofe Benches having only one Vote.

The Prelates are divided into two Benches, *viz.* of the *Rhine* and *Swabia*; but the Counts into four, of the *Weteraw*, *Swabia*, *Franconia*, and *Weftphalia*. Neither thefe Counts, nor their Minifter, attend at the Diet; they content themfelves with fending a Minifter for each Bench to maintain their Rights, and to give their Suffrages when demanded. The Archduke of *Auftria*, and the Archbifhop of *Saltzburgh*, are Directors of the College of Princes, and officiate alternately as the Subjects of their Deliberations fall out; and it is for this Reafon the Archduke of *Auftria*'s Minifter fits on the Right-hand Bench amongft the fpiritual Princes.

The third College is that of the free Cities of the Empire; and the Director of that College is the Minifter of the City, in which the Diet happens to fit. The two former Colleges are ftiled *Superior*; and indeed, as we fhall prefently fhew, they are in Effect the Diet.

In all thefe Colleges the Sentiment of the Majority is confidered as that of the Body, except in fome particular Cafes regulated by the Treaty of *Ofnaburgh*, in which the Confent of the whole is ftill neceffary. Thefe are, whatever concerns Religion, what relates to the Empire as a collective Body; and in a Cafe in which all the Papifts are on one Side, and all the Proteftants on the other; for here, as in many other Inftances, this, however unequal the Number of Voices may be, is notwithftanding looked on as an even Divifion. The Affair of Contributions was propofed to have been added to thefe Cafes, but was referred to the Diet, where it has never been fettled, and fo is much in the fame State as if it had been actually declared one of thofe Cafes.

When any Point comes before the Diet, it is firft deliberated and debated in the College of Electors, next in that of Princes: If thefe Colleges differ, they endeavour to reconcile them by a kind of *Free Conferences*, at which only the Directors affift, with fuch as the Colleges think fit to name in Conjunction with them. When by thefe Conferences the Colleges are brought to a Concurrence, then their joint Opinion is fignified to the third College, and they are invited to accede to it; but if they do not, the former is digefted and engroffed in the Chancery, and delivered to the Emperor's Commiffary,

with

with the Title of the Opinion of the Empire; only Mention is made at the Close of it, what was the Opinion of the third College.

It has been a Point debated with great Warmth, whether according to the *Germanick* Constitution, the Opinion of the Majority of the Colleges be properly the Sentiments of the Empire; a Question of Importance, no doubt, and therefore not like to be decided before the *Greek* Kalands; but in the mean time the Practice is as we have stated it.

After the Ceremonies before mentioned, this Opinion of the Colleges is transmitted to his Imperial Majesty, who gives it his Approbation, and then it is published in his Name, as a *Resolution* of the *Empire*, the States are exhorted to obey it, and all the Tribunals in the Empire are directed to consider it as such.

But after all that has been said, this Matter will yet remain in some measure obscure, if we do not explain the Subjects that come in this manner before the Diet. In the first place the Diet makes Laws, explains Laws, and decides ambiguous Cases; and therefore whenever the *Aulic* Council presumes to do this, they consider it as a real and dangerous Infringement; next they are to be consulted in making War, in which the Emperor can do nothing without them, even though it should be attended with Circumstances that ever so manifestly concern the Empire.

When War is declared, the Diet appoints the Field-Marshal who is to command the Army, and assigns him also a Council of War; nay, after War is declared, in any Case but for the Defence of the Empire, any Prince may notwithstanding remain neuter; as the Elector of *Bavaria* did in 1672, when the Empire entered into a War to save the *Dutch*, and in the last War occasioned by the Election of the present King of *Poland*. The Diet likewise settles the Expences of the Government; and the Quota which each Prince or State is rated at, is stiled the Contingent; these are governed by old Precedents, and the antient name of *Roman* Months is still in use, because of old these Subsidies were commonly given either to enable the Emperor to make War in *Italy*, or for his Journey to *Rome* to be crowned.

Lastly, the Diet enters into and makes Alliances with Foreign Princes, which are however commonly negotiated by the Emperor, who is empowered for that Purpose, and in the End, the Treaty so concluded is ratified by the Empire; and hence arise Wars, in which the Empire is obliged to take part, tho' not attacked; on this score likewise Foreign Princes

have

have their Minifters at the Diet, though the Empire fends no Ambaffador.

But in moft of the Congreffes for bringing about a Peace, where the Empire has joined in a War, fome Regard has been had to her Interpofition ; as at *Nimeguen*, where the Imperial Minifters had Power from the Empire ; at *Ryfwick* they named a fpecial Commiffion ; they fent Deputies on the fame Account to the *Hague*, when during the laft general War Conferences were held there about Peace ; they have alfo had fome Share fince in the Approbation of the Treaties of *Baden* and *Vienna*.

The Truth however is, and our Duty obliges us to fpeak it, that they have been exceedingly ill-ufed in all thefe Cafes, the Emperor making whatever Terms for them he pleafed, and only ufing their Authority to ratify them. This we may look upon (and juftify) as the Caufe of that Languor and Inactivity of the Diet, in regard to whatever has fo much as a diftant Relation to War ; for the States of the Empire knowing, as they very well do, that they have nothing to hope and all things to fear from a War, are unwilling to enter into it, and being embarked act but heavily from the fame Notion, which however unreafonable, is after all but natural.

The Peace of *Weftphalia* gave rife to the prefent Diet, and eftablifhed the *Germanick* Conftitution ; but the Diet paid dearly for the Advantages fhe gained, by confenting to yield fuch fine Provinces as fhe did to *France* and *Sweden* by that Treaty ; yet in all fucceeding Treaties fhe has had much worfe Luck, as lofing in each, and getting nothing by all of them. We need not wonder therefore if the States of the Empire are not fuddenly rouzed, fince both Reafon and Experience teach them, that while they can keep out of a War, they can lofe nothing, of which, whatever its Succefs be, they can never be fure any other way.

The great and powerful Princes of the Empire may, like other great Princes, be drawn to engage in Alliances and Wars by their Interefts and Private Views, and will then act with Vigour and Spirit as other Princes do, and upon the fame Motives of Gain and Advantage, having their own Minifters at every Congrefs to manage their Concerns ; but the *Germanick* Body being fo circumftanced as to be able to reap no Profit from fuch Negotiations, even at the moft favourable Conjunctures, but on the contrary, being often called upon and expected to make Satisfaction for what is given by Treaties to other Powers, we need not at all wonder at their Conduct.

But

But to proceed: There is nothing in reference to the *Germanick* Body, that deserves more Attention than their religious Distinctions, because these really divide the States as it were into two distinct Bodies, with different, and in some Cases even opposite Interests. All the World knows, that *Luther* began to preach the Doctrines of the *Reformation* first in *Germany*, and that his religious Sentiments were quickly embraced, not only by great Numbers, but even by the Subjects in general of several Governments in the Empire.

This having exasperated the Court of *Rome*, she left no Stone unturn'd to secure the Suppression of this Heresy (as she called it) by the secular Arm, which naturally induced the Protestants to make use of the same Method for the Defence of themselves and the Freedom of their Consciences. Hence arose the League of *Smalcald* in 1530, at the Head of which were the Elector of *Saxony* and the Landgrave of *Hesse*.

We have in the foregoing Article given the History of this and the succeeding Wars on the score of Religion, and shewn how little the Elector of *Saxony* got by trimming between the Protestants and the Emperor, and how near the latter was subverting the Reformation in *Germany*, as effectually as in *Bohemia*, and therefore we need not dwell upon it here.

It was the Treaty of *Westphalia* that, as it settled all other Disputes, adjusted this also, and put it in the Power of the People of *Germany*, of both Religions, to live quietly, as good Christians and good Subjects. But as these Stipulations could not have been long maintained, if some Method had not been found for the Protestants to meet, and take Measures in a Body for their own Preservation ; so the fundamental Laws of the Empire having once authorized this, the Method was not long undiscovered.

In the first Diet held at *Ratisbon* 1653, after the Conclusion of that Peace, the Protestant Princes and States resolved to enter into a close Conjunction with each other for their mutual Support ; and as no Body can act without a Head, they unanimously conferred that Honour upon the Elector of *Saxony*, at the House of whose Minister their Conferences have been ever since held ; and from this Conjunction or Confederacy arises what is called the *Evangelic Body*, which is the Guardian and Protectrice of the Protestant Interest in *Germany*, watches over the Laws provided for the Security of Religion, and in case of Violations, which from the natural Spirit of Popery are but too frequent, sets on foot Applications to the Imperial Throne, and thereby procures Redress and Satisfaction.

One

One would have imagined, that when the Elector of *Saxony* quitted the Proteftant Religion, he fhould of courfe have loft his Quality of *Head* of the *Evangelic Body*; but the contrary is the Fact, which the Reader muft admit is a very ftrange one; but for this, two Reafons are affigned: Firft, that the Elector of *Saxony*, confidering the Weight and Influence this Character gave him, was unwilling to refign it; and next, that the Proteftants finding his Change of Religion gave Force to his Reprefentations in their Favour to thofe of his own Communion, faw no Caufe to take their Affairs out of his Hand, which is however what they may do whenever they think fit.

There is, I think, only one Point more that is neceffary for me to confider, and that is, the Divifion of the Empire into Circles, which in a former Article I fhewed was a Regulation made in the Reign of the Emperor *Maximilian*, and in this I have mentioned the Reafon of that Divifion, which was for the Sake of adminiftring Juftice, and took place originally on the founding the Imperial Chamber. This Divifion, which was made in 1500, eftablifhed only Six, *viz. Bavaria, Franconia, Swabia, Saxony,* the *Rhine,* and *Weftphalia,* which are ftill called the antient Circles.

But the great Princes declining to bring their Dominions under the Form of Circles, that Emperor over-reached them, and by throwing the Dominions of the Houfe of *Auftria* into the Circles of *Auftria* and *Burgundy,* drew in the Electors of *Saxony* and *Brandenburgh* to follow his Example in the Circle of *Upper Saxony*; and the Elector *Palatine* and the Ecclefiaftical Electors did the like with Refpect to the *Upper Rhine,* which encreafed the number to *Ten.*

In each of thefe Circles there is a Director and a Chief, the firft for the Management of Civil, the latter for regulating Military Affairs; the Directors are fixed and permanent, but the Chiefs or Generals are elected by the Circles. It is to the Directors of the refpective Circles the Imperial Chamber commits the Execution of its Decrees, and from hence we fee how this Diftribution comes to be of ufe in that of Juftice, as alfo why the moft potent Princes were leaft inclined to it.

The Circles having many Affairs to manage, hold frequent Diets, in which their Directors prefide, and in which they take Meafures for their own Profperity and Security; and as fometimes thefe cannot be fo well purfued without the Concurrence of their Neighbours, they negotiate with the Diets of other Circles; and when this is done upon any particular

cular

cular Occasion, or with a View to a certain Point, they are ftiled *Confederate Circles*; but this being more frequent amongft the Circles of the *Upper* and *Lower Rhine* and *Weftphalia*, they are from thence denominated *Correfponding Circles*.

Thus in as narrow a Compafs as it is poffible, we have given the Reader a compleat View of the moft perplexed and complicated Government, ancient or modern, that ever exifted, and put it entirely in his Power to comprehend whatever is advanced in relation to it by any of our Orators or Politicians; and therefore we have nothing farther to add, but this Obfervation, that however particular Princes may act to promote their Interefts, the *Germanick* Body keeps conftantly in view the Maintenance of *Publick Liberty*, as founded on the Treaty of *Weftphalia*.

CHAP. X.

A Succinct View of the Hiftory of the FRENCH *Nation, fince they have been governed by the Houfe of* BOURBON, *explaining the Alterations that have been made in their Conftitution, the Progrefs of their Power, their Influence and Interefts.*

THE Memoirs of the two great Houfes of *Auftria* and *Bourbon* include almoft all that need be known of the general Hiftory of *Europe*, to underftand perfectly its prefent State and Condition, together with the Nature of thofe political Difputes which reign at prefent, or which, having difturbed paft Ages till laid afleep by fome happy Expedient, are in Danger of awaking again and kindling frefh Confufions.

We have already given the Reader the former Hiftory, which we were obliged to take pretty high, to make it the more evident how the *Auftrian* Houfe acquired by Policy, Marriages, and Accidents, fo extenfive Dominions as fhe once poffeffed; how fhe fixed the Imperial Dignity in herfelf, and how in confequence of her ambitious Projects and their Difappointments, fhe gave a fettled Form, a certain Authority, and an immutable Security to the *Germanick* Empire.

By the Nature of our Plan, we are next led to give as fatisfactory an Account of *France*, which confidering the narrow

Compaſs we are to do it in, is a very hard Undertaking ; but we are engeged and muſt go through ; only for the ſake of Perſpicuity it may be proper to ſay a Word or two of what we propoſe, and of the Method in which we are to proceed.

As to the firſt, we have three Things in View, *viz.* explaining the Change of the *Gallic* Conſtitution from what it was, into what it is at preſent ; ſhewing the Means by which the *French* have pulled down the Puiſſance of the *Auſtrian* Houſe, and rais'd one much more formidable of their own ; and exhibiting the true Syſtem of *Gallic* Policy, Influence, and Power, as it ſtands at this Day, and the Chances for and againſt her accompliſhing her great View, or of the King and his Miniſters, which in deſpotic Governments is all that can be ſtiled the Nation, of being the ſole Directreſs of *Europe.*

It will be allowed, that if we can tolerably accompliſh this, we ſhall not only furniſh the Reader with an entertaining and inſtructive Memorial in relation to one of the moſt important Points of Hiſtorical Learning, but alſo give him an Inſight into a political Myſtery of the higheſt Conſequence, which like the Popiſh Plot in our own Country, is believed by Multitudes and denied by Multitudes ; like it, ſubſiſted long before it was talked of, and ſtill ſubſiſts, and is like ſo to do ; and finally, has ſuch a Tendency to our Debaſement and Deſtruction, that we can be no longer ſafe than while we have our Danger in our Eye, and in conſequence of that the Means of preventing it in our Thoughts.

The only Method of doing this, and keeping within due Bounds, is to begin firſt with Facts, and bringing the *French* Hiſtory ſince the Acceſſion of the Houſe of *Bourbon* (which contains but four Reigns) into as ſhort a Space as can be ; repreſenting with as much Juſtice as poſſible the Spirit of each Reign, and of every Adminiſtration ; marking the conſiderable Acceſſions of Power at home, and of Territory abroad ; and laſtly, ſetting in a clear and full Light the State of *France* at this Day, in regard to Revenues, Power and Policy.

The Succeſſors of the Emperor *Charles the Great*, governed the Kingdom of *France*, for many Generations, from *A. D.* 814, in which that great Prince died, to *A. D.* 986, when *Hugh Capet* ſeized the Crown, and had his Right confirmed by the Nobility, Clergy, and People of *France*, upon the Death of *Lewis* V. to the Prejudice of *Charles* Duke of *Lorrain*,

Lorrain, who was the undoubted Heir of the *Carlovingian* Race.

Lewis IX. a direct Descendent from *Hugh Capet*, and who, on account of his various Expeditions against the Infidels, obtained the Sirname of *St. Lewis*, died *A. D.* 1270, and left two Sons, *Philip* and *Robert*. The latter espoused *Agnes*, Daughter of *John* III. Son to *Hugh* Duke of *Burgundy*, by the Heiress of *Archambault*, Signeur *de Bourbon*. This Lordship coming thus to *Robert* Count *de Clermont*, Son to *St. Lewis*, in right of his Wife's Mother, he thereupon assumed the Name of *Bourbon*.

His Family succeeded to the Crown about three hundred Years afterwards, on the Murder of *Henry* III. the last Monarch of the House of *Valois*, by *James Clement* a *Jacobin* Monk, in the Person of *Henry* King of *Navarre*, who was the Ninth in Descent from *Robert* Count of *Clermont*, and whose Claim to the Crown was clear, though on account of his being a Protestant, a great part of his Subjects were inclined to reject him ; and on his first taking the Title of King of *France* and *Navarre*, the City of *Paris*, not content with disowning his Authority, treated him with such Disrespect and Indignity, as few Princes but himself would have forgiven.

He came to the Regal Dignity *August* 2d 1589, in Circumstances extremely critical for himself and for his Kingdom. The Capital City and the greater part of the Provinces, were in the Hands of such as refused to acknowledge him, and who, to keep the better together, assumed the Title of THE LEAGUE, sheltered themselves under the Authority of the Pope, and were supported by the Assistance of *Philip* II. King of *Spain*. A great many of those who adhered to him were so divided between the Respect due to Principles of Loyalty, and the Care that was requisite to be had of the Catholick Religion, that he could scarce confide in them ; at the same Time his Army was but weak, and he had but very little, indeed, scarce any Revenue. Lastly, most of the great Powers in *Christendom* were averse to him.

The Emperor, both from spiritual and temporal Motives, was against him, as being desirous of weakening the Power of *France*. *Spain* was his declared Enemy, and even formed Pretensions to the *French* Succession ; all the Friends and Dependents of the House of *Austria* followed their Examples, as others also did, on Account of the Excommunication of the Pope, whose Prostitution of the Gospel to serve his wicked Design fign of extending his own Power, towards which he thought the Ruin of *France* neceffary, was one principal Source of the Troubles that ufhered in the Reign of *Henry* IV.

On the other hand, that brave and heroick Prince had alfo fome Circumftances that were not a little in his Favour, and which by his Prudence and military Skill he fo improved, as to bring his Enemies into fuch a State as forced them to fubmit. The LEAGUE was without a Head, or which comes to the fame Thing, had feveral, in regard to whom the Sentiments of thofe who were averfe to *Henry* were divided.

Some fuppofing that his being no Catholick, left him no Right, were for having Recourfe to the next Prince of his Blood, who was a Papift ; *viz.* the Cardinal *de Bourbon*, who was at that Time a Prifoner, and whom neverthelefs they proclaimed King, by the name of *Charles* X. Others favoured the Duke *de Mayenne*, who acted as Chief of the League in the Minority of his Nephew the Duke *de Guife*, to whom the Herd of Bigots were moft inclined, and laboured to perfuade him to fupplant his Uncle. The King of *Spain* confidering his Daughter the Infanta *Ifabella*, Grand-daughter to *Henry* II. as the neareft Relation to the deceafed King *Henry* III. was for having her owned (notwithftanding the *Salic* Law) Heirefs of the Crown of *France* ; and in that Cafe offered to give her in Marriage to any Prince the States fhould choofe.

This Diftraction of Interefts divided the Minds, and weakened the Forces of the Leaguers exceffively. Befides, the King was, in point of perfonal Abilites, in all Refpects, very much fuperior to any of the Faction that oppofed him. Thofe who ftuck clofe to him, efpecially his old Friends, were Men of great Probity and diftinguifhed Parts ; and many of them, the braveft men, and beft Officers in *France*. He had fome Allies alfo owned him in the worft Situation of Affairs ; and tho' that alone was a very confiderable Service, yet they afterwards affifted him to the utmoft of their Power ; fuch as the Queen of *England, Elizabeth* ; the Republick of *Venice* ; the Proteftant Princes of *Germany* ; and the States of *Holland*.

He found himfelf obliged to raife the Siege of *Paris*, which his Predeceffor had formed, and to retire into *Normandy*, in hopes of reducing that Province, and fecuring a Communication with *England*. The Duke *de Mayenne* followed, and came up with him at a Village called *Arques*, not far from

Dieppé,

Dieppe, where a Battle ensued, in which the King was victorious. He proceeded afterwards into different Parts of the Kingdom, and had the good Fortune to reduce them either by Force or Composition ; and then returned into *Normandy*, where he gained the famous Battle of *Ivry*, and defeated the Duke of *Mayenne* the second Time, who then sued to him for Peace. But the *Spaniards* entering the Kingdom, and Pope *Gregory* XIV. having excommunicated all who paid Obedience to his Majesty, both Clergy and Laity ; this embroiled Things again, and gave new Hopes to THE LEAGUE.

The King seeing clearly, that his Subjects would never universally acknowledge and submit to him, while of a different Religion, took a Resolution of professing himself of the Faith of the Church of *Rome*, which he did *July* 15th 1593, and the Year following he was with great Solemnity crowned at *Chartres*, the City of *Rheims* being not at that Time reduced. This Step produced, and very speedily too, all that the King expected from it.

The People of *Paris*, who had been his inveterate Enemies, and had shewn more Confidence and more Constancy than is usual in the Passions of the Populace, immediately changed their Minds, and in spite of the Duke *de Mayenne*, put the King into Possession of the Capital of his Dominions ; and by their Example made Way for his becoming Master of the whole Kingdom, and even of the bitterest and most powerful of his Enemies, whom he received to Mercy, and gave them no Cause to repent their returning to their Duty, and laying down their Arms, since he made no Distinction between his old and new Subjects.

But for all this, there wanted not some, who prompted by the violent and wicked Opinions taught by the Clergy and Monks in the time of the HOLY LEAGUE, desired the Death of the best Monarch that Generation had seen ; amongst these one *John Chastel*, the Son of a substantial Citizen of *Paris*, and himself a Boy of nineteen, actually attempted to murder that Prince, and aiming a Knife at his Throat, struck him in the Mouth with such Force, as to beat out one of his Fore-Teeth, for which, by the Judgment of the Parliament of *Paris*, he was torn to Pieces by wild Horses ; and the Jesuits, in consequence of whose Doctrine he did it, were banished for ever; which Edict the King, unhappily for himself, afterwards recalled.

As

As the Affiftance of the King of *Spain* chiefly fupported the LEAGUE; and as King *Philip*, under Colour of a Zeal for Religion, ftill continued to foment Sedition and Rebellion, *Henry* declared War againft him, as being better pleafed to contend with an avowed, than with a conceal'd Enemy; with one who was obliged to employ his own Forces, than with one who brought againft him none but his own traiterous Subjects.

This was a very wife and right Step, which the King profecuted with fuch Vigour, that King *Philip* became inclined to a Negotiation; and this ended in a Peace between the two Crowns, called from the Place where it was fign'd, the Peace of *Vervins*.

With this Treaty, tho' both Parties feemed very well pleafed, yet the Catholick King only diffembled, continuing his Intrigues with the Malecontents in *France*, and even debauching fome, who had the higheft Obligations to the King, from his kind Acceptance of their Duty. Amongft thefe Marfhal *Biron* was one, from whom King *Henry* had received many Services, in Confideration of which he pardoned him once, and advifed him to enter into no new Engagement of this kind, for fear he might not be difpofed to pardon him again.

But *Biron* was fo blinded with Ambition, and the Hopes of becoming an independent Prince by the help of *Spain*, that immediately after he relapfed into the fame illicit Correfpondence, which the King having difcovered, caufed him to be brought to Juftice, and by an Arret of Parliament he loft his Head on the laft Day of *July* 1602, in the *Baftile*, fhewing, thro' Guilt, little of that Courage in his laft Moments, for which he had been fo defervedly famous.

This King, who was one of the greateft Princes of his Age, both in the Field and in the Cabinet, was very unfortunate in his Family. He was firft married to *Margaret* of *Valois*, Sifter to his Predeceffor *Henry* III; a Marriage unhappy from its Commencement, which furnifhed Occafion for the Maffacre of *Paris*, one of the blackeft and moft barbarous Actions that ever deformed any Hiftory. This Princefs was not indifcreet only, but even diffolute in her Conduct, and the King was far enough from being faultlefs in his.

The Dutchefs of *Beaufort* was his favourite Miftrefs, and like others in her Condition, was fo proud of her Infamy, and abufed her Power with fuch extravagant Infolence, as made her generally hated. Upon her Death the Queen confented to a Divorce, which was quickly procured at *Rome*; and in confequence

quence of which *Henry* IV. espoused *Mary de Medicis*, Daughter to the Grand Duke of *Tuscany*.

But notwithstanding the great Inconveniencies that arose from his former Amour with the Dutchess of *Beaufort*, the King had fallen into another with Madam *d'Entragues*, afterwards Marchioness *de Vernueil*, to whom he gave under his Hand a Promise of Marriage, which afforded the Court of *Spain* an Opportunity of setting on foot a new Conspiracy in *France*, in order to alter the Succession, and instead of the Dauphin to raise *Cæsar* Duke *de Vendosme* (the King's natural Son by the Lady before-mentioned) to the Throne, which occasion'd much Trouble.

In respect to publick Affairs, *Henry* was a great and good Prince ; he loved his Subjects as his Children, promoted Trade, and maintained Justice throughout his Territories. He was not inclined to disturb or injure his Neighbours, but rather content with his own Dominions ; nay, so far was he persuaded, that a steady and unalterable Ballance of Power was for the common Benefit of *Christendom*, as in the latter End of his Reign and Life to form a Design of establishing it, and thereby cut off Pretences for Wars in succeeding Times, by Means of a perpetual Congress.

In order to this, he thought it requisite to lessen the Power of the House of *Austria*, by depriving it of those Dominions acquired without any just Title in *Italy*, which he proposed to have erected into separate Principalities, as most conducive to a general Peace, and the common Benefit of the Inhabitants. But while he meditated these great and glorious Projects for the Good of Mankind, and had assembled in *Champagne* a numerous Army, which was on the very point of marching to put them in Execution, a Period was put to his Days and Schemes by the Hands of *Raivillac*, an infamous Assassin, on the 14th of *May* 1610, in the 57th Year of his Age, and 22d of his Reign.

We have no very good Account of the Cause of this Assassination ; and some of the most esteemed amongst the *French* Historians give us very broad Hints, that it was never thoroughly inquired into ; however, various Circumstances have inclined the most impartial judges to suspect, that the Lady before-mentioned had a deep Hand in this Affair, and that the Partizans of *Spain* were far enough from being ignorant of it : At least thus much is evident, that his Death could not have happened more luckily than it did for that Nation, even if they had, as it is suggested they had, the appointing of it.

R

This

This great Monarch left behind him three Sons and as many Daughters, *viz.* the Dauphin ; the Duke of *Orleans*, who did not long survive him ; and *John Baptist Gaston*, then stiled Duke of *Anjou*, and after his Brother's Death Duke of *Orleans* ; *Elizabeth*, married to *Philip* IV. of *Spain* ; *Christina*, who espoused *Victor Amadeus* Prince of *Piedmont*, afterwards Duke of *Savoy* ; and *Henrietta Maria*, Consort to *Charles* I. of *Great Britain*. *Henry* IV. annexed to the Crown, *Bearne*, *Bigore*, together with the Counties of *Foix* and *Bresse*, which were his private Patrimony.

Lewis XIII. succeeded in the ninth Year of his Age, under the Tuition of his Mother *Mary de Medicis* ; and on the 17th of *October* 1610, was with great Solemnity crown'd at *Rheims* by the Cardinal *de Joyeuse*. The famous Marquis *de Rhosny*, at this Time Duke *de Sulli*, who had managed the Finances in the late Reign with so great Applause, resigned almost as soon as this began ; and tho' the Princes of the Blood, and great Lords, made very high Professions of Loyalty upon the King's Murder, yet the Court quickly fell into Confusions.

This arose in part from the ill Management of the Queen-Regent, entirely governed by an *Italian* Chamber-maid, whose Name was *Eleanor Galligai*, and her Husband *Conchino Conchini*, whom she had made Marshal of *France*, by the Title of Marshal *d'Ancre* ; and in part also from the boundless Ambition of the Princes and Grandees, who could not fail of laying hold of so favourable a Conjuncture as a Minority, to render themselves in a manner absolute in their respective Governments.

This bad Behaviour and immoderate Power of theirs, produced many and great Inconveniencies to the People, who, tho' less exposed than at present to the Oppression and Fleecing of the Crown-Officers, were nevertheless as much oppressed and fleeced by those Princes and Lords, who, tho' they sometimes mentioned them in their Speeches and Manifestos against the Court, yet never thought of them at any other Time, but compromis'd their Differences with the Administration on private and personal Conditions, without the smallest Notice taken of the Publick.

In this manner things went on till the Year 1615, when the young King espoused the Infanta *Anna* of *Austria*, at the same time his Sister married her Brother *Philip* IV. By this Match the Courage of the Court was so much raised, that they adventured to arrest the Prince of *Conde*, who was looked on as the Head of the Malecontents, even in the *Louvre* ; and how

how bold a Stroke this was accounted at that Time, may appear from hence, that *Themines* the Captain of the Guards who performed it, was for this Service immediately promoted to the Rank of Marshal of *France.*

The King was now, in the Eye of the Law, Major, and supposed to have the Direction of Affairs entirely in his own Hands; but they were much more so in those of Marshal *d'Ancre,* and none were suffered in the Royal Presence who were suspected of having Capacity enough to talk to their Master on proper Subjects. Yet these Precautions did not long avail. There was a young Gentleman about the Court, whose name was *Luynes,* who, by his Dexterity in Hunting, was mightily in the King's Favour; and this Qualification giving the Queen's Favourites no Umbrage, he was allow'd free Access to his Majesty, and even permitted to entertain him by his Bedside, in confidence that he would discourse only of Trifles.

But, as it often falls out, the Politicians quite mistook their Man. *Luynes,* instead of Horses and Hounds, talk'd to the King of the Distresses of the Kingdom, the Discontents of the Nobility, and his own unworthy Usage; all of which he imputed to the Marshal *d'Ancre,* hinting also, that as he had obtained it under one, he might think another Minority the most convenient thing in the World for securing or perpetuating his Greatness.

The King, who was naturally timorous, needed nothing more to drive him into Action, and therefore he resolved to be beforehand with the Marshal; with a view to which, Orders were sent by his Favourite *Luynes* to *Vitry* Captain of the Guards to arrest him, which he performed *April* 24th 1617, as he entered the *Louvre.*

The Marshal stepping back, as if he intended to have drawn his Sword, instantly received three Pistol Shots into his Breast, and dying on the Spot, his Corps was afterwards exposed to the Fury of the Populace; his Wife was condemned as a Sorceress, to have her Head cut off, which was executed in the *Place de Greve,* and *Vitry* made Marshal of *France,* for having so thoroughly executed the Commands of his Master.

We may from hence date the Administration of *Lewis* XIII. who had hitherto little more than the Title of King; and to say the Truth, it is almost all he was capable of having; but however, he thought Power was as well in the Hands of his own, as the Queen-Mother's Favourites; and therefore threw off Restraints of that Sort entirely. The Queen-Mother, who loved governing, or rather that those who governed her should

R 2

govern,

govern, was exceedingly difpleafed, and in the Year 1615 retired with the Duke *d'Epernon* into *Angoulefme*, which proved the Caufe, or at leaft the Pretence, for exciting frefh Diforders.

She was however quickly reftored to the King's Favour, by the Interpofition of the Bifhop of *Luçon*, whom fhe had brought into his Councils; and whofe Abilities and matchlefs Ingratitude to her who raifed him, made him fufficiently known afterwards when he obtained the diftinguifhed Title of Cardinal *Richelieu*.

All this Time *Luynes* continued the Favourite, obtained the Conftable's Staff, and was as powerful, and confequently as much hated, as ever Marfhal *d'Ancre* had been. The Bifhop of *Luçon*, as yet only Secretary of State, and who came but flowly into Credit with the King, contributed not a little to it, by writing, or at leaft caufing to be written, *The Life of the Conftable* DE LUNA, a *Spanifh* Favourite; in which not only *Luynes*'s Character was very freely treated, but the King himfelf had his Picture drawn, and his Temper and Capacity difplayed, in Terms not at all to his Advantage.

By thefe Arts, but moft of all by the Indifcretion of *Luynes* himfelf, who was ambitious, vain, and infolent, he funk in the King's Favour, who only looked for a fair Opportunity of humbling him, when Fortune fecured her Child from falling, by cutting the Thread of his Life when he enjoyed as yet the greateft Plenitude of Power.

It was from this Minifter that the King firft received that Plan which he afterwards fteadily purfued, for weakening and deftroying the Proteftant Party in his Dominions; as long as he lived, the Conftable affifted in the Profecution of it, and the laft Act of his Life was the Siege of *Monfleur*, towards the End of which he died; but the Notions he had put into the King's Head were far from dying with him; and notwithftanding thofe of the Reformed Religion had great Strength, and continued to defend themfelves vigoroufly, yet their Power gradually diminifhed, and they were very glad to accept of fuch Truces as the King would grant them, in order to recover themfelves and recruit their Forces.

In 1622, the Duke of *Rohan*, who was one of the principal Nobility of that Party, fubmitted to the King, after his Majefty had taken *Montpelier*, and reduced the greateft Part of *Guienne*. His Majefty then proceeded to *Avignon*, and exercifed there all Acts of Sovereignty, which had not been done by his Predeceffors for a long Time before. He went from thence to *Grenoble*, and fo to *Lyons* in the Month of *November* following, when the Bifhop of *Luçon* received the Cardinal's dinal's Hat, and was from thenceforward considered as Prime Minister; gaining in a short Time such an Ascendency over his Master, that the King was more distinguished by being the Instrument of his Minister's Projects, than as the Ruler of so great a Kingdom.

This Monarch was far from wanting Capacity, or even from being indolent, but he had a Weakness of Constitution, a natural Timidity in his Temper, and little or no Education, so that he was, generally speaking, sensible of his Unfitness to sustain the Weight of Government, and was glad to devolve it upon other Men's Shoulders; but then he was apt to grow jealous of their Authority, and repine at the Sight of that Grandeur of which himself, and that too for his own Sake, was the sole Author and Cause.

Hitherto he had been governed by a Favourite, of very limited Abilities; but his new Minister was a Man of quite another Cast. He had a Capacity as extensive as his Ministry required, and a Spirit capable of supplying the Defect of it in his Master. He laboured all he could to make the King easy and great; he indulged his Foibles, and extended his Authority; but in doing this, he never considered the Means, whether good or bad, or had the least Concern for the Consequences, whether salutary or oppressive.

He possessed his Master with an Opinion that his Government could not be either glorious or secure, till he had compassed three Points. The first was, the Suppression of the Protestants; for while they subsisted, and had strong Towns in their Hands, he was Master of only a Part of his Subjects, and not of his whole Kingdom. The second regarded the Princes of the Blood, and the great Lords who were intrusted with the Government, who, forgetting that they owed all those Marks of Distinction to the Favour of the Court, were very apt to pick Quarrels with the Ministry, and to turn the Force in their Hands upon their Benefactors. In the third place, he shewed the King that he could never be Master at home, while there was a Power superior to his own abroad, more especially if that Power was his Neighbour.

In short he insinuated, that ruining the Protestants, and abasing the Nobility, were the sole Means of making the King easy within his Realm, as reducing the Power of the House of *Austria* was a Point absolutely necessary to make room for the *Gallic* Monarchy, and to give it that Credit with the rest of the Powers of *Europe*, that it merited by its Situation and Forces.

The

The King saw this Project in the most advantageous Light possible; for it suited exactly his inclinations, and agreed in every respect with his manner of thinking. He had been bred with strong Prejudices against those of the Reformed Religion; he had very warm Resentments, from the Usage he had met with from his Grandees; and had Ambition enough to desire that his Reign should be signalized by Victories and Conquests.

He came therefore very readily into the Proposals made by the Cardinal; and conceiving rightly enough of his own Want of Strength, and of the bold, enterprizing, and yet solid Genius of his Minister, he resolved to put the Execution of his Plan entirely into his Hands, and to give him all the Assistance his Authority could supply, for bringing it in every respect to full Perfection.

He began with the Protestants, and the manner in which he treated them was such, that they saw plainly enough what they had to expect; and therefore exerted themselves to the utmost for their own Protection and Preservation. They knew they had a Title to their Privileges by the Laws, and when Force was made use of to overturn those Privileges, they thought it both reasonable and just to have recourse to the same Method for their Defence.

To render this more effectual, they found it necessary to apply themselves to their Neighbours of the same Religion for Assistance, which was promised them by King *Charles* I. of *Great Britain*, though he married his most Christian Majesty's Sister. The *French* King persisted however, in the Resolution to execute his, or rather the Cardinal's Scheme; and accordingly laid Siege to *Rochelle*, one of the strongest Places in the Hands of the Protestants, and a very convenient Port, by which, so long as it continued in their Hands, they might always have Succours from *England*.

This Siege lasted a whole Year, in which Time the *English* made two fruitless Attempts to relieve it; and the Place was at last taken by a Contrivance of the Cardinal's, who commanded the King's Army in Chief, and had two Lieutenant-Generals acting under him; for he found means to run a Dyke across the Canal, by which they received Provisions and Succours, tho' with infinite Labour, Expence and Trouble; and these being intercepted, the Inhabitants were forced to surrender, and submit themselves to the King's Mercy, who entered the Place in Triumph *November* 1, 1628.

By this Blow, the Protestants in *France* were brought so low, that many of their great Men were obliged to quit the Kingdom;

Kingdom; and some, despairing of their Cause, thought it best to embrace the prevailing Religion. Yet it was not judged expedient to proceed in this Matter with Violence, the Cardinal pretending the War was not carried on so much to make them good Catholicks as good Subjects; but he very well knew that when once their Power was gone, the Religion of the King and Court must by Degrees prevail.

The King was desirous that his Brother should marry the Princess *de Montpensier*, who was of the Blood Royal, and a very rich Heiress; but *Monsieur*, so the King's Brother is stiled in *France*, disliked the Match, and was rather inclined to marry some Foreign Princess; upon which, the Cardinal caused Marshal *d'Ornano*, and the Count *de Chalais*, whom he suspected to have given that Prince this Advice, to be arrested; the latter was soon brought to his Trial before a Court contrived for that Purpose, in which Faculty the Cardinal excelled, was condemned by them to lose his Head, and lost it accordingly; and it is supposed the former would have shared the same Fate if he had not died in Prison.

The Duke of *Orleans* was at first very angry, and shewed great Resentment at the Usage his Friends had met with; but at last he thought fit to fall into the Cardinal's Scheme, and married the Princess that had been judged fit for him. By this Step the Cardinal shewed what the great Lords of the Kingdom were to expect, when he made so little Ceremony of humbling the first Prince of the Blood, and the presumptive Heir of the Crown.

A War breaking out in *Italy*, the Cardinal went thither in Person, commanded the King's Armies in Chief, and the Marshals *Crequi*, *De la Force*, and *Schomberg*, acted under him; it is said he had in View the marching into the Neighbourhood of *Rome*, in Case the Pope, who was then sick, had died, in order to have forced the Cardinals assembled in Conclave, to advance him to that Dignity.

In the mean time a powerful Party was formed at Court against the Minister, of which the Queen was the Head; the Marshal *de Marillac*, his Brother the Keeper of the Seals, the Cardinal *de Berulle*, the Duke *de Bellegarde*, and the Marshal *de Basompiere*, were the principal Persons concerned. The King was at this Time sick at *Lyons*, and in a Council held by these great Men, several Methods were proposed of treating the Cardinal under the new Reign; but the King recovered, and the Minister having exact Information of every Man's Sentiments, to shew the full Extent of his Power, and at the

same

fame time and in the fame Proportion of his Refentment, pu-nifhed every one of them according to his Vote at that Council.

The Marfhal *de Marillac* he put to Death, the Keeper of the Seals loft both his Place and Eftate, the Cardinal *de Berulle* died of Poifon or Grief, the Duke *de Bellegarde* was removed from Court, and Marfhal *Bafompiere* imprifoned in the *Baftile*. This offended the Queen-Mother highly; but the King was fo far from fhewing any Concern for her Refentment, that he fent her Orders to retire to her Houfe; upon which fhe withdrew in Difcontent, and went foon after out of the Kingdom, carrying her favourite Son the Duke of *Orleans* with her.

It was not long before this produced an Infurrection, at the Head of which were the Dukes *de Bouillon* and *Montmorency*; but their Forces were defeated at *Caftelnaudari*, and the latter taken Prifoner. The King then offered his Brother his Pardon for what was paft, but he infifted upon the Pardon of the Duke, which was pofitively refufed. And he was foon after brought to *Thouloufe*, where he was condemned for High Treafon, and the 30th of *September* 1632, loft his Head publickly upon the Scaffold, tho' he was the laft of the Family, which was looked upon as the beft in *France*.

Upon this the Duke *de Bouillon* thought proper to withdraw into *Germany*; and the Queen-Mother, and the Duke of *Orleans*, who had returned again to Court, retired into the *Low Countries*, and put themfelves under the Protection of the Court of *Spain*. I have thrown all thefe Facts together, that the Reader may the better perceive with what inflexible Steadinefs the Cardinal profecuted the fecond Part of his Plan.

We are next to confider the Methods by which the laft Part of his great Project was carried on; and with Regard to this, we are to obferve, that the Cardinal perceiving the great Advantage the Situation of *France* gave him of acting at once againft both Branches of the Houfe of *Auftria*, continued to embarrafs *Spain* by a War in *Italy*, in which feveral of the little Princes of that Country were at all Times ready to offer their Service to *France*; and on the other hand he found Means to diftrefs the Emperor by fupporting the Proteftants in *Germany*, and calling in the King of *Sweden* to their Af-fiftance, at the fame time that he was deftroying them in *France*.

But all this could not be done without maintaining a con-fiderable Force, and acting on many Sides at once, which none of the former Kings of *France* had been able to do; but the Cardinal found Ways and Means to keep up numerous Armies, commanded by Officers entirely depending upon the

King,

King, or rather upon himself, which at the same time that they acted against the Enemies Abroad, kept the Discontented in Awe at Home.

Thus in 1635, when the King declared War against *Spain,* after acting against that Crown for several Years together under Pretence of assisting his Allies, he was obliged to have five Armies in the field, one in the *Low Countries,* another in *Germany,* a Third in *Italy,* a Fourth in *Franche Comte,* and a Fifth in *Roussillon,* besides two Fleets, one under the Command of the Archbishop of *Bourdeaux,* and another under several Officers.

It is very true, that these Fleets were far from being considerable; but however, it is rather wonderful that he had any Fleets, than that they were small; for, in fact, his Father had not so much as a Ship of War. But the Cardinal was the great Spring and Manager of all; he commanded the Armies of *France,* when it was necessary, with the Power of Constable; and he assumed the entire Direction of Naval Affairs, with the Title of Grand-Master in Chief, and Sur-Intendant-General of the Navigation and Commerce of *France.*

As he had thus, under one Title or other, the whole Power of the Kingdom in his Hands, he was the first that shewed the mighty Resources of *France;* and partly by Force, partly by Fraud, sometimes by the Help of numerous Armies, but more frequently by silent Intrigues, he so distressed and weakened both the Emperor and the King of *Spain,* that they saw they were in no Condition of continuing the War; and at the same time found themselves at a Loss how to extricate themselves by a safe and honourable Peace.

In former Times they had been able to create Diversions in *France,* by assisting such Lords as were discontented with the Court; they tried the same Method now, but not with their usual Success: For in the Year 1641, the Count *de Soissons,* a Prince of the Blood, and a most inveterate Enemy to the Cardinal, lost his Life in the Battle of *Sedan,* after he had obtained the Victory; and it is thought was assassinated by a Person employed for that Purpose by the Cardinal.

The Duke *de Bouillon,* who was also engaged in this Affair, retired into the strong Fortress of *Sedan,* of which he was Sovereign, and which in those days was looked upon as impregnable; yet scarce thinking himself in Safety there, upon the King's Approach he came out, and threw himself at his Feet, by which Means he received at that Time his Life, from a well-timed but dissembled Mercy,

But

But the Cardinal practised this Method with such Succcfs, in Favour of *France*, as not only produced immediate and important Effects, but such also as for ever weakened the Power of both those Potentates. Thus, on the Part of *Spain*, *Catalonia* was engaged to revolt, which drew the entire Attention of the *Spanish* Miniftry on that Side, and so made way for the Houfe of *Bragança* to mount the Throne of *Portugal*, and maintain itfelf on the other.

In *Germany*, befides bringing many Princes into a clofe League againft the Emperor, his own moft able and fuccefsful General, Count *Walleftein*, afterwards Duke of *Friedland*, was debauched from his Obedience, and encouraged to think of rendering himfelf Mafter of his native Country of *Bohemia*. And fo many Adventurers at the Head of mercenary Armies were fupported by *France* in the Empire, that the Chief of it knew not how to act ; and all the Members of the *Germanick* Body found themfelves obliged to let *France* dictate the Terms of Peace, which were the fole Contrivance of this Cardinal, tho' it was not till after his Demife, that this fubtil Scheme of his was executed in its full Extent by his Succeffor Cardinal *Mazarin*.

The Part that *Britain* might have taken in fuch a bufy Scene, was doubtful ; and therefore, by way of Prevention, or Precaution, the *Scots* were ftirred up againft King *Charles* I. and encouraged (to revenge the Succours he had given the *Rochellers*) to demand the Protection of *France* againft their natural Prince. This Humour fpreading Southward, produced the Civil War, in which the Cardinal held Intelligence with both Parties (that is, in the Beginning) and by infinuating evil Impreffions of one Side to the other, prevented all Poffibility of Reconciliation, which brought on the End.

In *Italy* and in *Holland*, the fame Methods were purfued ; and the mighty Honours paid by the *French* Ambaffadors to the then Prince of *Orange*, were calculated to kindle thofe Jealoufies and Heart-burnings, that were very near fubverting that Commonwealth. By Arts like thefe, Cardinal *Richelieu* in a very fhort Space of Time intirely changed the Face of Things ; and from overgrown Power, unreafonable Influence, and a kind of univerfal Monarchy, reduced the Houfe of *Auftria* to extreme Weaknefs on one Side, and to a very limited Authority on the other, drew over many of its Allies, and frighted the reft from fhewing any Affection towards that Family. So that we may from hence difcern what vaft Defigns one reftlefs and able Genius can effect, when it has its full Scope and fit Matter to work upon, which was precifely this Minifter's Cafe.

Thefe

These mighty Things performed for the Service of the *French* Monarchy, as well as enlarging the Power of the *King*, though they raised Cardinal *Richelieu* in the Opinion and Esteem of his Master, yet were they very far from gaining his Affection. We have already given the Reader his Character, and from hence it will appear that he was incapable of loving any thing, from the natural Timidity of his Temper; which prompting him to part with his Authority for the Support of his Government, at the same time inclined him to be extremely jealous and suspicious of those to whom he parted with it, though they managed it ever so much to his Advantage.

He had been governed in his Minority, and for some Years after, by the Queen his Mother, whom he treated in the remaining Part of his Reign with great Rigour, not to call it Inhumanity. He made Use of his Favourite the Constable *Luynes* to humble all that had been attached to his Mother, yet he conceived such Envy and Hatred towards him, as was absolutely unbecoming a Prince; for he was wont to complain, *that his Palace was not big enough to hold two Kings.* And when the *English* Ambassador went to confer with the Constable, who acted as Prime Minister, he said to them that were about him, *The Ambassador is gone to take his Audience of the King* Luynes. Nay, when the Constable came into his Presence, with many of the Nobility about him, he shewed his Uneasiness, and the Weakness of his Temper still more, by whispering to some that were near him, *Here comes the Court!*

He was afraid of the Bishop of *Luçon*'s Abilities, because he believed him devoted to his Mother, and on that Account removed him once from his Council; but when he perceived his Ambition was so great, as to extinguish all Sentiments of Gratitude for the Princess who had raised him, he honoured him with his intire Confidence, procured him a Hat from *Rome*, and made him as absolute both in Church and State, as it was possible for him to be.

Yet by Degrees he grew jealous even of him; and as his Power was infinitely superior to that of former Ministers, or to say the Truth, than that of former Kings, he hated him in the same Proportion. The Cardinal, who knew his Master's Temper exactly, and that he could no more be without a Favourite than a Minister, judged it convenient to give him one, a Man of an agreeable Behaviour, and under great Obligations to himself, to prevent a worse Choice.

The Person he pitched upon was M. *Cinquemars*, the Son of the late Marshal *d'Effiat*, whose Fortune he had made, and

of

of whose Fidelity therefore he thought himself secure. But the King corrupted his Favourite, by making him the Confident of his Aversion for his Minister. Besides, the Ambition of the young Man was as boundless as that of the Cardinal; and he had formed in his own Breast such Schemes of Greatness, as he was sensible could not be reconciled to the Views of *Richelieu*. It was natural for him therefore, according to the Policy of Courts, to wish the Destruction of a Minister, whose Power was incompatible with his Hopes.

He was sensible, that notwithstanding his Obligations to him, the King would not be displeased with the Cardinal's Fall; but he was sensible at the same time, that his Master wanted Spirit to accomplish what he desired; and this drove him to think of the desperate Method of depriving *Richelieu* of Life and Fortune at once by an Assassination. He remembered the Fate of the Queen-Mother's Favourite, and that it was the first Step to the Greatness of *Luynes*; and he had himself an Intrigue with a great Princess, whom he had Hopes of marrying, if he once arrived at the Dignity of Constable.

But by a Train of unforeseen Accidents, and that Confusion of Mind, which is natural to Men who are embarked in dark and dangerous Designs, he did not carry this Conspiracy against the Cardinal into Execution, in the Manner he intended; and the Consequence of this was, that in this Season of Delay, the Cardinal came to be informed of all that had been contrived against him.

He did not immediately take that Vengeance which might have been expected from a Man of his Spirit and Resolution, which was in some measure owing to the Circumstances of Affairs, but more to an Indisposition of Body; he kept therefore at a Distance from the Court, took the necessary Precautions for the Security of his Person, and very wisely waited to see what Time would produce.

M. *de Cinquemars*, who could not but perceive the Danger he was in, had recourse for his Security to Measures which ended in his Destruction. He knew that the Duke of *Orleans*, the King's Brother, hated the Minister as heartily as he did; he knew that the Duke *de Bouillon*, and others of the principal Nobility, were of the same Sentiments; he thought therefore if he could engage them in his Party, and draw them into a Treaty with *Spain*, they might make themselves sure of Safety, if not of Success; and in this Design he proceeded farther than in the former, for these great Men came

readily

readily into his Purpofe; and by the Affiftance of Mr. *Fontrailles*, the Treaty with his Catholick Majefty was actually concluded.

The principal Articles of this Treaty were, that the King of *Spain* fhould furnifh *Monfieur* with twelve thoufand Foot, and five thoufand Horfe, fhould fupply him alfo with four hundred thoufand Crowns for levying Soldiers in *France*, and twelve thoufand Crowns a Month towards their Pay. The Duke *de Bouillon* was to have a Penfion of forty thoufand Crowns, and M. *Cinquemars* the fame. The latter communicated the whole State of thefe Affairs to his Friend M. *de Thou*, a Man of great Worth and Probity, who diffuaded him from proceeding on this Scheme, and expreffed a juft Forefight of the dreadful Calamities with which, whatever Turn it took, it muft be inevitably attended.

The Cardinal's withdrawing from Affairs produced many Inconveniencies, which the King quickly perceived, and had Senfe and Penetration enough to difcover that the Ruin of *Richelieu*'s Power would be attended with that of his Authority, of which he was ftill more jealous than of his Minifter: This foon led to a Reconciliation; and the Queen, who hated the Cardinal as much as any of his Enemies, having been informed by the Duke of *Orleans* of fome Part of his Defign, and perceiving it would be attended with difagreeable Confequences to herfelf, in cafe of the King's Death, difcovered all fhe knew to the Cardinal, notwithftanding her Averfion to him. The King was no fooner acquainted with this, than he confidered it in the fame Light the Cardinal wifhed he fhould confider it, as a downright Confpiracy, and tending to a dangerous Rebellion.

The Duke *de Bouillon*, M. *Cinquemars*, and M. *de Thou* were feized; the Vifcount *de Fontrailles* took care to withdraw in Time, and thereby efcaped the Fate of his Friends. M. *Cinquemars*, and M. *de Thou* were condemned, the former for Treafon, and the latter for concealing that Treafon when difclofed to him, to lofe their Heads; and this Sentence was immediately put in Execution. M. *Cinquemars* was not much pitied, but the whole Nation was under a remarkable Concern for M. *de Thou*, who was the Son of the great Prefident of the fame Name, and was thought to have owed his Death to the ill Character defervedly given by the Prefident to the Uncle of the Cardinal, in his admirable Hiftory.

As for the Duke *de Bouillon*, though this was not either his firft or his fecond Offence, yet his Life was fpared upon his furrendering into the King's Hands the Citadel and Principality

pality of *Sedan*, which was his Property, and was a Place of very great Confequence. Thus ended a Confpiracy, which inftead of deftroying either the Perfon or Power of the Cardinal, contributed to the Security of the former, and, if poffible, to the enlarging of the latter, but very plainly to the Eftablifhment of both.

The Year 1642 was alike fatal to the Enemies of the Cardinal *de Richelieu*, and to himfelf. On the third of *July* the Queen Mother, *Mary de Medicis*, breathed her laft at *Cologn*, in the fixty-eighth Year of her Age, having fuffered a long Perfecution, and fpent fome Years in Banifhment, from the unnatural Severity of her Son, and the unrelenting Hate of the Cardinal, though fhe had been a moft tender Mother to the former, and a very kind Miftrefs to the latter, who was indebted to her for his firft Preferments, and for his Introduction to that Power, which with fo much Inhumanity he had exercifed againft her.

On the eleventh of *September* following, *Cinquemars* and *de Thou* loft their Heads at *Lyons*; and on the twenty-ninth of the fame Month *Sedan* was yielded into the King's Hands. Thefe great and happy Turns of Fortune feemed to reprieve the Cardinal from the Grave. He had long languifhed under a painful and dangerous Diftemper, which terminated at length in a Cancer in his Arm, which the Phyficians could not cure, and to the Anguifh which it created they could, with all their Skill, give little or no Relief.

His Strength decayed daily, and with it his Spirits funk fo much, that he was unable to rife; yet he quitted the City of *Lyons* the Day that thofe Gentlemen were executed, and was carried in a Litter on Mens Shoulders to *Fountainbleau*, where the King then was. He came thither in *October*, quitted his Bed, waited on his Majefty with as much Affiduity, and applied himfelf to Bufinefs with as much Vigilance and Activity as ever. But after Six Weeks Refpite his Diftemper attacked him again in fuch a Manner, as left him no Hopes of efcaping.

The King did him the Honour of a Vifit, and expreffed much Concern at the Condition in which he found him; but there is Reafon to doubt of the Sincerity of his Majefty's Grief, fince after the Cardinal's Deceafe, which happened on the fourth of *December* following, he appeared to be very well pleafed on finding himfelf delivered from a Minifter whofe Power he dreaded, and from whom he knew not how to take it away.

A ftronger

A stronger Proof of his Sentiments in this Respect was his setting at Liberty, and recalling to Court, such of the Cardinal's Enemies, as were either imprisoned or banished at the Time of his Demise; such as the Marshals *de Vitry*, *de Basompiere*, *d'Etrees*, and several others; who immediately returned to his Presence, and were well received. Such are the Virtues of some Ministers! and the Gratitude of some Kings!

It was not long that this Monarch enjoyed that Liberty with which he was so much pleased. He had suffered for four Years and upwards by a painful Distemper, which weakened him exceedingly, and which had several times reduced him to the very Point of Death. His bad Habit of Body, and his Neglect of all Regimen, made his Malady absolutely incurable; and the *April* following the Cardinal's Death, the King found his own approaching so hastily, that he thought fit to draw up a Declaration for settling, as far as possible, the Government of the Kingdom after his Decease.

The principal Points of this Declaration were these: That the Queen his Wife should be Regent during the Minority of his Son; that his only Brother, the Duke of *Orleans*, should be the King's Lieutenant throughout the Realm, and President of the Queen's Council, and, in case of his Absence, the Prince of *Condé*. This Council of Regency was to be composed of the Persons before-mentioned, the Duke of *Longueville*, *Julius Mazarin*, (for whom *Richelieu*, a little before his Death, had procured the Cardinal's Hat,) the Chancellor of *France*, the Sur-Intendant of the Finances, and M. *Chavigny*. The King caused this Declaration to be signed by the Queen, and by Monsieur. The Prince of *Condé* and the Chancellor carried it to the Parliament of *Paris*, where it was registered the twenty-first of *April* 1643.

The King survived to the fourteenth of *May*, and then died in excessive Agonies both of Body and Mind. He was chiefly troubled at his unnatural Severity to the Queen his Mother, to whom he had refused Leave to return into *France* when she made him the utmost Submissions, and when he had not the least Reason to apprehend any thing from her Return that could give him the least Uneasiness. He regretted likewise the Rigour of *Richelieu*'s Administration, and the Torrents of Blood that had been shed thereby.

He annexed the County of *Roussillon* to his Kingdom, and inlarged the Royal Authority far beyond its ancient and legal Bounds. This was the great, the distinguishing Characteristick of his Reign, which induced me to take so much Pains to shew in a narrow Compass, how so great a Change was brought about.

Yet

Yet after all that has been said, it can be but imperfectly understood, unless it be more particularly shewn what that Change was, which was thus made.

Before this time the Nobility were potent, and even the meaneſt of the People were in ſome meaſure free ; but at his Deceaſe the Royal Authority had almoſt ſwallowed up all ; and Mens Safeties and Fortunes, as well as Power and Preferment, depended on the Will of the King and his Miniſters. Yet ſuch was the abject Flattery, or rather ridiculous Folly of thoſe Times, that his Subjects beſtowed on him the Sirname of *Juſt* ; as if he had been more careful in obſerving the Laws, and maintaining the ancient and legal Conſtitution of *France*, than any of his Predeceſſors ; whereas in fact, he did more towards deſtroying it, than all the Kings that had reigned before him.

It is true, this did not proceed ſo much from himſelf as from his Miniſter ; but that Miniſter could have done nothing without the Aſſiſtance of his Authority ; and if he had preferred the Welfare of his Subjects to the Poſſeſſion of boundleſs Power, he would never have given into his Schemes. But ſo far was the King from diſapproving the Plan that *Richelieu* had laid down, or deſiring his Projects might be thrown aſide, that he provided to the very laſt, and even by the Declaration which he ſent to the Parliament, for the putting them in Execution, and that in their utmoſt Extent, by giving a Place in the Council of Regency to Cardinal *Mazarin*, the Creature and Diſciple of *Richelieu*, who purſued his Maſter's Inſtructions, if not with equal Genius, yet with much greater Cunning ; ſo that in the Space of thirty-ſeven Years, (for ſo long the Miniſtry of theſe two Cardinals laſted) the Deſign of rendering the Government of *France* (which in former Times reſembled the other Governments of *Europe*) an abſolute Monarchy, was brought to bear, not more to the Oppreſſion and Misfortune of thoſe, who from being Subjects only, were made Slaves thereby, than to the Terror and Confuſion of all *Chriſtendom* ever ſince.

It was thought requiſite to inſiſt longer, and to explain the Events of this Reign the more clearly, becauſe if the Reader will attentively conſider them, he muſt diſcern why *France* is much more formidable to her Neighbours now than ſhe was formerly, when perhaps her real Strength was greater, and with what Reaſon there is ſo much Jealouſy had of her Deſigns beyond thoſe of any other Power. We may likewiſe from the foregoing Account of this extraordinary Reign, deduce *three* Obſervations of the greateſt Conſequence in regard
to

in Government in general, and which ought to be perpetually in the Minds of thofe who defire their Pofterity fhould remain as free as themfelves have been, and confequently to have their own Memoirs revered, as juft Affertors of publick and fteady Liberty.

The *firft* is, That the Perfonal Characters of Princes are not of any great Confequence in altering of Governments. *Lewis* the *Juft* was, in Parts, very far inferior to *Henry* the *Great*, and yet he acquired much more Power by liftening to the Suggeftions of a Minifter who governed him, whereas his Father governed his Minifters as well as his Subjects. There are very great Qualities requifite in a Prince who aims himfelf at overturning a Conftitution ; but paffive Obftinacy is a Quality not hard to be met with, and this conducted by a defigning Minifter will do the Work to the full as well.

Secondly, There is nothing fo dangerous in any limited Monarchy, or mixed State, as fyftematical Adminiftrations, whether they are calculated to introduce Tyranny or defeminate Corruption ; which, in the Body Politick, differ from each other no more than an Inflammation from a Mortification in a natural Body ; that is, the former is more alarming, and the latter more, or at leaft equally, dangerous.

Thirdly, Such Alterations can never be wrought but by an artful Management of *Factions*, which are never fo dangerous to the Freedom of the People, as when they are connived at, and tampered with, by a Court. When the *Phyfician* and the *Difeafe* are agreed, the *Patient*, let his *Conftitution* be ever fo good, cannot *laft* long. But let us return now from Reflections to Hiftory.

Lewis XIV. fucceeded his Father at the Age of Four Years and eight Months, under the Tutelage of his Mother *Anne* of *Auftria*, Daughter of *Philip* III.ᵈ King of *Spain*. His long Reign, the Evennefs and Firmnefs of his Temper, the Variety of Opportunities that offered, and which, generally fpeaking, no Prince knew better how to turn to his own Advantage, enabled him to compleat what his Parent and Predeceffor had begun ; and therefore a juft and comprehenfive Idea of his Reign is abfolutely neceffary, to fuch as are inclined to be thoroughly acquainted with the Political State of *Europe*.

In order to contribute to this as far as is poffible, and yet keep as much within Bounds as fo fruitful and fo extenfive a Subject will allow, we fhall divide the general Reprefentation of this Reign into *five* diftinct Periods ; in each of which we fhall endeavour to point out the *ruling Maxim* that was purfued, the Means that were made ufe of for its

S
Accom-

Accomplifhment, and how far they were or were not attended with Succefs.

Thefe Periods fhall be from the Acceffion of the King in 1643, to the Peace of the *Pyrenees* in 1660 ; from that Peace to the Treaty concluded at *Nimeguen* in 1679 ; from the Peace of *Nimeguen* to that of *Ryfwick* in 1697 ; from the Peace of *Ryfwick* to that of *Utrecht* in 1712 ; from the Peace of *Utrecht* to the Death of *Lewis* XIVth in 1715.

By confidering the Events within thefe five Periods with proper Attention, we fhall be able to difcern how the Government of *France* was entirely modelled into as abfolute a Monarchy as ever exifted ; how the Power of that Crown has gradually increafed at the Expence of its Neighbours, to that formidable Greatnefs which rendered it the Terror of *Europe* at the opening of the prefent Century, and how it efcaped being reduced within reafonable Bounds by a grand Alliance, as happily conducted in the Courfe of the laft general War, as it was wifely concerted in the Beginning of it.

Thefe are Things of fuch Importance, that without a clear and perfect Notion of them, it is fimply impoffible to have any true and well-grounded Conceptions of the prefent State of *Europe*, and the refpective Interefts of its feveral Powers ; much lefs any Degree of Forefight as to future Events, and what the Confequences may be of the Increafe or Decline of the Power and Influence of this ambitious and all-grafping Crown.

We will begin then with a fuccinct Account of what paffed under the Regency of the Queen-Mother, whofe firft and fettled Maxim was to increafe and extend her Authority to the utmoft ; in order to which, fhe employed all the Arts natural to her Sex, to gain the Hearts, or at leaft the Voices of the principal Perfons of the Kingdom, during the laft Illnefs of her Confort ; fo that within four Days after his Deceafe, fhe obtained a Declaration from the Parliament of *Paris*, by which fhe was appointed folely and fimply Regent of the Kingdom during the Minority of her Son. And within four Hours after obtaining this Declaration, which intirely cancelled that of the late King figned by herfelf, and approved by the fame Parliament, fhe placed Cardinal *Mazarin* at the Head of her Council.

As this Minifter conducted the Affairs of *France* with great Variety of Fortune for eighteen Years, and as he is fuppofed to have given his Mafter that Plan of Policy purfued through his long Reign ; and which, for any thing that appears to the contrary, is ftill purfuing ; it will be neceffary to enter more particularly

cularly into his Character, and to shew by what Steps he rose from being a mere Adventurer, without any great Pretences to Family, Credit or Fortune, to the Rank of first Minister in a Kingdom where he was an utter Stranger till the time he was forty Years of Age.

He was by Birth a Gentleman of *Rome* ; his Enemies indeed have disputed this, and his Friends never contended for any thing more. He studied for some time in the University of *Salamanca* in *Spain*, but he neither was nor affected to be thought learned ; while he was at this University he had the Curiosity too common in all Countries, but most so in *Italy* and *Spain*, to have the Figure of his Nativity drawn and judged by a famous Astrologer of those Days, who very positively pronounced that he would one Day become Pope; which shewed his Ignorance, or rather his Fallacy of that pretended Art, by which all who put any Trust in it have been miserably deceived.

He was first the Creature of the House of *Colonna*, into which one of his Nieces afterwards married ; his next Patron was Cardinal *Sachetti*; then he became a Captain of Horse. Being taken notice of by Cardinal *Antonio Barberini*, he laid aside the Military, and assumed the Ecclesiastical Habit. He was made use of as an Agent by the *French* Court in concluding the Peace of *Casal*, which he performed at the Hazard of his Life, when both Armies were in the Field, in Sight, and ready to engage.

This recommended him to Cardinal *Richelieu*, who took him intirely into his Confidence, procured him a Hat from *Rome* at the Recommendation of his Master, and left him much in his good Graces at the Time of his Decease. *Mazarin* had a fine Person, an easy and insinuating Address, was possessed of all genteel Accomplishments, had an Air of Courtesy and Kindness, spoke sensibly of Affairs of Importance, agreeably and pleasantly on all other Topicks. In short, he was an able Statesman and a finished Courtier; but as for Religion, Virtue, Honour, Probity, or Regard for the People, they were (to speak without Envy or Prejudice) things out of his Way ; he did not either pretend to them himself, nor was he suspected of having any Acquaintance with them by others.

The Affairs of *France* were in a very flourishing Condition at the Time the Queen entered upon her Regency ; and her Majesty thought fit to continue the War with great Vigour for many Reasons, particularly for these two ; first, that she might satisfy the Princes of the Blood, and other great Persons in the Kingdom, by bestowing upon them the Command of

Armies;

Armies; the other, that she might keep the *Dutch*, the *German* Princes, and the *Swedes*, closely united to *France*, and thereby find the Enemies of that Crown so much Employment in defending themselves, that they should not either have Temptation or Opportunity to enter into any Intrigues with the Malecontents in *France*.

Her Views met with Success, the Duke *de Anguien*, Son to the Prince of *Condé*, and who afterwards bore himself that Title, gained a great Victory over the *Spaniards*, *May* 18 1643, in the Plains of *Rocroy*, where there were eight thousand killed and seven thousand taken Prisoners; and soon after he made himself Master of the strong Fortress of *Thionville*. The Duke of *Orleans* likewise took *Gravelins* by the Assistance of the *Dutch* Fleet. The Count *du Plessis-Pralin* pushed on the War in *Italy*, and the Duke *de Breze* defeated the *Spanish* Fleet at Sea; but in that famous Engagement lost his Head by a Cannon-shot. In *Germany*, though the Congress was then sitting at *Munster*, the War was carried on with great Vigour, but with various Success; and at home the Cardinal thought fit to remove the Chancellor of *France*, and Mr. *Chavigny* Secretary of State, from the Functions of their respective Offices, and excluded them from Council.

The Viscount *Turenne* having been beat in *Germany*, the Duke *de Anguien* was sent to his Assistance, and had great Success. *Tortenson* at the Head of the *Swedes* having defeated the *Imperialists* in *Bohemia*, struck excessive Terror into that Part of *Germany*, to increase which the Duke *de Anguien* advanced into *Swabia*, and on the third of *August* 1645, defeated Count *Mercy*, near *Nordlingen*, where that General, with near three thousand of his Men, lost their Lives. The Duke then carried his Army into *Flanders*, where he took some, and recovered many other Places; but things going very indifferently on the side of *Spain*, the Duke was recalled, and sent into *Catalonia* with the Title of Viceroy; but from various Accidents he had not the same good Fortune there, which, as things then stood, perhaps did not much displease the Court.

In the Year 1647 the City of *Naples* revolted, and the Duke of *Guise* went thither to put himself at the Head of the Rebels; but in this the Court of *France*, as usual, acted a very double Part, that is to say, they secretly encouraged the Duke in his Enterprize, and openly disavowed any Concern in it; which however was very lucky for him, since the Rebels being defeated in the succeeding Year, and himself made Prisoner, he saved his Life by pretending to be an Enemy to *France*.

In

In the beginning of 1648, the States General of the *United Provinces* concluded at *Munster* a Peace with *Spain*, by which that Crown acknowledged them for an Independent Republick, with which the Court of *France* was very far from being pleased.

The Viscount *Turenne*, assisted by the *Swedish* General *Wrangel*, defeated the *Imperialists* at *Summerhausen* on the seventeenth of *May* 1648, after which they pillaged all *Bavaria*. The Archduke *Leopold* had considerable Success with the *Imperial* Troops in the *Low-Countries*, where he made himself Master of *Lens* and other Places; but the Prince of *Condé* (formerly Duke *d'Anguien*) put a Stop to his Conquests, by defeating his Army near the Place last mentioned, on the 20th of *August* 1648; where the *Imperialists* lost seven thousand Men, thirty-eight Pieces of Cannon, and upwards of an hundred Standards and Colours.

On the twenty-fourth of *October* the same Year, the Treaties of *Westphalia* were concluded, which have been so often mentioned, and by which *France* gained the Sovereignty of *Metz*, *Toul*, and *Verdun*, of which she had been long in Possession, though by no better Title than that of Force. *Alsace* was likewise yielded to her by this Treaty, to the lasting Prejudice of the Empire; which gave up also the important Places of *Brisac* and *Philipsbourg*; so that the *French* were extremely well paid for any Assistance they had given to the Princes and States of *Germany*, in recovering their Liberties and securing their Constitution.

Thus the War ended on this Side as much to their Advantage as they could wish, and much more than they could with any Reason expect; since the Civil Dissentions were again broke out in *France* with more Heat and Fury than had ever happened in the last Reign, as we shall presently see; but the War with *Spain* still continued, tho' for that Reason on the Side of *France*, with very indifferent Success.

The Queen-Mother had hither conducted her Regency with Ease to herself, and Reputation to the Crown. But in 1648 a Party was formed against the Cardinal, in which the Parliament of *Paris* joined with the Prince of *Conti*, and the Princes of the House of *Lorrain*, and carried things to a very great Height; so high indeed, that the Royal Authority, which had been extended beyond all Bounds, was of a sudden strangely curtailed; and the Parliament, assisted by the Princes, began to take upon them the Supreme Authority.

If this had arisen from a real Spirit of Patriotism, or had been conducted by Men who meant well to their Country, it

might

might have been highly advantageous to the Nation; but as the Pretenders to Patriotism were Men as ambitious of Power as the Courtiers, and only took this Method to gain it, the Effects of their Proceedings were so far from being beneficial in any degree to the People, that on the contrary, they turned more to their Prejudice than the very worst Designs of the Court.

The Queen, who was a Princess of great Spirit, and who well remembered how *Richelieu* had supported his Authority, was inclined to follow his Steps; but his Successor *Mazarin* was of a milder Disposition, and knowing that his Adherents wished him no better in their Hearts than the most violent of his Enemies, used, or affected, such Moderation in his Conduct, as raised him many real Friends.

It was by his Advice that the King sent a Declaration to the Parliament, which was verified by them, to abate ten Millions in their Annual Taxes, two Millions in the Excises of *Paris*, and to establish the ordinary Court of Justice, so that no Man could be imprisoned or prosecuted, but by due Course of Law. If the Parliament had been contented with this, and had taken fair and legal Steps for establishing the Government on a just Foundation, Things might have continued to go well; but they were so exalted with their Success, and presumed so much on the Timidity of the Cardinal Minister, that in the Month of *January* following, the People made an Insurrection in *Paris*, and obliged the King, the Queen his Mother, and all the Royal Family, to retire with great Precipitation to St. *Germains*; two Days afterwards the Parliament declared the Cardinal an Enemy to the State, and a Disturber of the Publick Peace; at the same time that they endeavoured to raise an Army to support their Proceedings.

The Queen upon this recalled the Prince of *Condé* with his Army, which blocked up the City, and some Skirmishes happened wherein there was considerable Effusion of Blood. In about six Weeks Time, however, a temporary Pacification ensued; the Prince of *Conti*, and the Duke of *Longueville*, and the other Grandees, had Places given them; a general Pardon was published, and the Cardinal thereby for that Time bought his Peace.

At Bottom, however, the same Jealousies remained, or rather were increased; for the Parliament hated the Prince of *Condé* for having assisted the Queen, and despised the other Princes for deserting them. The Cardinal knowing this, and being sensible that his Authority could never be secure while the Princes of the Blood governed at Court, took this Opportunity,

and

and in the Beginning of the Year 1650, feized and imprifoned the Princes of *Condé*, and *Conti*, and the Duke of *Longueville*; a Meafure fo far from being difliked at *Paris*, that as foon as they heard of it the People made Bonfires in the Streets.

But long before the End of the Year Things came about again; the Nation in general fhewed great Concern for the imprifoned Princes; the Vifcount *Turenne*, with a Body of four thoufand Horfe, attempted to have fet them at Liberty, but fail'd; upon which the Duke of *Orleans*, the King's Uncle, put himfelf at the Head of the difcontented Party, who were diftinguifhed by the Name of the *Frondeurs*, which fignifies literally the *Slingers*, and like moft Party Appellations, ferved only to increafe the publick Confufion, which was already but too great.

The Cardinal finding the Torrent turned, and running violently againft him, fo that he could not avoid quitting the Kingdom, refolved to take a bold Step before his Departure; and accordingly went in Perfon to *Havre*, where the Princes were confined, and having fet them at Liberty, fet out immediately for *Liege*. The People of *Paris* were no fooner informed that the Princes were free, than they lighted Bonfires in the Streets, with as much real Zeal and Sincerity of Heart as they had done on the News of their Confinement.

This Tranfaction happened in *February* 1651, and during that whole Year Things went ftrongly againft the Cardinal, infomuch that the King was forced to publifh a Declaration excluding all Strangers from his Council, and even all *French* Cardinals, as too much addicted to the Pope. But this was fo far from giving Satisfaction, that the Prince of *Condé*, in Conjunction with the Duke of *Orleans* and other Princes of the Blood, proceeded to raife an Army, and to enter into fecret Engagements with *Spain*. The Court upon this feeing no Hopes of an Accomodation, and having more Need than ever of the Cardinal's Advice, refolved to recall him, of which the Parliament being informed, in the Month of *December* following fet a Price upon his Head; tho' in doing this they only fhewed how high on both Sides it was valued.

In the beginning of the fucceeding Year 1652, the Cardinal returned under an Efcort of fix thoufand Men, commanded by the Marquis *de Hocquincourt*, who for this great Service was made Marfhal of *France*. A new Civil War was now opened, and the King, though of Age to govern by himfelf, faw his Capital, and feveral other of the chief Cities in his Kingdom, declare againft him; the Prince of *Condé* had alfo an

Advantage

Advantage over the new Marshal, and if it had not been for the Prudence of the Viscount *Turenne*, now reconciled to the Court, had entirely defeated the King's Troops.

On the second of *July* another Battle was fought, when the Malecontents in their Turn had been totally routed, if the Daughter of the Duke of *Orleans* had not caused the Cannon of the *Baſtile* to be fired upon the King's Troops, and received the Army of the Prince of *Condé* into the City of *Paris*. The King upon this removed the Parliament of *Paris* to *Pontoiſe*, and in *Auguſt* Cardinal *Mazarin* was again so diſtreſſed that he retired a ſecond Time out of the Kingdom.

Things however took another turn towards the latter End of the Year. The Prince of *Condé* and the Duke of *Orleans* quitted *Paris*; the King went thither, the Parliament ſubmitted intirely, and in *February* 1653, the Cardinal returned in Triumph; the King and his Brother went two Leagues out of Town to meet him, the Magiſtrates went in a Body to compliment him, and the People by their Bonfires expreſſed their Joy for his Return. The Prince of *Conti* ſoon after married the Cardinal's Niece, and moſt of the Places that were held for his Brother the Prince of *Condé*, ſurrendered to the King.

On the twenty-eighth of *April* 1654, his Majeſty in Parliament declared that Prince a Rebel, and deprived him of all his Employments. On the ſeventh of *June* following, the King was crowned at *Rheims*, and at the ſame time took a ſolemn Oath never to pardon Duels. The War continued all this Time with *Spain*, and the laſt-mentioned Crown gained ſeveral Advantages, and had gained more if *Cromwell*, who then held the ſupreme Power in *England*, had not, contrary to all the Rules of Policy as well as Juſtice, aſſiſted the *French* both by Land and Sea, ſo much to the Prejudice of the *Ballance* of *Power* in *Europe*, that the Effects of his ill Conduct in this Particular are very ſeverely felt to this Day.

The *Spaniards* finding themſelves in no Capacity of maintaining a War againſt *France* and *England* at the ſame time, willingly liſtened to Propoſitions of Peace, which was concluded on the ſeventh of *November* 1659, and is that which is ſtiled the Peace of the *Pyrenees*; and on the ninth of *June* 1660, *Lewis* the XIVth eſpouſed the Infanta *Maria Thereſa*; in Conſequence of which the Prince of *Condé* obtained his Pardon, the Duke of *Lorrain* was reſtored to his Dominions, and *France* had a fair Proſpect of Quiet at Home and Abroad.

The Duke of *Orleans*, Uncle to the King, died about this Time, as the Cardinal did on the ninth of *March* 1661, leaving behind

behind him a prodigious Fortune to his Family, with this Advice to the King, *that he should never trust any Minister with the like Power*. It is certain he pursued steadily, though in a very different Manner, the Scheme of his Predecessor, but did it notwithstanding with the same Success. His Genius was exactly suited to the Times and the Circumstances of his Ministry. With this Disposition *Richelieu* had quickly been undone; and with *Richelieu*'s Temper *Mazarin* would have certainly ruined himself, and perhaps the Court also. Thus ended this Period.

The King was now in the twenty-third Year of his Age; and though he had not discovered in his Youth, either a strong Inclination or great Capacity for Learning, yet his Education had neither been neglected, as some have written, nor, as others have suggested, was the Care taken in this respect thrown away upon the King, whose Parts, if they were not quick, were however solid, and whose Want of some little Scholastic Accomplishments was abundantly supplied by the Evenness of his Temper, and the Strength of his Judgment.

The Cardinal observing the Weakness of his Constitution while a Child, was more careful of his Health, than of his Studies; and as that grew more confirmed, he caused him to be taught his Exercises, which he performed very gracefully, as he had a very fine Person. As he grew up, the Cardinal took Care to instruct him by his Conversation, to make him well acquainted with the Affairs of the Kingdom, and with the true Characters of all the considerable Persons in it; of which his Majesty was very capable, had naturally a Turn to Business, and could apply himself to it with Diligence, and transact it with all the Dignity becoming his Rank. He had a great Deference for that Minister, and the more so, perhaps, because he inspired him with a Diffidence for every body else.

Before the Death of the Cardinal, his Majesty was not so much considered as he ought to have been. The old Courtiers addicted themselves to that Minister, and to the Queen Mother; the younger ones applied themselves to the Sur-Intendant of the Finances, Mr. *Fouquet*, a Man of lively as well as great Abilities; and who flattered himself with the Hopes of succeeding the Cardinal, tho' he had declared himself pretty openly against him, and had engaged in some Intrigues that were afterwards fatal to him.

The King began his Administration with removing that Minister; and he did it with some Circumstances that were

only

only excufable in a young Man, that is to fay, he careffed him exceedingly to render him fecure, and went in Perfon to *Nantes* at the Time he was arrefted, as if that had been an Affair of Importance or Difficulty. The Queen-Mother was drawn to confent to this by a Lady who was much in her Favour; but fhe very foon repented it, for the King allowed her little or no Share in the Management of Affairs afterwards, tho' he treated her always with much Decency and Refpect.

Mr. *Colbert*, who, as himfelf affirmed, was of *Scots* Extraction, and a Creature of the late Cardinal's, fucceeded him in the Adminiftration of the Finances, with the Title of Comptroller-General, the Sur-Intendant being fuppreffed. This Man had great Parts, and a moft extenfive Genius: he perfectly underftood the King's Humour, and flattered it; he put him upon making himfelf abfolute in the utmoft Senfe of the Word; by his Advice he took from the Parliament of *Paris* all Power, but that of regiftering his Edicts, againft which they were for fome time allowed the Liberty of remonftrating after they were regiftered; but of this they were by Degrees deprived.

Thefe, and fome other Steps of a like Tendency, were taken at a Time of all others the moft favourable that could be wifhed for the King's Purpofes; there were few of the great Lords in *France* that retained any thing of their former Power; the Prince of *Condé* was but juft pardoned, and had Reafon to avoid reviving the Memory of paft Offences; the King's Brother, now Duke of *Orleans*, who had married the Princefs *Henrietta* of *Great Britain*, was young, and much addicted to his Pleafures, fo that there was no body left to oppofe the Defigns of the Court; and they were carried fo luckily, that the oppofing them became very foon totally impracticable.

The three Minifters then at the Head of Affairs were *le Tellier*, *Colbert*, and *de Lionne*, who had Addrefs enough, while they governed all Things, to perfuade their Mafter that they had nothing at Heart but the complete Execution of the Plan of the two Cardinals, which confifted in making their Countrymen Slaves, and extending the Power, or at leaft the Influence of their Mafter over all *Chriftendom*.

The King bought of *Charles* II. King of *Great Britain* the Port of *Dunkirk*, which the Cardinal had been forced to deliver up to *Cromwell*, the Importance of which was not well known, or at leaft confidered by the *Englifh* Court. This did not hinder *Lewis* XIV. from taking part with the *Dutch*

in

In the War they were engaged in againft *England*, and he did it with a View of weakening the Maritime Powers, having at that Time formed Defigns againft them both ; and in this he was but too fuccefsful ; for while they were ruining each other's Fleets, he was raifing and increafing his, which became quickly more confiderable than it had ever been under any of his Predeceffors.

In the Spring of the Year 1667, while this War continued, he fell very unexpectedly, as well as (the World thought) very unjuftly, upon the *Spanifh Low-Countries*, under Pretence of maintaining the Rights of his Queen, and took a great many ftrong Towns in a very fhort Space of Time. This effectually opened the Eyes of the *Englifh* and *Dutch*, who very foon compromifed their Differences by the Treaty of *Breda*, and quickly after concluded the famous Triple Alliance (the Crown of *Sweden* making the third Power) with a View of fetting Bounds to *France*.

This was indeed the wifeft and moft effectual Step that was taken for that Purpofe, in as much as the Allies declared roundly to the *French* Court, that they were refolved to take Part in the War againft her, if it was not fpeedily concluded by a fair and equal Peace. This well-timed and well-concerted Declaration produced the Treaty of *Aix-la-Chapelle*, which was concluded the 2d of *May* 1668, by which *France* gave up the *Franche Comte* which fhe had conquered, but fhe kept fome large Diftricts in the *Low-Countries*, and feveral Cities and Towns of great Importance ; fuch as *Namur*, *Charleroy*, *Aeth*, *Doway*, *Tournay*, *Lifle*, and many others.

But not long after the Conclufion of the Treaty, this Prince found Means to diffolve the Triple Alliance, and to engage the *Englifh* Court in a Defign of entirely deftroying the *Dutch* ; which was brought about, by his fending over the Duchefs of *Orleans*, who perfuaded her Brother King *Charles* the Second into it, and who at her Return to *France*, was poifoned in a Fit of Jealoufy by her Hufband, notwithftanding which, the Defign was ftill carried on by the two Crowns againft the *States*.

It broke out in the Spring of 1672, and in the Month of *May*, the King paffed the *Maefe* at the Head of one hundred thoufand Men, and pufhed the *Dutch* within a Hair's breadth of Deftruction by Land, while the *Englifh* with the fame unrelenting Fury attacked them by Sea. The generality of Hiftorians very falfly afcribe the Misfortune of that Republick to the ill Conduct of their famous Penfionary *John de Witte*, becaufe he had formerly drawn the *States* into a clofe Conjunction
with

with *France*; but in that he did no more than the Circumstances of the Times obliged him to; and if his Masters had been advised by him, and begun the War first, by burning the vast Magazines which the *French* King had raised at *Nuys*, and other Places in the Territories of *German* Princes, which it was in their Power to have done, all the Disasters that afterwards happened had been prevented, and they had gained Time enough to have provided for their own Defence. As it was, the Misfortunes of his Country proved fatal to that great Minister, who was barbarously torn, or at least murdered and cut to Pieces by the Mob.

The *French* King pushed on his Conquests as far as *Utrecht*, in which City he fixed his head Quarters; but the Prince of *Orange*, who was then very young, being put at the Head of the Army of the *States*, defended their Dominions so well, that their Allies had Time to come to their Relief, and the Parliament of *England* forced the King to make Peace with them, which soon altered the Face of Affairs.

But as the Emperor and *Spain* had declared in favour of the *Dutch*, the War was carried into their Territories, and a great many Places of Consequence were taken, several Battles fought; and the War had lasted longer, if the Parliament of *England* had not obliged the King to think in earnest of assisting the *Dutch*; this induced *France* to incline to Peace, which was negociated at *Nimeguen* under the Mediation of *England*; but the *French* and *Dutch* clapping up a separate Treaty on the 10th of *August* 1678, the Ministers of the mediating Power refused to sign it.

The Prince of *Orange* also being exceedingly displeased with this hasty Proceeding, fought the Battle of *Mons*, in hopes of frustrating the Peace, or of dissolving it in case it was signed; but the *French* were too wise for that, and so the Allies of the *Dutch* were forced to come in upon such Terms as they had stipulated, which were none of the best; for the Town and Territory of *Ypres*, the Town and District of *Menin*, the Towns and Dependencies of *St. Omer*, *Aire*, *Cambray*, &c. *Dinant* in the Bishoprick of *Liege*, and the whole *Franche Comte*, were given up to *France*, as was also the Town and Citadel of *Fribourg*, and in Effect, the whole Duchy of *Lorrain*.

Thus we are come to an End of the second Period; in which the Reader will perceive, that the Power of *France* was prodigiously augmented, and thereby the Terror of its Neighbours justly increased, all which was chiefly owing to that arbitrary Government which *Lewis* XIV. had introduced: From whence it appears, that Tyranny is scarce a greater Misfortune

to

to the State in which it prevails, than to its Neighbours, and consequently a Tyrant is not only an Enemy to his own Subjects, but also to Mankind in general. We need not therefore wonder, that henceforward the *French* King was generally distinguished by the Name of the *Common Enemy*, since it is plain he merited that Appellation.

The Character of Mr. *Colbert*, so far as was necessary in a Work of this kind, has been already given, but it is requisite for us now to speak of that of his Rival Mr. *de Louvois*. The former had given the King that Turn which proved destructive of the *French* Liberty, and this perhaps chiefly to secure his own Power; for he easily foresaw, that if the Princes of the Blood and the great Nobility came to have any Share in the Government, it would be very difficult, if not impossible, for him to preserve himself; and thus the *Interests* of a *whole Nation* were sacrificed to those of a *single Man*.

The latter however went far beyond him; he was Secretary of State and of War, and had great Abilities in his Office; but as those Abilities were of no Use in Time of Peace, he determined that during his Life there should be no such Thing; and he had so much Power over his Master, that he carried his Point. And thus the *Quiet* of all *Europe* gave way to *one* Man's *Convenience*.

The Method he took was very extraordinary. Under Pretence of settling the Limits of those Countries, which by the Treaty of *Nimeguen* were to be divided between the Kings of *France* and *Spain*, the former laid claim to whole Provinces, and tore away no fewer than forty Villages from the latter at once. Soon after Chambers of Reunion, as they were called, were set up at *Metz* and *Brisac*, and vast Countries were taken from their legal Owners, under Pretence that they were dependent upon Places yielded to *France* by the Treaties of *Munster* and *Nimeguen*.

As these outrageous Proceedings, of which every honest Man in *France* was ashamed, were carried on with Success; the *French* boldly seized *Strasbourg*, and blocked up *Luxembourg*, which they afterwards besieged and took, without any Declaration of War, as well as without any Colour of Right. The Prince of *Orange* indeed would have stirred to prevent this, but the *States* were afraid; and the Emperor and Empire were at that Time incapable of resisting this barefaced Injustice. *Spain* was in as low a Condition; and as for *England*, it was at this Time torn by Factions, and the Court so closely united to that of *France*, that no Good could be expected from it.

At

At the fame time that *Louvois* facrificed the Peace of *Europe* to his own Intereft and his Mafter's Ambition, he from the fame Principle, and to gratify the King's Paffion for Building, promoted fuch Expences, as made Taxes as heavy in Time of Peace as of War. The Palace of *Clagni* was built to gratify Madame *de Montefpan*, *Marly* for the Pleafure of Madame *de Maintenon*; but thefe were Trifles in Comparifon to the Palace built to pleafe the King himfelf, who delighted in rendering Defarts beautiful, and in having Abundance of Fountains in a Place to which Nature had denied Water.

In fhort, inftead of the Dignity and Magnificence of an *European* Prince, *Lewis* XIV. affected the Pomp, the Luxury, the devouring Profufion of an *Afiatick* Monarch; and his Grand Vizir *Louvois* took care to accommodate him in fuch Manner, that the Expence of his Palace and his Houfhold, with the Troops conftantly about him, were alone fufficient to impoverifh his Kingdom. And thus to render himfelf fomewhat more than a King, he degraded his Subjects into downright Slaves: Such was the *boafted* Eclat of LEWIS the GREAT, and fuch the *real* Merits of his fo much magnified *Minifters!*

But perhaps the worft is yet to come. We have fhewn, that the Conftable *Luynes* projected the Fall of the Proteftants, which was profecuted by *Richelieu*, as his Scheme was followed by *Mazarin*; but *Louvois* out-did them all; for he projected and executed the deteftable Defign of their Extirpation, which was begun by dragooning them into Apoftacy, and compleated by the Revocation of the Edict of *Nantz*, on the 22d of *October* 1684, the moft open and fcandalous Breach of Faith that was ever committed.

As unjuft and inhuman as this Action was, confidered in the Light of a religious Perfecution, it fell every way fhort of the Imprudence thereof, when confidered in the Light of an Act of State, and therefore did equal Injury to its Authors in their Characters, as Men of Rank and Confideration in the Court of the moft Chriftian King, and as Politicians of great Penetration, and Minifters of long Experience; for by this means there were eight hundred thoufand Perfons driven out of the Kingdom, and forced to take Shelter in foreign Countries, which, tho' in itfelf a prodigious Weakening to the State, yet was much more fo, from the Temper and Employments of the Perfons thus expelled, who were, for the moft Part, Merchants, Manufacturers, or Officers of a middle Rank in the Land and Sea Service; and, in a Word, the moft induftrious and ufeful People in the Kingdom.

We

We may eafily conceive from hence, that the Trade and Manufactures of *France* fuffered extremely, and we fhall have a clearer Notion of the Mifchiefs flowing from this impolitick Step, when we are told that thefe People carried out of the Kingdom, one hundred Millions of *French* Livres, or five Millions Sterling in ready Money, Plate and Jewels. Yet grofs and apparent as this Error was, fuch was the Meannefs and Servility of the *French* Nation, that the King was complimented upon it, as on the moft glorious Action of his Reign.

The Minifters however who contributed to exalt the King, in Point of abfolute Authority, fo much above his Predeceffors, were far from enjoying, without Difquiet, the Power they exercifed, and the Wealth they had amaffed. *Colbert*, the ableft, and, to do him Juftice, the beft of them, was fo much chagrined at fome ill Ufage he met with from his Mafter, that it broke his Heart ; and when a Letter from the King, written in a Fit of ill-timed Tendernefs, was brought him in his laft Moments, he refufed to read it.

By his Death *Louvois* expected to become entirely Mafter of the Court, but he was miftaken ; for Madame *de Maintenon*, who from the Widow of the Poet *Scarron*, and the Servant of Madame *de Montefpan*, was become the Miftrefs, and by a private Marriage the Wife of the King, hated him, and therefore brought into Bufinefs the Marquis *de Seignelaie*, the Son of *Colbert*, a young Man of no great Abilities, proud, vain, and debauched, who had the Title of Secretary of State, and the Affairs of the Houfhold and Marine committed to his Charge.

He had Wit enough to fee that his Competitor made himfelf neceffary to his Mafter, by embroiling him with his Neighbours, and gratifying his Paffion for Building ; he therefore refolved to take the fame Courfe, and employed immenfe Sums to render *France* a Maritime Power ; and that this might more clearly be demonftrated to all *Europe*, he engaged the King to pick a Quarrel with the State of *Genoa*, which gave this Minifter an Opportunity of going in Perfon with a Fleet, which threw into that fine City ten thoufand Bombs, and obliged the Republick to fend her Doge to afk Pardon at *Verfailles* of the proud Monarch, that conceived himfelf injured. By this Step the young Minifter raifed his Credit confiderably, which fo tormented *Louvois*, that it is believed he afterwards caufed him to be poifoned, though he did not enjoy above a Year the Satisfaction of feeing himfelf without a Rival.

There

There never was a Man of a more fierce and brutal Behaviour, or one whose personal Qualities did more Mischief to a State. His Pride induced him to treat with equal Insolence the Princes of the Blood at Home, and Sovereign Princes Abroad, even those who were nearest allied to the Crown of *France*.

He kept the Dauphin at a Distance from the Court, and in a State of Subjection scarce to be believed ; he took a Pleasure in persecuting the Prince of *Condé*, the Prince of *Conti*, the Duke of *Vendosme*, and his Brother the Grand Prior ; he took Advantage of his own Crimes to erect a Chamber of Poisons, or a particular Court of Justice to enquire after all who were suspected of such Practices ; by which he drove several great Persons from Court, and sent the Duke of *Luxembourg*, a Man of the greatest Quality in *France*, and one of her ablest Generals, to the *Bastile*.

He disobliged the Elector of *Bavaria* to such a Degree, that he became an Enemy to his Master, notwithstanding the Dauphin had married his Sister. His Haughtiness to the Duke of *Savoy* had the same Effect. He persuaded the King to treat the Court of *Rome* with the utmost Indignity. By refusing a Troop of Horse to Prince *Eugene*, he forced into the Service of the Enemies of *France* one of the greatest Captains of his Age ; and he sacrificed the unhappy King *James* II. partly to private Malice, and partly to his Ambition.

When the Prince of *Orange* was preparing to invade *England*, *Lewis* XIV. was advised to fit out a Fleet to obstruct his Passage, and to order his Troops to besiege *Maestricht*, *Louvois* prevented both ; he kept the *French* Navy, which was then more powerful than ever it was, or is like to be, in Port ; and he directed the Army to besiege *Philipsbourg*, which brought the Emperor and Empire into the War against *France*. I have thrown these Things together, that the Character of this Minister, or rather the Court of *France* under his Ministry, might be seen at one View.

The Conduct of the *French* Court, which produced this War, was so glaringly wrong and absurd, that it raised in a manner all *Europe* against her, and this entirely through her own Fault, without Reason and without Provocation. So that such as have represented the Policy of the *French* as very great and very refined, are undoubtedly mistaken ; for in the first place, the long Series of Injuries offered to the Emperor and Empire, were such, as must necessarily incline them to be revenged.

The

The *Dutch* had been wantonly attacked in the laſt War, and thereby rendered implacable; the Uſage given the King of *Spain* was intolerable; and the Meaſures ſuggeſted to the King of *Great Britain* not only coſt him his Crown, and thereby loſt *France* her moſt uſeful Ally, but warmly excited againſt her the whole *Britiſh* Nation; ſo that the War begun in 1688, might juſtly be ſtiled raſh and imprudent, and commenced rather thro' Haughtineſs than Policy.

It was managed alſo with great Indiſcretion; for as *England* was given away by the *French* not attacking the *Dutch* in time, ſo *Ireland*, after the War began, was loſt for want of proper Attention; and the War with *Savoy* was merely made to pleaſe Monſieur *Louvois*, and yet proved as troubleſome to *France* as any in which ſhe ever engaged.

It is true, that the Armies of *Lewis* XIV. were ſucceſsful in the *Low-Countries*; the Battle of *Fleurus*, which was ſought the firſt of *July* 1690, gained Marſhal *Luxembourg* great Reputation; and the taking of *Mons* after eighteen Days open Trenches, was very ſatisfactory to the *French* King, who commanded that Siege in Perſon; but theſe Advantages were very dear bought, and the King himſelf became very ſoon ſenſible of it. He owed this laſt Conqueſt, the greateſt in which he had perſonally any Share, to the Vigilance and ſurprizing Talents of *Louvois*, who underſtood the providing and ſupplying a great Army, the beſt of any Man in the World.

Yet the taking this City has by many been judged the Cauſe of his Death; for the King having been informed, that he attributed all to himſelf, was much diſpleaſed at it; and finding that he had rejected without his Knowledge the moſt ſubmiſſive Propoſitions from the Duke of *Savoy*, he expreſſed his Reſentment in ſuch ſtrong Terms, that the Miniſter went Thunder-ſtruck from his Preſence, and died immediately of Grief and Deſpair; tho' others ſay, that his Phyſician, *Seron*, was brib'd to furniſh him with a Paſſport for the other World, by a Prince I need not name.

However it was, his Death proved a very great Loſs to his Maſter, who brought his Son the Marquis *de Barbeſieux* into Power, tho' he was young, headſtrong, and had very mean Abilities. In the Year 1692, *Lewis* XIV. commanded in Perſon in the *Low-Countries*, and took *Namur*; and on the 3d of *Auguſt* the ſame Year, the Duke of *Luxembourg* obtained ſome Advantage over King *William* at *Steinkirk*; but to ballance theſe Advantages, the Duke of *Savoy* entered *France*, and took *Ambrun*; and the *French* Fleet was not able to look that of the Allies in the Face.

T

In

In 1693, he was more fuccefsful; the Duke of *Luxembourg* gained the Battle of *Nerwinde*, and feveral Places were taken in the *Low-Countries*. Marfhal *Catinat* entirely defeated the Duke of *Savoy*; but the Fleets of the Allies were victorious, and infulted all the Sea-Coafts of *France*.

In 1694, they did the fame, and had alfo confiderable Advantages in the *Low-Countries*. In 1695, *France* was fo exhaufted, that the King was forced to have recourfe to a general Poll-Tax, the moft grievous Impofition that any Country ever endured; and yet the War went on very indifferently for him; the important Fortrefs of *Namur* being reduced by King *William*, while Marfhal *Villeroy* looked on with a fuperior Army.

The next 1ear was not more fortunate; a Defign formed for reftoring King *James* mifcarried. *France* was reduced to act upon the Defenfive in the *Low Countries*, and at the fame time increafed her Taxes exceffively; fo that at the Clofe of the Year, the King found himfelf under an abfolute Neceffity of liftening to Peace, his Finances being entirely exhaufted. And accordingly a Treaty was concluded at *Ryfwick*, on the 20th of *September* 1697, whereby he gave up great Part of his Acquifitions, which was a plain Indication of the Senfe the King had of his own Weaknefs, which was chiefly owing to the great Faults in his Government.

His old Minifters and his old Generals being worn out, he fupplied the Places of the former by young Men, whofe only Merit was a blind Submiffion to his Will; they had boundlefs Power in their refpective Departments; and though nothing was more vifible, than that his Affairs fuffered exceedingly for want of a Perfon capable of fuperintending the whole; yet his Vanity was fo great, that tho' he plainly faw this, he could not bear the Thoughts of appointing a Prime Minifter.

His Generals were promoted by Court Intrigues, and the Favour of Madame *Maintenon*, who governed him entirely. His Naval Force, as it was raifed fuddenly, fo it funk as unaccountably, chiefly for want of Money to maintain it; his Armies were ruined, his Subjects exhaufted, and the Credit of *France* was entirely fupported by the Remembrance of that Power that was now in a great Meafure decayed. Such was the State of Things at the Clofe of this Period.

It might naturally be expected, that confidering the Situation of his Affairs after the Treaty of *Ryfwick*, *Lewis* XIV. fhould have contrived the moft effectual Means for eafing his Subjects, by improving his Country, and leffening the Expence of his Government; he did however quite the contrary, he kept up as

great

groat an Army in the Time of Peace, as would have been neceffary if the War had continued ; and he employed his Troops
in forming Camps of Pleafure, for the Inftruction of his Grand-
Children, as if the Art Military had been the fole Science
worthy of a Prince.

By thefe Methods, or rather Follies, he ruined the Officers,
from the prodigious Expence they were put to, and at the fame
time alarmed his Neighbours, who could not conceive that he
had no other Meaning in thefe Incampments than to wafte Money, and exhibit gaudy Spectacles to pleafe Boys. It is without
Queftion a deep Stroke in Politicks, to lull all the neighbouring
States into a profound Security, while a great Defign is in Contrivance, which might be eafily difconcerted if fufpected, and
fo bring the Difcovery and Decifion to the World's View at once.
But wantonly to alarm, and out of pure Vanity to keep all *Eu-*
rope in a Ferment, was the moft effectual Means to produce an
Oppofition greater than could otherwife arife ; and accordingly
it did produce a Confederacy, which fufficiently chaftifed that
Imprudence which gave Birth to it.

King *William*, from a fincere Concern for the Peace of
Europe, formed a Project for dividing the *Spanifh* Dominions,
to which the *French* King confented ; and this firft Treaty
of Partition was figned *October* 1, 1698, at the *Hague*, between the Kings of *Great Britain* and *France*, and the *States-*
General ; whereby it was agreed, that the Kingdom of *Naples*
and *Sicily*, the Places poffeffed by the *Spaniards* on the Coaft
of *Tufcany*, the Marquifate of *Final*, the Province of *Guipufcoa*,
the Towns of *Fontarabia* and St. *Sebaftian*, with Port *Paffage*,
fhould be given to the *Dauphin* ; the Duchy of *Milan* to the
Emperor's fecond Son, the Archduke *Charles* ; and all the
reft of the *Spanifh* Monarchy to the Electoral Prince of
Bavaria.

In a few Months after, this young Prince died at *Bruffels*, in
the feventh Year of his Age, which made a fecond Treaty of Par-
titition neceffary, by which laft Treaty, *Milan* was added to the
Dauphin's Share, upon Condition that it fhould be exchanged
for *Lorrain*, and the whole *Spanifh* Monarchy was given to the
Archduke *Charles*. This Treaty was figned the 13th of *March*
1699, and was fo unlucky as to give Satisfaction to nobody.

The Emperor refufed to accept it, the King of *Spain* was
extremely offended at it, and the *Englifh* Nation fell upon the
King's Minifters, though they knew that the whole Tranfaction
arofe from, and was conducted by the King himfelf. To fay
the Truth, it was a Project the beft calculated for fecuring the
Ballance of Power, and eftablifhing the Quiet of *Europe*, that

the Circumstances of Things would admit; and the Clamour against it was as *ill founded*, as the Opposition to it was managed with *ill Manners*.

The King of *Spain*, to prevent the Execution of this Treaty, and the dismembering of his Dominions, on the 2d of *October* 1700, signed a Will, by which he called to the Succession of the whole *Spanish* Monarchy, *Philip* Duke of *Anjou*, second Son to the *Dauphin*, after him his younger Brother the Duke of *Berry*, next the Archduke *Charles*, and then the Duke of *Savoy*, and died about a Month after. It was a great Question at the Court of *France*, whether the Will should be accepted, or whether his Majesty should adhere to the last Treaty of Partition; but at length a Resolution was taken to accept the Will, and the Duke of *Anjou* was declared King of *Spain*, by the Name of *Philip* V. in which it has been thought by some who take the Liberty of censuring even Kings, *Lewis* XIV. forgot his Duty as the Parent of his People, to follow his natural Affection as the Father of his Family.

King *William* and the *States* dissembled at first, by acknowledging and complimenting King *Philip*; but this seems to have been owing to the Nature of the Government in both Countries, which made it necessary to be secure of the Sentiments of the People, before their Rulers openly declared their own; and to speak my private Opinion freely, I believe this Conduct in their respective Governments, had no small Share in bringing the *English* and *Dutch* Nations to declare so warmly as they did for a War with *France*, into which their Governors very readily came, upon a Supposition that they should be supported therein with the same Unanimity and Spirit, by which they were excited thereto; and for some time they were not disappointed. Thus the Reader sees in a very narrow Compass, the true Grounds of that general War, which had so great an Effect on the Affairs of *Europe*, and which are so necessary to be thoroughly understood at present, in order to form a right Judgment of what we ought to hope or fear.

The World seems to be so universally persuaded of the great Wisdom and Policy of *Lewis* XIV. in laying his Schemes for securing the Crown of *Spain* to his Family, that it will be a very difficult Thing to persuade them, that this Notion is ill-founded; but the Truth will appear, from an impartial Consideration of Facts, which I shall endeavour to lay together in the succinctest Method possible; it being not either agreeable to my Purpose or Intention, to enter into a

particular

particular Detail of the War, which is too well known to need any such Account.

It must be acknowledged, that the Measures taken by the *French* King for putting his Grandson into immediate Possession of the extensive Dominions of the *Spanish* Monarchy, were well concerted and thoroughly executed. The Marquis *de Villars*, the *French* Ambassador at *Madrid*, had gained the Hearts of the *Spanish* Grandees ; the Prince of *Vaudemont*, and the rest of the Governors of the Provinces in *Italy*, were secured ; the Duke of *Savoy* having married one Daughter to the Heir Apparent of *France*, and another to the new King of *Spain*, could not avoid taking the same Side ; as for the *Low-Countries*, they were delivered up by the Elector of *Bavaria*, who had formed a strong Party for the *French* in *Germany*.

But still the Mischiefs remained that have been before mentioned ; that is to say, the several Branches of the Ministry were in the Hands of young Men of very mean Abilities ; and the Direction of the whole was in an old Lady, opposed and hated by the whole Royal Family, the King excepted. He had few General Officers of great Capacity, and those he had were not employed, and if employed, not trusted. His Marine was in a bad Condition, his Finances in a worse, and nothing but his absolute Power of taking every Shilling of Ready-Money from his Subjects, by altering the Value of his Coin, which he practised over and over with as little Ceremony as Conscience, could have enabled him to find wherewithal to defray those Expences ; for which it was impossible for him to run in Debt ; and through the whole Course of the War he defrayed no other.

As soon as the Grand Confederacy was formed, he saw many Courts act a very different Part from what he expected. As for Instance, *Sweden* entered into a Neutrality, *Denmark* and *Prussia* acted against him, nor was it long before his most useful and necessary Allies, such as the King of *Portugal* and the Duke of *Savoy* deserted him, and all his Schemes were broken.

The Duke of *Marlborough*, by the Victory of *Blenheim*, restored the Affairs of the Emperor and Empire ; he was so distressed in *Italy*, that he was glad to evacuate it to save *Spain*, and even there his Grandson was more than once driven from his Capital. In the *Low-Countries*, his Armies were continually beaten, all his strong Fortresses taken, and among the rest *Lisle*, the most valuable Place in his Dominions, after *Paris*, which, will Posterity believe it ! he once had Thoughts of quitting.

On

On the whole, after carrying on the War for feven Years, he found his Affairs in fo bad a Situation, that he would very gladly have accepted the Treaty of Partition, or even worfe Terms, if the Allies would have confented to them ; but all his Offers being rejected, the Defpair of his Subjects did more for him than he was able to do at firft with all his Policy and Power ; and yet it is very queftionable whether the Crown of *Spain* would ever have been left to his Grandfon, if the Death of the Emperor *Jofeph* had not rendered it a Thing difficult for the Allies to know where to beftow it better.

This produced the Peace of *Utrecht*, in which all that was either good or tolerable was copied from the two Treaties of Partition. It was figned in *March* 1712-13 ; and if the Allies had been unanimous in making it, might have been much better than it was ; but the Emperor perfifting in his Refufal, the War was ftill carried on againft him, and did not end till the Year afterwards, by the figning of the Peace of *Baden*, on the 7th of *June* 1714.

Thus ended this Period, when *France* was reduced far lower than fhe had ever been ; for not only her Armies were broken, her Fleets entirely ruined, and a great part of her former Conquefts yielded to other Powers ; but what was much worfe, the People were fallen into the moft abject Degree of Mifery, the Credit of the Crown was funk, the Succeffion depended upon the Life of a fickly Infant, the reigning Monarch was very infirm, and the Court divided into Factions : So that if *Lewis* XIV. had the Satisfaction of beholding the Rife and Progrefs of the *Gallic* Power, he had alfo the Mortification of feeing it decline, and was very, very, near looking upon its Ruin.

The Cares of *Lewis* XIV. after the Conclufion of the Peace, were fuch as ought to have been the Cares of his whole Life ; for they were bent to fecure the Succeffion of the Royal Family, and to reftore the Trade and Welfare of his Subjects ; as to both which he appeared now very follicitous ; nor did he make any Scruple of confeffing, that Experience had convinced him of the Error of his former Conduct, and the Follies of which he had been guilty, in preferring his own Grandeur to the Good of his People, and the Luftre of his Reign to the Safety of the State.

He gave all the Affiftance that was requifite to his Grandfon *Philip*, for extinguifhing the Remains of the *Spanifh* War, by the Reduction of *Catalonia*; he gave Satisfaction to the King of *Great Britain*, in reference to the Ports of *Dunkirk* and *Mardyke* ; and he executed very punctually whatever depended
pended

pended upon him in relation to the *Dutch*, from the Hopes of leaving *France* without any Apprehensions from her Neighbours at the Time of his Decease. He was very attentive also to what he thought might contribute to the domestick Quiet of his Subjects, as well as to the Establishment of his illegitimate Offspring.

In regard to the former, he constituted by his Will a Council of Regency, on purpose to exclude the Duke of *Orleans*, his Nephew, whose Fidelity he suspected, and of whose Ambition he was afraid: and he caused this Will of his to be deposited with the Parliament of *Paris*, who gave it the Sanction of that very small Authority which he had left them. He likewise caused an Edict to be registered, whereby he declared his Sons, the Duke of *Maine* and Count *Thoulouse*, Legitimate, and capable of succeeding to the Crown after those legally entitled thereto: And having thus put both his publick and private Affairs into Order, he did not seem much surprized at the Approach of Death.

In his last Moments he behaved like a Christian and a King; like a Christian in bewailing his Vices, and the bad Consequences with which they had been attended; like a King, in advising his Successor publickly to beware of following his Example, to study Peace, and to be truly the Parent of his People. In this Disposition of Mind, after enduring the sharpest Agonies in his Body, he expired *September* 1, 1715, N.S. in the seventy-second Year of his Reign, and when he wanted four Days of being seventy-seven Years of Age.

He was stiled Lewis the Great, with what Reason the Reader has seen. He was, tho' unlearned, a great Encourager and Protector of Learning, and more so of Flattery. He was no great Soldier, and yet loved War. His Courage was not very clear, but he had great Firmness of Mind. In Prosperity he was haughty, but not abject in Adversity. He was jealous of his eldest Son, but affectionate to his Family; he was a very faithful Friend, and a very kind Master. His Amours were numerous and scandalous; his Behaviour to his Queen civil, without Tenderness; to his Mother respectful, without Affection; to his Brother suspicious, but not indecent.

As a King, he was ambitious with respect to his Neighbours, arbitrary toward his Subjects, and boundless in both. With regard to the former he had no Tie but Interest; in reference to the latter, no Law but his Will. He intirely subverted the Constitution of his Country. He left the Princes of his Blood without Power, and his Parliaments without Autho-

rity.

rity. The Force of his Kingdom he reduced to a Standing-Army ; the Property of his Subjects he rendered precarious, and every Rank of them entirely dependent upon the Will of his Succeſſor.

In fine, he was a Rebel to the Court, and at the ſame Time a Slave to the Church of *Rome* ; he had a Paſſion for Glory, with ſcarce any Tincture of Virtue ; and with all the Vices and Weakneſs of a Man, had the Vanity to ſtile and think himſelf *immortal.* Such was the Character of *Lewis* XIV. when painted by the Pencil of Truth, how different ſoever it may be from the Pictures drawn of him by Foes or Flatterers.

This Prince married *Maria Thereſa* Daughter of *Philip* IV. King of *Spain*, *Anno* 1660, by whom he had Iſſue only one Son that lived, *viz. Lewis* Dauphin of *France*, who married *Mary-Anne-Chriſtiana*, Siſter to the Duke of *Bavaria*, by whom he had Iſſue three Sons, *viz.* I. *Lewis* Duke of *Burgundy*, born *Anno* 1682. II. *Philip* Duke of *Anjou*, King of *Spain*, born *Anno* 1683. III. *Gaſton* Duke of *Berry*, born in 1684, who died without Iſſue. *Lewis* the Dauphin died *Anno* 1711, whereupon *Lewis* Duke of *Burgundy* his eldeſt Son ſucceeded to the Title of Dauphin.

This Prince married *Mary Adelaide*, eldeſt Daughter to the Duke of *Savoy*, afterwards King of *Sardinia*, *Anno* 1698, and died 1712, leaving Iſſue of his Marriage three Sons, of which the two eldeſt, ſtiled Dukes of *Britany* ſucceſſively, died ſoon after him in their Infancy ; but *Lewis* his third Son, born *Anno* 1710, ſurvived them all, and ſits at preſent on the Throne of his Great Grandfather.

His natural Children by Madame *de le Valiere*, was *Mary Anne de Bourbon*, born in 1666, and married in 1680 to *Lewis* of *Bourbon*, Prince of *Conti*, who died without Iſſue by her.

By Madame *de Monteſpan*, I. *Lewis Auguſtus de Bourbon*, Duke of *Maine*, born in 1670, who by his Wife *Louiſa*, Daughter to the Prince of *Condé*, had a Daughter called Madamoiſelle *d' Aumale*, born in 1697, and two Sons ; *Lewis Auguſtus* Prince of *Dombes*, born in 1700 ; *Lewis Charles* Count of *Eu*, born 1701. II. *Louiſa Frances de Bourbon*, ſtiled Madamoiſelle *de Nantes*, born in 1673, and married to *Lewis* Duke of *Bourbon* 1685 ; whoſe Children were, Madamoiſelle *de Bourbon*, born 1690 ; *Lewis* Duke of *Enguien*, born 1692 ; *Louiſa* Madamoiſelle *de Charolois*, born 1693 ; and *Louiſa Anne*, called Madamoiſelle *Sens*, born in 1695. III. *Lewis Alexander de Bourbon*, Count of *Thouloufe*, born 1678,

late

late Admiral of *France*, whose Son, the Duke *de Penthievre*, now enjoys that high Office IV. *Frances Mary de Bourbon*, stiled Mademoiselle *de Blois*, born 1681.

His Majesty's only legitimate Brother was *Philip* Duke of *Orleans*, first married to *Henrietta Muria*, Daughter to *Charles* I. King of *England*, by whom he had one Daughter, married to the Duke of *Savoy*. He afterwards espoused *Charlotta Elizabeth*, Daughter to *Charles Lewis* Elector *Palatine*, by whom he had Issue, *Philip* Duke of *Chartres*, late Duke of *Orleans*, and Regent of *France*, who married *Frances Mary de Bourbon*, stiled Madamoiselle *de Blois*, by whom he had the present Duke of *Orleans*, *Lewis de Bourbon*, who by *Augusta Maria*, Daughter of Prince *Lewis* of *Baden*, has Issue, *Lewis Philip*, Duke of *Chartres*, born 1725, and married to *Louisa-Henrietta* of *Bourbon Conti*.

The Care that had been taken by the Great Monarch *Lewis* XIV. for the Security of his Infant Successor, and his Subjects, was just as ineffectual as the Pains taken by *Lewis* XIII. in settling the Regency at the Beginning of his own Reign, that is to say, the Duke of *Orleans* acted now the very same Part that the Queen Mother acted then, and by caressing the Parliament, for a Moment, and giving them Hopes of seeing their Authority restored, procured their Assistance to the single Act that could enable him to operate upon their Power at all.

This Point once managed, and the Duke of *Orleans* being declared sole Regent during the Minority of *Lewis* XV. the Government was compleatly restored, since the Regent governed from that Day as absolutely as ever the late King had done. He began his Administration, as all able Princes do, with Acts of Lenity and Mildness, and with a great Appearance of Zeal for the publick Good.

His Plan for foreign Affairs was the best laid, and best conducted, that the *French* had ever seen; it is indeed probable, that he was principally moved thereto by the Consideration of his particular Interest; but whatever his Motive was, his Conduct was right. He steddily adhered to the last Treaty of Peace, and he shew'd a Willingness to contribute as far as could be desired, to fixing a true Ballance of Power.

He was so far from dissembling, that he laid open to all the World the miserable State that *France* was in; and certainly in this he acted like a great Politician; for on the one hand, it justified his Measures at home, and on the other, it gained him Credit abroad; for by delivering her Neighbours from the Fear of *France*, he brought them to confide in his Promises, and

he

he made use of this Confidence to re-establish her Affairs upon a solid Foundation.

In respect to domestick Concerns he acted with the same Prudence and Moderation. He erected several Councils agreeable to the late King's Will, foreseeing the Confusion this would create, and the fair Opportunity it would give him of suppressing them ; and he restored to the Parliament their ancient Liberty of debating upon Acts of State, before they gave them the Sanction of their Authority. They were all very proper as well as popular Steps ; they served to settle his Authority, and to enable him to make use of it afterwards as he thought most convenient.

He had his Views, as all other Princes have ; and he shewed himself a great Prince, by taking the Precautions necessary to fix his Power, before he made his Schemes evident, from his Endeavours to accomplish them. In this indeed lay his Strength, he knew perfectly how to conceal his Designs under specious Pretences, to give these Pretences the highest Colourings possible, and never to bring his real Intentions into publick View, earlier than he was secure of trampling upon all Opposition.

When he had thus settled Peace abroad, and his Authority at home, he listened to the Cries of the People, and established a new Court of Judicature, for calling to an Account such as had the Management of the publick Revenue in the former Reign, and were almost the only People in the Kingdom that enjoyed affluent Fortunes under the present. The Pretence was specious ; and tho' this Enquiry might be conducted with a Severity that border'd upon Injustice, yet it answered the Purpose of the Court, and did not give general Offence.

He would have had recourse to healing Measures in the Church, but in that respect his good Designs were defeated ; and, as is but too frequent, those who by their Profession are of all others most bound to promote Peace, were those who by the Authority that Profession gave them, hindered it the most.

The Regent saw and understood perfectly the many mischievous Consequences that flowed from the frequent Variations that had been made in the Value of the Coin during the last Reign ; but what he most regretted was, that the People understood those so well, that it was impossible, as Things stood, for any Use to be made of this Expedient under his Administration.

To correct this Evil, and more especially to set his own Hands at Liberty; on the 12th of *October* 1715, he published an Edict. in which he set in a very clear Light the principal

Inconveniencies

Inconveniencies that followed this Practice, as well as the Advantages that must necessarily attend the remedying this Evil, and fixing the Coin on an equitable and immoveable Foundation, of which this Edict gave Hopes, by declaring that the Pistole or Lewis d'Or should for ever remain of the Value of fourteen Livres, at which it was then: But no sooner had this Edict produced its Effect, than the Regent issued another, by which the Subjects were required to pay their Money into the Mint at the Rate of sixteen Livres for a Lewis d'Or, which were issued out at the Rate of twenty.

I mention this Instance out of many, for two Reasons; the first is, that I may afford the Reader a View of the Distress of the *French* Government, and the Hardships it was obliged to impose upon its Subjects; and secondly, to give a Specimen of the Regent's Policy, which was of the same Stamp throughout; that is to say, he made no Scruple of professing any thing that might serve his Purpose, and acting with respect to those Professions, as if he had never made them. But this was only with regard to Transactions at Home; with reference to Foreign Princes, he was cautious how he entered into Engagements, but was afterwards punctual in performing them.

It is impossible, strictly speaking, to justify such a Conduct as the Regent pursued; but one may have leave to say in his Excuse, that he found the Government and Nation in a most ruinous Condition, with a Debt almost beyond Belief, since some have calculated it no less than three hundred Million Sterling, and this notwithstanding some considerable Spunges that had been made in the preceding Reign.

He saw that while the Government was in this Condition, it could not either act for its own Security, or for the Relief of the Nation, but must be obliged from time to time to lay heavy Burdens upon the Whole, in order to give some Satisfaction to that Part of the People who were become Creditors to the Publick. This it was that induced him to listen to a Project of Mr. *John Law*, a Native of *Scotland*, and a Man of a peculiar Cast of Mind, who knew how to apply those Schemes of Calculation, which hitherto had served only private and paultry Purposes, to the great Affairs of a Nation, and the extricating a Government from such Difficulties as that of *France* was then under.

The Patron and Projector were as well suited to each other as could be conceived. The Regent, had he been in a private Station, would probably have been the Contriver of this Scheme; the Projector, had he been vested with the Regent's Power, would have had Courage enough to have

executed

executed in its utmost Extent. The Colour that was given to this Affair was the erecting a new Company for carrying on a Commerce at *Louisiana*, or the River *Mississipi*; but the true Design was to pay the Debts of the *French* Government without Money, or with other People's Money.

I mean by other People's Money, the Money of Foreigners; and this Affair was managed with such Address, that in the Year 1719 the new Company offered to lend the Government fifteen hundred Millions of Livres. In the mean time however the Regent had been obliged to practise so many Methods of raising and falling Money, of stopping the Currency of Cash, forcing of Currency for Notes, and constraining such as had any Gold or Silver to part with it, whether they would or not; that he was obliged to stop short in the Execution of Mr. *Law*'s Scheme, and to drive him out of the Kingdom.

Yet, after all this, and notwithstanding the Disturbance, Clamour, and Confusion, which the Business of the Bank, the *India* Company, and other Expedients Mr. *Law* suggested, produced, the Government was a great Gainer upon the Whole, and a very large Proportion of the Debt was, if not paid, at least resolved into Waste Paper. It was certainly an iniquitious Scheme in its Nature, and such a one as no Man of Probity would have formed, or could have executed; but notwithstanding all this, when executed, it was as certainly attended with some good Effects.

While the Regent was thus struggling to free the Government of *France* from the Difficulties it was under, occasioned chiefly by the long War carried on to place *Philip* V. on the Throne of *Spain*, that Prince committed his Affairs to an enterprizing Minister, the famous Cardinal *Alberoni*, who died lately; and who, instead of submitting, as former Ministers had done, to the Measures prescribed by *France*, struck out a Plan of his own, which he would have obliged the Regent to follow; and which consisted in recovering all the Provinces that had been dismembered from the *Spanish* Monarchy by the late Treaties of Peace.

The Regent declared that he looked upon this as contrary to Justice; but it is certain that he considered it as not at all consistent with his Interest; and therefore, instead of promoting, he opposed it, agreeable to the Engagements he was under to the Imperial and *British* Courts. The *Spanish* Court, or rather the *Spanish* Minister, took this so ill, that he resolved to form a Party in *France*, and even to secure the Person of the Duke Regent; and as wild and extravagant as this Plot might

might feem, the Prince *de Cellemare*, then the *Spanish* Ambaffador at the Court of *France*, took his Meafures fo well, that he was very near carrying it into Execution ; it was however very critically difcovered, that Minifter arrefted and fent out of *France*, fome Gentlemen of *Bretagne* who were deepeft in this Scheme loft their Lives, and very foon after an open War broke out between the two Nations.

But as *Spain* could not fuftain herfelf without the Affiftance of *France*, much lefs againft the Power of that Monarch, join'd with the reft of her Opponents, Cardinal *Alberoni* was obliged to give way, the Crown of *Spain* acceded to the Quadruple Alliance ; and it was agreed that the young King of *France* fhould marry the Infanta of *Spain* ; and that the Prince of *Afturias* fhould marry one of the Regent's Daughters, and Don *Carlos* the other.

All Things being thus fettled, and the Peace of *Europe* for the prefent reftored, the Regent's Affairs wore a much better Afpect than they had done, and all the Powers of *Europe* faw with Surprize, but without Jealoufy, *France* daily recovering its Luftre. This is a Proof that the Regent's Conduct was agreeable to the true Intereft of the Kingdom he govern'd ; and that he much better underftood the Art of making *France* truly formidable, than thofe who affect at every Turn to make her appear fo. But to purfue the Thread of our Narration, and leave thefe Political Points to the Confideration and Decifion of the judicious Reader.

In 1722, the Regent caufed his Majefty to be crowned at *Rheims*, and in the Beginning of the following Year, he was declared of full Age in Parliament. The Regent knew well of what Confequence it was to preferve Forms, though he never meant by taking thefe Steps to relinquifh his own Authority. By his Advice therefore, his own Creature and Favourite, Cardinal *Du Bois*, was declared Prime Minifter, but did nothing but by his Royal Highnefs's Direction ; fo that the Duke had ftill the intire Adminiftration of the publick Affairs of the Nation without any Title or Office whatever.

He was very well fatisfied with this Situation of Things, but in the Month of *Auguft* following his Promotion the Cardinal died ; and the Duke of *Orleans*, too prudent to truft any other Perfon with the Title of Prime Minifter, afked the King for it, or rather affumed it himfelf. The Confufion that Cardinal *Du Bois* left his Papers in, and the delicate Nature of many of his Correfpondencies, obliged the Duke to apply himfelf with the utmoft Induftry and Diligence to putting them in Order, in which he was fo indefatigable, that

he

he fate up all the Night of the firft of *December* 1723, though
he found himfelf feveral times very near fainting, and the next
Day in the Afternoon he died of a Fit of the Apoplexy, with
great Projects in his Head, and, as many have thought, when he
was on the very Point of carrying fome of them into Execution.

Upon the Death of the Duke of *Orleans*, the Conduct of the
State devolved upon the next Prince of the Blood of an Age
fuitable to the Employment. This was the Duke of *Bour-*
bon, a Prince of great Parts, furprifing Quicknefs, and capable
of much Application. He found many Difficulties upon his
firft coming into the Adminiftration; to hinder thefe from increafing, he purfued the Plan of his Predeceffor very fteddily;
but the People were not much better fatisfied with him, than
they had been with his Royal Highnefs, becaufe the State of the
Finances were fuch as obliged him to make various Alterations
in the Coin.

He likewife preffed the Acceptance of the Bull *Unigenitus*,
both on the Laity and Clergy, which occafioned great Heats and
Animofities, and while thefe continued, the King was taken
fuddenly ill, which alarmed the Duke of *Bourbon* fo much, that
he refolved to fend back the young Infanta, who had been for
fome Time in *France* with the Title of Queen, in order to
marry the King to fome Princefs of riper Years; and accordingly his Majefty was foon afterwards married to the Princefs
Mary, Daughter of *Staniflaus* King of *Poland*, which gave great
Satisfaction to the People.

But the Court of *Spain* refented this extremely, and demanded in exprefs Terms, that the Duke of *Bourbon* fhould
be removed, to give his Catholick Majefty Satisfaction, as
Cardinal *Alberoni* had before been, at the Requeft, and for
the Conveniency of the moft Chriftian King. This being
refufed, threw the *Spanifh* Court into the Arms of that of
Vienna, which gave fuch a Face to the Affairs of *Europe*,
as differed much from that which they had worn for half a
Century paft.

It was not long, however, that the Duke of *Bourbon* was
able to maintain himfelf in Power; and the Thing that turn'd
moft to his Prejudice, was the raifing the fiftieth Penny
upon all Eftates throughout the Kingdom, which the Duke
judged neceffary for the Payment of the publick Debts, with
which after all this fpunging the Crown found itfelf ftill
over-charged.

There are fecret and dark Intrigues in all Courts, and
perhaps there never was any in which thefe have always prevailed more than in that of *France*. If we could abfolutely
depend

depend upon some Memoirs that have been written of these
Times, the Duke of *Bourbon* was deceived and outwitted by
his Successor, who first very gravely and conscientiously represented to him the many fatal Consequences that attended the
modern Method of paying, or rather not paying, publick Debts,
by Variation of the Coin, giving a Currency to Paper, and then
destroying its Credit: By which he so wrought upon the Duke,
that he resolved to abandon those Measures as unworthy of a
Government ; and then the crafty Priest lay in wait to represent him as a publick Oppressor.

The Duke, in the very Edict by which he imposed this Tax,
set forth the Reasons of it, giving a fair and full Account
of the Methods that had been hitherto taken in order to extinguish the publick Debt, their Consequences, and the Necessity
there still was of raising Money to pay off Incumbrances, which
stood the Crown in fifty Millions yearly for Interest, tho' they
paid but Two *per Cent.*

When the Murmurs began about this Tax, which, how just
and reasonable soever it might be in its Intention, was to a
People so exhausted, almost insupportable ; the ancient Bishop
of *Frejus* (so M. *Fleury* was then called) was the first to mention them to the King, tho' he had great Obligations to
the Duke ; and he did it in such a manner, and with the addition of so many Circumstances, that he who had always
regarded the Sayings of this Man as so many Oracles, resolved to part with the Duke of *Bourbon*, and declare this
Prelate first Minister ; which Resolution was no sooner taken
than it was executed, and the People, as is common enough
in all Countries, applauded the Change, chiefly because it was
a Change.

The Duke bore his Disgrace both with Patience and Dignity, and tho' he continued all his Life after a private Man,
and had very little Connection with the Court, yet he quickly
recovered his Credit with the Publick, and was as generally
esteemed to the Day of his Death as any of the Princes of his
House ever had been.

As for the Administration of Cardinal *Fleury*, it is so well
known here, that it would be needless to trouble the Reader
with a particular Detail of it. He was certainly a very artful
and a very ambitious Man, without any of those Talents that
are requisite to make an accomplished Statesman, or a great
Minister. It was the Ascendancy he had over his Master, that,
as it originally procured, kept him so long in Power ; as it
was a smooth and complaisant Behaviour to the Foreign Ministers,

nisters, that gave him so great an Interest, as he really had for many Years, in all the Courts of *Europe*.

He was very disinterested in respect to Money, was very far from being solicitous about his Family, talked continually of Moderation, and was very mild and affable in his Behaviour; yet there were many harsh Things done under his Administration, both with respect to Civil and Ecclesiastical Affairs. He had no settled Plan of Politicks, as appeared by his sometimes courting the Favour, and sometimes crossing the Measures of *Spain*. It was purely to please that Court, that he suffered his Master to enter into a War with the late Emperor *Charles* VI. but as soon as he saw an Opportunity of getting out of it, and of making so great an Acquisition to *France* as the Duchy of *Lorrain*, he resolved to embrace it; and as he had sacrificed the Honour, and was very near sacrificing the Life of the *French* Queen's Father, during the War, so he made no Scruple of sacrificing the Interest of *Spain* to the Peace.

The same kind of Temper was visible in almost every great Transaction while he was at the Head of Affairs. He made use of other Mens Capacities for contriving and executing Schemes that were above his Reach; but whenever he found himself pinched by those Schemes, he removed and ruined the Authors of them, to preserve or regain his own Credit; as is evident enough in the Case of Mr. *Chauvelin*, the Keeper of the Seals, whom he drove from Court, after he had made great Use of his much superior Abilities.

In respect to the late War, which began in his Life-time, he was drawn into it by those whom at that Time he trusted, chiefly from his apprehending that it would not be the Work of more than one or two Campaigns, and that the Allies of the House of *Austria* would be as passive in this War as in the last. But when he found his Mistake, and saw, or rather felt the Inconveniencies that followed from it, he had recourse to his old Expedient of shifting the Blame upon other People; but it was no longer in his Power to rid himself of them, as he had done of their Predecessors; Age, Infirmities, and approaching Death, obliged him to turn his Thoughts to other Matters.

He maintained his Power with, or rather Influence over, his Master to the very last, and like Cardinal *Mazarin*, had the Satisfaction of dying, in all outward Appearance, as great a Man as he had lived, and even of appointing, as it were, his Successor. But the Arts he made use of to keep his Master in a State of Dependence upon himself, have had such an Effect on all the Measures of the Court of *Versailles* since his Death, that it has been a perpetual Scene of Cabals, Intrigues, and Confusion,

Confusion, till the late Marshal Count *Saxe* gained the Ear of his Master to such a Degree, as to give Law even to the Ministers, at least in respect to all great Points, which was the Posture that Things were in a little before the Conclusion of the Peace.

We have in the Course of the preceding History made it our Business to shew the several Schemes or Systems of Government, which have subsisted since the Accession of the House of *Bourbon* to the Throne of *France*; and perhaps we shall run no great Hazard of misleading the Reader, by affirming that these may be reduced to Two. That of *Henry* IV. who was the Father of his People, and really somewhat more; for he not only meant honestly towards his own Subjects, but likewise to the rest of *Europe*. In short, he had the Happiness of the People at Heart in his own Dominions, and was for establishing a Ballance of Power abroad.

His Son and Successor *Lewis* XIII. aimed at making himself absolute at home and respected abroad; both his Successors have had the same Views, only instead of Respect, they have been for establishing a general Influence, from whence all the bad Consequences must flow, which are commonly dreaded from universal Monarchy. By this Means Monarchs are rendered so dependent as to differ little from Vice-Roys, and Republicks are ruined by the secret Encouragement given to their Rulers to arrogate an Authority to themselves, inconsistent with the Constitution of their Countries, and incompatible with their Interests. In short, the Safety and Grandeur of this great Power must be maintained by the Poverty, Weakness, Corruption, Discontents, and Maleadministration that prevails amongst her Neighbours.

Our present Business is to shew how far this has been effected, and upon what Grounds we affirm that the *Gallic* Constitution is changed, and that the Monarchy is absolute at present. In the first place, we are to observe, that the greatest Lawyers and best Historians of *France* agree, that the Power of their Kings was anciently restrained, not only within narrower Bounds than at present, but that in reality they were as much limited as any Monarchs' could be.

That in all Governments, supreme and absolute Power is, and must be lodged somewhere, we find generally agreed; that according to the old Constitution in *France*, this did not reside in their Princes, but in the general Assembly of the States of the Kingdom, as in all other *Gothic* Constitutions, is certain. Indeed the very Name of the People sufficiently proves this, since there cannot be a stronger Opposition than between *Francs*, (that is, Freemen) and Slaves.

U   But

But as it was found inconvenient to hold thefe general Affemblies very frequently, fo, to hinder the Incroachments of their Kings while they were not fitting, part of their Powers were transferred to certain Committees, which gave Rife to the Parliaments of *France*, and particularly to that of *Paris*, which was at firft Ambulatory, that is, attended the Perfon of the King; but in Procefs of Time, was fixed to that City for the Conveniency both of Prince and People.

The ancient Prerogatives of this Affembly plainly prove, that as Reprefentatives of the States, the Sovereignty was really in it, for amongft others they had thefe three. Firft, they judged the Peers and great Men of the Kingdom, over whom the King in this Refpect had no Power; but in cafe they were fufpected of failing in their Duty to the Conftitution, they were to be tryed by their Equals, according to the known Law of the Kingdom. Secondly, all the great Officers of State took their Oaths in Parliament; from which it is manifeft, that they were bound not to the Perfon of the King, but fwore to him in his Political Capacity, and for the general Benefit of the State. Thirdly, they had the Right of regiftering, approving, and promulgating the King's Edicts, without which they had not the Sanction or Force of Laws.

As thefe Inftances unqueftionably demonftrate, that according to the *Gallic* Conftitution, their Kings were not abfolute; fo there is nothing more requifite to prove that they are fince become fo, by overturning the Conftitution, than to obferve that all thefe Checks are now taken away. The Affembly of the States is a Thing no longer heard of; and as for Parliaments, they are but Shadows of what they were, or rather worfe, by which I mean, that they are now become the Inftruments of that Power they were inftituted to reftrain.

The Liberty of the Subject is intirely at the Mercy of the King; he imprifons whom he pleafes without giving any Account; and whenever he finds it requifite, appoints fuch Judges for the Tryal of Offenders as he thinks fit. The great Officers of State take their Oaths to and from him; fo that they now belong intirely to the King, who appoints, removes, extends, or retrenches their Authority as he pleafes. The regiftering of Edicts is become a mere Matter of Form; the Parliament of *Paris* does indeed fometimes remonftrate, but in the End the King's Will and Pleafure always prevails.

The whole Government of this great Nation having been, by the Arts of Cardinal *Richelieu* and his Succeffors, drawn
intirely

intirely into the Hands of the Crown and its Minifters, the utmoft Pains have been taken to reduce it into fuch a Syftem, as that this Power may influence the whole, and keep every Branch thereof in ftrict and conftant Dependence. As far as the Compafs of our Work will allow, we fhall endeavour to fhew how this is done.

We have heard much of the *Gallican* Church and of its Freedom; but from the Time of the Cardinal before-mentioned, this Freedom is become a mere Engine of State, by the Help of which the King has fometimes made ufe of the Power of the Clergy, and at other times of that of the Pope, to extend his own. It was with a View to this, that the *Proteftants* of *France* were in general expelled; and that the Remains of them in *France* are from time to time perfecuted, when they attempt in any Degree the public Exercife of their Religion.

The *French* Kings were refolved to make themfelves Supreme in Church as well as State; which is the true Reafon why they admit of no Diffenters; and they have carried this into Execution, nowithftanding the Nominal Authority of the Pope; which is often made ufe of by the King, and can never be turned againft him.

The Clergy of *France* are, however, a very great and confiderable Body; they confift at prefent of eighteen Archbifhops, and one hundred and thirteen Bifhops, all named and appointed by the King; who has likewife the Nomination of feven hundred and feventy Abbies, and of the Superiors of three hundred and feventeen Convents of Nuns. The Reader need not be told what Influence this gives the Crown over that Part of its Subjects, which were formerly the leaft attached to it.

The ordinary Revenue arifing from the Tenths of the Clergy, amounts to 1,200,000 Livres *per Annum*; befides which, in the General Affemblies of the Clergy, free Gifts are fo conftantly expected even in Times of Peace, that this additional Revenue is computed annually at two Millions; but in Time of War the extraordinary free Gifts render it much more.

As to the Civil Government, the King has a great Council of State, and twelve Parliaments, befides other Courts, fuch as Generalities and Intendancies, for the Management of his Revenue; of the former there are twenty-fix, and of the latter more. As for the Political Government, it is managed by feveral great Councils, or rather Committees of Council, of which there are at prefent four; which are ftiled the Council of State, the Council of Difpatches, the Royal Council of Finances, and the Royal Council of Commerce.

U 2

The

The firſt Civil Officer in *France* is the Chancellor, and the only Officer that is not removeable at the King's Pleaſure; that is to ſay, he cannot be removed without being brought to a Trial; but the King may, and frequently does take the Seals from him, and put them into the Hands of another Perſon, who has the Title of Keeper and the Power of Chancellor, who is removeable at the King's Pleaſure.

There is generally a Perſon at the Head of the Miniſtry, either with or without the Title of Prime Miniſter, and with more or leſs Authority, as the King pleaſes; at preſent this is conceived to be M. *de Machault*, Keeper of the Seals and Comptroller-General of the Finances, but without the Title. For the Management of Public Affairs, there are four principal Secretaries of State, who have each their ſeparate Departments. Theſe are at preſent; M. *de Saint Conteſt*, who is Secretary for Foreign Affairs, the Count *de Saint Florentin*, who has the Care of Domeſtic Concerns; the Count *L'Argenſon*, who is Secretary at War; and Mr. *Rouille*, who has the Marine in the Room of the Count *de Maurepas* lately diſgraced.

The principal Officer of the Revenue, is the Comptroller-General of the Finances, which Office is now in M. *de Machault*, who has under him a Multitude of Intendants, and other Officers, ſubject to the Direction of the Council of Finances, of which the D. *de Bethune* is Preſident. As to the ordinary and ſettled Revenue of the Crown of *France*, if we may believe their own Writers upon that Subject, it is not at all increaſed in its real, though it is conſiderably augmented in its nominal Value.

In 1683, it was computed at 116,873,476 Livres; and in 1730 it amounted to no more than 140,278,473 Livres, which make 5,844,937 Pounds of our Money. This ſhews that neither the general Wealth of *France*, nor the Income of the King, are near ſo great as is commonly imagined. It is indeed very true, that in time of War the King levies much larger Sums; but it is very plain, that even theſe muſt fall far ſhort of what ſome People would perſuade us they amount to; ſince there muſt be always a Proportion between the ordinary and extraordinary Revenue, and conſequently, if we know the one, we may very eaſily compute how far the other can be carried; becauſe, even under arbitrary Governments, ſome Meaſures muſt be preſerved, and ſome Regard had to the general Income of the People, which is leſs in Time of War, at the ſame Time that the publick Expence is greater.

As the Eccleſiaſtical and Civil Government of *France* was moulded in the Compaſs of two Reigns, into ſuch a Form

as

as made them wholly fubfervient to the Purpofes of the Crown; fo the Military Eftablifhment, as it now ftands, was intirely the Work of *Lewis* XIV. Before his Time a few Companies of Guards, and four old Corps, as they are ftill called, were all the ftanding Troops of *France*; neither were they exactly of the fame Nature with the Regiments that are now kept up, tho' this is not a proper Place to difcufs the Difference.

It is fufficient for us to obferve, that the Prince laft mentioned, finding every thing at home difpofed according to his good Pleafure when he took the Adminiftration into his own Hands, refolved to lay hold of that Opportunity to fecure the boundlefs Authority of which he was poffeffed in his own Dominions, and at the fame time to make himfelf formidable to his Neighbours. It was to this End that he eftablifhed firft under the Notion of Guards a very confiderable Force, which is now ftiled the Troops of the Houfhold; and afterwards, as Occafion ferved, raifed Regiment after Regiment both of Horfe and Foot, and kept them in conftant Service.

It was by the Help of this Standing Army, that he gained fo many and fo great Advantages over *Spain* and the reft of his Neighbours, and annexed feveral conquered Provinces to his Dominions; which at the fame time afforded him an Opportunity of increafing the Number of thefe regular Troops, and of covering his Frontiers on every fide with abundance of ftrong Fortreffes. By Degrees, other States in *Europe* found themfelves obliged, for their own Defence, to raife and maintain regular Troops likewife, which furnifhed that ambitious Prince with a Pretence for augmenting his to as great a Number as was poffible for him to maintain; and his Example in this, as well as in moft other Points, has been exactly followed by his Succeffor. So that immediately before the breaking out of the late War, the Standing Troops of *France* confifted of one hundred and twenty thoufand Foot, twenty thoufand Horfe and Dragoons, and between eight and ten thoufand Invalids; that is, in the whole, to about one hundred and fifty thoufand Men.

The keeping up fo large an Army, and the maintaining fo many Garrifons, is as ferviceable to the King as it is burthenfome and ruinous to the Kingdom, inafmuch as it keeps fo great a Proportion of able and active Perfons in a State of abfolute Idlenefs with regard to the Publick, at the fame time that heavy Taxes are raifed upon the laborious and induftrious Part of the People for their Subfiftence.

But it muft be allowed, that it finds Employment for the Nobility and Gentry of *France*, more efpecially as it is be-

U 3

come almoſt an indiſpenſible Cuſtom for them to ſpend their
Youth, at leaſt the firſt Part of it, in the Service; by which
they are brought inſenſibly into a Dependence upon the Court,
and have their Minds filled with falſe and ſlaviſh Notions of the
Glory of their *Grand Monarque*, which intirely gets the better of
the natural Paſſions that all Men of Birth and Breeding in other
Nations have for the Service of their Country. Thus the Reader
ſees, that the Church, the Law, the Civil Employments, and the
Military, being wholly at the good Pleaſure of the Court, the
far greater Part of the active People in this great Country have
their Lives and Fortunes at the Diſpoſal of the Crown, and
ſpend the beſt of their Days in the Maintenance of a Syſtem,
calculated to hold them in irrecoverable and perpetual Ser-
vitude.

The Reader will naturally expect, that we ſhould ſay ſome-
thing of the Marine, which in the laſt Reign was indeed extremely formidable, but was far from being ſo in this; ſince it
is very certain that at the Beginning of the late War, the whole
naval Power of *France* did not conſiſt of quite forty Ships of War
of all Sizes, which though it be very ſhort of what it was at the
Opening of this Century, yet is much ſuperior to any Force
the *French* had of that Nature before the Reign of *Lewis* XIV.
As to the Commerce of *France*, it was before the War began
very conſiderable, tho' certainly much ſhort of what has been
reported of it here.

The greateſt Evidence thereof that I have ſeen, is derived
from a Memorial now before me, which contains a Repre-
ſentation to the *French* Court of the Loſſes ſuſtained by the
War, which was drawn up at the Beginning of the Year
1747, and wherein they are ſtated at two hundred Millions of
their Money, which make above nine Millions three hundred
thouſand Pounds of ours. If this proves, as it moſt certainly
does, that the Trade of *France* was very much increaſed, and
even arrived at a ſurprizing Height; we have at the ſame time
the Conſolation of knowing, that it is now not only much
ſunk and impaired, but in many of its moſt important and
beneficial Branches almoſt ruined and deſtroyed; and this by
the Confeſſion of thoſe, who as they are employed therein,
muſt be beſt acquainted therewith, and who, in a Repreſenta-
tion of this kind, durſt not attempt to impoſe upon the Government.

We have likewiſe the Satisfaction of being informed from
the ſame authentic Memorial, that in the Judgment of the
mercantile Part of that Nation, if it were in the Power of the
Court

Court to maintain twenty Men of War at *Brest*, fifteen at *Cadiz*, and on the Coast of *Spain*, fifteen in *America*, and ten at *Toulon*, all the Branches of their Trade might be effectually protected : Whence it is evident that no such Force has been hitherto employed, and that the Merchants are doubtful whether if the Court was ever so well inclined, they could equip and maintain it.

In respect to the Interests of *France*, we are obliged to consider the Nature of the Government only, and the Views which the Court proposes to itself, since these are very different from, or, to speak the Truth, directly opposite to the true Interest of the Nation ; for considering the Soil, Climate, and Situation of the Country, and the Numbers of its Inhabitants, as they have no reason to fear, so they have no cause to disturb their Neighbours ; by whom, if they applied themselves industriously to Manufactures at home, and to foreign Trade, they might be very great Gainers ; and as the several Provinces of the Kingdom are full of great Towns, they might be all rendered populous and rich as well as the Country about them.

A Government therefore that consulted the Good of the People, and the general Benefit of its Subjects, should labour to preserve Peace, and be assiduous in cultivating the Arts of Peace, which perhaps would tend as much to increase the Power and fix the Security of such a Government, as the contrary Measures which are now pursued tend to strengthen and aggrandize that absolute Monarchy, which we have seen erected there on the Ruins of their Constitution, by the House of *Bourbon*.

But as a Scheme intirely opposite to this has been there carried on for at least a Century past, with great Steddiness and unusual Success, we have no Reason to expect, tho' Circumstances may induce them to dissemble, that the *French* Court will ever change their Measures ; and therefore looking upon Things in a Political Light, we must consider *them*, only, without having any Respect to the Interest of the People. The Grandeur of the Crown, which with some Impropriety is in that Country stiled the Glory of *France*, appears to be the ultimate Aim of the Policy of these Ministers, upon which they have fixed their own Attention so long, and have magnified it so much, that it seems at length to occupy solely the Cares and Attention of the Nation.

To speak impartially, it is on keeping up this Spirit that the Peace and Safety of the Government, as it is now administred, depends ; and it is impossible for the *French* Court to drop her Influence abroad, without manifestly hazarding her

Quiet

Quiet at home; so that to expect a *French* Monarch should adhere strictly to Treaties, and relinquish all Views upon his Neighbours, is to expect a Golden Age; a thing that may be wished even by the Wise, but which Fools themselves can never hope to see.

There is therefore no sort of Doubt, that so long as *France* enjoys her present Power, and is in a Capacity of preserving it, she will consider herself as the Head of the House of *Bourbon*, and as the first Potentate of the Christian World, to which high Titles she will not fail to add as many real Prerogatives as is in her Power. In order to this, she will study to continue *Spain* and the other Princes of her House in a close Dependence upon herself, by occasionally gratifying them in their Views; and as it is not easy to see how they can expect this any other way, there seems to be too much Probability that, for our Time at least, she will succeed in it.

It is also probable that she will persist in most of her other Schemes, such as keeping up a close Correspondence with the *Turks*, that she may have it in her Power to awe the House of *Austria* and the *Russian* Empire; that with the like View she will neglect nothing that may contribute to continue, and even to increase the Jealousies that have so long subsisted, and which still subsist in *Germany*; her Intrigues in all the Northern Courts, and her Correspondencies in *Italy*, where so long as she can preserve her Superiority, she will not fail to have the Court of *Rome* attached to her Cause.

In respect to the rest of *Europe*, the House of *Austria* will always remain the Object of her Hate, the Maritime Powers of her Envy, and *Prussia* of her Jealousy; whatever Professions under certain Circumstances, and to serve her own Purposes, she may make to the contrary; and upon which therefore those to whom they are made, can never depend but to their own Prejudice.

She may also, and it is highly probable she will, dissemble her real Views in Times of Peace in favour of her Trade, which there is no Question she will encourage and promote all that lies in her Power, that it may in some measure repair the Losses occasioned by her Wars; but there is no room to suppose that she will remain quiet for many Years together, because this must many ways indanger a Government like hers, by creating Factions in the Court, relaxing the Discipline of her Armies, and giving Time to her Neighbours to put themselves into a State of Security and Defence against her Power.

This

This is not a Picture drawn at Pleasure, or by the Hand of Prejudice, of the French Government, to render it odious and suspected, but from the Life and with strict Regard to Truth. The Reader has had the Evidence produced to him, which is sufficient to establish this, and it was with that View that we took so much Pains to produce it.

Without seeing the History of *France* since the Accession of the present reigning Family, and considering duly and impartially the principal Points therein, it would have been impossible to have set the Policy of the *French* Court in a true Point of Light; or if it had been possible, it could scarce have been expected that the Publick should have given Credit to it; but as the Case now stands, we may flatter ourselves that there are good Grounds to hope that the Justice and Impartiality of this Account will be conspicuous to every ingenious Reader, so as to convince him that this is a fair and equal Representation, given with no other End than to enable him to form a true Prospect of future Events, and of the Conduct of this Power in succeeding Times.

Before we quit this Article, it will be proper to observe, that notwithstanding the Truth of what has been said, yet there are no just Grounds to despair of preserving the Ballance of Power, tho' *France* and the rest of the House of *Bourbon* should pursue with the utmost Vigour their ambitious Schemes; and this we shall likewise make appear, by a few plain and natural Inferences and Deductions from the History and Remarks that have been already made.

It is very evident from these, that the *French* Power was at its greatest Height at the Time *Lewis* XIV. made the Peace of *Nimeguen*, or a very little after. The two succeeding Wars exhausted that Nation prodigiously, and more especially the last, which brought her so low, that notwithstanding the long Peace, and the many Advantages she has since enjoyed, it is very certain she is far from having recovered it, since her Revenue at this Day, tho' it makes a greater Number of Livres, falls short in Value of what it amounted to in 1683.

She has been likewise very much exhausted by the last War, in which she was defeated in most of her Views, found herself in no Capacity of keeping the Acquisitions she had made, and discover'd some signs of Weakness beyond what appeared even in the former general War. We know that whatever her Distresses may be, it is impossible for her to bring above 250,000 Men into the Field; perhaps it is impossible for her to do even that, and such an Army she cannot long maintain; or recruit, if she could maintain it. But supposing it to be possible, this Force will not

be

be sufficient to defend her, even against the last Confederacy, if she had not a Dependence upon *Prussia*.

Experience has shewn us, that without this Resource, she could not maintain an Army in the *Low-Countries*, and keep a Force sufficient to defend her Frontiers on the Side of *Alsace*. We may remember, for the Time is not long since, the Hurry with which *Lewis* XV. marched to cover that Part of his Dominions, had like to have cost him his Life, and very doubtful it is, whether he would have been able to have protected them at last, if a Diversion had not been made in *Bohemia*, which obliged the *Austrians* to repass the *Rhine*; and the Manner in which the *French* beheld that Retreat, fully shewed how highly satisfied they were at the Sight.

But suppose, as the Thing is indeed very practicable, such an Invasion were attempted at the same time, with an Irruption on the Side of *Provence*, and a Descent from *England* on *Bretagne*, or any other Part of their Coasts, where would Troops then be found to resist all these Enemies ? Yet there is Reason to believe, that *France* made a much better Figure in the late War, than she will be able to do in another, unless she is so lucky as to succeed as happily in her Intrigues at the Beginning of it, as she did in those she employed at the Commencement of this last, which, all Things considered, is very improbable.

Besides, in the Course of the last Quarrel, many Incidents happened that cannot fail of affecting strongly the general Interests of *Europe* for the future, no way to the Advantage of the Cause of *France*. As for Instance, the surprizing and unexpected Efforts made by the People of *Hungary* in Support of their Sovereign, which, as I have shewed in another Place, has introduced a new Power in *Europe*, and brought such an Accession of Strength to the House of *Austria* as saved her now, and must contribute not a little to render her respected hereafter.

The Devastation of *Germany* immediately after the War began, and more especially of the *Bavarian* and *Palatine* Dominions, must also have very good Effects in deterring those Princes from placing any Confidence in the Omnipotence of the *Grand Monarque*, or supposing the Success of a War must be determined on the bare Appearance of his Forces.

The heavy Misfortunes that befell the Duke of *Modena* and the *Genoese*, are also very discouraging Circumstances; notwithstanding the Restitution of their Dominions. We may therefore reasonably persuade ourselves, that in succeeding Times another Spirit will prevail; Princes and States will at last
perceive,

perceive, that by repeated Efforts, *France* has weakened her Force, tho' she preserves her Ambition to the full, is as vigorous as ever in her Views, tho' she wants Abilities to accomplish them.

All this may be the rather expected, because the Suggestions of *France* are commonly against the Interests of the Princes she tempts; and the Motives must consequently be very strong, the Persuasion of Success still stronger, to warp such Princes or States from their Interests, which they may pursue without Danger or Trouble. But after the Defeat of the Scheme laid at the Commencement of this War, what Insinuations can move, what Arguments appear conclusive?

But this is not all; if such a Check be once given to *France*, a new Spirit may arise, and those who have no Hopes of benefiting themselves by her Assistance, may incline to reap Advantages at her Expence. All *Europe* well knows how indifferent a Title she has to most of her Acquisitions, and with what Appearance of Justice her Possessions might be questioned; and who can tell what some time or other such a Spirit may produce?

It would be a very easy Matter to suggest various other Reasons to the same purpose; but I forbear at present, as having said enough to shew my Opinion, that the House of *Bourbon* will not, indeed, cannot relinquish her present System, which must always render her terrible to her Neighbours; but that on the other hand, there wants not a Power sufficient to render all her Intrigues abortive, and to defeat all her Enterprizes, tho' supported by her utmost Force.

I am very well aware that there are two Sorts of People who will be inclined to doubt of the Facts which I have advanced, and to dispute the Arguments which I have used upon this Subject. The first of these are the Admirers of that over-grown Power, those who look up not only with Surprize but Pleasure at the amazing Structure, which the Genius of *Richelieu* contrived, and the Labours of his Successors erected. In this there is indeed something strange and mean, and yet of these Sort of People there have been always some, to say the Truth, too many in the World; as appears by the *Greeks*, who in a Country of Liberty, were in their Hearts Friends to the *Great King*, though they knew him to be their common Enemy. The other Sort of People are such as fear *France* immoderately, and who have been so long used to frame horrible Apprehensions as well of the Force as the Designs of that Crown, cannot sufficiently divest themselves of their Panic, to enquire coolly and calmly whether there be any good Grounds for their Apprehensions or not.

It

It may, and very probably it will be urged by both thefe kind of People, that firft with regard to Facts, the Armies which *France* had on foot in the laft Year of the late War, were very much fuperior to what I allow fhe could poffibly form; and becaufe I know that this has been laid down with great Force, by fome who would be thought extremely well acquainted with the Military Eftablifhment in *France*, I have taken fome Pains to learn how far I was miftaken, which from thefe People I could never do, for they anfwered always in the general, that *France* was out of Comparifon ftronger than I imagined; that we deceived ourfelves here in thinking the contrary; and that the Troops in her Pay during the laft Campaigns, very far exceeded our Computations. But I am at prefent out of all Pain upon this Subject, having in my Poffeffion a compleat and authentic State of the *French* Military Eftablifhment in the Month of *May*, 1748; which is indeed a very correct and fatisfactory Piece of its kind, and in all refpects the fineft Detail of an Army I ever faw. I will give the Reader an Extract of the Totals, which will ferve fufficiently to illuftrate this Point.

S T A T E *of his Moft Chriftian Majefty's* LAND FORCES
in May 1748.

Infantry.	Battal.	Men.	Annual Pay.
Regular National Foot	356	261455	54854808 - 5 - 0
Foreign Regular Foot	84	59183	16099717 - 16 - 0
Irregulars	13	9569	2596073 - 2 - 0

Cavalry.	Squadrons.	Men.	Annual Pay.
Regiments of Horfe	301	47531	32130455 - 10 - 4
Regiments of Dragoons	85	13824	8064154 - 3 - 6
Irregulars	25	3120	2330728 - 16 - 0

Battal. 453		
Squad. 411	395382	116075937 - 13 - 4

My firft Obfervation upon this is, that fo far from fubverting my former Calculation, this State of the *French* Army very clearly eftablifhes it. In Time of Peace we have fhewn, that the ftanding Forces of *France* are about one hundred and fifty thoufand Men; and in Time of War, it may be very fairly computed, that about this Number is requifite for the Garrifons, the Security of the Coafts, and the Prefervation

of

of the interior Part of the Kingdom : Which will be ſtill more evident, if we conſider that one hundred and twelve Battalions of Militia, making upwards of eighty thouſand Men, are included in the foregoing State of the Army. I was not conſequently in the wrong, in ſuppoſing that *France* could not bring many above two hundred thouſand Men into the Field, even when ſhe exerted herſelf to the utmoſt. We have likewiſe ſeen, that great as this Force is, ſhe might have been attacked by the Allies, if their Engagements to each other had been punctually performed, with equal, if not ſuperior Armies.

My next Obſervation is as to the Expence, which the Reader ſees, for the bare Subſiſtence of the Troops, amounts to the whole ordinary Revenue of *France*, or ſomewhat more than five Millions *Sterling*. As to the Extraordinaries of War, the Subſidies to foreign Powers, the Expences of the Navy, the Charge of Colonies, and many other Particulars, they are totally excluded ; and I preſume noboby will think that the Computation is extravagant, if we conſider theſe as amounting to the like Sum. To all this we muſt add the Charge of the Civil Government, which in a Time of War cannot be at all leſſened ; and when we have done this, and brought into the Account the diſtreſſed Condition of their Trade, which maniffeſts itſelf more and more ſince the Concluſion of the Peace, when Traders attempting to draw their Money out of the Hands of thoſe who paid them Intereſt for it during the War, when they could not employ it in Commerce, has occaſioned innumerable Bankruptcies.

I ſay, when all this is taken into our View, and ſeriouſly reflected upon, we muſt, unleſs we will abſolutely ſhut our Eyes, perceive, that tho' the abſolute Power of the *French* Government enables thoſe who adminiſter it, to avail themſelves of the laſt Man and the laſt Shilling that Kingdom can raiſe, for the Support of their ambitious Projects, yet when this is done, no Policy, however refined, can repair that Waſte of Wealth, or reſtore their extenuated Strength, in a ſhort Space of Time.

Power may ſuperſede the Laws of Reaſon, Humanity and Juſtice ; but human Power cannot conſtrain the Laws of Nature. When a People are exhauſted, they muſt have Time to recruit ; and tho' it may be very well ſuppoſed, that in an abſolute Government, this will be ſo far from being prevented, that all imaginable Pains will be taken to further and facilitate their Recovery, yet a very little Penetration will ſhew us, that even this cannot be immediately done ; for thoſe who adminiſter ſuch a Government, being always jealous of their Neighbours, cannot turn their Thoughts inſtantly, or at leaſt not intirely, even to
this

this neceſſary Point; for tho' ſuch a Recovery is requiſite, yet Self-Preſervation remains ſtill the firſt Law, and conſequently Proviſion muſt be made for that.

When an abſolute Government is not preparing to attack her Neighbours, ſhe muſt be occupied in providing againſt any Danger, that may reſult from her being ſuddenly attacked; and therefore whatever the Bulk of the People, whatever thoſe who have the Intereſt of the People only at Heart, may wiſh or plead for, the Miniſters under ſuch a Government will attend to that, and will not ſuffer their Cares to be called off to any other Object, before what regards this, upon which their Power depends, is thoroughly ſettled.

We ſee that in Fact this was the Caſe in *France*, immediately upon the Concluſion of the War: The People took it then for granted, that the extraordinary Taxes ſhould ceaſe at once; they promiſed this to themſelves, and they had been promiſed it by the Crown; yet their Wiſhes and Expectations were not anſwered. The Parliament interpoſed in their Behalf; and it is amazing, that no Account was ever publiſhed here of the Subſtance of their Remonſtrances, which were in Effect to this Purpoſe: That extraordinary Taxes could only be paid chearfully upon extraordinary Occaſions, and from the Hopes of being ſpeedily delivered from them; and therefore to deprive Men of theſe Hopes, was to render them Bankrupts in their Fortunes, and deſperate in their Diſpoſitions: That to pay Debts was a good Thing in itſelf, and certainly tended to the Relief of the People; but this Relief being diſtant, and the People ſtanding in Need of immediate Eaſe, the latter was a more ſuitable Relief than the former: That Indigence was a Defence even againſt abſolute Power, and therefore it was to be feared, that if the extraordinary Taxes were paid, the ordinary Revenue of the Crown would be greatly diminiſhed, and conſequently new Debts be incurred faſter than the old ones diſcharged.

But did theſe Remonſtrances prevail? No; only inſtead of the Tenth, the Twentieth Penny was impoſed: For tho' it is highly probable the Miniſtry were ſenſible of the Force of this Reaſoning, and of the Diſtreſs of the Nation, yet being at the ſame time more ſenſible of the Wants of the Government, as concerning them more, they thought fit to poſtpone the Relief of the People to what they will certainly call the Intereſt of the State.

Thus I preſume it is made tolerably plain, that with all her Power and Policy, *France* cannot in a few Years recover the Loſſes ſhe has ſuſtained in the laſt War; nor will it be within the Compaſs of her Abilities, intirely to give thoſe Encouragements and Affiftances to her Allies, that very poffibly they were made to expect after the Conclufion of the Peace; and if this fhould happen, there is the higheft Probability, that thofe Allies will vary their Syftem as their Interefts fhall direct; and what the Confequences of this may be, I fhall not venture to foretell.

I fhall only take the Liberty of adding upon fo *nice* a Subject, that the part *France* has hitherto acted, both in the North and in *Germany*, renders it fufficiently evident that a *general War* upon *Terms*, any way like thofe of the *laft*, is by no means her Aim; which ferves to juftify what fome of her moft *able Statefmen* have upon certain Occafions declared; That the laft War was fo far from being of her Contrivance, that fhe was carried into it by Conftraint, and never comprehended the full Extent of her Engagements, till fhe was called upon to comply with them, and this under Circumftances that would not well admit of Refufal. We may therefore prefume fhe will fcarce bring herfelf into the *fame State* again.

We might very eafily carry our Reflections farther, and enter into a Multitude of entertaining as well as inftructive Difquifitions, on a variety of curious and important Subjects; fuch as the *ill* Treatment of a *Perfon* who had certainly deferved *well* from *France*; the incredible Pains ufed, and the immenfe Expence incurred to put her *Marine* not only on a fair, but on a formidable Footing; the bold Steps taken at home in humbling both the *Clergy* and the *Parliament*; the *vigorous* Meafures purfued in the *Eaft*, and her *artificial* Management in the *Weft Indies*; together with *another Event* more important than all of thefe. But we *forbear* from this fingle *Confideration*, that fince the Time of the celebrated Mr. BAYES, tho' the Arts of *Cyphering* and *Decyphering* have been greatly *improved*, yet we have entirely *loft* that more ingenious and ufeful *Art*—— of penning a *Whifper*.

To conclude, it feems highly probable, and it is to be wifhed that *Experience* may not confirm it; that if *France* has again recourfe to *Arms*, fhe will endeavour to do her Bufinefs *fingly*, fo as to avoid being drawn into a burthenfome and unfathomable Expence, in fupporting Allies, as well as of carrying on Wars in different Places. She will labour to *divide* before fhe attempts ftriking a *Blow*, and will practife every Art to hinder a *particular* from becoming a *general* Quarrel, and it is highly poffible, will give up with this View, that *Point* which it may be apprehended fhe has *moft* at *Heart*; in confequence of fome *Equivalent* either to herfelf or her *Allies*. I think a farther Explanation needlefs; if the *Reader* differs in Opinion, TIME before this Book comes to another Impreffion will decide the Difference, and it will afford me great Satisfaction to find the *Miftake* on my Side.

2   C H A P.

CHAP. XI.

The History of Spain, *under the House of* Austria; *the passing of that Crown into the Family of* Bourbon; *the Consequences of this Alteration, and the present Maxims of Government, true Interests, and political Connections of that Kingdom.*

WE are now to present the Reader with a succinct History of *Spain*, in order to give a clear Account of her political Interests and Connections. Every body knows how much it imports us to be acquainted with them, and many are by this Time sensible of the Misfortunes we have more than once brought upon ourselves, by not being sufficiently informed about them. The Crown of *Spain* is now one of the most considerable Powers of *Europe*, but it has not always been so. That great Country was formerly divided into several Kingdoms; and it was not till towards the latter End of the fifteenth Century, that most of them came to be united under *Ferdinand* and *Isabella*.

That King was reputed the wisest Prince of his Time, and his Queen, without being so reputed, was really the wisest crown'd Head in that Age. *Ferdinand* studied to extend his Power, *Isabella* laboured to make her Subjects great and happy. It was to him that his Successors, in a great measure, owe their being absolute at home, but it is to her they are indebted for the Figure they have since made abroad. In a Word, it was his Policy that made the Kings of *Spain* great, it was her Virtues that made the Crown so.

There were three Things that fell out under their Reigns, which intirely altered the Face of Affairs in *Spain*, and thereby changed the System of *Europe*. The first was the Junction of the Crowns of *Castile* and *Leon*, with the Dominions that belong'd to each of them; and this was brought about by their Marriage. The second was the total Exclusion of the *Moors*, which was effected by the Conquest of *Granada*, the last of those Principalities which they had erected in that Country; and which the Union of their Dominions put it in the Power of these Princes to accomplish. The third was the Dif-

covery

covery of the New World, and the annexing of it, when difcovered, to their Dominions; by which *Spain* may be said to commence her Maritime Power.

Thus in the Compass of about thirty Years, *Spain* became beyond all Comparison the greatest Power in *Europe*, which before was very inconsiderable. For this *Ferdinand* and his Queen *Isabella* began their Reign in 1472; the Queen died in 1504, and the King in 1516, after uniting the Kingdoms of *Naples* and *Navarre*, under various Pretences, to the rest of his already extensive Dominions.

This is a short Account of the Growth of the *Spanish* Power to the opening of the sixteenth Century, from which Time it is absolutely necessary that we should have more distinct Notions of its gradual Progress, greatest Height, and subsequent Declension, as well as of the great Change that has happened from its passing out of the House of *Austria* into that of *Bourbon*, which occasioned the last general War, and has been the Object of the principal Negotiations in *Europe* ever since.

That we may do this effectually, and at the same time keep as much within Bounds as possible, we shall first of all give a brief Description of the Power acquired by *Charles* V. who was at once Emperor of *Germany*, King of *Spain* and *Naples*, Master of a great Part of *Italy*, and Lord of the whole *Low-Countries*, as well those that now form the Republick of the *United Provinces*, as those which are stiled the *Spanish Netherlands*, and belong mostly to the Empress Queen of *Hungary*.

We shall next give a short View of the Reign of *Philip* II. who, if ambitious Princes are to be stiled so, was the wisest King, at least the greatest Politician, that *Europe* ever saw, and in that Quality bid the fairest for universal Monarchy; in his Pretensions to which, he was rather defeated by Providence than either by the Power or Prudence of those that opposed him, and yet he had to deal with some of the greatest Princes that ever ruled in this Part of the World.

We shall in the third place shew, how that mighty Power which he established dwindled away and sunk to nothing under his Successors; so that at last they were protected in the Possession of their Dominions, by those very Powers that had been raised upon their Ruin. A strange Revolution this! but of all that has happened in *Europe* the most worthy of Attention; because it shews us how the most potent Governments are infeebled and brought to Decay by all-grasping Princes; and how Providence counteracts human Policy, so as to draw Events

X   directly

directly contrary to their Intentions, from the Plans laid down and executed by the ableſt Stateſmen, to gratify the Deſires of the moſt ambitious Princes.

Laſtly, We ſhall give an impartial Account of the Manner in which this Kingdom changed its Maſters, and how all *Europe* came to acquieſce at laſt in its remaining in the Poſſeſſion of the late King *Philip* V. tho' a younger Branch of the Houſe of *Bourbon*.

We have in a foregoing Article relating to the Houſe of *Auſtria*, given an Account of the Deſcent of *Charles* V. who was the Grandſon of *Ferdinand* and *Iſabella* by their only Daughter, and who ſucceeded firſt to the *Low-Countries*, of which he was alſo a Native; and therefore it is no wonder that he retained for them a ſtrong Affection as long as he lived. It was this Affection, however, that render'd him diſagreeable to the *Spaniards*, who on the other hand were never very agreeable to him; and though by the Aſſiſtance of two very able Miniſters, he governed that Nation very quietly during the beſt part of his Reign, yet there never was any cordial Affection between him and his Subjects in that Kingdom.

It is true, that for the ſake of the prodigious Revenues which he drew from the *Spaniſh* Dominions in *Europe* and *America*, he behaved toward them always with great Civility and Condeſcenſion, and countenanced that Prepoſſeſſion in their Favour, which was ſhewn by his Son *Philip* even in his Infancy. On the other hand, the Fortune of the Emperor, who gained the higheſt military Reputation by a long Series of Victories, increaſed the *Spaniſh* Dominions in *Italy*, humbled the *French* Power, brought King *Francis* I. Priſoner to *Madrid*, and carried the Terror of his Arms into *Africa*, made him in ſome meaſure popular amongſt the *Spaniards*, naturally the moſt loyal People in *Europe*, and extremely charm'd with heroic Courage in their Princes.

But on the one hand the Emperor did not foreſee in the former Part of his Reign, the Impoſſibility of ſecuring all his Dominions to his Son, which if he had done, he would certainly have acted otherwiſe than he did, and have been more tender of the Intereſt of *Spain*, and more prudent in the Diſpoſition of that immenſe Wealth which accrued to him from the Poſſeſſion of it. He ſaw this in the latter Part of his Days, and then he changed his Scheme of proceeding; he endeavoured to augment his Maritime Force, and by the Marriage of his Son *Philip* with *Mary* Queen of *England*, ſought to eſtabliſh a new Connection between the different Parts of his Dominions, and at

the

the same time to surround *France*, and keep her in continual Dependence.

The *Spaniards* were as much deceived on the other hand in their Notions for the great Conquests and mighty Grandeur of the Emperor; as they were gained at their Expence, so they were kept by the same Means; and this exhausted *Spain* both of Men and Money, drew from her all the Wealth she derived from her *Indies* even faster than it came in, and by putting it into the Power of the Court to confer honourable and profitable Employments upon her Grandees, extinguished those Principles of Honour and Patriotism for which they had been formerly famous, and made them the Flatterers of Princes, and Dependents on their Ministers; which their free-born Ancestors would have despised.

It must be allow'd, that considering the End he aim'd at, this Monarch laid down a right Plan, and commonly speaking, pursued it steadily; he was also generally successful, and after the Battle of *Pavia*, stood very fair for carrying his great Design into Execution: But in the Decline of Life he was less fortunate, or rather he was better known; all the Powers in *Europe* were upon their Guard, and that fraudulent Policy, by which he had been so great a Gainer, grew not only useless, but was also turned upon himself.

Hence it was, that almost every where his Affairs began to decline. The Princes of *Germany* would no longer trust him; the Pope and the *Italian* Princes were continually plotting against him; *France* began to recover its Power, and even in the *Low-Countries*, which had been always the most favoured Part of his Dominions, he met with such Mortifications, as forced him to think of a Resignation, which he executed with Repugnance, and repented as soon as he had made it.

But it does not appear that he ever laid aside his Scheme of universal Monarchy; he was indeed satisfied, that it could never be brought to bear in his own Time, but he flatter'd himself to the last that it could not escape his Son. He knew the Disposition of *Philip* exactly, and tho' he was not so great a Hero, he was rather a more refined Politician than he; and therefore he took all imaginable Pains to infuse into his Mind the same Views, the same Passions, and the same Principles of Policy, that had governed himself.

It was to facilitate this, that at the Time of his Resignation he put into his Hands a System of the Art of War, and another of Government, of his own composing; both excellent in their kind, but fatal to his Pupil, and to the *Spanish* Nation. *Philip* received these Presents more respectfully than he had done

X 2

his Father's Dominions, and ſtudied them with ſuch Diligence, that he was ſoon in a Condition to have given the like Leſſons himſelf. The *Spaniards* even at this Time, retain the Memory of this Fact, and make uſe of it as a proverbial Expreſſion, *That in all great Emergencies, their Miniſters are wont to conſult the Spirit of* Charles V. which is but too true, for they proſecuted his Maxims till they wore out the Force and Riches of this opulent and potent Nation ; and came to be in that deplorable State in which we ſhall hereafter find them.

In 1558, the Emperor *Charles* V. died in his Retirement, diſſatisfied with the World, his Son, and himſelf ; but at the ſame time with a full Proſpect of *Philip*'s becoming Maſter of the greateſt Part of *Europe*, either by Force of Arms, or by Dint of his Intrigues. He left him, it muſt be acknowledged, a moſt formidable Prince ; for he had juſt triumphed over the *French*, by a deciſive Victory, had recovered all his Dominions in *Italy*, was in full Poſſeſſion of the *Low-Countries*, and had ſo much Power in *England*, as enabled him to employ the whole Strength of this Nation for his Service, directly againſt its own Intereſts.

To ſay Truth, if it had not been for the timely Death of his Conſort Queen *Mary*, there is hardly any Doubt to be made, that he would have carried his Point ; and have annexed this Crown, for ſome time at leaſt, to the reſt of his Territories, which as it would have been fatal to the general Good of *Europe*, would have been no leſs deſtructive to our Anceſtors in particular, as we ſhall perhaps have an Occaſion to ſhew more largely in another Part of this Work.

Philip II. began his Reign with much Reputation, and in the War which he entered into with *France*, had at firſt great Succeſſes, which were chiefly owing to the Fidelity and Virtues of his Subjects in the *Low-Countries*. It was not long, however, that he ſuffered his Affairs to continue in this Situation ; he was bent upon returning to, and living in *Spain* ; he preferred none but the Natives of that Country, and ſhewed himſelf fonder of their Cuſtoms, and Manner of Living, than was fit for a Prince, who had ſuch extenſive Dominions, and People of ſuch different Tempers, and Diſpoſitions, under his Obedience.

He attempted likewiſe upon their Liberties, and was deſirous of leaving *Spaniſh* Troops in their principal Cities, under the Command of the Prince of *Orange*, and Count *Egmont* ; but the People abſolutely refuſed to ſubmit, and ſoon after the Troubles in thoſe Parts began. The *Spaniards* miſtook their Intereſts in this Reſpect intirely ; they were pleaſed

at

at what had happened; they rejoiced at their having a King intirely *Spanish*; and looked upon the Revolt of the *Flemings*, as a Thing that must prove very advantageous to them, as it would afford the King, not only an Opportunity of curtailing their Privileges, but of confiscating their Estates, and bestowing them upon his Favourites, or in other Words, upon themselves.

But they were convinced by Experience of the Folly of these Notions; for the People of the *Low-Countries* were not to be frighted out of their Privileges, and therefore to deprive them by Force, Troops were continually to be sent from *Spain*, and to be maintained when sent in the *Low-Countries*, which instead of becoming, as *Philip* intended, a Place of Arms, from whence he might at Pleasure invade either *France* or *England*, they became in Reality the Theatre of a War, where at a very small Expence the *English* and *French* broke the Force of the *Spanish* Monarchy, while thus employed against its own Subjects. This was the first and great Mistake of his Reign, a Mistake which how much soever he might repent, he could never repair; a Mistake that was equally fatal to his own Power, and useful in creating a Diversion to his Neighbours, who but for this Mistake would have run a very great Hazard of becoming likewise his Subjects.

Another great Mistake committed by *Philip* II. was his considering in the Administration of Affairs, his own ambitious Projects only, without the least Attention to the Welfare of his Subjects. He saw his Dominions daily thinned by the Losses his Army sustained; he saw the Trade of his People decline, chiefly from the heavy Load of Taxes which he imposed; he saw likewise the naval Power of his Kingdom continually sink, from his employing almost all the Shipping and Seamen in his Dominions, in a Variety of Expeditions, many of which were unsuccessful, in respect to the Views that he proposed, and all of them were exceedingly ruinous to the *Spanish* Nation.

He had no Consideration of this, but acted as if his People had been Brute Beasts, in which he had a Property, without being under any Obligation to take care of them. He was so consummate a Politician, that he did nothing without a View, and thought of no other Views than his own; by which he stript his People of their Wealth, without providing for their Supply; which made an *Italian* Wit compare him to a bad Horseman, who rode his Beast hard, and seldom gave him a Meal's Meat. It was to this Principle, that he owed that Firmness, or rather Insensibility, for which he was so famous.

X 3

He

He shewed no Emotion on ill News, because he was careless of the Lives and Fortunes of his Subjects; and how much soever he might feel his own Disappointements, he had no Feeling at all for the Sufferings and Misfortunes of those whom he employed, but regarded the Loss of them as a Thing of course, and scarce worthy of his Notice.

A third Error in the Conduct of this great Prince, was the over-rating his own Power, which led him to undertake several great Projects, without giving himself Time to execute any one of them; by which he multiplied the Number of his Enemies, and put that in the Power of many, which could have been executed singly by none. As for Instance, he attacked *England* while he was engaged in subduing the *Low-Countries*; and in the Midst of the War this drew upon him, he broke with *France.*

Thus one Project embarrassed and confounded another, by which in the End they all miscarried, except the Conquest of *Portugal*, which he committed entirely to the Management of the Duke of *Alva*, who reduced the whole Kingdon in fifty-eight Days. This shews what he might have done, if he had proceeded always in that Method; as his sending the Duke of *Parma* to the Relief of the League in *France*, which gave the *Dutch* an Opportunity of recovering their Affairs, is an evident Demonstration that he failed in his other Designs, by undertaking more than one at once.

These Projects are all sufficiently well known to the World, as well as various Expeditions he caused to be undertaken against the *Turks*, and other Infidels, and some occasional Diversions made by his Forces in *Italy*. In respect to all these, the *Spaniards* pleased themselves with romantick Speculations, such as that the Sun never set in their Master's Dominions; that while he meditated in his Closet at the *Escurial*, the Plans were laid there, by which both Hemispheres were governed, and the Forces of *Spain* awed at the same Time both *Europe* and the *Indies*.

Delusive Dreams of boundless Grandeur! which made but very poor Amends for the dreadful Distresses that these ambitious Pursuits had brought upon their exhausted Country; and which serve to shew us, that the Examples of Princes are frequently as fatal to their Subjects as their false Politicks, by inspiring them with the same fond Passion for extensive Dominions, which swell their own Breasts, and so make that the Object of both their Wishes, which is equally destructive to both their Interests.

It

It muſt however be acknowledged, that towards the latter End of his Life this great Politician altered his Views, and out of Regard to the Peace of his Poſterity, began to think of ſecuring that of his Subjects. In order to this he gave the *Low-Countries* in Dowry to his Daughter *Iſabella-Clara-Eugenia*, whom he married to her Couſin the Archduke *Albert*, in Hopes that this might have drawn back the Inhabitants of the revolted Provinces to their Duty; and tho' this Contrivance failed, yet it muſt be acknowledged that it was very well contrived, and had a very fair Appearance.

He took care to diſpoſe Matters for a Peace with *England*, and if he did not conclude it, it was very probably in hopes of making better Terms with her Succeſſor, if Queen *Elizabeth* had died. But in regard to *France*, which he found recovered Strength on the Concluſion of the Civil War, and *Henry* IV. being peaceably ſeated on the Throne, he made haſte to compromiſe his Differences, that he might leave his Dominions quiet on that Side. As to *Portugal*, tho' he obtained it by Conqueſt, he ſought to preſerve it by a very mild and gentle Government, and laboured all that lay in his Power to make the People conceive it their Intereſt to continue united with *Spain*; which might probably have been effected, if he had not put his Son Don *Carlos* to Death, who was likewiſe the Son of *Mary* Infanta of *Portugal*. But the People were ſo averſe to the *Spaniſh* Dominion, that their Prieſts put into their Litanies a Petition to God to deliver them from the *Caſtilian* Yoke.

Thus it appears plainly, that Experience convinced *Philip* II. who was very juſtly eſteemed a conſummate Politician, of his former Errors, and in a manner forced him to ſee that the true Greatneſs of a King does not conſiſt in Conqueſts and extending his Dominions, but in governing thoſe wiſely which he juſtly poſſeſſes; and in making his Subjects rich and happy, rather than rendering his own Family great.

His laſt Error was committed when he was very near his End, and was of all others the moſt excuſeable. He flatter'd himſelf with the Hopes of governing the *Spaniſh* Monarchy after his Demiſe, and with that View drew up a Memorial for the Inſtruction of his Son. Vain and ambitious Thoughts! ſays the *French* Hiſtorian *Mezeray* very juſtly; for all Princes will govern according to their own Fancy, and have little or no regard to the Maxims of their Predeceſſors.

He died on the 13th of *September* 1598, after a long Reign, in which he obtained the Reputation of a great and wiſe Prince; tho', as we have ſhewn, he left his Kingdom much

weaker

weaker than he found it, and his Subjects impoverished to such a Degree as made their Recovery difficult, as the Conduct of his Successors rendered it impracticable.

His Son *Philip* III. was a Prince endowed with all the Virtues requisite to have rendered him happy in private Life; but without those Qualities which were necessary to make a great Monarch, or to reform the Errors of his Father's Government. He was naturally of a quiet and peaceable Disposition, and he had the good Fortune to confide in a Minister, whose Talents, if they were not great, were at least such as enabled him to do much Good.

This was the Duke of *Lerma*, during whose Administration a solid Peace was concluded with *England*, agreeable to the dying Counsel of *Philip* II. He also made a Truce with the *Dutch*, and laboured all he could to bring the Expences of the Government within some Bounds. But what is equally strange and remarkable, this happy Temper both in the King and his Minister was attended with an unforeseen Consequence, which rendered all the Expectations that might justly have been formed from thence vain and abortive.

It had been the Policy of his Father to lessen the Power and to abate the Credit of the Grandees, whom he hated, and who, no doubt, had as little Respect for him; but *Philip* III. pursued a contrary Conduct, he had an Affection for the *Spanish* Nation, and a sincere Respect for their Nobility, whom therefore he brought into his Councils, and employed in his Affairs; but it fell out, that their Notions were directly opposite to those of the Minister; they thought his Love of Peace a Weakness, and his forming no Plan for extending the Dominions of *Spain* derogatory from the Glory of the Crown; and by adopting the Sentiments of the Prince who had humbled them, and crossing the System of that Government under which they had recovered Credit, they made Way for new Mischiefs, and forced the King upon Measures disagreeable to himself, and destructive to his Subjects.

One of these was the most distinguish'd Transaction of his Reign, and at the same Time the most fatal; and that from which *Spain* derives part of that Misery under which she labours at present. This was the intire driving out the *Moriscos*, or the Descendents of the *Moors*, that inhabited the Kingdom of *Granada* and the Countries adjacent, to the Number of nine hundred thousand Persons, of all Ranks, Sexes, and Ages. The Pretence was, that they were disaffected and irreconcileable to a Christian Government, as being still *Mohammedans* in their Hearts.

In

In this, no doubt, there was a great deal of Truth; but when the fame Expedient was propofed more than once to *Philip* II. his Anfwer always was, *You muft find me fome other Method, for this is impracticable.* Yet under this Reign it was not only refolv'd upon but put in Execution; by which a vaft Tract of Country, and that too the moft populous in *Spain,* was left without Inhabitants, and from being beyond Comparifon the moft fruitful (becaufe the beft cultivated) Part of that great Kingdom, became and has continued ever fince almoft a Defart. For whatever thefe People were with refpect to Religion, in point of Morals and Induftry they were far from being the worft of his Catholick Majefty's Subjects; and this driving them over to *Barbary,* where they became his moft implacable Enemies, was one of the moft dangerous Miftakes in Politicks that Hiftory has recorded.

By Degrees the Nobility got the better of the Duke of *Lerma* in the King's Opinion; but that prudent Minifter forefeeing his Fall, took care to fecure his Head, which he knew was aimed at by his Enemies, by covering it with a Cardinal's Cap. After this Difgrace fome Troubles broke out in *Italy,* which proved very detrimental to the *Spanifh* Intereft; and it is highly probable that the new Miniftry would have engaged the King in a new War, notwithftanding his pacifick Difpofition, if he had not been removed by Death, which happen'd on the laft Day of *March* 1621.

Philip IV. fucceeded his Father in the Flower of his Age, and the firft Action of his Reign feemed to fpeak a much higher Genius for Government. He had interpofed, while Prince of *Afturias,* in Favour of a Gentleman condemned for Murder, and had obtained his Father's Promife for a Pardon, with which the Relations of the Criminal were fatisfied, and did not make hafte to take it out in Form. After the King's Death, the Profecution was renewed, and the new King directed Execution. Thofe who had follicited for the young Man were amazed, and reprefented to his Majefty the Inconftancy, as they conceived, of his Behaviour. His Anfwer was very remarkable, *While a private Man,* faid he, *there was Room in my Breaft for Compaffion, but now I am a King, it is intirely taken up with Juftice.* All Antiquity does not furnifh us with a Saying more fenfible or worthy of a Monarch; but alas! *cætera ad hanc formam non erant.*

He drove his Father's Favourites from Court, and among them the Duke *d'Uzeda,* the unnatural Son of the Duke of *Lerma,* and one of the warmeft Perfecutors of his Father. This was certainly right, but foon after he fpoiled the Cardinal-

Duke

Duke of all his Fortune which had been left him, even by the Avarice and Severity of the former Minifters; and this was furely wrong. If it had proceeded from a Diflike of Favourites, and a fettled Refolution of adminiftring the Government himfelf, it had been in fome meafure excufeable; but it very foon appeared that this was very far from being the Cafe.

He raifed *Olivarez* to the Rank of Prime Minifter, who is fo well known in Hiftory by the peculiar Title of the *Conde-Duke*, and delivered himfelf up to him intirely. It cannot however be denied that he was a Perfon of great Genius, which appear'd by the vaft Defigns he formed almoft as foon as he came into the Miniftry, or at leaft as foon as he was placed at the Head of it; but he had not Time to execute them, for as it fell out his Parts were better employed.

We have fhewn in fpeaking of the Affairs of the Empire, what were the Views of the other Branch of the Houfe of *Auftria* at this Time, and in our Account of the laft Reign, we have taken Notice, that a very ambitious Miniftry fucceeded the gentle and quiet Adminiftration of the Duke of *Lerma*, to which he muft now add, that among the firft Steps taken by the new Minifter, the fupporting the Emperor was one; the breaking the Truce with the *Dutch* another; and the moft fcandalous Breach of the Treaty of Marriage with our King *Charles* the Firft, then Prince of *Wales*, who made a romantick Voyage to *Spain* to fetch the *Infanta*, a third.

It muft however be confefs'd, that thefe Acts of Power were agreeable to the King and to his Council; fo that they cannot, ftrictly fpeaking, be intirely laid to the Door of the Minifter, tho' they afterwards were. Thefe Meafures having difobliged moft of the great Powers in *Europe*, occafioned in 1625, the League of *Avignon*, in which tho' there is little Mention of it in our Hiftories, we had our Share as well as in fuftaining the Affronts that occafioned it.

This League was the Effects of the ambitious Efforts of the Houfe of *Auftria*, to obtain an univerfal Monarchy; and the Defign of it was, to humble that Houfe to fuch a Degree, as to drive fuch a pernicious Notion out of her Councils, or at leaft to put the Accomplifhment thereof intirely out of her Power, by attacking her, and that, too, vigoroufly on all Sides at once. This was perfectly agreeable to the modern Doctrine of the Ballance of Power, which is in Truth the only political Doctrine that can preferve publick Liberty, and hinder one State from fwallowing up another, till fhe becomes too powerful to be withftood. Hence arifes the great Importance

of

of encouraging and commending whatever is written about it, since the very Rumour and Difcourfe of a Ballance produces fuch Conceptions even in common Minds, as have more than once contributed to preferve it.

It was in Confequence of this Plan that the *Dutch* attack'd *Brafil*; the King of *France* and the Duke of *Savoy*, the Republick of *Genoa*; the *Englifh*, *Cadiz*; the King of *Denmark* and the Proteftants of *Germany*, the Emperor's hereditary Countries; the *Venetians* too, tho' they did not declare openly, yet underhand affifted the Duke of *Savoy* and the *Grifons* in weakening the Power of *Spain* in *Italy*; *Bethlem Gabor* Prince of *Tranfilvania*, with the Affiftance of the *Turks*, fell upon *Hungary*, and the *Dutch* privately fupplied the *Moors* with Artillery and Engineers for attacking the Fortreffes of *Mamora* and *Larache*.

It is certain, that this Defign was very well laid, and what is not common where Alliances are made up of fo many Parties, almoft every Part of it was carried into Execution; fo that never any two Powers fuftained a greater Shock than the Emperor and *Spain* from this Confederacy. The Courage and Conduct of *Olivarez*, however, contributed chiefly to divert this Storm, and break its Force. He fent a Fleet in Time to *Brafil*, that recovered from the *Dutch* the Bay of *All-Saints*, and the Town of St. *Salvadore*; he affifted and deliver'd the *Genoefe* from the Danger that threaten'd them; his Emiffaries excited fuch Jealoufies of the *French* in the Minds of the *Grifons*, as determined them to make Peace with *Spain*, and to confent that the Popifh Religion fhould be eftablifhed in the *Valteline*, on Condition that it was reftored to them; the *Englifh* mifcarried in their Attempt upon *Cadiz*, the *Dutch* loft the important Town of *Breda*, the King of *Denmark* was beaten at the Battle of *Lutter*, and the *Moors* fail'd in the Siege of both the Fortreffes of *Larache* and *Mamora*.

This ought to have raifed the Reputation of the Minifter to the greateft Height; but the Envy conceived againft him was fo ftrong, and his Sufpicions and Jealoufies influenced him to that exceffive Degree, that he was fo very tenacious of Power, tho' not of Money, as by keeping it too much, and at the fame time too apparently in his Hands, he leffened his own Credit, and injured the Affairs of his Mafter.

But after all his good Fortune he really miftook the Cafe of that Government under his Care, and having fucceeded againft fo powerful a Confederacy, he perfuaded himfelf, that he might prevail in all the Schemes he had devifed, with-

out

out confidering how much the Strength of the Kingdom was weaken'd by formerly attacking and lately refifting fo many Powers ; Experience demonftrated his Miftake, for the Kingdom that recover'd by his Circumfpection, was ruined by his Ambition, juft as a Patient that gets over a Fever is fometimes loft by the Confumption that attends it, for want of Reft and Nourifhment.

If in this Time of Profperity the Minifter had given Peace to *Spain*, he had faved his Country, and fecured a lafting Fame ; but by neglecting this, and endeavouring to perform great Feats with an infirm and wafted Body, he made *Europe* fenfible of the Weaknefs of the *Spanifh* Monarchy, of which all Parties took their Advantage. The *Dutch* became utterly intractable, the *French* made Conquefts on both Sides of their Frontiers, the *Catalonians* revolted, the *Portuguefe* declared the Duke of *Braganza*, King. Great Troubles followed in *Italy* ; for a Fifherman's Boy at *Naples* fubverted that Government in three Days, and might have made himfelf abfolute Mafter of the Kingdom, if the Populace had been as eafily governed as they were inflamed.

So many Misfortunes upon the Back of each other, compelled the *Spanifh* Pride to fuit itfelf to the Circumftances of the Times ; in Confequence of which, a Peace was made with the *Dutch* upon their own Terms ; and they were acknowledged to be a free State, after *Spain* had fpent in ready Money, three hundred Millions *Sterling*, in labouring to reduce them, if their Accounts may be depended upon. The *French* made great Acquifitions in the *Low-Countries*, the War in *Catalonia* ruined that Province, the Subjects of *Spain* in *Italy* grew miferable, and the People of *Portugal* maintained their Independency.

The *Conde-Duke* all this Time kept his Mafter in fuch profound Ignorance, that he knew not the Diftreffes of his Government, when all *Europe* rung of them. But at laft this fell heavy upon the Minifter, for the Queen, at the Perfuafion of the Emperor, having once broke the Ice, Complaints againft *Olivarez* came from all Ranks of People, and all Quarters of the *Spanifh* Dominions ; fo that he was torn from the King, who directed him to retire a fmall Diftance from the Court ; he obey'd ; and if he could have been idle, he might have recovered his Power, for the King was inclined to recall him.

But he fpent his leifure Hours in writing an Apology for his Adminiftration, in which he fhewed more Wit in defending, than he had ever done Prudence in his Conduct ;

and

and this revived the Rage, and exafperated the Malice of his Enemies to fuch a Degree, that the King was forced to banifh him to a greater Diftance from Court, where his Anguifh and Difcontent foon killed him. In the Perfon of the Conde-Duke *de Olivarez* ended the Spirit of the Adminiftration, for none that fucceeded him were in any Degree equal to their Employment, or the Circumftances of the State.

The King had been fo long ufed to devolve the Cares of Government upon another Perfon, that he very foon made Choice of a new Minifter, *Don Lewis de Haro*, a Man of a very moderate Capacity, whofe Views reached no farther than maintaining the Government in its ufual Order ; and whofe only Ambition was, to keep his Place. The great Enemy of *Spain* was now dead, for Cardinal *Richelieu* had a particular Averfion to that Country and People; but his Succeffor *Mazarin* was of a milder Difpofition, and befides, the Queen Dowager of *France* was inclined to put an End to the Difputes between the two Kingdoms, which was precifely what the *Spanifh* Minifter moft earneftly defired.

The Truth is, the Kingdom of *Spain* could carry on the War no longer, her Armies were wore out, her Treafures were exhaufted, many of her Frontier Places loft, and moft of them run to Decay ; the *American* Commerce fallen much below what it was, and the dependent and tributary States in *Italy* falling off every Day. Upon this, Negotiations were fet on Foot between the two Crowns, but it was a long Time before they were perfected, and then the two Kings were to have an Interview, as the Minifters alfo had, upon the Frontiers of their refpective Dominions.

There was one Thing propofed at the Beginning of the Treaty, which made his Catholick Majefty very uneafy ; and this was the Marriage of his Daughter the Infanta *Maria Therefa* with the *French* King. He forefaw that this Marriage would fome time or other transfer the Monarchy of *Spain* from the Houfe of *Auftria* to that of *Bourbon* ; the Thought of which he could not bear. But as at this Time he had feveral other Children, his Minifters perfuaded him that this was an illgrounded Apprehenfion, and that nothing but this Marriage could render the Treaty in which they were embarked, folid and fecure.

Befides, the King was extremely fet upon reducing *Portugal*, and his Minifter made him believe, that a Peace with *France* would put that abfolutely in his Power, and that it was in vain to hope the Accomplifhment of it any other Way ; fo that at laft he was overcome, and confented to the Interview, and alfo the Marriage, both which foon after

took

took place; to which the War made against *Spain* by *Cromwell*, the Loss of the Island of *Jamaica*, and the Assistance he gave the *French* in the *Low-Countries*, greatly contributed.

This famous Treaty of the *Pyrennees* was concluded *November* 7th, 1659, by which the *French* were left in Possession of a great Part of their Conquests in *Flanders*, *Artois*, *Hainault* and *Luxembourg*; but most of the Sea Coasts were restored to his Catholic Majesty, the very important Port of *Dunkirk* only excepted, because it was then in the Hands of the *English*: The *French* likewise restored some Places they had taken in the *Milanese*, several Fortresses in the *Franche-Comte*, or County of *Burgundy*, and all that they then possessed in *Catalonia*. This was the most fair and equal Peace that was made in all the last Century, and those Politicians that annex true and just Notions to the famous Term of the Ballance of Power in *Europe*, mean with respect to these two Crowns, the Treaty of the *Pyrennees*; as with reference to *Germany*, they mean the Treaties of *Westphalia*; and in regard to the *North*, the Treaty of *Oliva*.

All Encroachments therefore upon this Treaty, by the Power of *France*, have been with Justice considered as destructive of that Ballance, which can never be restored any other way than by rendering the Crown of *Spain* independent of that of *France*, and bringing Things back to the State they were in. But notwithstanding this Treaty, *France* continued to assist underhand the *Portuguese*; so that notwithstanding the whole Force of the *Spanish* Monarchy was, during the Remainder of this Reign, employ'd against that Kingdom, yet it was to no Purpose, and served only to shew how much it was weaken'd and impair'd, and how little Proportion there was between its Strength then, and in the Reign of *Philip* II. when alone and without Allies, it was formidable to all *Europe*.

There is no Necessity that we should insist longer on what passed in the Time of King *Philip* IV. a Prince so weak in his tender Years, that is was generally believed he would not live to become a Man, and who notwithstanding reached to the Age of Sixty-one and upwards, and enjoy'd for the last forty Years a strong and vigorous Constitution. The Disposition of his Mind was the very reverse of that of his Body: for whereas in his Youth he discovered great Quickness of Parts, and unusual Penetration; in his riper Years, he addicted himself wholly to Pleasure, and in the Decline of his Life, fell into a State of Indolence, which differed very little from Insensibility, leaving all things to his Ministers; tho' now and then he shew'd that his Parts were not entirely extinguished, but that he had clearer

and

ind better Apprehensions of Affairs, than any of those by whom he was governed.

He died on the 17th of *September* 1665, after a Reign of forty-four Years and upwards ; during all which the Power of *Spain* had been gradually declining. He left behind him an only Son, under the Tuition of the Queen his Mother, and a Bastard by an Actress whose Name was *Calderona*, who afterwards made a great Figure in the World, under the Title of Don *John* of *Austria*, was the very last of that Family remarkable either for Courage or Abilities, and of whom we shall hereafter have occasion to speak more largely.

The Queen was very far from being beloved by her Subjects, because she retained so strong a Passion for her Country, that she scarce admitted any into her good Graces that were not *Germans* : Her Father-Confessor, a Jesuit, whose Name was *Nitard*, governed her absolutely ; and the first Thing she did was to raise him to the high Office of Inquisitor-General ; than which it was impossible for her to have done any thing more distasteful to the *Spanish* Nation.

Besides his being a Foreigner, and a *German*, there was another Circumstance, which made his Promotion both illegal and odious. It is an established Rule in Regard to the Holy Office, that down to the meanest Officer belonging to it, every one must have his Family free from Heresy, or even the Suspicion of Heresy ; whereas it was very well known, that Father *Nitard's* Parents were both Protestants.

One would think this was a very small Matter ; but in *Spain*, one may be sure it could not be considered in this Light, from the following Instance : A poor Priest of the Province of *Galicia*, who was never out of his Country in his Life, presented a Petition, desiring some Favour from *Philip* II. The Man's Name was *Martin Lotoro*, but unluckily for him, the Person who drew his Petition wrote it *Lutero* ; the King no sooner saw it, than he rejected it with Indignation. *A Man*, said he, *of such a Name, deserves no Favour.*

The great Hurry the Queen was in to promote this *German* Priest, brought a Cloud over her Administration in its very Dawn, which was never dissipated so long as she held the Reins of Government : For it is the Character of the *Spanish* Nation, that though they are soon offended, they are not soon reconciled ; and besides they are naturally averse to the Government of Women.

Charles II. the last King of *Spain* of the House of *Austria*, was not full four Years of Age at the Time of the Decease of the King his Father, who though he left his Widow *Mary Anne*

Anne of *Austria* Regent, appointed at the same time a Council, or as they call them in *Spain*, a *Junta*, without whose Advice she was to do nothing of Importance. This Council of State consisted of six Persons, four of whom had Seats therein, in Right of their Dignities. But the Cardinal of *Arragon*, being at that Time Archbishop of *Toledo*, and Inquisitor-General, the Queen prevailed upon him to resign the last of these two Places in favour of her Confessor Father *Nitard*, who thereby obtained a Place in the Council of Regency, and consequently had a large Share in the Government, which by Degrees he totally ingrossed.

The Queen, by her Influence over the King her Husband, had prevailed upon him on his Death-bed to take no more Notice of his natural Son Don *Juan*, than if he had not been in the World ; which, considering the Custom of *Spain*, where the Bastards of Kings have higher Rank, and greater Honours paid them, than in any other Country in *Europe*, was a strange thing, and at the same time the most impolitick Step she could have taken ; since after disobliging the People, by preferring Father *Nitard*, she should never have given them a Head, more especially such a one as Don *Juan*, who was already as much considered in the Kingdom, as if he had been the lawful Brother of the King.

It must be own'd that the *Spanish* History, and to say the Truth, scarce any History presents us with a more inactive or inglorious Reign, than this of which we are speaking. But for all that, the Events that happened under it were such as require it should be perfectly well known, as they had a strong Influence upon the Affairs of *Europe* ; and as for want of being acquainted with them, most of our Writers have given us false, or at least very imperfect Notions of the *Spanish* Government and Nation, at the Time of this Prince's Death, and the passing of the Crown into the House of *Bourbon*, which we have been made to believe was in Consequence of a forged Will, and against the general Inclinations of the People ; whereas, in Fact, neither of these were true, as will clearly be shewn to the attentive Reader of the following History, which we will begin with giving impartially the Characters of the principal Persons concerned therein, and pursue the same Method through the whole of this important Period.

The young King had a great deal of Wit and Spirit for a Child of his Age ; and though the Education given him was very indifferent, yet his Parts alone enabled him to discover a better Genius for Government, and a greater Capacity than either his Father or Grandfather. How he came to lose these

Parts,

Parts, and to grow equally feeble in Mind and Body, will be accounted for hereafter. His Mother, the Queen Regent, Daughter to one Emperor and Sister to another, was intirely devoted to the *German* Interest, ambitious to the higheſt Degree, fond of Power, which ſhe was far from knowing how to uſe, and as little capable of making a right Choice of thoſe to whom ſhe found herſelf obliged to confide it.

Don *Juan* was in the thirty-ſixth Year of his Age, of a middle Stature, an agreeable Perſon, had enough of the *Spaniſh* Gravity to pleaſe that Nation, but not ſo much as to diſguſt Strangers: He had an excellent Education, great Parts, was wiſe, brave, learned, and withal a very fine Gentleman. He had reduced the Kingdom of *Naples* when in Rebellion; had governed all the *Spaniſh* Dominions in *Italy*, with the Title of Vicar-General; had afterwards commanded againſt the *Portugueſe*; and at the Time of his Father's Death, was at the Head of the Privy Council, from whence the Queen removed him, with an Intent to have ſent him into *Flanders*; for which Country when ſhe concluded he was embarked, ſhe thought fit to cauſe his Favourite Don *Joſeph Malladas* to be apprehended and ſtrangled two Hours afterwards, by a Warrant under her own Hand.

Father *Nitard* was a Man of a very moderate Capacity, who knew how to govern the Queen, and to make his Court to ſome of the Grandees, by flattering them. One may gueſs at his Character by the Apology that he publiſhed for his Conduct, in which he thought he ſufficiently acquitted himſelf of the Death of *Malladas*, by alledging, that at the Time it happened he was ſaying his Prayers. Don *Juan* was at *Barcelona* when this was done, and was no ſooner made acquainted with it, than he returned from thence nearer to *Madrid*.

The Queen, who was extremely provoked, cauſed his Secretary to be ſeized, and baniſhed the Prince himſelf; but theſe Meaſures had a very bad Effect. The common People in *Spain* are born Politicians, and it is not eaſy to conceive with what Freedom, and with how much good Senſe they talk of publick Affairs, which however are no where worſe managed than in that Country. In all the great Cities, the common Diſcourſe of thoſe Times was, that they were an undone People, their King a Child, the Reins of Government in the Hands of a Woman, and by her committed to thoſe of a Stranger. One may well perceive, that theſe Diſcourſes were not very wide of Truth, and that Things could not go extremely well abroad, while they were in ſuch a Diſorder at

Y

Home;

Home; and the Fact is, that they went in such a manner as that it was hardly possible they should go worse.

A young Prince of the Abilities and Quality of Don *Juan*, knew very well how to manage the Temper and Discontents of the Multitude, so as to find his Interest therein; and therefore he took care to feed the Malecontents with Hopes, to give them private Informations, and to hint to them from time to time, Promises of Protection; till at last their Clamours rose so high, that he took occasion from thence to represent boldly to the Queen; the whole Kingdom was in a Ferment, Affairs both at Home and Abroad in a declining Condition, and that no Remedy could possibly be effectual, but the putting Things into a new Channel, which must be begun by sending her foreign Minister, Father *Nitard*, out of the Kingdom.

The Queen, as it might well be expected, took this very much amiss, and gave Don *Juan* such an Answer, as shewed plainly that she meant to insist upon her Authority, and to push this as far as it would go; a strong Proof of which she gave in causing *Patinho*, Don *Juan*'s Secretary, to be arrested, which had no better Consequence than making him lose all Temper; so that in the beginning of the Year 1669, he advanced very near *Madrid*, and sent the Queen such Messages, as gave her plainly to understand that he was resolved to carry his Point.

The Queen then laboured by fair means to divert him, but it was in vain. He had not about him above three hundred Horse, and yet with this inconsiderable Force he gave Law to the Government of *Spain*. About the middle of the Month of *February* Things came to a Crisis, by a very short Message he sent to the Queen, to this Effect: That if Father *Nitard* did not think fit to go out of the Gates of the Palace, by the twenty-sixth, he would come in Person and throw him out of the Windows.

It was then that the Queen saw, that notwithstanding her Title of Regent, she had little or no Power; for she attempted to put the City of *Madrid* in a State of Defence, and the People refused to obey her; so that much against her Will she was forced to send away her Confessor, as she did on the twenty-fifth; and he went directly to *Rome*, where she gave him soon after the Title of Ambassador from the Crown of *Spain*, and procured him a Hat from the Pope. Upon his Promotion, he wrote a very civil and even submissive Letter to Don *Juan*, in hopes of paving thereby his Way for returning into *Spain*; but that Prince never answered his Letter, and the Cardinal

very

very wisely drop'd a Design, that appeared to be impracticable.

The Queen, after taking this Step, in hopes to remove Don *Juan* out of her Way, and that she might find Means of supporting her Authority, thought proper to declare him Viceroy of *Arragon*; and this for some Time seemed very well to answer her Intentions, that Prince retiring thither, and applying himself with Diligence to discharge the Duties of his high Office. In the mean time the Queen found out a new Favourite, a *Spanish* Gentleman, whose Name was Don *Ferdinand de Valenzuela*, a Person that stood no way distinguished by Birth, Service, or any great Qualities.

He came to Court in no higher Rank than that of a Nobleman's Page; he made his Addresses to the Queen's Favourite, married her, and thereby came to have a large Share in her Mistress's Favour, rose by very quick Steps to the first Employments, and became as absolute, and as much hated a Favourite as Father *Nitard*. Several of the Nobility who were sincerely in the Queen's Interest, represented to her the bad Consequences that must naturally follow, from her too great Regard for such a Person; but it was in vain, the Queen remain'd fix'd in her own Sentiments, and these Remonstrances had no other Effect, than in making her endeavour to raise this Gentleman's Fortune so high, that it should not be easy to shake it.

In these Sort of Disputes, while the Affairs of the Kingdom were daily growing worse and worse, about six Years were wasted; so that on the 19th of *November* 1675, the King was declared Major, according to the Laws of *Spain*, having then acquired the Age of Fourteen. The Queen however took this Step merely for the Sake of Form, for she had not the least Intention to quit the Administration. On the contrary, she caused an Act to be drawn in the King's Name, declaring, that the Burthen of publick Affairs being too heavy for him to bear in his tender Age, he was desirous, as well out of Regard to the Welfare of his Subjects, as for his own Ease, to leave the Care of the Government in the Hands of the Queen-Mother and of the *Junta*.

She did not in the least doubt of the King's Consent; but when this Act was presented to him some Days afterwards for him to sign, he absolutely refused, with this remarkable Expression; " I hope that God, from whose Providence I re-
" ceive my Dominions, will be graciously pleased to give me
" the Capacity of governing the People he was committed to
" my Chage." This was was certainly well spoken, and it is

thought

thought the Actions of this young Prince would have been suitable to this Declaration; but we are told, that his Chocolate was *so prepared*, that in a short time he apparently declined both in Health and Parts, and consequently the Queen remain'd in full Possession of her Authority.

It is not to be imagined, that in so great a Kingdom there should not be some of the Nobility who preserved a just Regard for their Prince and for his People: Such as were in these Sentiments thought they could not take a more effectual Step, than to represent the State that Affairs were in to Don *Juan*, who had already received some Intimations of that Kind, and had written freely, but at the same time very respectfully to the Queen, beseeching her Majesty to take a just Care of the King's Education, to lessen the Taxes, and to provide for the Security of the Kingdom, which suffered exceedingly by the War, in which she was then engaged against *France*.

But all these Measures had very little Effect; the Queen valued her own Power beyond all things; and yet the raising and supporting *Valenzuela*, whom she made a Grandee of *Spain* of the first Class, was almost the sole Point that seemed to merit her Attention, and the only Effect of that Authority, which she so easily obtained, and was at so much Pains to keep. The Patriots therefore had recourse to another Measure; they applied themselves to the King, and having represented to him in general the Situation of his Affairs, they insisted more particularly on the Circumstances of his Person, which were such, that he was, properly speaking, very little better than a Prisoner, since the Marquis *de Valenzuela* suffered none to come near him, but those he knew, or at least took to be in his Interests.

These Discourses made such an Impression upon the King, that he readily demanded what Remedy could be applied? To which it was immediately answered, that the only way he had to deliver himself, was to withdraw secretly to *Buen Retiro*, send for Don *Juan* thither, and reform the Government by his Advice. They owned the thing was difficult, and they without Scruple or Reserve set forth the Difficulties attending it, that they might the better judge of the Spirit of their Prince. The King told them, that in spite of those Difficulties he would be free; and that on such a Day they might give Don *Juan* Notice that he expected to see him at that Palace.

They obeyed him, though at the same time they very much doubted whether the King would be able to keep his Word. The Evening before, he retired to his Apartment somewhat earlier than usual, and about the Beginning of the Night, attended only by one Gentleman, he wrapped himself up in

his

his Cloak, and walked on Foot to *Buen Retiro*. This signal Event happened in the Year 1677, when the King was about sixteen Years old.

It was not long after his Majesty came to the appointed Place, that Don *Juan*, who waited not far off, was admitted to his Presence, and was received with all the Joy and Satisfaction imaginable. A total Revolution ensued; the Queen-Mother was sent to *Toledo*, and there closely confined in a Convent; strict Search was made for the Marquis *de Valenzuela*, who withdrew for some time in hopes of escaping the Storm. He took Shelter in the Monastery of the *Escurial*, but falling sick, was discovered, first sent to Prison, next degraded from all his Dignities, and lastly transported as an Exile to the *Philippines*, from whence he was to go to *Peru*, and to be there treated as a Slave. He behaved better in his Misfortunes than he had done in his Prosperity, lived to recover his Liberty, and afterwards returned to *Spain*.

It is impossible to express how much Joy the Kingdom received from this Change of Affairs; and indeed it might have been highly advantageous to the Nation, if it had not wrought a Change in Don *Juan*, who having now the Royal Authority in his own Hands, thought of nothing so much as how to keep it, and to secure himself from any new Change. The Peace of *Nimeguen*, which was made so much to the Advantage of *France* and at the Expence of *Spain*, raised a great Clamour, tho' it was a necessary Step, the Kingdom being so exhausted, that the Loss must have been still greater if the War had continued. Yet the Grandees were much discontented, the People murmured, and Don *Juan* found himself, nor is it at all strange, more uneasy at the Head of the Administration, than while he was exiled from Court.

The King's Marriage was the next great Affair brought upon the Carpet, and the Princess intended for him by the Queen-Mother, was the Emperor's Daughter; but this being much against the Interest of Don *Juan*, he caused the Picture of a *French* Princess, Daughter to the Duke of *Orleans*, to be put into the King's Hands, with whom on the Sight of that Picture, he fell passionately in love. It is said that Don *Juan* afterwards repented of this, even before the Marriage took place, and inclined rather to have married the King to the Infanta of *Portugal*. But his Majesty adhered to his own Choice; and tho' Don *Juan* proposed in Council, that as this Princess was not the Daughter of a crown'd Head, it should be insisted upon, that some of the Places yielded by the last Treaty should be

restored

reſtored to *Spain*; yet the King, and the Grandees out of Reſpect to him, rejected this Propoſal, for fear it ſhould become
an inſurmountable Obſtacle to the Marriage.

This Point being carried againſt Don *Juan*, an Oppoſition
was quickly formed; and tho', ſo far as we can judge at this Diſtance of Time, his Power was his greateſt Crime, yet abundance
of Things were imputed to him, particularly one of a very high
Nature, which was, that he intended to get himſelf declared
Infant of *Caſtile*, which would have given him a Capacity of
ſucceeding to the Kingdom; but when it is conſidered that he
projected the King's Marriage, that he was himſelf ſingle, and
his Health declining, one can ſcarce ſee any Probability in a
Charge of this Nature.

Thoſe who were moſt forward in this Cabal againſt Don
Juan, formed another Project for recalling the Queen-Mother;
and notwithſtanding all that had paſſed, found means by the
Help of his Confeſſor to bring the poor eaſy King to reliſh this
Propoſal. The Marquis *de Villars*, who was now come a ſecond time Ambaſſador from the King of *France*, was alſo drawn
into this Party; and great Uneaſineſs he gave Don *Juan*, notwithſtanding he was ſenſible the Queen's Marriage was originally
of his propoſing.

The Chagrin which great Minds naturally conceive upon unexpected ill Treatment, wrought ſo powerfully upon that Prince's
Conſtitution, that it turned an Ague he caught in the Beginning
of Winter into a mortal Diſeaſe; ſo that he did not live to ſee
the Queen; whoſe Marriage had created him ſo many Mortifications. When it appeared that his Life was in ſo great Danger,
the King made him frequent Viſits, and lamented very ſincerely
a Loſs that was irreparable, and which he now clearly underſtood.

In theſe Conferences Don *Juan* talked to him very freely;
he ſhewed him the miſerable State of his Affairs, explained to
him the Means by which the Kingdom became ſo exhauſted;
ſhewed him what he had done for his Service, and how impoſſible it was for him to do more. He demonſtrated to him at his
Death, which happened on the 17th of *September* 1679, that all
his Enemies had publiſhed concerning his Deſigns were Calum-
nies and Fiction. For his Eſtate, which was not very large, he
left it intirely to the King; and his Jewels, which were much
more valuable in Proportion, he divided between the Queen
Dowager and the Queen Conſort.

With him expired the Genius of the *Spaniſh* Monarchy; or
at leaſt, of this Branch of the Houſe of *Auſtria*. There was now
no Prime Miniſter, indeed ſcarce any Miniſter at all; the Secretary of State for foreign Affairs was a Perſon put in by Don *Juan*

pro

pro Tempore, but he continued and acted as a Minister; because the Parties at Court behaved with such Violence against each other, that the King could not find himself at Liberty to appoint a Man of proper Rank to fill that Office.

The same kind of Disorder spread itself thro' the whole Administration; and as a Proof of the Weakness of their Councils, a Marriage (upon which the Fate of their own Kingdom, and indeed the Fate of *Europe* in some measure depended) was celebrated in a Village of about twenty Cottages, and in which there was not so much as one tolerable House. The only Sense their Grandees shewed upon this Occasion was, their endeavouring to hinder the *French* Ambassadors from being present, and even in this they did not succeed.

They were extremely pleased with their new Queen upon her first Appearance, who by the way was Grand-daughter to our King *Charles* I. and Niece to K. *Charles* II. then reigning. By Degrees however they grew out of Humour with that Princess chiefly because she had no Children; but this did not hinder their being more out of Humour with the Queen-Mother, for Reasons that have been before hinted, and which it does not become me more largely to explain.

The greatest Advantage that accrued to *France* from this Marriage, was the keeping at *Madrid* so able a Minister as the Marquis *de Villars*, who looked thoroughly into all the *Spanish* Affairs, and gave his Master so clear an Account of them, that he knew much better what *Spain* could do, than his Catholick Majesty and his Council, as appeared by the Measures he took. The Queen dying without Children, and a fresh War breaking out with *France*, the strange Weakness of the *Spanish* Monarchy became visible to all *Europe*; the *English* and *Dutch* Forces were employed in defending the *Spanish* Provinces in the *Low-Countries*; and the *English* Fleet for several Years together covered the Coasts of *Spain*, at which Time all her Ports were open to us, and *Gibraltar* and *Port-Mahon* were as much our own as they are now, abating only our Garrisons and our Expence.

The *Gazettes* of those Times, indeed, sometimes mention a *Spanish Armada*; but alas, it was no longer so much as the Shadow of what it once appeared. Five or six old Ships, ill manned, and miserably provided, were all that the *Spanish* Court could put to Sea; their Armies were in the same Condition, their Treasury in a worse; and therefore we may be satisfied, that the Terms procured for them by the Peace of *Ryswick*, were neither owing to their own Power, or the Moderation of *France*, but to the Wisdom and Steadiness of King *William*,

who

who remembering the Services that *Spain* had done him, considering the Ballance of Power in *Europe*, infisted upon what he obtained; and *Lewis* XIV. knowing the Value of a Peace at that Time, confented the more willingly to what was propofed, and executed what he confented to with unufual Punctuality; becaufe the Reputation of good Faith was of greater Confequence to him at that Juncture, than the Breach of it would have been.

It was for the very fame Reafon that he treated the Crown of *Spain* with more than ordinary Refpect, and made no Difficulty of paffing by fome Inadvertencies committed on his Frontiers, which he would have refented at any other Time. The *Spaniards* did not fee this, but attributed the Care of their Allies and the Complaifance of their Enemies to the Grandeur of their Crown, at a Time when it was fo far funk, that the King could not find Money for his ordinary Journies into the Country, and when they were infulted even by the fmaller States of *Europe*, of which we have given a furprizing Inftance in the Article of *Pruffia*. But this is not at all wonderful, fince in Kingdoms as well as in great Families, Pride rifes higheft when their Circumftances whom it poffeffes are at the worft.

The King, in 1690, had married a Princefs of the Houfe of *Neubourg*, by whom he had no Children, and his Health declining daily, all *Europe* fhewed more Concern for the Succeffion than was difcovered even in *Spain* itfelf. This had been the great Motive to the late Peace, which was quickly followed by the firft Treaty of Partition, in refpect to which the Sincerity of all Parties has been very juftly called in queftion. It is believed, and not without Foundation, that notwithftanding the Promife made by *France*, of keeping that Treaty a profound Secret, fhe gave private Notice of it to the *Spanifh* Miniftry, who were exceffively alarmed.

This produced an Enquiry into the Title of the Electoral Prince of *Bavaria*, which the *Spanifh* Lawyers held to be good, notwithftanding a Renunciation was made on purpofe to barr it; and this was the firft Blow given to the Hopes of the Imperial Family; and a very home Blow it was, for it decided two important Points: Firft, that Nearnefs of Blood ought to be confidered; and next, that no Renunciation could prejudice the Right that this gave.

The fecond Treaty of Partition, occafioned by the Death of that young Prince, was in like manner, and for the very fame Reafons, communicated to the Court of *Spain*, where it had the defired Effect; for his Catholick Majefty, and his Minifters, immediately took a Refolution to defeat this Scheme of a Division,

vision, and to preserve the *Spanish* Monarchy entire for the next Heir, tho' as yet they had not determined who that Heir should be.

It is certain that the King was inclined to the Imperial Branch of the House of *Austria*; and it was the Knowledge the Court of *Vienna* had of his Inclinations, that induced her to reject both the Treaties of Partition. But *France* had a powerful Party in the *Spanish* Court, who insinuated to the King, that these Treaties plainly proving the general Opinion of disinterested Courts, that the *French* Family had a Right, or at least a Colour of Right, they very easily prevailed that the Validity of the Renunciations by which this Right was supposed to be destroyed, should be examined and decided at *Rome*.

The Piety of the King drew him into this; and there was nothing at all in it repugnant to Policy or Justice, the Religion of all the Parties being considered. The Pope appointed a particular Congregation to examine this Affair, and notwithstanding the Exigency thereof, that Congregation went through it with all the Circumspection that its Importance seemed to demand. At last they came to a Point, and determined clearly that the Renunciations were void, at least with respect to the Posterity of the Princesses who made them; and for this Decision they gave many, and those very plausible Reasons.

The Determination of the Court of *Rome* did not arrive at *Madrid* before the Month of *August* 1700, when the King was thought by those about him to be very near his End. The Cardinal *Porto-Carrero*, who was at the Head of the Ministry, pressed his Majesty to lose no farther Time, but to fix this Point, on which the future Tranquillity of his People so much depended.

The Cardinal, and the whole Council, were inclined to prefer the House of *Bourbon* to the Imperial Branch of that of *Austria*, for various Reasons. First, because from the late Decision, the Right seemed incontestably in that House; next, because it seemed the surest Means of disappointing the Treaty of Partition; and lastly, because they had felt so many Inconveniencies already from the Dependence of *Spain* upon the Empire, that they could not by any means think of taking such a Step, as should at once increase this Dependence, and in all human Probability fix it upon them for ever, if it succeeded; and if it did not, leave *France* at liberty to dismember their Monarchy, while they had not so much as a Pretence to demand the Assistance of their Allies, who had in the most solemn

Manner

Maner acknowledged the Juſtice of the *French* Pretenſions by the two Treaties of Partition.

But though the *Spaniſh* Miniſtry agreed in this Point, yet they were extremely divided in another. Some were for calling the Duke of *Anjou*, the Dauphin's ſecond Son, to the Succeſſion; while others were better diſpoſed to the Duke of *Chartres*, eldeſt Son to the Duke of *Orleans*, afterwards Regent of *France* by that Title. The Reaſon upon which the former Party went was this, that the Right to the Crown of *Spain* being in the Dauphin, he might certainly, if he pleaſed, transfer it to his ſecond Son; and the great Argument urged by the latter, was, that the Duke of *Chartres* might very probably be agreeable to the Maritime Powers, and prevent any Diſputes about the Succeſſion. Yet the Conſideration of the Power of the *French* King, and the Improbability that he would employ this Power in favour of his Nephew againſt his Grand-Children, got the better of the laſt Reaſon; and the Members of his Catholick Majeſty's Council of State agreed to call the Duke of *Anjou* to the Succeſſion.

It was with great Difficulty that the King was brought to reliſh this Propoſition; but after reflecting on it ſeriouſly, he directed his laſt Will and Teſtament to be drawn, in the Preamble of which he recited the Invalidity of the Renunciations, and the inconteſtable Right of the Dauphin, whoſe ſecond Son he declared his Heir, requiring all the Subjects of the Crown of *Spain* in all Parts of his Dominions to acknowledge him as ſuch, immediately upon his Demiſe. In caſe of his Deceaſe without Heirs, his younger Brother the Duke of *Berry* was to be called to the Succeſſion, which failing, the Crown was limited to the Archduke *Charles*, and after him to the Duke of *Savoy* and his Children.

This Will was ſigned with all the requiſite Formalities upon the 2d of *October*, and this Fact was generally known, but the Contents of the Will were kept an abſolute Secret. The Imperial Miniſter Count *De Harrach* had no doubt that the Succeſſor appointed was the Archduke, and was therefore very well pleaſed the Thing was done. The *French* Miniſter Count *De Harcourt*, who had a much better Intereſt with the *Spaniſh* Grandees, received ſuch Intimations as kept him eaſy; and the Miniſtry, for their own Security, gave private Intelligence of this great Event to the *French* King.

After the Signing his Will his Catholick Majeſty grew better, and continued ſo for about a Fortnight, then relapſed, and expired on the 26th of *October* 1700, in the 39th Year of his Age, and the 35th of his Reign, which he had ſpent very unproſ-

unprofperoufly for himfelf as well as for his Subjects, and died very uneafy, as having a juft Forefight of the Mifchiefs that his Death muft inevitably bring upon his People. He was no fooner deceafed, than the Grandees affembled at the Palace in order to open his Teftament, and the Imperial Minifter went thither alfo; but was amaz'd to hear at his Arrival, that the Duke of *Anjou* was by the late King's Will declared his Succeffor, of which he gave his Mafter Notice as foon as it was in his Power.

The Regency appointed by the fame Will took upon them the Government, and difpatched inftantly Letters of Felicitation and Invitation to their new Monarch; but tho' they agreed in this, yet their Harmony lafted not long. The Queen Dowager and the Inquifitor-General, who were both of the Regency, began to cabal againft their new King; but Cardinal *Porto-Carrero* remained firm to his firft Principles, and laboured hard to perfuade all the Nobility of the Neceffity they were under of attaching themfelves unanimoufly to the Intereft of King *Philip:* Of the Confequences and Effects of his Exhortations, we fhall fpeak copioufly hereafter.

But before we quit this Subject, and enter upon the Hiftory of the next Reign, it may not be amifs to take Notice of fomething new which may be faid upon this Head, tho' often handled by the ableft Pens, and confidered over and over again by the greateft Politicians. The Reader will pleafe to obferve, that the War, to which an End was put by the Peace of *Nimeguen,* by which *Spain* loft fo many fine Towns and fair Countries in the *Netherlands,* was commenced by *France* under a Colour of that Right the King had by his Wife (notwithftanding all Renunciations) to thofe Places, and to many more which belonged to him by the fame Right.

This was faid to arife from the *Jus Devolutionis* which prevails in *Brabant;* and which in few Words is this: That where a Man has two Wives, the Heirs of his firft Wife, Male and Female, are Heirs to each other before the Children of the fecond Marriage; and therefore upon the Death of Prince *Balthazar,* his Catholick Majefty's eldeft Son, the moft Chriftian King claimed thefe Countries in Right of the Infanta *Maria Therefa,* Sifter of the whole Blood to Prince *Balthazar,* in Virtue of the *Jus Devolutionis.*

There have been whole Volumes written on each Side of this Controverfy, with which I fhall not meddle at all; but take it for granted, that the Right, as well as Power, was on the Side of *France.* I fhall alfo take it for granted, that the moft Chriftian King and his Son the Dauphin might refign,

fign, as they did to the Duke of *Anjou*, all their Rights; from whence it clearly follows, that *Philip* V. was the Reprefentative of the Infanta *Maria Therefa*, and had a juft Title to all her Rights; from whence I think there can be nothing plainer or more inconteftable, than that all the Countries and Places yielded to *France* by the Treaty of *Nimeguen*, belonged of Right to the late King of *Spain*, and belong now to his prefent Catholick Majefty, who, if he pleafed, might have refign'd them to his Brother Don *Philip*, and thereby provided him a Settlement, which would have contributed not a little to the general Tranquillity of *Europe*.

As foon as his moft Chriftian Majefty was informed of the Death of King *Charles* II. of *Spain*, and that his Grandfon the Duke of *Anjou* was called to his Succeffion; he prepared for maintaining him in the Poffeffion of that Kingdom, which he forefaw would be difputed by the Houfe of *Auftria* and its Allies. He called indeed for Form-fake a great Council, to confider whether he fhould accept the Will of the deceafed King or not; but from the previous Difpofitions on the Frontiers of *Spain*, and in the *Low-Countries*, it evidently appeared that he had long before refolved what Part to take.

Yet it was not till this Council had decided in Favour of the Will, that he acknowledged his Grandfon as the Heir of the *Spanifh* Monarchy, gave him the Title of *Philp* V. and confented to his going into *Spain*. It muft be allowed his Meafures were well taken upon this Occafion; and that the new King came into the full Poffeffion of the *Spanifh* Dominions, in a Manner that muft be no lefs furprifing to Pofterity, than it was to all *Europe* at the Time it happened. But it muft be allowed on the other hand, that this was in a great meafure owing to the intractable Difpofition of the Court of *Vienna*, where they looked upon the Succeffion to the *Spanifh* Monarchy as a Thing fo certain, that they would never confent to any Propofals made by their Allies for oppofing in time the Scheme of the Houfe of *Bourbon*.

The Maritime Powers were by this means put under the greateft Difficulties; the Elector of *Bavaria* admitted the *French* Troops into the *Netherlands*, of which he was Governor; and the Prince of *Vaudemont* declared for King *Philip* in *Italy*. It was this determined both *England* and *Holland* to diffemble for the prefent, and to acknowledge King *Philip*; and King *William* and the *States General* actually wrote him Letters of Felicitation upon his Acceffion, notwithftanding they at the
very

very Time were determined to contest his Title to that Crown.

It cannot be supposed that within the narrow Bounds prescribed to his Article, we should pretend to give the History of the War, occasioned by the Accession of *Philip* V. nor indeed is it at all necessary. We shall content ourselves with observing, that when the Grand Alliance was first formed, there was nothing farther proposed than the obtaining a proper Barrier for the *Dutch*, and a reasonable Equivalent for the House of *Austria*.

But after the Archduke *Charles* had assumed the Title of King of *Spain*, and the prodigious Successes of the Allies in the Beginning of the War had raised their Spirit and Hopes, they now projected no less than the entire Conquest of the *Spanish* Monarchy; and after the Battle of *Turin*, by which the *French* and *Spaniards* were obliged to evacuate *Italy*, there is scarce any Doubt to be made that they might have carried their Point, as by the Assistance of the *Portuguese* they were become Masters of a great Part of *Spain*, and even of the Capital; the *Austrian* Party in that Kingdom having done as much or more than, all things considered, could well be expected from them.

But no Care being taken in the Autumn of 1706, to send over proper Reinforcements to the Assistance of King *Charles*, King *Philip* began to recover Strength; and in *April* 1707 the Duke of *Berwick*, who commanded his Forces, obtained so total a Victory at *Almanza*, and pursued it with so much Spirit and Diligence, that before the End of the Year, the Face of Affairs was entirely changed in that Kingdom.

It is indeed true, that after this the Allies made a considerable Progress, and in the Month of *August* 1710, gain'd the Battle of *Saragossa*, which opened a Passage for *Charles* III. to *Madrid*, into which City he made his publick Entry in the Middle of the next Month; but the Dispositions of the *Spaniards* were now changed, and they adhered so firmly to King *Philip*, that before the Close of that Year, King *Charles* was again, after losing a Battle, driven back into *Catalonia*.

In the Month of *April* 1711, died the Emperor *Joseph*, and thereby left King *Charles* III. the sole Heir Male of the House of *Austria*, which altered the State of Things extremely, because it appeared now equally dangerous to give the *Spanish* as well as Imperial Dominions to this Prince, or to leave them to a Branch of the House of *Bourbon*; and there remained no Expedient that could be thought of, for preventing one or other of these Events.

The

The House of *Austria* was at this Time in Possession of the *Spanish Netherlands*, and all the Dominions that had belonged to that Crown on the Continent of *Italy*, which gave an Opportunity to the *French* Court to insinuate to the new Ministry in *England*, the Necessity as well as Expediency of putting an End to so long a War, upon Terms agreeable to the first Scheme of the Grand Alliance; and this in the End brought about the Peace of *Utrecht*, which was concluded in 1713.

By this Treaty King *Philip* yielded to *Great Britain* the Town and Castle of *Gibraltar*, and the Island of *Minorca*, for ever. The Kingdom of *Naples*, the Duchy of *Milan*, and the rest of the *Spanish* Dominions in *Italy*, together with the Island of *Sardinia*, and the *Low-Countries*, to the Emperor *Charles* VI; and the Island of *Sicily* with the Title of King to the Duke of *Savoy*.

It must be allowed that the Treaty of *Utrecht* was liable to great Exceptions; but however, the End of the Grand Alliance was in some measure answered by it. The Crowns of *France* and *Spain* were divided, the Power of the House of *Austria* considerably augmented, and the Ballance of *Europe* in some measure settled. But notwithstanding this, King *Philip* was not left in quiet Possession of his Dominions, to which the Emperor still kept up his Claim; and the Principality of *Catalonia*, and the Island of *Majorca*, though evacuated by the *Austrian* Troops, refused to submit, and were not reduced without a great deal of Trouble, and much Effusion of Blood; so that the Force of *Spain* seemed at the Conclusion of this War, exhausted to such a Degree, that there was not much to be feared from her, notwithstanding her being left in Possession of a Prince of the House of *Bourbon*.

It was the Policy of *Lewis* XIV. to match both his Grandsons, the Dukes of *Burgundy* and *Anjou*, into the House of *Savoy*; and tho' in the first Instance his Policy seem'd to be disappointed, since the Duke of *Savoy* took Part with the Allies throughout the whole War, yet his Daughter the Queen of *Spain*, by her engaging Behaviour, acquir'd the Affections of the *Spanish* Nobility, and thereby contributed not a little to maintain her Consort on the Throne.

She died the 14th of *February* 1714, and left behind her two Sons; Don *Lewis*, born in 1707, who became King of *Spain* by the Resignation of his Father; and Don *Ferdinand*, born the 23d of *September* 1713, who is the present King of *Spain*. By her Decease King *Philip* was left at Liberty to strengthen his Interest by a second Marriage, which he concluded in a few Months with the Princess *Elizabeth Farnese*,

Daughter

Daughter of the Duke of *Parma*, and Heiress not only of that Duchy, but also expectant Heiress of *Tuscany*, which Marriage was made with a View to revive the Interest of the House of *Bourbon* in *Italy*, which had been in a manner extinguished by the late Peace.

The new Queen brought her Father's Minister into Power, who was afterwards so well known by the Title of Cardinal *Alberoni*, who died lately. This Man, who must be allowed a great Genius, projected the Revival of the *Spanish* Power, and the Recovery of her *Italian* Dominions, at a Time when the former was thought very difficult, and the latter appeared totally impracticable.

It is true, that he did not absolutely succeed in this Scheme; but it is no less true, that he came much nearer it than any body could have imagined; for he put the Affairs of *Spain* into such Order, that she had Fleets and Armies capable of alarming her Neighbours, with which he actually recovered *Sardinia*, and would have recovered *Sicily*, if the *British* Naval Power had not interposed, and given such a Blow at *Messina* to his Catholick Majesty's Maritime Forces, as ruined all his Schemes at once; and which was still more, obliged his Master to part with him, and to accede to the Quadruple Alliance, which was set on foot to supply the Defects of the Treaty of *Utrecht*, and to fix the Tranquillity of *Europe* upon a more stable Basis.

By this Alliance *Sardinia* was given to the Duke of *Savoy* instead of *Sicily*; but at the same time it was agreed, that Don *Carlos*, his Catholick Majesty's first-born Son by his second Wife, should succeed to *Parma* and *Tuscany*. In 1721, a Marriage was concluded between the *French* King *Lewis* XV and the Infanta of *Spain*, which, as we have shewn elsewhere, did not take effect; but another concluded at the same time did, whereby *Lewis* Prince of *Asturias* espoused the fourth Daughter of the Duke of *Orleans* Regent of *France*.

Upon the Death of the Prince last mentioned, it is believed, that his Catholick Majesty entertained some Hopes of returning into *France*, and assuming the Government of that Kingdom in the Name of his Nephew; but whatever his Motive was, upon the 15th of *January* 1724, he actually resign'd the Kingdom to his Son Don *Lewis* Prince of *Asturias*, who is allowed to have had as great Abilities as could be expected in one of his Years, whose Manners as well as Birth endear'd him to the *Spaniards*, and who in the Beginning of his Administration gave great Hopes of his proving a wise and beneficent Monarch. But on the 30th of

August following he died, in the eighteenth Year of his Age, to the inexpreſſible Grief of his Father, as well as of his Subjects.

Upon the Demiſe of Don *Lewis* it was judged, that in the natural and legal Courſe of Things, his Brother Don *Ferdinand* ſhould have ſucceeded him in the Throne; but the Fear of a Minority, and perhaps ſome other Reaſons, induced the *Spaniards* to prevail upon *Philip* V. to reſume the Government, which he did, but with Reluctancy; whether real or feign'd, is hard to determine.

He apply'd himſelf very cloſely to Buſineſs, and being extremely provok'd at the ſending back of the Infanta from *France,* he began to meditate new and ſtrange Deſigns; or rather ſuch were infuſed into his Mind by the Queen and his Miniſters. It is generally believed, and not without good Grounds, that Cardinal *Alberoni,* who was then at *Rome,* contrived that amazing Scene which aſtoniſhed all *Europe;* at leaſt it is certain, that it was managed and tranſacted by one of his Creatures, a Man born to make a Figure in unquiet Times, and who, as he deſerted the Service of his Country, no other Prince ought to have relied on.

This was the famous *Ripperda,* who negotiated the Treaty of *Vienna,* by which the Emperor *Charles* VI. and King *Philip,* in whoſe Quarrel ſuch Rivers of Blood had been ſhed, and ſuch immenſe Treaſures expended, run into a cloſe Alliance for the mutual Support of each other's Intereſt, againſt thoſe very Powers which had ſacrificed ſo much for the Aggrandiſement of both. The true Motives to this ſingular Meaſure are by many held to remain ſtill ſecret; but it ſeems to be pretty evident, that the Views of the Emperor were immediate, and thoſe of *Spain* more at a Diſtance.

The former thought, that by this means he ſhould eſtabliſh his *Oſtend* Company, by which he hoped to revive the Trade of the *Low-Countries,* tho' at the Expence of his old Friends the *Dutch;* the latter conſented to the aggrandizing the Imperial Power, from the flattering Expectation that Don *Carlos* by marrying the eldeſt Archducheſs, at preſent Empreſs and Queen of *Hungary,* would become the Succeſſor to that Branch of the Houſe of *Auſtria,* as himſelf had been of the other, by which he ſeemed to renounce his Engagements with *France.*

This ſtrange Turn was more extraordinary, conſidering the Time in which it happened, when both *France* and the Maritime Powers were labouring to bring about in a rational and effectual manner, ſuch an Accommodation as theſe Monarchs haſtily and (if we may ſay it without Indecency) in-

conſiderately

considerately clapp'd up, with Views only to their private Advantage. To ballance this *Vienna* Alliance, *France*, the Maritime Powers, and *Prussia*, entered into the famous Treaty of *Hanover*, in order to provide for their own Interests, which they thought could never be safe, while this unnatural Conjunction subsisted.

The Emperor and the Catholick King, or rather his Queen (for she was at the Bottom of all this) seemed determined to persist in the Execution of Schemes from whence they expected to derive such mighty Advantages ; but the *Hanover* Allies took their Measures so effectually, that they were obliged, after some fruitless Attempts, to submit to the old Method of determining all Differences by a Negotiation, which produced the Congress of *Soissons*.

This Congress was opened the 14th of *June* 1728, but to very little Purpose, except that it served to shew the Ascendency which the *French* Minister Cardinal *Fleury* had gained by an Appearance of Probity, and an exterior Display of Equity and Moderation ; which demonstrates, that universal Monarchy might be attained by any powerful Prince, who really possest those Virtues. But this Situation growing tiresome to the *British* Nation, their Ministers entered into a secret Negotiation with the Crown of *Spain*, ending in the famous Treaty of *Seville* ; which it was expected would have determined all Differences, and put a Period to the Labours of the Ministers on both Sides. But this was so far from answering those sanguine Expectations, that the two next Years were taken up in contriving Expedients for carrying what was stipulated by that Treaty into Execution.

It is absolutely necessary that we should descend a little into Particulars. His Catholick Majesty's second Marriage was with a View to his Consort's Succession in *Italy*, and this was secured to him upon his acceding to the Quadruple Alliance ; that again was ratified by a subsequent Treaty, which was confirmed by the *Vienna* Alliance ; but for the Emperor's Security it was settled, that *Swiss* and not *Spanish* Troops should be sent into *Italy* to maintain Don *Carlos* in the Countries yielded to him by these several Treaties. But the Treaty of *Seville* altered this Method, and provided that *Spanish* Troops should be substituted instead of *Swiss*. To which the Emperor, as it might be reasonably expected, refused his Consent in the most positive and direct Terms.

It was to get over this Difficulty with him, that new Negotiations were necessary, and at length the Thing was brought about ; the Infant Don *Carlos* was sent to *Italy*

Z

with

with *Spanish* Troops, and received in Quality of Heir Apparent by the Grand Duke of *Tuscany*, which it was hoped would have contributed much, not only to the pacifying these Troubles, but securing the Peace of *Europe*, for the present Age at least.

But as the ablest Politicians are very liable to mistake; this last Step proved the Cause of a War, notwithstanding that the Maritime Powers had made a new Treaty with the Emperor, on purpose to facilitate it. The Infant Don *Carlos* arrived in *Italy* in 1731, and being in Possession of all the Dominions to which his expectative Right had created so many Disputes, his Mother formed new Schemes for enlarging his Power, and for enabling him to assume and maintain the regal Dignity. In order to this she set on foot Intrigues in *France*, to engage even the pacific Cardinal in a Measure directly repugnant to his System; and she endeavoured to engage the King of *Sardinia* to facilitate this Design, by the Promise of the Duchy of *Milan*. His Majesty had some Reasons to wish well to the *Spanish* Power, because of his being next in the Entail of that Monarchy; and he had stronger Reasons to dislike the Measures of the Imperial Court, which in respect to him were not altogether so just, and by no means so grateful or decent as they ought to have been.

These were the Motives to a new Confederacy, which upon the Death of the King of *Poland* in 1733, broke out into a War in *Italy*; and in the Year following Don *Carlos*, or rather the *Spanish* General *Montemar*, conquered the Kingdom of *Naples*, where he fought one decisive Battle at *Bitonto*, of which, to perpetuate the Memory of his Victory, he was made Duke.

As for the Island of *Sicily*, the Inhabitants, tho' not very remarkable for their Loyalty or Steadiness, had long shewn an Affection for the *Spanish* Government, which put Don *Carlos* in Possession of that Country without a Stroke. The Emperor, though he had no Assistance from his Allies, made a tolerable Defence in *Italy*; and the Circumstances of Things inclining the Court of *France* to a Peace, while it was in her Power to be well paid for it, *Spain* was forced to submit, and by this means publick Quiet was restored in 1735.

By this Peace Don *Carlos* remained King of the Two *Sicilies*, and thereby erected a third Monarchy in the House of *Bourbon*; but then he relinquished his maternal Succession, which was (considering the different Conditions of the Countries) perhaps a full Equivalent for it. His *Sardinian* Majesty, who had hazarded much, and whose Dominions had suffered excessively

by

by the War, gained very little, if we except his gaining fuch an experimental Knowledge of the good Faith of the Houfe of *Bourbon*, as will fcarce allow him to truft it again. *France*, who pretended to get nothing, got all; for fhe had *Lorrain* added to her Dominions, without any Colour of Right, except the moft inglorious abandoning King *Staniflaus*, chofen a fecond time King of *Poland*, could be fo called. This Treaty was concluded at *Vienna*, with which, except *France*, none of the contracting Powers either were, or had any Reafon to be fatisfied. After this King *Philip* might well be fuppofed to have nothing more in view than fo fpend the Remainder of his Days in Peace; and indeed this very probably might be all the View he had; but for his Queen, her Views were without End. She had made her eldeft Son a King, her third a Cardinal, almoft in his Cradle; and after all this *Europe* muft be once more embroiled, rather than her fecond Son Don *Philip* fhould mifs the being made an independent Prince. To influence *France* in his Favour fhe had married him to a *French* Princefs; and to bring the King of *Sardinia* into her Scheme, fhe promifed him any thing, but to no effect. She endeavoured likewife to cajole the Court of *Great Britain*, but to no Purpofe. She then caufed the King to turn a deaf Ear to the Complaints that were continually made of Depredations committed in the *Weft-Indies*, which produced at laft a War between the two Nations, extremely prejudicial to their mutual Interefts, and not lefs fo to her own, had fhe confidered them in a true Light; but Ambition is ufually blind, and the Defire of acquiring, defeats the Power of difcovering the Means of Acquifition.

Upon the Death of the Emperor *Charles* the VIth, the Enemies of the Houfe of *Auftria* having refolved to employ their utmoft Force to humble, at leaft, if not to deftroy it, the Crown of *Spain* entered into this Confederacy with a View of fpeedily carrying its Point in *Italy*, without the leaft Recollection of her Guaranty granted by the Treaty of *Vienna*, with all the Solemnity of which an Act of that Sort was capable. The Meafures taken for the Conduct of this War, tho' attended with an immenfe Expence, were, from the very Beginning, far from being fuccefsful. It was with infinite Difficulty that Troops were tranfported into the Kingdom of *Naples*, and when there, it was found no eafy Matter to provide for them Magazines, and, I was going to fay, a proper Train of Artillery, but that could not be provided at all.

The Duke *de Montemar*, the beft Officer in the *Spanifh*, and indeed one of the beft Generals in any Service, was put at the Head of this Army in the Summer of 1742, with Inftructions

to

to penetrate into *Lombardy*, through the Papal Dominions. He could not do this Time enough to save the Duke of *Modena*, whose Dominions were swallowed up by the Allies, and his Troops, to the Number of between five and six thousand Men, made Prisoners and disarmed. The *Austrian* and *Piedmontese* Army then marched to find out the Duke, who gave the last Marks of his Military Skill in making a very fine Retreat from a superior and victorious Enemy, in which he occasioned more Loss to them than he received. This, however, gave no Satisfaction to the Court of *Madrid*, who soon after removed him from his Command, to bestow it on a *Flemish* Officer of great Experience, the Count *de Gages*, who continued to command it with no great Success indeed, but with very high and just Reputation to himself during the whole War.

It is not at all necessary to our Design to enter here into a Detail of the Operations in *Italy*, of which we shall have Occasion to speak more at large elsewhere; and therefore it shall suffice to say, that after five Campaigns, in which there perished at least Fourscore Thousand Men, and for the Expence of which the Crown of *Spain* did not disburse so little as one hundred Millions of Pieces of Eight, Things fell into the most desperate Condition imaginable. The King of the two *Sicilies*, after suffering a Kind of Siege in his Camp, where he remained to cover his Kingdom from an Invasion, was at length obliged to have recourse to another Neutrality; the Infant Don *Philip*, after risking a desperate Battle at *Rottofreddo*, which with the Hazard of his Life opened him the Means of Flight, abandoned *Italy*; and the Republick of *Genoa*, which had embraced the *Spanish* Cause, was left to the Mercy of the *Germans*, who became Masters even of the Capital.

Under these Misfortunes, and worn out with Age and Infirmities, *Philip* the Fifth departed this Life on the 29th of *June* 1746, in his Grand Climacteric, and in the 46th Year of his Reign. He was a Monarch endowed with few great Qualities, but at the same time blemished with still fewer Vices. He was governed by his two Queens, and owed entirely to them the different Circumstances in which at certain Periods of his Life he found his Affairs. They were both *Italians*, both Princesses of great Abilities, but of very different Tempers. His first Queen, the Daughter of the late King of *Sardinia*, and the Sister of the present, was the most amiable Woman in the World in her Behaviour, and by engaging the Hearts of the *Spaniards* preserved the Throne to her Husband. The second formed by the Lessons of Cardinal *Alberoni*, knew likewise how to raise a strong Party to herself among the *Spanish*

Grandees;

Grandees; and tho' it was generally believed that fuch as were not in her Intereft were far fuperior in Number, and that the Death of the King would have entirely demolished her Power, yet Time has fhewn the contrary; and that notwithftanding what the *Spaniards* have fuffered by purfuing her Pretenfions in *Italy*, they ftill preferve a very high Refpect and Efteem for her Perfon, or at leaft affect it, on account of her having ftill fo good a Reverfionary Right to Power.

The King at his Deceafe, befides the Prince of *Afturias* of the firft Bed, left behind him, by his fecond Confort, three Sons and three Daughters, *viz.* Don *Carlos*, who with vaft Expence and Trouble he had feated on the Throne of the *Sicilies*, efpoufed to a *Saxon* Princefs; the Infant Don *Philip*, married to the eldeft of the *French* Princeffes, the Cardinal Infant Don *Lewis*, Archbifhop of *Toledo* and of *Seville*. The Infanta *Mary-Anne-Victoria* Queen Regent of *Portugal*; the Infanta *Maria-Terefa* married to the Dauphin of *France*, fince deceafed; and the Infanta *Maria-Antonietta-Ferdinanda*, then in her 17th Year, at prefent Duchefs of *Savoy*.

Ferdinand the VIth fucceeded his Father in the 33d Year of his Age, having married *January* 8, 1729, the Infanta *Mary Magdalena* of *Portugal*, near two Years older than himfelf, by whom he has no Iffue. It was generally believed upon the Acceffion of this Monarch that Things would have taken entirely a new Turn in the Court of *Spain*, and his Catholick Majefty, or at leaft his Minifters, took fome Pains to keep up this Opinion, from whence they reaped very confiderable Advantages. The War, however, was carried on with Vigour, becaufe, as the new King publifhed in his Manifeftoes, it was very earneftly recommended to him by his Father; and t athe fame time it was given out, that his Catholick Majefty looked upon it as a Point of Policy, as well as of Duty, to procure his Brother an Eftablifhment in *Italy*; fo that it was very quickly difcerned that a Peace was not to be had without.

The Supplies given to the State of *Genoa* were very confiderable, and the *Spanifh* Forces in *Savoy* were thoroughly recruited and fomewhat augmented; in fhort, every Step was taken, upon the Entrance of the new Prince, that might give his Subjects equal Hopes of his being defirous to reftore their Tranquility, and at the fame time refolved to fupport the Dignity of the Crown of *Spain*. The Reports that prevailed, as if the *French* Intereft was now at an End, had no other Foundation than the Opennefs with which the Populace difcovered their Refentment againft the *French* Nation. Wife People very quickly faw, that no great Alteration either could or would

Z 3 happen;

happen; and those who were the fartheft from that Character, had Proofs fufficient to convince them that at this Juncture thefe Conjectures, however ridiculed, were but too well founded.

In the Negotiations that were carried on for Peace, the Court of *Madrid* relied implicitly upon that of *Verfailles*, which was the more extraordinary as they had all that Time a Minifter at *London*; but it may be very well fuppofed that the Nature of his Inftructions could be no great Secret to the *French* Minifters, fince it does not appear that they ever took any Umbrage at this Part of his Catholick Majefty's Conduct. The Marquis *de Soto Major* acted as the *Spanish* Plenipotentiary at *Aix-la-Chapelle*, where the feventh Article regarding the Ceffions made to the Infant Don *Philip*, was indeed the moft important, and by very much the moft difputed in the whole Treaty; and tho' it was not adjufted entirely to the Satisfaction of the *Spanish* Court, which preffed for a general Settlement of the Duchies of *Parma*, *Placentia* and *Guaftalla* upon the Royal Infant and his Iffue without any Reftrictions, yet by the Influence and Steadinefs of the *French* Miniftry, thofe important Ceffions were not only procured upon as good Terms as could be reafonably expected, confirmed by the moft authentick Acts of the Emprefs Queen and the King of *Sardinia*, but the Execution likewife preffed with equal Vigilance and Vigour.

As to the Article which regarded the Differences between this Court and that of *Great Britain*, nothing was regulated thereby, except the Right of the *South-Sea* Company to four Years of the *Affiento* Treaty, and the reft of the Differences were tacitly referred to the Negotiation before mentioned; fince that, the *Affiento* has been fold by a Convention; to which, by way of Appendix, a Treaty is ftill carrying on, as to the Event of which, we as yet know nothing. By this Means his Catholick Majefty was extricated out of an expenfive and deftructive War, (which had continued feven Years, and in that Time had drawn upon his Subjects inexpreffible Hardfhips) had an effectual Eftablifhment provided for his Brother Don *Philip*, honourable Provifions made for his Allies, the Duke of *Modena*, and the Republick of *Genoa*; and a Way opened to reduce his military Expences, and bring the Domeftick Concerns of his Adminiftration into Order, which while the War lafted could not be done. Befides the War with *Great Britain* which had begun fomewhat earlier was likewife ended; and in a Manner too with which the Court of *Madrid* had many Reafons to be pleafed; but none greater than its removing the Impediments to the Return of that vaft Mafs of Treafure which had been collected in the *Weft-Indies*, of which the *Spaniards* were in great Want, and for which even at this Time they were not altogether without Fears.   We

We have since seen all the Advantages that *Spain* could promise herself from this Treaty obtained in their full Extent; the Infant Duke is in Possession of the Countries yielded to him, the Duke of *Modena*, and the Republick of *Genoa*, have had their Territories restored, and the Wealth expected from the *Indies* has been safely brought home. What the Issue will be of so great and so happy a Change in her Circumstances, is in the Womb of Time; but without all doubt, the present Season is very critical, and the future Welfare or Misery of the *Spanish* Nation depends, in a great measure, upon the Turn his Catholick Majesty's Councils shall take at a Juncture, when it is entirely in his own Power to make them take what Turn he pleases, and to render himself as great and independent a Prince as any of his Predecessors.

We might have entered into many other Particulars, and descended to the Consideration of various Matters of Fact, if these were not beside our Purpose, which is to exhibit a Picture of the present State of *Spain*, or rather the present State of the Politicks of the Court of *Spain*, towards which a few great Strokes are sufficient, and all the little Trimmings and Niceties of an historical Abridgment would be destroying a Likeness. It is indeed very true that the Out-lines are only marked, and that the Piece wants heightening, and even Colour; but in respect to this, we must be excused, where in Reality we are restrained. The greatest Part of this Work was written and published too, during a War, when the Noise of Arms rendered the Writer less attentive to certain Scruples; but now Peace is restored, we must no longer express ourselves with so much Freedom. We must therefore be content with laying Things down in general Terms in many Cases, and leaving them to the Interpretation of the Ingenious. Heretofore we have been wont to conduct the Reader to his Journey's End; and if we now only point him out the Road, it does not arise either from Weariness or want of Civility, but because we cannot travel it in the same Manner; for tho' he may pursue the Journey very effectually in his Mind, yet if we do it, it must be upon Paper.

But we are now, according to the Method that hitherto has been followed, to speak of the Interests of this Monarchy, which we shall do in such a Manner as will in a great measure remove every Difficulty that might lie in the Way of deciding with Probability on the future Conduct of the *Spanish* Ministers. For if the real Interests of the Nation be thoroughly explained, it will not require much Penetration to discern whither they are pursued. It must indeed be observed, that this decides nothing

with

with respect to the Abilities of Ministers; for Men may pursue wrong Measures with great Skill and Address, and perhaps those Statesmen have acquired the highest Characters in that Capacity, who have employed their Talents to none of the best Purposes. In such Cases they are responsible who give the Bias; for Princes must be served in the Way they will be served, tho' it frequently happens, that when their own Inclinations have brought them into a Labyrinth, they make no Scruple of extricating themselves at the Expence of their Servants, and so sacrifice the Instrument to the Resentment of those who are hurt by it, without considering where the Offence really lies, or distinguishing between the Intention of giving the Wound, and the Hand, which from a Principle of Duty, perhaps, gave it.

Yet this, as it is the common Lot of Ministers, tho' it is just in one Sense, is grievous in another; for tho' the Victims to national Fury are commonly abandoned, either through Want of Courage, or Want of Gratitude, yet they are seldom abandoned to any Punishment greater than they have deserved. He who to gratify his Appetite to Profit, Pomp, or Power, undertakes to do what either he does not well consider, or which well considered he knows ought not to be done, gratifies his Passions at his own risk; and tho' when he feels the Effects of his Ambition or his Avarice, he may with some Reason complain of his Master, yet he cannot with the least Shadow of Equity declaim against that Stroke of Justice which sooner or later may reach him from the Sense of the People. The most absolute Princes must have their Counsellors and their Ministers; and if these make their Court, either by saying or doing Evil, it is at their Peril; and if they deceive themselves with the Hope that either Things will last for their Time, or that they shall be able to cover themselves by the Authority of the Prince against the just Hate of his Subjects, they can blame nothing but their own Want of Foresight, if their Expectations fail them.

Instances of both kinds, that is, of Ministers praised, and Ministers punished, occur frequently in the *Spanish* as well as in other Histories; but it may fall out there, as well as elsewhere, that Praise and Punishment too may be misapplied; and to judge of this rightly, not only in Times past, but likewise in Times to come, we must have right Apprehensions of that Rule, which can alone distinguish in such Matters; that is to say, we must know what are the true Interests of the Nation, and what those Biasses are, to which Ministers are liable from the false Notions and the false Interests of the Court; and these

may

may be very fairly and fully explained, from what able and disinterested Pens have written before us upon this Subject.

At the Conclusion of the Peace of *Utrecht*, when the Title of *Philip* V. as King of *Spain* and the *Indies*, was acknowledged by the High Allies, there were two kinds of Securities taken, for preventing those mischievous Consequences, which were but too justly apprehended from the leaving such vast Dominion in the Hands of the younger Branch of a Family already become too powerful, and too formidable in respect to the rest of *Europe*.

The first of these was the Renunciations made by King *Philip*, and the Princes of his Family, to the Succession of the Crown of *France*, in favour of the House of *Orleans*; and the other, the yielding *Gibraltar* and the Island of *Minorca* to the Crown of *Great Britain* in the Nature of Cautionary Places, or Securities for the Performance of what was stipulated by that Treaty.

This was then held necessary on both Sides; for as the Allies very justly dreaded the too close Conjunction of the Crowns of *France* and *Spain*, so the *Spaniards* themselves were very sensible of the Inconveniencies resulting from their Dependence upon that Crown; and were desirous enough of being freed from them for the present, and secured against them for the future; and all this very plainly appeared, from the readiness with which they gave those Renunciations the most solemn Sanction, that it was in their Power, as a Nation, to give.

It was the Interest also of the Royal Family, the Ministry, and the People of *Spain*, to have adhered religiously to this Treaty, and to have been content with every thing that was stipulated therein and thereby. It was this that secured the Dignity of King *Philip*, and made him truly a King, and not a Vice-Roy: It was this that put it in the Power of the *Spanish* Ministry to reform the Disorders in, and to restore the Credit and Force of the Kingdom; and it was this that enabled the People to reap the Pleasures and Profits of Peace, and the Advantages secured to them by the sole Possession of the *Indies*, which they had never possessed in so great Tranquility before.

But it very quickly appeared, that as clear and self-evident as these Maxims were, they had no great Influence on any of the Parties concerned. His Catholick Majesty was entirely governed by his Grandfather as long as he lived; and after his Decease he turned his Views so thoroughly toward his native Country,

as

as to act in a manner equally inconsistent with the Interests of his Crown, and with the Treaties by which he had acquired it. His Ministers made no Difficulty of falling into his Views; and the natural Pride and Ambition of the *Spaniards* drew them to wish the Recovery of their *Italian* Dominions at least, tho' the Possession of them was never of any great Service, but might be esteemed rather a Burthen to them.

After the King's second Marriage, this wrong Turn of Politicks began to display itself more fully, and the *Spaniards* endeavoured by Force of Arms to recover *Sicily*, and were also inclined to attack *Gibraltar*. This forced the Maritime Powers to adhere closely to the House of *Austria*, and to take such Measures for destroying the naval Strength of *Spain*, as could only be justified by that Necessity upon which they were plainly founded.

By the Accession of *Spain* to the Quadruple Alliance, and the Advantages stipulated for her therein, a new Opportunity was offered of establishing her Peace and Prosperity upon a lasting Foundation; and it looked for some time as if she intended it, but this lasted not long. The *Vienna* Alliance was contracted upon false Principles; for it tended to destroy the Ballance of Power in *Europe*, and to force *Gibraltar* and *Minorca* out of the Hands of *Great Britain*, which can never be effected by War, because every War proves the Possession of them by this Crown to be for the common Benefit of all the independent Powers in *Europe*.

From that Time the *Spanish* Ministry introduced a trimming kind of Politicks, pursuing sometimes one Scheme, sometimes another; but never affecting that Independency and Care of their own Concerns, which can alone render their People happy at home, and their Power respected abroad. Yet it is certain, that both *Alberoni* and *Ripperda* very well understood the Interest of *Spain*, to which they always gave the second Place in their political Projects. Happy had it been for themselves, the *Spaniards*, and all the rest of *Europe*, if they had constantly given it the first! That they were both Foreigners, and both the Sons of Fortune, was and must be their sole Excuse.

The Ambition of the two first Princes of the House of *Austria*, and the Inactivity of the three last, threw the Affairs of the Crown of *Spain* into such Disorder, and brought the People into such Indigence, that it certainly became their Interest, at least for the Space of a Century, to endeavour at re-peopling their Country, recovering their Trade, and restoring
their

their Constitution and ancient Government ; for the effecting of all which, they had every Means and every Opportunity they could wish, and many more than they had any just Reason to expect.

They ought therefore to have laid aside all Thoughts of recovering their Dominions in *Italy*, since though they served well enough to enrich particular Families, sent thither in Quality of Vice-Roys, or other high Officers, yet to the Nation they were burthensome, as requiring a much greater Expence to preserve and defend them, than those or any other Advantages accruing to private Persons could ballance in any Degree. It was of no less Consequence for them, to promote their Commerce in the *West-Indies*, which if duly attended to, would most certainly have produced the Means of setting up useful and valuable Manufactures at home, and thereby have brought such immense Treasures into *Old Spain*, as would soon have enabled them to have recovered all their past Losses, and to have put every Fortress in the Kingdom, as well as their Navy, into a proper State of Defence.

But if the *Spanish* Punto, and the Honour that is the Humour of the Nation, was to be preferred to all Things, and the Dominions torn from their Crown by the last War recovered at any Rate, still it was their Interest religiously to have observed the Peace of *Utrecht*, and above all things to have courted the Friendship of the Maritime Powers. The *Spanish* Prudence in former Times was wont to gain, rather than lose, by Delay ; and if the King and his Ministers, instead of taking the Steps they did, had steadily adhered to the Faith of Treaties, they might have found Opportunies, even without Bloodshed, and at a very trivial Expence in Comparison of what it has cost them since, to have carried all their Points.

If *Spain* had been absolutely detached from, and no way dependent upon *France*, her Power would not have been the Object of Envy to the rest of *Europe* ; and the Establishment of the younger Princes of her Family in *Italy* might have been promoted instead of being so vigorously opposed by certain Potentates, that do not act either from Ambition or Caprice, but are influenced purely by Motives of Self-Preservation, and a just Regard for the Maintenance of that Commerce, that is and must be the Basis of their Power.

Spain and the *Indies* may be considered as two great Empires under the Dominion of one Monarch, and the Happiness of both depends upon a reciprocal Regard for the Welfare of
each

each other. To preferve her *American* Dominions, and to reap the utmoft Profits from them, it is the Bufinefs of *Spain* at all Events to maintain Peace, at leaft till fhe has recovered fuch a maritime Force as will enable her to fend Supplies, and to bring home her Galleons in fpite of any Power with whom fhe is at War.

On the other hand, the *Spanifh* Government in the *Indies* might he put under fuch a Regulation, as to make all her Subjects there infinitely more eafy and happy than they could be under any other Crown ; and at the fame time procure from them all the Advantages that either the Government or the *Spanifh* Nation could reafonably expect; and this too, not only without the Envy, but with the entire Satisfaction of moft of the Kingdoms and States of *Europe*, who have very near as great an Intereft in preferving the Poffeffion of the *Indies* to *Spain*, as *Spain* itfelf.

But then it is both reafonable and neceffary, that on the one hand the *Spaniards* fhould endeavour to make the moft of their Plantations, and not fuffer them by mere Negligence to fall to Ruin and Decay ; and on the other hand, that they fhould punctually fulfill their Engagements, and allow certain reafonable Advantages in Trade to their ancient, natural and ufeful Allies. Thefe Maxims once made the Rule of their Conduct, their own Commerce would revive, and of courfe become daily more extenfive and more profitable, their *American* Dominions recover their former Luftre and Profperity, and the Power of *Old Spain* rife as high as ever it ftood in the Days of the Emperor *Charles* V. No wonder therefore, if the Purfuit of contrary Meafures produces contrary Effects.

As to the Interefts of *Spain* with regard to her Neighbours, without doubt it confifts in maintaining a fair Correfpondence with them, without forming any Pretenfions on their Territories. Her Differences with *France* are now extinguifhed, and as fhe has Reafon to look upon that as an Advantage, fo it is a natural Motive to Peace and good Neighbourhood, that they are governed by Monarchs of the fame Blood ; but at the fame time, a King of *Spain* ought to confider, that he owes it to his own Dignity, and to the unfhaken Loyalty of his Subjects, to govern them as their own Monarch, not as the Subftitute or Deputy of another Prince.

He ought to confider this as the Error chiefly to be guarded againft in his Government, becaufe there is none that he can commit will be attended with fo bad Confequences, inafmuch as it cannot fail of creating Jealoufies and Uneafineffes at home,

2

at the same time that It sinks his Credit, and disposes other States to be his Enemies abroad. Besides, in point of Trade, and even of Dominion, the *French* alone can have Views upon him, as appears by their Attempts to trade directly to the *South-Seas*, and to obtain the entire Dominion of *Hispaniola*; which whenever they acquire, the *Spanish* Territories in *America* will be at their Mercy.

In regard to the House of *Austria*, the great Cause of Dispute has been in the *Italian* Dominions; and evident it is, that this Spirit of Disputing is the Effect of *Italian* Counsels, which we have too great Reason to fear will influence that Court for a long Series of Years to come; unless some *Spanish* Minister of true Genius should arise, and convince his Master of the Necessity of setting Bounds to that Spirit. This alone can contribute to the Peace and Grandeur of *Spain*, to the Quiet and Safety of *Italy*, and to the general Tranquility of all the rest of *Europe*.

To the Grandeur of *Spain*, by keeping her out of those tedious and destructive Wars that exhaust her People, which she can so ill spare, and her Treasures already brought very low. To the Welfare of *Italy*, by maintaining the Ballance of Power, which is essentially necessary to the several States of that Country, and which can never be subverted, if the *Spaniards* would act with Moderation, and consult their true Interest in this particular. To the Tranquility of *Europe*, all the Powers of which are so much concerned both by Interest and Treaty, in the Preservation of the System in that Country, that it is impossible for them to suffer any Variation without having recourse to Arms, in order to set the Ballance right again.

In reference to *Portugal*, it is certainly the Interest of *Spain* to live well with her, and in the closest Correspondence possible; because though that Power can be no formidable Enemy by herself, yet in case the Enemies of this Crown enter into a Confederacy against *Spain*, she is able to give her more Uneasiness than any other Potentate; as appeared plainly in the last general War, when the Allies became once Masters of *Madrid*, purely by being engaged in Treaty with the *Portuguese*.

It must indeed be owned, that the Situation of *Portugal* is such as must naturally tempt an ambitious Prince on the Throne of *Spain* to aspire to the Conquest of it; yet even ambitious Princes, if they are wise, will weigh the Risk they run against the Advantage they seek; and it will scarce ever happen, that a

Spanish

Spanish Monarch shall find himself in such a Situation, as to be able to undertake the Conquest of *Portugal*, without running the Hazard of bringing the War into the Heart of his own Dominions ; which is such a Hazard, as certainly no prudent Prince will run, for the Sake of any Advantage whatever ; even if it were not, as in this Case it must be, attended with the most manifest and flagrant Injustice.

The Emperor of *Morocco*, and the Piratical States of *Barbary*, have always been considered as hereditary Enemies of the Crown of *Spain*, and perhaps they are the only Enemies against whom the *Spaniards* can exert their Force ; and that compatible with the Circumstances of their Affairs at home, agreeable to their own Interest, and without exciting the Jealousy of their Neighbours. The Crown of *Spain* is already in possession of *Ceuta*, *Oran*, and some other Fortresses upon that Coast, which she has hitherto found it difficult to preserve ; and though she has made frequent Attempts, yet has she never been able to make any considerable Addition to her Conquests.

It may perhaps be hereafter in her Power to do something more considerable on this Side ; but in all human Probability, if this is ever done, it must be by a Naval Force, in which as she would meet with no Opposition from any of the *European* Powers, so she might hope for the Assistance of *Portugal* and the *Italian* States ; and any Impressions she could make on that Side, would certainly answer valuable Purposes, and particularly the securing her Coasts, the preserving her Commerce, and the reviving the Reputation of the *Spanish* Navy, which for a Century past has been almost as low, as for the Century preceding it was both formidable and famous.

The Face of Affairs in *Spain* has been greatly changed by the Accession of the present Family to the Throne, who without doubt reaped vast Advantages from the prodigious Efforts made in their Favour by the *French*, who yet made those Efforts in favour of a younger Branch of their own Royal Family, and not as the natural or even political Allies of the *Spanish* Nation ; and it is certain that they have been very well paid for it since. But the Condition to which *Spain* was reduced both in *Europe* and *America*, at the Time of the Death of *Charles* II. is a Proof that there cannot be a greater Misfortune to any People, than for their Princes ever to entertain Thoughts of universal Monarchy, whether by actually subduing, or by maintaining a general Influence over other Nations ; for the former Method will infallibly leave them with-

without Men, as the latter muſt neceſſarily leave them without Money.

Indeed *Spain* at that Time was left without either; there were not in the important Fortreſs of *Gibraltar*, twenty Pieces of Cannon fit for Service; and the Garriſon did not conſiſt of one hundred effective Men; yet in all Probability it was not in a worſe Condition than the reſt. In ſhort, at that Time the Nation was quite exhauſted; and if the Duke of *Anjou* had not ſucceeded by the King of *Spain*'s Will, *France* muſt very probably have increaſed her Power and Dominions by the Conqueſt of a conſiderable Part of the *Spaniſh* Monarchy. This ought to prove a Leſſon, even to that ambitious Nation: Her People cannot always hold out, her Treaſures muſt be ſome time or other quite drained; and if in ſuch a Situation they ſhould have either a weak Prince on the Throne, or a long Minority, we might ſee *France* in as low a Condition as *Spain* was in at the Death of *Charles* the Second; for the ſame Cauſes will every where produce the ſame Effects.

Before the *Spaniſh* Princes were infected with the Spirit of univerſal Rule, we find *Ferdinand* the Catholick, with an Army of twenty thouſand Horſe, and fifty thouſand Foot, beſieging the City of *Granada*, when that Kingdom was under the *Moors*, and when *Arragon* refuſed to take any ſhare in the Quarrel. This ſhews how powerful *Caſtile* was before the Addition of ſo many Kingdoms and Provinces, and before *America* was diſcovered. Yet it would be very raſh to conclude from thence, that *Spain* has been ruined barely by Acceſſion of Territory, and by her ſending Colonies to the *Weſt-Indies*. When ſhe acquired the former, they were very well peopled; and ſhe has been fully paid in every reſpect for all the Expences ſhe has been at about the latter. The true Deduction is this, that vaſt Territories and immenſe Treaſures cannot ſecure a Nation from feeling want of Strength, and ſinking into downright Beggary, if ſhe is governed by weak and ambitious Counſels.

In the midſt of all her Grandeur, the *Spaniſh* Territories were ſeparated at a vaſt Diſtance one from another: If ſhe had maintained a conſtant Peace, and had lived in Harmony with her Neighbours, ſhe might have kept them all, for no ſingle Power how potent ſoever durſt attack her. Inſtead of this, ſhe graſped at all, made War on every Side, and forced thoſe ſhe injured to make themſelves both rich and powerful, by contributing to her Ruin. It was the Ambition and Injuſtice of *Spain* that raiſed raifed up the Maritime Powers, as it was the Ambition and Injuftice of *Spain* that loft her many of her Dominions, and exhaufted the reft. Thefe are very weighty political Reflections; and by attending to them, we fhall come to conceive clearly both of her paft and prefent Condition. In reference to the former, we have faid enough; in refpect to the latter we fhall obferve, that as fhe has ftill great Advantages, fo fhe ftill labours under fome Inconveniencies.

It is, or at leaft it might be, a great Advantage to *Spain*, that fhe alone of all the *European* Powers poffeffes Dominions both in the *Eaft* and *Weft-Indies*, that have a direct and immediate Correfpondence with each other. If this were properly attended to and improved, fhe might raife her Revenues much higher than it is poffible under their prefent Circumftances for any other Power to do. She might by encouraging her Commerce, fucceed in a great meafure to that Share in the *Eaft-India* Trade, which *Venice* has loft fince the Difcovery of the Paffage of the Cape of *Good-Hope*; for by tranfporting the Commodities of the *Eaft-Indies* to *Acapulcho*, and from thence to *Vera-Cruz* over Land, fhe might bring them from thence into *Spain* by her Galleons, at as cheap a Rate, and in as fhort a Time, as the *Englifh* or *Dutch*; more efpecially if fhe allowed her Subjects either in the *Eaft* or *Weft-Indies*, an open unreftrained Navigation.

It is true, that as things ftand at prefent, the *Philippines* do not yield any tolerable Profit to the *Spaniards*; but this is entirely their own Fault; fince if we confider the Situation of thofe Iflands, it muft be allowed that they might eafily come in for a very large Share of the Commerce of the *Eaft-Indies*, or at leaft for the moft valuable Part of it. Some Correfpondence they have already with *China*, and might have a greater; no Country lies fo conveniently as they do for the Trade of *Japan*; and there is nothing wanting to put them in Poffeffion of all this, but withdrawing thofe Reftraints that are laid upon their Subjects in the *Eaft-Indies*, and adding another Galleon to carry the Produce of their Trade to *Mexico*. The fame Advantage might be reaped by rendering *Vera-Cruz*, the *Havannah*, or even *Buenos-Ayres* a free Port to their own Subjects; for this would draw fuch a Trade thither, as would make the Intercourfe between the two *Indies* before-mentioned both practical and eafy in a fhort Time.

This would be more advantageous to *Spain*; becaufe it would give little or no Umbrage to foreign Nations; which

would

would carry on their Trade to *Old Spain* as they do at present; it would occasion a greater Vent for their Commodities and Manufactures, and consequently it would still make it more their Interest to maintain and support the *Spaniards* in their Possessions. It might also, at least in Time, restore some of their decayed Plantations. As for Example, if the *Havannah* was made the Staple of such a Trade, for which it lies very conveniently, this would not only prove highly beneficial to the Island of *Cuba*, but would revive the Industry of the Inhabitants of *Hispaniola* and *Porto-Rico*; and though it is very probable, that the *English* and *Dutch* might come in for a Share by an illicit Trade, which is one of the Inconveniencies to which *Spain* will be always exposed, yet even this would be ballanced by the additional Concern, that both the *English* and *Dutch* would have in preserving to the *Spaniards* what produced, tho' in a clandestine way, an immediate and considerable Gain to themselves.

Besides these Advantages abroad, they have also others at home, by which I mean in *Europe*; for as they have no longer any Provinces in *Flanders*, they are wholly exempt from all the Trouble and Expence, which was entailed upon them by those Provinces while in their Possession. They are also Gainers, or might be Gainers, by the Change of Affairs in *Italy*, where, as Things now stand, distinct Principalities in the Hands of Descendents from the Crown of *Spain*, may be as advantageous as Provinces annexed to the Kingdom, and be supported at much less Expence; indeed without any Expence at all, if those Princes pursue only their own Interest, remain well-affected to the Ballance of Power in *Italy*, and maintain a fair Correspondence with their Neighbours, who will be always willing to live upon the best Terms imaginable with them. Another great Advantage is their being free from any Apprehensions on the Side of *France*; to which we may add, their having it absolutely in their own Power to be as free from Danger on the Side of the House of *Austria*; for without Allies she has not the Power of hurting them; and if *Spain* will be content with minding her own Business, the Allies of the House of *Austria* would become hers. All these Advantages are so clear, that we need spend no more Time about them.

The Inconveniencies that *Spain* labours under, are chiefly those which she has brought upon herself. The first is the Want of People, which is the Reason that both the inland and foreign Trade is in a great measure driven by Strangers,

of

of which also for the most part her Armies are composed. Another great Inconvenience which results from this, is the Poverty of their Country, which is not occasioned by the Barrenness, but from the Want of Cultivation. A third Inconvenience is the exceffive Number and unproportionable Wealth of the Ecclefiafticks, fecular and regular ; of which, as great Bigots as this Nation have been always held, they are now become very fenfible, and would willingly find a Remedy for it if they could. Their late Plenipotentiary at *Breda*, Mr. *Macanas*, projected fuch a Remedy, which though it was not received in the late Reign, may be fome time or other accepted, and could not but be attended with very happy Effects.

But after all, the capital and moft dangerous Inconvenience is their Court's not being governed by *Spanish* Counfels; for all true Politicians will agree, that there is no Curfe can be fo heavy upon a People, as to be made Tools and Beafts of Burthen to any other People. For the firft twenty Years after the Acceffion of the late King *Philip*, *Spain* was in effect no better than a Province to *France*; and her Condition for more than twenty Years fince that, has been much worfe; fhe is become a Province to thofe which fhe takes for her own Provinces, I mean the *Italian* Dominions; for which fhe has already paid ten times more than they are worth, and has alfo remained under a Dependence on *France* for the greateft part of that Time. In fhort, the Queen Dowager governed the King, and by fo doing governed *Spain*, with a View only to the Intereft of *Italy*; and this Paffion was fo ftrong in her, that all the Kingdoms and Provinces of the *Spanish* Monarchy have been exhaufted, beggared, and facrificed to the Love fhe has to her own little Duchies of *Parma* and *Placentia*.

Whenever this Inconveniency is taken away, the reft will be eafily removed : *Spain* will then become an independent and powerful Kingdom : *France*, inftead of giving Laws to, muft court her ; the Houfe of *Auftria* would fee her flourifh without Envy ; and the Maritime Powers, inftead of regarding her as an Enemy, would behold her in the amiable Light of their Benefactor, and their Friend. All this fhe may be, and that foon ; and if fhe will not be this, it cannot be long before fhe is totally undone. For fuch muft be the Fate fooner or later of all Nations, that are obftinately bent upon purfuing Meafures diametrically oppofite to their own Interefts. Political Conftitutions are indeed ftronger than Natural Ones, but, like them,

if

if they are continually harralled, they will at laft be moft certainly wore out.

It may indeed be objected, and furely it concerns the modern Politician to confider the Objection, that fince the Conclufion of the War the Affairs of *Spain* are much altered, her Power on the Continent is augmented, an immenfe Treafure has poured in from the *Indies*; and when once her Marine fhall be reftored, fhe may pafs for one of the moft formidable Powers in *Europe*. It is farther ftill infinuated by fuch as make this Objection, that whatever Weaknefs there might be in the Politicks of *Spain* in attaching herfelf fo clofely heretofore to the Intereft of *France*, there may poffibly fome Event fall out, which will make a full Amends for all this; and which is more, may make the Continuance of the fame Meafures pafs for found Policy even in the Opinion of the beft Judges.

But in anfwer to this Objection, now in a good meature removed by Providence, we muft obferve, that it is founded in a Diftinction between the Interefts of the Crown, or rather the Interefts of the Royal Family, and the Interefts of the Nation, which is a Diftinction that ought never to be made, which notwithftanding has been too often made; and to which the Interefts of many Nations, but of none fo remarkably as this, have been facrificed. We therefore maintain, that allowing all that is contended for in the Objection fhould happen, it would never alter the Nature of Things, or juftify that new and ftrange Method of governing, which facrifices Interefts natural and permanent, to thofe which are temporary only and fluctuating. In fhort, we affirm that the Acceffions of Territory made by the two laft Wars can be rendered beneficial only by purfuing the Principles before laid down; and that the real Strength, Grandeur, and Profperity of the *Spanifh* Crown muft be the Work of Peace; and of that mild, juft, and equitable Government, to which his prefent Catholick Majefty King *Ferdinand* the Sixth is naturally inclined; and for the Truth of this we appeal to Time and the Judgment of Pofterity.

We are next to fpeak of that Kingdom, which was once but a Province of the *Spanifh* Monarchy, which of all the Acceffions of Territory fhe ever made, it moft imported her to have kept, becaufe the keeping of it would have added Luftre to the Crown, and Strength to the Nation. An Acquifition made by one of the wifeft Princes that ever fat on the *Spanifh* Throne; an Acquifition, the Importance of which was thoroughly known, and an Acquifition which never could have

been

been loft, but from thofe Errors in Government which we have before laboured to fhew, ought of all others to be exploded. Thofe ambitious and all-grafping Meafures weakened the Power of *Spain* to fuch a Degree, that *Portugal* of a Province became once more a Kingdom; and tho' moft cruelly harraffed, weakened and exhaufted, while under the Dominion of *Spain*, retained ftill Strength enough to refume, defend, and eftablifh its Independency; and is at prefent in fuch a Condition as to deferve the higheft Regard from its potent Neighbour, to whom it may be always a moft ufeful Ally; and to whom, how much inferior foever in Power, it is capable of being the moft dangerous Enemy.

C H A P. XII.

The advantageous Situation, modern Hiftory, prefent State, political Interefts and Connections, of the Kingdom of PORTUGAL, *fince the Acceffion of the reigning Houfe of* BRAGANÇA.

IN order to give the Reader a diftinct Notion of the prefent State and Condition of the *Portuguefe* Nation, it is neceffary to fay fomewhat of the Situation of their Country, which is very pleafantly extended on the Coaft of the *Atlantick* Ocean, about three hundred Miles, or fomewhat more in Length, from South to North, but fcarce any where one hundred Miles in Breadth from Weft to Eaft. The Climate is very fine, and the Air efteemed as wholefome as any in *Europe*, notwithftanding it lies fo far South, the great Heats being commonly tempered by the Sea Breeze. As for the Soil, it would be every where extremely rich and fruitful, if the greateft Part of the Country were not mountainous; but notwithftanding this, they have, confidering the Quantity of arable Land, a vaft deal of excellent Corn in the Vallies; the Sides of the Hills produce in great Plenty the richeft Fruits; and from the Bowels of the Earth they dig almoft all Sorts of Metals, Gold and

Silver

Silver not excluded ; of the laſt mentioned they are believed to have the richeſt Mine in *Europe*, which is that of *Guacaldana*, for this yields one Year with another, Silver to the Value of two hundred thouſand Pounds. There are alſo three great Rivers, that after watering the adjacent Provinces, empty themſelves into the Sea in this Country, *viz*. the *Dueroro* or *Douro*, the *Tajo*, and the *Guadiana*.

After this Deſcription, the Reader will eaſily believe that for its Size this Kingdom is much more populous than *Spain*, and the Inhabitants alſo beyond compariſon more induſtrious. Some Writers would perſuade us, that the *Portugueſe* are, generally ſpeaking, a very corrupt and bad Sort of People ; according to the common Proverb, " Take a *Spaniard*, ſtrip him " of his good Qualities, which are but few, and you make " him a *Portugueſe*. " Theſe kind of national Reflections are, generally ſpeaking, as ill-founded as they are ill-natured, and ought never to be repeated but with a View to refute them. In their Diſcoveries, which led the Way and ſuggeſted the Deſign to *Columbus*, they ſhewed themſelves a penetrating and enterprizing People ; their Conqueſts in the *Indies*, though the beſt Part are now low loſt, are yet Proofs of a Courage and Conduct that deſerved better Fate ; their reviving Naval Power in *Europe*, and carrying it to ſo great a Height as they did in a few Years, ought to procure them, with us at leaſt, a better Character. But there is one Circumſtance relating to the *Portugueſe*, the Truth of which cannot be diſputed, and which is alone ſufficient to wipe off all the Imputations of their Enemies : They have always been remarkable for their ſteady Loyalty to their Kings, as on the other hand their Monarchs have been no leſs diſtinguiſhed by their Juſtice, Moderation, and ſincere Affection for their Subjects.

Philip II. of *Spain*, under Colour of Right, ſeized this Country, and annexed it to the reſt of his Dominions, in 1580 ; but the People were equally diſſatisfied with his Title, and averſe to the *Spaniſh* Government, which was, to ſay the Truth, the immediate Cauſe of the Ruin of their Country. It was this that gave Occaſion to the *Dutch* to deprive them of their Settlements in the *Indies*, on the Coaſt of *Africa*, and, in a great meaſure, the *Brazils* ; for the *Spaniards* looking upon this as a conquered Kingdom, took but little Care of their Concerns ; and the *Portugueſe* Nobility, who had formerly ſhewn ſo much Courage and Conſtancy in the Service of their native Princes, were far from exerting themſelves in the

ſame

same Manner for the Support of Strangers, who they plainly saw did not either use or with them well.

At last, tired out with the bad Behaviour of such as were sent to govern them by the Court of *Madrid*, they resolved to throw off the *Spanish* Yoke at all Events; and it so fell out, in 1640, that a fair Opportunity offered itself of carrying into Execution what they had so long designed. *John* Duke of *Bragança*, Grandson to that Duke who was Competitor with King *Philip* for the Kingdom, was prevailed upon to hazard his hereditary Estates, which were very little short of one third of the Kingdom, in asserting of his Title to the Whole, and the People supported him so unanimously, that there is no general Revolution recorded in ancient or modern History to have been more effectually, or more secretly brought about, or with less Effusion of Blood, than this, from whence he was raised to the Throne of *Portugal* by the Title of *John* the Fourth. His Subjects were no less steady and constant in supporting him upon the Throne, than they had been universally willing and ready to raise him to it, though the *Spaniards* maintained a long War, in hopes of recovering this Kingdom, and though the *Dutch*, notwithstanding they were then fighting for their own Liberties against the same Crown, prosecuted their Designs in the *Indies*, and in *Brazil*, against the *Portuguese*.

It is true, that they lost several of their remaining Settlements in *Asia*; and that it was with great Difficulty they preserved *Goa*, *Bombay*, *Diu*, and a few inconsiderable Places on the Continent; but in the *Brazils* they had better Fortune, the People preferr'd their Government to that of the *Dutch*, and in a short time they recovered all that they had there lost.

We must observe that while the *Spaniards* were Masters of *Portugal*, their Maxims of making the most of the Kingdom while in their Hands, ruined the Trade, sunk the naval Power, and brought the *Portuguese* Plantations almost to nothing. An equal and just Government is necessary, not only to raise, but to preserve these Advantages to any Nation, since whenever that is wanting, they droop, dwindle, and decay, like Plants that remain unwater'd, or Children trusted to a mercenary Nurse, that soon lose their Flesh and Colour, which were the Result of the Pains taken with them by an affectionate Mother. To judge from Effects may be a bad Maxim in Morality, but in Politicks it seldom fails.

John

John the IVth died in 1651, without seeing an End of that War which his Accession had occasioned. He left his Dominions to his Son *Alphonso* VI. then a Child, under the Tutelage of the Queen Dowager his Mother. This gave the *Spaniards* a great Advantage, and nine Years after they obtained, in Appearance at least, still a greater ; for at the Conclusion of the Peace of the *Pyrenees*, the *French*, who had hitherto been the warm and almost the sole Allies of *Portugal*, engaged to give that Crown no farther Assistance ; but their great Regard for their own Interest, induced them, in direct Violation of that Article, to send the *Portuguese* greater Assistance than they had ever done, under the Command of Marshal *Schombergh*, an Officer of such Capacity, that it might be truly said, his single Person was equivalent to a small Army.

He reformed many Abuses, and introduced a new Discipline among the *Portuguese* Troops ; so that notwithstanding they had the whole *Spanish* Force to deal with, yet they bravely defended their Liberties, and gained two such signal Victories at *Estremos* and *Villa Viciosa*, as convinced their Enemies, that the Desire of Freedom may over-ballance Superiority of Numbers. At last in 1668, the *French* King *Louis* XIV. falling, contrary to the Faith of Treaties, with a great Army into the *Low-Countries*, the *Spaniards* found themselves under a Necessity of making Peace with *Portugal*, which was done under the Mediation of King *Charles* II. of *Great Britain*, who had married the Infanta *Catharine*, Daughter to King *John*, and Sister to King *Alphonso* ; by this Treaty the Crown of *Spain* renounced all her Claims and Pretensions on that of *Portugal*, and solemnly acknowledged the Rights of the House of *Bragança*, which put an End to a disputed Title, and restor'd Peace to this Country, after a War, or at least the Interruption of Peace, for the Space of twenty-eight Years.

Alphonso VI. having attained the Years, tho' not the Discretion of a Man, resolved to take the Government of his Dominions into his own Hands, tho' his Mother had ruled with great Prudence, and himself could not but be satisfied of his own Incapacity, which is said to have been owing to a long Indisposition, that so much weakened his Abilities, both in Body and Mind, as to render him equally unfit for the Duties of a King, and of a Husband. But his Favourites who had persuaded him to remove his Mother (who is said to have died of Grief in a Year after) from the Administration of Affairs, advised him likewise, from Views of their own,

to

to marry without Delay; and accordingly a Princess of *Savoy Nemours* was thought of for his Queen, whom he actually espoused. Those who had pushed him upon these Designs, and who had no other View than that of governing the Kingdom at their own Will under his Name, began next to infuse Jealousies of his Brother Don *Pedro*, the presumptive Heir of the Crown; and are also said to have engaged him in such other low and shameful Intrigues, as obliged the Queen, after she had cohabited with him for six Months, to retire to a Convent for the Preservation, as she affirmed, of her Honour and her Life.

The Infant Don *Pedro*, considering the Incapacity of his Brother, the confused State of publick Affairs, and his own great Peril, determined by the Advice, and with the Assistance and Consent of the principal Nobility, to secure the Person of the King, and to take upon himself the Administration of the Government. This was accordingly done, and not long after the Queen left her Convent, and a Dispensation having been obtained from the Court of *Rome* for that Purpose, espoused the Prince Don *Pedro*, who removed *Alphonso* to the Island of *Tercera*, where he kept him confined under a strong Guard; but caused him to be treated with the Tenderness which he owed his Brother, and the Respect that was due to a King. However, some malicious Tongues, in a few Years, reporting the contrary, the Prince caused him to be brought back to the Castle of *Cintra*, within a Day's Journey of *Lisbon*, and there, under an easy Custody, he was served and respected as a King. The Prince was persuaded by many to have assumed that Title himself, but he inflexibly declined it, contenting himself with that of Regent till his Brother died, which was in 1683.

This is the best Account, that, from comparing the most authentick Relations, we have been able to obtain of this Affair; for as to the fine-wrought and amazing Stories that are found in some secret Histories and private Memoirs, they seem to be destitute of all Foundation in Truth, since if Don *Pedro* had been inclined to get rid of his Brother, and to make himself Master of the Kingdom at any Rate, he might most certainly have done it in the Confusion of the first Revolution, or not long after he was sent to *Tercera*; but as he did neither, but showed himself in all other Respects a religious and virtuous Prince, there is no Cause for giving Credit to any of those Suspicions, which fanciful, ill-informed, or malicious Writers have published,

King

King *Pedro* had by his first Queen, who had been his Brother's Wife, only one Daughter, and for some time before her Mother's Death, she was considered as the Heiress of the Kingdom, and while she was so considered, a Marriage was treated for her with the young Duke of *Savoy*; nay this was carried so far, that the *Portuguese* Fleet was actually sent to the Coasts of *Italy*, in order to bring over the intended Bridegroom; but that Prince changing his Mind, the Fleet returned without him, and the Infanta dying soon after this Disappointment, the People of *Portugal* violently sollicited their Sovereign to think of a second Marriage, which induced him to espouse the Princess *Maria Sophia*, Daughter to the Elector *Palatine*, by whom he had Issue *John* Prince of *Brazil*, and also the Infants Don *Francis*, Don *Antonio*, and Don *Emanuel*.

The King continued for many Years to govern his Subjects with great Justice and Moderation; and as a long and cruel War had wasted his People and his Treasures, during the Reign of his Brother, he was very careful to preserve Peace, to encourage Agriculture, and to promote the Commerce of his Subjects. A little before the Peace of *Ryswick*, he offered his Mediation to *Louis* XIV. but received such an Answer, as showed plainly enough that *France* was resolved to reject it with a kind of Disdain. The *Portuguese* Monarch thought fit to pass by the Affront for the present; but it afterward cost *France* dear. So dangerous a thing it is for Princes, though ever so powerful, to treat with any Degree of Contempt such as are confessedly equal to them in Rank, though for the present it may be inferior in some other, and those too accidental Respects.

When *Philip* V. mounted the Throne of *Spain*, the Friendship of *Portugal* became not only expedient, but necessary. Upon this Occasion, *Louis* XIV. was as obliging and civil, as he had formerly shewn himself haughty and proud; and tho' Don *Pedro* had already resolved on the Part he was to take, yet considering how soon, and how easily he might be crushed by the Forces of the two Crowns, he entered into an Alliance with King *Philip*, and this for various Reasons. In the first Place, it gained Time, and delivered him from present Danger; in the next, it gave an Opportunity of gaining good Terms, which might be of Use to him on another Occasion; and lastly, he obtained by it some present Advantages, which were very beneficial to his Subjects. Yet notwithstanding this Treaty, he refused, though warmly pressed by the *French*

King,

King, to acknowledge the Title of the Son of King *James* to the Crown of *Great Britain*; which showed plainly enough, that in making this Treaty he had followed his Interest rather than his Inclination.

As soon as the general Confederacy was formed against *France*, and it clearly appeared that the Allies meant to set up another King of *Spain*, the *Portuguese* Monarch demanded of the *French* King, pursuant to the late Alliance, a Fleet of thirty Sail of the Line, and a large Sum of Money. He knew well enough, that as Things then stood, those Demands could not be complied with; but he wanted a Pretence for breaking that Treaty, without breaking Faith, and this did his Business very effectually; for as soon as the Fleet of the Allies appeared upon his Coast, he thought fit to declare himself neuter, and not long after made a Treaty with *Charles* III. whose Claim they supported to the whole *Spanish* Monarchy. By this Treaty he stipulated for himself very great Advantages; for the new King was to espouse the Infanta of *Portugal*, though but a Child of seven Years old; several Places were to be yielded to him on the Frontiers of *Spain*; some Concessions were likewise to be made in the *Indies* and *America*; and he was to have the Assiento of Negroes, which had been also granted him by the former Treaty with King *Philip*.

In consideration of these Terms, he agreed to receive King *Charles*, and to assist him with Forces, for the Recovery of his Kingdom, for which, however, he was to have large Subsidies from the Maritime Powers, and a good Fleet to protect his Coasts. A few Days before King *Charles* arrived at *Lisbon*, died the Infanta, who was to have been his Queen; but this made no Alteration in the Measures that had been concerted, his *Portuguese* Majesty resolving to prosecute the War as he had promised; but before any Steps could be taken for this Purpose, he was removed by Death, *December* 9, 1706, when he had lived fifty eight, and from the Death of his Brother, had reigned twenty-three Years.

John V. the Father of the present King of *Portugal*, succeeded his Father, and pursued his Steps very exactly, notwithstanding the *Spaniards* surprized the Town of *Alcantara*, and made the Garrison Prisoners of War, almost before he was warm in the Throne. The Assistance he gave the Allies, brought the *Spanish* Monarchy twice to the Brink of Ruin; and though most of our Accounts say, that the *Portuguese* Soldiers behaved but indifferently in that War, yet this ought not to be

under-

understood as a national Reflection, farther than as long
Peace, great Wealth, and much Luxury, are capable of cor-
rupting any People. And it may not be amiss to inform the
Reader, that the greatest Part of the young Nobility, who
were Officers at this time in the Army, were but Fresh-water
Commanders, and who from leading indolent and debauched
Lives at *Lisbon*, were come to make their Fortunes by their
Commissions. It was no great Wonder therefore that they
behaved but indifferently, or that the poor People who obeyed
them followed their Examples. But that this was the sole
Cause of their Misbehaviour appears from hence, that after
the fatal Battle of *Almanza*, many *English* Officers were obliged
to fill up, and some raised their whole Corps afresh amongst
the *Portuguese*; and from the Mouths of those Officers I have
heard, that such Men, when in our Pay, behaved in Time of
Action as well as any Men could do, and were besides so sober,
so diligent, and so attentive to their Duty, that what was
at first done from Necessity, became Matter of Choice. This I
thought it was but Justice in me to mention, as the calumnious
Reports to the Prejudice of their Reputation are already common
enough in Print.

At the Close of the War, King *John* raised very high Demands upon the Crown of *Spain*; for he knew well enough
that Abatements might be made at any time, and very rightly
judged, that by asking a great deal he should be sure to get
somewhat, as he really did, both in *Europe* and in *America*,
besides a Compensation for the Loss of his Negro Contract.
But after all, it fell very short of what he had stipulated with
King *Charles*, though perhaps the Peace he made with King
Philip, in 1715, might be very near an Equivalent for what
would have been allowed of his Treaty, if King *Charles* had
succeeded, and become the peaceable Possessor of the *Spanish*
Monarchy; as there is a wide Difference between what Princes
may be brought to promise in their Distress, and their Readiness to perform, when it is in their Power to dispute the Performance.

While the War continued, the Commerce of the *Brazils*
began to grow much more considerable than in former Times,
by the working of the Gold Mines; and as there was at that
Time a great Intercourse between the two Nations, the *British*
Traders obtained a large Share of that Gold for the Commodities
and Manufactures with which they furnished the *Portuguese*.
King *John* could not help seeing this with Concern, he
thought it hard they should have but a Sight of the vast Wealth
                                                    derived

derived from their own Settlements, and that it should immediately vanish, as it were, out of *Portugal* into another Country. His Ministers were exactly of their Master's Opinion, and many Consultations were held about finding a speedy and effectual Remedy for what they considered as the greatest Grievance. At length it was concluded, that the only Method could be taken was to prohibit the Wear of foreign Manufactures; and this had certainly been put in Execution, if Lord *Galway*, the Commander of our Forces in that Country, tho' a *Frenchman* by Birth, had not prevented it.

He was a great Favourite with his *Portuguese* Majesty, and esteemed to be, as he certainly was, a very honest Man. To him therefore, as to a Friend, and under the strictest Injunction of Secrecy, the King communicated this Affair, and asked his Advice about it. His Lordship told him fairly, that the Remedy would be worse than the Disease; that the same Providence which had given his Subjects Gold, had bestowed Commodities and Manufactures upon the *English*; that the Exchange therefore was not so injurious as he imagined; and that by prohibiting Commerce, he might force those that were now his best Friends to become his Enemies, and to employ their Naval Power, which he knew to be so much superior to his own, in taking that by Force for which they now gave a proper Equivalent.

He farther represented, that whatever turn the War might take, *Portugal* must always stand in need of the Friendship of *England*, to prevent becoming dependent on the House of *Austria* or the House of *Bourbon*; and therefore it was much better that his Subjects should trade with those from whom he had so much to hope, than with other Nations from whom he had all things to fear. The King, who was both a reasonable and a just Prince, and who in his Business acted solely from a laudable Affection for his Subjects, comprehended the Force of these Arguments, and immediately laid aside a Project, which how plausible soever in its first Appearance, was certainly at the Bottom neither equitable nor practicable. Happy for the World if all Kings meant as well, deliberated as coolly, and were as ready to receive and follow good Advice!

The next remarkable Point in this Reign was, the Quarrel between his *Portuguese* Majesty and the Pope, about the Affair of the Nuncio *Bichi*, an Incident too inconsiderable in itself to be mentioned in a Work of this Nature, if it did not contribute to explain a political Article which is very well worth the ingenious Reader's Time perfectly to comprehend; because

because on the one hand, it shews the Connection between the Catholick Powers and the Head of their Church; and on the other hand, it explains the Manner in which these Powers act when they believe themselves at any time ill used by the Pope. Signior *Bichi* was sent to the Court of *Lisbon* so early as the Year 1710, and at first the Court was very far from being pleased with him, but by Degrees he got over the Aversion, and in a short time afterwards the King recommended him to *Clement* XI. for a Cardinal's Hat; which was refused, under Pretence that his Nomination was opposed by the Imperial Court; which, whoever, was not strictly true. *Innocent* XIII. confiding in the known Piety of the King of *Portugal*, ventured to use him worse than this Predecessor had done; for he not only refused absolutely to make the Nuncio a Cardinal, but recalled Signior *Bichi*, and sent another Prelate to succeed him. But the King of *Portugal* would not submit to this Indignity, and therefore sent Word to the new Nuncio, not to set Foot in his Dominions, and refused likewise to let the old one go, till he was assured that Respect would be paid to his Nomination.

Upon the Death of *Innocent* XIII. succeded *Benedict* XIII. who went a Step farther than his Predecessor, by commanding positively the Nuncio *Bichi* to quit the Court of *Lisbon*, which accordingly he did, and returned by the Way of *Madrid* into *Italy*. But this Treatment provoked the King of *Portugal* to such a Degree, that he recalled his Subjects from *Rome*, broke off all Correspondence with that Court; and if the Pope had lived a little longer, would very probably have set up a Patriarch. Cardinal *Corsini* succeding Pope *Benedict*, by the Title of *Clement* XII. found himself under a Necessity of putting an End to this Quarrel, which had now lasted almost twenty Years, and in his second Promotion in 1731, bestowed the long-expected Hat upon *Bichi*, who was then upwards of Sixty.

There is no doubt the Court of *Rome* hoped that, in the Course of this Dispute, either the King or the Nuncio would have died, and then it would have dropped of course, in a manner honourable to the Holy See; but failing in this, the late Pope was forced to make the best of a bad Bargain, that he might avoid driving things to Extremities.

In the Year 1729, a double Marriage was concluded between the Courts of *Spain* and *Portugal*; the Prince of *Asturias*, now his Catholick Majesty, espoused the Infanta of *Portugal*, and the Prince of *Brazil*, now King of *Portugal*, the Infanta of *Spain*, formerly stiled Queen of *France*. The Exchange of the Princesses

was

was made with great Solemnity, and their Catholick and *Portuguese* Majesties had an Interview on the 23d of *January*, in the Island of *Pegon* in the River of *Caya*, about a League from *Badajoz*. But notwithstanding this Alliance, the two Courts were very near coming to a Rupture in 1735; and it is thought, that the sending a *British* Feet under the Command of Sir *John Norris* to *Lisbon*, was what chiefly prevented it, and saved *Portugal* from an Invasion.

The two Crowns were not reconciled thoroughly till the Year 1737, from which Period they became every Day more united, which gave much Satisfaction to some Courts, and no Umbrage to any. Through the Course of about thirteen Years more, the King prosecuted steadily the same Maxims of Government to which he adhered in his Youth, which would have turned more to the Advantage of his Subjects than they did, if he had not consumed such immense Sums in erecting religious Houses, decorating Churches, and causing a Chapel to be built, the Ornaments and Furniture of which surpassed all Example, and almost exceeded Computation. A Stroke of the Palsy, under which he laboured for many Years, and by which his Faculties were very much impaired, threw publick Affairs in a great measure into the Hands of Priests, as little agreeable to the Inclinations as it was to the Interests of the People. In this Situation of Things, a Treaty was made in 1750 with the Court of *Madrid*, by which *Nova Colonia* on the River of *Plate* was yielded to his Catholick Majesty, to the great Regret of the *Portuguese*, as well on Account of the Value of that Settlement, as because they apprehended their Possession of the *Brazils* would by this Cession be rendered precarious. On the last of *July* the same Year, this Monarch, worn out by his Distemper, deceased, in the sixty-first Year of his Age, and in the forty-fourth Year of his Reign.

Don *Joseph*, Prince of *Brazil*, succeeded his Father, to the universal Satisfaction of his Subjects, and with as great Expectations as ever any Monarch that mounted the Throne. It was generally believed that he would make considerable Alterations, in which he did not disappoint the Hopes of the Publick; and yet they were done so slowly, with such Moderation, and with so many Circumstances of Prudence, as hindered all Grounds of Complaint. Amongst other new Regulations, the Power of the Inquisition suffered some Restriction; the King directing that none of their Sentences should be put in Execution, till reviewed and approved by his Privy Council. But as in the Reign of his Father he

had

had confented to the Treaty with *Spain*, he ratified it after his Acceſſion, and has ſince actually carried it into Execution upon this noble Principle, that no Conſiderations of Intereſt ought ever to induce a Monarch to break his Word.

The Progreſs of his Reign has been of a Piece with its Beginning; and the Allies, as well as the Subjects of the Crown of *Portugal*, have had juſt Reaſon to eſteem themſelves happy in ſo good a Prince. One Circumſtance only occupies the Attention of the former, at the ſame time that it excites the Fear of the latter. His *Portugueſe* Majeſty is without Iſſue Male, his Uncles and his Brother unmarried. This might afford room for many Speculations of a delicate Nature, and for that Reaſon, at this Juncture more eſpecially, improper. We may be ſure that the King and Queen cannot but have this Matter at heart, in which their People and their Poſterity have ſo near and ſo great a Concern, and therefore we may hope that ſome Proviſion will be made, conſiſtent alike with the true Intereſts of *Portugal*, and the Tranquility of *Europe*. We have had too recent an Example of what happened upon the Death of the Emperor *Charles* VI. notwithſtanding all the Care that could be taken, and we know how very near that was to deſtroying the Ballance, which perhaps would have taken place, but through the Defect of Force in that Prince to whom they gave the Title of Heir. This Error, no doubt, will be avoided here, and the Succeſſion ſo ſecurely ſettled as to put it into their Power to maintain themſelves with the Aſſiſtance of the Nation's Affections, and the Support of Crowns which are naturally bound to reſpect *Portugal*, and to manifeſt the Truth of their Profeſſions by their Deeds.

As for the Intereſts of *Portugal*, they may be divided into Political, which regard their Poſſeſſions in *Europe*, and Commercial, which reſpect their Dominions in *Aſia*, *Africa*, and *America*. As to the firſt, there is no doubt that it conſiſts in maintaining Peace; a Point to which his late Majeſty remained always well inclined, and thereby preſerved Quiet to his Subjects in the midſt of all the Broils of *Europe*. There is no doubt the Power of the Houſe of *Bourbon* has been, and there is no Reaſon to ſuſpect that it will not remain, formidable to this Kingdom; and hence ariſes the Neceſſity that *Portugal* is under, of living upon good Terms with the Maritime Powers, and more eſpecially with *Great Britain*. It is indeed ſaying no more than Truth, that there is ſcarce any Inſtance in Hiſtory of a more laſting and ſincere Friendſhip, than has ſubſiſted, for near

a Cena Century paſt, between the two Crowns; and as it is their mutual Intereſt that it ſhould ſubſiſt, there ſeems to be no Ground to ſuſpect it will not do ſo. While this continues, and while *Great Britain* maintains her Superiority at Sea, *Portugal* can hardly ever be in danger.

As for the Northern Crowns, ſhe has very little to do with them, or they with her; and as for the *Italian* States, it is not eaſy to conceive how any Differences ſhould ariſe between them and his *Portugueſe* Majeſty; and if there ſhould, it is very eaſy for him to do himſelf Juſtice. There were formerly long and bloody Wars between the Subjects of this Crown and the *Moors*; but as their Cauſes are now ceaſed, their Conſequences are ſunk with them. We muſt however except the piratical States of *Barbary*, which are in conſtant War with *Portugal*, becauſe they are conſtant Gainers by it; but whenever a martial and active Prince ſhall be ſeated upon that Throne, he will not find it a very difficult Matter to put his Navy in ſuch a Condition, as may impoſe Reſpect upon theſe thieviſh People, whoſe Depredations are a Scandal to all the *European* Powers, who might eaſily cruſh them at once, inſtead of continuing to pay Tribute to an inſignificant Race of Rovers, that owe their Impunity merely to the Negligence and Want of publick Spirit in thoſe, who ought long ago to have deſtroyed them, and may do it whenever they think fit. Let us now deſcend to the ſecond Particular.

As to to the Commercial Intereſt of *Portugal*, it lies now chiefly in the *Weſt*, as it did formerly in the *Eaſt-Indies*; and in reſpect to *Brazil*, their Strength is ſo great, that they have no Reaſon to apprehend any thing from their Neighbours; the only Danger to which they are expoſed, is from an Inſurrection of their own Negroes, which might indeed have very bad Conſequences. In the preſent State of Things, this Colony is the moſt profitable in the World, ſince, conſidering the Proportion between the two Kingdoms, *Portugal* draws more Profit from her *Brazils*, than *Spain* from both *Mexico* and *Peru*. It is otherwiſe in regard to *Aſia*, where from an Empire of almoſt incredible Extent, the *Portugueſe* Dominion is in a manner ſhrunk within the narrow Bounds of the little Peninſula at the Point of which ſtands the City of *Goa*.

It has often been deliberated in the Council at *Liſbon*, whether they ſhould not deſert even that, ſince in ſome Years it coſts more to maintain it than it is worth. But of late we were told, that a Project has been formed, not for recovering their Dominions indeed, but for reſtoring their Trade, and extend-

ing

ing their Commerce in the *East-Indies*, by reforming the Abuses under which it has long suffered. If ever this is carried into Execution, it must be at a Time when the other *European* Powers, that have Dominions in those Parts, are at War with each other; and therefore they could never expect a more favourable Juncture than the past War, which they neglected. If they had embraced it, there is no doubt that foreign Merchants would have been ready enough to secure their own Effects, trading under *Portuguese* Colours; and a very few Years Practice of this kind would have changed the Face of their Affairs in *India*, and might possibly have encouraged their Government at home to think seriously of giving them all the Assistance in their Power; the want of which has been most apparently the principal Cause of their Decline.

Before the Kingdom of *Portugal* was annexed to that of *Spain*, her Monarchs were remarkable for their Attention to naval Power, to the Support of their Colonies, and whatever might extend their Commerce; and to this extraordinary Care of their Princes, the quick Growth of their maritime Force, and their amazing Progress in *India*, was chiefly due. But while a Province to *Spain*, all this sunk as fast as it rose, and before the *Portuguese* could extricate themselves from this Dependence, they were almost undone. The defending their own Country next, and the recovering of *Brazil*, employed all their Care, and these are their Excuses for neglecting the *Indies*. But as all those Burdens are now removed, as they have no secret Enemies to fear, no avowed Enemies to oppose them, they may certainly, by a timely and steady Application, restore the Face of Things in this Country; but to delay this, will very probably put it for ever out of their Power.

Upon the whole it may be truly said, that under the present and the last Reign, the Kingdom of *Portugal* has had Time to recruit and recover its internal Strength, which was much exhausted by so long a War, as followed the raising the House of *Bragança* to the Throne. If the Advantage therefore of this Conjuncture be not lost, but the *Portuguese* avail themselves some way or other of an Interval that leaves them entirely at Liberty, there is no Question that they may make a different Figure in the next Century, from what they did in the last, or do at present. But if, as I said, they let this Occasion entirely slip, and stay till *Europe* settles upon its old Foundation, when their Dependency on

Spain

Spain will be again felt, they may continue as inconsiderable as some Writers have taken a Pleasure to represent them.

But this will be their own, that is, the Fault of their Government. For when the great Powers are embarrassed, then the lesser States have an Opportunity of becoming, by some bold Measure, which may be taken before any of their Neighbours are well acquainted with their Views, powerful and independent. If a Plan for regulating what little belongs to them in the *Indies*, had been fixed a Year after the War began, they might have been, by this time, as formidable there as any, except the *Dutch*; and the *French* would have connived at and assisted them as the weakest Side, till they made them more considerable than the rest, and then they would have repented of their good Offices, and endeavoured to ruin them. Yet their first Run of good Fortune might well enable them to stand firm, and the Remembrance of past Misfortunes inspire them with just Principles.

This being conceived, and attentively promoted, is a very feasible Scheme for reviving their past Glory, and restoring naval Power to the *Portuguese*, who must attempt somewhat of this kind, if they really mean to raise up their Heads again, and rival that Reputation they had before Don *Sebastian*, by invading *Barbary*, destroyed himself, his Army, and the Interest of his Subjects, which it had cost his Ancestors so much to acquire. It is true this might have been undertaken with much greater Probability of Success while the War continued, at which Season these Conjectures were first advanced; but it is far from being too late, even now, if Things are maturely considered before they are carried into Execution, and are then executed without Precipitation. It is a Point of great Consequence to those who would understand the Interests of *Europe*, to reflect on past Events, and to speculate freely upon what may possibly happen in time to come.

We have an Instance of this, with respect to the Country of which we are now treating, that ought not to be passed over in Silence. A Resolution was taken a little before the late King's Death in the Councils of *Portugal*, and carried into Execution, by which, under colour of repressing Luxury, some severe Edicts have been published, which have a bad Effect upon Trade. This shewed that his *Portuguese* Majesty either forgot or changed his Sentiments on the Point formerly discussed with the Lord Viscount *Galway*, which sooner or later, they may have Occasion fion to repent. There is no doubt at all to be made, that the capital Maxim in Government is the Welfare of the People: but as the Neglect of this is criminal, so Miftakes about it may be fatal. A Prince can never be too much commended for keeping that Maxim conftantly in View, but at the fame time it is of the utmoft Importance to him, that it be thoroughly underftood. We will not enter into a long political Differtation upon fo felf-evident a Point, but content ourfelves with applying what has been already laid down, and which cannot be difputed, to the Matter before us, becaufe this will at once contribute to the Information, and to the Entertainment of the Reader.

It has been already demonftrated, as far as things of this kind will admit of Demonftration, that the Safety, Independency, and Profperity of *Portugal*, muft depend either upon her maintaining a ftrict Conjunction with her natural Allies, or upon her acquiring a Strength fufficient to fuftain herfelf, without having recourfe to any foreign Affiftance. But as the latter is a thing very difficult to do, fo beyond all Queftion till it can be brought about, it will never be good Policy in this Crown to run any hazard as to the former. Now we have likewife fhewn, that till *Portugal* fhall have acquired a naval Force fuperior to that of her Neighbours, fhe muft, in fome meafure, depend upon that of *Great Britain*, and therefore it is directly contrary to her true Intereft to take any Step whatever that may be either prejudicial to that Force upon which her own Safety depends, or which may weaken thofe Ties Experience has fhewn to have been hitherto ftrong enough upon any Emergency to intitle her to that Affiftance. Whatever affects the Commerce between *Great Britain* and *Portugal*, operates to the Difadvantage of the laft mentioned Crown, as well by leffening our naval Force, which depends upon Trade, as by weakening the Connections that unite the two Nations, and are of equal Confequence to both

It may indeed be pretended, that if this new Scheme of Politicks fhould not leffen the *Portuguefe* Commerce in general, it will be of no great Confequence to that Crown, tho' there fhould happen fome Variation in the Manner of carrying it on; yet when this fhall be maturely and candidly confidered, it will be found there is no Ground at all for fuch a Pretence. The Kingdom of *Portugal* muft be furnifhed with Commodities and Manufactures from other Countries; but it does not follow from thence, that it is a Matter indifferent from what Countries fhe derives them. It may be, that a Part of her Trade may

fall

fall to the Share of the Subjects of a Crown, the natural Interests of which are contrary to her own; or they may fall into the Hands of a People, who have no Regard to any body's Interest but their own; and in such a Situation of Things, it certainly behoves the *Portuguese* to be attentive rather in keeping up their Commerce with those who will, for that very Reason, consider the Interests of *Portugal* as their own. If this Method of arguing be not conclusive, in a Point of this Nature, there is nothing that can be so; for Commerce is no longer a Blessing to a Country, than the Consequences of it are beneficial to that Country.

We must indeed allow, that suppressing of Luxury, encouraging Frugality, and providing for the Stay of Riches amongst the Body of a People, in whatever manner they acquire them, are Points that deserve the Attention of a Government, and more especially of a Government true to its own Interests. But these can never be properly attended to, if all the Consequences that may follow them are not foreseen and provided for. When Luxury is purely the Effect of prodigious Wealth, it requires much Circumspection in providing a suitable Cure for it; but when Luxury proceeds from an unequal Distribution of Wealth, Industry with proper Encouragements will work an easy and an effectual Cure. On the other hand, forced Frugality may have very bad Effects, and produce in a short Time Evils attended with worse Consequences than those that are apprehended from Luxury. It may, indeed it must create a very unequal Distribution of Wealth; for if those who are possessed of Money, are forced to save it whether they will or not, Numbers will be driven to downright Want, who would otherwise have subsisted very well upon that Dissipation, which was looked upon as a Calamity. These are Things that merit very serious Reflection in all Countries, but more especially in *Portugal*, where if the Minds of the noble and rich are not to be taken up with splendid Trifles, it is a thousand to one that they are occupied by worse Objects. An historical Instance will set this Matter in a very full and proper Light.

When the Inhabitants of *Portugal* had just thrown off the Yoke of *Spain*, the Conde Duke *d'Olivarez* consulted with a noble *Genoese*, who had great Credit with him, as to the Means by which this Country might be reduced, For now, said that great Minister, the King must recover his Rights by the Sword, and add to his other Titles that of Conquest; but the Business is where to begin, and what Measures we ought to take, in order

order to weaken the Enemy moſt? To this the crafty *Genoeſe* anſwered, The beſt Method is to leave them in Peace; there are many of the noble Families in that Country immenſely rich, and if theſe are not alarmed by the Apprehenſion of common Danger, they will infallibly fall out amongſt themſelves and do your Buſineſs; there is a Reſtleſſneſs in the Spirit of that Nation, which will not ſuffer them to enjoy their Wealth in Peace. The Conde Duke followed this Advice, tho' it did not ſucceed; but it was ſo very near ſucceeding, that it ſhewed plainly he that gave it had judged right.

It is very probable that what this Man ſaid of the *Portugueſe* then, may be ſtill true; for while their Government continues the ſame, the Humours of Nations ſeldom alter. If therefore this reſtleſs Temper is allowed to ſpend itſelf in Dreſs, Furniture, Equipage, Diverſions, and ſuch other Articles of Expence; this may contribute to the publick Tranquility, and muſt of Neceſſity diſperſe the Riches of the Great among the meaner ſort of People, and of theſe the moſt induſtrious will, as it is fit they ſhould, have the greateſt Share. But if a ſudden Check is given to this before ſuch as laviſh their Money have taken another Turn in employing it, this may become the Source of deſtructive Factions among the Great, and of as deſtructive Indigence among the Mechanicks and lower ſort of People; the former will find themſelves on a ſudden too rich to be quiet, and the latter will become poor enough to venture upon any thing that may procure, or even bid fair for a Subſiſtence.

It may be ſaid in anſwer to this, that in many Countries ſumptuary Laws have had very good Effects; which is certainly very true; but then the Cauſes of this muſt be looked for in the Nature of the Government, under which the Inhabitants of thoſe Countries lived, and the Diſpoſition of the People. Where the Wealth of a Nation ariſes from annual Importations of intrinſick Riches from their Colonies, it will be a hard Matter to inſpire Induſtry, at leaſt ſuch an Induſtry as ſumptuary Laws are calculated to promote; and therefore it is unnatural and impolitick to venture laying legal Reſtraints upon ſuch a People; for the true Way to moderate Luxury amongſt them muſt be by encouraging Expence of another Kind, and of publick Utility.

If therefore the Court of *Portugal*, inſtead of thoſe Edicts, had encouraged the Nobility to intereſt themſelves in Expeditions to the *Indies*, for improving their Settlements on the Coaſt of *Africa*, or to fit out Squadrons againſt the *Barbary* Corſairs; this would have done effectually what the other either will not

do,

do, or if it does, will introduce Diſtempers infinitely more dangerous and deſperate than the Diſeaſe it was calculated to remove.

In dwelling ſo long upon this Subject, we have been influenced chiefly by two Motives, the firſt general, and the latter particular. In general, it is a Point of great Conſequence to have a true Notion of Matters of this Nature, with which State Empirics are much inclined to meddle, and with which if they are ſuffered to meddle, they ſeldom fail of creating Confuſion; for it is no ſuch eaſy Matter as ſome imagine, to rectify the Manners of Mankind by Laws, though it may be ſafely and advantageouſly done by Examples. In Countries that derive their Wealth from Trade, or from the Produce of their foreign Settlements, ſuch Attempts are moſt dangerous, as the Mechaniſm of their Conſtitutions is very complicated, and ought therefore never to be tampered with, for fear that while the Correction of ſome ſmall Inconvenience is endeavoured, the whole Machine ſhould be put into Diſorder, and what was intended for publick Service, become unexpectedly the Ground of publick Diſturbance.

As to the particular Motive, we have a ſingular and ſpecial Intereſt in whatever regards the Welfare of the Crown of *Portugal*; its Subjects are our old, our natural, and our uſeful Allies; we have been benefited by our Commerce with them, and they have derived great Advantages from our Friendſhip. Beſides, the Crown of *Portugal* is one of thoſe Powers, that while it regards its own Intereſts muſt remain attached to the Common Cauſe, by which I mean the Liberty and Independency of *Europe*, the preſerving to every Kingdom and State its juſt Right of purſuing its own Welfare, according to its own Conſtitution, which as it is a common Benefit to all, is very properly ſtiled the Common Cauſe, in Oppoſition to thoſe arbitrary Syſtems whereby ſome overgrown and deſpotick Crown, or ſome ambitious and overbearing Family is made the Center, about which other ſecondary States muſt move, as the Planets do about the Sun; with this Difference, that as the one is according to the Law of Nature, ſo the other is in direct Defiance of it, as the Conſequences in both Caſes plainly prove.

C H A P.

CHAP. XIII.

A succinct Description of ITALY, *the Powers subsisting therein at present, their Forces, Revenues, and Trade. The Nature of the* BALLANCE *in that Country; whence it has been so often in Danger; and why those Powers of Europe interest themselves so much for its Preservation, which are not connected with* ITALY *by any of the usual Ties.*

THE great and fruitful Country of *Italy* has been, as high as History records, either the Seat of Empire, or the Theatre of War. According to the earliest Account we have, this extensive and beautiful Peninsula was then in the same Situation that it now is, cantoned out into various little States and Republicks, all living in Distrust, at least, if not in War with each other. The *Roman* Commonwealth changed the Face of Things by swallowing up all, and making herself the Head and Mistress of *Italy*. The Division of her Empire proved the Ruin of it, and the Provinces adjacent to *Italy* being lost, the barbarous Nations that conquered them very soon became Masters even of the Imperial City of *Rome*, and divided *Italy* once more into separate Principalities, all of which have been extremely subject to Revolutions, sometimes from the superior Power of foreign Invaders, and as often from the Effects of intestine Commotions; so that no History is fuller of Events, and consequently more capable of gratifying the Curiosity, and fixing the Attention of a Reader, than that of this Country. But to enter into this is not our Business; it would be a Work of great Extent, and prodigious Variety, highly entertaining and highly useful. All we aim at, is to make such a Representation of its present State, as may enable every Reader clearly to comprehend the Grounds of the high Attention that is paid to the Ballance of Power there; by shewing as briefly as we can, how it is divided, what are the Titles of its present Possessors, their comparative Force and Interests, with other Circumstances of a like Nature, that may set in a proper Light the Disputes that have been lately composed,

and

and those latent Pretensions, which it is suspected may produce in our Times further Disturbances.

We have different Computations of the Extent of *Italy*, according to the different Notions that ancient and modern Authors have entertained of the proper Bounds of this Country. But not to trouble the Reader with Geographical Niceties, which have scarce any thing to do with our Design, and would contribute little or nothing to his Information, let it suffice, that from the Frontiers of *Switzerland* to the Extremity of the Kingdom of *Naples*, it is about seven hundred and fifty Miles in Length ; and from the Frontiers of the Duchy of *Savoy* to those of the Dominions of the State of *Venice*, which is its greatest Breath, about four hundred, though in some Parts it is scarce a fourth Part so broad. As to its Situation, it is bounded on the West by the *Alps*, which separates it from the adjacent Provinces of *France*; on the North it is likewise bounded by the *Alps*; and on the East by the Dominions of the House of *Austria* ; on the one Side it is washed by the *Mediterranean*, from the County of *Nice* to the Coasts of the Kingdom of *Naples*; and on the other by the Adriatick and the Gulph of *Venice* ; a narrow Streight divides it from the fruitful Island of *Sicily*, which however has been in all times reckoned a Part of it. The Soil and Climate, in different Parts, are as opposite as can well be imagined. In *Switzerland*, and the Country of the *Grisons*, the Mountains are as high as in any Part of *Europe*, the Earth barren, and the Air bleak and sharp ; the Plains of *Lombardy* again, are justly stiled the Garden of *Europe*, as well on Account of their Fertility, as the Serenity and Pleasantness of the Climate; in the Dominions of the Church, and in the Kingdom of *Naples*, the Heat in Summer is excessive, to which however they are indebted for the richest Fruits, and the most odoriferous Flowers, as well as Oyl, Wine, Silk, and other valuable Commodities.

There are few Countries in the World better watered than this, in respect to Springs, Rivulets, small and great Lakes, as well as large Rivers. Thus bountifully dealt with by Nature, it has also, from the Ingenuity and Application of its Inhabitants, been esteemed the Mother of Arts and Commerce, in respect to the rest of *Europe* ; its Reputation is still so high with regard to the first, that the Tour of *Italy* is considered as the necessary Conclusion of a polite Education ; and in reference to the latter, though the Trade of *Italy* is now nothing to what it was, yet the Ports of *Genoa*, *Leghorn*, *Naples*, and *Venice*, to say nothing of those in *Sicily*, make still a

very

very great Figure, and derive vast Advantages to the Sovereigns in whose Dominions they are situated. Besides all this, the several Countries of *Italy* have such Funds of natural Riches, and the People are so happy at improving as well as inventing Manufactures, that they stand in need only of some favourable Juncture to revive their ancient Spirit, and to make as great a Figure as their Ancestors did in comparison with other Nations.

There is no kind of Government subsisting in any Part of *Europe*, of which something of the like Kind is not to be found in *Italy*. As to the Sovereignty of the Pope, it is peculiar to this Country, as it is vested in a spiritual Person, and yet is altogether a temporal Power exercised as absolutely, and, as is generally supposed, with more Policy than in any other Monarchy. The Dominions of those two crowned Heads (for as yet there are no more) that lie within its Limits, are those of his *Sardinian* Majesty at one End, and of the King of the *Two Sicilies* at the other. The Duchy of *Milan*, once the largest and richest in this Part of the World, together with the Duchy of *Mantua* and its Dependencies, belong to the august House of *Austria*. His Imperial Majesty is considered as one of the *Italian* Powers, not only in that Capacity by which he claims a Title, paramount to the greatest Part, if not the whole, but particularly also as Grand Duke of *Tuscany*. The Infant Duke of *Parma* is at length in Possession of a Settlement, composed not only of that Duchy, and of *Placentia*, which was the Patrimony of his Ancestors by the Mother's Side, but likewise of *Guastalla*. His Serene Highness the Duke of *Modena* holds that Duchy and *Reggio*, together also with the Duchy of *Mirandola*; and besides these, there are some other lesser Princes who would take it ill if they were not stiled Sovereigns. The Republick of *Venice* is an unmixed Aristocracy, still venerable for the Wisdom of its Government, as heretofore formidable by the Extent of its Dominions as well as a great naval Force. The Republick of *Genoa* is an Aristocracy also, but not quite so pure as that of *Venice*. The *Swiss* Cantons, the *Grisons* their Allies, and the City of *Geneva*, are so many different Republicks, each having its particular Form of Government, but owing their Strength to their Confederacy, which renders them truly great and formidable. There are, besides these, two free States, the Dominions of which are surrounded by those of Sovereign Princes, to whom notwithstanding they owe no Obedience, or even Homage; the first of which is the Commonwealth of *Lucca*

in

in the Neighbourhood of *Tuscany*, and the latter the Republick of St. *Marino* in the Midst of the Pope's Territories.

Such is the Distribution of Power in *Italy*; and in the supporting this Distribution, and maintaining each of these Princes and States in their respective Rights, so as to prevent their encroaching upon each other, or being overborn by a foreign Force, consists the Preservation of the Ballance in *Italy*. A Term very significant in Policy, and originally invented here, where it is perfectly well understood, though not always practised; for if it were, the Powers in *Italy* need not the Assistance of Foreigners to keep it steady, since how small or weak soever some of them may appear when considered separately, yet the Conjunction of their Forces would be at all Times found sufficient to defend this Country from Invasions.

This may appear strange, and perhaps incredible, considering the Figure that *Italian* Princes have generally made in the Wars that have happened in our Time. The Fact is nevertheless true. For first with regard to Troops, though the Militia in many of the Principalities are very indifferent, and the regular Forces much fitter for Show than for Use; yet this ought to be reputed the Effects of Luxury and bad Government; for in former Times, as the most authentick Histories shew, these Countries bred as good Soldiers as any in *Europe*. In the next place let it be observed, that there is hardly any foreign Service in which *Italian* Officers have not distinguished themselves; and if we look into the Records of the two last Centuries, we shall find the Names of *Italian* Heroes, who in Point of Courage and Conduct were little inferior to those of Antiquity.

To say the Truth, most of the great Houses in *Italy* were founded by illustrious Soldiers, and there is no doubt that if a true Spirit of Liberty prevailed, they would very soon become famous again. As it is, the *Swiss* and the *Grisons* furnish in other People's Quarrels as good Infantry as any in the World; his *Sardinian* Majesty's Troops have acquired a just Reputation in the three last Wars, and the Insurrection of the *Genoese* Peasants shew what might be expected from the Valour of those who knew what they were fighting for. All the Strength of *Italy* collected, is rather under than over computed at one hundred and forty thousand Men, which in their own Country and for their own Defence, those Princes and Powers that raise them might very well maintain, since if it were not for a vain Affectation of Show and Magnificence, and a still vainer Propensity to costly Superstition, the Subjects of the *Italian* Potentates

tentates would be very far from wanting wherewith to defray such an Armament for the general Security.

But after all, notwithstanding that the Ballance of Power is the common Interest of all these Princes and States, notwithstanding that they know this better than Strangers possibly can do, and are as well satisfied of it as can be wished, yet so it is, that with all their Penetration and Prudence, some or other of them are continually deluded by specious Views and flattering Promises, to act against what they are convinced is their true and great Interest, which would certainly appear a Thing monstrous and absurd, if it happened no where but in *Italy*, and must on the contrary appear very natural and probable to any impartial Politician who is well acquainted with the Nature of Mankind, and who is sensible that notwithstanding all their Circumspection and Gravity, the Inhabitants of *Italy* are Men like their Neighbours, Men having the same or perhaps stronger Passions, and consequently very capable of being wrought upon when the Hopes of gratifying those Passions are placed in a full, though at the same time in a fallacious Light. In their Writings and in their Discourses, you see the Benefits of the Ballance perfectly explained, and the Errors of their Ancestors in calling now the *French*, then the *Spaniards*, often the *Germans*, into *Italy*, very judiciously exploded, while the same thing is practised by themselves to this very Day. Nor can the strongest Foresight discern, when this Infatuation will cease.

The Truth of the Matter is, that the Influence of the two great Houses of *Austria* and *Bourbon*, have in our Days chiefly contributed to keep the Scale in almost constant Motion, and whenever there has been any little Recess, it has lasted no longer than till the silent Intrigues of the Partisans of one or other of these Houses have been able to pave the Way for new Disputes. Sometimes it has been thought for the Interest of *Italy* to rid themselves entirely of one House by the Assistance of the other, and when this has been in a good measure effected at the Expence of much Bloodshed and Confusion, Experience has shewn them their Mistake, in consequence of which they have entered into a new War to set Things right again. Other Nations more at a Distance, find themselves strongly interested in the Preservation of the Ballance from a Variety of Motives, but principally from these two ; first, because their Trade in the *Mediterranean* must suffer exceedingly if the Ballance in *Italy* be destroyed ; and secondly, this Ballance is attended to, because a Diversion on the Side of *Italy* proves often

often a Thing of the laſt Conſequence in the Caſe of a general War, the very Apprehenſion of which keeps a very conſiderable Part of the Forces of each of the contending Houſes from being employed where they might be of moſt Prejudice to thoſe Powers, who for this Reaſon make the Ballance of *Italy* ſo much their Concern.

Whatever there may be, either dark or difficult, in theſe ſhort and general Reflections, will be rendered very perſpicuous by what follows ; for we will now treat of theſe *Italian* Potentates ſeparately and diſtinctly, in order to give the Reader a competent Idea of their comparative Strength, the Nature of their particular Intereſts, and the Means by which they have been wrought upon from the Deſire of bettering theſe, to ſacrifice from time to time that Safety and Security, which would certainly reſult from adhering to their general Intereſt of preſerving the Ballance, which being built upon this Principle, that Princes and States be content with their own, and purſue the Good of their Subjects without Prejudice to their Neighbours, is a thing always to be wiſhed, but at the ſame time hardly ever to be expected.

S E C T.   I.

The modern Hiſtory, political Intereſts, and Connections, of the Dukes of Savoy, *Kings of* Sicily *and* Sardinia.

THE Dominions of his *Sardinian* Majeſty, conſidered as Duke of *Savoy*, and Prince of *Piedmont*, have been always regarded as the Key of *Italy*, on the Side of *France* ; and in latter Times this Prince has been juſtly looked upon as the natural Maſter of the Ballance in *Italy* ; not that his Dominions even now, when by various Acquiſitions they are become much ſuperior to what they were under any of his Anceſtors, qualify him to give Law to his Neighbours, or even to ſecure himſelf from the bad Effects of a general Alliance againſt him ; but upon the Score of its being his Intereſt to affect Peace rather than War ; and becauſe while he remains firm to his own Intereſt, Reaſon and Experience ſhew, that he will never want Allies willing to give him all the Aſſiſtance he needs for the Preſervation of his own Territories, and maintaining

maintaining that Syftem, upon which their Security and his own Grandeur muft always depend.

To trace the Family of *Savoy* to its Origin, and to enter into a long Detail of what has happened to its Princes in Times paft, would not contribute much to the Performance of what we have promifed to the Reader; and therefore we fhall afcend no higher than *Victor Amadeus* the Second, the Father of his prefent *Sardinian* Majefty, and who in his Life-time was efteemed one of the greateft Captains, as well as one of the ableft Politicians in *Europe*. He was likewife of all the Princes of his Time beft verfed in the Bufinefs of Negotiation, which therefore he never trufted at all to his Minifters, who were feldom acquainted with his Treaties till they came to figning, and fometimes not then. His whole Study was the Ballance of *Italy*, which he perfectly underftood and fteadily purfued. His Situation made this requifite, his Penetration brought this very early to his Notice, and having once conceived its Importance, it became his Rule of Action to his Life's End.

He fucceeded his Father Duke *Charles Emanuel*, in the Year 1675, and that by a very furprizing Accident. He was then a Boy, and had juft begun his Exercifes; his Father, who had a true Forefight of his great Qualities, was extremely fond of him, and coming one Day to fee him ride, the young Prince had the Misfortune to be thrown from his Horfe, with fuch Violence that thofe about him cried out he was killed, which affected Duke *Charles Emanuel* to fuch a Degree, that he fainted upon the Spot, and died in a few Days of the Fright. His Mother, the Duchefs Dowager of *Savoy*, governed his Dominions during the Minority of *Victor Amadeus*; and when he had attained to an Age fit for Marriage, fhe negotiated a Match for him with the Infanta, who was then efteemed Heirefs of the Kingdom of *Portugal*, which was carried fo far, that the Duke de *Cadeval* came with a *Portuguefe* Squadron to *Nice*, in order to have carried his Highnefs to *Lifbon*.

But the young Prince fufpecting that he might lofe his hereditary Countries, and poffibly mifs of the foreign Crown he was feeking, changed his Mind fuddenly, and broke off the Marriage. It would carry this Article into too great a Length, otherwife we might from this brifk Refolution in fo young a Prince, and the Confideration on which it was founded, fhew how very early in fome Minds the Seeds of political Prudence appear, and that Faculty of judging (as it were) by a fingle Glance, on which Side the Advantage lies, a Thing hardly ever to be taught. But to proceed; fome time after

he

he efpoufed *Anna Maria* of *Orleans*, the eldeft Daughter of
Philip of *Orleans*, only Brother to the late *Lewis* XIV. by
Henrietta Maria, Daughter of our King *Charles* I. So that
he became nearly allied to our Royal Family; and his Son
the prefent King of *Sardinia*, is the firft Prince of the Popifh
Line, after the Heirs Male of the Houfe of *Stuart*, but excluded from this Succeffion by the Act of Settlement.

It was in virtue of this Marriage, that in the Beginning of
his Reign the Duke of *Savoy* went into the Meafures of *France*,
and at the Inftigation of *Lewis* XIV. began a violent Perfecution
againft his Proteftant Subjects in the Vallies, about the Year
1685, which threw his whole Country into Blood and Confufion. But it was not long before he perceived his Error, and
that nothing could be fo fatal to a Prince as depriving himfelf
of a great Part of his Subjects. He was alfo convinced that
the *French* Monarch meant him no better than the reft of his
Neighbours; and therefore when the firft Grand Alliance was
formed at the *Hague* in 1690, he took care to be included in
it, and ventured fo far as to ftake his Dominions, to preferve
his Independency.

His Succefs in that War was but indifferent; his Troops
were not fo well difciplined as thofe of *France*, and he had not
himfelf acquired that Experience in the Art of War, for which
he became afterwards fo remarkable. He perfifted however in
his Purpofe, tho' he loft the Battle of *Staffard*, and moft of the
ftrong Towns in his Dominions that Year. But in the next
the *French* were baffled before *Coni*; and the Duke, to fhew
that he was not fo defpicable an Enemy as the Grand Monarch
imagined, made an Irruption into *Dauphiny*, where he took
Gap and *Ambrun*, and then returned into his own Dominions.
This Incurfion had its Effect; for in 1693, *Lewis* XIV. propofed, and the Duke accepted a feparate Peace, by which *Nice*,
Sufa, *Villafranca*, and *Montmilian*, were reftored to him, as
was alfo *Pignerol*, but the *French* thought fit to demolifh it
firft. He obtained alfo three Vallies, and a very confiderable
Sum of Money, as a Compenfation for the Lofs he had fuftained by the War.

To attach him more firmly to his Intereft, the *French* King
confented that the Duke of *Burgundy*, his eldeft Grandfon,
fhould marry the eldeft Daughter of the Duke, and that his
Highnefs fhould command his Troops in *Italy* againft his old
Allies. After the general Peace, there happened fome new Differences between him and *France*, which were compromifed by
another Treaty in 1701, when the moft Chriftian King thought
nothing

nothing could ftrenghen the Intereft of *Philip* Duke of *Anjou*, whom he had declared King of *Spain*, fo much as marrying into the Houfe of *Savoy*; and therefore he confented to his Match with the fecond Daughter of the Duke; and it was at the fame time agreed, that in cafe of a War, his Highnefs fhould be Generaliffimo of the Army of the two Crowns in *Italy*.

By this Step the Politicians at *Verfailles* imagined that they had carried two great Points, that of fixing the Houfe of *Savoy* for ever in its Dependence upon the *Bourbon* Family, and providing for the Defence of the *Spanifh* Dominions in *Italy*, by putting them under the Protection of the only Power whereby they could be hurt; and it is very highly probable that this Scheme of theirs would have taken place in its full Extent, if *Louvois*, who had then the greateft Credit with *Lewis* XIV. had not overturned it. He had conceived an unreafonable and a very unaccountable Diftafte to the Duke of *Savoy*, and from the Brutality of his own Temper, was fo far from concealing, that he expreffed it in Terms fo grofs and fo abufive, that no Gentleman could have borne, and which therefore it was impoffible that a Sovereign Prince fhould not refent.

Victor Amadeus confidered, that if his clofe Alliance with the Houfe of *Bourbon* could not defend him from fuch Treatment, his Succeffors, when the Power of that Houfe fhould be more extended than it was, would fink into a Degree of Dependence, more uneafy and not lefs difhonourable than downright Subjection; he took therefore the glorious Refolution of forgetting the Ties of natural Affection for his Daughters, that he might fupport the Dignity derived to him from his Anceftors, and leave his Pofterity as free as, in fpite of the Difficulties they had to ftruggle with, thofe Anceftors had left him. Such were the Motives that threw him into the fecond Grand Alliance, though at the Beginning Things did not feem to go much better than when he entered into the firft. The *French* were every where fuperior, he was furrounded by them on all fides, his Friends were at a Diftance, and it required a good deal of Time before they would be able to act. No Prince could know this better than he, yet he profecuted his Plan, and what he had concerted with the Wifdom of a Politician, he fupported with the Magnanimity of a Hero.

The *French* King was no fooner acquainted with, or rather no fooner fufpected his Royal Highnefs's Defign, than he caufed a great Body of his Troops which had joined the

French

French Army to be seized and difarmed; he sent the Duke *de Vendome* into *Piedmont*, who took *Verceil* on one Side, while another Body of *French* Troops became Masters of *Sufa*; all *Savoy* was conquered, and the important Fortress of *Montmilian* demolished. The County of *Nice* was reduced soon after, and the greatest Part of *Piedmont* by degrees; at last *Turin* was invested, and the Duke saw himself upon the very Point of losing every Foot of Ground he had. He bore his Misfortunes with Patience, he took his Measures with Prudence, and with great Generosity of Soul rejected the Terms that *Lewis* XIV. would have prescribed, with this remarkable Expression, *that it was better for a Prince to starve with Honour than reign with Shame.* The Imperial Army designed for the Relief of *Turin*, was commanded by a Prince of his own House, the Great *Eugene*. His March appeared wonderful both to Friends and Enemies, and when he arrived in *Italy*, his Army was so much inferior to that of the Enemy, that the *French* boasted he had taken so much Pains, and run so many Hazards, merely to sacrifice them.

Their Triumph was but short; the Prince attacked the Duke of *Orleans* in his Lines before *Turin*, beat him, and by a single Victory recovered *Piedmont*, and saved *Italy*. This was in 1706; the very next Year the Duke invaded *France* in his Turn, forced the Passage of the *Var*, marched directly thro' *Provence*, and formed the Siege of *Toulon*, which miscarried by Accidents it would require too much room to relate. One Thing is remarkable, the *French* with a Fury more than barbarous, had destroyed all his fine Walks, and cut down all his fair Plantations near *Turin*; he had an Opportunity of returning this Compliment in *Provence*, by destroying their Mulberry, their Olive Trees, and their Capers; but he disdained it, and on the contrary, took all the Pains imaginable to preserve them. He continued the War with his own Forces, and obliged the *French* to keep an Army on that Side constantly to prevent his Irruptions, which weakened their Forces elsewhere, and convinced them he was no contemptible Enemy.

At the Conclusion of the Treaty of *Utrecht*, the late Queen *Anne* insisted upon the Cession to him of the Kingdom of *Sicily*, and took care that the Crown of *Spain*, failing the Heirs of *Philip* V. should be entailed upon this Prince. *France* restored to him the Duchy of *Savoy* and the County of *Nice*, and yielded to him likewise in Perpetuity the Valley of *Pragelas*, with the Forts of *Exilles* and *Fenestrelles*, with the Vallies of *Oux*,

Oux, *Bardonache*, and *Chateau Dauphine*; but on the other hand he yielded the Valley of *Barcelonetta* to the Crown of *France*. His most Christian Majesty likewise confirmed the Cessions that were made by the Emperor, of a Part of *Montferrat*, the Provinces of *Alexandria* and *Valentia*, the Countries between the *Po* and the *Tenaro*, the *Lomelin*, the Valley of *Seffia*, and the Equivalent that was to be given for *Vigevanasco*.

All this contributed to make the King of *Sicily*, as he was now stiled, a very considerable Prince, and he would have soon become much more considerable, if he had remained longer in Possession of *Sicily*, where he began to make himself very agreeable to the People, by supporting the Authority of the Civil Government against the Clergy, who made use of their too great Wealth and Privileges to oppress and pillage the People. He had not time, however, as we have hinted, to bring his Designs to bear; the *Spaniards*, on the one hand, could not endure that he should keep that Island, and the late Emperor *Charles* VI. on the other, kept up his Claim to it, and resolved to take the first Opportunity that should offer of re-uniting it to his Kingdom of *Naples*.

The Lovers of secret History have reported, that *Spain* offered to King *Victor Amadeus*, an Expedient for extricating him from these Difficulties, which was the driving the *Imperialists* out of *Italy*, and then granting him all that he could desire or expect; but they say likewise, that *Spain* insisted upon having the Prince of *Piedmont* delivered as a Hostage, which the King excused, upon account of the Tenderness the Queen his Mother had for that Prince; but at the same time offered the Prince *de Carignan* in his stead, which was accepted; but when the Time came for the Delivery, it was said, that Prince had made his Escape, and was retired into *France*, which so irritated the Court of *Madrid*, that they immediately resolved upon the Invasion of *Sicily*.

That there was a Negotiation set on foot between this Monarch and the *Spanish* Court, I do not at all doubt; but as to the Tale of his giving Hostages, I look upon it as a Chimera. *Victor Amadeus* was of another Temper, than to sacrifice the Safety of his Heir Apparent, or any Prince of his Family, in such a manner. The Use he made of that Treaty was to amuse the *Spanish* Ministers, and gain 'Time to take the best Measures possible, which, after mature Deliberation, he judged was striking in with his old Allies, who about this Time concluded the Quadruple Alliance. All he could obtain was the Exchange of *Sicily* for *Sardinia*, which tho' a

C c   very

very great Loſs, was better than nothing; but in a little Time it ſeemed very doubtful whether he would be able to obtain even this, the *Spaniards* making themſelves entirely Maſters of that Iſland, at the ſame time that they attacked and conquered a great Part of *Sicily*. Theſe Events paſſed in the Year 1718, when the Affairs of this Monarch wore but an indifferent Aſpect, till Sir *George Byng* having entirely deſtroyed the *Spaniſh* Fleet, put it in the Power of the *Imperialiſts* to make themſelves Maſters of *Sicily*; and ſo far check'd the Ambition, and humbled the Power of the Catholick King, that he was once more content to abandon *Sardinia,* which in conſequence of the Alliance before-mentioned, was delivered up to *Victor Amadeus,* who bore ever after the Title of his *Sardinian* Majeſty, and continued alſo in Poſſeſſion of that Iſland, ſituated very near his own Dominions, very far from being an inconſiderable Acquiſition; though certainly much inferior to the noble Kingdom of *Sicily,* that for the preſent fell under the Dominion of the Emperor *Charles* VI. and continued ſo many Years after, till in conſequence of the Reſentment of his preſent *Sardinian* Majeſty, it was once again recovered by the *Bourbon* Family, remains ſtill, and is like to remain, in their Poſſeſſion.

As ſoon as the King found himſelf in ſome meaſure free from thoſe Troubles and Diſputes, with which his Reign had hitherto been embarraſſed, he ſet about the Execution of a Project which had been long floating in his Mind; in ſhort, he compiled, or cauſed to be compiled under his Direction, a compleat CODE or *Body of Laws* for the Uſe of his Subjects, which he ordered to be publiſhed in 1723, by which he in a great meaſure freed his People from trivial and vexatious Suits, and from the running into a tedious Length of ſuch as were more neceſſary. The Lawyers were ſomewhat diſpleaſed with this, but the King told them, " what they loſt " would be a Gain to their Poſterity, and that in Dominions " ſo narrow as his, and ſome of them not over fruitful, it " was inconſiſtent with common Senſe to grant an Indulgence " to any one Set of Men to eat up the Produce of all other " Men's Labours." By his royal Edict therefore, and without any further Ceremony, this CODE divided into five Parts (the ſixth not being then publiſhed) making a Volume of 644 Leaves, was declared the Meaſure of Civil Right throughout his Territories.

It is certain that he had projected other Regulations, and ſeemed wholly bent upon ſuch Meaſures as might tend

to

to the Improvement of his Country, and to better the Condition of his People, when he found himself under a Necessity of taking a very extraordinary Step, which however it is highly probably he had very maturely considered before he took it, tho' he was so secret therein, that nobody either in his own Country, or in any of the Courts of *Europe*, had the least Intelligence thereof, before it appeared in the Gazette of *Turin*. In conducting which important Design as he did, his Majesty had in view the confirming and establishing that great Character he had obtained through *Europe*, by observing the same Conduct to the last, as well as to secure those great Advantages for the Sake of which this amazing Step was taken, and which would have been infallibly lost, if it had been discovered or disclosed.

This singular and surprising Measure was the Resignation of his Crown in favour of his Son the Prince of *Piedmont*. He was moved thereto from various Considerations, but particularly three. In the first Place he found himself so extraordinarily pressed by the Emperor on one Side, and by *France* and her Allies on the other, that he could scarce determine with himself which Side to take, and therefore inclined to make a Chasm in the Government, rather than take either, in hopes of gaining Time for his Successor. He was so sensible, in the second Place, that many Reasons might be alledged against the Execution of several Schemes he had formed, in relation for the most part to the Ecclesiastical and Civil Government of his Dominions, that he judged they might be better managed by his Son. He was, thirdly, much worn with the continual Fatigues of a long and active Reign, and was desirous therefore of passing a few Years in repose with the Countess St. *Sebastian*, whom he married when a private Man, and retired with her to *Chamberry* in *Savoy*.

This Resignation took place in the Month of *September* 1730; it was made with great Solemnity, in the Presence not only of the great Ministers of his Court, but also of almost all the Nobility and Persons of Distinction in his Dominions. He reserved to himself an Annuity of one hundred and fifty thousand Livres *per Ann.* and having recommended Moderation to his Son, and Fidelity to his Subjects, parted with his Crown with the utmost Appearance of Satisfaction.

CHARLES EMANUEL II. his Son and Successor, mounted the Throne which his Father had quitted, in the Flower of his Age, being then in his thirtieth Year. He had married in the Year 1722, a Princess of the House of *Neuburgh*, and
upon

upon her Demise he espoused in 1724, a Princess of *Hesse Rhinfelds*. He had given great Hopes from his most tender Years, of making a mild and gracious, as well as a gallant and wise Prince; and at his Entrance into the Government he met with so many and so unexpected Crosses, that Posterity will learn with Wonder how he extricated himself from them without Blemish to his Character, and without Prejudice to his Administration.

In short, the old King, at the Instigation of the Lady he had made his Wife, but not his Queen, grew dissatisfied with his private Condition, and began to form Designs of resuming his Dignity, which he prosecuted in a manner suitable to so wild and inconsistent a Project, and to the Disposition of the Person at whose Instance he was weak enough to attempt it. The young King acted a very wise and discreet Part, he called together the great Officers of State and the Nobility, and having acquainted them with the Necessity he was under to secure his Father's Person, he demanded their Advice; and they were unanimously of Opinion, that as well for the Sake of his Subjects as himself, he should continue to administer Affairs with the same Spirit, Œconomy, and Prudence, which he had shewn from the Time he mounted the Throne.

In following their Advice, he shewed himself a true Father to his Country; for there is nothing more certain, than that it was with the utmost Reluctance and Concern, that he took the only Measure that was left for him to take, that of confining the old King to his Palace at *Montcalier*, where he remained to the Day of his Death, which was the last of *October* 1732, in the sixty-seventh Year of his Age.

But if the Situation of this Monarch's Affairs at home continued all this time uneasy and perplexed, the Concerns he had with foreign Powers were not at all less embarrassed. The Imperial Court had afforded many Occasions to his Father of Complaint; and those Occasions were not removed under the Reign of the Son. Whether this proceeded from Design or Inadvertence is yet undecided, but from whatever it proceeded, its Effects were fatal. His *Sardinian* Majesty acquainted the late Earl of *Essex*, then the *British* Minister at his Court, with the Nature of his Grievances, and the Reasons which led him to suspect that they were not very sincere at *Vienna*, in reference to the Concessions that had been made him, the rather because that all the Titles and Records of the *Montferrat*, which was yielded to him by Treaty, were withheld; and he could not help regarding this, and the forming some Pretensions upon certain Districts, as if they were dependent on the Duchy of *Milan*,

Milan, as Signs that he was no longer to retain the Possession of those Territories, than till some fair Opportunity should offer for resuming them.

The *British* Court having just Apprehensions of what happened, laboured earnestly with his late Imperial Majesty *Charles* VI. and his Ministers, to remove these Obstacles, to a close and cordial Correspondence with the Court of *Turin*; but the Dilatoriness which had been but too observable on all such Occasions, hindered them from taking those Steps which perhaps they were inclined to take, and which might probably have given his *Sardinian* Majesty Satisfaction. So that while they were negotiating and trying a variety of Methods, to oblige this Prince to let fall some of his Pretensions, the general Affairs of *Europe* took such a Turn, as proved by no means favourable to their Views.

In the beginning of the Year 1733, died King *Augustus* of *Poland*, which, as we have shewn elsewhere, gave Occasion to a Rupture between the Houses of *Austria* and *Bourbon*, and together with the ill Conduct beforementioned, afforded the latter an Opportunity of detaching his *Sardinian* Majesty intirely from the former. In pursuing this extraordinary Measure, that Monarch acted with all the Secrecy and Address which have been the constant Characteristics of his Administration. He signed on the twenty-sixth of *September*, with the Marquis *de Vaugrenant*, an offensive and defensive Alliance with *France*, to which *Spain* afterwards acceded. The true Design of this wise Prince in making this Treaty, was that expressed in his Manifesto, *viz.* restoring the Ballance of Power in *Italy*; where he thought the House of *Austria* had acquired too great an Ascendancy.

It is at least certain, that many of the *Italian* Potentates had just Reason to complain of the Conduct of the Court of *Vienna*; and that notwithstanding this, their Complaints were very little regarded, which joined to his own particular Grievances, induced his *Sardinian* Majesty to believe, that if the Plan laid down in this Alliance could be carried into Execution, the Affairs of *Italy* would not only be put into a better Condition for the present, but that all things might be properly settled on a right and solid Basis for the future. When the *French* Army began to pass the *Alps*, Count *Traun*, at that Time Governor of *Milan*, was so little apprised of the true State of Things, that he offered his *Sardinian* Majesty all the Assistance in his Power, to impede their Passage; to

which

which the King anfwered coldly, *That they did not come as Enemies.*

Marfhal *Villars* commanded the *French* Army, and his *Sardinian* Majefty having joined his Troops, with thofe under his Orders, the Conqueft of the *Milanefe* was very foon atchieved. The King made this Campaign in Perfon, as he likewife did the next Year ; but the Queen falling dangeroufly ill, he was conftrained to return to *Turin* in the latter End of the Month of *June* 1734, and during his Abfence was fought the famous Battle of *Parma.* Count *Merci* commanded the *Imperialifts* ; he was extremely ill of the Gout, but that did not hinder his taking Poft on the Right of the firft Line of his Infantry in his armed Chair, where with great Coolnefs and Intrepidity he gave his Orders till he was mortally wounded. The *French* General was *Monfieur* fince *Marechal de Coigni,* who having been lately deceived by the *Imperialifts* paffing the *Oglio,* and penetrating into the *Parmefan,* which he thought impracticable, he was the more concerned to recover his Reputation by gaining a Battle. This rendered the Difpute very obftinate and very bloody ; for fome People fay, that there never was an Action in which the Bufinefs was determined by fmall Arms that lafted longer than this, except the enfuing Battle of *Guaftalla.*

The *Imperialifts* were obliged to retire ; but Prince *Lewis* of *Wirtemberg,* who fucceeded Count *Merci* in his Command, brought his Forces in very good Order to *Reggio,* and the late Field-Marfhal Count *Koningfegg* coming to take the Command, it was not long before he made the *French* fenfible of his fuperior Capacity ; for on the fifteenth of *September* 1734, he paffed the *Secchia,* furprized a part of the *French* Army, and obliged Marfhal *Broglio,* who was a Horfe-Officer, and ought to have known the Fords better, to make his Efcape without his Breeches.

This brought on the Battle of *Guaftalla,* which was fought on the nineteenth, and therein the King of *Sardinia* commanded in Perfon. He had already gained a great Character in publick and private Life : He was the Father of his Family and of his People, enjoyed in his Court the Pleafures of a regular and amiable Oeconomy, at the fame time that he was revered and adored by his Subjects ; he had fhewed a Reach in Politicks much fuperior to his Age, but his Behaviour in the Battle of *Guaftalla* obfcured all that he had hitherto performed ; and the Splendor of that Victory, which was entirely owing to his perfonal Courage and Conduct, threw all his former great Actions into Shade, fince all *Europe* rung now with his Praifes as a Hero.

In

In the Beginning of the next Year died his Queen, which however did not hinder the King from appearing again in the Field, where Count *Koningsegg* found himself obliged to yield to the great Superiority of the Allies, and the Skill of the *Spanish* General the Duke *de Montemar*, one of the ablest Proficients in the Art of War then in *Europe*. All the *Imperialists* had to do was to preserve their last Stake, the important City and Fortress of *Mantua*, and this they did till the Preliminaries were settled and signed at *Vienna*.

On this Occasion his *Sardinian* Majesty had a convincing Proof of the Steadiness, good Faith, and upright Intention of the Court of *France*; for the *British* Ministry having concerted with the Court of *Vienna* a Plan of Peace, by which *Tortona* and the *Tortonese*, *Novara* and the *Novarese*, together with the *Vigenavasque*, were to be detached from the Duchy of *Milan*, and annexed for ever to *Piedmont*; the *French* Court, by a clandestine Negotiation, deprived him absolutely of one of these Districts, and only left him his Choice of the other two, in which Situation he preferred the former. These Preliminaries were signed *October* 3, 1735, and were in every respect favourable to *France*, Injurious to her Allies, fatal to the House of *Austria*, and destructive of the Ballance of *Europe*.

By them, under Colour of King *Stanislaus*'s Right to the Crown of *Poland*, *France* obtained *Lorrain* for herself, contrary to repeated Declarations, that she meant to gain nothing by this War; for this *Spain* was obliged to give *Tuscany* as an Equivalent, and *Parma* and *Placentia* were also yielded to the Emperor in lieu of *Sicily* and *Naples*. The King of *Sardinia* well understood the ill Usage he had met with, and saw clearly how little he had to hope in favour of the Ballance of *Italy*, from either the Justice or the Policy of the House of *Bourbon*. But the Preliminaries being signed, there was no drawing back, and therefore he acceded to them on the 16th of *August* 1736, at *Turin*, fully satisfied, that he had exposed his Person and his Dominions, only to aggrandize a Power already but too formidable to all its Neighbours, and particularly so to him.

It was from this Time that his Majesty pursued with the greatest Steadiness his original System, of restoring and preserving, to the utmost of his Power, the Ballance of *Italy*, by preventing the Incroachments of either of the two great Families, whose Quarrels have so long disturbed the Peace of that Country, and indeed of all *Europe*. I call it the original System

of

of this Prince, becaufe it was really what he aimed at by this War; fo that when our minor Politicians glance at his In-conftancy, and affect to be witty upon his having been on both Sides, they fhoot very wide of the Mark, for he never was but on one. I mean by one, his own natural, rational, and invariable Intereft, that of the Ballance, from which his Wifdom will never allow him to depart, and which it is hop-ed his other heroic Qualities will always enable him to fuf-tain.

It is not however to be expected, that this Difpofition fhould bind him infeparably to either of thofe Houfes; his Principle is Independency, not for himfelf only, but for the other Powers of *Italy*, in whofe Caufe he fights as well as his own; and this is not his Intereft fingly, but ours; and therefore he is, with great Propriety, ftiled our natural, as from his unalterable Steadinefs to the common Caufe he is with equal Propriety called our faithful Ally. But to return from Reflections to Hiftory.

At the preffing Inftances of his Subjects he confented to a third Marriage, and in the Month of *March* 1737, efpoufed the Princefs *Elizabeth Therefa*, Sifter to the prefent Emperor, then Duke of *Tufcany*, a Princefs who joined all the Accom-plifhments that are amiable in her Sex, to all the Virtues that were requifite to adorn her high Station. She made her Entry into *Turin* on the 22d of the Month laft mentioned; and as there never was a Marriage more agreeable to the Maxims of true Policy, fo never was there any more happy with refpect to the Parties themfelves; for with regard to the Conjugal State, it may without Flattery be affirmed, that their *Sardinian* Ma-jefties were a Model to their Subjects. On the 3d of *May* 1739, his prefent Imperial Majefty, at that time Great Duke of *Tufcany*, made a Tour to *Turin*, where he was received with all the Refpect and Affection imaginable.

A little after, the definitive Treaty of Peace was proclaimed there. I mention this particularly, becaufe it was attended with a Declaration from the King of *Sardinia*, by which it plainly appeared that fome Doubts had been ftarted about the Town of *Saravalla*, whether it was to be regarded as a part of the *Tortonefe* or not; and from thence it alfo appeared, that the Records beforementioned were not even then delivered up, but the King figns upon an exprefs Condition, that they fhould be delivered to him in fix Months Time, purfuant to the Treaty of 1703. This very clearly fhews how much Reafon this Prince has had to act with great Caution and Circum-

fpection,

fpection, in respect to whatever Ceffions have been made him since; but with Regard to the Uprightness of his Intention, and his fincere Defign of maintaining the refpective Powers in *Italy* in the juft Enjoyment of their Rights, no part of his Conduct has given the leaft Caufe to doubt it.

After the Death of the late Emperor *Charles* VI. when *Spain* was determined to pufh her Pretenfions in *Italy* by Force, and had alfo fecured the Affiftance of *France* for that Purpofe, no Stone was left unturned to bring his *Sardinian* Majefty into their Meafures, and Threats and Promifes were employed with all the Addrefs of which their ableft Minifters were capable, and yet to no manner of Purpofe. We are however to confider, that at no that Time his Majefty's Affairs were in a very embarraffed Situation; the Queen of *Hungary* was pufhed to the utmoft in *Germany*, her Forces weak in *Italy*, and as yet there was no Treaty of Subfidy fettled with *Great Britain*. On the other hand, the Duke of *Modena* was actually arming in favour of the *Spaniards*, they fucceeded perfectly in their projected Defcent upon the Coaft of *Tufcany*, and the *Neapolitan* Forces were ready to join them, when there was juft Reafon to fear that *France* would invade *Italy* on the other Side.

In thefe perplexed Circumftances the King of *Sardinia* fhewed himfelf equally firm and prudent. He was determined to act in favour of the Queen of *Hungary*; but in fuch a Situation of Things, it was not either requifite or convenient that he fhould declare his Intention. He publifhed therefore a Manifefto, afferting his own Rights to the Duchy of *Milan*, which he laid down as the Foundation for his defending that Country againft a *Spanifh* Invafion. Soon after this he entered the Duke of *Modena*'s Dominions, and upon his Serene Highnefs's refufing to difarm his Troops, and retiring to the *Spanifh* Army, his Majefty made no Difficulty of reducing *Modena* and *Mirandola* by Force; and by a wife and well-conducted Oppofition, forced the *Spanifh* Army under the Duke *de Montemar* to retire towards the Frontiers of *Naples*.

But the *Spaniards* having a furer Game to play, and marching another Army through the South of *France*, the King found it neceffary to return to *Turin* to provide for the Defence of his Country on that Side; and this he did fo effectually, that the Enemy, after attempting to force his Retrenchments at *Villa Franca*, were obliged to abandon their Defign of penetrating through the County of *Nice*; and they were alfo defeated in another Attempt they made through the Valley of *Barcelonetta*. It is true that in the Winter they fell upon the Duchy of *Savoy*,

Savoy, and made themselves Masters of it ; but the King soon drove them out again, and covered that Country till towards the Close of the Year, when by Dint of superior Force they became Masters of it again.

By this Time the Face of Affairs was somewhat chang'd in *Europe*, and his *Sardinian* Majesty was more at Liberty to avow his real Intentions ; which when he found himself secure of being supported by his Allies, he did without Scruple, and his Troops had a very considerable Share in the famous Battle of *Campo Santo*, which was fought in *February* 1743, in which Count *Aspremont*, who commanded his Forces in Chief, lost his Life. It is very true, that after the Court of *Vienna* thought fit to recall Marshal *Traun*, and send Prince *Lobkowitz* towards the Frontiers of *Naples*, his Majesty did not appear extremely vigorous in supporting that Measure ; but the Reason is very plain, and was no other than this, that he suspected his own Dominions would be again attacked, as they accordingly were in the most unlikely Season of the Year, by the *French* and *Spaniards* in Conjunction.

His Majesty took the Command of the Army, upon this Occasion, in Person, in the Month of *October* ; and though he was seized with a violent Cold, so that his Head and Face were swelled to a great Degree, yet he visited his Retrenchments himself, and contributed not a little by his Presence to the Defeat of the Enemy at the Village of *Pont*, where they lost five thousand of their best Troops, and were obliged to abandon all Hopes of penetrating into *Piedmont* for that Year. These Transactions are demonstrative Proofs how defensible the Entrances of the Dominions of this Prince really are, when he is able to defend them, and how impossible it would be to force him if his Power and Revenue were somewhat greater than they yet are, though in both he is far superior to his Ancestors.

It was about this Time that his *Sardinian* Majesty, as the strongest Proof of his constant and unalterable Resolution to support the common Cause, and preserve the *Austrian* Dominions in *Italy*, concluded with that Princess, and his *Britannick* Majesty, the famous Treaty of *Worms*, the only clear and explicit Alliance entered into during the War ; by the eighth Article of which he obtained certain Concessions in return for what he had already done, and in consideration of what by that Treaty he undertook to do, and which he afterwards most punctually and faithfully perform'd.

By the *ninth* Article the Queen of *Hungary* yielded to him any Right she might have in the Marquisate of *Final*, then in
the

the Poſſeſſion of the *Cemeeſe*, who were to receive an Equivalent for it, and excluſive of the general Benefit that was to reſult to all *Italy* from its being made a free Port, and from its opening a Communication by Sea to the Dominions of his *Sardinian* Majeſty, who from the Terms of this very Treaty, became the perpetual Protector of the *Italian* Liberties. By the *tenth* Article it was agreed, that no Peace or Truce ſhould be made till his Majeſty was reſtored to thoſe Parts of his Dominions, of which he had been diſpoſſeſſed by the common Enemies, and of which they continued poſſeſſed, till they were totally eaten up and impoveriſhed.

There is no doubt that the Advantages ſtipulated in favour of this Prince by the Treaty beforementioned were very conſiderable ; but when it is remembered that he had already dearly earned them, that what was given him was as much for the good of the common Cauſe as his own, and after loſing a great Part, he was ſtill to riſk all the reſt of his Dominions in defence of this Cauſe ; it is impoſſible for any ſenſible Man to think that what was thus granted him was too much. It is the more neceſſary to clear up theſe Points, becauſe many Miſtakes have been made about them, and becauſe without having a right Idea of them, it is impoſſible this Subject ſhould be thoroughly underſtood.

There is another Circumſtance which we muſt not paſs over in Silence, and it is this ; at the very Time the King of *Sardinia* concluded this Treaty, he was offered higher Terms, in reſpect to his private Advantage, by the *French* and *Spaniards* ; which ſhews the Importance of his Friendſhip, and proves the Reaſonableneſs of granting him a juſt Equivalent for the extraordinary Expences to which he was put, by adhering to this Cauſe. There were however ſome Difficulties made in the Execution of this Treaty, but they were at laſt got over, and his *Sardinian* Majeſty reaped the Benefit of it in its full Extent during the War, ſo far as depended upon the Queen of *Hungary*.

The Campaign of 1744 afforded new Proofs of his *Sardinian* Majeſty's Abilities, and of the Significancy of his Friendſhip. In the very Beginning of the Year, the *Spaniſh* and *French* Army, commanded by the Infant Don *Philip* and the Prince of *Conti*, aſſembled on the Frontiers, and as ſoon as the Seaſon would permit paſſed the *Varr*, and took Poſſeſſion of the Town of *Nice* upon the firſt of *April*. His *Sardinian* Majeſty's Forces, under the Command of the Marquis *de Suza*, remained in the Retrenchments thrown up in the Neighbourhood

hood of *Montalban*, where on the twenty-second of the same Month the Enemy attacked them, and bought at a very dear Rate (*viz.* the Loss of six thousand Men, exclusive of Officers) a very small Advantage.

But however, this enabled them to penetrate into *Piedmont*, and to lay all the Country waste in their Passage ; and yet they found so many Difficulties in this Expedition, that when they seemed to have in a manner accomplished it, they were glad to abandon all they had taken rather than venture a Battle ; and turning off into the *French* Territories, took the Rout of *Chateau Dauphine*, which in five several Attacks, from the seventeenth to the nineteenth of *July*, they could hardly master ; after which, however, they reduced *Demont*, and so forced a Passage on that Side into *Piedmont*, in which Country, when once they came into it, they lived with all the Humanity and Politeness of *Tartars*.

As late as it was in the Year, they besieged the Fortress of *Coni*, in which there was a small Garrison commanded by Baron *Leutrum*, who notwithstanding defended it with the utmost Resolution, and interrupted the Progress of the Besiegers by such well-timed and such well-concerted Sallies, as gave the King his Master leisure to come to his Relief, which he attempted the thirtieth of *September*, with great Intrepidity, attacking the *Spaniards* and *French* in their Lines, which however were so well defended, that he retired with some Loss, but not without finding an Opportunity of letting the Governor know, that he would very soon adventure another Engagement; for which however there was no Occasion, since the *French* after a general Storm, in which they lost near three thousand Men, found themselves in no Condition to carry on the Siege, and therefore raised it on the nineteenth of *October* following, burying at their Departure many Pieces of Cannon, and suffering in their Retreat to such a Degree, that not one half of their Army returned into *France*.

In 1745, the *Spanish* and *French* Courts having concerted Measures with the Republick of *Genoa*, made very little doubt of overpowering the King of *Sardinia*, more especially as they were certain that the *Prussians* would employ the whole Forces of the Queen of *Hungary* in *Germany*; neither at the Beginning was it at all unlikely that they should have succeeded to the utmost of their Wishes, since they had by a vast Superiority, penetrated through the Dominions of the Republick as they proposed, united all their Forces, which hitherto they never had been able to effect, and having received their Auxiliaries

and

and a Train of Artillery from *Genoa*, began to attack the moſt conſiderable Places in his *Sardinian* Majeſty's Dominions, ſuch as *Tortona*, *Alexandria*, &c. which were ſo well defended, that before they could be reduced, the Army of the two Crowns was leſſened by a full Third. All this Time the *Auſtrians* were acting upon the Defenſive, Things had taken a very bad Turn in *Germany*, and the Rebellion was at its greateſt Height here.

In ſuch Circumſtances, and after a Battle which brought their Forces within Sight of *Turin*, the *French* ſet on foot a new Negotiation with his *Sardinian* Majeſty, in the Courſe of which they made him greater Promiſes than ever, and at laſt offered him his own Terms ; but the King remained firm to his Engagements, and diſcovered the ſame Activity, Diligence, and Spirit, as in the former Campaigns. In this he followed his Father's Example, and ſhewed that while his Allies kept the Terms ſtipulated with him, he was incapable of ſetting on foot a ſeparate Treaty, and thereby making himſelf eaſy at their Expence, though he might have pleaſed Neceſſity with as great a Colour as any Prince ever did or could. But all the uſe he made of this Conjuncture was to ſet a good Example, and to ſhew that Alliances deliberately made, were to be religiouſly kept.

In the Spring of the ſucceeding Year, when the Circumſtances of the Queen of *Hungary* allowed her to reinforce her Armies in *Italy*, his Majeſty very early exerted himſelf, and by a moſt ſurprizing Stroke of military Courage and Conduct, drove the *French* out of moſt of the Places they had taken in his Territories, and afterwards joining the *Auſtrian* Army, ſhut them up in the City of *Placentia*. This brought on the famous Battle of *Rottoffredo*, in which they opened a Paſſage for a Flight out of *Italy*, abandoning *Genoa* to the Reſentment of her Enemies, and retiring with Precipitation into *France*, whither they were ſoon after followed by the Allies.

His *Sardinian* Majeſty took this Opportunity, and availing himſelf of his good Fortune, reduced *Savona* and *Final*, which remained in his Poſſeſſion to the cloſe of the War. Theſe glorious and inconteſtable Proofs of his Wiſdom, Valour and Probity, received the next Year a noble Addition, by the almoſt incredible Victory gained at *Exilles*, by which the beſt-laid Plan the *French* and *Spaniſh* Generals ever form'd, was entirely diſconcerted, and the Flames of War hindered from ſpreading again into the Heart of *Italy*.

The

The different Attempts that were made for reducing the City of *Genoa* after its Revolt, had all the Affiftance and Countenance given them by this Monarch that could be expected, confiftent with his Safety, tho' he had many Reafons to be difpleafed with the Ufage he met with in the original Capitulation. Yet Surmifes there were, as if fomewhat of Indifference had appeared in his Conduct in this Point, which if true, muft have been prejudicial to the common Caufe. We are not, however, obliged to credit any fuch Story, without the flighteft Degree of Evidence, more efpecially when it is remembered, that his *Sardinian* Majefty defired to have a military Minifter conftantly refident in his Court during the War on the Part of the Crown of *Great Britain*, who might affift in Councils, and fee the Corps that were employed every Campaign, that it might appear he fulfilled in every Refpect the Terms ftipulated on his Part by the Treaty of Subfidy ; which Punctuality his Majefty confidered as the moft efficacious Means for preferving the Friendfhip of *Great Britain*, even when the War fhould be at an End; and in this there is no doubt but he will find his Account.

In the Negotiation carried on at *Aix la Chapelle*, for the definitive Treaty of Peace, his Majefty employed the *Chevalier d'Offorio*, and the Count *de la Chavannes*. By the fixth Article of the Treaty concluded there, he was obliged to reftore to the Republick of *Genoa*, and to the Duke of *Modena*, whatever had been taken from them; fo that by this Means he loft both *Savona* and *Final*, and confequently all that had been ftipulated in his Favour by the Treaty of *Worms*, as to the laft mentioned Place; but by the fame Article the Duchy of *Savoy*, and the County of *Nice*, were reftored to him by the Houfe of *Bourbon*. By the feventh Article he made a folemn Refignation of that Part of the Duchy of *Placentia*, which had been yielded to him by the Emprefs Queen, by the Treaty beforementioned. But by the twelfth Article, the Poffeffion of all his former Acquifitions, as well as thofe that were left to him in Confequence of the Treaty of *Worms*, were recognized and fecured, and he likewife obtained the general Guarantee eftablifhed by that Treaty for thofe Provinces, as well as for all the reft of his Dominions wherever fituated, or in what manner foever acquired.

We well now take a fhort Survey of the Territories of this Monarch, as they ftand fince the Conclufion of the Peace, diftinguifhing the modern Acquifitions from the hereditary Eftates defcended from his Anceftors. The Ifland of *Sardinia* is, is, next to *Sicily*, the largeſt in the *Mediterranean* ; it is about forty-five Leagues In length, and twenty in breadth, has ſeveral good Ports and large Towns, very populous for its Size, though the Air is reputed not very wholeſome to Strangers. It produces a coarſe ſtrong Wine, and a conſiderable Quantity of Oil, but the Staple Commodity is Corn, of which in a very plentiful Year there has been exported to the Value of two hundred thouſand Pounds Sterling. The People are rough and unpoliſhed, live in a kind of barbarous Plenty, which affording them much Meat and little Labour, they look upon their own Iſland as a Paradiſe, out of which they are drawn with great Reluctancy. We have ſhewn that the late King *Victor Amadeus* was obliged to accept this Iſland inſtead of *Sicily* ; and as it is now managed, it affords a tolerable Revenue, more eſpecially when the King's Circumſtances permit him to receive it in Corn.

The Duchy of *Savoy* is a large but very far from a fruitful Country ; however, the Inhabitants are a hardy and laborious People, and by their Induſtry ſubſiſt tolerably well. The Principality of *Piedmont* is a very large, and the beſt Part of it a very fertile and well-cultivated Country, much leſs expoſed than *Savoy*, on Account of the difficult Entrances into it, very ſtrong by Nature, and moſt of them well fortified by Art. *Turin*, which is the royal Reſidence, is a very large and beautiful City, ſtanding on the River *Po*, and admirably well fortified. The County of *Nice* is leſs fruitful, but of great Importance, at it is almoſt the only part of the King's Dominions on the Continent, which lies upon the Sea, Theſe Countries are the ancient Patrimony of his Majeſty's Family, but the Additions made to them are very conſiderable. The *Montferrat* is a Duchy that was formerly annexed to that of *Mantua*, but the Houſe of *Savoy* had an old Claim to it, which was revived when the laſt Duke of *Mantua* was put under the Ban of the Empire in 1708, when the preſent King of *Sardinia*'s Father obtained the Inveſtiture of it from the Emperor, which was confirmed to him by the Peace of *Utrecht*. The Diſtricts which from time to time have been acquired at the Expence of the Duchy of *Milan*, have augmented very conſiderably both the Power and Revenue of his *Sardinian* Majeſty, and have alſo extended his Influence in ſuch a Manner, as to make his Friendſhip very eſſential to the Safety of all his Neighbours ; ſo that he is juſtly eſteemed one of the moſt conſiderable Potentates in *Italy*, excluſive of his Expectancies, which if any of his Family ſhould come to enjoy, would render them one of the moſt conſiderable Powers in *Europe*.

The

The Commerce of these Countries was heretofore so very inconsiderable as to be scarce worthy of Notice, but by Degrees, and under the two last Reigns more especially, Things have been very much changed. The Staple Commodity of *Piedmont* is a kind of Silk indispensably necessary in many Manufactures, and his *Sardinian* Majesty has put this under such Regulations as make it rise to the highest Amount possible. The Navigation of the *Po* enables the Inhabitants of *Turin*, and the adjacent Country, to carry on a confiderable Trade to *Venice*. There is a little (and but a little) Traffick stirring at *Alexandria* and *Villafranca*. Besides all these, his *Sardinion* Majesty has gradually and silently possessed himself of all the Passages by which the inland Trade is carried on between *France* and *Italy*, and having it by this Means in his Power to lay what Duties he thinks proper, derives from thence an additional Revenue, which is not only of great Consequence in itself, but the more so by keeping the neighbouring States in a kind of Dependence, through Fear of the Injuries he might otherwise do the Commerce of their Subjects.

This Account, concise as it is, sufficiently demonstrates the Power of his *Sardinian* Majesty, and the Truth of what we at first laid down, that it is both natural and expedient the Ballance of *Italy* should be held by him. His Interests seem to direct, the Situation of his Country demands, and even without the least Suspicion of Flattery, we may add, the Conduct of the present King deserves it. Whatever Addition of Territory he receives from any Quarter, is not more an Acquisition to him, than to the common Cause ; and we have Reason to wish his Power increased, because we see the whole of his Power has been exerted for the noblest Purposes, in preserving the Freedom and Independency of *Italy*, which without Question will be always at his Heart, and in his Eye.

The Doubts and Suspicions which weak and narrow Minds have been, at certain Seasons, too apt to suggest with Reference to this great Prince's Conduct, are in Reality as idle and improbable, as they are false and groundless ; because it is impossible that the House of *Bourbon* should ever give him any Security for the Performance of the Promises they may be induced to make him. A little Consideration will set this in the strongest Point of Light. The Offers they made him have been almost without Limits, which, at the same time that it shews his Importance, must convince him, that unless they had mighty Views for their own Advantage they would never make them. But what are these Views ? The establishing a
superior

superior Power in the House of *Bourbon* in *Italy*. If we put this into other Words, it means neither more nor less than proposing to give him a Master; which is such a Proposition, as no Offers whatever can tempt a wise and brave Prince to listen to with the last Attention.

It was to avoid this, that in the earliest Part of his Reign he entered into an Alliance with those very Powers, which gave him an Opportunity of knowing their Maxims so well, while they professed themselves his Friends, that it is the greatest Absurdity to suppose he can ever be brought to trust them, after having had them so long, and to such a Degree, his Enemies. It was to prevent his having a Master, that he engaged in the late War, and run so many risques in the Course of it. This was manifestly the Basis of the Treaty of *Worms*, the whole Scope of which was to render him independent, and to give him the Power of supporting that Independency.

To depart therefore from this Plan, for the Sake of any thing that could be offered by the *Spaniards* and *French*, would be such a manifest Sacrifice of the Substance to the Shadow, that considering the Knowledge we have of his *Sardinian* Majesty's Character, ought never to be suspected. The smallest District granted him by the Queen of *Hungary*, under the Guarantee of his other Allies, is of more real Consequence to him, than half the Duchy of *Milan* given him by the House of *Bourbon*, admitting they should have it in their Power to give it; because they can never have this Power, without having at the same time the Power of taking it again, which would not only render the Possession of that, but of all his other Dominions, precarious.

It is very apparent, that even as Things stand now, the Territories of this Monarch are very far from being extensive; but it must be allowed that they are very populous, and the People of *Savoy*, and of the Valleys, are naturally martial; so that under these two last Reigns a very considerable Army of regular Troops has been constantly kept up, and the King can never be at a Loss to bring forty or fifty thousand Men into the Field, when Occasion requires it. This Force is indeed nothing in Comparison of that of *France* and *Spain*; but it will appear very considerable, when compared with the Strength of other *Italian* Princes. Besides this, the Fortresses of *Piedmont* are in so good Order, that his *Sardinian* Majesty can always make a Stand till he is supported by the *Austrians*,

D d
which

which he muft be fo long as they defire to preferve their Dominions in *Italy*.

Upon thefe Principles therefore we may fafely lay it down, that though his Revenue is not fo large as that of the Great Duke, yet he is one of the greateft Powers in *Italy*, and is juftly efteemed fo by his Neighbours, his Allies, and his Enemies. His Claim upon the City of *Geneva*, and the Attempts made by fome of his Predeceffors to become Mafters of it, will be hardly ever forgot by that little Republick, which however is fufficiently covered from either his Ambition, or his Refentment, by its ftrict League with the *Swifs* Cantons, as well as by the Protection it may always expect from the *French* Crown.

The Pretenfions he inherits from his Anceftors to feveral Places poffeffed by the Republick of *Genoa*, will probably hinder him, at leaft for fome Years, from living in any ftrict Degree of Harmony with that Commonwealth, which is naturally jealous of him, and will probably continue fo ; though if they knew their own Intereft, they would certainly compromife their Differences with this Prince, which would be a Thing of great Confequence to both. His taking the Title of King of *Cyprus*, and fome other Circumftances, has created a Coldnefs between this Monarch and the Republick of *Venice*, though it is certainly for their mutual Good to forget old Injuries, and to affift each other.

There have been formerly high Difputes between his Majefty's Predeceffors and the Pope, which have been renewed in the laft, and even in the prefent Reign, but they feem now buried in Oblivion, as they ought to be, confidering that his Holinefs muft be long ago convinced by Experience that the Thunder of the *Vatican* has loft its Efficacy, and Excommunications will do very little, either with this Prince or his Subjects ; and as to the temporal Power of the Pope, it is not to be compared with that of the *Sardinian* Monarch.

The Territories of the King of the *Two Sicilies*, if we confider him only in the Light of an *Italian* Potentate, lie at too great a Diftance to create any Differences between them ; but confidered as a Prince of the Houfe of *Bourbon*, the King of *Sardinia* cannot but be jealous of any Augmentation of his Power. But to fay the Truth, the great Point which this Monarch muft always keep in View, is the ballancing the Power of that Houfe and the Houfe of *Auftria* ; to the latter

of

of which, notwithſtanding his near Relation in Blood to the former, it is more natural for him to adhere.

As Things ſtand at preſent, it is far from being probable that the Court of *Vienna* will incline to Meaſures that may juſtly provoke a Prince, to whom ſhe has ſo many Obligations, for whoſe Aſſiſtance ſhe muſt ſo often have Occaſion; and who in that Caſe, would eaſily find Reſources ſufficient to defend himſelf againſt all Attempts. On the other hand, while from a due Regard to their reſpective Intereſts, a good Correſpondence is kept up between them, the Light of Experience plainly ſhews, that their Enemies will find it very hard to make any Impreſſion upon either; and in Proceſs of Time it is highly probable that ſuch Alterations may happen in *Spain*, as will render their Capacity of defending themſelves ſtill greater than they are at preſent.

But with reſpect to the Houſe of *Bourbon*, though it will be always decent and proper for his *Sardinian* Majeſty to preſerve for it a juſt Meaſure of Reſpect and Complaiſance; yet as his Safety muſt perpetually depend upon the Greatneſs of his own Strength, and the Limitation of their Power, ſo it can never become either requiſite or agreeable to him to enter into any cloſe Alliance with that Family, the aggrandizing of which muſt be always, if not at his Expence, at the riſque of his Security. There are alſo good Reaſons to believe, that *France* will not eaſily be drawn to quarrel with a Prince, who keeps as it were the Gates of her Dominions, and who may be juſtly ſtiled a Terror to her, while ſhe is ſo to all the reſt of her Neighbours; for, without doubt, if the King of *Sardinia* were thoroughly provoked, and the Houſe of *Auſtria* at full Liberty to ſupport him, he might carry his Arms either into *Dauphiny* or *Provence*, or perhaps into both at the ſame time, more efficaciouſly than in the laſt, or the preceding War; in both which, however, Irruptions on this Side have brought the *French* Monarchy into Circumſtances of very great Diſtreſs.

As for the Maritime Powers, they are, though at a Diſtance, the natural and conſtant Allies of the Monarch of whom we are ſpeaking; becauſe their Intereſts and his are the ſame: And if a good Port could be made in the County of *Nice* capable of admitting Men of War, he would be quickly able not only to maintain his own Freedom, but alſo to protect the Liberty and Independency of *Italy* againſt all Invaders: And though he would not be even then in a Capacity of giving Law to others.

It

If once the Affairs of this Part of the World were put into such a Situation, the Benefits refulting to the People there, as well as to all the reft of *Europe*, would be fo great and fo evident, that his *Sardinian* Majefty would have no room to apprehend any new Confederacy formed againft him, fince his Neighbours would be then as willing to defend that Syftem, as for want of confidering it properly, they formerly feemed averfe to receive it.

We have dwelt the longer upon this Article, becaufe, with refpect to the *Britifh* Nation, there is no Power in *Italy* with the Strength and State of which it imports us fo much to be well acquainted as the Crown of *Sardinia*. Befides, from the manner in which we have treated this Point, many Things have been faid which relate to the general Intereft of that Country, as well as to the particular Concerns of feveral of the *Italian* Powers, which confequently we fhall be under no Neceffity of repeating again. But there is one thing very requifite to be obferved before we conclude, which is this, that nothing can be of greater Importance to the Trade of this Nation, than the preferving the Ballance in *Italy*, which, if loft, muft neceffarily throw all that valuable Branch of Commerce in which we have prefent fo large a Share, and from which we derive annually a confiderable Profit, into other Hands, and which is worft of all, into the Hands of the *French*; a Thing againft which we have as much Reafon to guard as a trading Nation, as the King of *Sardinia* himfelf has Caufe to oppofe, as far as poffible, the Growth of the *French* Power, out of regard to his own Safety. This fufficiently fhews, that our Interefts are really mutual, and that there is nothing of political Art in what we have been told, of the Expediency of fupporting this Monarch againft all his Enemies, though at a large Expence to ourfelves.

S E C T.

SECT. II.

The Present State of the Dominions of the House of AUSTRIA *in* Italy.

THE great Point which the Maritime Powers had in View at the Death of *Charles* II. King of *Spain*, the laft Heir-Male of the eldeft Branch of the Houfe of *Auftria*, was to divide his Territories in fuch a manner between the remaining Part of the Houfe of *Auftria*, and the Defcendents of the Dauphin of *France*, as might preferve the Tranquility of *Europe* at that Time, and the Ballance of Power for the future. It was to anfwer this End, that by the Treaties of *Utrecht* and *Baden*, all the *Spanifh* Dominions in *Italy* were fecured to the Emperor *Charles* VI. and the Quadruple Alliance, and all the Negotiations founded thereon, were built upon the fame Principle

By this Means his Imperial Majefty became poffeffed of the Kingdom of *Naples* and *Sicily*, the Duchy of *Milan*, and all its Dependencies, together with the Duchy of *Mantua*, which was feized upon the late Duke *Charles* IV's adhering to *France* in the preceding War, and dying in Exile at *Venice*. The Duchies of *Parma* and *Placentia* were yielded to him by the Treaty of *Vienna*, as an Equivalent for *Naples* and *Sicily*, though in the Opinion of the Court of *Vienna*, but a poor one

The noble Duchy of *Milan*, which has been defervedly efteemed one of the fineft Principalities in *Europe*, is above two hundred and forty Miles in Length, and eighty in Breadth. It is generally divided, together with the Countries annexed to it, into thirteen Diftricts, *viz.* The *Milanefe* Proper. The *Pavefe*. The *Lodefan*. The *Cremonefe*. The *Comafco*. The County of *Anghiera*. The Vallies of *Seffia*. The *Novarefe*. The *Vigevanois*. The *Lomeline*. The *Alexandrin*. The *Tortonefe*. And the Territory of *Bobbio*. But of thefe feveral have been ceded to the King of *Sardinia*, fome by the Emperor *Charles* VI. and others by the Emprefs Queen now reigning, as we have already fhewn in another Place ; but notwithftanding this, what remains to the Houfe of *Auftria*, may be ftill confidered as one of the faireft and fineft Countries in her Poffeffion.

It

It lies in a moſt excellent Climate, and is bleſt with as fruitful a Soil as any in *Europe*, watered by the noble Rivers *Po*, *Teſſin*, *Adda*, and *Seſſia*, beſides the famous Lakes of *Maggiore*, *Lucano*, and *Como*. But to come to the moſt material Point, the Revenues that are drawn from it amount to at leaſt three hundred thouſand Pounds Sterling a Year, beſides its furniſhing Subſiſtence for thirty thouſand Man, and enabling the Court of *Vienna* to provide with Governments and Preferments, Eccleſiaſtical, Military, and Civil, Numbers of her Dependents, and that too, which is no very eaſy Matter, even to the Extent of their Hopes and Wiſhes.

The Duchy of *Mantua* is alſo a very fine Country, about fifty Miles in Length, but ſo unequal in Breadth, that there is no ſaying any thing of it with certainty. The Capital is very large, and withal one of the beſt Fortreſſes in *Italy*, both by Art and Nature; the Country abounds in Corn, Fruit, Flax, Silk, and Cattle, and the Revenue is uſually computed at about a fourth Part of that of *Milan*.

At the Concluſion of thoſe Treaties which followed the long War upon Account of the *Spaniſh* Succeſſion, the Emperor engaged himſelf to give the Duke of *Guaſtalla* a competent Satisfaction for his Pretenſions to the Duchy of *Mantua*, which were thought to be pretty well founded, but what that Satisfaction amounted to, or when it was given, no Author I have ever yet met with mentions; but this is very certain, that when his Serene Highneſs *Joſeph Maria Gonzagua*, Duke of *Guaſtalla*, died in 1746 without Iſſue Male, Poſſeſſion was taken of his Dominions on Behalf of the preſent Emperor. It will be very proper to mention here, that his preſent Imperial Majeſty has by Deſcent a better Title to the Succeſſion of *Guaſtalla*, and perhaps I ſhould not err, if I ſaid *Mantua* too, than any other Prince in the World; and therefore it was no more than his Right.

It is very eaſy to conceive, even upon this ſlight Survey, of how great Importance the *Italian* Dominions were to the Grandeur of the Houſe of *Auſtria*, and how much Reaſon the Empreſs Queen had to take every Step poſſible for preſerving them at the Beginning of the late War, ſince at that Time, and in the Courſe of it, they conſiſted of five fine Duchies, *viz.* *Milan*, *Mantua*, *Guaſtalla*, *Parma*, and *Placentia*, yielding a clear Revenue, if they could have been kept, of very little leſs than ſix hundred thouſand Pounds a Year, beſides accidental Advantages, and the great Conveniency of providing the Princes and Princeſſes, or as they are ſtiled at *Vienna*, the Archdukes and Arch-

Archduchesses of that august Line, with Governments, in which they might have resided with Dignity and Magnificence, little inferior to that of sovereign Princes. It is true, that in order to be in a Condition to defend these Dominions, it was necessary to make considerable Cessions to the King of *Sardinia*; but then it is likewise true, that by making these Cessions, those Dominions were actually preserved; and after a bloody and expensive War of several Years Continuance, there was not a Foot of them lost, but on the contrary, the whole Duchy of *Modena* and its Dependencies, together with a Part of the Territories of the Republick of *Genoa*, were actually conquered, and remained in the Possession of the Empress Queen and his *Sardinian* Majesty, at the Conclusion of the Peace.

By the Treaty of *Aix la Chapelle*, a provisional Establishment was made for the Royal Infant Don *Philip*, which swallowed up the Duchies of *Parma*, *Placentia*, and *Guastalla*, and consequently reduced the Dominions of the House of *Austria* to the Duches of *Mantua* and *Milan* only; and the latter of these severely dismembred. Yet notwithstanding these Misfortunes, the Territories still preserved are very considerable, more especially if we consider two Advantages with which they are attended; the first is, that they are capable of maintaining a Force sufficient for their own Defence; and next, that upon any Emergency, the Court of *Vienna* can pour what Reinforcement she pleases into the Duchies through the *Tyrolese*; so that notwithstanding the Power and the Ambition of the House of *Bourbon*, there is good Reason to hope that these Countries, in the Condition they now are, will remain in the peaceable Possession of their august Sovereign, not only from the Force of the general Guaranty contained in that Treaty, but from the Interest of the other Powers in *Italy*, to preserve the House of *Austria* in its present Condition, as a Point essentially necessary to the Ballance.

There has been, ever since the Conclusion of that famous Treaty, a Rumour of a Congress to be held for composing amicably the discordant Interests in *Italy*; for whatever the Treaty of *Aix la Chapelle* might be, with respect to the other Parts of *Europe*, it was very far from being definitive here, since it has left Things in such a Situation as it is impossible they should continue long. But then this Defect is attended with a Circumstance, whether owing to the Penetration of those able Politicians who negotiated it or not, we will not presume to determine, which in a good measure ballances that

Defect.

Defect. That Circumstance is this ; all the Potentates whose Interests were regulated by that Treaty, are equally diſſatisfied and diſtreſſed, which will probably have this good Conſequence, that they will concur in making ſuch Alterations for their mutual Convenience, as may procure a definitive Eſtabliſhment of their reſpective Territories for the reciprocal Benefits of the ſeveral Parties. Something of this ſort has been long in Agitation ; and when by ſecret and ſilent Negotiations, the principal Points are ſettled, it is thought that a Congreſs will be held at *Piſa* for adjuſting leſſer Matters, and putting all Things into form. When this is over, and not till then, we ſhall have a clear and diſtinct View of the Diſtribution of Power in this Part of the World, and therefore what has been already ſaid, and what we have farther to ſay, muſt remain ſubject to the Conſequences that may reſult from any Exchanges or Alterations which ſhall be then made.

In the mean time it is certainly the Intereſt of the Houſe of *Auſtria*, with reſpect to her Dominions in *Italy*, to preſerve a ſtrict Friendſhip with the King of *Sardinia*, and a fair and equal Behaviour towards all her Neighbours. This would have been at all Times exceeding proper and advantageous, but at preſent it is indiſpenſably neceſſary. For though it may ſeem a Paradox to maintain, yet in Time it will be found a political Truth, that the Loſs of *Power* in *Italy* may prove the Means of augmenting the *Influence* of the Houſe of *Auſtria*. A moderate, firm, and juſt Conduct, will not only excite Veneration and Eſteem, but will by Degrees beget Confidence and a ſtrong Attachment, ſince now all jealous Apprehenſions are removed, and the Protection of that Power may be ſought without any Fears that this may give Occaſion to dangerous Incroachments.

Whenever this ſhall be brought about, it will promote a ſincere and an extenſive Union, founded upon a mutual Reſpect, and a Concurrence of natural Intereſts, which will afford a much higher and more effectual Security than any diſtant Guarantees. It may poſſibly be ſuggeſted, that this being the Conjecture only of a private Perſon, cannot deſerve much Regard. But if this Conjecture be founded in the Nature of Things, and ariſes from a ſerious Contemplation of Facts that cannot be denied, it may be juſtified by Conſequences let it be whoſe Conjecture it will. For after all, it will be found that private peculatiſts in Politicks have ſeen as far into future Events as more elevated Politicians ; for being neither blinded by their Paſſions, nor miſled by falſe Lights,

Lights, they derive as many Advantages from thence as great Statesmen do from their private Intelligence, since Negotiations and Intrigues, howsoever so well contrived, or how secretly soever managed, rarely reach the Ends proposed by them, but are counter-acted by Circumstances neglected or overlooked by their Authors; and yet obvious enough to those who content themselves with studying things, instead of listening to the Projects of Men.

There was great Reason to hope, and the Publication of this Edition was for some time deferred, on Account of that Hope, that by a Convention lately concluded, as it is said, between the Courts of *Vienna*, *Madrid* and *Turin*, all Disputes were settled from the Principles above suggested; but notwithstanding this is still affirmed and generally believed, yet as no such Convention has appeared, it is impossible to state the Terms or to give any Opinion about it.

SECT. III.

A concise Account of the Grand Duchy of Tuscany; *the Manner in which it is possessed by his present Imperial Majesty; the Advantages derived from thence to the* Austrian *Dominions; and the Reasons which particularly interest the Maritime Powers in the Preservation of it in the same Condition in which it at present subsists.*

THE Grand Duchy of *Tuscany* is composed of the Territories that formerly belonged to three small but potent Republicks, *viz*. those of *Florence*, *Sienna* and *Pisa*. It was about the middle of the fifteenth Century that *Cosmo de Medicis*, who had the glorious Sirname of the Father of his Country, assumed the supreme Power. *Alexander de Medicis*, his Descendent, was made Duke of *Florence*, by the Emperor *Charles* V. in 1531. He was succeeded by his Cousin *Cosmo*, who had the Title of Grand Duke bestowed upon him by Pope *Pius* V. in order to raise him to a Rank superior to the Princes of *Italy*, though he had the Stile only of Serene Highness, whereas that of Royal Highness was given to the Duke of *Savoy*. About the Beginning of the present Century the Grand Duke *Cosmo* the Third, finding the Title of Royal Highness given by the Emperor *Leopold* to the Duke of *Lorrain*, applied himself likewise to his Imperial Majesty in order to obtain the same Favour, which was accordingly granted.

This

This Prince, after a long and happy Reign, deceased *October* 31, 1723, and was succeeded in his Dominions by his Son *John Gaston de Medicis*, the last Heir Male of his Family. The Infant Don *Carlos*, at present King of the *Two Sicilies*, was declared his Heir, and soon after his Arrival in *Italy* assumed, with the Consent of the Grand Duke, the Title of Hereditary Grand Prince of *Tuscany*. But upon the Conclusion of that War by which he acquired the Kingdoms he now enjoys, it was stipulated by the Treaty of *Vienna*, that the Grand Duchy of *Tuscany* should be given to *Francis* Duke of *Lorrain* in Exchange for that Duchy, which was yielded to his most Christian Majesty after the Demise of King *Stanislaus*.

The Bounds that are generally ascribed to *Tuscany*, **are the** River *Tiber*, the *Apennine* Mountains, and the River *Magra*. The whole Extent of this Country from South to North is about one hundred and thirty Miles, and about one hundred and twenty from East to West. It is washed on the South and on the West by the *Mediterranean*, and with respect to Strength and Convenience, it has all the Advantages from Situation that can be wished. As to the Soil of this Country, it is in some Parts mountainous, where there are Mines of Copper, Iron, Silver and Allum, and Quarries of fine Marble, Alabaster and Porphyry. In other Parts it abounds with pleasant Hills which are covered with Vines, Oranges, Lemons, Olives, and other Fruits, and in some Places there are Vallies which produce abundance of Corn and Grass.

It has many little Rivers, but the Chief of them is the *Arno.* The other Commodities besides those already mentioned, are Wool, Flax, Saffron, Serges, Woollen Cloths, Silks, Tapestries, gilt Leather, Earthen Ware, Perfumes, &c. There is no Country in the World where the People are, generally speaking, better adapted to mercantile Affairs, or where they know better how to make this Disposition of theirs turn to Account. All the Princes of the House of *Medicis* were themselves Merchants, and by their Example Commerce has been always thought there what it ought to be thought elsewhere, a thing not at all incompatible with Nobility.

The **Country** round about *Florence* is excellently cultivated, and the City itself so rich and beautiful, that it is stiled at home and abroad FLORENCE *the Fair*, according to the *Italian* Humour of bestowing Epithets upon all their great Cities. The other two Parts of the Grand Duke's Dominions, *viz.* the *Pisan* and the *Siennois*, tho' the Country is not at all inferior to the *Florentine*, are far from being so well peopled, and consequently

quently from being so much improved. On the contrary, in some Places they lie almost waste for want of Inhabitants, which has been owing chiefly to the Jealousy of their Princes. As this Humour is now pretty well wore out, there is good Reason to hope that these Countries may recover, at least to a tolerable Degree, tho' not to their ancient Splendor in the Times when *Pisa* and *Sienna* were Republicks, and either of them very capable of making Head against *Florence*. This shews the different Effects of Government, and that Places may derive from Liberty almost as great Blessings as from Nature.

But the great Glory of *Tuscany*, and the true Source of her Power and Wealth, at least in modern Times, has been her famous Port of *Leghorn*, or, as the *Italians* call it, *Livorno*, obtained in Exchange for *Sarzana* from the *Genoese*. The Country about it was formerly a vile Morass, or rather Quagmire, the noxious Steams of which rendered the Air unwholesome ; but by the Skill and Pains of an *Englishman*, Sir *Robert Dudley*, Son to Queen *Elizabeth*'s potent Favourite the Earl of *Leicester*, and himself created Duke of *Northumberland* by the Emperor, the Soil was rendered habitable, the Air much less unwholesome, and the Port improved so as to become the best in *Italy*.

By his Advice also it was made a free Port, that is, the Duties inwards are very easy, and upon Exportation there are no Duties at all. This has rendered it for about a Century past the great Magazine of the *Levant* Trade, and drawn thither Merchants from all Parts, more especially *Jews* and *Armenians*, of whom many reside there, and have great Privileges allowed them. But after all, the greatest Part of the Commerce was and is carried on by the Subjects of the Maritime Powers, who for that Reason have their Consuls resident there, and interest themselves upon all Occasions in its Favour.

On this Account Care has been taken to stipulate in all the Treaties since the Quadruple Alliance, that the Port of *Leghorn* should remain in its present Situation, in whose Hands soever it was left ; which however to some may appear almost a needless Precaution, since it is of such very high Importance to the Sovereign of *Tuscany* that it should so remain. It is in Truth the great Wheel which gives Motion to the Trade of that Country, and attracts thither the richest Commodities and the most valuable Manufactures of *Italy*, from whence vast Advantages arise, not only to the Subjects of the Grand Duke, but also to the Prince himself ; whence one would be tempted to suppose, that Respect to his own Interests might supersede the Necessity of any such Interposition.

Besides,

Besides, the Friendship of the Maritime Powers is a thing of so great Consequence to whatever Prince is in Possession of *Tuscany*, that the bare Consideration of that seems to be a Motive more than sufficient to secure all the Immunities granted to the Port of *Leghorn* from the smallest Violation. However, in Matters of so tender a Nature nothing ought to be neglected, and therefore we have the greater Reason to persuade ourselves, that a thing so perfectly agreeable to the Interests of all Parties will never become the Subject of any kind of Dispute.

John Gaston de Medicis, Grand Duke of *Tuscany*, having had the Mortification to see his Territories disposed of in his Lifetime to Strangers, notwithstanding all the Opposition he could possibly give to that Measure, left this World *July* 9, 1737, and his Royal Highness the Duke of *Lorrain* succeeded him without the least Dispute, in Consequence of the fourth Article of the Preliminaries signed at *Vienna* in 1735. Throughout the whole Course of the last War, the Grand Duchy of *Tuscany* was considered as a neutral Country, as indeed it ought ; for his Imperial Majesty holding it in Exchange, and under the same Rules of Succession with those of his hereditary Countries of *Lorrain* and *Barr*, there could be no Pretence formed to his Prejudice, or that could so much as afford any Colour for disturbing or distressing his Subjects.

It is to be hoped that this Precedent will be exactly followed, in case any future Disturbances should break out in this Country, and it is very easy to perceive what real Advantages are derived from so valuable a Privilege, more especially when it respects a Country which subsists in a great measure by Trade, and which in consequence of this Privilege must always prove, as it did in the last War, the Asylum of such as have no other Desire than to live by the Fruits of their own Industry.

It is now time to speak of the Revenue and Forces of this Principality. The Grand Dukes of *Tuscany* were always remarkable for their prudent Œconomy, which rendered them without Comparison the richest Princes in *Italy* ; they were great Patrons of Industry and Arts, very attentive to what might promote the Welfare of their Subjects, and omitted nothing that might engage Strangers of Merit to settle amongst them. Yet the Politicians of *Italy* had always a Notion, that though in all other Respects these Princes made very good Shepherds, they were nevertheless apt to shear their Flock a little too close. However that Matter may be, it was never thought an extravagant Computation when the Revenues of this Grand Duchy were estimated at beween three and four Millions of Crowns yearly,

yearly, one half of which, at leaft in Times of Peace, remained late in the Coffers of the Grand Duke, or if it found its Way out, was employed in Trade, or lent to his Subjects at a good Intereft. Whether the Savings are altogether as great now as in former Times, may poffibly admit of fome Doubt, but there is none with Regard to the Income, which is as great as ever.

The Grand Duke had alfo commonly thirty thoufand Men in Pay, or rather inrolled; but as they were feldom called to Service, fome have fufpected that inftead of cofting him any thing, his Troops might poffibly contribute to the Increafe of his Revenue. In the Situation that Things are now, there is a fmall regular Force, and but a very fmall one, maintained by the Grand Duke, but the Militia either are, or might be, put upon the fame foot as in former Times. The Princes of the Houfe of *Medicis* had likewife a confiderable maritime Force, by which is meant a confiderable Force in refpect to their Neighbours, which tho' in itfelf no great Matter, yet the Grand Duke's Squadron of Gallies, in Conjunction with thofe of *Naples*, and the Pope, kept the Sea clear of Privateers, and the Inhabitants of the Coaft without Apprehenfion of being infulted by the Corfairs of *Barbary*. In a word, the Grand Dukes of *Tufcany*, through their Wealth and their Power, under the Direction of a right Plan of Policy, maintained a high Reputation, and were efteemed and treated by their Neighbours as the greateft Princes in *Italy*; as in Return, they were never wanting either in good Offices, or in any other Affiftance towards fuch of their Neighbours as were oppreffed, or feemed to be in Danger of Oppreffion. This therefore, as far as it is practicable, ought to be the Policy of modern Times.

Before the Treaty of *Aix la Chapelle*, the Communication between *Tufcany* and the Dominions of the Houfe of *Auftria* in *Italy*, was open and eafy, but as Things now ftand, it is quite otherwife; for all the Dominions of the Infant Duke of *Parma*, as well as Part of thofe of the Duke of *Modena*, lie between the Grand Duchy and that of *Milan*; and the Duchy of *Modena*, and the Dominions of the Church, interpofe themfelves between *Tufcany* and the Duchy of *Mantua*. This will explain to the Reader the true Reafon of the Pains that is taken to make a large and convenient Road from the Frontiers of *Tufcany* to *Bologna*, which would indeed facilitate a Communication with *Mantua*, but then it muft be through the Dominions of other Princes. This is a great and vifible Inconvenience, and fo much the more mortifying, as there feems to be no Poffibility of finding a Remedy, becaufe it is not any

Parcel

Parcel or Corner of a Country that interposes, but the whole Length of one, and the whole Breadth of the other, which in Time of War at least, will render all Correspondence precarious, if not impracticable, and without doubt is a Matter which deserves Consideration.

But however troublesome and inconvenient this Change may be for the present, yet assuredly neither the Grand Duchy of *Tuscany*, nor the Dominions of the House of *Austria*, are in any imminent Danger from it, or the Ballance of *Italy* much affected thereby. The Grand Duchy, as we have already shewn, belongs to the Emperor by such a peculiar Right, that while there is any Faith, any Honour, or any Shame in Princes, it can never be attacked. On the other hand, as his Imperial Majesty succeeds the House of *Medicis* in all their Prerogatives, and is from the very Nature of his Tenure obliged to pursue their Maxims of Government, that is to say, avoiding as much as may be, all Disputes with his Neighbours, we may well expect that the interior Strength of his Dominions may prove a sufficient Security to him, as it did to them. We may add to this, that the Sea must remain always open, and considering the Interest that the Maritime Powers have in the Port of *Leghorn*, as well as the Guarantee they have granted to the Grand Duchy, there is no room to fear that they would be remiss in sending a speedy and sufficient Naval Force to his Assistance.

As to the *Austrian* Dominions, their Safety cannot be endangered through the Want of a direct Communication with *Tuscany*, because Experience has shewn us in the last War, that they may be very well defended, tho' the Grand Duchy maintained a strict Neutrality. Besides, if contrary to all Appearances, *Tuscany* should be attacked on both Sides, that is, by the King of the *Two Sicilies*, and the Infant Duke of *Parma*, or any of their Successors, a powerful Diversion might be made from the *Austrian* Dominions, and a new Communication quickly opened. As to the Ballance in *Italy*, there is not the least Colour to suspect that it should suffer at all by this Means, for the Safety of that ever did, and ever will depend upon the several Governments that subsist there, attending to their respective and several Interests, without incroaching upon or disturbing their Neighbours; so that whatever contributes to this, may be very reasonably considered as advantageous to that likewise. But tho' this is a great deal to this Point, yet it is not all.

For

For we muſt conſider at the ſame time, that if the Eſtabliſhment of the Royal Infant, and the Duchy of *Modena*, lie
between the *Auſtrian* Dominions and the Grand Duchy of
Tuſcany, the Grand Duchy of *Tuſcany* at the ſame time lies
alſo not only between them and the *Two Sicilies*, but alſo between them and the Sea, which is a Point of very great Conſequence, I mean to the Tranquility of *Italy*, and to the Ballance of Power there; becauſe it puts both the Houſes of *Auſtria*
and *Bourbon* under equal Difficulties, in caſe of their forming
any Projects to the Prejudice of each other, or of any of the
reſt of their Neighbours, which in whatever Light they may
regard it, cannot certainly be diſpleaſing to other Powers, who
have no other Intereſt or View, with reſpect to this Part of the
World, than to ſee it remain quiet, and the ſeveral Princes
therein employed in promoting the Welfare of their reſpective
Subjects, which if they would do, they might be all rich and
happy, and free from the Fear of ſeeing ultramontane Armies
in its Bowels.

It is plain from what has been ſaid, that there is very little
Probability, and no ſort of Neceſſity, of ſuch a Change as has
been long rumoured of this Grand Duchy, for the new Eſtabliſhment of the Infant Duke, with a Sum of Money equivalent to the Difference of the Revenues produced by the two
Countries. Such an Exchange it is true would remove the Obſtacle beforementioned, would reſtore the Connection between
the *Auſtrian* Dominions and thoſe of his Imperial Majeſty,
and make the Royal Infant Sovereign of Territories, that confine not indeed upon his Brother's Dominions, but upon thoſe
of the Church, through which his Armies might always
command a Paſſage. It may however be doubted, whether
this Plan would be acceptable to the other Princes of *Italy*, as
well as whether it would be really productive of any extraordinary Advantage to the Parties intereſted therein, for the Reaſons that have been already given. The Point however ſeemed
worth explaining, becauſe notwithſtanding the Noiſe this Project
made, there were but very few at this Diſtance who ſeemed to
have a true Notion of the Motives upon which it was
founded.

To conclude, the plain Intereſt of his Imperial Majeſty, in
Quality of Grand Duke of *Tuſcany*, is to maintain the ancient
Form, and to purſue the old Maxims of Government in that
Country, to take every Meaſure requiſite for preſerving, encouraging, and extending the Commerce of his Subjects, and
cultivating with all poſſible Care a ſincere Friendſhip with the
neigh-

neighbouring Powers. Such Measures cannot fail of procuring the desired Effects; that is, cannot fail of making the Grand Duchy rich and flourishing, which is the only Means to secure its Sovereign a great Revenue, while his Subjects enjoy the greatest of temporal Blessings, Plenty and Peace.

SECT. IV.

A brief Account of the Family, Dominions, and political Interests, of his Serene Highness the Duke of Modena.

THE House of *Este* is not only allowed by the best Historians to be without Controversy one of the most ancient and illustrious in *Italy*, but also in *Europe*. This Family derives its Descent from *Azon*, Lord of *Este*, which is a small but pleasant Town in *Lombardy*, not far from *Padua*, who flourished in the tenth Century. His Descendents became very considerable Princes, and so continued down to *Alphonso* I. who was Duke of *Ferrara*, *Modena*, and *Reggio*. This Prince had three Wives. the first *Anne* Daughter to the Duke of *Milan*, by whom he had no Issue: The second, *Lucretia*, natural Daughter to Pope *Alexander* VI. by whom he had Issue three Sons; *Hercules*, who succeeded him in his Dominions; *Hypolito*, Cardinal of *Este*, the greatest Prelate of his Age; for he was Archbishop of *Milan*, *Auch*, *Arles*, and *Lyons*, Bishop of *Autun*, Abbot of *Flavigni*, &c. and *Francis* Marquis *de la Massa*: His third Wife was *Laura Eustochia*, the Daughter of a Citizen of *Modena*, by whom he had *Alphonso de Este*, Marquis *de Montechio*.

Hercules II. succeeded his Father, and married the Daughter of the *French* King, *Lewis* XII. by whom he had *Alphonso*, and *Lewis*, stiled Cardinal of *Ferrara*. *Alphonso* II. succeeded his Father, and having no Issue, called to the Succession of his Dominions, *Cæsar de Este*, Son to *Alphonso de Este*, Marquis of *Montechio*, and died in the Year 1597. Pope *Clement* VIII. resolved to lay hold of this Opportunity of uniting the Duchy of *Ferrara* to the Dominions of the Church; and accordingly, under Pretence that *Alphonso de Este* was illegitimate, he marched in Person with an Army into the Territory of *Ferrara*, and by Force of Arms drove out the new Duke. This Transaction must be entirely attributed to Ambition, supported

ed by Violence, since the Pope had no Colour of Right: For, first, *Alphonso de Este* was no Baftard, his Mother, tho' much inferior in Degree, being lawfully married to the Duke his Father: In the next Place, he was exprefly legitimated by the Emperor, to remove all Objections: And, thirdly, if he had been a Baftard, he might have fucceeded in that Duchy by a Cuftom fanctified, if not introduced, by Authority of the Holy See. It is therefore not without Reafon, that the Dukes of *Modena* always infift on their Right to the Duchy of *Ferrara*.

Cæfar de Este, however, tho' he loft the Duchy of *Ferrara*, received the Inveftiture of *Modena* and *Reggio* from the Emperor *Rodolph* II. He married *Virginia*, Daughter to *Cofmo* I. Grand Duke of *Florence*; and having reigned thirty Years, deceafed in 1628. He was fucceeded by his Son *Alphonso* III. who had married in his Father's Life-time the Princefs *Ifabella*, Daughter to the Duke of *Savoy*, for whom he had fo tender an Affection, that upon her Death he renounced the World and became a *Capuchin*, leaving the Government of his Dominions to his Son *Francis*, who became Duke of *Modena* in 1629. This Prince was thrice married; firft to the Daughter of the Duke of *Parma*, by whom he had his Succeffor *Alphonso*, and feveral Princeffes; fecondly, to her Sifter, by whom he had an only Daughter, who died an Infant; and laftly, to the Daughter of the Prince of *Paleftrina*, by whom he had a Son *Rinaldo*, honoured with a Cardinal's Cap from *Rome* in 1686.

Alphonso, by fome reckoned the fecond, by others the fourth, fucceeded his Father in the Year 1658. He married *Laura Martinozzi*, Niece to Cardinal *Mazarin*, by whom he had a Daughter *Mary Beatrix Eleanora*, who efpoufed *James* the fecond, King of *Great Britain*; and *Francis*, who fucceeded him in his Dominions while a Child in his Cradle in 1662. This Duke married in 1692 the Daughter of the Duke of *Parma*, and dying without Iffue in 1694, his Uncle the Cardinal of *Este* laid afide his Purple, and affumed the Title of Duke of *Modena* and *Reggio*.

Rinaldo de Este attached himfelf from the Beginning of his Reign to the Houfe of *Auftria*, and remained firm to thofe Engagements fo long as he lived. He efpoufed in 1695 *Charlotta Felicia*, Daughter to the Duke of *Hanover* and Sifter to the Emprefs, which very probably fortified his Zeal to the Imperial Family, which difcovered itfelf at a Time when it was far from turning to his Advantage, that is, upon the breaking out of the War occafioned by the difputed Succeffion to the Throne of *Spain*; which induced *Lewis* XIV. towards the Clofe of the Year 1703 to difpoffefs him of all his Dominions, and to unite them to the Crown of *France*. The Duke of *Modena* had fome

Time

Time before retired to *Bologna*, and went from thence to *Rome* in order to follicit the Pope's Interpofition with the Eldeft Son of the hurch in favour of a Prince, whofe Crime was of no deeper Dye than acknowledging the Archduke *Charles* for King of *Spain*; but except fpecious and delufive Promifes, his Serene Highnefs reaped nothing from this Journey.

The moft Chriftian King however perceiving, that tho' the Duke of *Modena* could not defend his Dominions, yet the Manner in which he had treated him was univerfally offenfive to the *Italian* Princes, and did him much more Hurt than the Poffeffion of *Modena* and its Dependencies could do him Good, thought proper to renounce all Title to his new Conqueft, declaring it to belong to his Grandfon the King of *Spain*, and uniting it to the Duchy of *Milan*. In this Situation it continued till Prince *Eugene* with the Imperial Army entered *Italy* in 1706, when in the Night between the 19th and 20th of *November* the City of *Modena* was taken by Storm, or rather by Surprize, and the greateft part of the *French* Garrifon cut to pieces. The fmall Remains of that Garrifon retired into the Citadel, which they not only threatened to hold out to the laft Extremity, but even pretended to bombard the Town and reduce it to Afhes, which his Serene Highnefs Prince *Eugene* prevented by acquainting the Governor, that if he proceeded in his brutal Defign, he would infallibly caufe him and every Man under his Command to be hanged upon the Walls. This gave a new Turn to Things ; for Monfieur *de Bar*, the *French* Governor, being informed that the Duke of *Modena* was returned from *Bologna* to his Capital, fent him a very polite Meffage, importing, that he defired to have the Honour of delivering up the Citadel into his Hands, as to its lawful Mafter ; which Propofition was immediately accepted, and the Duke entered again into the Poffeffion of his Countries, which had been miferably harraffed and exhaufted by his Enemies, who treated his Subjects with inexcufable Severity out of Hatred to their Sovereign.

His Serene Highnefs, in 1708, had fome Hopes given him, that after fuffering fo much by the War he might at length be a Gainer by it, fince his Brother-in-law the Emperor falling out with the Pope feized the County and Caftle of *Comachio*, to which the Duke of *Modena* had the fame Right as to the *Ferrarefe*, and it was generally thought that he would have reftored both Duchy and County, as he might very eafily have done, to its lawful Owner. But his Imperial Majefty having carried his Point with the Pope by a Treaty figned *January* 15, 1709, left the Decifion of the Duke's Claim to a Congregation of Cardinals, who to be fure were moft equal Judges between the Pope and

and any Prince whatever; but in the mean time the Emperor kept *Comachio* in his own Hands by way of Sequeſtration. In this Situation Things remained, very little to the Satisfaction either of the Pope or of the Duke, till by a Treaty between *Benedict* XIII. and the Emperor *Charles* VI. dated at *Rome November* 24, 1724, *Comachio* was reſtored to his Holineſs, but with an expreſs Reſervation of the Rights of the Empire and of the Duke of *Modena* upon that Fief, and a Proviſo that this Reſtitution ſhould have no Operation whatever in favour of the Pope's Title.

But if his Serene Highneſs of *Modena* failed in his reaſonable Expectation of being once more put into Poſſeſſion of the Patrimony of his Anceſtors, he had however the Satisfaction of receiving a noble Equivalent for the Loſſes he had ſuſtained by his Fidelity to the Houſe of *Auſtria*. For the *French* King having given the Example of transferring the Dominions of one *Italian* Prince to another, his Imperial Majeſty made no Difficulty of granting to the then hereditary Prince, and now reigning Duke of *Modena*, the Inveſtiture of the Duchies of *Mirandola* and *Concordia*, their Sovereign of the Houſe of *Pio* having thought fit, a little imprudently, to declare himſelf very early in favour of the two Crowns, which by thoſe valuable Duchies were united to the Dominions of *Modena*, and have continued Part of them ever ſince.

The Tranquility of *Europe* being in ſome meaſure reſtored by the Treaties of *Utrecht* and *Baden*, his Serene Highneſs thought fit to provide for the Succeſſion to his Dominions, by marrying the Hereditary Prince in the Month of *June* 1720, to *Charlotte Aglae d'Orleans*, Daughter to the Duke Regent of *France*. This Marriage ſoon after it was celebrated, became, from Cauſes the World has never been acquainted with, the Source of ſome Family Diſcontents, upon which the Hereditary Prince and Princeſs quitted the Court of *Modena*, and endeavoured to mitigate the Senſe of this Diſaſter by Travelling. The old Duke in the mean time remained firm to his original Syſtem, and in the War which broke out upon the Death of the King of *Poland*, adhered ſteadily to the Intereſts of the Houſe of *Auſtria*, which coſt him as much Trouble and ill Uſage in the very Decline of Life, as he had experienced in the Flower of his Age. He had however the Satisfaction of ſurviving his Misfortunes, and of returning from *Bologna* (which he had again choſen for his Retreat) to his Capital of *Modena*. His Imperial Majeſty *Charles* VI. in Gratitude to the Virtues of this great and good Prince, made him a Preſent of a moſt noble Lordſhip in *Hungary*, and entailed it upon his Family. After paſſing through ſuch a Variety of Fortunes without the leaſt Diminution of

Character,

Character, this venerable Duke departed the World in Peace in his own Palace *October* 26, 1737, aged eighty-three.

Francis Maria de Este succeeded his Father in his Dominions, but having married a Princess of the Blood of *France*, by whom he has a numerous Issue, he entered into Engagements with the Crowns of *France* and *Spain*, tho' with great Secrecy, before the breaking out of the last War, raised Forces, and fortified all the strong Places in his Dominions. His *Sardinian* Majesty, however, taking Advantage of the Difficulties the Duke of *Montemar* who commanded the *Spanish* Forces in *Naples* was under, entered the Dominions of his Serene Highness with a superior Force, and upon his withdrawing to the *Spanish* Army, seized and reduced them, having first disarmed his Forces. After this, all the Territories of this Prince in *Italy* were administer'd by the Authority and for the joint Benefit of the Empress Queen and the King of *Sardinia*. The former likewise confiscated and disposed of his Estates in *Hungary*, to which however, as well as to all his Dominions in *Italy*, his Serene Highness was re-stored by the Treaty of *Aix la Chapelle*, and is in full Possession of them at this Time. He has already begun to restore Things to their former State, by directing the strong Citadel of *Miran-dola* to be repaired and fortified, and that he may appear no less careful of his Subjects Interests than of his own Security, has abolished various Duties and Impositions that were injurious to Commerce, and is meditating other salutary Resolutions, amongst which it is said a cordial Reconciliation with the Court of *Vienna* is one of the chief. This is so much the more probable, as there is no Prince in *Italy* to whom the Friendship of the Emperor and the House of *Austria* is of so great Consequence as to the Duke of *Modena*. The Truth of this will manifestly appear from the following Description of his Territories.

The Dominions of his Serene Highness the Duke of *Modena* are composed, as the Reader has already seen, of various Terri-tories acquired at different Times, and held by different Titles. If we compare the present State of the House of *Este* with its original Condition, it will seem to be greatly improved ; but if we reflect upon the Condition of this Family when the Duchy of *Ferrara*, and the County of *Comachio*, as well as the Duchies of *Modena* and *Reggio*, were in its Possession, we shall find it far short now of what it was. However the present Duke of *Modena* is a much more considerable Prince than his Grandfather, whe-ther we consider the Extent of his Dominions, or the Amount of his Revenues ; neither is it at all impossible, in case of any future Alterations in the Distribution of Power in *Italy*, this Prince

or

or his Succeffors may be Gainers, as well as his Predeceffors were in Times paft.

The Duchy of *Modena*, properly fo called, comprehends one of the faireft and moft fruitful Countries in *Italy*, abounding with Corn, Wine, Oil and Fruits, very populous, and inhabited by an ingenious and induftrious People. The fmall County of *Frignano* bordering on the *Bolognefe*, is annexed to it on one Side, and Part of the Country of *Carfagnano* on the other, the reft belonging to the Republick of *Lucca*. It is very mountainous, but far from being defpicable for all that, fince in thefe Mountains there are Mines of great Value, and the Inhabitants are a Race of People robuft, hardy, and brave, as any in *Italy*. The Duchy of *Reggio* lies Weft from that of *Modena*, and is by fome accounted the more confiderable Duchy of the two, and indeed fo it is, if we confider its Dependencies, fuch as the Principalities of *Correggio* and *Carpi*, the former heretofore poffeffed by the Princes of the fame Name, and the latter belonging to the Family of *Pio*. In the North-weft Corner of this Duchy, ftands *Bercello* upon the *Po*, formerly a Place of great Strength, yielded by the late Duke of *Modena* in 1701 to the Imperialifts, to facilitate their military Operations in *Italy*, and for that Reafon, befieged, taken, and entirely demolifhed by the *French* in 1705, nor has it been ever fince reftored to its ancient Condition.

The Duchy of *Mirandola*, including that of *Concordia*, is about twenty Miles in Length, and five in Breadth ; it is a very beautiful and a very plentiful Territorry, full of Villages, and the Country round about them thoroughly cultivated. *Mirandola* is ftrong by Situation, and has been formerly well fortified. The City of *Concordia* ftands on the *Secchia*, at the Diftance of fix Miles from *Mirandola*, between which Cities there is a fine Canal called the *Navilio*, which facilitates the Commerce of both. Thefe Duchies were very great Acquifitions to the Family of *Efte*, fince their Revenues are moderately computed at one hundred thoufand Crowns a Year. Having fpoken of thefe Countries feparately, we will confider them next as they lie together, and make the Patrimony of this Prince, now fettled and confirmed, as well as guaranteed, by the greateft *European* Powers.

The whole Eftates of the Duke of *Modena* have the Duchies of *Mantua* and *Guaftalla* on the North ; the Grand Duchy of *Tufcany* on the South, together with the Territories of the Republick of *Lucca*; the *Bolognefe* and the Duchy of *Ferrara* on the Eaft ; and the Duchy of *Parma* on the Weft. The Extent

of

of these Countries from South to North, is about fifty-six *English* Miles, and they are about fifty Miles in Breadth from West to East. The Duke of *Modena*, in time of Peace, enjoys a Revenue of about one hundred thousand Pounds a Year at least, with which he maintains a very splendid Court, and when his Circumstances render it requisite, can keep up a Body of eight thousand regular Troops. The greatest Inconveniency in the Situation of his Country is, that it has no Communication with the Sea, which might be easily removed, if he could recover either by Treaty or Force the Duchy of *Ferrara*, which lies upon the Gulph of *Venice*.

It is to be observed, that the Western Part of the Duchy of *Reggio*, intervenes intirely between the Duchy of *Parma* and that of *Guastalla*, so that they can have no Communication but by the River *Po*; as this is very inconvenient for the Infant Duke, it has been surmised that he would restore to the Empress Queen a Part of the Duchy of *Guastalla*, in order to engage her to grant the Duke of *Modena* an Equivalent for this Part of his Country; and if this Negotiation is ever brought to bear, that Equivalent will be easily found, since the Country of *Novellara*, which is likewise a Part of the *Mantuan*, lies in the midst of the Estates of the Duke of *Modena*, and would be very convenient for him. On the other hand, there has been a Rumour as if his Serene Highness was desirous of exchanging for it the Countries that he holds in *Hungary*, which to him no doubt would be very acceptable, but will hardly appear in the same Light to the House of *Austria*. Upon the whole, it is plainly the Interest of his Serene Highness (if he proposes to continue an *Italian* Prince) to resume his Father's System, and to attach himself closely to that Family, which will be always able to protect him, and from which alone he can expect any Assistance, in reference to the old Claims of his Family, which if they could be brought to bear, would alter his Condition very much.

Since our former Edition, the Prospect with respect to this ducal House is much altered by the Death of the Cadet Prince of *Este*. The present Duke is old, and the Duchess also, who resides in *France*. The Hereditary Prince, upon whom the Continuance of this illustrious Family depends, is not on the best Terms with the Princess of *Massa-Carrara*, by whom as yet he has only a Daughter. So that considering the Nature of Fiefs in *Italy*, the Fate of so considerable a Succession may excite much political Confusion.

SECT.

SECT. V.

The Power of the Pope considered as the Head of all Christians who hold Communion with Rome; his Grandeur as a Temporal Prince; the Maxims of his Government; the general Interest of the See of Rome with regard to the Princes and States of Christendom, and particular Interests, in reference to the Princes and States in Italy; including also an Account of all the Temporal Dominions of the Pope, their Situation, Extent, Revenues, &c.

THE Design of this Work makes it absolutely necessary to examine the Nature of the Papal Power, for many Reasons, but more especially as it has a very great Influence on the Ballance of Power in general, as well as a very particular Relation to that of *Italy*. It would indeed require much more Room than we have to spare, and lead us at the same time beside our Purpose, to treat this Matter in its full Extent, and to enter into an express Deduction of the Means by which the Spiritual Authority of the Popes was gradually raised to such a Height, as that with which it was exercised in the Times immediately preceding the *Reformation*; neither is it at all necessary that we should enter into any express Detail of the Means by which the Popes have acquired the several Parts of their Temporal Dominions. What we chiefly aim at, may be accomplished by a succinct View of the Nature, Prerogatives, and Influence of this Spiritual Monarchy, so far as it respects the Christian Powers, and a short Description of those Territories, from the Possession of which the Pope is considered as a Temporal Prince, and as one of the most considerable Potentates in *Italy*, which will be found highly useful towards obtaining a thorough Comprehension of the Interests of *Europe*.

If we consider that the Popes rise to that Dignity from very inferior Stations, were heretofore frequently, and are still sometimes of mean Families, without any Support from Kindred or Relations, deriving a great Part of their Revenues from the

Sub-

Subjects of other Princes, and this in Virtue of their claiming a Share in their Allegiance, exercising an Authority grounded only in Opinion, and frequently assuming a Superiority over those to whom they have not only been themselves in Obedience, but have also rendered them domestick Offices in the Nature of Servants : When, I say, we consider all this, with a Multitude of other Particulars, that every intelligent Reader's Memory will furnish, we cannot help wondering that this *Ecclesiastical Empire* has stood so long, grown up to so great a Height, and continues yet to enjoy a green old Age, that does not seem to betray any Symptoms of a speedy Dissolution.

But upon a nearer and closer Inspection, we shall find that this *Spiritual Monarchy*, like some of the leaning Towers that have made so much Noise in *Italy*, tho' it seems to carry evident Marks of Weakness, is in fact a Structure very strong in itself, contrived with great Skill, as well as erected with much Art. If in other Monarchies Princes have pretended to a *Divine Right*, the Pope goes still farther, and claims a kind of *Divine Power*, by which he is raised as much above other Princes, as those Princes are above their People. This Claim, together with the Title of *Holiness*, having the Recommendation of a long Prescription, cannot but excite an high Veneration in the Minds of such as believe it. The *Papal* Character being given with the greatest Ceremony by those who are presumed to be the best Judges of Religion and religious Interests, seems in the Opinion of the Multitude to alter the very Nature of him who is adorned therewith, and to transform him from a Man of like Passions with themselves, into a *Sacred Person*. It is true, that in Protestant Countries, as nothing of this is believed, so it is very hard to be understood. Yet the Fact is beyond Dispute, and whatever wiser Persons in Popish Kingdoms may conceive, the Bulk of the People have the highest Reverence for the Holy Father.

The close Connection between the Clergy in all Popish Countries and the Court of *Rome*, joined to the occasional Benefits that Monarchs themselves may receive by Bulls from the Holy See, makes them unwilling to interpose, or break off that Commerce which their Subjects have with *Rome*, that upon certain Occasions they made derive Favours from thence, which may easily procure what otherwise might with Difficulty be forced by their own Authority. The Subjection of the Clergy to a foreign Head makes them sometimes more tractable to their natural Sovereigns than they otherwise would be, since

the

the Good-will and Friendſhip of a *ſingle Perſon* is more eaſily
attained, than the Direction of *many*, and beſides in thoſe
Caſes there can be no Appeal to the People, becauſe in all ſuch
Diſputes they think an implicit Submiſſion the Duty of the
Clergy. We may add to this another Reaſon, which is, that
the Popiſh Princes cheriſh the *Spiritual Power* of the *Pope*, as
the Means of preſerving Unity in Religion, and thereby preventing religious Diſputes, which very ſeldom diſturb the
Church, without diſturbing the State alſo. Thus it appears,
that independent of Enthuſiaſm and Superſtition, political Principles have no ſmall Share in promoting that Adherence to the
See of *Rome*, which at firſt Sight ſeems ſo irreconcileable to
the abſolute Authority of *Sovereign Princes*, and which notwithſtanding by their dextrous Management is often made to
co-operate therewith.

As to the *interior* Strength of the Papal Government, we
need only reflect that the Advantages of Birth are well ſup-
plied by the great Parts, and other Qualifications with which
a Man muſt be neceſſarily endow'd, who is promoted to this
Dignity. His being obliged to Celibacy is another Point of
great Conſequence, in as much as it prevents the changing this
elective into an hereditary Sovereignty, which would be entirely repugnant to the fundamental Maxims of this Conſtitution. We may add to this, the Precautions taken in electing
commonly a Perſon far advanced in Years, which leaves no
room for attempting to alter the ſettled Principles of the Government; and all great Politicians allow, that it is the ſacri-
ficing theſe to the Intereſts of a Family, or to the private Advantage of the reigning Prince, that opens a way to the Ruin
even of the beſt digeſted Syſtems. It has been alſo an old Rule
in the Conclave, never to elect two Popes of the ſame Family, Faction, or even of the ſame Diſpoſition, in immediate
Succeſſion, for the ſame Reaſon. It would indeed be endleſs
to enter into all their Refinements upon theſe capital Points,
from whence the Character of the Court of *Rome*, in reſpect
to Policy, has always ſtood ſo high, as to be thought the beſt
School for breeding Miniſters in all the Popiſh Monarchies,
from whence alſo it draws great Advantages.

We muſt not however imagine from hence, that becauſe the
fundamental Maxims of the See of *Rome* have been always the
ſame, the Adminiſtration of the Government has been exactly
uniform; ſince conſidering the vaſt Variation in Men's Tempers and Habits in different Ages, this muſt appear a Thing
abſolutely impoſſible. Neither ought we to imagine, that any

Con-

Constitution could be so framed, as to extinguish in the Minds of Princes all natural Affection for their Families. But on the one hand, such has been the Skill and Capacity of these Spiritual Monarchs, that from Time to Time they have made such prudent Alterations in their exterior Conduct, as hath perfectly kept up that Relation between the *Church* and the *Court* of ROME, upon which their Authority depends. They have likewise on the other reduced their Family Tendernesses into a kind of System, by which the *Nepotism* of the *Roman* Pontiffs has been in many Reigns made subservient to the Interest of the State, as well as agreeable to the Inclinations of the Popes, who thought they could never trust their Affairs in so safe Hands for themselves, as with those who must be conscious, that their Wealth, their Influence, and their Power, must in a great measure determine with the Life of him from whom they were received, and that besides they must from that Moment lie open to the strictest Inquiries possible into their past Conduct.

One may with great Truth and Impartiality venture to assert, that the whole Scheme of the *Romish* Religion is admirably well adjusted, to maintain in every respect the Power of the supreme Head. He is reputed infallible that his Decisions may have the greater Weight; the Traditions of the Church, which with the Members of it pass for the Rule of Faith, are subject to his Controul; all religious Doctrines are liable to his Censure; the Power of Absolution, even in the highest Cases, is attributed to him; he dispenses the Treasures of the Church, I mean Spiritual Treasures, such as Pardons and Indulgences; he grants Dispensations of all Kinds; he regulates Fasts and Feasts at his Pleasure: In a word, being reputed the Successor of St. *Peter*, and the visible Head of the Christian Church, he has Prerogatives without Bounds, and without Number; so that it is no surprizing thing at all, that so much Power, directed by so great Policy, should be able to perform such mighty Things, and to preserve itself for so many Ages.

But our Draught would be extremely imperfect, if we did not take notice of the several Ranks and Orders of Men subject in an especial Manner to the Holy See, and which without any great Impropriety in the Term, may be stiled the Spiritual Forces of his Holiness. In the first Class of these stand the *Cardinals*, who are acknowledged *Princes* of the Church, and pretend to be next in Dignity to *Crowned Heads*. They were originally no more than the Parish Priests of *Rome*, and their Number sometimes greater, sometimes less,

but

but now it is fixed to seventy-two, in Allufion to Chrift's Difciples. Heretofore a Cardinal was content to be ftiled his *Excellency*, but now they affume the Title of *Eminence*, which was formerly given to Princes, and thereupon the latter took the Title of Highnefs. The Cardinals are of all Nations, that the Influence arifing from the Hopes of this Dignity may be the more extenfive; the Nomination to *Hats* by crowned Heads is a new Stroke of *Roman* Policy, which heightens the Dependence upon the *Holy See*, while it feems to leffen the *Papal* Authority. The Majority, however, are always *Italians*, to prevent the Throne from being filled by a Stranger, and it is provided that in all Elections the Perfons chofen fhall have the Voices of two Thirds of thofe who enter the Conclave, that there may never be a ftrong Faction againft the Pope, amongft the Cardinals, which might be attended with ill Confequences. All the fubordinate Dignities in the Church, may be confidered as the Nobility in the Pope's fpiritual Empire.

But in all others, fo in this, the Strength of the Monarchy confifts in the Number of its Subjects, and if we take into our View the fecular and regular Clergy in the Church of *Rome*, the former bound by the moft facred Ties, and the latter not by Vows only, but by their Interefts, to the Obedience of the Holy See, we cannot but entertain a high Idea of its Power, fince long ago it was the Calculation of a certain Sovereign Pontiff, that in *Europe* he had three hundred thoufand Parifhes, and fifty thoufand Convents fubject to his Jurifdiction. The conftant Refort of all thefe to *Rome* upon different Occafions, muft carry thither annually an immenfe Treafure, and tho' Prelates fometimes complain of the Expence attending their *Bulls*, yet it is obferved, that fince the Reformation gave them Apprehenfions of feeing Ecclefiaftical Eftates fecularized, they have been lefs frequent in their Remonftrances, and chofe rather to fit down under thofe kind of Burthens, than expofe the Value of their Preferments to all the World, and thereby encourage that Spirit of Envy which they find ftrong enough already, without any fuch Inducement.

It is very eafy to difcern, that nothing has been neglected which could poffibly contribute to render the Foundations of this Monarchy firm and ftrong. That moft important Truft of educating Youth is intirely in their Hands, who are devoted to the Service of the Holy See. The Jefuits are particularly famous for their Application in this refpect; and when they have received the firft Tincture of Literature, fuch as are fent to compleat their Studies at the Univerfities meet with the fame

Doctrine

Doctrine and Discipline, and whatever the Science be to which they apply, Veneration for the Pope is a Thing so frequently insisted upon, and so strongly impressed, that it is almost impossible they should ever lose it while they remain constant to their Religion. The Offices of the Church, by which I mean Ecclesiastical Benefices of all sorts, are so numerous, and afford such ample Maintenance and such agreeable Prospects to Men of all Ranks and Tempers, in conjunction with the Canon Law which is peculiar to this Spiritual Monarchy, that the most effectual Provision is made for a constant Succession of Persons bound to support that Interest, which is the Support of themselves and all their Pretensions.

As these are bound by Affection, and by finding their own Account, to a constant Submission, so the proper Methods have been taken for subjecting the Laicks in that Church also to such an Obedience as they cannot well break through. Amongst these we may reckon Auricular Confession, Masses for the Dead, the Direction of Female Consciences, the Opportunities they have of working upon Persons in their dying Moments, and many more. So that judging according to those Rules of Probability, which hold in other Cases, there is no great Reason to expect that the Papal Authority will decline much more than it has already done; especially if succeeding Popes imitate the Moderation of their immediate Predecessors, and endeavour to maintain themselves rather by Address than by the Force of Ecclesiastical Censures, which is a sort of Artillery than no longer does the Execution it did in the darker Ages, when the little Learning there was remained intirely among the Priests and Monks.

The Reader will apprehend this more clearly, if he takes a short View of the *European* Powers that still profess Obedience to the See of *Rome*. In *Poland* the Clergy are numerous, and well provided for, have a great Share of Power allotted them by the Constitution, and are for the most composed of the younger Sons of the Nobility. In *Germany*, it is visible that the Popish Religion rather prevails than declines, and the Ecclesiastical Electors and other Prelates are so formidable a Body in the Diet, as not to be apprehensive of any future Secularizations. It is besides the Interest of several great Houses to support the Church as it is now constituted, on the score of the Preferments which are in a manner entailed on the younger Sons of their Families, so as not only to afford them noble Establishments, but also render them capable of supporting the Head of their House, instead of being a Burthen upon him, as would be the Case if these

Dignities

Dignities were fecularized. The hereditary Countries of the House of *Auftria* remain ftrictly attached to the See of *Rome*. The *Gallican* Church has always claimed a kind of Freedom, which having been improved by the Struggles that have been heretofore made againft them, the modern Popes have wifely had recourfe to another Method, which feems to have had a better Effect; and while the Courts of *Rome* and *Verfailles* agree, both will find their Account in the reciprocal Support of each other's Power. In *Spain* and *Portugal* the Papal Authority ftands upon a much ftronger Foundation, as appears from the amazing Wealth of the Clergy in the former, and the Joy with which the Sovereign of the latter accepted very lately from the Pope the Title of *Moft Faithful*. In *Italy* the Influence of the Pope extends every where; and he is fo able to make either his Favour or Refentment felt, that all the Princes and States of his Communion find it their Intereft to live upon good Terms with his Holinefs, and as none underftand their own Interefts better, are like to continue in the fame Inclinations received from their Anceftors in that refpect.

It has been generally fuppofed, that one of the Maxims of the See of *Rome* has been attaching itfelf to the fuperior Intereft, and always courting that Power moft which was uppermoft; and in proof of this much has and may be faid: but at the fame time it is very certain, that the true Intereft of the Holy See confifts in fupporting the BALLANCE of POWER, becaufe it's Influence depends chiefly upon an Equality among the Princes of that Communion: and if any of thefe fhould gain an entire Afcendancy, the See of *Rome* could not fail of feeling the firft Effects of it. This is not only evident from Speculation, but from Experience likewife. When the *Spaniards* were in the Zenith of their Power, the Pope felt the Weight of it. And in much later Times, when *Lewis* XIV. thought himfelf in a Condition to give Law to *Europe*, his profeffing himfelf the Eldeft Son of the Church did not reftrain him from treating the Holy Father very undutifully; upon which the wifeft Proteftant Politicians did not in the leaft hefitate at giving the Article for making his Holinefs Satisfaction a place in the Grand Alliance. The Truth is, that while the Court of *Rome* continues famous for its Policy, for which it is like to continue famous as long as it continues at all, we can never fufpect its falling from this Maxim. For as in Decency it imports the Holy Father to fhew an equal Affection for all who profefs themfelves his Children, fo it is his Intereft to be really indifferent; and tho' fome Cafes may happen that require a temporary Sufpenfion of that Appearance,

pearance, yet wife Men will not be deceived by the Conduct of Popes under such Circumstances. But it is now Time to speak of the Temperal Authority which the *Roman* Pontiff enjoys in consequence of his Dominions in *Italy* and elsewhere; and in treating of these we shall be as succinct as the Subject will allow.

As an *Italian* Prince, the Pope would be very powerful if the Number and Wealth of his Subjects bore any Proportion to the Extent of his Dominions, which lie in the very middle of *Italy*, and go quite across from the Gulph of *Venice* to the *Mediterranean*, which is an Advantage that (except the King of the *Two Sicilies*) no other Prince in that Country enjoys but himself. We will speak of the several Provinces into which they are divided, or rather of the several Territories of which they are composed, in their natural Order, beginning with the Country that lies farthest to the North-West, which is the Duchy of *Ferrara*. This, which was formerly one of the finest Principalities in *Italy*, lies stretched upon the Gulph of *Venice*, the River *Po* running through it, and falling there into the Sea. The Climate was formerly good, and the Soil fruitful, producing Corn, Flax and Hemp, and other valuable Commodities, which made the Duke rich and the People happy; but now Things are quite altered; for the Country lying low, and being thinly inhabited, the Inundations of the *Po* have rendered a great Part of it a Morass, and *Ferrara*, from being one of the finest in *Italy*, now scarce deserves the Name of a City. The Town and County of *Comachio* is no better than a Fishing Village, surrounded by unwholesome Marshes. The *Bolognese* is still a very fine Country, and retains something of its ancient Freedom: The Capital is stiled *Bologna*, or *Bononia the Fat*, from the Fertility of its Territory in Corn, Wine and Flax: Fort *Urban*, which stands ten Miles from *Bologna*, is a Fortress built to cover the Pope's Frontier on this Side: The *Bolognese* is an Inland Country, but as it lies between *Tuscany* and the Duchy of *Mantua*, the Road through it creates some little Trade. The Country of *Romagna* is next, it lies upon the Gulph of *Venice*, and is very pleasant and fruitful, watered by several fine Rivers, and enriched by its Salt Mines: The Capital is *Ravenna the Old*, as the *Italians* call it, and indeed its Appearance speaks it so, for it is now fallen very much to Decay. The Duchy of *Urbino* lies also upon the *Venetian* Gulph, and though it was formerly reckoned a fine Country when under Princes of its own, there is nothing more certain than that the Air is very unwholesome, and the Soil

extremely

extremely barren; the beft Place now is *Pefaro* on the Coaft of the *Adriatick*, from whence it enjoys fome Trade, and is tolerably well built. The Marquifate of *Ancona* lies alfo on the fame Gulph; the City from whence it receives its Name was formerly famous for its Port, now in a very low and poor Condition; but *Loretto*, which ftands about ten Miles from it, is famous for its Riches acquired by the worft fort of Trade.

The Territory of *Citta de Caftello* is fmall, and derives its Name from that Place which ftands on the River *Tiber*, and is pleafant and well built. The *Perugiano* lies next, and abounds with excellent Wine and very good Corn. The Capital is *Perufa*, enriched by its famous Lake well ftored with excellent Fifh. The *Orvietano* lies next, fo called from its Capital *Orvieto*, a fmall but beautiful Country, rich in Corn and Wine, and enjoying the beft Air in the Pope's Dominions. Adjoining to this Province lies the Duchy of *Caftro*, belonging formerly to the Dukes of *Parma* and *Placentia*, but rejoined to the Holy See partly by Ufury, and partly by Violence: The Pope's Poffeffion was quieted by a Treaty with the Emperor *Charles* VI. in 1724, but it is poffible the old Title to it derived from the Dukes of *Parma*, on a favourable Occafion may yet be revived.

The Patrimony of St. *Peter* lies on the *Mediterranean*, and is fruitful in Corn and Wine, and famous alfo for its Allom Mines: The Capital of it is *Viterbo*, anciently a fine Place, now little better than a Heap of Ruins: *Porto*, formerly (as its Name fignifies) a noble Haven, now capable only of receiving Barks: But *Civita Vecchia* has ftill a fine Port, and would be a very confiderable Place, if the Unwholefomenefs of its Air did not render it thinly peopled, and the Lazinefs of thofe People who dwell in it did not contribute to the Unwholefomenefs of the Air by leaving their Country uncultivated. *Umbria*, or the Duchy of *Spoleto*, is a Country well watered, and much diverfified in its Appearance, in fome Parts mountainous, in others marfhy, but intermixed with Plains fruitful in Corn, Wine, Oil and Fruits: The Capital is *Spoleto*, and there are fome other good Towns in this Country, which is owing to a little Trade ftirring there. The Province of *Sabina*, which takes its Name from the *Sabines*, is fmall, but very fruitful and pleafant. The Country about *Rome*, called *Campagna di Roma*, would be wholefome and fruitful if well cultivated, but at prefent it is neither, efpecially in fome Seafons of the Year, when that Capital becomes a kind of Defart, being alike abandoned by Strangers and its beft Inhabitants, for the fake of enjoying a purer Climate.

The

The whole Dominions of the Holy See that lie thus all together, and compose what the *Italians* call *Stato della Chiesa*, are bounded on the North by the Territories of the State of *Venice* and the *Adriatick* Sea, on the East by the Kingdom of *Naples*, on the South by the *Mediterranean*, and on the West by the Dominions of the Great Duke and the Duchies of *Modena*, *Mirandola*, and *Mantua*. The greatest Length of this Country, computed from *Francolino* in the Duchy of *Ferrara* to *Terracina* in *Campagna di Roma*, which is in a Line from North-East to South-West, may be about two hundred and forty *Italian* Miles; as to the Breadth, from *Civita Vecchia* in the Patrimony of St. *Peter* to *Ancona*, it is about one hundred and thirty Miles, but in many other Places it is not near so broad. We have already taken notice of the Advantage of its Situation, from which tho' the Pope derives no great Benefit, yet ought it to be considered as a Point of very great Consequence in treating of the Importance of his Countries. Upon the whole it may be affirmed, that after the two crown'd Heads, the Pope is the most considerable Power in *Italy* in point of Dominions, and might be in every other respect, if any thing like the same Policy was discoverable in the Conduct of his Temporal Estates that is shewn in the Management of his Spiritual Authority. As it is, his Subjects are the hardest used, and yet his Revenue is below that of any other Prince, the Extent of his Territories considered; for it has never been computed at above two Millions of *Roman* Crowns, whereas *Tuscany*, that is not half as big, produces twice as much to the Grand Duke. His regular Troops are now only fit for Show, hardly any of his Fortresses in a State of Defence, and tho' the Gazettes sometimes mention the Pope's Gallies, his naval Power is very inconsiderable. We must however in Justice to some of the last Popes allow, that they have endeavoured to correct the Errors of their Predecessors, and that their Subjects have lived much easier under them; but then these Amendments have extended no farther than to keep Things from growing worse, and much more must be done before they can be expected to grow better.

Besides these the Pope has other Dominions, as well in *Italy* as elsewhere. The Kingdom of *Naples* is held from him by an annual Tribute. The Duchies of *Parma* and *Placentia* were Part of the Patrimony of the Church, but by the famous Quadruple Alliance, they are declared to be Fiefs of the Empire, and are like to be considered in that Light for the future. The Principality of *Masseran*, belonging formerly to

the

the Family of *Fiefque*, and at prefent to the King of *Sardinia*, is held in like manner from the Pope. Other Dominions he has in Poffeffion, which are held from other Princes, fuch as the Territory of *Benevento* in the Kingdom of *Naples*, the Archbifhop of which is the fecond Ecclefiaftical Dignity In that Kingdom; and the County of *Avignon*, in the South of *France*, in which, while they were deprived of *Rome*, the Popes themfelves refided, who ftill govern it by a Vice-Legate, and this in every refpect is a very confiderable Acquifition, of which the Popes are particularly tender, and which is the only Part of their Poffeffions obtained in the way of a fair Purchafe.

After having thus fairly and clearly ftated the juft Extent of the Papal Dominions, and the Nature of their Government, which is truly defpotic, the Reader will eafily fee, that as an *Italian* Prince, the Sovereign Pontiff is obliged to keep great Meafures with moft of his Neighbours. The King of the *Two Sicilies*, tho' he confiders him as his Subject, is neverthelefs a very powerful Prince; and as we have lately feen by his blocking up *Benevento*, not at all afraid of refenting any Injury that may be done him by the Court of *Rome*. The Grand Duke was alfo to be managed for many Reafons; and tho' the Dukes of *Parma* and *Modena* were never formidable from their own Power, yet they feldom wanted fome very puiffant Protector. With the Republick of *Venice* the Popes have generally fpeaking endeavoured to live well, and when at any time they have departed from this falutary Maxim, Experience has quickly taught them to recur to it for their own Safety. They have always kept fair with the Duke of *Savoy*, or at leaft endeavoured it, as knowing that he held the Paffages into *Italy*; neither have they often differed with the Republick of *Genoa*. On the other hand, the Princes and States of *Italy* having more frequent Occafion than other Potentates to follicit Favours from his Holinefs, in temporal as well as fpiritual Concerns, have very feldom been wanting in Teftimonies of Duty and Refpect, and this tho' they have fometimes had Jealoufies of the perfonal Conduct of particular Popes.

As a temporal Prince, every wife Pope confiders the Ballance of *Italy* as his moft important Concern, and therefore labours as far as in his Power lies, to preferve the Tranquility of that Country, and to provide as much as may be against a Revolution, becaufe he is fure that in time of War his Countries muft fuffer, and he is very far from being fure, confidering the many Flaws in the Titles by which he holds many of them, that fome part or other will not be taken from

F f   him.

him. Besides, nothing exposes his Weakness so much to the World, as a War in *Italy*, when he is often able to do but little by Intreaty, and always incapable of doing any thing by Force. Upon these Principles the Popes endeavour to keep all the *Italian* Princes in a State of Equality as much as possible, and are also very attentive to prevent either the House of *Austria*, or the House of *Bourbon*, from gaining the Ascendancy there, which may be fatal to the Independency of other Powers, and consequently destructive of the Pope's Influence, which thereupon entirely depends. The same Maxim governs the Cardinals in the Choice of a Pope, so that they not only avoid electing a Subject of either of those powerful Houses, but are likewise very cautious in raising to the Papal Throne any Cardinal who has shewn himself warm in either of their Interests.

The Pope is jealous and afraid, not without good Reason, of the *Turks* and of the pyratical States of *Barbary*, his Coasts being very liable to Descents from the one, and to Insults from the other. It has indeed been suggested, that from a refined Stroke in Politics, the Countries seated on the Gulph of *Venice* and on the *Mediterranean* have been suffered to lie waste and uncultivated, that the Unwholesomeness of the Air, and the Poverty of the Inhabitants, might take away all Temptations from an Enemy that might otherwise prove irresistible. If one could imagine any Truth in this, it must give a strange Idea of his Holiness's Councils; but as the *Italians* have been always esteemed subtile Politicians, so there have never been wanting a certain Class of Writers, willing to attribute the grossest Mistakes in Government to some mysterious Design far above the Reach of ordinary Capacities; which in plain *English* is refining to a Degree that is palpably ridiculous. But after all, the real Source of the strange Conduct in the Administration of civil Affairs in the Dominions of the Church, is the known Consequence of Industry, Wealth and Commerce, which is Freedom of Thought, and a Liberty in acting; Principles that are not at all compatible with that kind of Sovereignty; and this alone very fully accounts for that otherwise surprizing Opposition between the Dexterity with which every thing relating to the spiritual Monarchy is managed, and that negligent Stiffness which appears so manifestly in the Direction of civil Affairs.

The Reader may probably wonder at finding these *Italian* States so fully and particularly described, and therefore it may

not

not be amifs to give the true Reafon of that Attention in this
Place, which is, that new Difputes in *Italy* may in all Probability create the next general War in *Europe*; on which as it is
not at all impoffible that we may have our Eye, fo it feems to be
very reafonable that we fhould be able to form fome Notion of
the Merits of the Caufe, and of the Situation of Places in that
Country, that at the Beginning will be, in all Appearance,
the Theatre of the War. We have already feen how the
Auftrian Dominions are feated, how the Territories of the
Duke of *Modena* are blocked up by the Pope, what fine Countries belong to the Holy See, and how far he is from making
the beft ufe of them. We will next apply our Thoughts to the
folid Eftablifhments that have been made fince the Peace
of *Utrecht* in favour of the Houfe of *Bourbon*.

SECT. V.

The Pretenfions and Dominions of the Houfe of BOUREON *in* Italy.

WE have heretofore mentioned this Subject occafionally, in order to explain other Matters which we were
treating; but we will now take the Opportunity of going
to the Bottom of it, and of ftating the Rife and Progrefs of
that Eftablifhment, which has chiefly occupied the Attention
of the *European* Powers fince the Conclufion of the laft general
Peace, at *Utrecht*. By that Treaty the Emperor was put in
Poffeffion of the Dominions of the Houfe of *Auftria* in *Italy*,
and it was thought this Difpofition had fecured the Ballance of
Power in *Europe*, in fpite of almoft all Events. But it very
often happens, that when Politicians have fome one great and
important Object in View, they neglect or pafs by unobferved
what merits their Attention; fo in this Cafe, the Care they had
of the Ballance of *Europe* made them intirely forget the Ballance
of *Italy*, which was abfolutely overturned by this very Settlement.

It is indeed true, that *Sicily* was given to the Duke of *Savoy*;
but as this proceeded from the pure Affection of Queen *Anne*,
fo the giving him that Kingdom was not attended with fuch
an Augmentation of Power as might enable him to keep it; for
at this time, the Emperor was not only Mafter of great Dominions in, but to fpeak truly, was Mafter of all *Italy*. He
had

had the Kingdom of *Naples* and the Duchy of *Milan*, together with the Island of *Sardinia*, as his hereditary Countries; the Duchy of *Mantua* he kept as an efcheated Fief; and in virtue of his Imperial Dignity, he had, or claimed, fuch Rights over the *Italian* Princes and States, as gave moft of them infinite and intolerable Uneafinefs.

Before the Death of *Lewis* XIV. they had entered into fome fecret Negotiations with the Court of *France*; for it was evident enough that the Houfe of *Bourbon* only could afford them the Protection they wanted; and upon the Death of the Queen of *Spain*, the Marriage of *Philip* V. with the Heirefs of the Houfes of *Farnefe* and *Medicis*, gave them no fmall Hopes of feeing a Turn in their Favour. By this one fees how ill the Imperial Minifters took their Meafures, who beginning early to fet forth the Claims of the Head of the Empire on the *Italian* Fiefs, perfuaded the Politicians on that Side the *Alps*, there wanted only a fair Opportunity to deprive them all by Degrees of their Territories, as has been the Fate already of the Dukes of *Mantua* and *Mirandola*. This converted them at once; fo that now they were as defirous of recalling the *Spaniards* as they ever were to fee them expelled.

His Catholick Majefty had two very different Interefts in *Italy*; one founded on the Pretenfions, which as Succeffor to the Houfe of *Auftria*, he had on the Kingdom of *Naples* and *Sicily*, and the Duchy of *Milan*, which he had renounced by force; and another in Right of his Queen, his Iffue by her being intituled to the Succeffion of *Parma*, *Placentia*, and *Tufcany*. The Emperor was jealous of both thefe Rights, and was very earneft with his Allies to provide againft them; which might have been very effectually done, the Pope having a Claim to the Duchies of *Parma* and *Placentia*, and his Imperial Majefty at leaft a Colour of Right to difpofe of the Grand Duchy of *Tufcany*, upon the failing of the Male Line of the Houfe of *Medicis*.

The Quadruple Alliance, however, was concluded foon after, with a View to remedy the Defects of the Treaties of *Utrecht* and *Baden*; but the Regent of *France* could not be brought into that Alliance, without ftipulating in favour of his Catholick Majefty the eventual Succeffion of *Parma* and *Placentia*, by which there was a formal Decifion againft the Rights of the Pope, and in Favour of the Prerogatives of the Emperor; but then the latter were only acknowledged, to fupport his Power, in giving thefe Duchies away. There is no doubt, that the Proteftant Powers interefted in that Alliance, acted very confiftently, becaufe they deny all the Claims of the Pope, but the fame

cannot

cannot be said of the Catholick Princes ; yet this was afterwards solemnly confirmed by Cardinal *Fleury* : so much stronger with Politicians is *Interest* than *Principle*.

The Emperor, without doubt, foresaw all the Inconveniencies that would attend this Concession ; but the immediate Advantages which he derived from that Alliance, by the Exchange of *Sardinia* for *Sicily*, induced him to consent to it, though it is very certain that he did it with Reluctance, and that he expostulated the Point with his Allies to the utmost. It is also very likely, that the Succession to *Parma* and *Placentia* being eventual only, and attended with many Contingencies, was what chiefly prevailed upon the *British* Ministers to go so readily into this Scheme. It looked as if they had judged right upon the Death of *Francis* Duke of *Parma*, Uncle to the Queen Dowager of *Spain* ; for his Brother *Antonio Farnese* no sooner succeeded to the Duchy, than, contrary to every body's Expectation, he married the Princess *Henrietta* of *Modena*, by whom if he had been fortunate enough to have had any Issue, the Succession of the King of *Spain*'s Children by his second Marriage had been defeated, and this Duke's Descendents would have been the Heirs, not only of his Dominions, but also of those of the Grand Duke.

But he dying in *January* 1731, without Issue, the Infant Don *Carlos*, in virtue of a Multitude of Treaties, which having been mentioned in their proper Places need not be repeated here, became intituled to that Succession, and according to the Stipulations in the Treaty of *Seville*, was actually put into the peaceable Possession of *Parma* ; and in Consequence of a Negotiation with *John Gaston*, the last Duke of *Tuscany*, was by him also acknowledged for the Heir Apparent, and had the Title of *Grand Prince*. It was now thought that the Views of *Spain* were intirely accomplished, and that both the King and the Queen would be content with seeing their Son so amply provided for, and his Possessions so well secured to him as they were by several Treaties. The *Italian* Princes also were very well satisfied, because they were at length sure of Support in case they entered into any Alliance amongst themselves, to set Bounds to the Power of the House of *Austria* in that Part of the World, which was all they wished.

But upon the breaking out of the War, occasioned by the Death of the late King of *Poland*, the Face of Affairs in *Italy* intirely changed, and his Catholick Majesty having already obtained all that he could pretend to in Right of his Queen, began to revive the Claims which he had renounced in Right of

his

his Crown, and in the Month of *March* 1734, the Infant Don
Carlos having penetrated through the Ecclesiastical Dominions,
arrived with a *Spanish* Army, commanded under him by the
Count *de Montemar*, on the Frontiers of the Kingdom of *Naples*.
The Count *de Visconti* was at that Time Viceroy of the Kingdom for the Emperor *Charles* VI. and had the Misfortune to succeed his Predecessor in the general Hatred of the People, who revolted almost unanimously as soon as the *Spaniards* entered their
Country; upon which the Viceroy quitted *Naples*, after plunder-
ing all the Mounts of Piety; Funds, which had been accounted
sacred in all former Revolutions. The only Cities that were in
a Condition to make Resistance, were those of *Gaeta* and *Capua*,
and in these there were pretty good Garrisons. The Imperial
Troops that kept the Field were about nine thousand Men, and
they retired to a very strong retrenched Camp, under the little
Town of *Bitonto*, where they were attacked and forced by the
Count *de Montemar*, who gained the most signal Victory recorded in the *Neapolitan* History, for which he was deservedly rewarded with the Title of Duke of *Bitonto*; which however I
do not find that he used, but was afterwards stiled in *Spain* and
by Foreigners, Duke *de Montemar*.

The Infant Don *Carlos* Duke of *Parma* and *Placentia*, and
Hereditary Grand Prince of *Tuscany*, as hitherto stiled by this
Revolution, became King of the *Two Sicilies*, in virtue of the
Cession made to him of his Father's Rights; which Rights
however he had renounced over and over, in Favour of the then
Emperor. Having so good a Title, he was pleased to constitute
the Duke *de Montemar* the Year following Viceroy of *Sicily*,
who made the Conquest of that Island in as short a Time as of
the Kingdom of *Naples*, if indeed it could be called a Conquest,
where the People rose in every Province to favour his Expedition, as having been always fond of a *Spanish* Government in the
same Proportion that they hated that of the *Germans*. Upon this
Don *Carlos* went over thither, made his publick Entry into *Messina* with all the Magnificence imaginable, and after having done
the same at *Palermo*, where he was crowned, he returned to *Naples*,
which was to be the Place of his Residence.

By the Revolution in these two Kingdoms, and by the other
Losses which the Emperor had sustained in *Italy*, where he had
nothing now left but the City of *Mantua*, the Ballance was again
altered, and the *Italian* Princes had then as much to fear from
the House of *Bourbon*, as they apprehended a very few Years before from the House of *Austria*. But things did not long wear
this Face. *France* was resolved to get out of the War, and to
get

get something for going into it ; she compromised Matters therefore with the Emperor at the Expence of her Allies. Instead of the Duchy of *Milan*, the King of *Sardinia* was forced to be content with two very small Districts, tho' the Emperor would have given him three. The Duchies of *Parma* and *Placentia* were bestowed upon his Imperial Majesty, as an Equivalent for the *Two Sicilies*, which was rather a worse Equivalent than had been given the House of *Savoy* by the Quadruple Alliance.

As for the eventual Succession to *Tuscany*, it was given to the Duke of *Lorrain*, according to the old Plan of *France*, which many Years before had offered to exchange it for the Duchy of *Milan*. By this Treaty of Peace, to which Don *Carlos* was obliged to accede in *December* 1736, the Dominions of the House of *Bourbon* were reduced to the Kingdom of the *Two Sicilies*, and the Fortresses on the Coast of *Tuscany*.

All the World knows how much the Court of *Madrid* was displeased with this Distribution of Things, and how soon the Queen of *Spain* began to revive her Pretensions to her hereditary Dominions in Favour of her second Son the Infant Don *Philip*. It was to pacify her, and to give a kind of Security, that on the first proper Occasion, *France* would assist in obtaining her new Demand, however unjust and unreasonable ; that a Princess of *France* was given to Don *Philip*, which the Cardinal *de Fleury* hoped would have quieted Things for his Time, as in all Probability it would, if the sudden Death of the Emperor *Charles* VI. had not obliged him to abandon his pacific System. I mean by this, that it put an End to all his Expedients, and forced him much against his Inclinations upon a new War, for which he seemed to have provided, but was really in hopes that some lucky Event would have afforded him the Means of disengaging himself from the Measures he entered into for the Sake of gratifying the Court of *Madrid*, or rather the Ambition of the Queen of *Spain*.

The Consequences attending these Measures, together with the Progress of the last War in *Italy*, have been so often and so fully considered in other Parts of this Work, that there is no need of running them over again here ; and therefore it shall suffice in this Chapter to take notice of the Effects of this War with respect to the King of the *Two Sicilies*, as in the next Chapter we shall shew the Nature and Value of that Establishment, which by the definitive Treaty of Peace was stipulated in Favour of the Royal Infant Don *Philip*, in whose Cause perhaps more Men have bled, than there are living Souls in those Territories, which have been at last given up to him. These

Remarks

Remarks will compleatly anſwer our Intention, and exhibit a conciſe, but at the ſame time a clear Account of the *Italian* Territories in the Hands of the Houſe of *Bourbon*, ſo as perfectly to comprehend not only the Acceſſions made to them in the two laſt Wars, but alſo the preſent Proſpect of Things in that Part of the World, and the Danger there is that even in our Times the preſent definitive Diſpoſition of Property may be again violated, upon Pretences as idle and trifling as gave Birth to that War which ended but the other Day.

His Majeſty of the *Two Sicilies* ſeemed at firſt diſpoſed to embrace a Neutrality, but when it was judged that Affairs were ripe enough, he declared himſelf, at leaſt by his Actions, a Party. This Conduct of his, however, did not turn at all to his Advantage, but on the contrary irritated thoſe Powers that had contributed moſt to his Eſtabliſhment in *Italy*, drew upon his Subjects inexpreſſible Diſtreſſes, and expoſed both his Crown and his Perſon to very great Hazards. In the Courſe of that War, he had the Mortification to ſee his Troops defeated, almoſt as often as they came to Action, to have his Coaſts inſulted, his Ports blocked up, and even his Capital menaced by *Britiſh* Squadrons. His Subjects alſo gave frequent and open Teſtimonies of Diſaffection to his Government, which obliged him to take many diſagreeable Precautions, which ſerved only to increaſe the Malady they were meant to remove. The *Auſtrian* Forces ravaged a Part of his Dominions; he was obliged to put himſelf at the Head of an Army deſtined to repel theſe Invaders; and tho' he had the good Fortune to prevent their penetrating into the Heart of his Territories, which would probably have been attended with a total Revolution, yet this could not be accompliſhed without feeling great Inconveniencies, and expoſing his Perſon in a Manner that could not fail of giving him much Chagrin. After all this, inſtead of reaping either Conqueſts or Laurels from theſe Dangers in the Field, he was again conſtrained to have recourſe to a Neutrality, which was procured for him chiefly by the Neceſſity that the Powers in War were under of temporizing with the Father of his Conſort, in which Situation, as little pleaſing as it was honourable, he ſaw the repeated Defeats of his Allies, and in the Midſt of Troubles and Anxieties, ſpun out the Remainder of the War, from which after all that he had ſuffered, he did not acquire either the leaſt Honour or Advantage.

The Kingdoms of which this Prince is in Poſſeſſion, are in themſelves as rich, as fruitful, and as happily ſituated, as even the moſt ambitious Monarch could deſire. They abound not
only

only with all the Necessaries of Life, but with a Variety of useful Commodities that might serve to entertain an extensive Commerce, for which both Kingdoms were formerly famous, and for the carrying on of which they are furnished with capacious and convenient Ports. His Subjects are numerous, and under a better Government might be rendered industrious. But the Prerogatives of the Crown are of such a Nature, the Authority of the Nobility over their Vassals so exorbitant, and above all, the Power and Property of the Clergy so excessive, that there are hardly any Countries upon the Face of the Globe, where the Bulk of the People are most dissolute in their Morals, or more wretched in their Circumstances, which is the true Reason that in the Midst of so many natural Advantages, the Crown of the *Two Sicilies* is regarded in a Light so little favourable to it, by most of our Politicians, and their Opinion from time to time confirmed by that Impunity with which both its Commerce, and its Coasts, are insulted by the *African* Privateers.

Yet it must be acknowledged, that since this Country has been restored to the Possession in some measure of an independent Government, and that Providence has been pleased to bless his *Sicilian* Majesty with Male Issue, there might be probable Grounds to hope, that in Time, and by Degrees, many Inconveniencies might be ʼremoved, the real Power of the Crown increased by a wise Circumscription of Rights, rather terrifying than useful, by a strict Execution of Justice, and by obliging all Ranks of People to submit to such Laws as are for the common Benefit. But then this is not to be expected till the Administration is delivered from all Cares, but those for its own Safety and Welfare, and released from the Consideration of any Interest but that of the Crown of the *Two Sicilies*, and its Subjects. These are Objects that might sufficiently employ the Attention even of able Politicians, and from a due Care of which, very considerable Advantages would arise to these Countries in particular, and in their Consequences to *Italy* in general.

But while Doubts are still remaining, in spite of an occasional Settlement, as to the future Fate of these Kingdoms, while the Councils of the Court of *Naples* receive their first Impressions from that of *Madrid*, while the Ambition of making fresh Acquisitions is the ruling Passion in Breasts where the Study of their People's Happiness should alone take place, there is little Reason to wonder that a Change so apparently

bene-

beneficial, as that of a King for a Viceroy, has not hitherto been attended with greater Effects, and still less Grounds to expect that the Monarch of the *Two Sicilies* should retrieve the ancient Splendor of that Diadem, and make the Figure that some of his Ancestors in past Ages have done, as the most puissant Prince upon the Continent, and the greatest Maritime Power in *Italy*, of which his Territories however are still as capable as ever, and will be found so when their King shall have nothing else either in Will or in View, but to extend his own Authority by cultivating the Arts of Peace, and promoting Industry and Trade amongst his Subjects.

SECT. VI.

A succinct Account of the present Establishment of the Royal Infant Don Philip *in* Italy ; *including also a clear and concise Deduction of the Pretensions of the Queen Dowager of* Spain, *as Heiress of the Houses of* Farnese *and* Medicis ; *with other Points of great Consequence.*

IT has been already observed, that at the Time the Quadruple Alliance was form'd, the late King of *Spain*, *Philip* the Fifth, had two very different Pretensions to certain Dominions in *Italy*, neither of which could be said to be over-well founded. As King of *Spain*, by a mixt Right of Descent, and the Will of *Charles* the Second, he conceived himself to have an indefeasible Right to all the Dominions in the Possession of that Prince, from which therefore he could not bar himself by any Renunciations. His other Claim was in Right of his Wife, in case she or her Issue became Heirs to the reigning Duke of *Parma*, and the Grand Duke of *Tuscany*. On the first of these Rights he insisted before his Accession to the Quadruple Alliance, in consequence of which he actually conquered *Sardinia*, and attempted the Conquest of *Sicily*, notwithstanding his former Renunciations. Upon his Accession to that Treaty, his Catholick Majesty once more renounced those Rights, in consideration of the eventual Succession to the Duchies of *Parma*, *Placentia*, and *Tuscany*, being secured to his

his Children of the second Marriage, which was done at the Requett of the Regent of France by the Quadruple Alliance. All these Pretensions were actually realised by the famous Treaty of Seville, when it seemed to be understood by all the contracting Parties, that the Succession of Don *Carlos* in the Manner prescribed by that Treay, should terminate all Disputes, and extinguish all Rights, except those that were settled thereby.

But when the next War broke out, it appeared that the King of *Spain* had no such Meaning, but that after engaging the Emperor to grant the Investiture of the Dominions claim'd in Right of his Wife, he was resolved to keep up still his other Claim against the Emperor himself in Reference to the Countries formerly bolonging to the Kings of *Spain*, or the House of *Austria*, and in consequence of this Don *Carlos* invaded and possessed himself of *Naples* and *Sicily*. Then came the Treaty of *Vienna*, by which those Kingdoms were left to that Prince, *Parma* and *Placentia* given up to his Imperial Majesty, and *Tuscany* exchanged for *Lorrain*. But notwithstanding this last Treaty, upon the Demise of the Emperor *Charles* VI. his Catholick Majesty revived his old Claims to the Duchy of *Milan*, as Heir of the House of *Austria*, and to *Parma* and *Placentia*, as belonging to his Queen and her Children, and hence arose the Pretension of procuring a Settlement for Don *Philip*, which after a long and bloody War, was at length obtained by the Definitive Treaty of *Aix la Chapelle*, which has put that young Prince in Possession of *Parma*, *Placentia*, and *Guastalla*, upon certain Conditions.

In order to understand how and why he holds these Countries, as well as the Consequences of his having this Establishment given him in *Italy*, it is absolutely necessary to give the Reader a succinct History of the House of *Farnese*, from which he is supposed to derive his Right; for without some Knowledge of this, and of the Situation of the Countries he possesses, it is absolutely impossible that we should have a distinct Conception of the present State of Things in *Italy*, or frame any tolerable Opinion of the new Claims that are already become the Subject of Discourse, will in all Probability serve for the Foundation of new Treaties, and it is not at all impossible may sooner or later become the Causes of another War. But these Points being once settled, this Matter which is at present so very obscure and perplexed, will appear as plain and perspicuous as can be, and we shall have the
same

same Facility in judging of the Controversies that may arise in *Italy*, as in those which have been agitated in the North and in *Germany*, and that very possibly may again require our Attention, since where-ever the Spark of War may first fall, it will not be long before the Flame communicates itself into all Quarters.

At the Time the *Lombards* acquired by Force of Arms a very considerable Kingdom in *Italy*, and threatened to extend their Dominions still farther, many Cities finding their Liberties in Danger, and having no Hope of Protection from the *Greek* Emperors, tho' they still retained the Name of Sovereigns, confederated together for their joint Preservation, and with the same View put themselves under the Protection of the Pope, among which Cities were *Parma* and *Placentia*. When the Holy See lost both Power and Credit, and the Popes themselves were forced to retire to *Avignon*, *Parma* and *Placentia*, as well as other Parts of their Territories, suffered a long Succession of miserable Revolutions, sometimes under one Race of Tyrants, sometimes under another, till at length, when most of these were extirpated, the Cities and the Duchies belonging to them, were again annexed, in the Beginning of the Sixteenth Century, to the Dominions of the See of *Rome*, and were peaceably possessed and enjoyed by *Leo* X. *Adrian* V. and *Clement* VII. in a Manner as absolute and independent as any of their other Temporal Estates whatever, not barely without Molestation, but with the full Knowledge and express Consent of the Emperor *Charles* V. Let us now see how they were detached from the Pope's Territories.

Authors are divided as to the Original of the House of *Farnese*, but amongst several Opinions, there is none more probable, than that they were Lords of *Castello Farnese*, in the little State of *Castro*. *Alexander Farnese*, Head of this House, having insinuated himself into the good Graces of Pope *Alexander* VI. obtained from him, while a very young Man, the Legation of *Ancona*, which for him was a great Preferment. He fell in Love there with a Lady of the noble Family of *Raffini*, which brought him under great Difficulties, since if he married, his Hopes were at an End, and on the other hand, he could not be happy without the Lady. In order to extricate himself, he took a Method not very uncommon in those Times ; that is, he married, and kept that Marriage a Secret. By this Lady, he had two Sons, *Peter-Lewis*, and *Alexander*, and a Daughter whose Name was *Constance*. Upon his Return to

Rome,

Rome, as the secret Hiſtory of that Capital reports, he gained the Favour of the Pope beforementioned in ſo high a Degree, by appearing ignorant of a certain Amour, that in 1493, he was honoured with the Purple at the Age of twenty-four. Whatever were the Foibles of his Youth, all Authors allow, that in his more advanced Years he diſcovered Qualities truly worthy of his Dignity, inſomuch, that on the Death of *Clement* VII. when he was advanced to the Age of forty, he was elected his Succeſſor, and took the Name of *Paul* III.

He governed fifteen Years with great Reputation, and in that Space having taken great Care of the Affairs of the Church, he thought it no Diminution of his Character to take ſome of his Family. His Anceſtors had lent very conſiderable Sums to the Apoſtolick Chamber, and were in Poſſeſſion of *Nepi* and *Fraſcati*. The latter being at the very Gates of *Rome*, and affording a Sanctuary to Bankrupts and other flagitious Perſons, it was very inconvenient to the Holy See, the Pope therefore propoſed to give up theſe Places, and to extinguiſh all Debts due to his Family, in caſe the Cardinals would conſent to grant the Duchies of *Parma* and *Placentia* to a certain Perſon he ſhould name, who ſhould reſide in one of thoſe Cities, and hold it as a Fief of the Church; which being aſſented to in a Conſiſtory, his Son *Peter-Lewis* had the Inveſtiture of thoſe Duchies on the 12th of *Auguſt* 1545, to hold to him and his Heirs Male for ever, and was inſtalled on the 19th of the ſame Month, in the Cathedral Church of *Placentia*, by Cardinal *Marino Grimani* the Apoſtolick Legate. It may not be amiſs to obſerve, that before this young Prince attained theſe Duchies, his Father had beſtowed upon him thoſe of *Caſtro* and *Cammerini*, which lie within the Eccleſiaſtical State, as we have already ſhewn, in ſpeaking of the temporal Dominions annexed to the Popedom; but theſe, as they were acquired, ſo they were loſt by Uſury, one of his Succeſſors borrowing a large Sum of Money from the Apoſtolick Chamber, and by computing Intereſt upon Intereſt the Debt was at laſt raiſed ſo high, that the Church re-entered for Want of Payment, and annexed theſe Countries once more to the Papal Domains.

This Misfortune befell the Houſe of *Farneſe*, under the Reign of *Ranuccio* II. the direct Deſcendent of *Peter-Lewis* beforementioned. He was a wiſe, and in other Reſpects, a fortunate Prince, governing his Subjects with great Moderation and Mildneſs. He was thrice married, firſt to *Margaret* or *Savoy*, by whom he had no Children; Secondly, to *Iſabella* of
Eſte,

Efte, by whom he had a Son *Edward,* and two Daughters; laftly, to *Mary* of *Efte,* his fecond Wife's Sifter, by whom he had *Francifco* and *Antonio. Edward,* hereditary Prince of *Parma,* married *Dorothea Sophia* of *Newburgh,* Daughter to the Elector *Palatine,* in 1690, by whom he had an only Daughter, *Elizabeth,* born *October* 25, 1692, and on the 5th of *September* following died, in the Life-time of his Father. *Francifco,* Prince of *Parma,* married his Brother's Widow, who became thereby Duchefs of *Parma,* upon the Demife of her Father-in-law, which happened in 1694, and the new Duke brought up his Brother's Daughter as his own.

Francis I. Duke of *Parma* and *Placentia,* was a Prince of his Father's Temper, and by a wife and prudent Adminiftration of his Affairs, kept his Dominions in a great meafure from fuffering as the reft of *Italy* did, during the long War on Account of the *Spanifh* Succeffion; but after the Peace of *Utrecht,* and the Death of the Queen of *Spain,* he liftened with great Satisfaction to the Propofal of a Marriage between *Philip* V. and his Niece and adopted Daughter the Princefs *Elizabeth,* who was looked upon as the Heirefs of *Parma* and *Tufcany,* her Great Grand-mother being *Magaret de Medicis,* Daughter to Duke *Cofmo* II. and this notwithftanding Prince *Antonio Farnefe* was living, becaufe it was believed that he had an invincible Averfion to Marriage, to which, if there be Truth in fome *Italian* Conjectures, this Manner of difpofing his Niece might contribute. However that Matter might be, the Succeffion was looked upon as a Thing out of Difpute at leaft on that Side; for it was known that the Peope intended to queftion it, and that it was not very agreeable to the Emperor.

But upon the Demife of *Francis* Duke of *Parma* in 1727, and the Acceffion of Prince *Antonio,* Things changed their Appearance. The new Duke was no fooner poffeffed of that Dignity, than he declared his Diflike of Marriage atofe from the Narrownefs of his Circumftances, while he was a younger Brother, but that now he was a fovereign Prince, and the laft Heir Male of his Family, he judged it incumbent upon him to prevent the Extinction of the Houfe of *Farnefe.* He married accordingly *Henrietta de Efte,* Daughter to the Duke of *Modena,* but had notwithftanding the Misfortune to die without Iffue, *January* 20, 1731, though upon his Demife it was given out, that the Duchefs his Relict was with Child; but this being quickly found to be without any Foundation, the Royal Infant Don *Carlos,* eldeft Son to his Catholick Majefty

by

by the Princess *Elizabeth*, Heiress of the House of *Farnese*, entered into the quiet Possession. The old Duchess Dowager *Sophia Dorothea*, Relict of Duke *Francis*, and of his elder Brother Prince *Edward*, Mother to the Queen Dowager of *Spain*, and Grandmother to the Royal Infants *Carlos* and *Philip*, and of the Cardinal *Bourbon*, died about the Close of the last War, in a very advanced Age. As for the younger Dowager, Widow of *Antonio Farnese*, the last Duke of *Parma*, she married in 1740, Prince *Leopold* of *Hesse Darmstadt*, with whom she resides at *Placentia*.

As to the Extent, Situation and Value of the Countries which form the Settlement of the Infant Don *Philip*, we are to consider the following Particulars. The Duchies of *Parma* and *Placentia* form together a very considerable Sovereignty; in Length, from West to East, they are about sixty *English* Miles, and their Breadth from South to North is about forty. On the West they are bounded by the Dominions of the Empress Queen and the King of *Sardinia*; on the South, by the Territories of the Republick of *Genoa*; on the East by the Duchies of *Modena* and *Reggio*; and on the North they are divided by the River *Po* from the Duchies of *Mantua* and *Milan*. As to the Climate it is without Exception, being equally healthy and pleasant; and with this the Soil likewise corresponds, which is wonderfully fruitful; the Vallies abound with all Kinds of Fruit, with rich Pastures and excellent Vineyards; and in the Mountains they have both Copper and Silver Mines; the Inhabitants have prodigious Herds of black Cattle, and also numerous Flocks of Sheep; the first enable them to make the best Cheese in *Italy*, and, in the Opinion of many, in *Europe*; and the latter furnish them with vast Quantities of very fine Wool. The Cities of *Parma* and *Placentia* are the only Places of any Consequence in the Royal Infant's Dominions; the former is an old irregular Place, and not very large, meanly fortified, but commanded by a Castle of some Strength; the latter is larger, better situated, more beautiful, and fuller of People, within a very small Distance of the *Po*, which is a great Convenience.

While these Countries were held from the See of *Rome*, the Dukes of *Parma* paid an annual Acknowledgment of ten thousand Ducats; at present they are considered as Fiefs of the Empire, and their Possessor applies for and receives his Investiture from his Imperial Majesty in the same Manner with other Princes. The Revenues have been formerly computed at six hundred thousand Crowns, but it may be doubted, whether in
their

their prefent Situation the People can raife above two Thirds of that Sum; yet a few Years of Peace, under a gentle Adminiftration, would quickly reftore them to their former Condition. It is fuppofed that thefe Duchies may maintain a regular Force of about fix thoufand Men, without any great Detriment either to Prince or People.

As to the additional Duchy of *Guaftalla*, we have already fhewn how it came into the Hands of the Emperor by the Death of the laft Duke of the Houfe of *Gonzagua*. It is in Truth nothing more than a Diftrict of the Duchy of *Mantua*, which was given as a Provifion for a younger Branch of the ducal Houfe, and is confequently a Thing of no great Importance. It is, as we obferved before, feparated from the reft of the Royal Infant's Dominions by a Part of the Duke of *Modena*'s Country, but notwithftanding this, the Commucation by the *Po* is always open. *Guaftalla* is a very neat and flourifhing Place, and the Country about it both fruitful and pleafant; the Revenue is computed at fifty or fixty thoufand Crowns. Thefe are all the Territories that the Royal Infant poffeffes in *Italy*; and though in themfelves they may be juftly reckoned very confiderable, yet when we reflect on the Royal Birth, the high Pretenfions, and illuftrious Marriage of his Royal Highnefs, one cannot help admiring at the ftrange Profufion of Men and Money with which this inconfiderable Settlement was purchafed.

This appears ftill ftranger, when we remember that all thefe Territories are inland Places; nay, that there is not fo much as a fingle navigable River in the Dominions of this Prince, the *Po* excepted, and that only wafhes them. From hence one may be eafily tempted to fufpect, that when this Eftablifhment was accepted for the Royal Infant, it muft have been under fome Expectation of freeing it from thofe Reftrictions with which the Ceffions contained in the Definitive Treaty of *Aix la Chapelle* were made; enlarging it either by Purchafe or otherwife, and thereby opening a more direct Correfpondence with *Spain*, than it is poffible to carry on at prefent through the Territories of the State of *Genoa*; though for the facilitating this, it is faid, that a great Road is making through the Mountains from the Duchy of *Parma* directly to *Seftri de Ponente*, which may be a good temporary Expedient, till fomething better can be contrived, or till fome lucky Opportunity makes way for its being carried into Execution. It is indeed true, that joining as it does to the Territories of *Modena* on one Side, and to thofe of the Republick
before-

beforementioned on the other, the Royal Infant might eafily receive, In cafe of need, whatever Affiftance thefe Neighbours of his would be inclined to give; but then all their Force taken together, would be infufficient to cover fo open a Country againft the Troops of the Houfe of *Auftria*, if upon any Occafion a Rupture fhould happen hereafter.

We have thus given a general Sketch of the Situation that this Prince is in, and many of our Readers may poffibly look upon that as fufficient. But Time will quickly convince them of the contrary, and that nothing deferves to be more maturely weighed, than what may be expected from the Fermentation that ever fince the Peace has been, from its Effects, apparent enough in *Italy*; and to fay the Truth, moft of the Troubles that have difturbed *Europe* fince the Conclufion of the Treaty of *Utrecht*, have been hatched in that Quarter. Should we incline to penetrate the Reafon of this, it would not be found difficult to find, and which is ftill more to our Purpofe, it would appear to fubfift and act as ftrongly now as ever; neither ought this to furprize us, if we reflect on the great Events that have happened in our own Time, where the next News from this Part of the World, upon the making and executing a Peace, has ufually been new Claims, new Negotiations, and in a fhort Space of Time, new Preparations for the Commencement of a frefh War. It may therefore be very expedient to make a Trial, whether it may not be poffible to difcover fomething of thefe Matters before they are conveyed to us in foreign Gazettes.

Firft with refpect to the Reftrictions by which the Royal Infant Don *Philip* is, or may be thought cramped in his Poffeffions. We know that at *Aix la Chapelle*, the *Spanifh* Plenipotentiary expreffed very clearly the Diflike of the Court of *Madrid* to thofe Refervations, that eftablifh a Reverfionary Right in the two Crowns, to the Ceffion made of this Settlement for Don *Philip*; and though this Difficulty was then got over, yet we are no Strangers to the Interpofition in confequence of which it was got over; nor is at all inconfiftent with the Lights of Reafon or Experience, to believe, that it was got over by the Suggeftion, that tho' an abfolute Poffeffion could not be gained at that Time, yet it might be procured by a fubfequent Negotiation. Of this we have had many broad Hints fince, and therefore we may take it for granted, that unlefs fome unforefeen Change fhould happen in the Syftem of certain Courts, this Point

will

will certainly be pursued till it is accomplished some way or other.

But this is not all, there has been a Protestation in Form upon a late Occasion, as well as upon others, in favour of the See of *Rome*, from whence, as the original Right of the House of *Farnese* was derived, it is not easy to see how its Claim to these Duchies has been vacated. On the other hand, such is the Spirit of a certain Court, that we have no great Cause to suppose she will suffer these Pretensions to subsist, for fear that some time or other an Opportunity should offer for enforcing them. It is true indeed, that there is no Prospect of any such thing at present, but the Politicks of the Court of *Rome* are deservedly famous, and the very Care that the Popes have taken to keep up this Claim upon every Occasion, sufficiently indicates that they would not suffer an Opportunity to slip, in case any such Opportunity should offer. The Desire therefore of emancipating this dear-bought Settlement even from this dormant Pretension, is a Point that will hardly escape the Eye of a Court, that has been ever famous for Jealousy, in a Degree not at all inferior to its Ambition.

We are yet farther to consider, that it was purely to avoid this Claim of the See of *Rome*, that *Parma* was acknowledged to be a Fief of the *Roman* Empire. Duke *Francis*, Uncle to the Queen Dowager of *Spain*, when the Emperor levied Contributions from his Dominions, upon Pretence of their being Fiefs, exclaimed against it as an Act of Violence and Injustice, the Pope also protested against it upon the same Motives. Since that Time his Successors have seen things in quite a different Light, or rather have been under a Necessity of admitting what their Predecessor so warmly disputed. As things now stand, there can be no Dispute that Homage is due to the Emperor, and that his Investiture is necessary to the Possessor of these as of other Fiefs. But possibly there may come a Time when this may be accounted either a Grievance, or at least an Inconvenience, unless in the ensuing Congress at *Cremona*, or where-ever else it shall be held, some Method can be found to settle it to the mutual Satisfaction of all Parties; and tho' this may be a thing far enough from being impossible, yet one may venture, without fearing to sin against Truth, to hazard a Suspicion that it will not be without its Difficulties.

In the next place, the Augmentations of this Settlement which may be endeavoured, deserve our particular Notice. We have

have very good Reason to apprehend at least, that after such violent and repeated Struggles, so long and bloody a War, and since the Conclusion of the Peace, such a Train of secret and silent Negotiations, some Enlargement of the Royal Infant's Territories is a Point still at Heart with those who procured his Settlement, and who in going so far to obtain that, however unequal to the Cost with which is was obtained, gave an Earnest to the World that they meant to go further, and not to desist from their Enterprize, till attended with a Success proportionable to their Characters who have embarked in it. Let us then consider, whether from the Lights afforded us by these historical Memoirs, and the Hints that have been given us as to the Tendency of those secret Negociations beforementioned, we may not be able to form some Guess as to the Nature of these Arguments, and the Methods which may be possibly practised in order to compass them ? It is very unlikely that we should be able to go to the Bottom of this Matter, or to point out exactly, and in their proper Order, the very Steps that will be taken in this Business: But tho' we should not do this, yet we need not despair of giving the Reader some Satisfaction, since in pointing out most of the Roads that are possible, we can hardly miss those that the active Politicians will think practicable, and what may not be atchieved in our Times, it is very likely may occupy the Attention of Posterity; at least we have past Experience on the Side of this Conjecture.

The Royal Infant's Settlement was hardly fixed, before it was observed that some Alterations, Cessions, and Exchanges would be necessary, in order to accommodate things between that young Prince and his Neighbours. We have touched upon this Subject before, and shewn that a Part of the Duke of *Modena*'s Dominions would be exceedingly commodious, and that it might not be impracticable to assign his Serene Highness an Equivalent with which he might be well contented. Something of the like Sort might be expedient also with respect to the Empress Queen, there being a small Portion of the Duchy of *Guastalla* that cannot well be separated from her hereditary Countreis, and it is certainly of much too little Consequence to be worth disputing about; these, taking them altogether, though they may be convenient and even necessary Things, are of no mighty Importance, and there is nothing very unlikely in supposing, that for the Sake of mutual Ease and Security, such Matters may be settled in a Congress to the Satisfaction of all Parties.

But

But there has been an Augmentation mentioned of quite another Nature, and that is the Island of *Corsica*, which was for some time looked upon as the Fiction of Gazette-Writers: The *French* were lately in Possession of that Island; the Malecontents seem to be determined in their Resolution, never to submit again to what they stile their old Yoke. On the other hand, indeed, there has been a Regulation settled between the Republick and the *Corsicans*, under the Mediation of his Most Christian Majesty, with great Care and Deliberation; yet if this should prove unacceptable to either Party, or if Objections should be made to it on both Sides, the admitting of a Treaty of Purchase, in order to the Republick's parting with its Sovereignty, may be thought a proper Expedient, or at least it could never have been introduced in a less exceptionable Way. In that Case, however, some further Stepts must be taken before it can be connected with the Royal Infant's present Settlement; but if this grand Purchase is once made, that will not be absolutely impracticable. There is a small Tract of Country between the Duchy of *Parma* and the Sea, that would in such a Case be a very valuable Acquisition; and this, no doubt, would be obtained by Contract or Exchange; and thus the Royal Infant would acquire a large, and, in part, an independent Settlement, and it may be a more splendid Title; yet as we have seen strange Changes, it may not perhaps be a chimerical Conjecture, that after all these Junctions and Purchases, the whole might be thought a proper Equivalent for another Territory in *Italy*, of which his Brother Don *Carlos* once wore the Title of hereditary Prince.

Before we quit this Subject, it may not be amiss just to hint, that the former Dukes of *Parma* thought themselves very ill treated by the Pope in the Affair of *Castro*; and once by the Interposition of the Crown of *France*, that Affair was brought so far, that upon Payment of the original Debt and Interest, the Pope engaged himself to restore those Territories, tho' upon a Tender of the Money he disengaged himself again, alledging that it was not in his Power. I have before observed, that this Business was compromised by Treaty with the House of *Austria*, when the Duchies of *Parma* and *Placentia* were in the Possession of the late Emperor *Charles* the Sixth; but now they are in other Hands, that Claim may be revived, and perhaps enforced, when other Points of greater Consequence are settled. Thus we have taken a View of the several possible Systems of Augmentation, and of the Methods by which they must be acquired, Time will speedily shew us which will be first brought on the Carpet; and by Degrees there is very little Doubt that we shall

hear

hear of all the reft, for one Augmentation will facilitate another, and Pretenfions that might have been ridiculous for a little Duke to make, will appear of great Confequence, when confidered as the Demands of a very confiderable King.

Thefe political Difquifitions on the prefent State of the Dominions and Pretenfions of the Houfe of *Bourbon* in *Italy*, will affift us much in forming an Idea of that new Sçene of Negotiation that is at prefent on foot, and which at this Juncture is fo great a Myftery, that very few feem to know what to make of it, but by Degrees it will open, and expand itfelf, fo as to become very perceptible, and then we fhall be no longer in the Dark as to our Concern in it. The Ballance of *Italy* will always retain its Connection with the Ballance of Power in *Europe*; fo that it is a vain Thing to imagine, that it can be either altered by a War, or fettled by a Peace, without Prejudice to the Maritime Powers, and confequently without their being obliged to trouble themfelves about it. It is true indeed, that it is, and muft be the Intereft of the King of *Sardinia*, more efpecially to keep a fteady Attention to that Ballance; and if the Treaty of *Worms* had been effectually executed, that alone would have been a fufficient Security; he muft have taken care of our Interefts, becaufe it is certain he will never defert his own. But the Cafe is much altered now, and remains ftill in a State of Alteration, which when or where it will ftop, is not in the Breaft of Man to determine.

Let us next proceed to the Republicks in *Italy*, upon the State of which we fhall be much more concife; and, that what we have to fay may be with the more Eafe retained, we will take them in the Order of Time, in which they were erected.

S E C T. VII.

The Prefent State and Political Interefts of the Republick of VENICE.

THE Glory of the *Venetian* State is at prefent indeed much inferior to what it was, when without Affiftance fhe was a Match for the whole *Ottoman* Power by Land and Sea, and loft nothing of her Courage, and but very little of her Territories, by the famous League of *Cambray*, when rather out of Envy, than from any better Caufe, the greateft Powers in *Europe* were allied againft her.

But

But tho' it be true, that the Republick is not what she has been, that her Dominions are reduced within narrower Bounds, so that except what she possesses on the *Terra Firma* of *Italy*, in *Dalmatia*, and a few inconsiderable Islands, she has nothing left of those extensive Territories that contributed to enrich her Subjects by their Trade, and gave her so considerable a Rank amongst the Powers of *Europe*; yet she is still Mistress of enough, not only to deserve Notice, but also to be regarded as one of the most considerable Potentates in *Italy*, and most illustrious Republicks in *Europe*.

It is highly to the Honour of this State, that for upwards of twelve Centuries she has preserved her Freedom, and for a great Part of that Time has lived under the same Government, without suffering any of those dreadful Revolutions by which many of her powerful Neighbours have been involved in Blood and Confusion. This has justly given a high Reputation to the Wisdom of her Senators, who by their great Policy and wonderful Secrecy, have been able through so long a Track of Time, to guard with equal Diligence and Success against foreign Confederacies and domestic Conspiracies, many of which they have defeated, when laid with the deepest Cunning, and supported with no inconsiderable Strength.

Her very Losses are so far from reflecting Discredit on the Republick, that on the contrary, they do her the greatest Honour in the Sentiments of those who are capable of forming a right Judgment of History, and know how to distinguish properly in respect to Causes and Events. The long War in Defence of *Candia* against the *Turks*, exhausted the Treasures, and weakened the Power of this State to a Degree, that she has not been able to recover; but that War was continued for many Years against the whole Strength of the *Ottoman* Empire by Sea and Land, and was almost as fatal to the *Turks* as to her; for they too have been declining in Power and Reputation ever since: So that she might be truly stiled in that respect the Bulwark of *Europe*, to the Safety of which she contributed much more than she suffered by the Losses, that by the Fortune of War she sustained during that famous Contention.

The common Opinion that she continues still to decline, and that the very Being of the Republick is in Danger from a slow Consumption, has been perhaps taken up without due Attention, and for want of having just Notions of the wise and solid Maxims by which her Government is conducted. For tho' it be true, that she is in no Condition to maintain such a War

as

as that of *Candia*, yet it is no lefs true, that as Things are now circumftanced, fhe has very little Reafon to fear it.

In the two laft Wars with the *Turks*, fhe fufficiently demonftrated, that tho' her Forces were much weaken'd, fhe was far from having loft her former Spirit, or from wanting fuch a Power as was neceffary for her Defence; and the noble Statue erected to the Honour of the late Field Marfhal *Schulemberg* in the great Square of *Corfu*, which he fo glorioufly defended, will remain a perpetual Monument of the Bravery of her Troops, as well as of her Zeal and Gratitude to that intrepid Officer, which it may be hoped will not a little contribute to procure a Succeffion of Generals as worthy and as fortunate.

Befides all this, it ought to be remember'd, that fhe is now better fecured againft the *Turks* by her perpetual Alliance with the Houfe of *Auftria* than in former Ages; and if we alfo reflect, that in cafe the latter at any time break with the *Turks*, in virtue of that Alliance, they are fure of being fupported by the *Ruffians*, it will be fufficiently evident, that the *Venetians* have much lefs to fear than they had in former Days. Since the Peace of *Paffarowitz*, therefore, which was concluded on the 10th of *July* 1718, they have remained very quiet; and as they have very wifely avoided taking any Share in thofe Difputes that have perplexed *Europe*, they at the fame time have thought it proper to keep up a numerous Body of Forces, in order to render their Neutrality refpected.

That the Reader may perceive, what we have advanced in relation to this Republick is founded in Truth, it may not be amifs to give a fhort Account of the Countries fhe poffeffes. In the firft place, the noble City of *Venice*, and the Iflands about it, which are fo populous, have fo many Manufactures, and ftill carry on fo great a Trade, more efpecially whenever the other Powers of *Italy* are at War, and the Subjects of the Republick enjoy the Benefit of her Neutrality, that the Revenue drawn from them by the State, amounts annually to three Millions of Ducats.

On the *Terra Firma* or Continent of *Italy*, fhe poffeffes the *Trevifan*, the *Paduan*, the *Vicentin*, the *Veroneze*, the *Bregamafc*, the Territory of *Brefcia*, the City of *Crema* and its Diftrict, and the *Polefin*; they have alfo a great Part of *Friuli*, of *Iftria*, of *Dalmatia* and *Albania*; and they ftill preferve the Iflands of *Corfu*, *Zante*, *Cerigo*, *Finnes*, *Curzola* and *Cefalonia*: All thefe Countries are rich and fruitful, and the Inhabitants drive a very great Trade in the *Levant*, as well as in other Parts of *Europe*.

The

The entire Revenue of the Republick is computed at about eight Millions of Ducats, and the annual Expence does not commonly exceed half that; so that in Time of Peace they are constantly laying up large Sums. Before the fatal War of *Candia* they had in their Treasury fifteen Millions of Ducats in ready Money, exclusive of the famous Gold Chain, to which they annually added some Links, which forty Porters could hardly carry, and which on certain Festivals was extended crofs the Square of St. *Mark*, for the Entertainment of the People. As they have now enjoyed Peace thirty Years, it may be presumed that their Coffers are again pretty full, so that upon any emergent Necessity, they would be able to make much greater Efforts than is commonly imagined.

As to the Government of *Venice*, it is so well known, that we need not describe it. We shall only observe, that it is a pure Aristocracy, and though the Duke has the Title of Prince, yet the Majesty of the Republick resides in the Senate. The great Maxim of this wise Body, is to manage the Government with the utmost Frugality, to encourage Trade as much as possible, and to preserve Peace as long as they are able.

They have always a constant Eye upon the *Turks*, and have excellent Intelligence even in the Seraglio itself; so that they can hardly be surprized; and in Time of Peace they carry on a prodigious Commerce in all Parts of that Empire. They are jealous of the *Pope*, with whom they have many ancient Grounds of Dispute, which is the Reason that they exclude all Ecclesiasticks from their Counsels. They are obliged to live in strict Friendship with the Emperor, tho' it is certain, that they are not at all desirous of seeing the Power of the House of *Austria* extend itself in *Italy*. They were heretofore jealous of the Crown of *Spain* for the same Reason; and very probably this Spirit would revive, if Don *Philip* should gain by Purchase any more considerable Establishment in that Country; for the keeping even the Ballance of which, they are as much or more concerned than any other Potentate.

In former Times the Republick was strongly inclined to favour *France*; the Ambassador of this Crown received very high Honours at *Venice*, and generally speaking, the *Venetian* Cardinals joined those of the *French* Faction in the Conclave; yet there is no Reason to presume, as some do from hence, that the Republick is governed by these Notions still, for the Circumstances of Things being changed, according to the settled Rules of their Policy, the Conduct of the Republick must change also; and the very same Principles that induced her to

f . .

fide with the *French* in the Conclave, will engage her now to act against them, and in Favour of the House of *Austria*, because the Family of *Bourbon* is become too potent.

It may indeed be surmised that this State, affecting Peace so much as she does, might be awed by the Power of *France*; but of this there is no sort of Appearance. For when *Lewis* XIV. about 1711, declared at *Rome*, Cardinal *Ottoboni*, a Subject of the Republick's, Protector of the Crown of *France*, and his Eminence had accepted that Dignity, contrary to the Maxims of the *Venetian* State, which never permits any that have been in their Service, to enter into that of other Princes; they proceeded without Delay, and without Ceremony, to deprive him and all his Relations of the Privileges of Nobility, and to banish them their Dominions. We may therefore take it for granted, that the Grandeur of this House will be very far from being acceptable to the *Venetians*.

They have always maintained, and very probably will continue to maintain, a close Friendship and strict Alliance with the *Swiss*, there being a mutual Connection between their Interests; and each of them having frequent Occasions, from the Vicinity of their Territories, to ask and receive Favours from the other.

They are likewise bound to live in good Intelligence with the Monarch of the *Two Sicilies*, and with the Grand Duke of *Tuscany*, on Account of the Difficulties to which their Commerce would be unavoidably liable, in case of a Rupture, or even a Difference with either. There was heretofore a great Coolness between the Republick and the Dukes of *Savoy*, on account that the latter assumed the Title of King of *Cyprus*; to which also the Doge of *Venice* pretends: And it is difficult to believe how much this slight Punctilio kept these two Powers at a Distance. But since the Duke of *Savoy* has become King of *Sardinia*, and the Situation of Things in *Italy* is so much changed, that the Balance is almost constantly in his Hands, the *Venetians* have altered their Measures; and it is certain, that at present there is a very good Correspondence between that Monarch and the Republick.

The long and warm Disputes that have happened heretofore between this Republick and that of *Genoa*, has occasioned such an Inveteracy as is scarce to be conceived; grounded also upon a Punctilio, the latter desiring to be regarded as an Equal, and the former treating her upon all Occasions as an Inferior. This Spleen was carried farther, during the fatal War with *Candia*, than one would have expected from the *Venetian* Prudence; for when the *Genoese* offered very considerable Assistance at a Time when *Venice* wanted it most, upon Condition that an Equality should subsist for the future, they rejected the Proposition with Disdain,

and

and chose rather to run the Hazard of total Destruction, than to receive Assistance upon such Terms.

Yet even this Quarrel seems now to be laid asleep, if not extinguished; for during the last Distress of the *Genoese*; it is very certain that the *Venetians* interposed not only with much Civility, but with great Earnestness at the Court of *Vienna*; and if we may depend upon the Reports that have been current in *Italy*, the *Genoese* received pecuniary Supplies of a Nature that sufficiently declared the Depth of the Purse from whence they were drawn, though it was not held convenient to embark openly in their Quarrel.

Thus by a brief Enumeration of Facts, we have shewn, that notwithstanding what has passed heretofore, the Republick of *Venice* is still in a Condition to support herself, and in no Danger either from the Power of her Enemies, or of her Neighbours; that if she loves Peace it is from wise and prudent Motives, and not from Timidity; that as she forms no Pretensions upon her Neighbours, so she is inclined to live with them in the greatest Harmony imaginable; and in a Word, that as she has no Views of Conquest for herself, she is bound by Interest as well as led by Inclination to give all the Opposition possible to such as from ambitious Motives disturb the Peace of, *Italy*.

The Consideration of this to those who maturely weigh Things of so important a Nature will appear of no small Consequence. For as no Government in the Universe understands its own Interests better, or pursues them more closely than the *Venetian* Senate, so it is a mighty thing to be secure, that no Temptation will ever engage this State to violate Justice, or aim at increasing her Wealth or her Dominions at the Expence of any of her Neighbours. Besides there is a moral Certainty that if the BALLANCE in this part of Christendom should be apparently in Danger, this Commonwealth would take the Part of the Oppressed, and venture all for preserving the Freedom of *Italy*. Add to this, that the *Venetian* Ambassadors in the several Courts of *Europe* never want the Means of insinuating their Sentiments to the Ministers, and giving such true Lights in respect to the Concerns of *Italy*, as may prevent false Steps being taken, and powerfully persuade the taking those that are true, neither of which would otherwise be brought to pass.

SECT.

SECT. VIII.

The Present State and Political Interests of the Republick of Genoa.

THIS Republick made anciently a very good Figure, not only confidered as a free State of *Italy*, but in refpect to *Europe* in general. Her Dominions were large, her Commerce extenfive, and her Naval Power extremely formidable. But according to the Nature of all Commonwealths, Fluctuations and Revolutions in Government have been very common here; and to them it has been chiefly owing, that *Genoa* has fallen from what fhe was, and been driven at feveral times to fubmit herfelf, not only to the Emperors and Kings of *France*, but to the Marquiffes of *Montferrat*, the Dukes of *Milan*, and other little Princes.

In fhort, the Characters given by ancient Writers of this Nation under the Name of *Ligurians*, have been always, and at all times, but too applicable to the *Genoefe*; who from a factious Difpofition, and almoft perpetual Difaffection to the Form of Government under which they lived, have kept themfelves in continual Difquiet, and loft unaccountably the Advantages derived to them from their Trade, and from their Situation, which might otherwife have enabled them to attain what feems after all to have been the utmoft Extent of their Wifhes, a Power as great, and an Eftablifhment as folid, as that of their Sifter Republick, *Venice*.

As to their prefent Condition, by which I mean the Form of Government they are now under, they owe it entirely to the Virtue of *Andrew Doria*, who in 1527 refcued them out of the Hands of the *French*, and refufing the Sovereignty offered him, fixed their Condition as a free State, regulating their ancient Nobility, to as to confift in twenty-eight Families, and their new Nobles in twenty-four. It is not neceffary for us to enter into the Particulars of their Hiftory from that Time, becaufe they are well known; and therefore we fhall content ourfelves with faying, that if it had not been for the Factions between their old and new Nobility, which in 1573 rofe fo high as to occafion a Civil War, and their Difputes with the Duke of *Savoy*, which engaged them in feveral Wars, they might have from that Period to this enjoyed Peace and Plenty.

In

In 1684 they were severely chastised by *Lewis* XIV. on account of some Offence he had taken to their Conduct, or rather from a Vanity of shewing his Naval Force by bombarding *Genoa*, and obliging the Doge, and four of the principal Senators, to repair to *Versailles*, and make a Submission as little honourable to him as to the Republick. In the War occasioned by the *Spanish* Succession they were but indifferently treated by the Allies, and by the *French*; but at the Close of it, they made themselves some amends by purchasing from the late Emperor *Charles* VI. the Marquisate of *Final*, to the Possession of which they had long and ardently aspired.

We have heard so much of this Matter already, and it is possible may hear so much more of it hereafter, that it is requisite we should say something of it here; and as we have no kind of Prepossession in favour of either Party, we shall state the Fact in few Words, and as fairly as it is possible. The *Genoese* had very old Pretensions upon this Country, in Right of a Mortgage by the Princes to whom it belonged; but under colour of a Felony committed by one of those Princes, it was seized by the House of *Austria*, and belonged to the *Spanish* Branch of that Family. It was by this means that it came with the rest of the *Italian* Dominions of that House into the Hands of the late Emperor, and on his Behalf the Duke of *Savoy* put a Garrison into it. But upon the Sale of this Marquisate by his Imperial Majesty in 1713, the *Piedmontese* Garrison in *Final* evacuated it, and three hundred *Corsicans* took Possession of it for the *Genoese*, who kept it till the last War.

But it is also necessary to observe, that the Dukes of *Savoy* had likewise Pretensions upon this Marquisate, though they were not in a Condition to assert, or make them good; and therefore on the Conclusion of the Treaty of *Worms*, as we have shewn in another Place, his *Sardinian* Majesty stipulated, that upon giving the *Genoese* Satisfaction for the Money laid out in the Purchase of this Country, it should belong to him. This the Republick considered as so great an Injury, that they entered into a Treaty with the *French* and *Spaniards* for their own Security, and for the Preservation of their Dominions; the Consequences of which are very well known.

But with respect to this Marquisate, and the Disposition of this Country by the Treaty of *Worms*, there are three Points that deserve well to be considered. The *first* is, That whatever Rights the Dukes of *Savoy* had to this Country, they could not be prejudiced by the Emperor's Sale of it to the
Genoese;

Genoese; and therefore there was no Injuftice in the King of *Sardinia*'s taking Advantage of that critical Conjuncture to avail himfelf of the Pretenfions of his Family.

The *fecond* is, That the *Genoefe* were to have a Satisfaction for this Marquifate; and tho' it might be true, that both their Interefts and their Inclinations led them to prefer the Poffeffion of *Final* to any Equivalent that could be given them for it, yet this ought not to be a Rule to other Powers, whofe Interefts and Inclinations were on the Side of his *Sardinian* Majefty. This will appear ftill plainer, if we confider that it is not out of any real Affection for the Republick of *Genoa*, that the Houfe of *Bourbon* contended for maintaining her in the Poffeffion of this Country, but for the Sake of keeping her in Dependence, and keeping at the fame Time *Final* from the King of *Sardinia*. The Allies therefore, who had the fame Reafon to wifh this Country in the Hands of that Prince, had the fame Right to employ their Power for the Accomplifhment of their Wifhes in this Refpect.

The *third* Point is, That the Defire of making this Alteration was not, as has been fuppofed, either wanton or arbitrary; on the contrary, it appears to have been founded upon Principles of good Policy; for on the one hand, as it would have immediately opened a Communication between the Dominions of his *Sardinian* Majefty and the Maritime Powers, which is apparently of the higheft Confequence for the Prefervation of the Tranquility and Ballance of Power in *Italy*; fo on the other hand, it was provided that it fhould be equally beneficial to Commerce, by an exprefs Stipulation that *Final* fhould be made a free Port, in the fame Manner, and for the fame Purpofes, as *Leghorn*.

But none of thefe Confiderations weighing with the *Genoefe*, they ventured the Subverfion of their State for the Sake of preferving this Territory, which neverthelefs was taken from them by the Chance of War, together with *Savona*, which is another fine Port, that they have long ago filled up and rendered ufelefs, for the Sake of confining the Commerce of that Part of *Italy* to their own Harbour; which, how confiftent it is with the Law of Nations, and the general Interest of other trading Countries, I fhall not take upon me to determine. One Thing however is very clear, that a State which confiders nobody's Interest but her own, has no great Reafon to expect that other States would confider her Interest more than their own.

The

The Dominions of this State confist of the Countries extending along the Sea-coaft, on both Sides, from the City of *Genoa*, which are ftiled the Eaftern and Weftern *Rivieras*. This Word in *Italian* fignifies a *Strand*; and indeed the Country is very little better, having high, craggy, and almoft impaffable Mountains behind it. Thefe however are not fo barren as they are reprefented, every little Valley, and indeed every Spot of Ground that will admit of it, being cultivated and improved to the utmoft; fo that Fruits, Oil, and Silk, are raifed here to great Advantage.

The Ifland of *Corfica* belongs alfo to this Republick; it is reckoned three hundred and twenty-five Miles in Circumference. It abounds with all Sorts of Provifions; the Wines are thought tolerable, and if long kept, are little, if at all inferior to thofe of *Spain*. Honey, Wax, and Salt, are the ftaple Commodities of the Country: There are feveral good Fifheries upon its Coafts, and fome Iron Mines in the Heart of the Ifland. The Severity of the *Genoefe* Government on one fide, and the feditious and turbulent Spirit of the Natives on the other, have hitherto hindered *Corfica* from making any Figure in *Europe*; which, if thefe Obftacles were removed, it might certainly do.

The Revenues of the Republick are very far from being confiderable, nor is the Trade thereof near fo great as it was; however both are ftill capable of being recovered. The private Perfons in this City, of great Families, are commonly rich, and have large Eftates, fome in *Naples* and *Sicily*, others in *Spain*, and not a few in the *Italian* Dominions belonging to the Houfe of *Auftria*; which is attended with great Inconveniencies, as throwing them into Interefts inconfiftent with, or directly oppofite to thofe of their Country.

The Conftitution of *Genoa* is of a mixt Nature, but feems from Experience to be but ill-contrived, as having fo much of an Ariftocracy as to make the People uneafy, and yet fo much of a Democracy as to keep up a continual Ferment. The *Doge*, or Duke, is elected every two Years, during which Time he refides in the Palace, is maintained at the publick Expence, has Guards and other Enfigns of Princely Dignity, and twelve Counfellors continually about him, ftiled the *Seignory*, in whom the Majefty of the Republick refides; but with regard to the *Dernier Refort*, or Legiflative Power, it is vefted in the great Council, which confifts of four hundred. And this, in few Words, is a clear Detail of that Gouvernment, which

which some Writers have affected to obscure by long and perplexed Accounts, that are very little to the purpose.

The ruling Maxim in this State, is the maintaining good Government at home, and Peace with all its Neighbours, which if steadily pursued would speedily change the Face of her Affairs; and though there is very little Probability that she should ever recover her former Power or Greatness, yet she might certainly rise to such a Measure of it, as might free her from many Apprehensions of her Neighbours. Her Situation for Trade is so convenient, and in Time of Peace Money is to be had there at so low Interest, that without doubt their Merchants might carry on a much greater Commerce than they do, if they were not so fond of Banking, which though in some measure advantageous, is in other respects very inconvenient to the State. Her Disputes with the King of *Sardinia* has been always detrimental to her Interests, and of late had well nigh been destructive. The Peace of *Aix la Chapelle* has compromised, or rather silenced those Disputes for a Time, which however may possibly make way for some new Alliance truly definitive in that respect, since without it one Power cannot be long easy, or the other secure.

S E C T. IX.

A succinct Account of the Swiss *Cantons, their Allies and Subjects.*

THERE are very few Nations that are less, and yet hardly any in *Europe* deserve to be better known than the *Swiss*. They are placed in a Country which, though surrounded with Rocks, and in a manner inaccessible, yet is very considerable, and of great Consequence from its Situation, as will very fully appear from as succinct a Description of it as can be given.

Their Dominions are bounded on the North by part of *Alsace*, the *Black Forest*, and the Circle of *Suabia*; on the East by the Country of *Tyrol*; on the South by the Duchies of *Savoy* and *Milan*, by the Territories of *Bergamo* and *Brescia*; and on the West by the *Franche Compte*, or, as it is commonly stiled, the County of *Burgundy*.

It appears from hence that they have for Neighbours the Subjects of the House of *Austria*, those of the Crown of *France*, the King of *Sardinia*, and the State of *Venice*. We need no other Account to give us very high Notions of the Force and

Bravery

Bravery of this Nation, than the bare Obfervation, that they have not only preferved their Freedom in Spite, but have been alfo always formidable to the moft potent of their Neighbours: Yet their Country is very far from being large; in Length fome-what lefs than three hundred, and in Breadth very little more than a hundred Miles.

Before we proceed farther, it will be requifite to give fome Account of the Diftribution of thefe People. The Inhabitants of *Switzerland* then may be divided into three Parts: *Firft*, the *Swifs* properly fo called, or the thirteen Cantons; which ftand in the following Order. 1. *Zurich.* 2. *Bern.* 3. *Lucern.* 4. *Wic.* 5. *Switz.* 6. *Underwald.* 7. *Zug.* 8. *Glaris.* 9. *Bazil* or *Bafle.* 10. *Friburg.* 11. *Soluthurn.* 12. *Schaffhaufen.* And 13. *Appenzel.* Of which the Proteftant Cantons are *Zurich, Bern, Bazil,* and *Schaffhaufen,* with above two Thirds of the Canton of *Glaris,* and more than half of *Appenzel*; the People in the reft are all *Roman* Catholicks.

Secondly, The Subjects of the *Switzers* which are either fuch Towns and Bailliages as belong to them all, or to feveral in common, or that depend upon feveral Cantons. Of the for-mer they reckon nine; *viz.* the County of *Baden,* the *Free Villages,* the Counties of *Turgovy, Sargantz,* and *Rhintal,* and the four *Italian* Bailliages of *Lugano, Locarno, Mendrifco,* and *Valmodia*; to which we muft add the three Cities without Ter-ritory, *viz. Boemgarten, Mellingen,* and *Rapperfwail.* The four Bailliages of *Lugano, Locarno, Mendrifco,* and *Valmodia,* were difmembered from the Duchy of *Milan,* and belong to all the Cantons except *Appenzel,* which at that Time was not ad-mitted into the Alliance. Three other Bailliages in *Italy, viz. Bellinzona, Valbrima,* and *Riviera,* were conquered by the Can-tons of *Zurich, Switz,* and *Underwald,* from the Dukes of *Milan.* The little Territory of *Alfax,* and the County of *Werdenbergh,* both feated on the *Rhine,* belong, the former to the Canton of *Zurich,* and the latter to that of *Glaris.* The Bailliage of *Gaf-teren* belongs to the Cantons of *Switz* and *Glaris*; and the Can-tons of *Bern* and *Friburg* poffefs the four Bailliages of *Morat, Gremton, Echelens, Swartzenburg,* which they conquered from the Dukes of *Savoy.*

Thirdly, The Allies of the *Switzers* are the *Grifons,* who are divided into three Leagues, that of the *Grifons,* of the *Houfe* of *God,* and of the *Ten Jurifdictions.* They are partly Proteftants, and partly Papifts, and have alfo a confiderable conquered Country that belongs to them. The Town and County of *Neufchatel,* of which we have fhewn elfewhere the

King

King of *Pruffia* is Sovereign; the Abbot and City of St.
Gall, the little Republick of *Wallais*, which the *Germans* call
Wallis-Land; the City and Republick of *Geneva*; the Town
of *Bienne* or *Biel*, which is allied to the Canton of *Bern*; and
the Town of *Mulhaufen* not far from *Bafil*, to which it is
allied.

It is not to be expected that we fhould enter into a long Detail either Hiftorical or Political, concerning thefe People, for
that would require a confiderable Volume, whereas what we
have to fay about them muft be confined within a very narrow
Compafs. There is hardly one of the Cantons, States, or Cities
beforementioned, that agrees with another in point of Government; and indeed every kind of Government that ever was invented, is to be found amongft them; yet they are all maintained under their refpective Forms, and in their refpective Rights,
from that common Love of Freedom and Juftice, which prevails
generally among the whole Nation.

The greateft Part of their Country is the moft rugged in
its Appearance, and naturally the moft barren in its Soil of any
in *Europe*; and yet by Dint of Labour and Cultivation, they
render it tolerably fruitful. All their Cities are well built, populous, and moft of their Inhabitants live pretty much at their
Eafe, which is owing partly to their Induftry, and partly to their
Frugality. The Gentry of *Switzerland*, notwithftanding what
is commonly reported of them, are, generally fpeaking, tolerably
educated, and from their feeing foreign Countries, commonly
well bred. Their Traders have great Privileges, and fome of
them are in wealthy Circumftances; and as for their Peafants,
they are very hardy and laborious. As their Women are juftly reputed very honeft as well as very good Houfe-wives, fo
they are generally fpeaking very prolifick, and their Country
being but narrow, this lays them under an abfolute Neceffity of
fending out Numbers every Year to feek their Bread in foreign
Countries.

As they are naturally of a martial Difpofition, and accuftomed to Arms from their Youth, they ufually feek fome foreign Service or other; thofe of the Popifh Cantons go into
the *French* and *Spanifh* Pay; thofe of the Proteftants, and not
a few of the Popifh likewife, into that of the *States General*;
but wherever they are, they have the Honour to be accounted as good Troops as any in the World. After fome Years
Service more or lefs, according to their Contracts, the private
Men return home, though their Corps remain ftill in foreign

H h

Service,

Service, and are from time to time filled up with fresh Recruits.

It is owing to these People that have served abroad, both Officers and Soldiers, that the *Swiss* are never at a loss for as large and well disciplined an Army as any Government in *Europe* can raise, which are at the same time the Guardians of their own Liberty, and the Protectors of their Neighbours Freedom. Neither is their Power grounded only on Opinion, for they have defended themselves at different Times against most of the great Powers in *Europe*, and though they have been sometimes outwitted, yet they were never beaten, or reduced to demand Peace by any Power whatever; so that they may be justly considered, taking in their Situation and their Militia, as the most unconquerable People in *Europe*.

It is very difficult, perhaps hardly possible, to make a just Computation of the Force of the *Swiss*. Some say, that the Canton of *Bern* alone can bring into the Field one hundred thousand Men; but those who say this allow, that they could not maintain them for any Time. Things are much changed with this Nation from what they were formerly; for they have now several good Fortresses, though heretofore they had none. Many of the Gentry of *Switzerland* are very able Statesmen, as well as experienced Officers, and such in former Times were very scarce. Several of the Cantons are now very rich, and besides vast Sums that they have locked up at home, have also great Wealth in foreign Banks, and particularly in our Funds. Every great City is well furnished with Artillery, and at *Bern* and *Zurich* they have Field and Battering Trains of Brass Cannon, than which there are few better in *Europe*.

Yet with all this Force they are not in the least formidable to those that live near them, since they are without doubt the very best Neighbours in the World; so void of Ambition, that they have no Idea of Conquest, such Lovers of Justice, that the very Report of Oppression will bring them to the Relief of the Distressed. By this means the City of *Geneva* has been often, and will probably be always protected against two very formidable Powers, one the most enterprizing, and the other the most ambitious in *Europe*.

Those who have treated of the Interest of the *Swiss*, seem to think that they may be some Time or other in Danger from *France*; but of this there seems to be at present very little Appearance. For in the first place, it is not easy to conceive why
the

the *French* should quarrel with them, since as themselves allow, and indeed all the World knows, the *Swiss* Troops in their Pay make the Flower of their Infantry. It is in the next place very difficult to apprehend why the *Swiss* should quarrel with the *French*, from whom it is certain they receive considerable Advantages. It is true, that the *Swiss* are open on the Side of the *Franche Compte*; and it has been thought a great Oversight in this Nation to let the *French* become Masters of it; but in all Probability they depended upon their natural Strength; and within less than half a Century, when *France* talked very big, and threatened in relation to the Sovereignty of *Neufchatel* and *Valingen*, the *Swiss* were so far from showing any Concern about it, that they were ready to have taken up Arms, if *Lewis* XIV. had not immediately changed his Language.

As for the House of *Austria*, they will never attack or offend the *Swiss* for fear of throwing them into the Arms of *France*, and there is no other Potentate in Condition to disturb them. The only Point of their Interest which they seem not perfectly to understand, is the Power they have of protecting *Italy*; for if the Princes of this Country could be brought to enter into a Treaty of perpetual Neutrality, and could prevail upon the *Swiss* Cantons, in Consideration of an annual Subsidy, to join in it, and keep up a constant Body of Troops, to give Weight to that Neutrality, the Ballance there might be effectually settled; but private Interests, and the ambitious Views of small Princes as well as great, render this a Thing not so much to be hoped for as wished.

Thus we have made the compleat Tour of *Italy*, and have taken a View of all the Kingdoms, Principalities, and Republicks, of which it consists, *Lucca* and St. *Marino* excepted, which are not of Consequence enough to claim a Place in a Work of this Kind. We have seen the comparative Strength, and the natural Interests of all these Powers, from whence it manifestly appears, that every one of the Potentates have in reality but one great Object which ought to absorb all their Views, and that is the Maintenance of the Peace of *Italy*, which they have Force sufficient to accomplish, and which if they could agree upon a general Treaty of Neutrality and Guaranty, might very probably be maintained without any Force at all, that is without keeping up Land Forces for that Purpose, distinct from those, which every Power will judge it requisite to keep on foot, for the Safety of its own Dominions. This would enable them to turn the Cares of their respective Go-

vern-

vernments to their proper Subject, the Welfare of their People, by employing them in the Improvement of the Countries they inhabit, and reviving that Commerce, which was once, and might be again the Glory of *Italy*. This the Reader ought not to regard as the visionary Scheme of a private political Writer, unacquainted with the Manners, Notions, and Designs of the *Italian* Powers, since it is really a Thing in which their own Authors agree, and which in its Nature is as capable of Demonstration as any thing of this Kind can be, and therefore ought to be taken as a certain and established Truth, to which, however repugnant the Practices of Men have been, or may be, it yet remains, and will ever remain unaltered in itself, and consequently worthy the Attention of those, who from a rational and well-grounded Principle of true Policy, wish well to Mankind, and desire rather to see them easy and happy, than poor and oppressed, and their Countries rich and flourishing, than barren and uncultivated, contrary to the Laws of God and Man.

We have likewise seen what indeed could be seen no other way, from a succinct Deduction of their respective Interests, from History, what the real Sources are of that Conduct which has hitherto counteracted, and will probably continue to hinder their Concurrence in establishing this plain and salutary System. We have seen in *Italy* what may also be seen in the *North*, in *Germany*, and indeed every where else, that the Ambition of Princes, the Desire of aggrandizing certain august Families, the pernicious Inclination of pursuing private and particular Views, inconsistent with Universal Prosperity, and consequently inconsistent with themselves, have seduced those who have the Power of commanding others, to enter into Confederacies upon plausible Appearances, and generally speaking with a fallacious Promise of supporting that Equality, Independency, and Tranquility they were really calculated to destroy; and we have seen to how little Purpose long and bloody Wars have been carried on, immense Treasures squandered, the real Welfare of the People neglected, till through downright Weakness and Weariness, all Parties have been content to let their Quarrels rest, till they recovered Strength, and compassed the Means of reviving them again; we have seen that as fatal, and as fruitless, as these Contentions have been, the Seeds of them still remain, and we have too much Reason to fear will shoot once more even in our Times. We have seen this, but to what Purpose? To despair perhaps of ever seeing it otherwise, but not to despair of seeing

that

that Ruin of the Ballance of Power, that total Confusion, and entire Subjection of this fine Country to the Lusts of an ambitious Family, prevented; if not from a generous Zeal for Liberty, yet by a dextrous Management of repugnant Interests, and combining the Views for private Advantages so as to answer, in some measure, the Ends of a virtuous and publick Spirit.

To see, and to understand this thoroughly, still is, and always has been a Point of very high Consequence even to those who have no other Concern in Matters of this Kind, than to know when they go wrong, and when they go right, what political Measures are undertaken upon just, prudent and practicable Principles, when entered upon without due Consideration, to answer some immediate, and yet unnecessary End, or upon Grounds false or studiously misrepresented; this I call not only an entertaining, useful, and noble Part of Knowledge, in comparison of those little mean and trifling Studies that frequently take up a great deal of Time, without adorning or elevating the Mind, but also a weighty and important Science, because it puts it in our Power to be a Check upon those who have the Direction of our Finances and naval Power, to discover their Mistakes, or their wilfully sacrificing national Concerns to ministerial Interests, and on the other hand gives us the Capacity of exploding the plausible Harangues of false Patriots, who by a theatrical Delivery, and pathetick Diction, distract the Minds of the Vulgar, and excite their Passions against those whose Conduct, for want of proper Lights, it is impossible for them to understand. We may therefore be convinced, that how vain a thing soever it may be to hope, that political Perfection from Men in publick Office, which is never to be expected among them, considered in their private Capacities, yet it is really worth while to know wherein that Perfection consists, and the Methods by which it may be approached, tho' not absolutely attained.

But to resume our Subject. Those who have truly at Heart the maintaining the Ballance in *Italy*, must be sure to have it constantly in their Eye, and to watch carefully all the Steps that may be pursued to subvert it. It is true, that Steps of this Kind may be taken without any direct Breach of Treaties, and in that case, it may not be possible to prevent them, perhaps not prudent to intermeddle with them; but it may be very reasonable to remonstrate to such of the *Italian* Powers as are neutral in such Transactions, the Consequences that may attend them, to which those Powers would willingly

hearken,

hearken, because it is their true and natural Interest; and it is also very far from being improbable, that they may in return suggest Methods proper and effectual for the Prevention of such Evils as are justly feared from them; for as they are first to be exposed to them, so it is impossible that they should be the last in considering and comprehending them. This may in Time produce Treaties of another Nature than this Age has seen, founded not on Views of private Interest, or Ambition, but on the solid Basis of publick Utility, not hastily negotiated to serve a particular End, but thoroughly weighed, and maturely considered before they are concluded.

History will inform us, that heretofore, and even so late as the last general War, occasioned by the *Spanish* Succession, the Commonwealths of *Venice* and *Genoa*, the Pope, and the Grand Duke, were always neutral, and other Princes would have been so if they could. It must be confessed, that Things have since changed their Appearance; but if this proves something against our Notion in one Respect, it proves more for it in another, for as they have changed, they may change again. There is a certain great Prince of *Italy*, whom upon this Occasion I will not name, that may find it expedient to make a Semblance of changing his Maxims, for doing which, he cannot be made responsible by his former Allies, since they settled and changed their Plan without him; but beyond question that Prince will go no farther in a bad Road than Necessity carries him, and whenever he sees a tolerable Provision made for the Support of the true Interests of *Italy*, he will follow the Example of his Ancestors, and recur to the Interests of his true Friends, and the Maintenance of the old Cause with Pleasure. There can be no question that the *Swiss* Cantons and their Allies would countenance such a Design to the utmost of their Power; and if it should be suggested that they thrive by Wars, the Answer is obvious, provided those Wars are at a Distance, and consequently not in *Italy*. A defensive Alliance like this might have always Strength sufficient to keep the Ballance even, by joining their Forces to those of the weaker Side, disclaiming all ambitious Designs of Conquest, and prescribing as the settled Terms of Peace, every State's being contented with its own Dominions. One successful Trial of this Sort would be sufficient; for when certain restless and ambitious Powers saw an Alliance subsisting upon such Principles, they would judge it proper not only to submit to, but also to fulfil their Treaties, a Thing otherwise not to be expected.

The

The only formidable Objection that can be made to this Scheme, is the Want of external Assistance of Force and Money, because Experience shews, that the best disposed States in *Italy* are not inclined to risque their own Safety, by entering into a League for these salutary Purposes, to countenance which, however, some successful Precedents might be mentioned in former Times. But the true Solution of this Difficulty must arise from shewing, that there are in *Europe* certain Powers, that have no other foreign Interests but that of supporting the Ballance, and that in this they have so near a Concern, as to render them always willing to venture both their Forces and their Treasures to preserve the Freedom and Independency of their Neighbours and Allies. And this fully obviates the Objection, and plainly proves that it is not only possible, but practicable, to preserve the Peace and promote the Prosperity of *Italy*, in case those *Italian* Potentates that have no private Interests incompatible with that of the Publick, will exert themselves, and concur to make such Measures effectual as are requisite for their own Preservation. To be Spectators of Mischiefs they cannot prevent, is a great Misfortune, yet no Crime; but to look upon a Fire at its first breaking out, without using the Means to quench it which are in their own Hands, till the Conflagration becomes irresistible, is Madness and Folly, and therefore not to be suspected in those Governments, which have been for Ages celebrated for a steady Adherence to wise Maxims. But it is now high Time to leave *Italy*, the Interests of which have been so largely discussed for Reasons already assigned, and which to the ingenious and well-meaning Reader cannot but prove satisfactory; and to proceed without Delay to what remains, in order to compleat our political View of the Interests of Christendom.

This leads us to speak of the *Maritime Powers*, and first of that *Republick*, who tho' the last erected, is by far the most powerful in *Europe*, the UNITED PROVINCES, and then, by Way of Conclusion, of the *foreign Interests of* GREAT BRITAIN. These were designed to be the last Chapters of the Book, because our Intention was not barely to amuse and entertain the Reader with historical Relations and political Remarks, but to make them subservient to more useful Purposes, by inspiring a true Sense of what is meant by PUBLICK LIBERTY, the INDEPENDENCY of EUROPE, and the COMMON CAUSE; Terms that ought by no means to be confounded with the *Cant Words* of a *Party*, calculated to amuse the Minds, bewilder the Understandings, and inflame the Passions of the

Vulgar; but decent and proper Expreffions of Things that concern the Peace, the Safety and Profperity of MANKIND, which it behoves thofe who aim at diftinguifhing themfelves from the *Herd*, clearly to comprehend, thoroughly to digeft, zealoufly to maintain, as far as their *Sphere* of *Action* extends. Happy the Man! who in an Age like this could fet fo glorious a Subject in a Light fo true, as that it fhould be generally feen, and as generally comprehended. We might then hope to fee that divine Spirit revived, which once enabled us in the very *Dawn* of our *Maritime Power*, to break the Chains of *Europe*, to *burn* the *Beard*, as Sir *Francis Drake* pleafantly called it, of that *Catholick King* who formed the wifeft Plan of *univerfal Empire*; to baffle, with the Affiftance of Heaven (ever to be expected in confounding BABELS) his *invincible Armada*, and to protect the *Poor Diftreffed* STATES of HOLLAND, till they became *High and Mighty*. And how this came to pafs, will be fhewn in the enfuing Chapter.

C H A P. XIV.

A fuccinct Account of the Rife, Progrefs, and Eftablifhment of the Republick of the United Provinces; *the Sources of the amazing Succefs of its Subjects in Commerce, and the quick Growth of their Naval Power; the Nature of their domeftick Government truly ftated, and their real Interefts with regard to the reft of the Powers of* Europe *impartially confidered.*

UPON the Declenfion of that Empire which *Charlemagne* erected in the Weft, the Countries of *Lower Germany*, which had made a Part of it, fell under different Modes of Government, in refpect to the Title of the fupreme Magiftrate, and fome Points of Form in regard to the Adminiftration of Affairs, but with refpect to the fundamental Principles of Rule, the fame. That is to fay, the Governors under various Names took upon them the fupreme Dignity, by the Confent of the People, to which they were equally indebted, both for their Power and for their Titles, there being nothing clearer

in

in History, than that the Inhabitants of these Countries had ever high Notions of Liberty, and would no farther submit to Rule, than they thought requisite for their own Good. It was with this View, that they were content to have one supreme Magistrate, who was to preside in their Councils in Times of Peace, and to be at the Head of their Forces in the Field when they were obliged to make War ; but the Regulation of civil Affairs, by repealing old, and making new Laws, and the Power of giving, raising, and appropriating the publick Revenues, was in the General Assembly of the States, composed of the Nobility, Clergy, and Cities.

These Provinces, according to the common Computation, were seventeen in Number, *viz.* four Dukedoms, *Brabant, Limburg, Luxemburg,* and *Gueldres* ; seven Earldoms, *Flanders, Artois, Hainault, Holland, Zealand, Namur,* and *Zutphen* ; five Lordships, *Friesland, Malines, Utrecht, Overyssell,* and *Groningen* ; and *Antwerp,* which has the Title of Marquisate of the *Roman* Empire. These Provinces were anciently ruled, each by its Prince or Lord, but afterwards several of them were either by Inheritance, Marriage, or Contract, united together, till most of them fell to the Share of the House of *Burgundy,* from whence they came to the House of *Austria,* by the Marriage of *Maximilian* I. who had espoused *Mary* the only Daughter of *Charles* sirnamed the *Hardy* ; and were afterwards all united under *Charles* V. who governed them in Peace and Prosperity. He was a Native of *Ghent,* and had both a paternal and fraternal Affection for the People of the *Low-Countries,* and therefore met with a reciprocal Return of Duty and Loyalty from them.

His Son and Successor to the Crown of *Spain,* and the Possession of the *Low-Countries, Philip* II. was by no means of his Disposition, but beheld in the Light of Sedition whatever crossed his absolute Will and Pleasure ; though in forming his Resolutions he had shewn ever so little Regard to the Laws and Liberties of his Subjects. He conceived the highest Prejudice against the Inhabitants of the *Low-Countries* before he quitted them, for he was there at the Time of his Father's Resignation, on Account of the Application made to him by the States, that he would withdraw the foreign Troops, confide the Defence of the Fortresses to the national Forces, and bestow all Places of Trust and Profit upon the Natives. He is acknowledged to have been a consummate Politician ; but such as allow him this Character, must of necessity except his Conduct in the *Low-Countries,* which was certainly the very reverse. He dis-

obliged

obliged the People to such a Degree, as to spread amongst them a universal Spirit of Disaffection, and at the same time gave them a. Head, by maletreating the Prince of *Orange* in such a manner, as no Man of his Rank could endure. Those who love refined Strokes in Government, have suggested that King *Philip* did all this by Design, in hopes of becoming absolute Master of the Provinces, and enjoying besides the confiscated Estates of the Prince, which were very large, and of great Value. If it was possible to believe this true, it might with Justice be said, that the King was as much disappointed as he deserved to be. The Severity of those he intrusted with the Government, drove the People to take up Arms; and the Prince of *Orange*, who could not see his Country ruined, and his Countrymen destroyed without Regret, resented at last their ill Usage and his own with so much Spirit, as laid the Foundation of the People's Liberties, and of the Grandeur of his Successors.

William of *Nassau*, the first of that Name, Prince of *Orange*, to whom Cardinal *Grenvelle* gave the Sirname of the *Silent*, may be justly stiled the Founder of this Republick. He was endowed with great Qualities by Nature, which were improved by constant Study, and an excellent Education, in which he had the Emperor *Charles* V. for his Tutor, who took him for his Page when he was twelve Years old, whom he served for nine Years, and by whom he was trusted with the greatest Secrets of State, at an Age when others could have scarce comprehended them. He preferred him at the Age of two and twenty to all his old Generals, and gave him the Command of an Army when his Affairs were in the most critical Situation. If it was surprizing that so wise and great a Monarch should have such a Confidence in a Person so young, it is still more surprizing that he should justify that Confidence by his Behaviour, more especially when he had to do with the ablest and most experienced Officers of that Age. He was born to a great Succession in *Germany*, the *Low-Countries*, the County of *Burgundy*, and in *France*, and coming early to so large a Fortune, he lived with that Magnificence with which it enabled him to live, and added Lustre to the Court from which he received the Honours due to his Birth, and nothing more. He had a Magnanimity that neither Prosperity could elate, or Adversity depress; his Wisdom enabled him to act in all Situations; he was never wanting in his Duty to his Prince, till his Prince rendered that Duty a Folly, by withdrawing his Protection, and laying Snares for his Life; his Courage,

his

his Conſtancy, his Sincerity, attracted the Friendſhip of the Nobles; his Probity ſecured him the Reſpect, his Affability gained him the Affection of the People. All Ranks and Degrees of Men looked up to him in their Diſtreſs, as the only Perſon who could protect them; he repaid their Confidence by a generous Contempt of Danger, and ſacrificed his hereditary Fortune for their Preſervation. With all theſe Virtues he could not eſcape Envy; but he did more, he triumphed over it; he bore with the calling in the Archduke *Matthias*, and then with a Prince of the Blood of *France*, as willing to yield to any thing that might ſave his Country from Deſtruction; and when theſe Hopes were found vain, he was content to take up things, deſperate as they were, and by his Prudence laid the Foundation of the publick Freedom, by engaging the Provinces of *Gueldres, Holland, Zealand, Frieſland,* and *Utrecht,* to aſſociate for their mutual Safety in 1579.

The great Difficulty in rendering a People free, who have felt the Weight of Tyranny only for a ſhort Time, does not conſiſt ſo much in perſuading them to hazard their Lives and Fortunes, by taking up Arms againſt their Oppreſſors, as in prevailing on them to ſubmit to ſuch Regulations as are abſolutely neceſſary for conducting their Affairs to a happy Iſſue. The Prince of *Orange* experienced this from the very Beginning of the Civil Wars in the *Low-Countries,* to the Time of his Demiſe. He felt it however moſt towards the Cloſe of his Life, when the Duke of *Alencon,* by his raſh and perfidious Attempt upon *Antwerp,* excited the People to abhor the *French* as much as they had ever done the *Spaniards.* In the Aſſembly of the *States General* at *Dort,* it was with extreme Difficulty that he prevented them from diſcovering their Reſentment without reſerve, by repreſenting that it was not only impoſſible for them to think of reſiſting both the *French* and *Spaniards,* but likewiſe, that the only probable Means of defending themſelves againſt the latter, was by ſecuring the Friendſhip and Protection of the former. Some mention was made in this Aſſembly of giving the Title of Count of *Holland,* with all the Prerogatives annexed to it, to the Prince of *Orange;* but the States were too fond of their Sovereignty to liſten to any ſuch thing; and thoſe who were Enemies to his Serene Highneſs and his Family, have taken care to repreſent this to Poſterity, as a direct Proof of his boundleſs Ambition, which conſidering the limited Authority of thoſe Princes, and the extreme Danger the People were in of being reduced by Force of Arms under the abſolute Power of the King of *Spain,* is a very unjuſt Imputation,

putation, perhaps we should not carry things too far, if we stiled it a groundless Calumny. All that he could obtain of that Assembly, was to send an Ambassy to the Duke of *Alencon*, with Instructions to negotiate an Accommodation that they might not be totally deprived of the Assistance of *France*, and while at his Request they thus happily temporized, Providence delivered them from their Fears on this Side, by the Death of that Duke, which happened on the 10th of *June* 1584.

The News of the Duke of *Alencon*'s sudden if not violent Death was brought to the Prince of *Orange*, by a Person who assumed the Name of *Francis Guyon*, and pretended to be the Son of one *Peter Guyon* of *Bezancon*, who had been put to Death on the Score of his being a Protestant, to which Religion this young Man appeared to be a zealous Bigot. His Highness had employed him in several Affairs of Importance, in which he had discharged his Trust with great Diligence and Integrity. His true Name was *Balthazar Gerhard*, a native of *Burgundy*, and about the Age of twenty-seven, a Man of a determined Spirit, deep Dissimulation, and a furious Papist. He took the Advantage when the Prince was just risen from his Dinner, in his Palace at *Delft*, and was calling for a Standish in order to sign a Passport for this Man to take another Journey, to discharge a Pistol laden with three Bullets directly against his Highness's Breast, of which Wound he immediately died without speaking a Word. The daring Assassin had taken his Measures for his Escape with great Sagacity, and was very near effecting it. Being seized, he avowed the Fact, and affirmed, that if it was to do again, he would perform the same Thing; and in this he not only persisted throughout all his Examinations, but even in the Midst of those Torments, in which he ended his miserable Life, without ever owning a Syllable of the Conspiracy of which he was barely the Executioner. Most of the *Dutch* Writers charge this Murder upon the *Spaniards*, and indeed not without Reason, since by an Edict dated *March* 25th, 1580, *Philip* II. had proscribed the Prince of *Orange*, branded him with all the Crimes imaginable, expressed in the grossest Language, and promising Pardons, Honours and Rewards to any who would dispatch him. But others, considering the Juncture in which he died, believe, that *Balthazar* received his Instructions in a Language more familiar to that Country than *Spanish*. However that Matter may be, it is certain that the Death of this great Man, who was always the Darling of the People, and whose Maxim it was that Happiness ought to be extended to all Ranks and Degrees, that the

Con-

Confciences of Men fhould be free, and that whatever was raifed on the Publick fhould be fpent in the publick Service: I fay, it is very certain, that his Death was equally agreeable to the Partizans of *Spain*, and to the high Republicans; that is, to fuch as difdained to have any other than a King for a Mafter, and to fuch as defpifed the Thought of having any Mafter at all. The poor People who had loft their Protector, their Patron and their Friend, the Soldiers who had loft an Officer, who without Severity maintained moft ftrict Difcipline, and the Friends to rational Liberty, who in lofing him were apprehenfive they had loft all, deplored him with unfeigned Tears. Such was the End of *William* the firft Prince of *Orange*, *July* 10, 1584, in the fifty-fecond Year of his Age.

The *States General*, as foon as the Prince of *Orange* was dead, declared themfelves Sovereigns of the *United Provinces*, and after thus opportunely fecuring the fupreme Authority, in Condefcenfion to the general Grief of their Subjects celebrated the Funeral of the deceafed Prince with great Solemnity, and decreed the higheft Honours to his Memory. His Highnefs had been four times married, and had Children by each of his Wives. By his firft, *Anne* Daughter to Count *Egmont*, he had *Philip* Count *de Buren*, and a Daughter *Mary*, who married Count *Hohenloe*. By his fecond, *Anne* Daughter of *Maurice* Elector of *Saxony*, he had Count *Maurice*, and a Daughter *Emilia*, who married *Emanuel*, Son to Don *Antonio*, whom the *Spaniards* deprived of the Kingdom of *Portugal*. By his third, *Charlotte de Bourbon*, of the Houfe of *Montpenfier*, he had fix Daughters. And by his laft Wife, *Loulfa de Coligny*, Daughter to the Admiral of *France*, he had a Son *Henry Frederick*, whom he left in his Cradle. *Philip* Prince of *Orange* at the Deceafe of his Father was a Prifoner in *Spain*; Count *Maurice* about the Age of eighteen, was taken from his Studies, and declared Governor of *Holland* and *Zealand*, and the Nephew of the Prince of *Orange*, *William de Naffau*, was declared Stadtholder of *Friefland*, from whom the prefent Stadtholder of the Union is lineally defcended. The *States General* found the Authority they had affumed, in a fhort time very feverely fhaken, by the Progrefs which the Duke of *Parma* made, in taking many Places of Importance, and at length befieging *Antwerp*, which he reduced after a long Blockade. Thefe Misfortunes, which were very near overturning their new Republick, taught them how great their Lofs was in that Prince, whofe civil Skill and military Prudence was the real Source both of their Power and Safety. In this Diftrefs they were as ready to part with their

Sove-

Sovereignty, as they had been to affume it, and were now willing to fubmit to any Mafter except their old one. With this View they applied themfelves once more to *France*, but the moft Chriftian King found his Affairs too much embarraffed at home, to think of defending Subjects at a Diftance; they next offered themfelves to Queen *Elizabeth*, from whom they had already derived very great Affiftance, but fhe too, for Reafons of State, rejected that Propofition; yet to prevent their total Ruin, condefcended to their Requeft of having one of the principal Noblemen in *England* fent over to fupply the Place of the Prince of *Orange*, and to adminifter the fupreme Power, both civil and military.

This Nobleman was *Robert Dudley* Earl of *Leicefter*, the chief Favourite, the great Confident, and the principal Minifter of Queen *Elizabeth*, whom the *Spanifh* and *Dutch* Writers fay, was fent over out of the Queen's Affection for him, and her Defire to raife and diftinguifh his Character; but *Camden*, who was likely to know thefe Things better, infinuates that he was fent over to *Holland* by a Stroke of his own Policy; that is, thofe Members of the Privy Council who were moft forward in advancing him to this Charge, wifhed him the leaft Good. It is certain, that the *States General* did not underftand the Thing at all in this Light, but believing that he had an abfolute Power over the Queen, endeavoured to make their Court to him, by granting him almoft an abfolute Power over their Subjects, which difpleafed his Miftrefs, and very foon grew troublefome to themfelves. The Earl of *Leicefter* was a compleat Courtier, and a great Statefman, where he knew his Ground, but either never knew, or had long before forgot the Art of War. So that upon the whole, he made but a very indifferent Figure here, tho' he fhewed great Abilities in raifing, extending, and maintaining as great Power as any Favourite ever had in *England*. His Campaign in 1586 was far from doing him any Honour, the Duke of *Parma* carried every thing before him, baffled all the Attempts of *Leicefter*, and relieved *Zutphen*, after a fharp Action, in which Sir *Philip Sidney* was mortally wounded, in a manner that raifed his Reputation in the fame Degree that it depreffed that of the *Englifh* Stadtholder. The Earl of *Leicefter* finding his Conduct difliked, as it might well be, by the *States*, fell to flattering the Minifters, and cajoling the People, in which his counterfeit Piety wrought fo ftrongly with the former, and his diffembled Patriotifm had fuch Effects on the latter, as threw every thing into Confufion; and when Matters were in this State, he returned

turned to *England*, leaving the *Dutch* Affairs in a much worse Condition than he found them.

As soon as the Earl was gone, the *States General*, at the Perfuasion of their Penfionary *Barnevelt*, declared Prince *Maurice* their Captain-General, and made his Brother-in-law Count *Hohenloe* his Lieutenant, which gave great Offence to the Court of *England*, but was undoubtedly a very right Step with regard to their own Affairs. But *Leicester*, who had still as great Credit as ever with the Queen his Miftrefs, and was very fond of the Title of Excellency, and the Power he enjoyed in *Holland*, refolved to return thither the next Year, which the *States*, who depended upon Queen *Elizabeth*'s Affiftance, could not prevent, and were therefore forced to admit him, and reftore him in a great meafure to his Authority, which he managed worfe than before, and thereby confirmed the Sufpicions which the *States* had entertained, on account of fome of his Creatures betraying the Places with which he had entrufted them to the *Spaniards*. He made two or three unfuccefsful Attempts to relieve *Sluys*, and the fame ill Fate followed him in all his Undertakings; fo that he quite loft his military Character, if indeed he was ever efteemed a good Officer. By this Time the *States* had difcovered their Miftake, and that their Complaints againft him would not want powerful Patrons, which encouraged them to deal roundly with him, and plainly with his Miftrefs, who thereupon recalled him, and appointed the Lord *Willoughby*, an honeft Man, and a good Officer, to command her Forces in the *Low Countries*. All Hiftorians agree, that a little before his Departure, *Leicefter* encouraged a Confpiracy at *Leyden*, which coft fome People their Lives. He is accufed by fome foreign Writers of attempting to make a Peace between *Spain* and *England* at the Expence of the *Dutch*, but the Proofs of this have not been as yet produced. There is yet another Charge in *Camden*, which I fhould not mention, but for its not appearing in any of the Tranflations of his Annals, or even in any Edition of the original *Latin*, except that of *Hearne*, printed from a Copy corrected with the Author's own Hand. This Charge is, that he had framed a Defign of feizing Prince *Maurice* of *Naffau*, and the Penfionary *Barnevelt*, and fending them Prifoners over into *England*. Whatever the Faults of this *English* Stadtholder might be, the *English* Troops, and the *English* Money, did the *States* moft ufeful and acceptable Service, as themfelves very fully acknowledge, and in fome meafure repaid, when by a Stratagem in 1588 they contributed not a little to the Deftruction of the *Spanish* invincible Armada, in which they were true to our Interefts and their own.

The

The Neceſſity they were under of having a Perſon of diſtinguiſhed Character at the Head of their Armies, and the Inſtances that Count *Maurice* of *Naſſau*, for ſo he called himſelf while his Elder Brother lived, though he is generally ſtiled by Hiſtorians Prince *Maurice*, induced the *States General* to confide their Armies to him in the ſame manner as to his Father. He was indeed the true Succeſſor to his Virtues and Abilities; which is not at all ſtrange, ſince from his firſt Appearance in the World, he made it his ſole Study to copy that noble Character, agreeable to his Device, which was a Tree cut to the Stumps, with a Shoot growing out on one Side, with this Motto, *Tandem fit ſurculus arbor*. It has been already obſerved, that he entered into the publick Service at ſeventeen, and at the Age of twentyone he had the ſupreme Command. He ſhewed himſelf at that Time not at all inferior to the Duke of *Parma*, who had been ſo long eſteemed the beſt Officer in *Europe*; and which is very ſingular, though no Man gave greater or more frequent Teſtimonies of perſonal Courage, yet he diſtinguiſhed himſelf very early by Stratagems of War, which are commonly the Effects of deep Judgment and long Experience. He was at the ſame time a very enterprizing and a very cautious General; enterprizing, as he often undertook things deſperate, and in Appearance impracticable; cautious, as he never failed to execute them with ſo much Circumſpection, as to ſhew that he did not depend either upon Fortune or Force, but upon military Skill. He ſtudied old Authors carefully, and more eſpecially the Writings of *Cæſar*, upon which it is ſaid, that ſeveral of his Expeditions might be conſidered as Commentaries. His Succeſs was anſwerable to his Courage and his Abilities; in the Space of twenty Years he took forty Cities and Towns of Conſequence, and beat the *Spaniards* thrice in the Field with great Diſproportion of Numbers, and under ſome other Diſadvantages. As his Father laid the Foundation, ſo this Prince raiſed the Fabrick of the *Dutch* Republick, delivered them from the Fear of their Enemies, and gained them the Title, as well as gave them the Power, of a free and independent State.

In his Time, however, thoſe Diviſions aroſe which ſubſiſted ever after, and which many think are not yet extinguiſhed in that Commonwealth. As there is no forming any Idea of the Domeſtick Intereſts of the *United Provinces*, without having juſt Notions of the Principles to which both Parties have pretended, during theſe long Diſputes; it will be neceſſary to treat this Matter freely and fully, at leaſt ſo far as is conſiſtent with the Bounds that are preſcribed to this Work; and without any Prejudice

judice against one, or Prepoffeffion in favour of the other Party, both having in certain Circumftances fhewn themfelves equally to blame.

The Civil War in the *Low-Countries* having now lafted full forty Years, and brought inexpreffible Miferies as well on the Subjects of the *States General*, as on thofe who remained under the Obedience of the Houfe of *Auftria*, the wifer and better Part of the People on both Sides were inclined to an Accommodation. This was by no means agreeable to Prince *Maurice*, who apprehended a Diminution of his Power was the principal Object aimed at, by thofe who were for pacific Meafures among the *Dutch*. At firft the *French* King *Henry* the Fourth was againft this Pacification, but the Penfionary *Barnevelt* having reprefented to him by the Minifters of the Republick at *Paris*, that they were no longer able to carry on the War, without running every Year in Debt, that by Degrees the very Intereft of thefe Debts muft become a heavy Burthen, from which it was impoffible to deliver themfelves, as many had lent their whole Fortunes to the Publick, and had no other Subfiftence than by receiving their Intereft regularly; the *French* King being convinced, promoted that Meafure all he could, fo that a Truce was concluded in 1609 for twelve Years, by which the Republick was left free, and in full Poffeffion of thofe Dominions which had been acquired during the War. After this, the Difputes between Prince *Maurice* with thofe who adhered to him, and the Penfionary *Barnevelt* and his Party, rofe very high, his Highnefs being extremely jealous of his Authority, and fuch as oppofed him no lefs anxious for the Prefervation of their Liberty, which they confidered as equally loft, whether they fubmitted to the Sovereignty of one of their own Countrymen, or a Stranger.

It happened very unluckily for the publick Tranquility, that at this Time there arofe religious Difputes about the Doctrines of Grace and Predeftination, which divided the whole Nation into two Parties, under the Title of *Arminians* and *Gomarifts*. The Penfionary *Barnevelt* was in the Sentiments of the former, but out of regard to the Peace of his Country, was inclined to have ftifled thefe Difputes by a publick Edict, which Prince *Maurice* and his Party who took the contrary Side prevented ; and laying hold of this Opportunity, inflamed the Minds of the Populace to the higheft Degree, by reprefenting the *Arminians* as fecretly inclined to the *Spaniards* ; and under thefe and other Pretences, making ufe of the Attachment of the Army to his Perfon, the Prince ventured to make fome bold Alterations in the

Civil

Civil Government, by changing the Magiftrates of Cities at his Pleafure, fo as to gain an abfolute Afcendency in the Affembly of the *States General*.

The Death of *Philip* Prince of *Orange* in 1618 without Iffue, having added to the Titles the Credit and the Fortune of the Stadtholder, he refolved to pufh Things to Extremities againft his Adverfaries, and therefore caufed Penfionary *Barnevelt* to be arrefted; as alfo, Mr. *Huguerbeets* Penfionary of *Leiden*, *Hugo Grotius* Penfionary of *Rotterdam*, and the Sieur *de Leedenberg* Secretary to the *States* of *Utrecht*, all Perfons equally diftinguifh-ed by their Capacities, and by their Probity. Of thefe, *Barnevelt* only was made a Sacrifice, being accufed of the moft enormous Crimes, before Judges who acted by Commiffion from the *States General*, who in reality had no legal Jurifdiction over him, if he had been ever fo guilty, the *States* of *Holland* being his fole Judges; but they having taken him under their fpecial Protec-tion, were not like to ferve the Purpofes of his Enemies, who procured him to be condemned by the Judges beforementioned, and executed him the next Day. Tho' he was upwards of feven-ty, he died with the fame Calmnefs and Courage he fhewed in all the Actions of his Life, and his Death produced the direct contrary Effect to that which was expected from it.

Prince *Maurice* of *Orange* found his Authority more generally difliked than ever, and by none fo much as thofe who had affifted violently in the Perfecution of the Penfionary. He faw that he was no longer popular, and upon the breaking out again of the War in 1621, he perceived that he was forfaken by his good Fortune. An Attempt which he made for furprizing *Antwerp* failed, though he thought the Defign fo well laid as to fay, that God only could difappoint it; he faw his own Town of *Breda* taken by *Ambrofe Spinola*, the Relief of which he attempted with-out Succefs; and by reflecting on his Reverfe of Fortune, he firft loft that even Temper for which he had been always famous, and then his Health; fo that broken with Care and Sicknefs, he breathed his laft in the Spring of the Year 1625, in the fifty-third Year of his Age. His Enemies allow this Prince to have had great Virtues; and, except his Ambition and Averfion to Marriage, few or no Vices. He left behind him a natural Son Mr. *de Beververt*, who was Governor of *Bolduc*, a Gentleman of great Parts and Courage, who lived and died with unfpotted Reputation; one of whofe Daughters married the Earl of *Offory*, by whom fhe was Mother to the late Duke of *Ormond*, and the prefent Earl of *Arran*; and the other *Henry* Earl of *Arlington*, Secretary of State in the Reign of King *Charles* the Second.

Prince

Prince *Henry Frederick*, the youngeſt Son of *William* the firſt Prince of *Orange*, ſucceeded by the Death of his Brother *Maurice* to all the Eſtates, Titles, and Dignities of his Father, being at that Time about forty Years of Age, having ſerved the *States* in their Armies in a manner from his Childhood, and yet having riſen no higher than a Colonel of Horſe, till he ſucceeded to the ſupreme Command. He had in the Time of his Brother's Adminiſtration given frequent Teſtimonies of his Courage and Conduct, and yet it does not appear that thoſe who were in the Government had any Idea of his being near ſo great a Man as he really was. It is ſuggeſted by *De Witt*, and the Obſervation is worthy of ſo great a Man, that the Difficulties the two Brothers *Maurice* and *Henry* had to ſtruggle with in their Youth, and that Circumſpection with which they were obliged to behave, had very good Effects, and was a principal Cauſe of their acquiring thoſe great Accompliſhments, by which they raiſed their own Credit ſo high, and rendered ſuch uſeful Services to their Country. In 1626 the Prince of *Orange* took *Oldenſeel*, and the ſame Year Vice Admiral *Hein* made himſelf Maſter of the *Spaniſh* Fleet in the Bay of *All Saints* in *Brazil*. In 1627, the Prince took *Grol*, in the Sight of a *Spaniſh* Army, who durſt not attack him in his Intrenchments; and towards the End of the ſame Year, the Vice Admiral beforementioned took the whole *Spaniſh* Plate Fleet, with five Millions Sterling on board. In 1629, the Stadtholder reduced *Bolduc*, a Place of great Strength as well as Importance, which Prince *Maurice* had attempted in vain; and this notwithſtanding the *Spaniards* made an Irruption into the Country about *Utrecht*, which engaged the beſt Officers in his Army, as well as the *States* themſelves, to deſire him to raiſe the Siege; but he was of Opinion that a ravaged Country was not loſt, whereas a good Fortreſs gained was a great Acquiſition; beſides, by ſurprizing *Wezel*, where the *Spaniards* had all their Magazines, he compelled them to retire in haſte, and to the Character of an excellent Officer, added that of a General happy in his Enterprizes; a thing of the higheſt Conſequence, inſomuch that the *Roman* Dictator *Sylla* choſe rather the Surname of *Fortunate* than *Great*.

Henry, Prince of *Orange*, married *Amelia* Daughter of the Count *de Solms*, by whom he had a Son, Prince *William*, and four Daughters. In 1631, the *States General*, to ſhew their Reſpect for, and Confidence in the Prince Stadtholder, granted the Survivancy of all his Employments to the Prince his Son, and preſented him with the Patent in a Gold Box, tho' he was not then quite five Years old, which was an extraordinary

Stretch

Stretch of Complaifance, and far beyond any thing they had done for his Father and Brother, which was the Effects of his real or feeming Moderation; and as fome Writers fay, this proceeded from the Counfels of his Mother-in-law the Princefs Dowager of *Orange*, who had been always a true Friend to *Barnevelt*, and had thereby a great Influence over his Party. In 1632, he took *Ruremond*, *Venlo*, and *Strale*, befieged *Mae-ftricht*, and having beat *Pappenheim*, made himfelf Mafter of that important Place. The next Year he took *Rhinberg*. There was indeed fcarce a Year during the Continuance of his Life, which was not diftinguifhed by fome remarkable Event, and amongft thefe we may reckon his Ufage of the powerful Cardinal *de Richlieu*, who debauched the Sieur *de Walkemberg* from his Duty, and engaged him for a Sum of Money to deliver up the Citadel and Principality of *Orange*, of which he was Governor; the Prince having Intelligence of this, fent one Colonel *Knut* to *Orange*, who killed *Walkemberg* in a private Houfe where he went to Dinner, and then produced the Prince's Orders, and took the Command of the Caftle, by which that Contrivance was defeated. After this he gave the Cardinal repeated Marks of his Refentment, which in fpite of all his Pride he was forced to diffemble and digeft, and having engaged in an offenfive Alliance with the *States*, gave Inftructions to two Marfhals of *France*, upon their Junction with the *Dutch* Army, to obey the Orders of the Prince of *Orange*. In 1637, the *French* Ambaffador in a fet Speech gave him the Title of *Highnefs* inftead of *Excellency*, and his Example was followed by the Ambaffadors of all the other Courts of *Europe*. The fame Year he recovered by a vigorous Siege his own Town of *Breda*, in which Siege the *French* Ambaffador, who to fhew his Refpect for the Prince Stadtholder, ferving at the Head of his own Regiment, was unfortunately killed. In 1639, the *Spanifh* Fleet was defeated and deftroyed on the Coaft of *England* by Admiral *Tromp*.

In 1641, Prince *William* married the Princefs *Mary*, Daughter to *Charles* I. King of *Great Britain*, with great Pomp and Splendor, and in Honour of this Marriage he had the Province of *Friefland* added to his Government, or rather to the Survivorfhip. In 1644, Prince *Frederick Henry* made himfelf Mafter of *Sas-van-Ghent*, and the Year following he took *Hulft*, which in thofe Days was looked upon as a Place of great Strength and Importance. In a word, his whole Adminiftration was equally glorious from the Beginning to the End, and might have been ftill more fo, if thofe who envied his Power

2   and

and Greatnefs, had not taken all imaginable Care to prevent his extending his Conquefts in Proportion to his Inclinations and Abilities, and particularly hindered him from reducing *Antwerp*; which was of all Things what he moft defired. He died *March* 14, 1647, and was buried with great Magnificence, as one who had deferved well of his Country, who had added Glory and Influence to that Liberty which it received from his Father, and that Security which refulted from the Labours of his Brother. *De Witt* informs us, that there were fome who reproached him with his Profufenefs and Luxury, after he came to the Poffeffion of the Principality of *Orange*, and the vaft hereditary Eftates of his Family, as alfo with his Lewdnefs, in which he did not ufe much Diffimulation; and above all, his Ambition, which induced him to keep up a great Army, that he might extend his Glory by his Conquefts, and maintain his Power by the Continuance of the War. It is true, that having the Title and Revenues of a Prince, he kept up his Dignity, but this being at his own Expence, was a Benefit rather than a Prejudice to the Publick. He left behind him a natural Son, the Sieur *Zuyleftein*, whofe Defcendents are at this Time Peers of *Great Britain*, and fecured to his only lawful Son the Honours that had been enjoyed by his illuftrious Predeceffors.

In the Year following the Death of Prince *Frederick Henry*, the *States General* concluded at *Munfter* a Peace with the Crown of *Spain*, without any regard to the Endeavours of the *French* King and the Prince of *Orange*, to diffuade them ; which is believed to have been owing to the Sufpicions they began to entertain of both, apprehending very much the Confequences of having *France* for a Neighbour, and the Spirit of the young Stadtholder, who had been accuftomed to Authority, and to Magnificence from his very Cradle, and who befides had married the Daughter of a King. It was not long before thefe Jealoufies rofe on both Sides very high ; for the zealous Republicans, that is, the Remains of *Barnevelt*'s Party, were for taking Advantage of the Peace, and difbanding, or at leaft reducing the Army, which the Prince of *Orange* oppofed. It is fuppofed that he did this merely to preferve his own Power, by moft of the *Dutch* Hiftorians, but it is certain that he gave other Reafons for it, which brought over a Majority of the *States* to his Opinion. He faid it was ungrateful, becaufe they were fafe at prefent, to difmifs thofe who had purchafed that Safety with their Blood ; that this was ftill more imprudent, confidering the War continued between *France* and *Spain*, who might take Advantage of them in that defencelefs Con-

tion.

tion. He farther obferved, that hitherto they had been pitied, but that now they had Reafon to fear the Envy of moft of the States of *Europe*, and that as their Tranquility was procured, fo it would be beft preferved by keeping up their old Troops, which if they did not recruit, would with lefs hazard to them diminifh faft enough of themfelves.

But tho' his Eloquence prevailed upon the *States*, it was not at all relifhed in the Provinces, or by the great Cities; upon which his Friends propofed, that he fhould vifit them himfelf, againft which the City of *Amfterdam* petitioned, as having at that Time no Inclination to the Honour of his Highnefs's Company, which the Prince took for fuch a Mark of Contempt, that he caufed Mr. *De Witt* Burgomafter of *Dort*, and five other Members of the *States General*, to be fent to the Caftle of *Louveftein*, and gave Orders to a Body of Troops to advance towards *Amfterdam*; but the Poft-boy from *Hamburg* paffing thro' his Army, gave Notice of it to the Citizens, who in order to exclude it, made no Difficulty of laying all the adjacent Country under Water. Thefe Differences were afterwards compromifed, and Burgomafter *De Witt* and his Fellow Prifoners fet at Liberty; yet from their Imprifonment, the Party to which they adhered, from the Place of their Confinement, took or received the Name of *Louveftein*. In all Probability thefe Differences would have been revived, if the Prince of *Orange* had not foon after fallen ill of the Small-pox, which proved fatal to him; and fome Months after his Deceafe, *November* the fourth, 1650, his Widow the Princefs was delivered of a Son, called after his Father *William*, who became in Procefs of Time, Stadtholder, and King of *Great Britain*.

We will here make a fhort Paufe, in order to confider the Government, Commerce, and Strength of this Republick, and then refume our Hiftory, the rather becaufe it is generally believed the *United Provinces* came to the Height of their Profperity not long after the Death of Prince *William II.* and in reviewing thefe Points, we will be as clear, as concife, and as impartial as is in our Power, which is fo much the more necef-fary, becaufe few of the many Writers who have already mentioned this Subject, have treated it in this Manner, but have either given way to their Prejudices, or have thrown together Facts and Dates, without giving themfelves much Pain, as to their Importance or Connection; whereas in order to render a Work of this Kind ufeful, it is abfolutely requifite that due Attention be paid to both, and Matters not only

stated

stated as they really are, but in such an Order as may shew the Relation that one Thing has to another.

At the Entrance of this Chapter, we described the original Form of Government that prevailed in these Countries, which Form continued likewise when they became a Part of the Dominions of his Catholick Majesty; for as the Prince of *Orange* justly observed in his Apology, whatever Title that Monarch might assume, either in *Spain* or in the *Indies*, he was no more than Earl of *Holland*, or of *Flanders*. At the Time *Philip* II. left those Provinces, he constituted the Prince of *Orange* Governor of four of them, the *Flemish* Word is Stadtholder, which is precisely the same thing with Lieutenant, and the *States* had that Power, with which they were vested by the Constitution. When therefore they threw off the Yoke of *Spain*, the Question was, whether they should retain their old Form of Government; which if they had done, they must have chosen another Earl, and to this those were inclined who were most attached to the Prince of *Orange*. Indeed the Generality of the People were best pleased with the old Form, and this induced them to think of the Archduke *Matthias*, the Duke of *Alencon*, and afterwards of the *French* King and Queen *Elizabeth*; but at last those who had Seats in the Assembly of the *States*, began to think of securing the Sovereignty to themselves, which was actually changing the old Constitution into that of a Republick. It is true, that for their own Conveniency they were disposed to give the Title of Stadtholder to a single Person, as they actually did to the Earl of *Leicester*; but tho' the Title continued, the Office was changed; for the Lieutenant of a Prince is an Office easily conceived, but the Lieutenant of an Assembly, such as the *States General*, is not so readily comprehended, because it imples the Representative of those who were but Representatives themselves; and this was the very Reasoning that *De Witt* used for abolishing that Office also after the Death of *William* II.

The Treaty of Union concluded in 1579, at *Utrecht*, was a Confederacy of so many different Republicks, as there were Provinces that entered into it, and the *States General* were properly and distinctly the *States* of all these Provinces taken together; but because such a Meeting was inconvenient, and for other Reasons likewise, a kind of Committee composed of Deputies from each of the *States* was appointed to sit at the *Hague*, and these have been since stiled the *States General*, tho' in Reality they are rather the Representatives of the *States General*, in whom the Majesty of the Republick resides. They

have

have pursuant to the Form of their new Constitution, such Powers as are requisite for the Management of publick Affairs, and have also the Government of those Towns and Districts that belong to the Republick, and yet are not within any of the confederated Provinces, and many other Prerogatives; and for the better Management of such a Variety of important Concerns, they commit Part of the Administration to a Council of State. But whereas in the Assembly of the *States General* there are no more Votes than there are Provinces, whatever the Number of Members may be who compose that Assembly; in the Council of State, it is otherwise, and tho' some Provinces send there two Deputies, and others but one, yet every Member has a distinct Vote. But after all, with respect to the great Points of Sovereignty, they still remain in the States of each Province, who make War and Peace, coin Money, and raise Taxes within their own Territories, as they think fit. As each Province has its own *States*, so each has also a Council of State, and the same Kind of Government prevails likewise in the Cities, so that they are all in some measure independent Republicks. From this View of the Government in the *United Provinces*, one would naturally conclude it a Democracy, and so it really is with respect to its Form, but by Degrees Things have suffered great Changes. The Senate or Council in all the Cities, are, and were always for Life, but upon the Demise of any Member a new one was chosen by the Burghers, which being found very inconvenient, the Right of filling up such Vacancies was either yielded to, or assumed by those Assemblies; and this small Alteration has in Process of Time produced an Oligarchy, which shews how much Care should be taken in changing or tampering with the first Springs of Government.

We have at the Beginning of this Work given a succinct historical Deduction of the Progress of Commerce through the different Parts of *Europe*. To which let us add, the vast Trade of *Holland* arose chiefly from the Destruction of *Antwerp*, which, when the Civil Wars in the *Low-Countries* broke out, was, and had been long the Center of Traffick in *Europe*. The Troubles in *France*, the Wars in *Germany*, and the religious Persecutions set on foot in other Parts of *Europe*, contributed to fill the *United Provinces* with People, merely because here they might enjoy their Consciences, and the Fruits of their Industry, in Peace. Those who resorted thither were such as had wherewithal to live upon, or were acquainted with some Manufacture or Mystery, by which a Living might be obtained. Both were welcome, and both Sorts of People were very soon at their Ease; new Munufac-

tures

tures were every Day set on foot, and Trades too big even for a wealthy Purse, were managed with Facility, and to great Advantage, by joint Stocks ; the Fisheries were annually improved, new Branches of Commerce were continnally opened, and in the Compass of twenty Years, their Villages swelled into fair Towns, and those that were good Towns before, rose into rich Cities. At first the Inhabitants of those Provinces carried on a large Trade to *Portugal*, from whence they received great Quantities of *Indian* Goods ; but when *Philip* II. became Master of *Portugal*, he put an End to that Trade, which instead of proving a Misfortune, was in reality of high Advantage to the *Dutch*, by forcing them to attempt opening a Trade to the *East-Indies*, which in the Compass of a few Years they did with Success beyond their Hopes ; and this Commerce being managed by a Company with great Prudence, Frugality, and Industry, produced within the Period of which we have given the History, prodigious Advantages. This encouraged them to set up a *West-India* Company, and that too became no less flourishing in a very short Space of Time. The Subjects of the *States* likewise, by the Recommendation, and under the Protection of the *French* King *Henry* IV. obtained Leave to trade in all the Ports within the Dominions of the Grand Seignior ; so that their Commerce in the *Levant* became also within this Period very considerable. Taking therefore their Fisheries, Manufactures, and foreign Trade together, we may easily account for the Growth of their Naval Power, the Increase of their Wealth, and the Possibility of their sustaining that infinite Variety of Taxes, Customs, and Excises, which were necessary to support so long and so expensive a War, as that by which their Liberties were established and secured.

We ought likewise to observe, that the Situation of Affairs in *Europe* through this whole Period were remarkably favourable to the Growth of this new Republick. The overgrown Power of *Spain* was equally dreadful and dangerous to most of the Potentates in *Europe*, which induced them openly or secretly to give all the Assistance possible to the Inhabitants of these Provinces upon their Revolt ; and the intestine Disturbances in several Countries, but more especially in *Germany* and *France*, prevented their meeting with any Rivals ; and though it be true that *England* began at that Time to extend her Commerce, and increase her Naval Power, yet this was so far from being any Detriment, that it was in reality of very great Service to the *Dutch*, with whom they acted conjunctly in warlike Expeditions, and from whom, by the Temptation of high Wages,
they

they drew Numbers of experienced Pilots, and able Seamen, who were extremely useful to them in their early Voyages both to the *East* and *West-Indies*. The Quarrel between *England* and the *Hanse Towns* turned also very much to their Advantage; and in short, before any Spirit of Envy or Emulation arose, the Republick was not only beyond the Reach of Danger, but infinitely superior in every respect to any that could through Envy aim at lessening her Grandeur, the Progress of her Prosperity being not barely quicker than either Expectation or Experience could suggest, but beyond any thing which either ancient or modern History records, and which by Posterity will be very hardly believed.

But that we may not seem to deal wholly in generals, tho' this might be excused from the narrow Bounds to which we are confined, we will enter into a few Particulars, from whence the Reader will very easily discover the Truth of what we have already advanced, as to the sudden and immense Growth of the Commerce of this Republick. The original Fund or Capital of their *East-India* Company, was in their Language sixty Tons of Gold, by which Phrase of a Ton of Gold, is understood One hundred thousand Florins, or about Ten thousand Pounds Sterling, so that this Capital was very little above Six hundred thousand Pounds of our Money. In the Space of Six Years, deducting all their Costs and Charges, which were very great, and their Dividends, which were extremely high, the Fund or Capital of that Company increased notwithstanding to Six hundred Tons of Gold, that is, to upwards of Six Millions Sterling. It is indeed true, that the *East-India* Trade has not kept any thing like this Proportion since, but in Point of Wealth, Extent of Dominions, and real Power, the *Dutch East-India* Company is at this Day, not only beyond any Comparison with all other Commercial Establishments, but might be esteemed a very potent State of itself, if it was independent of their High Mightinesses. The Governor General, who resides at *Batavia*, and is Supreme in civil and military Affairs, has the State, the Court, and the Appointments of a Sovereign Prince; makes War and Peace at his Pleasure, can assemble an Army of Twenty or Thirty thousand Men, and if Occasion should require, could put to Sea a Fleet of fifty Sail of the Line of Battle, without building a Ship. A Power superior to any thing Trade ever produced elsewhere!

The *West-India* Company was at the Beginning as great and as fortunate, but they ruined themselves by making too large Dividends, and by neglecting Trade, that they might attend to their Conquests, which however was very excusable, while they

were

were Masters of *Brazil*, of which they might have continued Masters, if they had pursued the Example of the *East-India* Company, and had confided in Count *Maurice* of *Naffau*, to whom they stood in a great measure indebted for those important Conquests. But tho' they are now very inconsiderable in respect to what they were, or in regard of the *East-India* Company, yet they are still possessed of several important Places in *Africa*, of some Islands that yield a great Profit in the *West-Indies*, and of the valuable Settlement of *Surinam*, with many new Establishments upon the Continent of *South America*.

If therefore we reflect upon the Grandeur of these two Companies, and take into our Consideration also the vast Extent of the *Dutch* Commerce besides in the early Days of this Commonwealth, when the Trade of *Italy* was sunk, the maritime Power of *Spain* and *Portugal* in a great measure ruined, the Vigour of the *Hanse Towns* in *Germany* vastly declined, the Commerce of *Great Britain* in its Infancy, and hardly any Trade at all in the *North*, we may very easily conceive how the Subjects of the *United Provinces*, at the Beginning of the last Century, came to have more Shipping than all the rest of *Europe* together. We may likewise, by reviewing in our own Minds the Changes that have since happened in the Affairs of *Europe*, the great Application of this and other Nations, to the promoting Industry and encouraging Commerce, comprehend without any Difficulty how this Proportion has been altered to the Degree which has been set forth in the Beginning of this Work ; notwithstanding which, the Republick of the *United Provinces* still is, and has still the Capacity of maintaining the Rank of, a very great Maritime Power.

But besides the Reasons before assigned for the speedy Progress of this Republick in Power, Wealth, and Trade, there are a few Points that ought not to be omitted, because they have been less observed than those beforementioned, by most of the Authors who have treated this Subject. The Barrenness of the Soil and want of Subsistence in *Holland*, and *West-Friesland*, was a principal Cause of Industry and Wealth ; for People not being able to live there with the Practice of ordinary Labour, were compelled to join that of their Head with their Hands, and to make Frugality the Steward of what was acquired by both ; which soon strengthened into such Habits of Thinking, Working, and Saving, as rendered those Countries famous, and drew thither all who had a little Money to live upon, and were willing to improve it to the best of their Power. In the next place, a great Part of the People that were drawn into these Provinces by the Reputation of the Liberty enjoyed there, and the Mildness of the Government,

came

came thither from the *Walloon Provinces* which remained subject to the King of *Spain*, which gave them a double Advantage, by diminishing the Wealth and Power of their Enemy, in the very same Proportion that it strengthened themselves. Add to all this, that their Government in those Days had really great Advantages, for their military Power by Land and Sea being wholly under the Direction of their Stadtholders and Captain Generals, they derived from thence all the Benefits, without feeling any of the Inconveniencies sometimes borne in a Monarchy ; and the *States General* having all Civil Affairs entirely under their Direction and Management, they were very wisely conducted : for the Safety and Power of the Governors depending every where upon the Success of their Measures ; Probity and Prudence were so much their Interest, that it was next to impossible they should neglect them. And thus private Views concurring with publick Spirit, things for the first forty Years were in all Respects carried to as high a Degree of Perfection, as the Power of human Wisdom could provide, or indeed that human Abilities could reach.

But upon the Demise of *Willam*, the second Prince of *Orange*, the *States General* assumed the executive as well as legislative Power of the Government into their Hands, and conceiving the most violent Apprehensions of falling again under the Dominion of a single Person, made it the capital Object of their Policy to provide against it, which had very bad Effects. In 1651, they held another General Assembly, in which the Union of *Utrecht* was ratified. After this, the *Louvestein* Party projected the perpetual Edict for abolishing the Stadtholdership, that is, for destroying the Constitution which had been the Parent and Nurse of their Liberties ; they dismissed their best Officers, they disbanded their old Troops, and gave the Command of those that were necessarily kept up, to their own Friends and Relations. In short, their ruling Maxim was that which upon some Occasions they made their Motto, *Peace and a good Government* ; things very compatible for a Time, but which can never subsist long together.

For Peace, in process of Time, introduces Effeminacy and Corruption, which of course debase and infeeble a Government to such a Degree, as to render it incapable of resisting external Invasion, or intestine Commotions ; the former of which it invites, and seldom fails to kindle the latter. But though these Mischiefs might have been obvious enough to able and disinterested Politicians, yet Concern for private Advantage, hid them from the Eyes of the prevailing Faction in these Provinces, who with all their Zeal and Industry laboured to possess
them-

themselves of the Government, which they very speedily effected, to the most absolute and incontroulable Degree.

When I say they possessed themselves of it, I would be understood to mean, they filled by Degrees all Posts of Honour, Trust, and Profit, with those of their own Party, excluding such as were well affected to the Family of *Orange*; notwithstanding that Numbers of them had served their Country with equal Fidelity and Reputation. This produced here what it has ever produced in all Countries, where any thing of the like kind has happened, Envy, Discontent, Jealousies, Heats and Animosities, equally destructive of private Peace and publick Welfare. Those in Power treated such as they had excluded, as if they had been Enemies to their Country, and those that were oppressed regarded all in Possession of Employments, not as their legal Governors, but as so many Tyrants, who violated those Laws they pretended to administer, and treated as Slaves, those whom they stiled their Subjects.

At this Juncture, as we before remarked, the Republick was at its greatest Height in Respect to Power, to Wealth and Reputation; and this tempted the great Men then at the Head of Affairs, to signalize their Administration by entering into a War with *England*, which was suddenly become a Republick also What they hoped would have added Strength and Fame to that Authority, of which they were just become absolute Masters, had the quite contrary Effect, for it exhausted their Naval Power, and by its unfortunate Issue lessened their Credit extremely. This they ascribed to the Disaffection of some Officers they were obliged to employ, and to the Contagion of their Principles among the Seamen, which acquired some degree of Probability, by their managing with much better Success a second War with that Nation, after the Restoration of its Monarchy, and when the *Louvestein* Faction employed none but their own Creatures. Their good Fortune, however, as it made them insolent, so it rendered them hated; for tho' *John De Witt* who was at the Head of Affairs lived very modestly, and acted with great Moderation, yet his Brother *Cornelius*, tho' he too a brave and able Man, had such a Tincture of Vanity, and conducted every thing with such an Eclat, as raised the Envy of the better Sort, as much as it excited the Jealousy and Aversion of the Populace.

This Situation of their Affairs, and the extraordinary Power of *Lewis* XIV, made it necessary for the Governors of the Republick to court him, which tho' they sometimes did, yet such was the haughty Spirit of their Administration, that by a wanton Display of what they took to be the Effects of their great Wisdom and good Fortune, they provoked this great Monarch to

enter

enter into a Confederacy, which aimed at no less than the Destruction of the Republick. This produced the Invasion of 1672; and as that appeared to the People the mere Effects of the oftentatious Pride of their Rulers, it brought about a sudden, and in some Respects a bloody Revolution, the two *De Witts* being murdered by the Mob, the *Louvestein* System entirely dissolved, and *William* the third Prince of *Orange*, by the Abolition of the perpetual Edict, restored to the high Offices which his Ancestors had discharged with so much Glory.

The great Courage and Prudence with which he conducted that War, and extricated his Country from Difficulties very little inferior to those against which his Great Grandfather struggled, procured him the stable Possession of those Honours which the Inclinations of his Countrymen had bestowed, and fixed his Authority upon a firm as well as legal Basis. When that great Prince raised himself to the Throne of the *British* Dominions, he still retained the Dignity of Stadtholder, which in case he had been blessed with Children, was before that Time declared hereditary; but wanting this Support, and being obliged to be often absent, his Power was actually, tho' secretly diminished, while in outward Appearance it was at its greatest height. The Remains of the *Louvestein* Faction, partly by Compliance, and partly by dint of the great Interest of their Families, crept again into Employments, so that at the Demise of King *William*, they became once more in some measure Masters, and being taught Prudence and Moderation by Adversity, strengthened themselves imperceptibly, and at length settled their oligarchic Sway upon a much broader Foundation than it had ever stood before.

It is not known to many People, but the matter of Fact is nevertheless true, that the protracting the last general War, and the continual Opposition given by the Field Deputies of the *States* to the Duke of *Marlborough*, more especially at his first Entrance upon his Command of the Army of the Allies, was owing entirely to this State of Things. The *Louvestein* Faction were afraid, that if either a Battle should be lost, or their Troops removed at any Distance from their Frontiers, the Inhabitants of the great Cities would discover that Dislike, which they knew they bore to their Proceedings. The happy Progress of that War made them easier by Degrees, more especially after the unfortunate Death of his Serene Highness the Prince of *Orange* and *Nassau*, Father to the late excellent Stadtholder, who was drowned in his Passage at *Moredyke*, *July* the 14th, 1711, as he was coming to the *Hague*, to settle all Points in difference between the King of *Prussia* and himself, in relation to the Succession of

the

the late King *William* the third ; the Prince being Heir by Will, and the King by Defcent.

By this deplorable Accident in fo critical a Seafon, when the Claim of the Houfe of *Orange* defcended a fecond Time to a pofthumous Child, the Steps taken to fupport them were rendered abortive, and at the fame time it ruined in a manner all the Hopes of thofe who were either attached by Inclination, or connected by their Circumftances to that illuftrious Houfe. The dominant Party taking the Advantage therefore of this favourable Opportunity, exerted their utmoft Skill and Power in difpofing of all Places, in fuch manner as might render them for ever fecure, and prevent fo much as the glimmering of a Recovery to their Opponents, in which if they did not act as worthy Citizens, they certainly behaved wifely upon Party Principles ; and for fome time their Scheme was attended with all the Succefs they could wifh, as in other Countries is generally the Cafe, till Party Succefs turns upon itfelf.

In this State things continued for many Years ; and this Continuance encouraged fuch as were Mafters of Power, to believe it a thing inherent to them, that they had an exclufive Right to enjoy it, and that whoever fought to rife without their Confent, tho' he fought it in ever fo honourable a manner, was to be regarded as a public Enemy. A Man might be learned, induftrious and rich, might live in what manner he would, build Palaces, fet up Equipages, keep Affemblies, or even Operas in his own Houfe unmolefted ; but if fuch a Man lived frugally, was kind to his poor Neighbours, and took pains to be acquainted with the better Sort at the fame time, he was held in Sufpicion, and if he attempted to get into the Magiftracy, he was accounted a dangerous Man. Thefe Apprehenfions, grounded upon the known Difcontents of the common People, had fuch an Effect upon the Grandees, that inftead of regarding the Welfare and Honour of the Republick, they ftudied only to preferve it in Peace ; and this becaufe they faw plainly, that whenever War was declared or entered into againft any Enemy, but againft *France* more efpecially, it would fooner or later make a Breach in their Syftem, through which the Stadtholder would certainly enter and bring in his Friends with him, which they dreaded as much as they did the laft Day.

I may fafely appeal to the Hiftory of *Europe* in general, and to that of this Republick in particular, for the Proof of what I fay. Treaty after Treaty was made for the fake of preferving, or rather patching up of Peace ; the military Eftablifhment was fuffered to run into great Diforder, their maritime Power

dwindled

dwindled extremely, and in short every thing sunk, except Taxes, Debts, and the private Fortunes of these great Rulers and their Friends. By this means it came to pass, that in a short time it was no Secret the Strength of the State was greatly declined, she was in no Condition to undertake any thing extraordinary to deliver her out of this Plight, but rather obliged to attach herself some way or other to her Neighbours, so as to be sure of Support, and to be kept out of Danger of taking up Arms. Yet even in these Circumstances there wanted not Men bold enough to profess themselves Patriots, to compare the present Condition of the Republick with the past, and to testify their Wishes, that the Face of Affairs might change, so as to resemble what they were in former Times.

In 1722, the *States* of *Gueldres* chose the late Prince of *Orange* their Stadtholder, notwithstanding all the Opposition that could be given to that Measure by the Province of *Holland*; and this alarmed the prevailing Party excessively. They saw that this would give Life and Spirit to the Patriots, and that as his Serene Highness grew up, and displayed upon all Occasions the hereditary Virtues of his Family, the Number of his Adherents would increase, and those who disliked their Management would not be without a Head, as had been the Case for many Years; and this heightened their Aversion to every thing that had the least Appearance of Vigour, or of Spirit, at the same time it drove them into that Complaisance for a certain powerful Neighbour, which was so detrimental to the true Interests of *Europe*.

When in spite of all their Care, and after a long Series of temporizing and negotiating, they found themselves obliged to take a part in this last War, their Conduct was so fluctuating and irregular, that it gave no small Dissatisfaction to both Parties. On the one hand, the Allies knew not how to depend upon them; and, on the other hand, notwithstanding all the Service they rendered to the *French* by their Fickleness and Irresolution; they also were at a loss how to deal with them. In the first place, they tried by the Intrigues of *Fenelon*, and his Successor, to engage them in a Neutrality, to which they shewed at once an Inclination and a Reluctance. The former was the Effects of the true Spirit of their Government, which was to take care of themselves, and let what would become of the rest of the World; the latter proceeded from their Fear, for it was now evident enough that the People abhorred so dishonourable a Measure, and were inclined to hazard any thing, rather than sink into so shameful a

State

State of Dependence on that Power, which of all others they had moft Reafon to fear.

To bring the Matter therefore to fome Iffue, the *French* Court took the Refolution of making ufe of Force, and this induced them to transfer the War into the *Low-Countries*, and to attack the Barrier, which certainly was no Part of their original Defign, and which neither could, or did contribute much to the facilitating their Views. In this Invafion they had all the Succefs they could defire in the Field, but none at all in the great Point of the Neutrality, which by this time was become more difficult, and more dangerous for thefe great Statefmen to undertake; fince their Syftem was now thoroughly manifeft, and from the ftrange manner in which the War had been conducted, their Forces were fo much weakened, that they were as little able to impofe by Violence upon their Subjects, as to oppofe their Enemies. In the mean time, the Length of the War grew infupportable to the *French*, and they found themfelves under an abfolute Neceffity of coming to Extremities, and trying what might be done by falling upon the Territories of the *States*, which hitherto had been refpected. There is but too much Caufe to believe, that this was not altogether unforefeen in *Holland*; and the *French* Generals, from the natural Infolence and Impetuofity of that Nation, made fo little a Secret of the Expectations of their Court, when they fell upon *Dutch Flanders*, that the Populace, who had long before opened their Eyes, were tempted by Defpair to open their Mouths too, and to declare in plain Terms againft that Government, which either by Connivance or Contrivance had facrificed them.

The only Expedient they could have recourfe to, was fetting up his Serene Highnefs the Prince of *Orange* and *Naffau* for Stadtholder; and therefore there is no kind of Wonder, that they had recourfe to it. But, however, the Spirits of the Nation were funk to fuch a Degree, that whatever Figure the Mobs might make, that brought this important Event about, in our Gazettes, I can affirm that they were in themfelves very inconfiderable, and that two or three good Troops of Horfe might have difperfed them with great Eafe. The Reader muft have a care of conceiving from hence, that thofe who wifhed well to this Revolution were only the Dregs of the People, for there is nothing lefs true; but thofe who wifhed well to it, contented themfelves with thofe Wifhes, and were afraid to give any publick Signs of their Satisfaction till it became dangerous not to do it; and then feeing the Strength

of

of their own Party, they were amazed it had not been brought about long before. Yet they suffered themselves to be imposed upon by Appearances, and to believe, that the Facility with which this great Change had been instantaneously produced, was a good Omen of its proving as effectual as they could desire it; and therefore either from a Return of Indolence, or an unreasonable Timidity of acting against those to whom they had so long submitted, they left the Accomplishment of this great Work to the Populace who had begun it. Accordingly the Prince was declared Stadtholder of the Union, *June* $\frac{4}{15}$, 1747.

It is very certain, that if these poor People had known as well how to go about their Affairs, as they knew what they would have been at, they would have performed the whole Business of a Revolution to a Miracle; and as it was, they procured those Resolutions which have been the Basis of all that has been done since, and which will in the End become the fundamental Principles of the *Belgic* Liberty, either by a Restoration of the old Constitution, or the constructing it a-new. But how upright soever their Intentions might be, the boisterous Manner in which they pursued them, was manifestly inconsistent with any kind of Government, and therefore instead of countenancing them, the Prince Stadtholder found himself under a Necessity of restraining them.

This very necessary Step had two very unlucky Consequences; the first, that it encouraged the fallen Party to form new Schemes, and the next, that it not only damped the Spirits of the Populace, but induced those who secretly approved their Proceedings, to suspect that things would take another new turn, and that the old Faction would avail themselves of the Stadtholder's Authority. These Notions floating in People's Heads, produced for some time a Confusion that no Words can describe, and of which it is impossible that any should form an Idea, except those who saw and observed its Effects. By degrees all Ranks of People returned to their original Sentiments, the Patrons of the old System found themselves rather frighted than hurt, they were still in the quiet Possession not only of their private Fortunes, but of their Posts in the Government, and this tempted them to make their utmost Efforts to procure such a Countenance to their former Proceedings, as might make it appear both at home and abroad, that what they did was with the Consent of the Nation.

While they had this great Point in view, they forgot the Promises which they had made the People in the Beginning of the Year, and to the Performance of which they expected it

would

would be impossible to call them, on the Score of a very dangerous Distemper, with which his Serene Highness was then afflicted, the Issue of which being very doubtful, kept the Hopes of some, and the Fears of others in suspense; by which, as the domestick Oeconomy of the Republick suffered exceedingly, so it is to be feared the common Cause met with irreparable Damage, by the neglect of a War, as important in its Consequences, as in its Nature it was just and necessary.

Human Policy may be compared to the Image of *Janus*, except that the Eyes in the Head looking backward, are infinitely better than those that respect present or future Events. It is very certain that good Patriots at this Juncture, were under violent Apprehensions, and I dare say there was not a single Man in *Holland*, who foresaw the strange Effect of this dull and indolent Supineness, at a Season that required the utmost Activity, as well as the greatest Circumspection. It had, however, good Effects; for the People's Patience being quite wore out, and no Sign of the Performance of what had been promised them, they resumed the Work of Reformation, and resolved to demolish the Farms. When once this Humour broke out, it spread like Wildfire. Publicans were ever hated in all Countries, and by all Nations; that is, those who spoil their Neighbours under Colour of executing the Laws, but in reality to enrich themselves. This was plainly and undeniably the Case of the Farmers, from the greatest to the least; and whatever Authority they might derive from the Laws, there is no doubt that their Insolence, their Luxury, and their Profusion, was their own; and for these they were most justly punished.

One would have imagined that the shortest and most natural Way of putting a stop to these Disorders, had been to have complied with the Promises made to the People in the Month of *January*; and this was the very Method to which the Magistrates in some Cities were inclined to have recourse; but the Lovers of the old System, who could not bear the thoughts of losing the Farms and the Farmers, which afforded at once a large Revenue, and a numerous Militia, interposed, cancelled the publick Acts of those Magistrates, and endeavoured to maintain, as essential to the Government, what was become an insupportable Burthen upon the People; towards which they made a very free Use of his Serene Highness's Name, endeavouring to entrench their own Measures behind his Titles.

This, tho' well contrived, proved but a very feeble Expedient. Weak and infirm as his Highness was, he shewed the true Spirit, and generous Resolution of his illustrious Family; he came in Per-

son and offered that Proposition, which gave new Life to the
Republick, by shewing the Plan upon which he meant to proceed, and that he was in earnest resolved to put the Government upon its old and right Foundation, the Love, the Fidelity,
and Confidence of all its Subjects.

His Highness's subsequent Behaviour, in regard to the Tumults
at *Amsterdam*, the Pains taken to satisfy the People of *Friesland*
and *Groningen*, his Care in reference to the Disturbances at *Leyden*, his being content to undergo the Fatigue of holding the
supreme Direction of Affairs belonging to the *East-India* Company, and discharging it in such a manner, as to excite a Desire in the Proprietors of the *West-India* Company to vest the
like Measure of Authority in his Hands, plainly proved that
he inherited the Virtues and great Qualities of his illustrious
House, and seemed to be raised up by Providence to deliver the
Republick from the Jaws of Corruption (a Monster less hideous
indeed, but more subtle, and to the full as inexorable as
Tyranny herself) by his Wisdom and Virtue.

The whole of this Prince's Administration might, without
Partiality, and with great Propriety, be stiled a continual Display of his Affection for his Country, and for his Countrymen, and a clear Demonstration that his high Dignities were
no otherwise pleasing to him, than as they afforded him an Opportunity of removing Evils and doing good to the People. It
gave him inexpressible Concern, that with indefatigable Attention, and the best Inclination in the World, he could do but
little. Like a Husbandman employed in the Cultivation of
a degenerate Soil, he ploughed and sowed without receiving
any Return, or at least a very small one, in the Harvest. Under
these Difficulties his Spirit rather rose than fell; and he was always offering some new Expedient for the Benefit of the State,
or for the Service of the People, notwithstanding they were almost always rejected. He pushed with the most Vigour the
Performance of those Promises that had been made to the Publick; and in all human Probability he would at length have
prevailed so far as to have seen them executed in their utmost
Extent, of which the present Generation have now but weak
Expectations.

At the Time when, for certain Reasons, he thought proper
to make a Tour to *Aix la Chapelle*, he caused the great Scheme
for the REVIVAL of TRADE to be laid before the *States* in
his Absence, that they might deliberate freely upon it, and
take what Share of Merit to themselves they pleased. If
this had been the only shining, as it was almost the last *Act*

of his *Adminiſtration*, it ought to have rendered his Memory immortal, as it was indubitably one of the worthieſt and nobleſt Actions his high Dignity enabled him to perform. He could not be ſuppoſed to underſtand Commerce, as a Merchant; he never affected any kind of Knowledge that did not become him. He underſtood it however as a Prince, he knew that it was the ſole Foundation of Maritime Power, he ſaw that the State roſe as it roſe, and that it declined as it decayed. He judged therefore, and he judged wiſely, that the moſt ſpeedy, certain, and effectual Method to reſtore the Affairs of the Republick, was to revive Commerce; and having formed this great and ſalutary Project, he did next what Princes are leaſt inclined to do, he ſought, he obtained, and he followed the *beſt Advice*.

It had been glorious for him, and happy for his Country, if he had lived to purſue and perfect this great Deſign, which procured him the ſolemn Thanks of the City of *Amſterdam*, and the univerſal Attachment of the whole mercantile Intereſt in *Holland*. But Providence otherwiſe decreed; and tho' at his Return from *Aix la Chapelle*, his Highneſs appeared in a better State of Health than for many Years before, yet he ſoon after fell ill of a Fever, which in a very ſhort Time bereaved the *United Provinces* of their *Beſt-beloved* Stadtholder; for that was the Epithet beſtowed on him by the Voice of the People; and deprived *Europe* of a Prince, whoſe Virtues added Luſtre to his Dignity, in the Prime of his Life; for he was but in the fortieth Year of his Age; and when he was moſt in a Condition to execute the great and good Deſigns he had ever meditated for the Benefit of the Republick.

Immediately upon his Death the *States General* chearfully, punctually, and honourably executed the conſtitutional Settlement, in acknowledging the Count *de Buren* his Son for their Hereditary Stadtholder, and her Royal Highneſs the Princeſs of *Orange*, his Widow, in Quality of Governeſs General during the Minority. What will follow is in the Womb of Time, and may it bring forth propitious Events to the Peace of this Country, the Proſperity of the Proteſtant Intereſt, and the Independency and Tranquility of Chriſtendom!

All the ſenſible and diſintereſted Part of the *Dutch* Nation, are by this time convinced, that the Notion of a perfect Democracy, and a Form of Government founded on an Equality of Wealth and Power, is mere Deluſion, invented and preached up by ſuch, as mean to poſſeſs themſelves of as much of both as

they

they can poffibly grafp, and then cover themfelves and their Affociates with the fpecious Title of the Rulers of a free People, when they are in Fact no more than Leaders of a certain Faction. The Nation muft be fatisfied from Experience, that fuch a Regimen as this, participates of both Extremes, of Tyranny and Anarchy; inclining to the former in a Seafon of full Peace, and declining towards the latter in a Time of Trouble. The *Dutch* Nation muft by this time apprehend, that the only natural Poize in their Conftitution is the Power of a Stadtholder; in whom an Excefs of Authority can never be apprehended, while that innate Love of Liberty, for which they have been ever famous, continues to glow in their Bofoms, and whofe Authority will by Degrees extinguifh thofe Attempts, that crafty and feditious Men may infpire their Tools to make, in order to create frefh Confufions. Harmony and Perfection are the Works of Time, as well as Wifdom, and the Continuance of Peace will without doubt bring them to that Maturity, which will effectually reftore the domeftick State of their Affairs.

As to the foreign Interefts of this Republick, they confift in living upon good Terms with her Neighbours, in the ftrict Performance of Treaties, and in the Maintenance of the Ballance of Power. A good Correfpondence with her Neighbours is an effential Point of Policy with refpect to this State, becaufe the chief Dependence of her Subjects is on Commerce, which is incompatible with an unfettled State of Things. This Maxim however muft not be adhered to, without due Deference for the other two, fince Peace, like Gold, may be bought too dear, and nothing can be fo prejudicial to Commerce, as to make it a Pretence for betraying the Dignity, and finking the Credit of the State, by which it muft in time be weakened, and in the End loft. Alliances and Treaties of a defenfive Nature are to be made with great Deliberation, but are facred when once concluded, and muft be at all Events fulfilled, that the Republick may have a clear Title to the Affiftance of her Allies whenever her Circumftances may require it. But that Peace may produce thofe Fruits that are expected from it; that the Endeavours of the Republick may prove fuccefsful in the Caufe of her Friends; and that her Allies may never be deterred from complying with their Engagements in her Favour; it is abfolutely neceffary that the Ballance fhould be preferved. For this Maxim, as it gave Being to the Republick, which was fupported in its Infancy, in order to leffen the exorbitant Power of *Spain*; fo if ever the Ballance fhould be loft, it is fure to feel the bad Effects

of

of it firft, and in the moft imminent Degree. As thefe are Truths, which may be demonftrated from Reafon, fo they have been more than once juftified by Experience, fince the Affairs of *Europe* were never at a Crifis in this refpect, but thofe of the *United Provinces* were in the utmoft Danger, as the Reader has already feen from a Deduction of Facts.

In the *North*, it is apparently the Intereft of *Holland* to fupport the Independency of the feveral Powers in that Part of *Europe*. Her wifeft Statefmen have always maintained this, and when her Affairs have been beft managed, fhe has acted accordingly. Her Fleets have more than once fecured the Kingdom of *Denmark* from being totally overwhelmed; and fhe has frequently felt in Return, the good Effects of her wife and laudable Concern for the *Danes*. At the Clofe of the laft Century, fhe joined with *Great Britain* in fending a Fleet under the Command of Sir *George Rooke*, to the Affiftance of the *Swedes*, upon which Occafion fhe acted againft the *Danes*; and this too was a wife and prudent Meafure, which anfwered very effectually the End it was calculated to anfwer, and prevented that Defign from taking Effect; which was contrived to weaken, if not to fubvert the Ballance in the *North*, which can never fuffer, but the Commerce of *Holland* muft fuffer likewife.

It is impoffible to reflect on the Situation of the Territories of the Republick, without perceiving how great an Intereft fhe has in preferving the Ballance between the Houfes of *Auftria* and *Bourbon*, and of what Importance it is to her Safety, as well as Profperity, that the former fhould not be oppreffed. She is likewife obliged to have a conftant Attention to the Princes of *Germany*, who on the other fide have very powerful Reafons to live upon good Terms with her, and when her Affairs require it, to yield her any Affiftance that fhe wants. But above all, fhe is bound to maintain a perfect Friendfhip with his *Pruffian* Majefty, as well on account of the vaft Acceffion of Power which that Monarch has obtained, as his being her near Neighbour, in Confequence of having Part of *Guelderland* yielded to him by the Treaty of *Utrecht*; the Duchy of *Cleves*, by his Treaty of Partition with the Elector Palatine; the Diftricts that fell to him as joint Heir of King *William* III; and the Principality of *Eaft Friefland*, which is acquired by the Extinction of the Line of its ancient Princes. With all thefe Powers, the Republick is under Engagements by folemn Treaties, and it is by an exact Performance of thefe, that fhe muft maintain her Rank, her Reputation, and the Benefits

which

which refult to her Subjects, from the Conftitution of her Government; which in virtue of thofe Treaties, all thefe Powers are bound to maintain.

In reference to the Ballance in *Italy*, fhe has alfo confiderable Intereft; refulting from the large Share of Commerce which her Subjects enjoy in the *Mediterranean* and the *Levant*, and which will always depend on the preferving the Independence of the Princes and States in that Part of *Europe*; fo that fhe is bound to promote that, as far as in her lies; and in Times paft, has fhewn a due regard to this Obligation. She has befides, fome particular Engagements with the *Swifs Cantons*, and their Allies; and has for a long Courfe of Years, had a confiderable Corps of their Infantry in her Service, who with great Courage and Fidelity have fought in fupport of her Liberties, whenever they were in Danger.

Laftly, there is nothing clearer, than that it is her true Intereft to live in perfect Harmony with *Great Britain*; in as much as both Countries have continually reaped the greateft Advantages, when this Union has fubfifted; and have both felt and ftill feel the bad Effects of being fet at Variance, and employing their Maritime Forces againft each other, through the Intrigues of their common Enemies. It is indeed true, that each of thefe Powers have an equal Intereft in Commerce; but while they live upon good Terms, and confult their refpective Interefts only, they can without any Difficulty regulate the Views of their Subjects, fo as to prevent their clafhing with each other, and for the common Benefit of both, which in the prefent Situation of Things is far eafier than in former Times; and perhaps too of greater Confequence than ever, confidering the new Schemes that are every Day formed, and are ftill forming in different Parts of *Europe*, with a Tendency equally prejudicial to the Trade of both.

CHAP. XV.

Of the true Interest of Great Britain, with respect to the other Powers of Europe.

THE gradual Changes that have happened in the Circumstances of this Nation, may be very rationally supposed to have had a strong Influence upon its Interests, and yet this does not seem to have been sufficiently considered; for if it had, we should scarce find so many People as there really are, who adhere to the old Notions laid down by some of our Patriots in the Beginning of the last Century, that the true Interest of this Nation consists in keeping their Affairs as distinct from those of the Continent, as their Country is removed from it by Nature, who by surrounding it with the Sea, seems to have made it a World by itself. It must be confessed, that many plausible Things have been advanced in Support of this Doctrine, as well as great Authorities alledged, more especially that of the learned Antiquary Sir *Robert Cotton*, who wrote a Treatise to this Purpose in the Reign of King *James* I. with a View of convincing *Henry* Prince of *Wales*, that he ought not to pay any respect to the Arguments which had been insinuated to him, against the pacifick Measures that were then in Fashion, but ought to regard whatever was said of foreign Wars, and foreign Acquisitions, as calculated to gratify the Spirit of ambitious Men, at the Expence of their Country, which had been often exhausted, but never received any real Benefit from such Kind of Expeditions, as he undertook to shew from History and Records.

But whatever Truth there might be in this Doctrine, as it is laid down by him, and how well soever it might be supported by the Instances which he has produced, it has nothing to do with the present State of our Affairs; and the only Use that can be made of it, is so far to examine it, as that we may be convinced of the Truth of this Observation. The Expeditions made by our ancient Princes for the Maintenance of the Countries they possessed in *France*, or in Support of their Claim to that Crown, might very probably impoverish this Nation, and how much soever their Successes might enlarge the Power, or exalt the Glory of those Monarchs, they might be far enough from be-

ing

jng ufeful to their Subjects. It is however very poffible that they might be in fome meafure neceffary, as our Conftitution then ftood; and we fhall have the more Reafon to credit this, if we confider that fuch of our Princes were always moft popular at home, as made themfelves renowned by their victorious Arms abroad, and that fuch as purfued a contrary Conduct, were very feldom free from domeftick Infurrections, or foreign Invafions.

The only Objections that can be raifed to this Pofition, muft be taken from the Conduct of *Henry* VII. who was indeed a very wife Prince, and yet is reported to have meddled lefs with foreign Affairs than moft of his Predeceffors. Yet upon a more ftrict Examination it will be found, that his Happinefs refulted chiefly, not from the confining his Cares entirely to his own Dominions, but from his prudent Management of that Share he thought proper to take in the Transactions of the Continent. It has been thought, that as a true Politician he fhould have prevented the *French* King from annexing the Duchy of *Bretagne* to his Crown, but it does not appear that this was at all in his Power. He made ufe, however, of the Jealoufy which the Nation conceived upon this great Acceffion to the *French* Power, and actually engaged in a War againft *France*, for the Profecution of which he had vaft Supplies granted him by Parliament. Yet he did not after all this carry on that War in the Manner that was expected, but contented himfelf with making, from the Terror of his Arms, a Peace upon very advantageous Terms, that lafted during his Life, by which he fecured to himfelf an annual Tribute from two *French* Monarchs fucceffively, and which left them at full Liberty to purfue their Defigns in *Italy*, that exhaufted their Treafures, and weakened their Forces as much as a War with *England* would have done, and proved confequently more to his Advantage. He took care likewife during that Peace this Meafure procured, to enter into a ftrict Alliance with the Houfe of *Auftria*, which was a very right Connection at that Time, cemented that Alliance by a Marriage, and married his own Daughter to the King of *Scots*, which, as he forefaw, united in Procefs of Time the whole Ifland into one Kingdom. The true Inference therefore from his Conduct is this, that the intermeddling more or lefs with the Affairs of the Continent is right or wrong, according to the Judgment the Prince who intermeddles forms of the Situation and Circumftances of Things.

The

The Figure that *Great Britain* makes at prefent in *Europe*, arifes from her being in a Situation very different from that fhe held in Times paft ; but we owe our prefent Greatnefs to Maxims very different from that of neglecting every thing that paffes without the Bounds of our own Ifland. The wife Queen *Elizabeth*, who laid the Foundation of that Wealth and Power which we now poffefs, acted upon quite different Principles, and was fo far from paying no Attention to foreign Affairs, that it plainly appears they were never fo well underftood or managed as in her Time. She it was that prevented *Philip* II. from accomplifhing his Scheme of univerfal Empire, not barely by providing for the Security of her Dominions at home, but by employing both Money and Men to occupy him with perpetual Diverfions abroad. She prevented *France* from becoming a Province to *Spain*, which muft have been fatal to the Liberties of *Europe* ; and fhe afforded that Affiftance to the *States* of the *United Provinces*, that enabled them to become an independent Republick, which has in fucceeding Times contributed fo much to preferve the Independence of the *European* Powers againft the ambitious Views of the Houfe of *Bourbon*.

It is true, that fhe likewife promoted the Navigation and Commerce of her Subjects, opened a Paffage for them into both the *Indies*, and excited that Spirit which afterwards induced us to make Settlements in the moft diftant Parts of the Globe; and by a wife and happy Conjunction of our Labours both there and in *Britain*, at once extended our Wealth and Power, without the leaft Diminution of our People, contrary to the Effects of Plantations made from other Countries, which have fuffered at home, by aggrandizing themfelves abroad ; whereas our domeftic Power is conftantly augmented, in Proportion to the Advantages derived from our Settlements abroad ; and to this Circulation of our Commerce it is in reality oweing, that our Strength is fo much greater, our Lands fo much more valuable, and our intrinfic Wealth fo much increafed, as it is fince that Time ; and this, in fpite of long Wars, and other intervening Accidents, not at all favourable to our Interefts.

This may look like a Paradox to fome, and there may be others who perhaps will regard it as a thing taken upon Truft. But in reality the Facts are abfolutely certain, and it is to the wonderful Growth of our Plantations that we owe the Strength and Populoufnefs of this Ifland, which could never otherwife have attained its prefent Condition. A very little Attention will make this plain. The Commodities and Manufactures of any
Country

Country have a certain Limit, beyond which it is impossible they should extend without an Alteration of Circumstances, that is to say, when they are carried so high, as that no new Markets are to be found, domestick Industry can proceed no farther. Now it is owing to our Colonies, that hitherto we have not been very sensible of this Truth ; for the People settled there, from a Variety of Causes, into which I have not room to enter at present, take off much greater Quantities of our Commodities and Manufactures, than if they had remained at home. So that one of our Countrymen established in *America*, finds full Employment for several Hands here ; and as full Employment will always draw People, it plainly follows from thence, that our Settlements abroad must increase the Number of People at home. As this Method of arguing shews the Reason of the Thing, so the Truth of it may be likewise demonstrated from Experience. It is certain, that the Number of People in the City of *London* is about five times as great as at the Death of Queen *Elizabeth* ; and tho' it cannot be supposed, that the Number of People in this Island hath increased in the same Proportion, yet it is certain that they have very much increased, as is apparent from the Growth of other great Cities, the swelling of small Villages into large Towns, and the raising on our Coasts of many new Sea Ports. It may indeed be objected, that if People remove out of the Country into great Towns, this augments the Number of their Inhabitants, but not that of the Nation, but then the Fact must be proved, which is a thing impossible ; for such as dwell in great Towns consume a larger Quantity of Provisions, and all other Necessaries, than such as live scattered up and down the Country, they must consequently be supplied with these, and therefore the Growth of Towns must increase the Number of People in the Country about them. Thus the farther we trace this Matter, the clearer and the more certain it appears, and therefore what is deduced from it cannot be rationally called in question.

We may from hence likewise discern how the other Parts of the *British* Dominions have also increased in the Number of their Inhabitants, as well as *England*, and have reaped a proportionable Benefit from so happy a Change in their Circumstances ; which as it demonstrates how much they owe to that excellent Constitution under which they live, so it is likewise an evident Proof that it is the Interest, and ought to be the Care of such as are intrusted with the Administration of the Government, to see that every Part of the *British* Empire enjoys to the full the Advantages derived from the Laws, and that glorious Freedom which is the Result of their being maintained

tained in full Vigour. The Subjects as well as the Soil are ever to be taken into our Notion of the *British* Empire; and as Obedience is expected from such as are ever so remote, as well as those who are near the Center of Government, so they are entitled to the same Protection and Encouragement; which while they receive, there is no doubt that our Affairs will continue in a flourishing Condition, and the Fears which many have entertained, that some of our distant Colonies may some time or other throw off their Obedience to their Mother Country, will be but Dreams and Vapours; for in the Body Politick, as in the Natural Body, while the vital Parts are strong and found, the Circulation will be every where brisk and lively, and the Effects of it perfectly felt, to its very Extremities. In Theory this looks very fair and probable, but it is our peculiar Felicity, that through the Piety, Virtue, and Wisdom of our Ancestors, we know that this may be, and is reduced to Practice. We need only look into the State of our Affairs at present, compare them with what they were in times past, and reflect on the manner in which these Alterations have happened, to be convinced this is all Reality, and not Vision.

It is the maintaining the *British* Empire in this Situation, and thereby providing for the Happiness of this Nation, that as I said ought to be the sole Point of View to our Statesmen and Patriots, as of old among the *Greeks* and *Romans*. Our Constitution like theirs is of a mixt Nature, but one may without Partiality or Vanity affirm, that it is more happily compounded, so that Majesty and Liberty trespass not at all upon each other, the Prerogative of the Prince being without Restraint, where it may be exerted for his Subjects Good, and the Paramount Prerogative, being this, that the Crown can do no hurt at all. It is most evident therefore, that at this Day our Princes can have no Temptation to enterprize Wars of Conquest as in former Times; so that a true Spirit of Patriotism can never be shewn, in opposing Projects that will never be set on foot; and in this lies our great Happiness, that having no Views or Pretensions upon our Neighbours, there is no solid, indeed not so much as a plausible Ground for us to hate them, or they us. This is the true fundamental Principle of our Policy; that in respect to the Affairs of the Continent, we are not to be governed by any of those temporary or accidental Conveniences, which very often, and that justly too, pass for reasons of State in other Kingdoms; but by this single Rule, of their acting in Conformity to our natural Interests, so far as is consistent with their own.

There

There is a Diſtinction often made, chiefly by Foreigners, between the Intereſt and the Commerce of *Great Britain*; but in reality this is a Diſtinction without a Difference; for the Intereſt and the Commerce of the *Britiſh* Empire are ſo inſeparably united, that they may be very well conſidered as one and the ſame. For Commerce is that Tie, by which the ſeveral, and even the moſt diſtant Parts of this Empire, are connected and kept together, ſo as to be rendered Parts of the ſame Whole, and to receive not only Countenance and Protection, but Warmth and Nouriſhment from the vital Parts of our Government, of which, if I may be indulged ſo figurative an Expreſſion, our Monarchy is the Head, and our Liberty the Soul. Whatever therefore aſſiſts, promotes, and extends our Commerce, is conſiſtent with our Intereſt; and whatever weakens, impairs, or circumſcribes it, is repugnant thereto. We may eaſily, conſidering Things in this light, (and if we conſider them in any other, we ſhall deceive ourſelves) derive from thence a true Notion of the Intereſt of *Great Britain*, with reſpect to the other Powers of *Europe*; and be able to judge when that Intereſt is really purſued, and when it is either neglected or abandoned.

The firſt Point dictated by our Intereſt, is the maintaining others in their Rights, or to make uſe of a more known Term, to ſupport the Independency of the Powers of *Europe*; becauſe the engroſſing, ſubjecting, or ſubduing ſeveral Countries under one Potentate, naturally and even neceſſarily contributes to leſſen the Number of Inhabitants, to extinguiſh Induſtry amongſt them, and conſequently to enfeeble and impoveriſh them, which muſt be detrimental to us, if we correſpond or trade with them.

Another Point is, the ſtipulating with foreign Nations proper Terms of Security, Indulgence, and Reſpect for our Subjects, and for the Effects which from time to time they ſhall carry into thoſe Countries, in return for which we muſt covenant on our parts, to do and perform what ſhall be thought reaſonable. When theſe Kind of Alliances are made with due Deliberation, they become ſacred Ties with reſpect to us, and we are bound to fulfil them punctually; ſo that whatever different Form Appearances may wear, the true Intereſt of *Great Britain* is always to comply exactly with her Treaties.

A third Rule is, to reſent Wrongs done us, vigorouſly and without delay, more eſpecially where it is in our Power to do it by employing our maritime Force, ſince in this Caſe it anſwers a double End; firſt, it redreſſes the Miſchief, whatever it is, for the preſent; and next, it raiſes our Reputation for the future,

future. We ought likewife to be ready to affift any Nation that is unjuftly attacked, or in any Danger of being oppreffed, that it may be feen we are true Lovers of Freedom, and are as unwilling to behold the Necks of others put under a Yoke, as to fubmit our own.

Thefe Rules conftantly attended to, are fufficient to keep us upon good Terms with all the World, and to make it the Intereft of every Potentate and State in *Europe*, to court as well as to refpect our Friendfhip; which ought to be freely beftowed, and not either purchafed or proftituted. It may fometimes happen, that a ftrict Compliance with thefe Rules will interfere with fome Branch or other of our Commerce; neither in fuch a Cafe muft that be regarded, for it is not this or that particular Branch of Commerce, which coincides with the general Intereft of this Nation, but the whole Circle of our Commerce; and therefore there is nothing abfurd or contradictory in affirming, that the Whole muft take place of a Part, any more than it is ridiculous to affirm, that whatever refpects the Intereft of a Nation, becomes worthy the Concern of a Monarch, let its Nature be what it will. And therefore they are in an Error, who think the Royal Character any way leffened, by being obliged to attend to Trade, a Thing already acknowledged in many Parts of *Europe*, and which by Degrees will be found true in all; to which let me add another Truth, that Trade is a mean and inconfiderable thing, in thofe Countries only where this Error ftill prevails.

It appears in fome meafure from our Hiftory, and much more from our Records, that we have always interefted ourfelves very much in the Affairs of the *North*. Our old Treaties with *Sweden*, *Denmark*, and *Poland*, fpeak this plainly, and our Alliances with *Ruffia* are elder than thofe of moft other Powers. We have, as Occafion required, acted either as Mediators or Allies, in favour of all thefe Powers. The *Swedes* in particular have been frequently indebted to us for Affiftance, and in the laft Century, they detached themfelves in a great meafure from the Interefts of *France*, for the fake of our Friendfhip, which was a Meafure very beneficial to all *Europe*. At prefent we are clofely connected with *Ruffia*, and with very good Reafon; neither can our Alliance ever be flighted by the Northern Potentates, while the *Baltick* remains open to our Fleets, that is, while we remain a Maritime Power. This Confideration, joined to thofe important Points beforementioned, will always hinder us from entering into improper or inconfiftent Treaties, cannot fail of keeping up our Reputation in this part of the World, and confequently preferving that Refpect to thofe Privileges,

vileges, and that Attention to our Demands, which the Situation either of our Affairs or theirs may require. For as we can never have any Interest superior to, or inconsistent with the Care of the Ballance in the *North*, so that must also remain the great Object of all the Potentates there, and is not likely therefore to suffer any great Alteration within the Compass of that Period, to which human Foresight or human Policy can extend.

As to the Affairs of the *German* Empire in general, and of the several Princes in particular, we have always maintained a fair Correspondence with them, and manifested when it was necessary, a just Concern for their Liberties; the same Conduct will be ever incumbent upon us, so long as we preserve a Respect for the Protestant Religion, and for that great Principle of Independence, which has been no where cultivated so much as in *Germany*, and where it still continues to make a considerable Figure. It has been thought also the Interest of this Nation, to shew an extraordinary Zeal in favour of the House of *Austria*, notwithstanding the Rectitude of that Measure hath been at different times controverted, if I mistake not, by both Parties. It is indeed true, that in reference to our Commerce we have no less Connection with the House of *Austria*, than with many, I may say with most of the great Powers in *Europe*; as also, that we have supported her in times past, at a very large Expence to ourselves, without any visible View of reaping any immediate Advantage from the Effects of those Subsidies, which were so liberally granted. To this it has been added, that by this wonderful Attachment, we have greatly promoted the Power and Influence of that House over the *Germanick* Body, which how useful soever it might be to the Sovereigns of that illustrious Family, might turn in some measure to our Prejudice, as it could not fail of giving Offence to many of the Princes in *Germany*, who for that very Reason had recourse to another Power, at a time when if we had dealt more equally, they would have relied solely upon us.

But notwithstanding all this, if we consider that the House of *Austria* is on one Side the great Bulwark of Christendom against the *Turks*, and on the other, the natural Ballance against *France*, and also a near Neighbour to us in Part of her Dominions, it is no Wonder at all, but rather an Honour to us, that we have adhered so closely to our Engagements. In supporting that august Family in three several Wars, we justified our Fidelity to our Treaties, which in itself is a

Point

Point ever of the higheſt Conſequence, as it is a Kind of national Honour, which once loſt can hardly ever be regained. As to the Judgments of Parties, they are not always to be relied upon, but if they were, it would be no difficult thing to ſhew, that all Parties have in their turns approved this Meaſure, which when prudently purſued, is certainly right; and tho' immediate Advantages may not ſpring from it, yet if there be no other way than this of ſupporting the general Ballance of Power, and maintaining that Independence which is the primary Point in our foreign Syſtem, we acted well and wiſely in ſuſtaining it ; neither could any Offence be juſtly taken at this by any of the *German* States, ſince if they had conſidered it in a true Light, it was as much their Intereſt as ours ; and many Inſtances might be produced to prove, that they have injured and weakened themſelves by a contrary Conduct. If indeed our Partiality to the Houſe of *Auſtria* had ever carried us into the Breach of Treaties with other Powers, or put us upon ſupporting the ambitious Schemes of that Houſe, or any other Houſe, to the Prejudice of their Neighbours, the Charge would be juſt, and the Adminiſtration culpable that had led us into thoſe Meaſures.

An inveterate Hatred, or a perpetual Oppoſition to *France*, is a Maxim that never was laid down by any wiſe *Engliſh* Miniſter, and ought never to be received or countenanced. In Queen *Elizabeth*'s Time we aſſiſted the preſent reigning Family, and Medals were ſtruck with the Arms of *England*, *France*, and *Holland*, as Powers whoſe Intereſts were thoroughly united, and ſo at that Time they were; and our Regard for the *French* as well founded then, as that which we teſtify for the Houſe of *Auſtria* is now. But preciſely at that Juncture, when our Conduct ought to have changed, we miſtook our Meaſure, and *Cromwell*, by embracing the Intereſts of that Crown, facilitated the Execution of Schemes that have been ſince ſo detrimental to *Europe* in general, and this Nation in particular. The Miſtake was quickly diſcerned, but not ſo ſoon rectified ; on the contrary, two of our Princes perſiſted in that Miſtake, as well againſt the Intereſt, as againſt the Voice of the Nation. When we recovered from our Error, we found it very difficult to retrieve what had been loſt by this ill Conduct ; we managed a long and very expenſive War with little apparent Succeſs, but this War however weakened, and wore out the Strength of *France* ſo much, as to make way for the glorious Victories that were obtained in that which quickly ſucceeded it, which is ſufficient to conſole us for Loſſes and

Ex-

Expences in a juft Caufe. It is that Caufe that we fupport, and not an innate, hereditary, and groundlefs Averfion to the *French* Nation; for whenever their Statefmen fhall abandon that Plan which is dangerous and deftructive in its Nature to themfelves as well as others, they will infallibly difarm us, and extinguifh that Animofity which their boundlefs Ambition, and not our Obftinacy or Perverfenefs, has excited. There have been, within the Memory of the prefent Generation, certain Seafons, in which the *French* Minifters either really or feemingly laid by thofe Schemes, and affected to act upon other Principles, that very foon produced an Alteration in the Conduct of other Powers towards them, which fully juftifies this Obfervation; and therefore their Politicians have no juft Grounds for imputing to the Fiercenefs of our Manners, that Alacrity we have fhewn in entering into all Alliances againft them, but ought rather to afcribe it to that Rectitude of Judgment which is natural to a free People, and which will always appear amongft us as long as we continue free.

The Ballance in *Italy* is thought to concern us more remotely, notwithftanding which, we have hitherto fhewn a juft and laudable Regard to that likewife; and indeed Diftance in this Refpect is of little Confequence, more efpecially to a Maritime Power. Our Commerce in the *Mediterranean*, and in the *Levant*, is of very high Importance, and we cannot but be fenfible, that whatever Alterations have been felt in the *Italian* Ballance, have likewife affected thofe Branches of our Commerce in a very fenfible Degree; fo that whatever Steps we have taken, either during the Continuance of Peace by Negotiations, or in Time of War, by fupporting the only Prince in *Italy* who declared for the common Caufe, and was true to his own Interefts, which were likewife ours, were right and juft Meafures, and have no doubt left thofe Impreffions which will never be effaced by any Arts or Intrigues, whatever may be given out to ferve their own Purpofes, at certain critical Junctures, by fuch as wifh they may.

The recent Injuries our Merchants have fuftained, and the great Infults offered to the Nation by the Corfairs of *Barbary*, will not allow us to doubt, that it is our true Intereft to keep the *Italian* States firmly united to us, that when Occafion requires they may afford us all the Conveniencies in their Power towards chaftifing thefe Infidels, as our ufing vigorous Meafures in fuch Cafes, and fending a powerful Fleet into the *Mediterranean*, will contribute not a little to make us refpected by the *Italian* Potentates, as well as to obtain Juftice from thofe pyratical

pyratical Governments, tho' for the prefent Things have been adjufted by milder Meafures.

Our Affairs with the Crown of *Spain* have been long in a perplexed Situation, notwithftanding that it is generally thought the *Spanifh* Minifters have fuch true Notions of their own Intereft, as to be perfuaded that nothing concerns them more, than to live upon good Terms with *Great Britain*. Without any Queftion it is our Intereft likewife to live in a perfect Correfpondence with that Court, and therefore no Pains ought to be fpared that are requifite to remove all Jealoufies and Difcontents on both Sides. It was hoped, that this would have been effectually done by the Definitive Treaty of *Aix la Chapelle* ; but it feems that the Neceffity of reftoring the Tranquility of *Europe*, made it requifite to conclude that Treaty without adjufting the Differences between the *Britifh* and *Spanifh* Courts, which were left to a particular Negotiation, which in part has taken place, and in part is ftill depending. It is from this remaining Negotiation that we are yet to expect an abfolulte Conclufion of this important Bufinefs, which as it has proceeded flowly, we have good Ground to apprehend, whenever it is brought to a Determination, will fettle the Terms of Correfpondence to the mutual Satisfaction of both Nations. Delays are very difagreeable in all Points of national Concern, but more efpecially fo in Points of great Confequence, fuch as this undoubtedly is both to us and to them. Yet after all, if by bearing with thefe Delays, Things can be entirely adjufted, fo as to leave no Grounds for future Difputes ; inftead of patching up expedient Agreements to ferve a prefent Turn, which never afford Content to either Party, and are feldom long obferved, we fhall have good Caufe to excufe thofe Delays, and to be well pleafed with the final Iffue of them. In the mean time we have the Comfort of knowing, that at length the Syftem of Expedients is exploded ; for if there had been the leaft Intention of returning to that Sort of Practice, we might have had a Convention long ago. It was certainly better to treat with Clearnefs and Dignity, to explain and go to the Bottom of Grievances on both Sides, that both old and frefh Wounds might be thoroughly healed, and not fkinned over, and that fucceeding Minifters may have a full, explicit, and well-concerted Treaty for their Guide, upon which the Subjects of both Crowns may rely, without any Doubts as to the Senfe of the refpective Articles, or any Fears of their not being punctually executed.

We

We have lived so long, and in so strict a Friendship with the Crown of *Portugal*, that I mention it here only for the Sake of shewing, that there still subsists an Instance of that kind of Connection which it is most our Interest to have with every foreign Court. Our Subjects trade largely with those of *Portugal*, to their mutual Benefit and Advantage ; we have all the Privileges there that we can reasonably desire in favour of our Merchants ; the *Portuguese* are considered here, upon all Occasions, as our faithful Friends and Allies. These have been the Rules of Behaviour to both Courts in Times of perfect Tranquility, and when nothing farther was necessary to evince the Cordiality of Esteem on both Sides. But when a Difference arose between the *Spaniards* and the *Portuguese*, which swelled so high, as that the latter were threatened with an Invasion, we made no Difficulty of sending in due Time, and without any Delay, such a Fleet to *Lisbon*, as served to protect the Subjects of the King of *Portugal* from any Insult.

We seem at present to be universally persuaded, that it is our Interest to live not only on good Terms with the Republick of the *United Provinces*, but also in the closest and most perfect Harmony, in which it is certain that we act conformable both to the Lights of Reason and Experience. TRADE is indeed the common Mistress of the Maritime Powers, but at the same time they have many other Rivals, of whom they have no grounds to be afraid, while a strict Union subsists between them ; and a due Sense of this ought to induce them to prefer the joint Interest of both, to the private and particular Views of either. Another strong Reason for their living always upon good Terms, is the Sameness of their foreign Interest, that is to say, those who are Friends or Enemies to one, are likewise Friends and Enemies to the other ; which is a Point that ought to be kept always in View, by such as are entrusted with the Administration of either Government. In a word, the Conformity that there is between the Religion, the Constitution, and the natural Inclinations of the Inhabitants of both Countries, is sufficient to demonstrate to any intelligent and disinterested Person, that nothing can contribute so much to their joint Happiness, as supporting each other upon all Occasions, and that nothing can bring about their Destruction so soon, as sowing the Seeds of Dissention and Division between them.

The many Alterations that happen daily in the World, afford, and will always afford sufficient Reasons for our exerting ourselves,

felves, not without Hazard and Expence, in favour of fome or other of our Allies ; which however muft be done, and done with Spirit and Chearfulnefs, if we will remain a free, a great, and a refpected People. It is in vain to hope to maintain our Characters by a felfifh and furly, or by a lazy and inactive Behaviour ; if we reafon ever fo little with ourfelves, we may be fatisfied of this ; if we confult Hiftory, Hiftory will convince us ; if we have recourfe to Experience, Experience will read us the fame Lecture. Neither ought we to confider what we do as any Burthen or Inconveniency, fince it arifes from the Rank and Figure we make in the World, from thofe Connections which have been the Fruit of our Significancy, and by which that is upheld and fecured. In fhort, when we fuccour our Neighbours, we do it from a Principle of Juftice to ourfelves ; we flourifh, in part, from the Commerce that we have with them ; and having thus a Stake in their Welfare, it is really confulting our own Intereft, when we fulfil thofe Engagements that were entered into, on account of that Stake ; and therefore inftead of repining that we are obliged to it, we ought to rejoice that it is in our Power, and fhew by our Alacrity how much it is in our Will.

These are the general Principles of *Britifh* Policy, deduced from thofe Tranfactions, which after having been often and ferioufly examined in the wifeft and greateft Affemblies, have received repeated, as well as publick Sanctions ; fo that if private Men err in adopting them, it will be very difficult to eftablifh another Rule attended with clearer Evidence, and fupported by better Authority.

THE
CONTENTS.

CHAP.

CONTENTS.

CHAP. IX.

CHAP. X.

CHAP. XI.

CHAP. XII.

CHAP. XIII.

SECT. I.

SECT. II.

SECT. III.

CONTENTS.

FINIS.